Happy 50th
hunny bunny! I
you continue to be
a 'nonconformer'! ♡
Love Kallie
5-20-22

NON
CONFORM
ERS

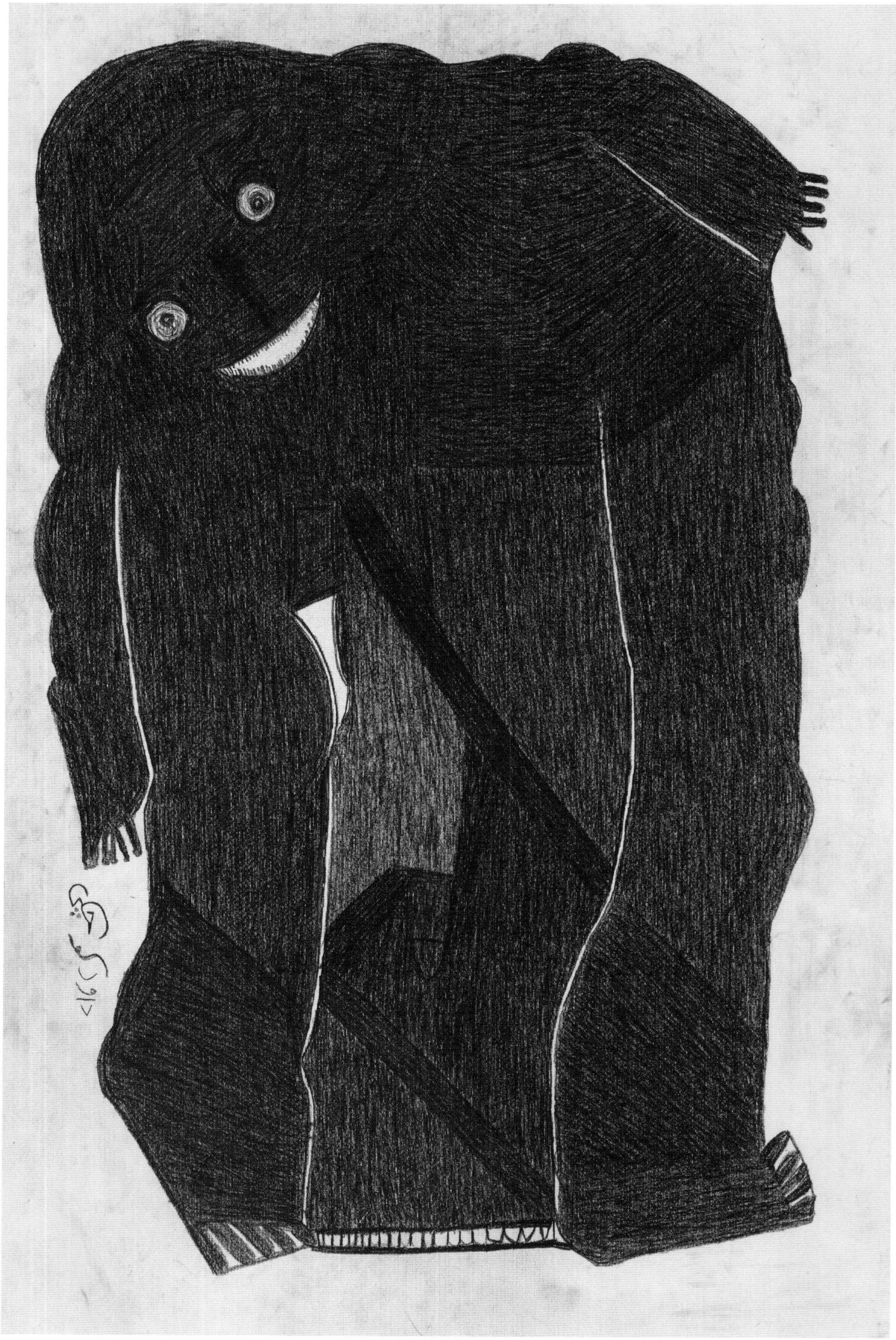

Davood Koochaki (1939–2020), untitled, *2019, graphite on paper, 39 × 27½ in (100 × 70 cm). Courtesy Gallery Outsider Inn.* Exuberant and uncanny, Koochaki's pencil drawings feature hybrid forms. Working as an automobile mechanic in Tehran, Koochaki only became dedicated full-time to his creative practice when he was in his 60s.

NON CONFORM ERS

A NEW HISTORY OF SELF-TAUGHT ARTISTS

LISA SLOMINSKI

Yale UNIVERSITY PRESS

New Haven and London

CONTENTS

PART 3:

HERE I AM: AGENCY, AWARENESS, AND AUDIENCE

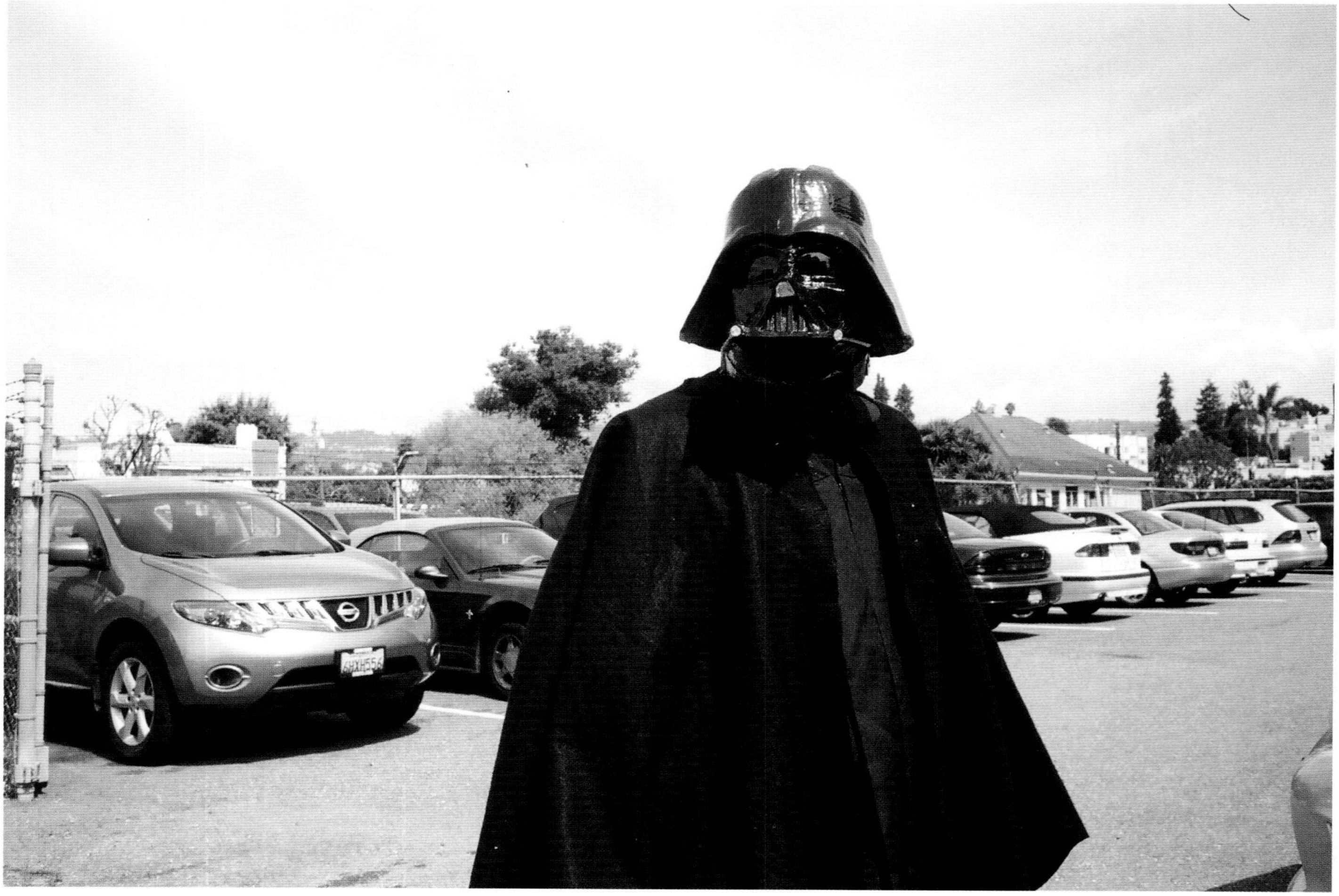

William Scott (b. 1964), 2013, photograph by Cheryl Dunn. Courtesy of the Artist and Creative Growth Art Center. Here, Scott is featured wearing one of his artist-made masks of Darth Vader. Creating various masks are part of Scott's larger art practice. His video and performance work often incorporates mask-wearing.

Nonconformers is an effort to reframe and advance the recognition of artists and dialogue often prefaced by the descriptor "self-taught."[1] Applied broadly, this blunt definition for not having formal academic training in the arts is layered with presumptions of a segregation from cultural influence; a lack of creative agency; an unsophisticated aesthetic or process; and operation in a separate trajectory to the established art world.[2] *Nonconformers* reframes the featured artists and creatives by demonstrating that they continually defy and challenge these prohibitive characteristics. As nonconformers, they, in fact, do not fit or conform to these categorical presumptions. Here, we examine the unique circumstances of each artist, including how their individual situations often presented predetermined cultural and personal conditions, such as racial oppression, poverty, mental illness, and disability. This recognition poses that discriminatory positioning for many was more complex than the concept of being self-taught. Through this reexamination, a pedagogy for addressing difference and adversity that is both critical and necessary is adapted. These shifts are a revelatory, albeit at times subtle, progression in the evolving framework on how to present, discuss, and describe the oeuvre of artists currently prefaced as self-taught.

Nonconformers critically examines the overwhelming dominance of the term "Outsider Art." Cultivated and perpetuated by dealers, gallerists, and collectors, this ubiquitous branding of self-taught was assigned to artists and prescribed to the mainstream. In response to a discourse that has historically left the artists themselves out of the conversation, interviews with living artists about their practice and their identity within the art world are included. It includes an examination into the historical architecture in which self-taught was constructed via four categorical attempts; followed by a selection of compelling but disparate themes falling under the 21st-century definition of the term "self-taught" demonstrating its impossibility to act as a cohesive framework. In collaboration with nine contributors, each with specific art historical and curatorial knowledge, *Nonconformers* also provides a survey of current points of view. This preface gives an overview of how *Nonconformers* is structured, how difference and biography are approached, and sets forth the paradigm of characteristics intrinsically linked to self-taught.

Composed in three parts, *Nonconformers* first examines how self-taught artists were presented and categorized (by curators, institutions, and historians) in 20th-century European and American art history. Its chapters, *Modern Primitives, l'Art Brut, Outsider Art*, and *Black Folk Art,* are introduced by a leading art historian and provide the reader with an understanding of some of the genre-defining moments in the field, while the chronological framework demonstrates the evolving and restrictive taxonomy. In *20th-Century Origins and Representation* the artists included were defined by the language of their respective chapters to allow critical consideration of an artist's historical placement.

Disparate Boundaries purposefully exemplifies the outstretched nature of the proposed categorical fence that attempts to contain self-taught artists. The chapters in this section, *Clandestine*, *Renegades*, *Environments*, and *Ability*, each introduce a particular circumstance, setting, or motivation for artmaking. Jarring juxtapositions are made between chapters, such as one featuring monumental built environments and one focusing on artists with disability, therein illustrating the nebulous perimeters of commonalities. The concepts are explored by four contributing essays, while the curated chapters are composed of international artists and include practices active into the 21st century.

The final chapters, in the third part of the book, *Compositions*, propose a movement away from historical categorizations and attempts to define artists via flimsy and often oppositional characteristics, offering instead to hit "refresh." By adopting thematic explorations via a classical compositional framing: *Abstraction*, *Landscapes*, and *Figuration*, the artist's direct voice is made accessible, and substantiated by extensive interviews. Establishing *Nonconformers'* conclusion, *Compositions* introduces new modes and aesthetics of interpretation, as well as direct conversations with the artists to propose a much-needed shift in empowering artists to define themselves.

Addressing difference and adversity is important, especially when presenting a problematic historical framework to aid in a current evaluation. My approach is to acknowledge these circumstances through a multifaceted presentation of each artist that is practice-led and steps away from previous biographies guilty of the "fetishizing of difference."[3] This approach does not focus on "difference as separation" but on "difference as visibility."[4] Asserting that "difference" need not assign an individual as "other," "separate to," or "outside of," *Nonconformers* discusses biography judiciously, and respectfully refrains from "biographical reduction" and discovery narratives. These critical parameters are examined in depth through eight artists in focus: William Edmondson, Aloïse Corbaz, Madge Gill, Bill Traylor, Henry Darger, Lee Godie, Nek Chand, and Judith Scott. Each is unique in their practices and circumstances, further demonstrating the lack of cohesion in attempting to link self-taught artists together. The artists in focus further assert individual perspectives and demonstrate creativity not void of cultural influence.

Characteristics of artists historically segregated as self-taught—a lack of agency and position of cultural isolation, including operating "outside" of the art world—are often erroneously presumed. However, the majority

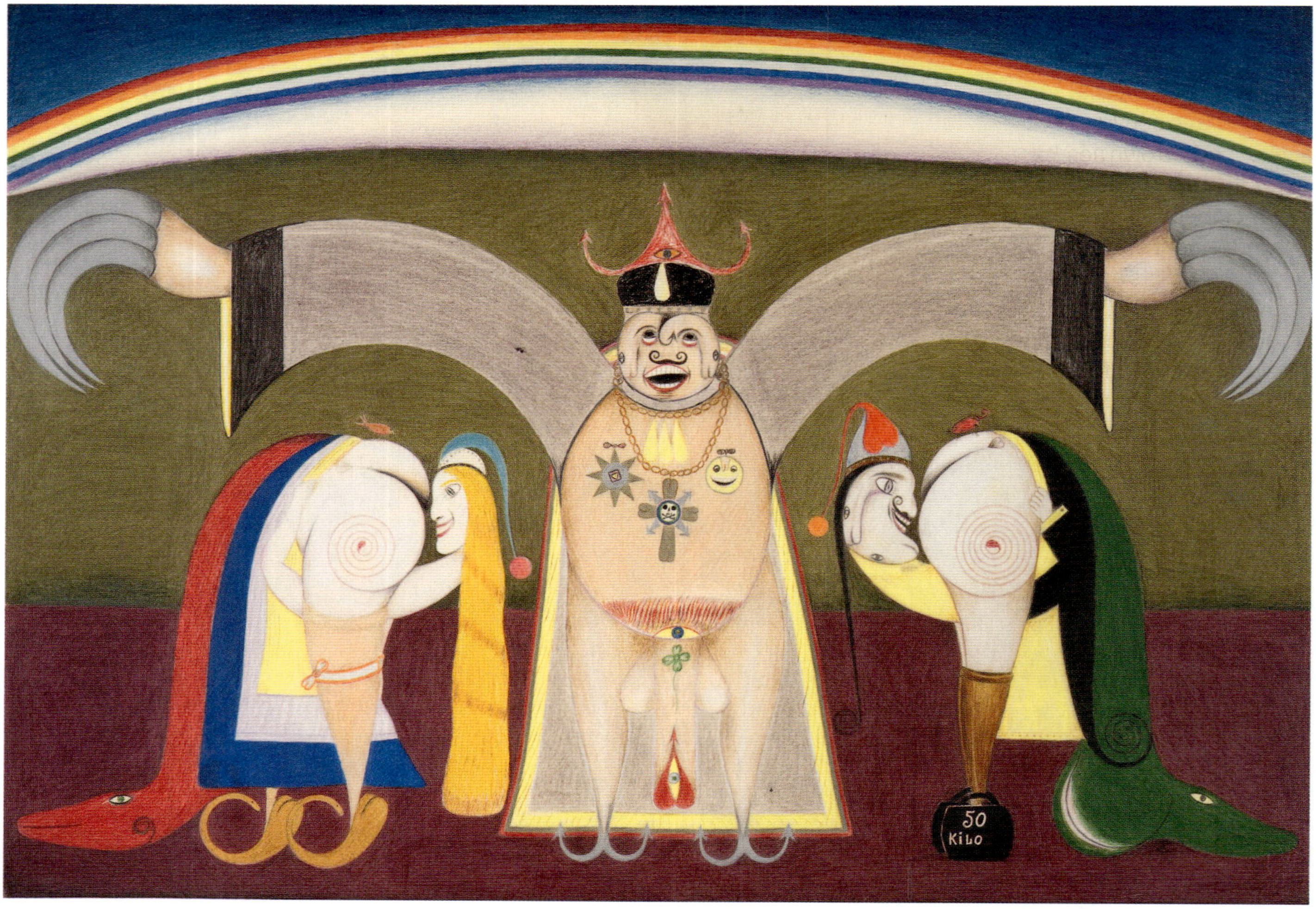

Friedrich Schröder-Sonnenstern (1892–1982), Trilogy of the Search for Truth, *1953, colored pencil on cardboard, 20 × 28¾ in (51 × 73 cm). Courtesy Galerie Brockstedt.* This surreal and irreverent drawing by Schröder-Sonnenstern has a central male figure with exposed genitalia and implied authority through his scale and accessories of medals and badges. Smaller figures left and right are skewed and stretched, repositioned to be in view of their own backsides.

of artists presented in *Nonconformers* are (or were) indisputably engaged in cultural dialogues. And this engagement, in fact, is at times of reciprocal authority: artists influenced by culture, culture influenced by artists. Prolific artist Henry Darger's reclusive tendencies are often cited, yet his astute collecting of contemporaneous printed material and fondness for literature, including Harriet Beecher Stowe's *Uncle Tom's Cabin,* are abundant throughout *Realms of the Unreal*. Guo Fengyi's meditative drawings were informed by her practice of Qigong and her studies of *Book of Changes (I Ching)*, an ancient Chinese divination text. Conversely, artists considered self-taught are impacting mainstream culture; Nek Chand's *Rock Garden* is India's second-most visited cultural site. Howard Finster created album cover artwork for both R.E.M. (*Reckoning*, 1984) and Talking Heads (*Little Creatures*, 1985). More recently, Tomoyuki Shinki designed one of the official posters for the 2020 Tokyo Olympics.

This consideration of a two-way influential relationship can also be applied within the historical canon of art, proving that the traction of self-taught artists is not limited to a separate trajectory, nor occuring in isolation. In 1950, shortly after deciding to be an artist, Friedrich Schröder-Sonnenstern began attending bi-weekly art lectures/forums in Berlin organized by artist Juro Kubicek.[5] Around the same time, British mediumistic artist Madge Gill was in correspondence with a journalist, Louise Morgan, and wrote of her admiration for the work of American artist Grandma Moses. Moses, in her own right, may be the most culturally ubiquitous artist in *Nonconformers*, with her paintings licensed by Hallmark for greeting cards and her appearance on the cover of *Life* magazine for her 100th birthday.

Schröder-Sonnenstern's participation and presence among art circles in Berlin exemplifies a specific and notable influential exchange between the artists in *Nonconformers* and contemporaneous artists. In 1961, Georg Baselitz was gaining admiration for Schröder-Sonnenstern, and even invited him to contribute to his *First Pandemonium Manifesto*.[6] As explored further in the chapter *l'Art Brut*, the idiosyncratic oeuvre collected by Jean Dubuffet directly influenced his own aesthetic. These artists and creatives that informed Dubuffet's work, as well as American artists Janet Sobel and Morris Hirshfield, were significant within the movement of surrealism. Similarly, the Chicago Imagists, a group of artists associated with the School of the Art Institute in the 1960s and 70s, were influenced by, and interested in, artists considered self-taught, and formed a relationship with fellow Chicago-based artist Joseph E. Yoakum. Conceptual artist Ed Ruscha commemorated his admiration for Sam Doyle's work in his 1985 painting, *WHERE ARE YOU GOING, MAN? DO YOU DIG ME? (*WASS A GUIN MON? U DIG ME?).[7] More recently, in 2019, artist Alvaro Barrington was invited to curate an exhibition of artists that directly influence the way he works at Thaddaeus Ropac, London. Titled *Artists I Steal From*, it included Jean-Michel Basquiat, Joseph Beuys, and Louise Bourgeois alongside Thornton Dial, Mary T. Smith, Derrick Alexis Coard and Purvis Young.[8] Another extremely influential exhibition, *Outliers and American Vangard Art* (2018–2019) curated by Lynne Cooke, explored the intersections of mainstream and self-taught artists in American history.

Preconceived characteristics for self-taught artists transfer from cultural positioning to creative motivations and a singular aesthetic. *Nonconformers* contradicts these assumptions by confirming a diverse aesthetic and creative agency, asserting from the outset that the practices presented do not commonly share a raw aesthetic, or a process of secretive frenetic production. The intricate detail and sublime symmetry in the compositions of Augustin Lesage contrasted with Andrew Omoding's performative and participatory practice demonstrate otherwise, for example. Furthermore, artists particularly of the American South, including Sister Gertrude Morgan and Lonnie Holley, are (or were) active in their local communities, contradicting assumptions of solitude.

Returning to the discussion of biographical detail, the complex and teetering navigation of the relationship between an artist's biography and an autonomous reading of their work should be recognized. The delivery of biographical details, particularly by a dealer, historian, or curator, is crucial for maintaining a non-reductive reading of the oeuvre, as opposed to an emphasis on traumatic events or "wacky life stories"[9] that overshadow the integrity of the creative output. Yet historically, select artist narratives, principally those prefaced as self-taught, have been presented with "discovery" and "mythic" attributions that restrict a multidimensional appreciation of the individual, while simultaneously inviting the potential of a marginalized gaze. *Nonconformers* contends that elements of personal biography can have the capacity to inform a deeper reading of a work of art. Considering that producing (art) work is personal, which arguably it is (as part of the human experience, we are all products of our environment and circumstance), then we could contend (self-taught artist or not), that aspects of an artist's life are very much relevant to discussing the art itself, if done in a respectful manner.

Charles A.A. Dellschau, whose illustrated notebooks were discovered in a garbage disposal site some 40 years after his death, is one of the rare exceptions where the word "discovery" is accurate. The anti-discovery approach considered for *Nonconformers* does not discount the important role of advocates, champions, and collectors; all of whom play a distinctive role in the legacy of any artist. Sidney Hirsh, and Alfred and Elizabeth Starr were certainly influential figures in William Edmondson's narrative and creative legacy, but in relation to being discovered, it is worth acknowledging that Edmondson already had his sculptures publicly displayed throughout his yard.

Nonconformers operates within the ideological framework that the individuals featured are validated as artists and do not require justification. This is not an attempt to legitimize practices in comparison to modern or contemporary peers, but rather a presentation of biographies, ideas, and interviews that disrupt the broad assumptions and stigmas applied throughout the categorization of self-taught. Artists are discussed within the broader art historical/contemporary canon with the intention of, where possible, demonstrating their placement—be that exhibition, publication, or collection—beyond the perimeters of the self-taught remit.[10]

The paintings of Mary T. Smith, which she displayed across her property in Southern Mississippi, contained personal messages and proclamations. Smith, who was born with a severe hearing impairment, often felt dismissed or overlooked by her peers in her formative years. Of her multitudinous messaging, her most remembered affirmation is: Here I Am, Don't You See Me. With this phrase, Smith's insertion of her voice within the public sphere echoes the sentiment and approach of this book. A single act emblematic of claiming agency, awareness, and audience.

Poster for l'Art Brut *exhibition at the Galerie René Drouin, Paris (1949). Collection de l'Art Brut, Lausanne.* Featuring 200 works by 63 creators, *l'Art Brut* was Jean Dubuffet's first exhibition of this material in the gallery's main space. It featured works by Aloïse Corbaz (Aloyse), Marguerite Sirvins (Demoiselle Sir.), Auguste Forestier, and Fleury-Joseph Crépin.

TERMINOLOGY: TASTES, GATES, LABELS, AND SUITS

Defining tastes and unlatching the gate

The European origin of the genre Outsider Art is often attributed to the publishing of *Artistry of the Mentally Ill* in 1922. This significant book by German psychiatrist Hans Prinzhorn (1886–1933) featured a selection of drawings[11] by patients from psychiatric hospitals and institutions; among them were the remarkably detailed drawings of Adolf Wölfli, a patient of the Waldau Clinic, Bern. Concerned with the relationship between art and psychiatry, Prinzhorn's publication was one of the first efforts to analyze the creative output of individuals impacted by mental illness. In 1942, via the work of Prinzhorn, French artist Jean Dubuffet also became intrigued with artwork created outside of museums and academies. The boundaries of Dubuffet's interest expanded beyond medical facilities to include mediumistic producers, such as Fleury-Joseph Crépin. Dubuffet defined this composition of artists as *l'art brut*. Its translation: "raw or uncooked." In 1947, he launched in Paris a series of impactful exhibitions and contemporaneously critical publications initially under Foyer de l'Art Brut (which became Compagnie de l'Art Brut from 1948). Dubuffet constructed a legacy for his definition of Art Brut, particularly through decades of collecting works, which are now housed in Lausanne, Switzerland, at the museum Collection de l'Art Brut.

In 1972, Art Brut (which as a term still operates in close proximity to "Outsider") informed the research of British art historian Roger Cardinal (1940–2019), for his book titled, *Outsider Art*. He set out to write in regards to, and within the framework of, Dubuffet, and to introduce the concept of Art Brut to an English-speaking audience. In 1979, the exhibition *Outsiders: An Art Without Precedent or Tradition* at the Hayward Gallery, London, curated by Cardinal and Victor Musgrave (1919–1984), featured European artists established in Dubuffet's *l'art brut,* including Johann Hauser from Gugging, as well as British mediumistic artist Madge Gill. It also presented American artists Henry Darger and Martín Ramírez. Their inclusion aligned with the European interest in Outsider as an examination of the link between creativity and mental illness, and artists considered firmly planted in isolated or anti-cultural positions. The inclusion of Chicago artist Joseph E. Yoakum, however, speaks to the adjacent emergence of self-taught artists in America and their placement within the Outsider framework.

Juxtaposed to this European focus on psychiatric institutions, in 20th-century America, interest in artists without academic training was being curatorially shaped by the genre of folk and of "primitive" artists' relationship to modernism. This context of "folk art" was linked to tradition, communal processes, and often craft; but unlike the origins of Art Brut and Outsider Art, it was not generally defined by the creativity of individual makers.[12] Curator Holger Cahill (1887–1960) organized the first American folk art exhibitions at the Newark Museum, and later, as temporary acting director of the Museum of Modern Art (MoMA), New York, he organized *Folk Art: The Art of the Common Man in America, 1750–1900* (1932). MoMA became a key institution for shaping the emergence of the self-taught genre, in the most part under the supervision of its first director, Alfred Barr, Jr. In 1938, during Barr's tenure, MoMA presented *Masters of Popular Painting: Modern Primitives of Europe and America*, the country's first significant survey under the remit of self-taught. MoMA cultivated the language and context of the modern primitive and under this lexicon, painters including Morris Hirshfield, John Kane and Horace Pippin were exhibited. From 1941 to 1944, MoMA presented the permanent collection installation *Modern Primitives: Artists of the People.*

Prior to this, in 1937, MoMA had presented *Sculpture by William Edmondson.* A self-taught artist from Tennessee, Edmondson was the first African American to receive a solo exhibition at MoMA. The following decades brought further national interest in vernacular art, specifically toward the American South and by people of color. Sister Gertrude Morgan, Bill Traylor, and Sam Doyle were among the Southern African American artists that constituted the 1982 seminal exhibition *Black Folk in America, 1930–1980*, which debuted at the Corcoran Gallery, Washington, D.C., and traveled internationally, including to the Brooklyn Museum and the Institute for the Arts in Houston.[13] Curated by John Beardsley and Jane Livingston, this exhibition raised several criticalities: for African American artists, it amplified the debate surrounding the placement of their artwork's context under an art historical or anthropological framework (art or artifact?).[14] While in relation to the terminology it further questioned the increased appeal of African American artists labeled as "folk" to white audiences, and more broadly suggested a redefinition of "folk" through its presentation of artists with idiosyncratic styles, methods, and individual messaging.

Key figures played oscillating roles as "gatekeepers" and "tastemakers": Prinzhorn, Dubuffet, and Cardinal set forth the paradigm of individuals cultivating a genre from the outside, while the *Modern Primitives* presentations at MoMA and the *Black Folk Art* exhibition showed gates were being selectively unlocked through institutional validation. Around the turn of the 21st century, as a genre defined by others, this notion of tastemakers became increasingly integral to the notoriety of the genre. Significantly, the role of dealer and gallerist emerged as perhaps the most powerful propellant, with key dealers including Phyllis Kind, Carl Hammer, John Ollman, and Henry Boxer. In regards to terminology, Cardinal's Outsider Art has undeniably transpired as the dominant label in the 21st century. It has encompassed the evolution (and merging) of the categorical framework of artists considered self-taught—the existing Art Brut, folk, primitive, vernacular titles—and following the development of supported studios in the 1970s, the term today often includes artists with intellectual and developmental disabilities.[15] With consideration for the international categorical attempts to demonstrate historical ramifications and adaptations, the following examination is focused on the contemporary dialogue between Outsider Art to artist, audience, and messenger.

Manufacturing a label

American sociologist Gary Fine points out that labels are absolutely necessary, stating that "institutionalization of cultural practices depends on terminology, however imperfect."[16] However, with Outsider Art's current ambiguity and perimeters controlled by enthusiasts rather than by the artists, how culturally effective and respectful could the term be? Examining the relationship between the label "Outsider Art" to those who defined it and to those defined by it, polemic factors are raised. These factors are present in the positioning of the Outsider Art by gatekeepers and tastemakers, raising the label's relativity to context and effectiveness. Such relativity asks the questions: Are those operating within the administration of Outsider Art hoping to merge the creatives within the existing artworld framework or is it being cultivated in direct opposition to that same framework? And secondly, do we measure cultural recognition through the accomplishment of exposure alone, or do we factor in the marginalized gaze and/or problematic context where relevant?

In its broad application, Outsider Art attempts to encompass those with little to no connection to the art world or no formal artistic training; those with psychiatric conditions; intellectual and developmental disability; and, at large, those considered on the margins of society. Predetermined connotations often also imply the artist is not influenced by society and their creative endeavors are without knowledge or understanding of the larger art world exchanges. Their individual circumstances often present predetermined cultural and personal conditions—racial oppression, poverty, mental illness, and disability—that may have contributed to their "Outsider" positioning. The oeuvres within this categorization are often described as having pure and transcendent qualities, argued by some as not possible within the mainstream art remit. Yet, this categorization can have problematic connotations, for example, when assigned to someone who would otherwise be categorized as an emerging contemporary artist—only redefined as an "Outsider" because of an intellectual disability.

With contemporary consideration, categorizing an artist as an "Outsider" could have potential justification within a historical framework, particularly those artists who were closely connected to Cardinal's research. Art historian David Maclagan suggested setting a historical framing of Art Brut, using 1900–1950 to place the artists and oeuvres, favoring a "cultural rather than natural phenomenon" and affording works created outside of their own respective "cultural and sociological situation."[17] With attempts to provide an accurate label that crisscrosses globally, morphs aesthetically, and has the ability to time travel, the assessment of "Outsider" therefore becomes one of identity and circumstance. Furthermore, as a label not cultivated by the artists themselves, its malleability may speak more to the tastemakers and gatekeepers appealing to collectors and audience than an attempt to critically elevate a cohesive stable of artists.

This notion of malleability for an audience or adapting tastes can be illustrated through the subtle evolution of the naming of the American Folk Art Museum. The New York museum first opened in 1961, officially titled the Museum of Early American Folk Art, but following a rising interest in contemporary makers, in 1966, the name was updated to the Museum of American Folk Art. In 2001, subsequent to the museum's pursuits to include international artists and broader genres (with exhibition titles including *Photo | Brut* and *Six Decades Collecting Self-Taught Art*, and a history serving as an official sponsor and beneficiary of the Outsider Art Fair), they entered their current taxonomy, the American Folk Art Museum.[18] Though this brief example considers the implications of defining "folk" rather than "Outsider," the

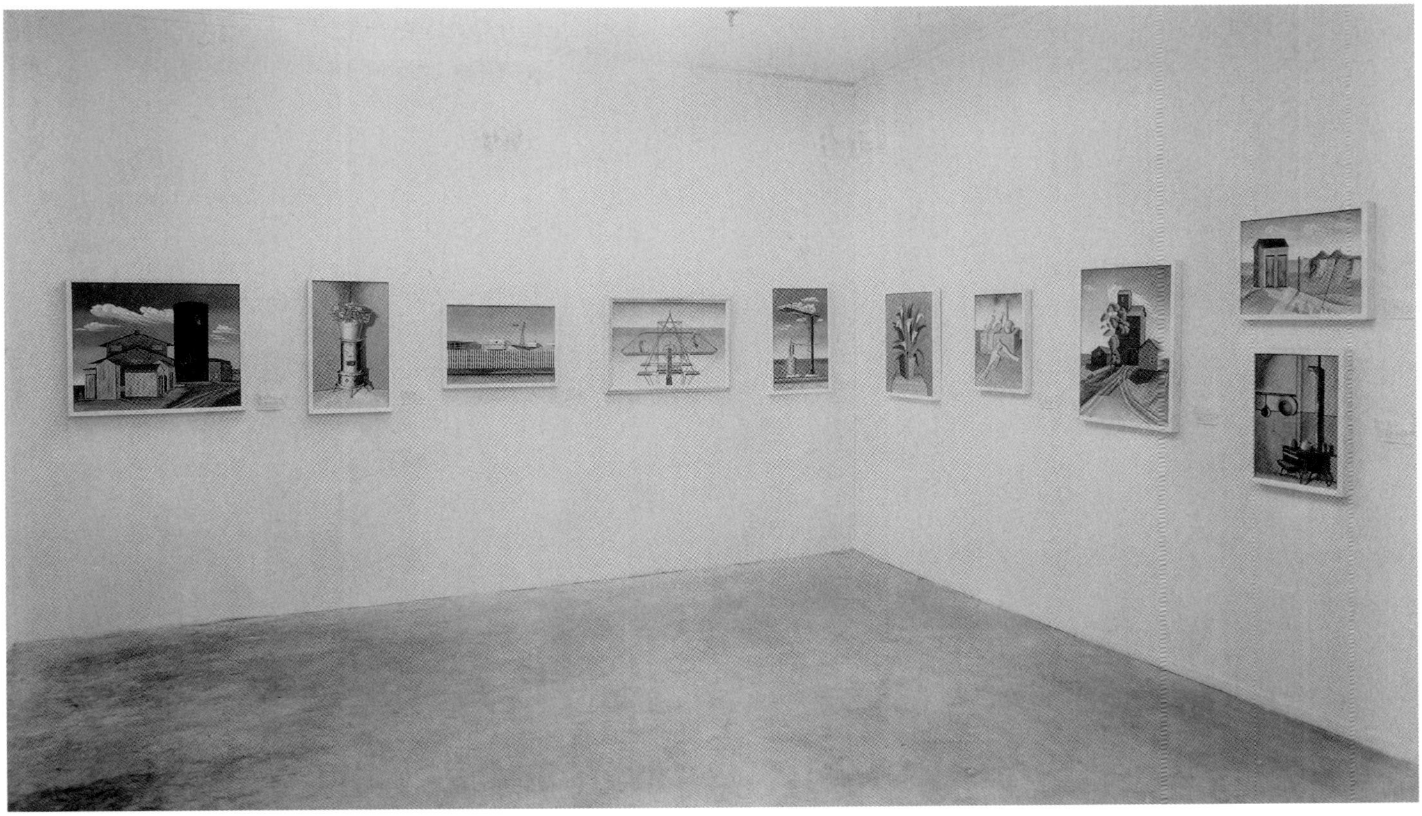

Installation view of the exhibition Masters of Popular Painting: Modern Primitives of Europe and America, *Museum of Modern Art, New York (April 27, 1938–July 24, 1938). Museum of Modern Art (MoMA), New York.*

This view shows a presentation of artist Pedro Lopez Cervántez, including his paintings *Los Privados* (1937) and *Bovina Elevators* (1937). Of the 22 artists featured, Cervántez was the only Latinx artist included.

concept is still applicable. These incremental name changes illustrate how a wider genre aims to expand to meet popular and cultivated interests.

As outlined above, the terminology associated with artists considered self-taught, from modern primitive to Art Brut to the now ubiquitous Outsider, has always been defined by those interested in cultivating a genre, not by those defined within the genre. One of the more complicated aspects of this positioning is the hedging of Outsider Art's placement within the wider art context. On the one hand, many in the field are critically asking (some actively trying to rectify) the artworld gatekeepers: Why have these artists been separated from the mainstream or academic artworld? On the other hand, the genre is continually and strategically marketed as being "different" or "alternative"—purposefully cultivating an isolation. There seems to be tension here between a sentiment of active resistance to the art world establishment and simultaneous disgruntlement of noninclusion (or separate treatment) within the same establishment. If Outsiderism was cultivated by dealers and enthusiasts with a resistance to standard artworld practice, then I would query why mimic the structure so closely by establishing distinct museums, galleries, art fairs, auctions, and publications developed to operate separately to those already mainstream? In Outsider Art's position as a non-statically defined genre, the aspirations are not fixed either. With the sculptures of Judith Scott as part of both the Collection de l'Art Brut, Lausanne, and MoMA, New York, is one of these respected positions more coveted or marketable by those leading the field?

The propagating of Outsiderism is unarguably successful for the market and to the legacy of artists defined within. This success of exposure by those pushing an Outsider agenda (inclusive of the terminological precursors mentioned previously) has significantly raised the profile and awareness of artists beyond the white male narratives that are outlandishly dominant in art institutions and history. Therefore, the reckoning question poses: Does the act of elevating artists and creatives from marginalized circumstances, contributing to the diversity of perspectives

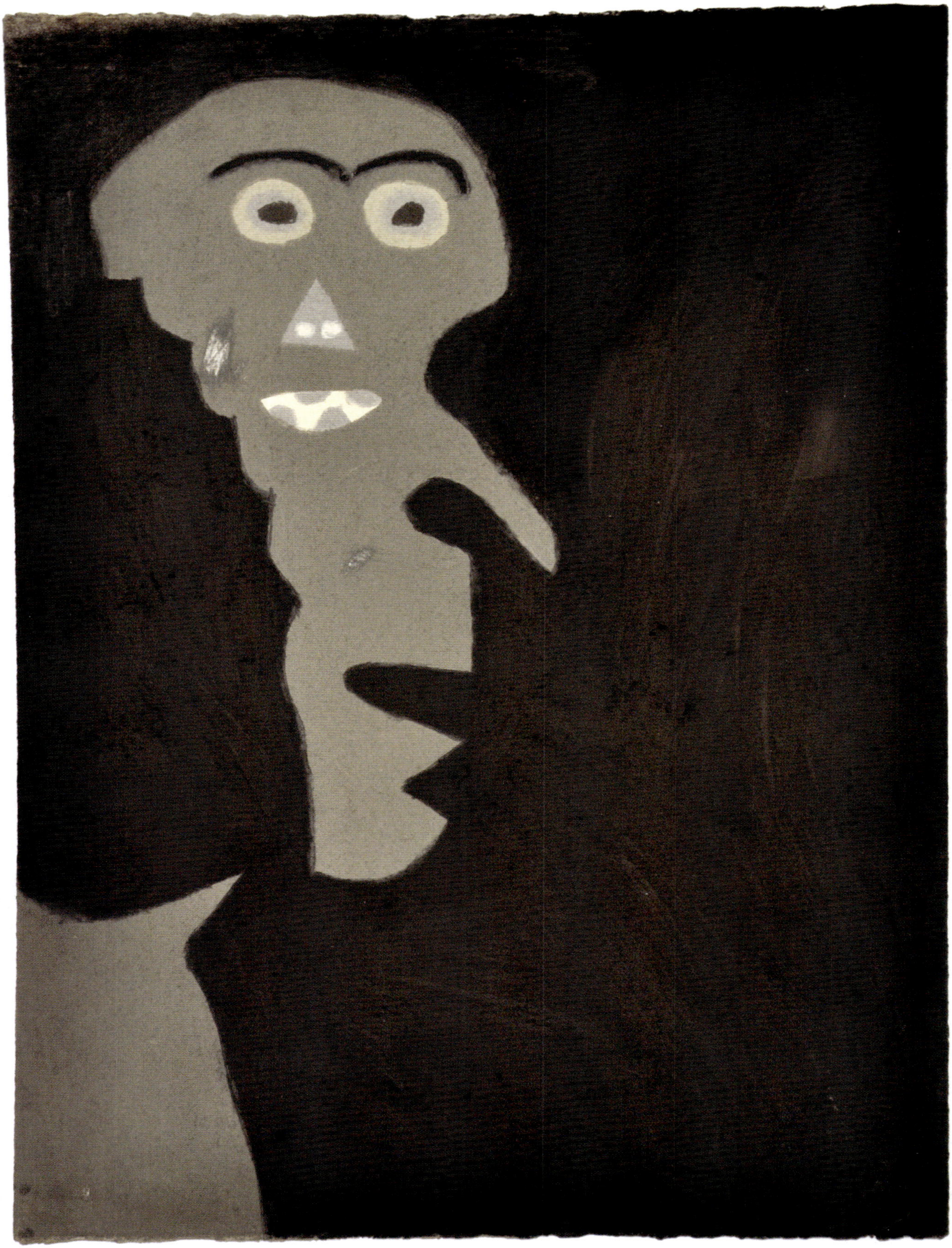

Julian Martin (b. 1969), untitled (Mr. Keating)*, 1992, pastel on paper, 15 × 11 in (38 × 28 cm). Courtesy Arts Project Australia.* Martin works with Arts Project Australia, a studio supporting artists with intellectual disabilities in Melbourne. While his work has been exhibited at the Outsider Art Fair, it is also in the collection of the National Gallery of Victoria. This early work, playing with perspective, depicts the former Australian prime minister, Paul Keating.

expressed in the artworld, outweigh the potentially problematic or restrictive lens in which they are presented?

Curators, historians, artists, and even dealers, have raised issues with the term Outsider Art as discriminatory and restrictive for decades. Art critic Roberta Smith said it "is a somewhat vague, catchall term for self-taught artists of any kind. Its exact borders are frequently debated, but generally it includes art made by patients in mental hospitals, by recluses, naives, and visionaries, by rural laborers saying they receive instructions from God, by suddenly creative retirees."[19] That description was part of Smith's 1994 review of the Outsider Art Fair, New York, where she went on to acclaim the oeuvres of Grandma Moses and Thornton Dial, acknowledging that while the labeling can be problematic, it doesn't necessarily hinder the appreciation of the art. This demonstrates Smith's ability to navigate through the dichotomy of assessing an imperfect context for accessing artists from less traditional or privileged circumstances, while also recognizing the quality of their practice.

The dichotomy of recognition via a restrictive label, becomes further layered with connection to the market woven in. Eponymous opportunities such as the Outsider Art Fair (founded in 1993 by Sanford Smith and bought by Andrew Edlin in 2012), which currently takes place annually in both New York and Paris, have undeniably provided a voice, audience, and financial market. The fair can be applied as a paradigm for the marketability of the term Outsider, while also demonstrating complexities of operating commercially with aggregated relationships to the label. Participation in an event such as the Outsider Art Fair, which irrefutably promotes and develops an artist's career and legacy, is also intrinsically linked to the presenter's financial gain, bringing attention to the role and responsibility of the dealer or gallery. These tastemakers need to consider how the artists they represent will benefit or be restricted by promotion under the Outsider label. Even if they are dubious about the title, does the financial gain from the Outsider Art market and recognition achieved override the potential prohibitive appeal? While we need critical voices discussing outdated and restrictive labeling, is it fair to expect the dealers or gallerists to become the activists, when abstaining from particular commercial events may have severe financial consequences? They have landed in a powerful but delicate position.

Tom di Maria, who became director of Creative Growth in 2000 (America's most renowned studio supporting artists with disability, founded in 1974), notes, "While the words 'Outsider Art' are not embraced by Creative Growth, there are advantages for artists with disabilities to align themselves with the collectors and galleries that do use the term," stating that venues like the Outsider Art Fair have been beneficial.[20] Di Maria continues, "The term can be useful, however, the word also has negative connotations as it denotes how the maker, in this case, a person with a disability, can be seen as being 'other'."[21] This clarifies a thoughtful but complex position of embracing Outsiderism for the development of artists (in the case of Creative Growth, a stable of predominantly living artists) with acknowledgment of concerns. Creative Growth's founder Elias Katz wrote that the studio's method is to "create new works specifically for exhibition and sale, make frequent visits to local galleries and museums, and have regular access to artist mentors who assist them in developing new approaches and techniques."[22] In this definition, it could be considered that their intent was, in fact, the antithesis of Cardinal's original definition of Outsider Art, but perfectly suited for the commercial venue of the Outsider Art Fair.

Suit alterations, and what do we wear next?

It is established, whether through a marginalized gaze or careful branding of Outsider Art, that there is wider recognition and a market for artists within the considered remit of self-taught. There is also progress with artists and exhibitions successfully blurring and defying barriers, but at the same time, the broadening elasticity of Outsider to serve multiple purposes gives rise to inconsistent boundaries. How do these barriers shift with an artist's agency?

When Southern American artist and musician Lonnie Holley (b. 1950), who is known for his resonant assemblages incorporating found objects, was asked in an interview about being referred to as an "Outsider" he said, "I didn't want to be outside of nothing. We been considered to be outside quicker than we been considered to be artists of America. I wanted to be an American artist. All these titles fitted me like an ill-fitting suit. I've worn them proudly because that was the only thing I had to wear. But otherwise I want people to see that I'm hopefully one of America's greater artists."[23]

Artist George Widener (b. 1962), who is recognized internationally for his mixed-media drawings of complex calculations and data, has acknowledged that he used to relate to the term "Outsider," but asserts he no longer identifies with it: "People can make of it what they want. You can't control that or whatever people are going to think of me. I just do my work and try to stay true to myself and that's it . . . I have evolved and I have explored things that were interesting for me. And now I interact with galleries and I'm aware that people see my artwork. And, you know, it's true that I'm somewhat influenced by that. I don't think you can have an audience and not be influenced."[24]

Conversely, in 2017, when I was present at a major art fair, a well-dressed (probably mid-50s) white man approached me during the VIP preview to tell me that while he had a professional career, he also painted in his spare time, concluding that (because he didn't go to art school) he thought he could be an Outsider Artist. He continued to show me his paintings saved on his iPhone, aesthetically comparing them to Francis Bacon. I found this encounter baffling on several levels. Here was an individual, present at an elite and world-leading commercial venue for the artworld, attempting to validate his artistic output through appropriating a typically marginalized gaze, which, as described by Holley and Widener, many artists (if aware of their Outsider positions) have aspirations to transcend.

This appropriation can be examined further. Dubuffet became aware of artist Gaston Chaissac in 1944, leading to his inclusion in the seminal *l'Art Brut* exhibition in 1949. A year earlier, in 1948, Chaissac wrote to French art critic Michel Ragon stating, "I think we should go in the direction of *brut* and untrained art because painting in our era is encouraged too little for the artist to allow himself a sufficiently sustained education and development in order to achieve mastery."[25] More recently, such interpretations have been used as a promotional device, transparently manifested by actor Jim Carrey presenting his drawings at the Outsider Art Fair in 2018. Presumably this was used as a marketing tool, but nonetheless, if Carrey qualifies as an "Outsider" for being self-taught and coming "to art without career aspirations,"[26] then couldn't we apply that same perimeter for NFT artist, Victor Langlois, aka FEWOCiOUS (undoubtedly well immersed with society and popular culture, but self-taught), who, in 2021, at the age of 18, had a dedicated online auction at Christie's of his digital animations and paintings that made over $2 million?[27] And if the definitive characteristic of lacking art world awareness (making for an audience) is held at the forefront of the term, then wouldn't that forfeit Lee Godie's post as a quintessential "Outsider"? In 1968, Godie positioned herself on the steps of the Art Institute of Chicago as a self-proclaimed "French impressionist." She performatively sold her paintings to museum curators and art students alike. A student recalled acquiring a painting for $5.00, while in contrast, a seemingly hyperaware Godie charged a curator from the Art Institute $100.00 for a very similar work.[28]

It is important to clarify that this discussion of the problematic and ambiguous properties of "Outsider" is not a condemnation of the development of the field; or of individuals who have or still embrace this term, which has elevated a canon of artists that perhaps would have lacked due recognition otherwise because of personal or social circumstance. Rather, by returning to Holley's analogy of the label of "Outsider" to an ill-fitting suit, it navigates the proposition that instead of perpetuating a terminological evolution and marketable branding, it might be time to retire it, if it no longer fits? With its vague perimeters: it is a suit jacket too large and bulky for some; its suit pants too tight and restrictive for others (while a few have made alterations to try and make it fit); and with its potential negative connotations, it is a predesignated uniform that some artists would prefer not to wear at all.

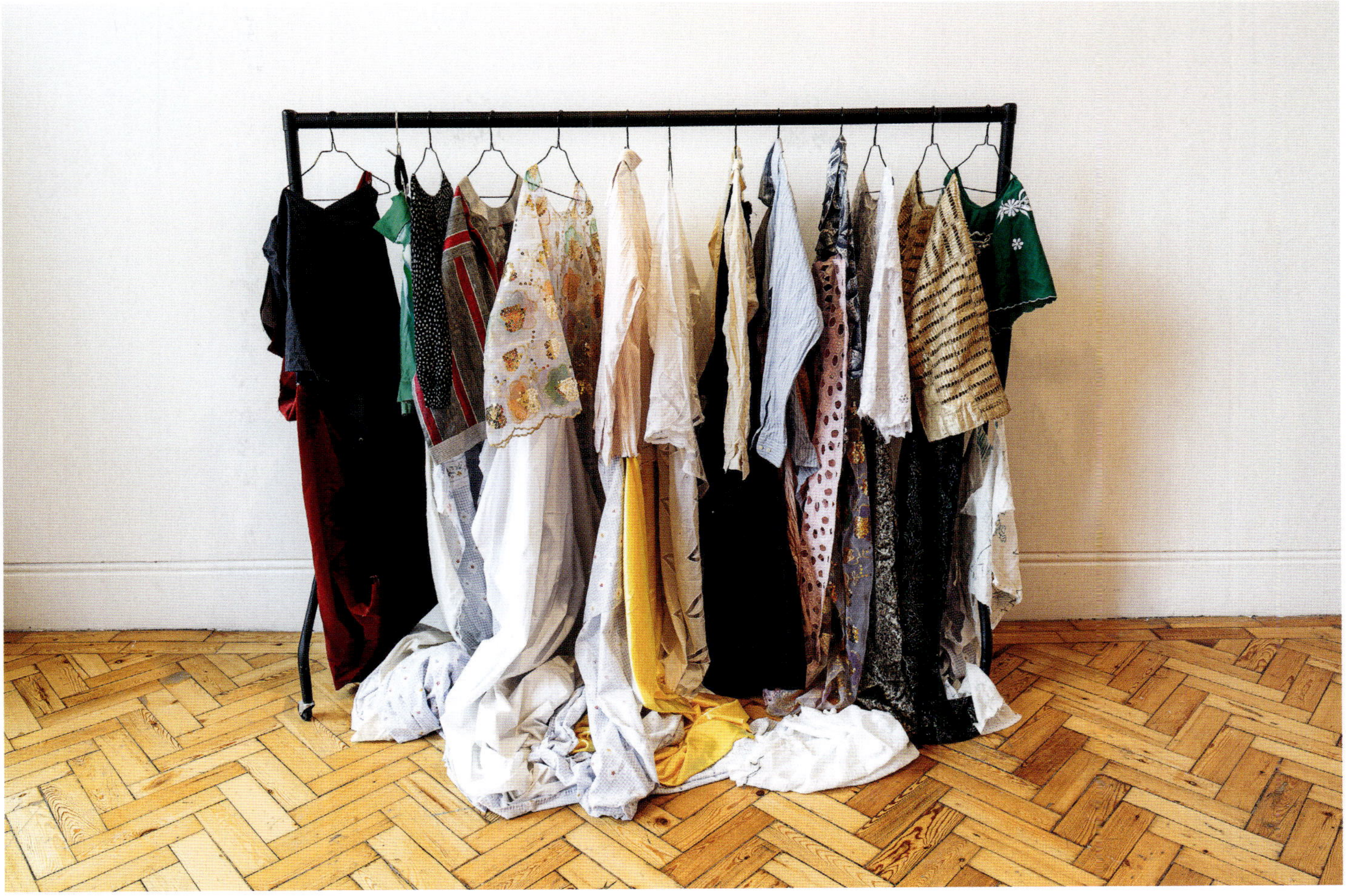

Andrew Omoding (b. 1987), installation detail of It's my work, come see, come see, *2019, Camden Arts Centre, London. Courtesy the Artist and ActionSpace.* Echoing the analogy of a suit for artistic identity—whether embraced, restricted, or explored—Omoding's practice often involves creating bespoke costumes, inviting both his peers and members of the public to wear them and perform improvisationally alongside him.

PART 1: 20TH-CENTURY ORIGINS AND REPRESENTATION

20th-Century Origins and Representation examines four key moments that presented and attempted to define self-taught artists in Europe and the United States. *Modern Primitives* examines the Museum of Modern Art's initial exhibition pursuits, followed by an exploration of Jean Dubuffet's endeavors to cultivate his interest in undefined creative agency in *l'Art Brut*. *Outsider Art* discusses Roger Cardinal's incidental title that shaped the legacy of a genre, and the chapter *Black Folk Art* is framed by the 1982 exhibition to consider the complex aims of presenting self-taught African American artists.

Each chapter is contextualized by an art historian, followed by a focus on a significant artist historically presented within the chapter's framework. Studies of William Edmondson, Aloïse Corbaz, Madge Gill, and Bill Traylor are succeeded by additional presentations of historical artists and their relationship to the chapter. *20th-Century Origins and Representation* demonstrates the evolving, pliable, and complex nature of self-taught terminology.

CHAPTER 1

MODERN PRIMITIVES: MOMA EXHIBITS THE SELF-TAUGHT (1932–1944)

ONCE SEEN AS MODERN

Katherine Jentleson

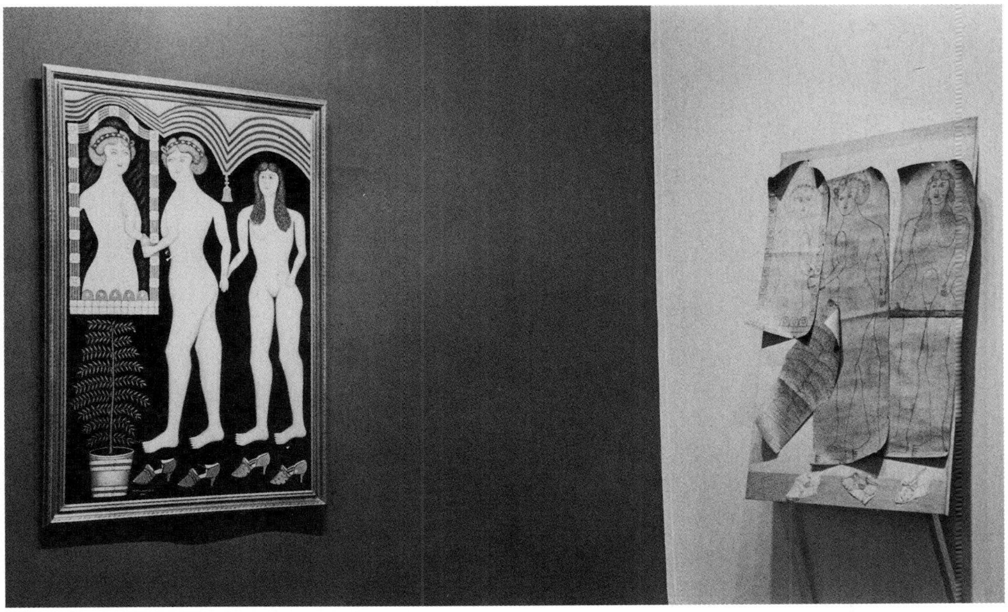

Installation view of the exhibition, The Paintings of Morris Hirshfield, *Museum of Modern Art, New York, June 23, 1943–August 1, 1943. Museum of Modern Art (MoMA), New York.* Following the exhibition *Modern Primitives: Artists of the People* (1941), this solo presentation of Morris Hirshfield's work was a significant moment for MoMA's engagement with self-taught artists.

During its first decade and a half of existence, New York's Museum of Modern Art (MoMA) made the work of self-taught artists a fixture within its program of modernism. This began with *American Folk Art: The Art of the Common Man in America, 1750–1900* (1932), which included paintings as well as utilitarian and decorative objects drawn from the collection of founding trustee Abby Aldrich Rockefeller, who had made her acquisitions under the advisement of the show's curator, Holger Cahill. Cahill had been organizing exhibitions on folk painting and sculpture at the Newark Museum, and worked with the trailblazing New York dealer Edith Halpert, who added an annex specializing in American folk art to her Downtown Gallery in 1931.[1] Halpert's joint efforts to promote contemporary American and historical folk artists evidenced how the two groups became intertwined in this era. Artists like Charles Sheeler and Yasuo Kuniyoshi, who connected with folk art in rural retreats like Buckstown, Pennsylvania, and Ogunquit, Maine, embraced not only how formally innovative so much folk art seemed, with its often quite schematic distortions of reality and expressive color, but also how it served as an index of national character: proof that artistic originality had existed in the United States for centuries, despite the longstanding presumption that American artists had been, and continued to be, overly reliant on their European peers.[2]

MoMA's presentations of self-taught artists in the 1930s and early 1940s were less concerned with ideas about the distinctly national character of this material, although with Cahill curating some of them, such narratives were often present. The insistence of MoMA's founding director Alfred Barr, Jr. that "recognition of the achievements of naive or self-taught artists" was essential to "contemporary taste" was more grounded in his awareness of the debt that modern innovation owed to art outside of Western academic traditions. When Barr conceived of his now infamous chart outlining his ideas about the development of modern art, for instance, "Negro Sculpture" was one of the tributaries that led to cubism, as was "Rousseau," a reference to the French autodidact, Henri Rousseau (see page 32).[3] Developing a kinship with other artists operating outside of academic authority, such as Alfred Jarry and Pablo Picasso, Rousseau's reputation grew posthumously, especially in New York. After Alfred Stieglitz honored him with a memorial exhibition at his modern art gallery, 291, his works appeared at The Armory Show in 1913, and the Whitney Studio Club celebrated him with an exhibition in 1924.

Around the same time that Barr included Rousseau as a cubism influencer, he began showing the artist's work at MoMA, beginning with a small summer show of private collections in 1935, then within the exhibition *Fantastic Art, Dada, Surrealism* (1937), and finally as one of the lead artists in the first major survey of self-taught artists in the United States, *Masters of Popular Painting: Modern Primitives of Europe and America* (1938). This groundbreaking exhibition included a freshly organized group of North American artists, that was credited to Cahill but relied on significant contributions by MoMA curator Dorothy Miller and MoMA trustee and New York gallerist Sidney Janis.[4] Each "master" was represented by multiple works, but Rousseau was afforded a king of grand master status matched only by the American painter John Kane (see page 36): the two dominated the show, with 19 and 20 paintings, respectively. A Scottish American immigrant who developed his artistic skills painting boxcars and houses, Kane had been gaining traction as the American Rousseau since 1927, when he succeeded in placing his work, *Scene from the Scottish Highlands* (ca. 1927) in the Carnegie Museum of Art's annual International exhibition of contemporary art. The International's acceptance of Kane's jaunty scene of two children jigging at one of the Scottish American ethnic festivals he enjoyed attending at Pittsburgh's Kennywood Park revealed to Kane that he could find success painting the things that were dear to him, namely his Scottish heritage and scenes elevating the industry and infrastructure that he labored to build in his adopted city.

Barr maintained the comparability of Kane and Rousseau in a 1941 permanent collection installation that placed Kane's self-portrait alongside Rousseau's iconic *The Sleeping Gypsy*. Barr titled the gallery *Modern Primitives,* terminology used in the subtitle of *Masters* and throughout MoMA's press releases and other texts related to living self-taught artists at this time.[5] The repeated use of this oxymoronic term reinforces how the appreciation of these artists was grounded in the much larger movement of modernist primitivism that began early in the century, attracting artists to work made outside of Western academic traditions. But "modern primitives" was by no means the only way of referring to untrained artists during this period. In fact, authorities like Janis, were as turned in circles by terminology as we remain today: "The confusion caused by the various descriptive terms for *self-taught artist* leads one to ponder the problem of a name that will convey without ambiguity his place in the world of art," Janis wrote in 1942.[6] However, the prevalence of "modern primitive" in this period importantly reveals how the related catchall category of the "primitive" became a powerful Trojan horse that completely invaded and transformed existing canons, despite being cast in monstrous opposition to Western sophistication.

Breakthroughs that were otherwise anomalous in the interwar art world occurred as a result. In October of 1937, for instance, Nashville artist William Edmondson (see page 24) made history by becoming the first African American artist to have a solo exhibition at MoMA, when the museum opened a small exhibition of a dozen of his limestone carvings. The reduced, disarming forms of his resulting sculpture were deeply resonant with what was being done by contemporary artists associated with the direct carving movement. Yet the enthusiasm for self-taught artists in this period predominantly centered on painters, hence the medium-specific focus of *Masters of Popular Painting*. Despite the exclusion of Edmondson, *Masters* did defy the norm of segregation that dominated exhibitions in this era by including two artists of color: Pedro Lopez Cérvantez (see page 48), a painter whose crisp scenes of vacant streets, domestic interiors, and agricultural architecture in New Mexico had already debuted at MoMA in *New Horizons in American Art* (1936); and Horace Pippin (see page 44), an African American artist who had returned to his childhood

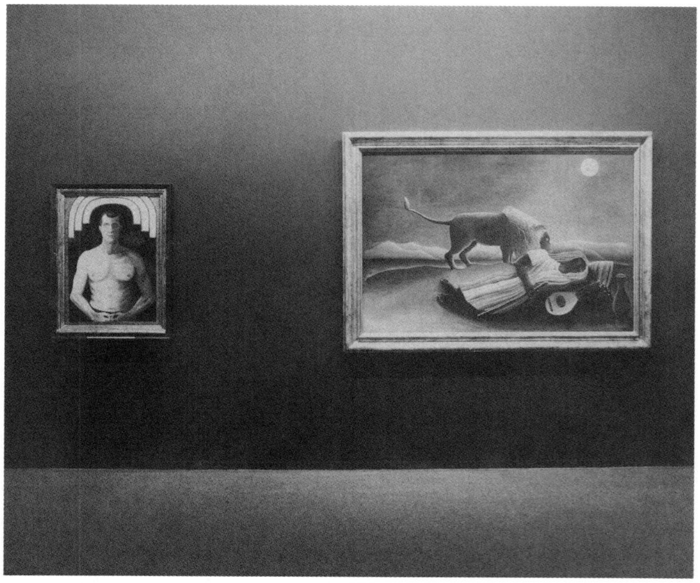

Installation view of the exhibition, New Acquisitions: Modern Primitives; Artists of the People, *Museum of Modern Art, New York, October 21, 1941–April 30, 1944. Museum of Modern Art (MoMA), New York.* This collection display features 19 artists including Pedro Lopez Cervántez and Morris Hirshfield. This installation detail features John Kane's *Self-Portrait* (1929, left) and Henri Rousseau's *The Sleeping Gypsy* (1897, right).

love of painting after suffering trauma during World War I and would go on to achieve great access not only in exhibitions of self-taught art, but also the many survey exhibitions of New Negro art that flourished in this era. Although the other painters in *Masters* would be considered part of the racial category of whiteness today, the majority of them were recent immigrants from countries that were reviled by xenophobic groups with a stronghold in American politics of the previous decade.[7] With the exception of the French artist Séraphine Louis, *Masters* was entirely male, but several women artists advanced careers in its wake. Following the discovery of her paintings in an upstate New York drugstore in 1938, Anna Mary Robertson "Grandma" Moses (see page 330) was featured in MoMA's *Contemporary Unknown American Painters* (1939), a small exhibition curated in the member's lounge by Janis. And Josephine Joy, another artist employed by the Federal Art Project (FAP), a branch of the New Deal[8], broke the gender glass ceiling at MoMA when she became the first woman painter to have a solo exhibition there in 1942.

During his defining tenure as director at MoMA from its founding in 1929 to 1943, Barr often took a serial approach to his exhibitions, positioning single events within larger goals. *Masters*, for instance, was the third in a series of exhibitions that Barr "intended to present some of the major divisions or movements of modern art," which had begun with two aforementioned shows, *Cubism and Abstract Art* (1936) and *Fantastic Art, Dada, Surrealism* (1937).[9] *Americans 1943: Realists and Magic Realists*, an exhibition that included self-taught artists such as Patrick Sullivan and Patsy Santo alongside trained artists like Ben Shahn and Peter Blume, was likewise part of a series focused on art produced in the United States, further demonstrating Barr's view that "certain of our self-taught painters can hold their own in the company of their best professionally trained compatriots."[10] Shortly after that exhibition closed, however, a solo show for the Brooklyn painter Morris Hirshfield (see page 40) upset Barr's inclusive treatment of self-taught artists. Critics such as Peyton Boswell, who had been welcoming to Kane a decade earlier, ripped the show apart, criticizing Hirshfield's approach to the human form and certain decisions made by the guest curator Sidney Janis.[11] "While serious, professional artists fight for the recognition that means life to them," wrote Boswell, "the Modern fiddles away its resources building a precious cult around amateurism."[12]

This complaint, that self-taught artists were essentially taking up too much space within a pluralistic and highly competitive landscape of American modernism, was echoed by other critics in the postwar period, especially as the art of Grandma Moses soared in popularity.[13] Following her highly publicized appearance at the Gimbel's department store Thanksgiving Festival in 1940, Moses became a household name through both her mass media appearances and merchandise reproducing her idyllic paintings of rural New England. In 1950, an exhibition of Moses's work toured five European cities and drew more admiration from critics abroad than the concurrent US pavilion at the Venice Biennale. This outraged critics like Aline Louchheim, who wrote: "Europeans like to think of Grandma Moses rather than [John] Marin as representative of American art. They praise our naiveté and integrity (especially in rodeos and Westerns), but they begrudge us a full, sophisticated artistic expression. Grandma Moses represents both what they expect of us and what they are glad to grant us." [14] Robert Goldwater who had dedicated a section to the "modern primitive" in his 1938 book, *Primitivism in Modern Painting,* was among the other notables who seemed to turn on self-taught artists during this period. As the Moses show remained on view at the American Embassy early in 1951, it coincided with an exhibition of Hirshfield's work at Galerie Maeght, creating a profile of American art in Paris that Goldwater felt, "can only strengthen the Parisian's tendency [. . .] to think of the United States as a land of auto- and tank-producing peasants."[15]

Ironically, the self-taught artist's example of humbly and unconventionally achieved excellence that had ignited so much interest within the American art world after World War I, and fueled it through the Great Depression, became cause for concern after World War II. While self-taught artists hardly disappeared in the postwar period, their presence as a branch within the ever-growing tree of 20th-century modernism snapped under larger pressures around how to best represent American art at home and abroad. The repair of this break is still ongoing.

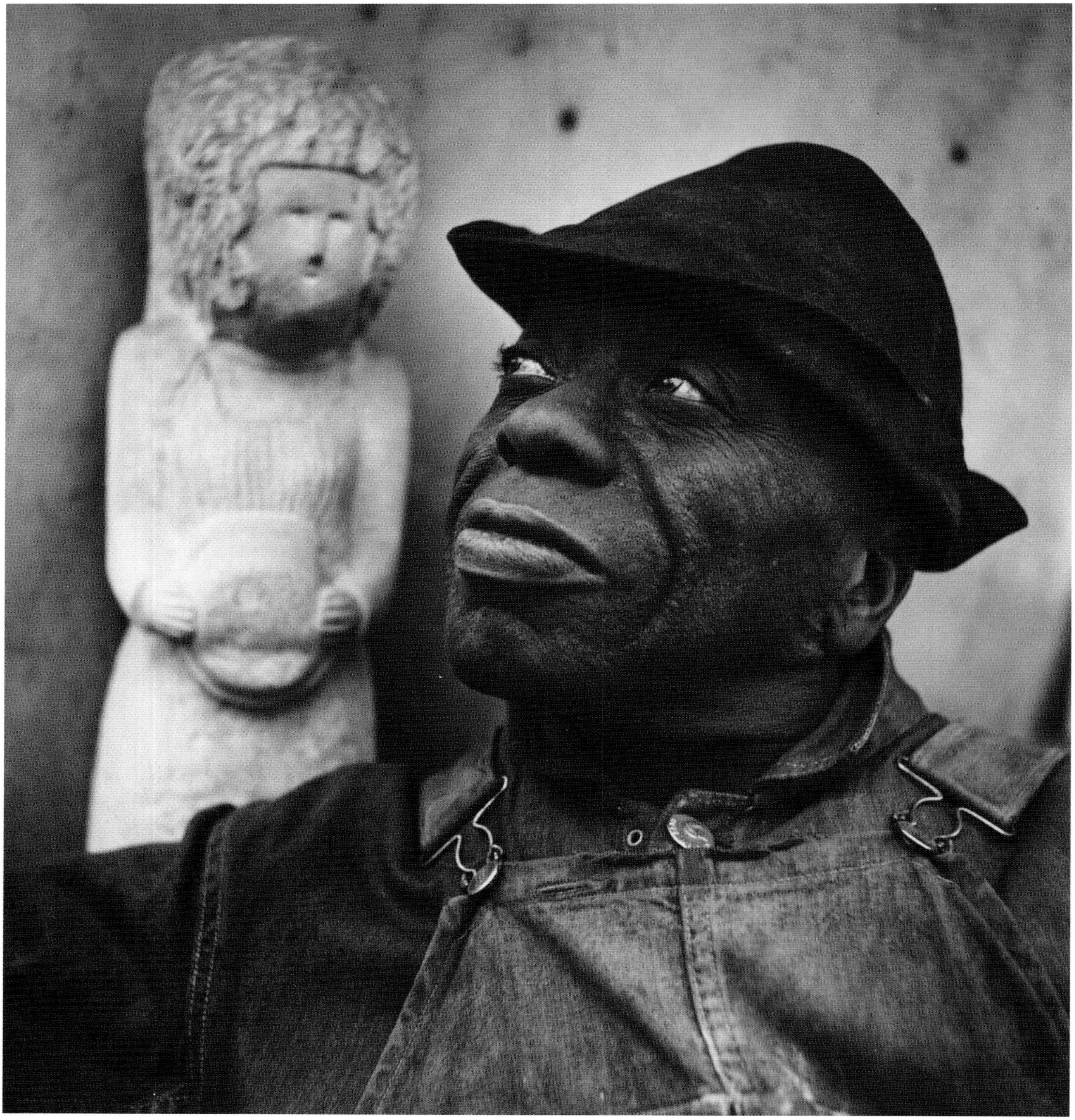

William Edmondson, 1937, photograph by Louise Dahl-Wolfe (American, 1895–1989). Center for Creative Photography. This is one of several portraits of Edmondson taken by Dahl-Wolfe in 1937, which she submitted for a *Harper's Bazaar* feature. The feature was unpublished but this portfolio, including this portrait, introduced Edmondson's work to MoMA, New York.

WILLIAM EDMONDSON

(1874, Davidson County–1951, Nashville, Tennessee, USA)

In 1931, after working as custodian and caretaker between a college and hospital for 25 years, William Edmondson received the divine inspiration to carve tombstones from a vision of God in the sky. Soon thereafter, he expanded from tombstones to garden ornaments and sold them from his Nashville property. A son of freed, formerly enslaved parents, Edmondson was born on a Tennessee plantation in the emergence of the Jim Crow era in the American South. Unknowingly aligned with the modernist aesthetic of direct carving, his limestone sculptures often included motifs derived from Black burial traditions and Christianity, as well as community and animals. In 1937, Louise Dahl-Wolfe photographed Edmondson and his sculptures for *Harper's Bazaar.* The magazine declined to publish the feature, allegedly because he was African American, but Dahl-Wolfe's portfolio introduced his work to the Museum of Modern Art, New York (MoMA), resulting in the presentation, *Sculpture by William Edmondson* (1937). Curated by Dorothy Miller, Edmondson was the first African American artist to receive a solo exhibition at MoMA.

The Museum of Modern Art's first director, Alfred Barr Jr., introduced pioneering thought in relation to artists within the contemporary canon of "self-taught." Prior to *Masters of Popular Painting: Modern Primitives of Europe and America* (1938), MoMA presented *Sculpture by William Edmondson,* (1937), asserting him as the first artist associated with the term "modern primitive."[16] More importantly, in this landmark exhibition, Edmondson became the first African American to receive a solo exhibition at MoMA.

The categorical strife into which Edmondson was born and raised certainly has invoked a mythic inheritance upon his narrative. His artistic legacy into the 21st century was astoundingly achieved under restrictions of race and circumstance, and this has contributed to his mythology. Edmondson's narrative was often communicated via a lens of marginalization. Hence, a more multifaceted account is required for a better understanding, contextualized by his history. Edmondson's solo exhibition was monumental, but it is imperative to acknowledge that it was not without the effects of the inherent and systemic racism of interwar America.

William Edmondson was born around 1874,[17] in Davidson County, Tennessee. His parents were enslaved until 1865 when Congress passed the 13th amendment abolishing slavery. Liberated from Compton Plantation, the Edmondsons continued to work the land for their previous owner. Raised on the plantation, Edmondson recollected that he was working in the cornfields as a teenager when he had his first divine vision of a flood. The flood concept emerges later as a motif in his practice, specific to its biblical significance. Following his father's death, his mother moved Edmondson and his siblings to Nashville in around 1900, in search of better opportunities. Along with his brother, Edmondson found work with the Nashville-Chattanooga and St. Louis Railroad until he was injured in 1907. Edmondson then worked several trades before securing long-term employment between a teacher's college and a white women's hospital. Records affirm that, by 1913, Edmondson was a property owner on 14th Ave in Nashville's mixed-race neighborhood of Edgehill. He further purchased the adjacent plot where his mother was residing. In 1922, following the death of his mother, his sister moved in and was followed eventually by their niece. There was an extended family community among the property. The strife of the Great Depression caused institutional closures throughout

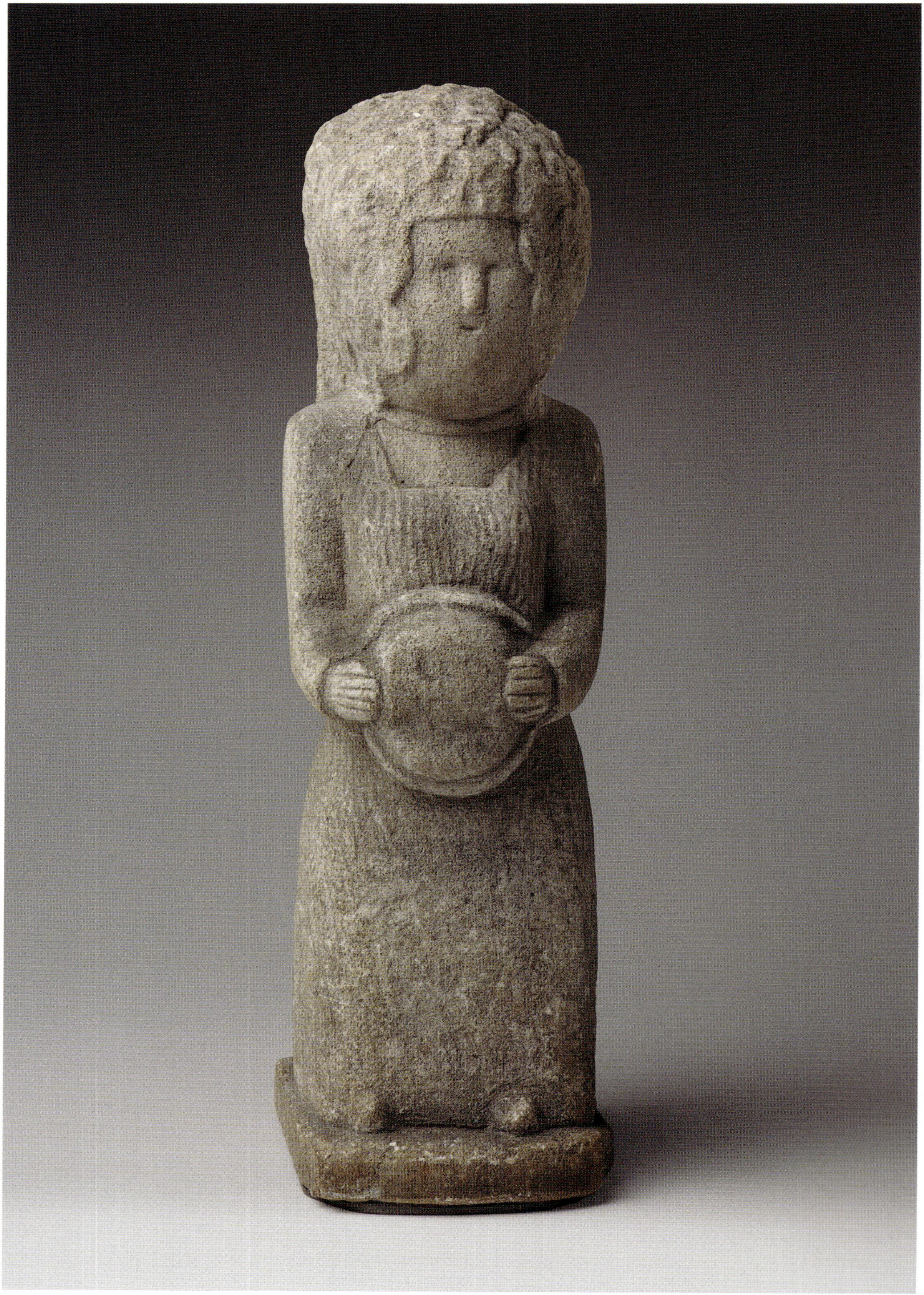

William Edmondson, Miss Louisa, *1933, limestone, 20 × 5¾ × 7½ in (50.8 × 14.6 × 19 cm). Philadelphia Museum of Art.* Often memorializing his local community, this carving is of Edmondson's neighbor, Miss Louisa. Carving regularly from Nashville's repurposed paver stones, the limestone's existing shape likely informed the narrowness of this sculpture.

Nashville, rendering Edmondson unemployed in 1931. At nearly 60 years old, following a few short-term employments (including assisting a stonemason), Edmondson stopped working when: "I was out in the driveway with some old pieces of stone when I heard a voice telling me to pick up my tools and start to work on a tombstone. I looked up in the sky and right there in the noon daylight He hung a tombstone out for me to make."[18]

Edmondson, newly converted, embarked on his new vocation of carving tombstones and subsequently—whether inspired by divinity or confidence in his creativity—ornamental sculptures. Visions and divine influence are important to his creative practice, but it is key to consider his personal heritage, memory, and culture as fundamental influences.[19] Edmondson's oeuvre converged religion, experience, and history—in particular, a sublime amphibology that merged the visual culture of Christianity and his local lived culture. Amid his subjects and symbols, his archetype of the dove assists in an examination for select interpretive context. Its emergence in his tombstone carvings echoed the mourning dove symbolism that materializes within Black burial traditions. The emblematic dove also was a signifier for liberation in African American Southern culture. A further connection can be drawn between carvings of paired doves that infer the biblical parable of Noah's Ark and the preparation of coupled

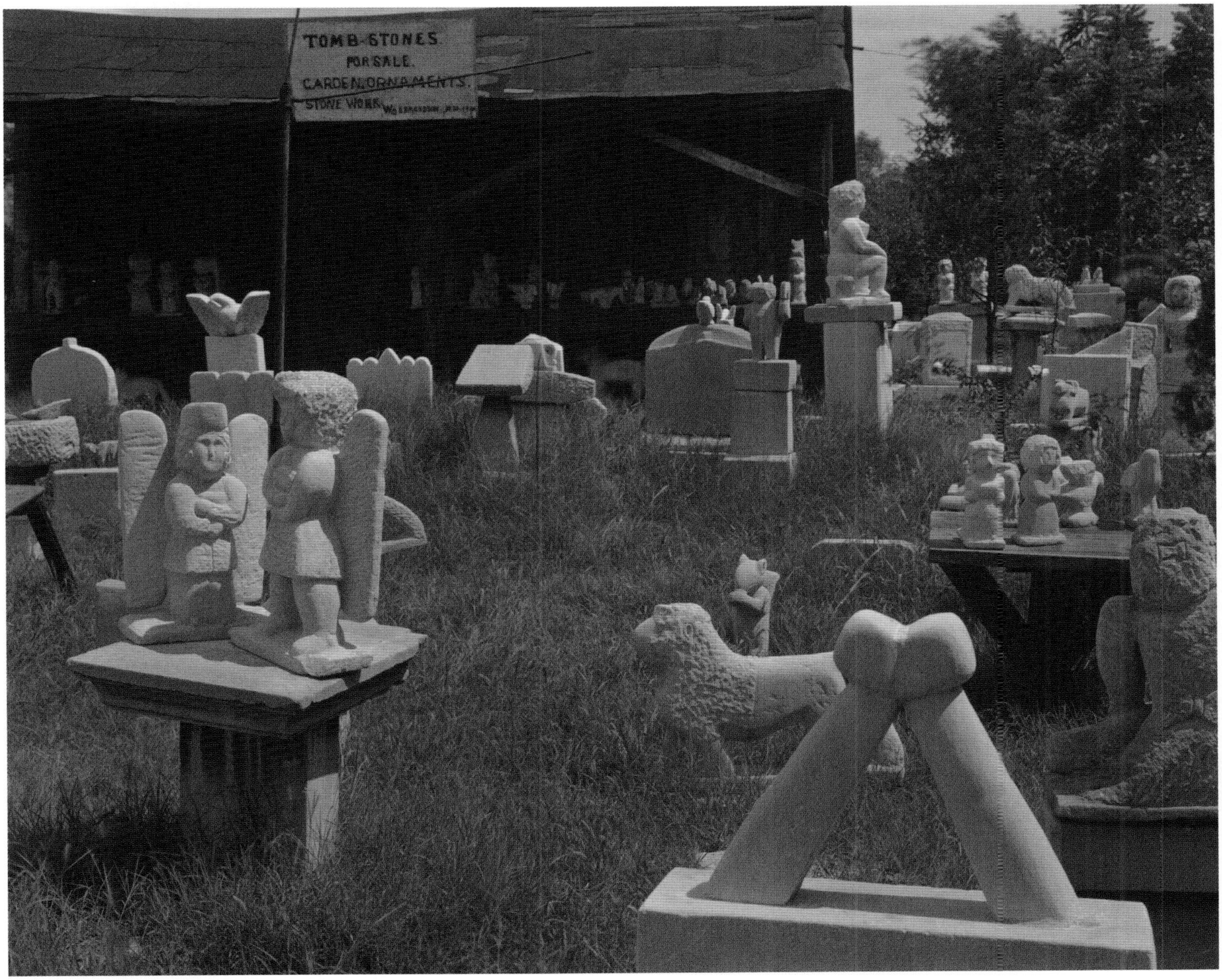

William Edmondson, 1941, photograph by Edward Weston (American, 1886–1958). Center for Creative Photography. This photograph of Edmondson's yard in his Edgehill neighborhood, taken in 1941 by Weston, shows the abundance of carvings on view for visitors and passersby, from tombstones and animals to figures. His display includes a sign that reads: TOMB-STONES. FOR SALE. GARDEN. ORNAMENTS. STONE WORK. Wm EDMONDSON.

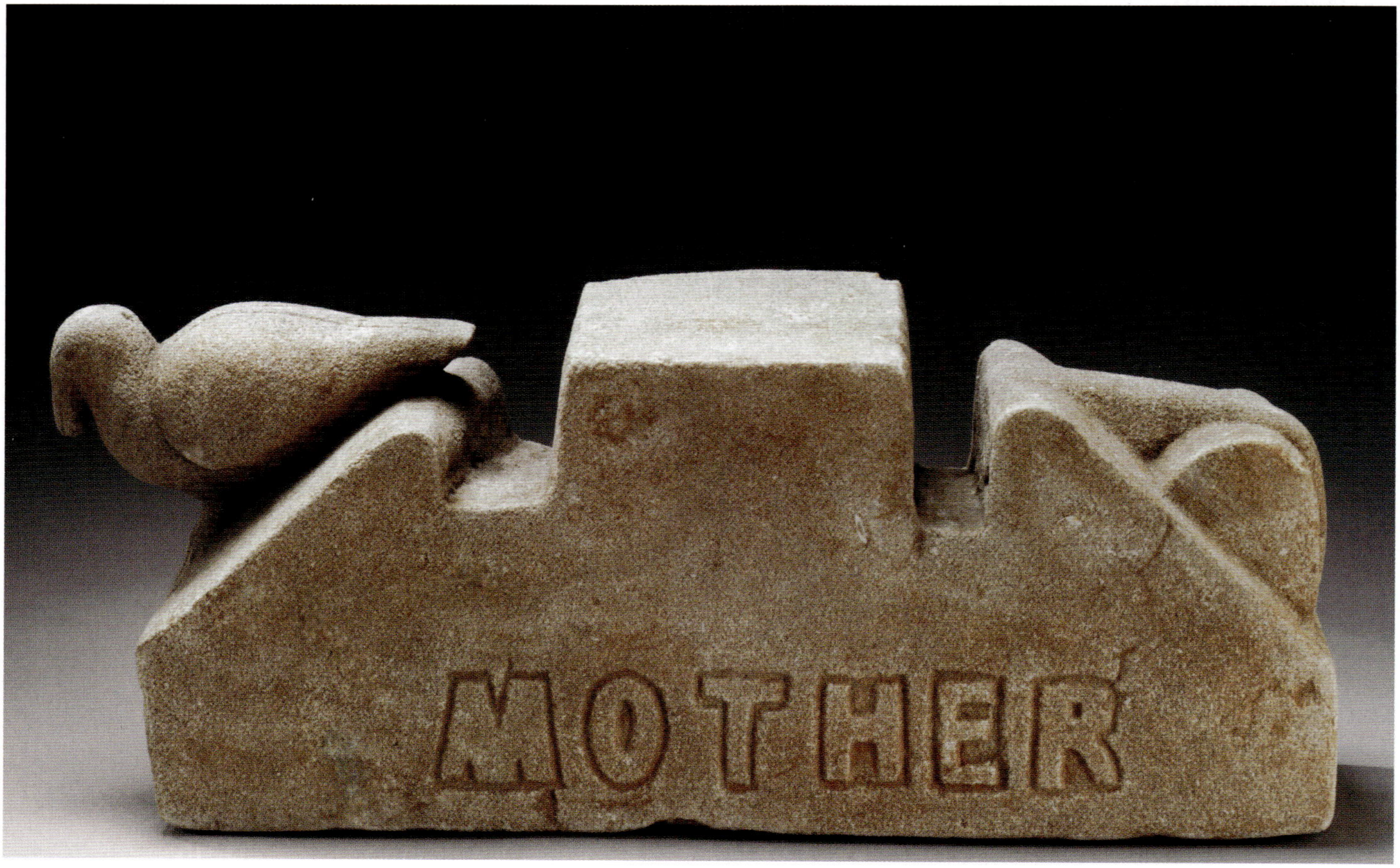

William Edmondson, Tombstone with Bird, *1934–1941, limestone, 6⅝ × 18¾ × 5¼ in (16.8 × 47.6 × 13.3 cm). The Newark Museum of Art.* Edmondson's sculpting began with the carving of tombstones, as seen here in a grave marker with distinct play between symmetry and asymmetry. This piece also introduces two key visuals in his sculptures: doves and his outlined engraved font, here stating MOTHER.

animals for the Great Flood, as Edmondson envisioned as a child.

Alongside his carvings of animals, which also included squirrels, turtles, and rams, his figurative depictions further emoted religious, personal, and cultural influences. He carved his neighbors *Miss Louisa* (1933) and *Bess and Jo* (ca. 1930–1937) and referenced a biblical narrative concerning two sisters in *Mary and Martha* (ca. 1930–1939). Like *Miss Louisa*, Edmondson memorialized his community and women he had worked with. Of the female characters, a celestial but authoritative angel is another motif. He also carved icons of African American culture, including his portrait of Eleanor Roosevelt—a primary political figure in the interwar popular culture for African Americans. Likely with Edmondson in attendance, she had visited Nashville on 18 November 1934.

One of the initiatives of President Roosevelt's New Deal was the reconstruction/modernization of the South. As a result, limestone walkways were being replaced with cement. These old paver stones were accessible and served as raw reused material for many of Edmondson's sculptures. His allowance of the inherent shape of sourced blocks to inform his aesthetic—often attributing the narrowness of his sculptures—aligned his process with adjacent concepts of Modernist sculpture. Those trends included returning to natural, found materials, and cutting or altering the material directly (as opposed to casting or molding). Using a hammer and chisel directly to the limestone, Edmondson had an incredible technique to capture texture, specifically observable in the tactile quality of the fur and hair. The inadvertent placement within the dialogue of Modernist sculpture lent an aesthetic desirable to the white art world.

Edmondson developed his creative skills and presented his practice publicly. Though it is not known if he had a community of fellow artists, he was not in a reclusive

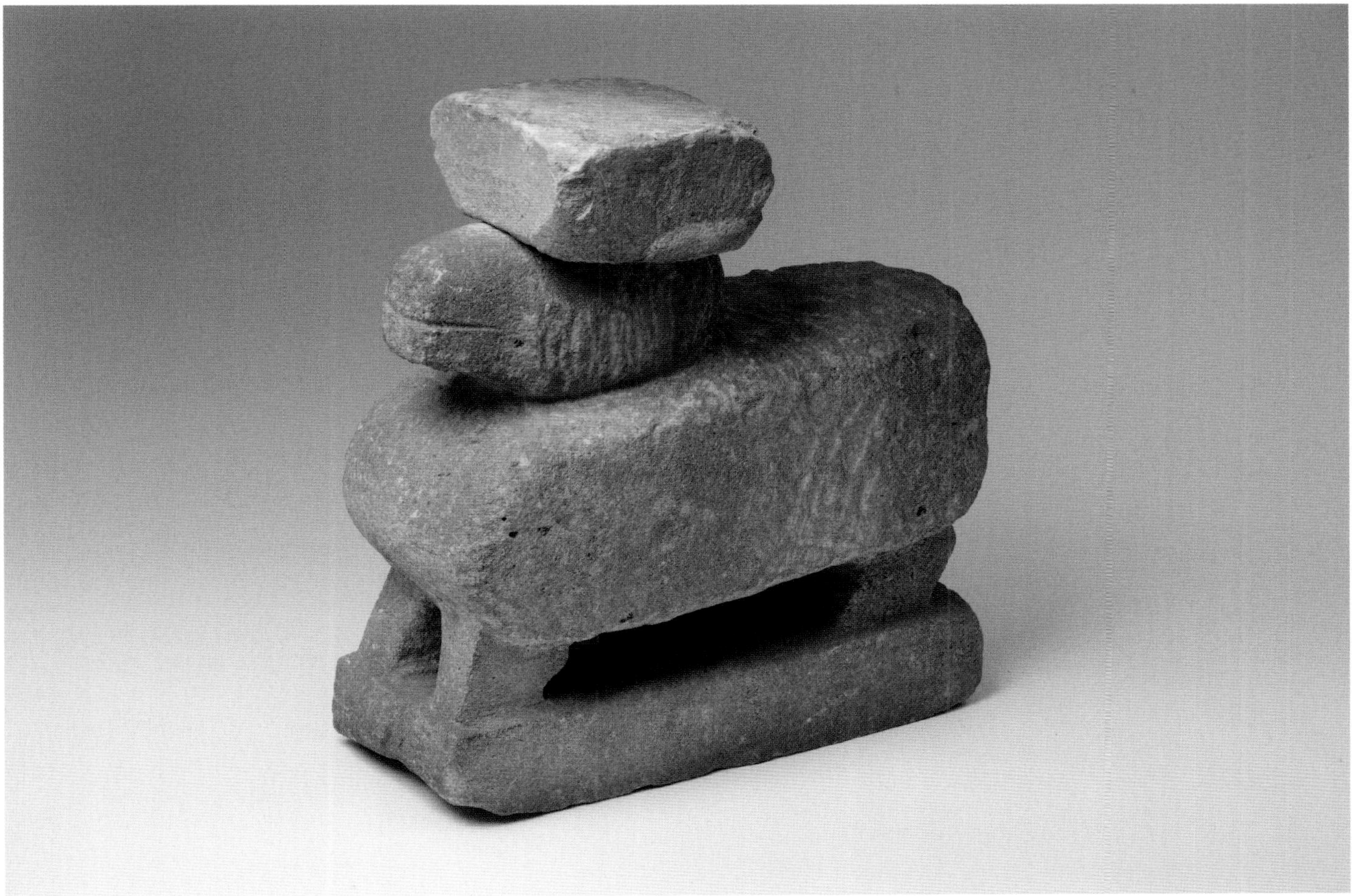

William Edmondson, Sheep, *n.d., limestone, 13½ × 12½ × 5½ in (34.3 × 31.8 × 14 cm). Philadelphia Museum of Art.* Edmondson had a penchant for sculpting animals, as seen here with his depiction of a sheep. This work is an unusual example in which he has placed a second piece of limestone on top of the main carving, creating a more complex physical composition.

or isolated position. Edmondson had local African American and white patrons buying his carvings. He assembled his yard for the community to encounter his work, punctuated by a wooden sign announcing his tombstones and garden ornaments were for sale. This point is key to the anti-discovery narrative for Edmondson explored in the following paragraphs.

In 1935, Sidney Hirsh, a white Nashvillian, visited Edmondson's home display of carvings. Hirsh was already a keen collector. Shortly after his initial visit, he introduced Edmondson to Alfred and Elizabeth Starr, who established themselves as significant supporters within Edmondson's lifetime. Their support came via acquisitions, an available stipend, and promotion of his work among progressive whites; the Starrs introduced him to photographers Edward Weston and pivotally, Louise Dahl-Wolfe. While both her and Weston's photographs have served as primary documentary archives for Edmondson, it was the circuitous route of the Dahl-Wolfe photographs of Edmondson in 1937 that would advance his position as the first African American to receive a solo exhibition at MoMA. Certainly, these white advocates facilitated the path to his landmark exhibition and deserve recognition for their support and promotion; however, their actions should not qualify as a heroic *discovery.*

Dahl-Wolfe was a staff photographer for *Harper's Bazaar,* where her editor showed interest in publishing Edmondson's portfolio; discouragingly, its publication was allegedly thwarted by racial prejudice[20]. The photographs found themselves with interim director of MoMA, Thomas Mabry, who, along with the Starrs, shipped 31 sculptures to New York and facilitated Edmondson's first exhibition. On October 20, 1937, *Sculpture by William Edmondson* opened in MoMA's temporary gallery at the Rockefeller Center. Agreed by Barr and curated by Dorothy Miller, it featured

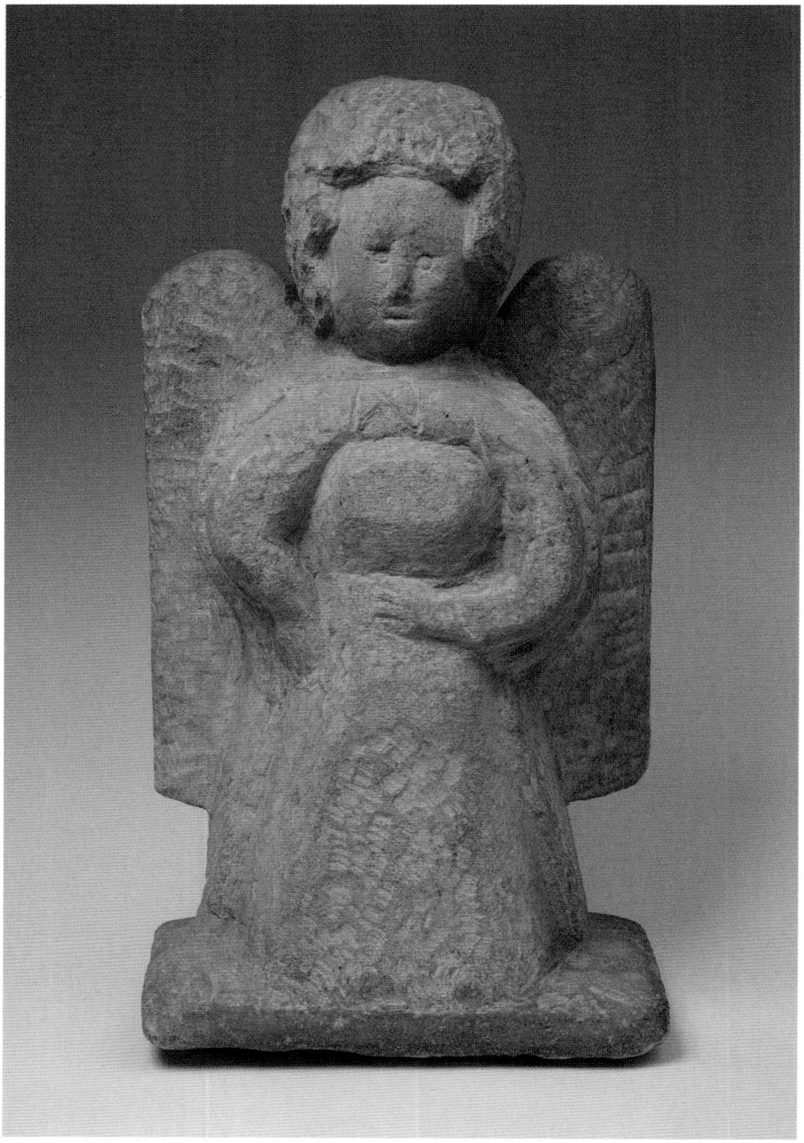

William Edmondson, Angel, *n.d., limestone, 22 × 12½ × 7 in (55.9 × 31.8 × 17.8 cm). Philadelphia Museum of Art.* The depiction of angels is a recurring motif in Edmondson's carvings, identified as celestial beings by their wings. His archetypal angels are characteristically frontal facing, often with forward-facing arms in a protective yet authoritative position. Further exuding strength is this angel's intense stare and textured wings.

12 sculptures and raised Edmondson's profile to national attention. The majority of research strongly indicates that he never made it to his exhibition.

There was a marketable racist lens to MoMA's presentation of Edmondson in 1937 that portrayed him in an overtly reductive tone. The presumption in the press release that "he has probably never seen a piece of sculpture not his own" is most likely inaccurate when taking into consideration Nashville's cultural landscape that included a full-scale replica of Athens' classical Parthenon. Also, given his years working for the railroad company, he presumably would have entered the city's union station, which featured ornate European reliefs, and given his vocation of carving tombstones he presumably visited the local cemeteries, which were teeming with sculptural forms. The press release also presented an extended phonetic quote to amplify his Southern dialect and the implication of Edmondson's illiteracy, seemingly to enforce further othering of Edmondson for his white audience. "Dies here sont n' all those out there in de yard—come from God. It's de word in Jesus speakin' his mind in my mind . . . These here is Mikels (miracles)"[21] These references and tone fed the wider press and marketing of Edmondson, pushing an agenda of an "unspoiled" isolation narrative[22], whereas, Edmondson's circumstance was not one of isolation. This is not to discount the contemporaneously progressive decision by MoMA to put forth the exhibition by an artist of color in New York, but it is important to understand it is not of mythical perfection.

Following the MoMA exhibition, *Mary and Martha* traveled to Europe for the *Museum of Modern Art: Three Centuries of American Art,* at the Musée du Jeu de Paume, Paris (1938). Edmondson was also employed by Tennessee's Federal Art Program between 1939 and 1941. He was included in *American Negro Art: 19th and 20th*

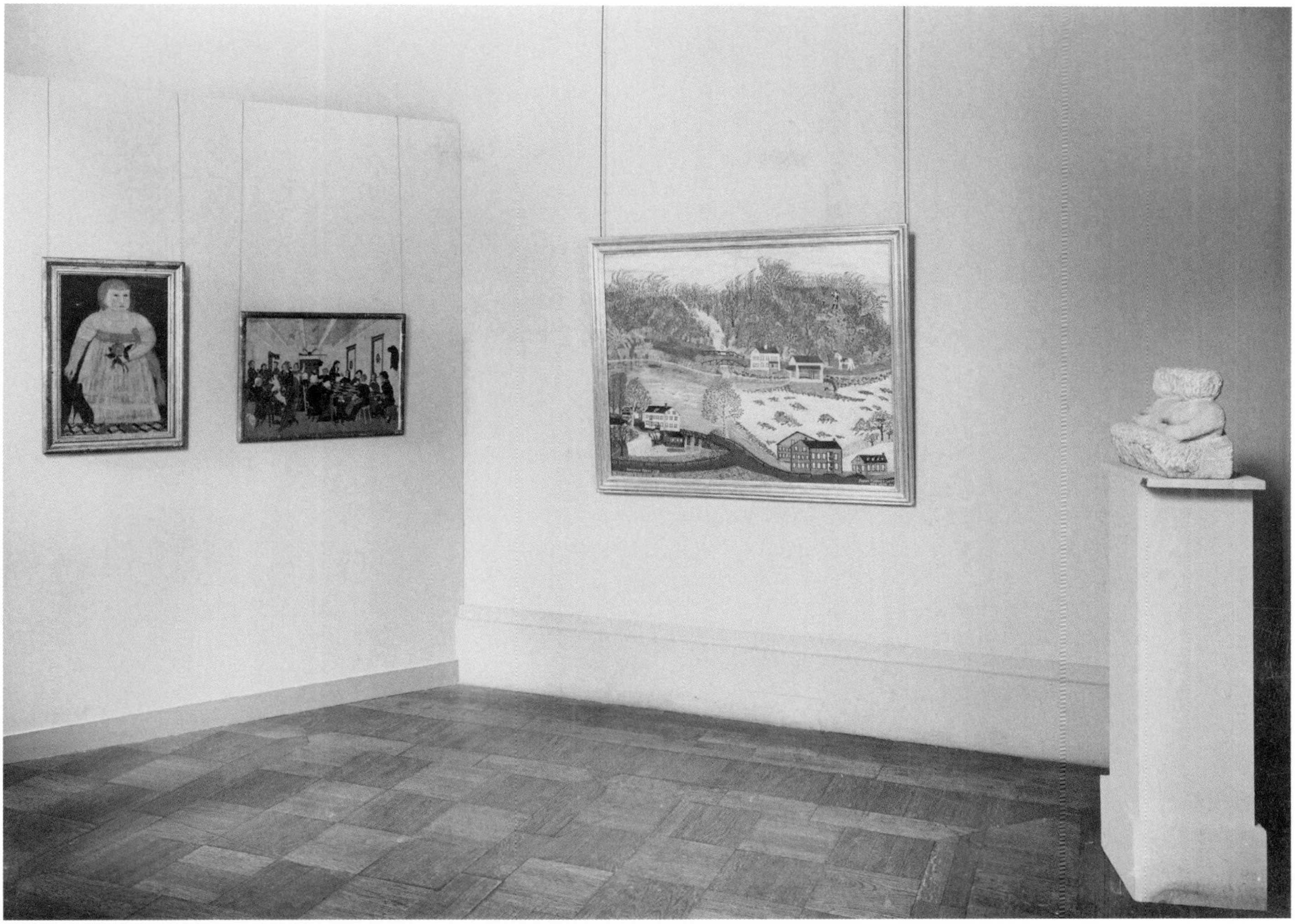

William Edmondson, installation view of the exhibition Three Centuries of American Art, *the Musée du Jeu de Paume, Paris, organized by the Museum of Modern Art, New York, May 24, 1938–July 31, 1938. Museum of Modern Art (MoMA), New York.* Following his solo exhibition at MoMA, New York (1937), Edmonson's sculpture, *Mary and Martha* (ca. 1930–1937), pictured here to the right on a plinth, was exhibited internationally in *Three Centuries of American Art*.

Centuries, Downtown Gallery, New York (1941), organized by Alain Locke and Edith Halpert. However, Edmondson was widely absent from institutional exhibitions toward the end of his life. He continued carving until 1950, when he became too ill to continue and passed away at the age of 76, in 1951.

Edmondson's posthumous resurgence commenced with his solo exhibition at the Fine Arts Center at Cheekwood, Nashville (1964), and his inclusion in *Black Folk Art in America, 1930–1980*, at the Corcoran Gallery, Washington, D.C. (1982). Into the 21st century, his practice has re-established itself as an important part of the dialogue of American art history, and his work is now in esteemed collections worldwide, with significant holdings by Cheekwood Botanical Garden and Museum of Art, Nashville; Newark Museum of Art, Newark, and the Philadelphia Museum of Art, Philadelphia. Edmondson is currently buried in an unmarked grave at Mt Ararat Cemetery in Nashville. Unfortunately, accounts such as this are not uncommon for African Americans amid the Jim Crow era. Edmondson left an emphatic legacy through the prominence of his carvings that wove together personal, cultural, and biblical histories.

HENRI ROUSSEAU

(1844, Laval–1910, Paris, France)

Historically referred to as the insiders' first "outsider," Henri Rousseau's vivid paintings were seductive to European avant-garde artists and American modernists alike. Nicknamed *Le Douanier* (French for customers officer, though he was actually a municipal inspector), he only dedicated himself to painting after retirement in 1884. Rousseau began exhibiting shortly after with his inclusion in the Parisian exhibition *Salon des Indépendants* (1886), which was open to any participant, academically trained or self-taught, who paid a fee of 15 franc. This became a key platform for Rousseau, which led to his recognition among avant-garde artists including Max Weber and Pablo Picasso. His oeuvre of landscapes and portraits stemmed from visual reality but was laden with, perhaps unintentionally, audacious humor. After Rousseau's death, Weber organized a presentation in 1910 of his paintings at Alfred Stieglitz's New York gallery. While he became a key figure for MoMA's formation of modern primitives, Rousseau had exhibited at the museum before, including *Cubism and Abstract Art* (1936) and *Fantastic Art, Dada, Surrealism* (1937), followed by *Masters of Popular Painting: Modern Primitives of Europe and America* (1938).

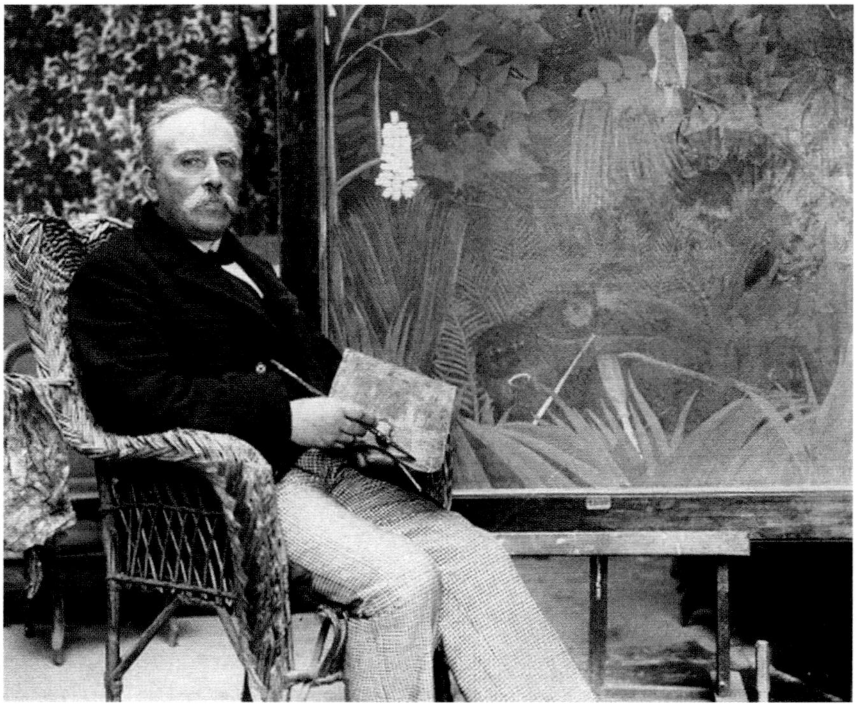

Henri Rousseau, 1907, photograph. This portrait of Rousseau in his studio features one of his jungle paintings, *Merry Jesters*. His first jungle painting was in 1891, but following a hiatus from this theme he recommenced on exotic motifs in 1904, possibly after seeing the Tahitian paintings of Paul Gauguin.

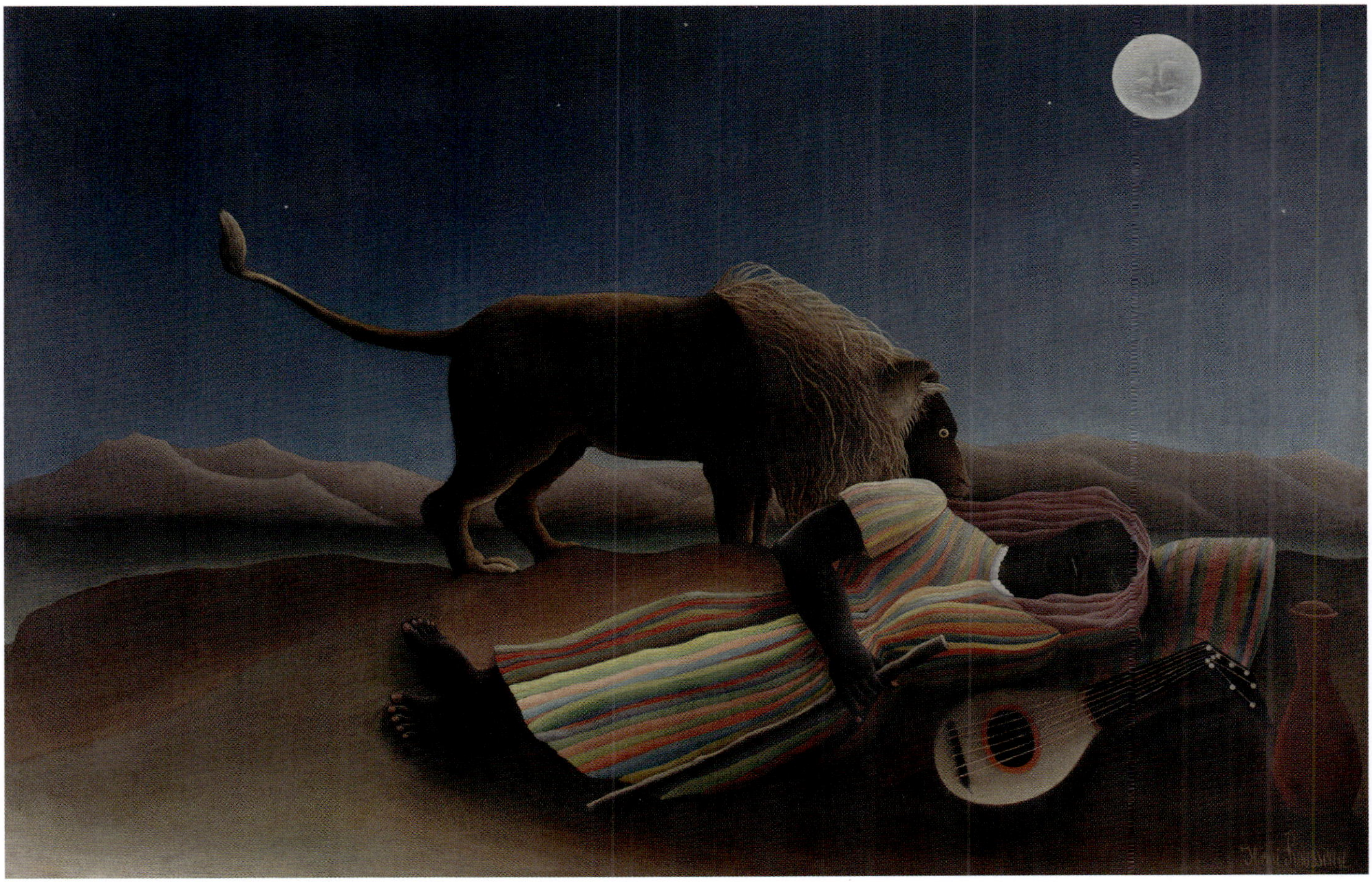

Henri Rousseau, The Sleeping Gypsy, *1897, oil on canvas, 51 × 79 in (129.5 × 200.7 cm). Museum of Modern Art (MoMA), New York.* This painting has a dreamlike and surreal quality through Rousseau's use of flat perspective with undulating horizontal lines and the juxtaposition of elements.

Rousseau, along with many of his creative peers took great interest in the Romany people known as *bohémiens* in France, contemporaneously referred to as wandering gypsies.

Though Henri Rousseau, as a self-taught artist, was accepted and acclaimed among the European art world elite during his lifetime, the aesthetic power of his paintings was inherent to their naive quality or imperfect technique. Rousseau combined visual cultural references familiar to him, using these as a tool to form his compositions and subjects. Among the most distinct of his themes are his jungle paintings. Rousseau never traveled outside of France, so his fantastical jungles are imaginary collages of his accessible references: the zoo, botanical gardens, magazines, and publications. Rousseau's oeuvre navigated a curious occupation within the representational genres of landscape and portraiture from where he departed. This precipitous position within these traditions was playful and sublime, especially when compared to his academically trained peers.

Whether it was to embrace whichever path led to success or an inner turmoil, historical accounts question whether Rousseau embellished the characteristic of naivety within his personality. His autobiographical notes suggested he longed to be a painter from a young age but without the means for academic training, he felt inferior to engage artistically. Regardless of his methods, his intentions for artistic success were clear, and with his paintings being appreciated shortly after he began painting in 1884, the start of the 20th century marked incredible notoriety for the artist in Europe.

Following his posthumous growing success in America and institutional exhibitions in the 1930s, MoMA's first director Alfred Barr Jr. acquired Rousseau's *Sleeping Gypsy* (1897) for the museum in 1939. The painting also took the most prominent view for MoMA's permanent collection installation dedicated to modern primitives (1941–1944).

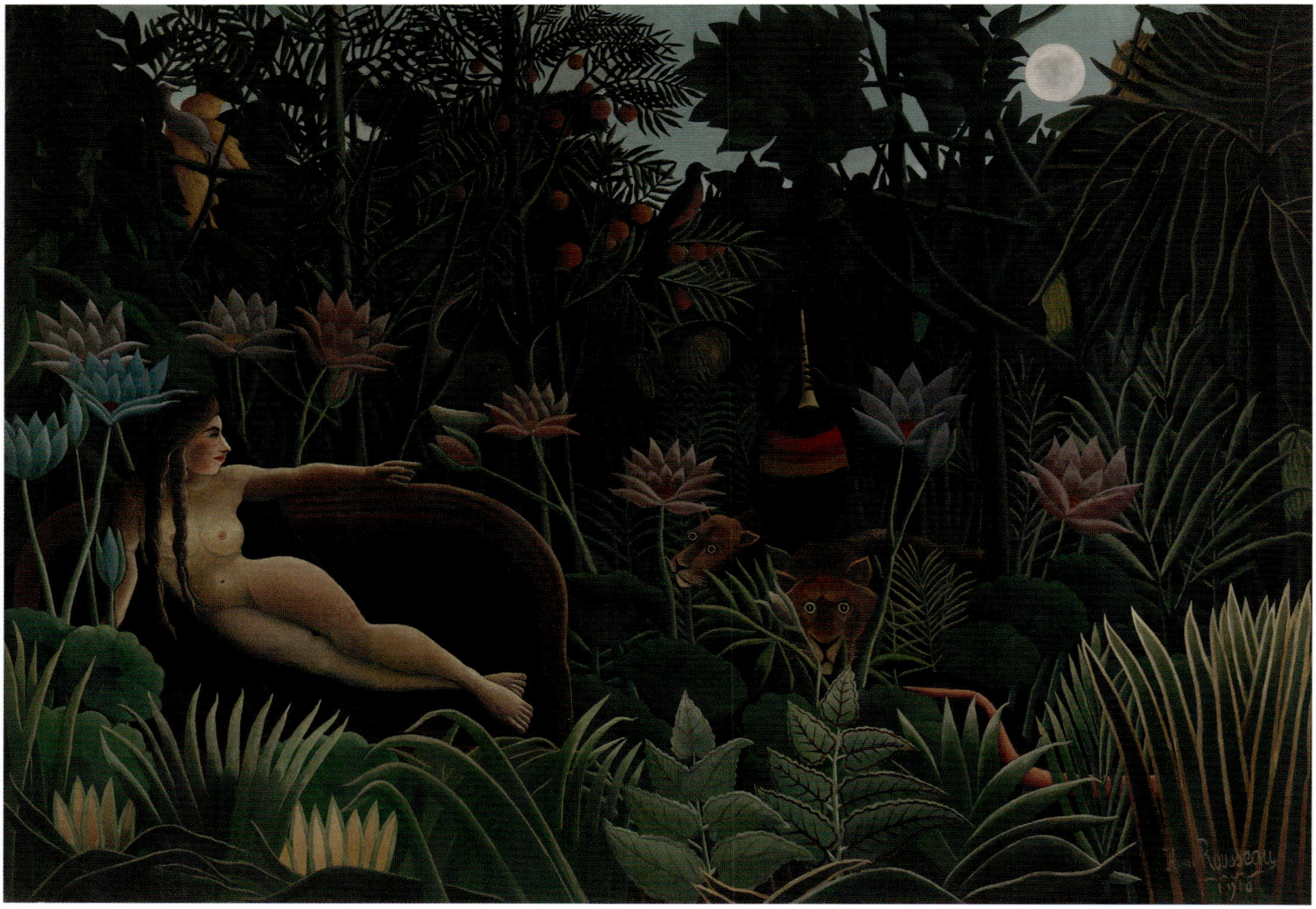

Henri Rousseau, The Dream, *1910, oil on canvas, 80½ × 117½ in (204.5 × 298.5 cm). Museum of Modern Art (MoMA), New York*. Rousseau's jungle paintings were influenced by the Jardin des Plantes, a Parisian zoo and botanical garden. An archetype of this oeuvre, Rousseau said of this painting: "The woman asleep on the couch is dreaming she has been transported into the forest, listening to the sounds from the instrument of the enchanter."

Henri Rousseau, Carnival Evening, *1886, oil on canvas, 46³⁄₁₆ × 35¼ in (117.3 × 89.5 cm). Philadelphia Museum of Art.* This early painting by Rousseau depicts an eerie wintry forest-scape and was selected for the *Salon des Indépendants*, Paris (1886), his first exhibition opportunity. Indicated by the title as a night scene, the central two figures in carnival costume illuminate as if lit from within, rather than by moonlight.

"Nothing makes me so happy as to observe nature and to paint what I see. Just imagine, when I go out into the countryside and see the sun and the green and everything flowering, I say to myself, 'Yes indeed, all that belongs to me!'" – Henri Rousseau[23]

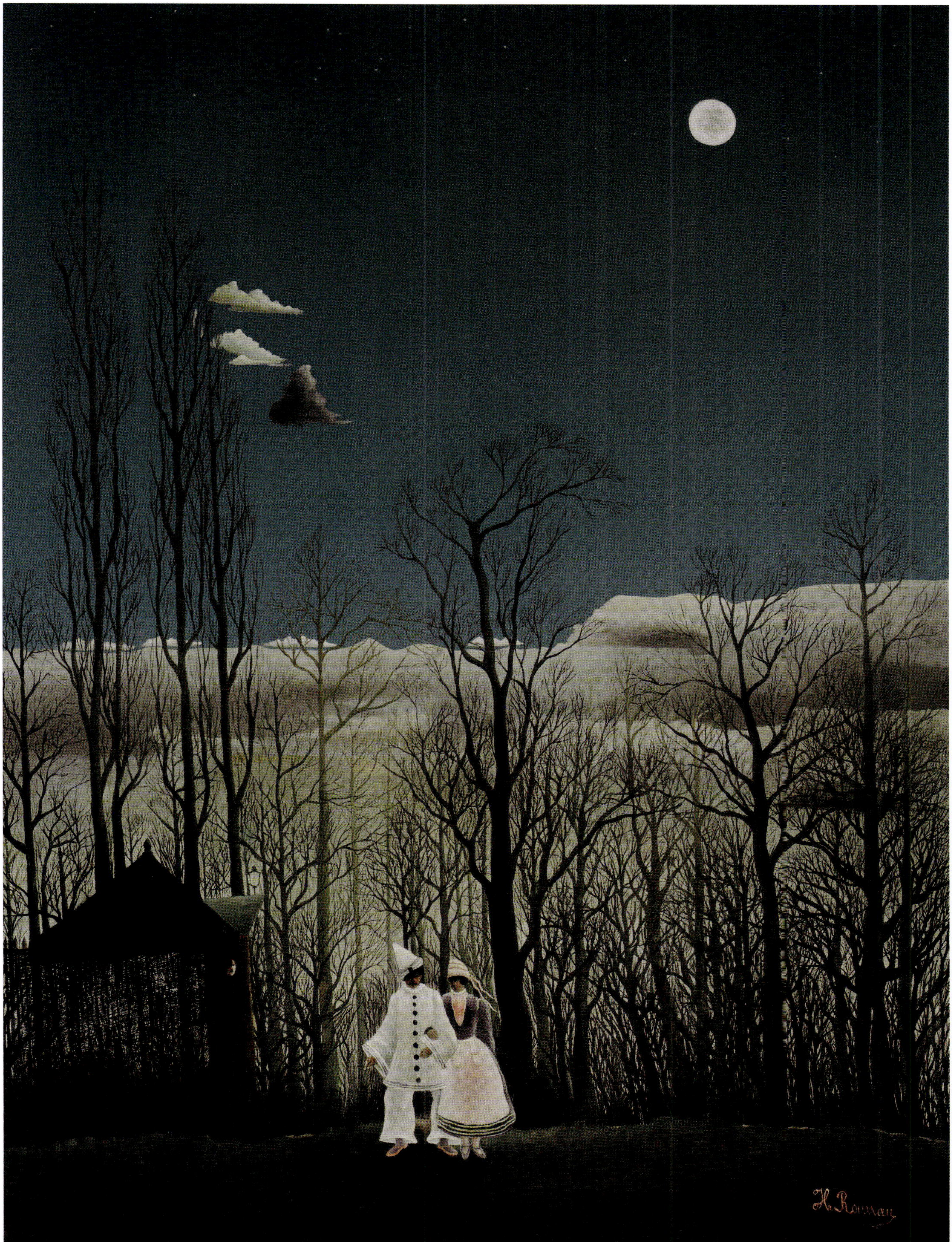
H. Rousseau

JOHN KANE

(1860, West Calder, Scotland–1934, Pittsburgh, Pennsylvania, USA)

John Kane became the foremost celebrated self-taught artist of his time following his institutional debut at the Carnegie International, Pittsburgh, PA (1927). Kane, who was painting by trade, was a controversial inclusion to the juried exhibition as a nonacademic artist. Born in Scotland to Irish parents, he emigrated to America at the age of 18 to work in the mines. However, after a train accident that resulted in his leg being amputated, his physical labor opportunities were limited. Completing approximately 150 paintings in his lifetime, he became most widely known for his poetically disproportionate landscapes, particularly of Pittsburgh, which held a dichotomy of pastoral and industrial. Challenging the parameters of self-taught artists from 1927 until his death, Kane exhibited regularly in Pittsburgh and was lauded by prominent collectors and patrons. Posthumously, 1938 marked a significant year for Kane, as he was featured in *Vogue*'s "Four American Artists Look at America" alongside artist Edward Hopper and furthermore, his paintings were included in *Masters of Popular Painting: Modern Primitives of Europe and America* at MoMA and *Three Centuries of American Art*, Musée du Jeu de Paume, Paris, France (1938).

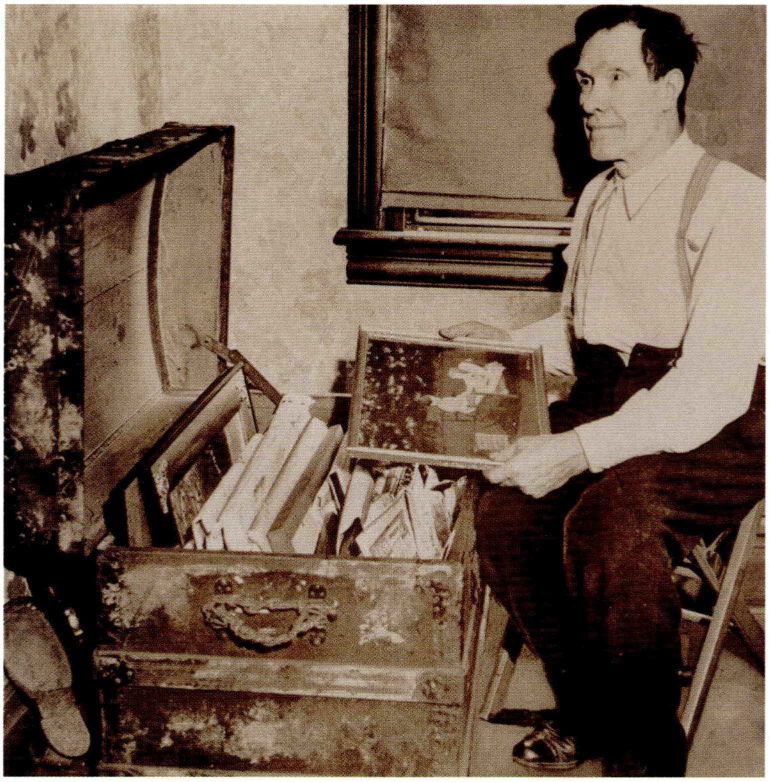

John Kane, n.d., photograph. Carnegie Museum of Art. This early-20th-century portrait of the artist shows Kane posing with a trunk of paintings.

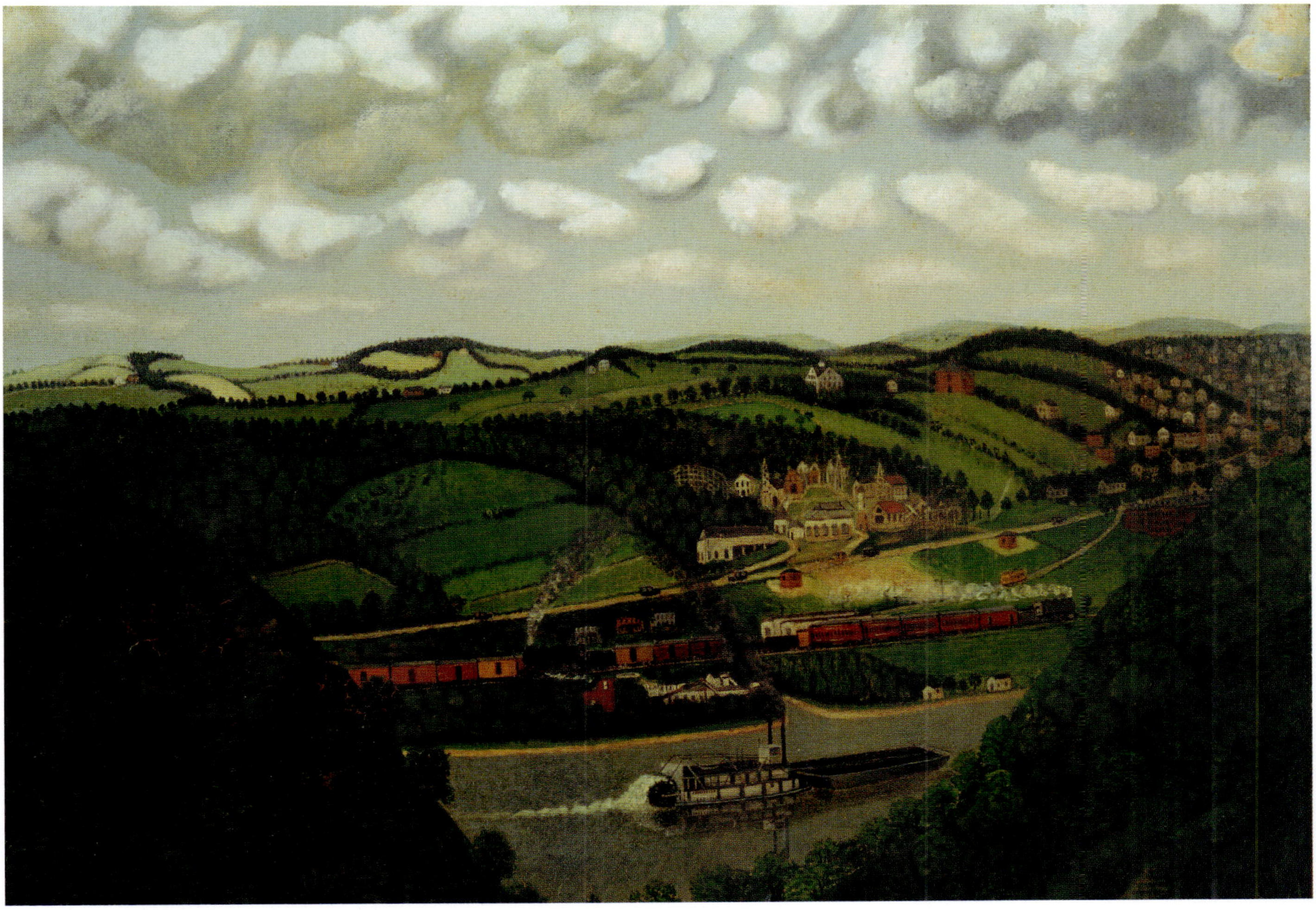

John Kane, Through Coleman Hollow up the Allegheny Valley, *ca. 1928, oil on canvas, 30 × 38⅝ in (76.2 × 98.1 cm). Museum of Modern Art (MoMA), New York.* Although originally omitted from the 1929 Carnegie International with the jurors' selection of Kane's painting *Homestead* (ca. 1929), *Through Coleman Hollow up the Allegheny Valley* was the start of his archetypal paintings featuring locomotives and industrial transport interwoven with pastoral hills.

Prior to settling in the United States, John Kane had been working in the Scottish mines since the age of nine. Manual labor continued to be his means of working in America until his disability from a train accident in 1891 reduced his employment opportunities. With his physical limitations, he found work painting for a Pennsylvania car company in 1897. Though decades before the Carnegie International, it was here that Kane began experimenting with painting as a medium—testing out techniques of shadowing and mixing colors. As Kane established his own aesthetic, his personal identity as a working-class Scottish American immigrant served as a departure point in both overt and subvert ways.

Kane was called the Poet Laureate of Pittsburgh[24]. His eminent landscapes were recognized for re-introducing pastoral notions of the Midwest among the contemporaneous industry of Pennsylvania. His anti-precision, or "lack of technique," presented a rugged but

"I helped to build its steel mills and homes; I paved its streets, made its steel, and painted its houses. It is my city; why shouldn't I paint it? ' – John Kane[26]

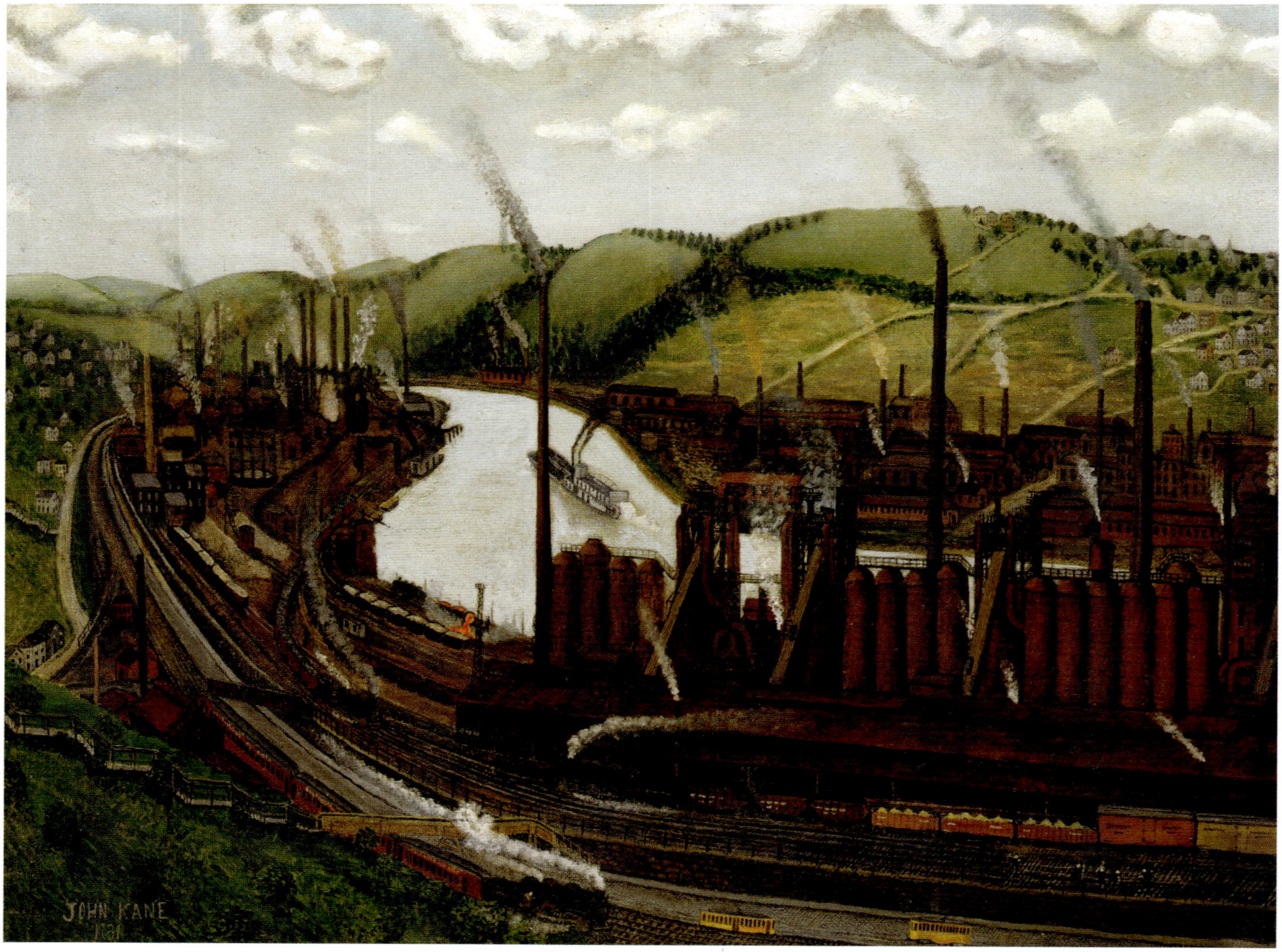

John Kane, The Monongahela River Valley, Pennsylvania, *1931, oil on canvas, 28 × 38 in (71.1 × 96.5 cm). Metropolitan Museum of Art, New York.* This painting is an exceptional example of Kane's pictorial amalgamation of industrial and pastoral in a single scene. Railroads, trains, boxcars, and steamboats all invigorate the painting with a celebratory nod to industry while the rolling hills are also rendered with respect in the background.

John Kane, Self-Portrait, *1929, oil on canvas over composition board, 36 ⅛ × 27 ⅛ in (91.8 × 68.9 cm). Museum of Modern Art (MoMA), New York.* This self-portrait, with its raw reality, is considered one of the most impactful paintings by Kane. The blunt depiction of bare chest and aging face is framed with ornamental decoration presenting his portrait for display. *Self-Portrait* was exhibited in both *Musée du Jeu de Paume*, Paris (1938) and *Modern Primitives: Artists of the People*, MoMA, New York (1941–1944).

poetic reality to the landscapes. As noted by art historian Katherine Jentleson in an examination of his tactics of precision: "Kane both deviated from and stayed true to his subject."[25] Furthermore, there is a polarization between the serenity of how Kane painted an industrial Pittsburgh and considerations of what he, as an immigrant miner at the end of the 19th century, would have experienced first hand.

Though Kane was primarily revered for his depictions of Pittsburgh, one of his most iconic paintings is a self-portrait from 1929. In this haunting work, Kane addressed the industrialization of his Midwest environment via the autonomous lens of self-portrait. He presented himself as the American working man, staring into a mirror with an enduring gaze and exposed emotions.

"Rarely has an artist revealed himself so unflinchingly. At the same time, by the curious canopy and the strange formality of the pose (as if he were a priest or dead), the artist has given his lean, aging nakedness an austere, even awe-inspiring dignity."– Alfred Barr Jr., art historian and the first director of the Museum of Modern Art (New York) on Kane's *Self-Portrait*.[27]

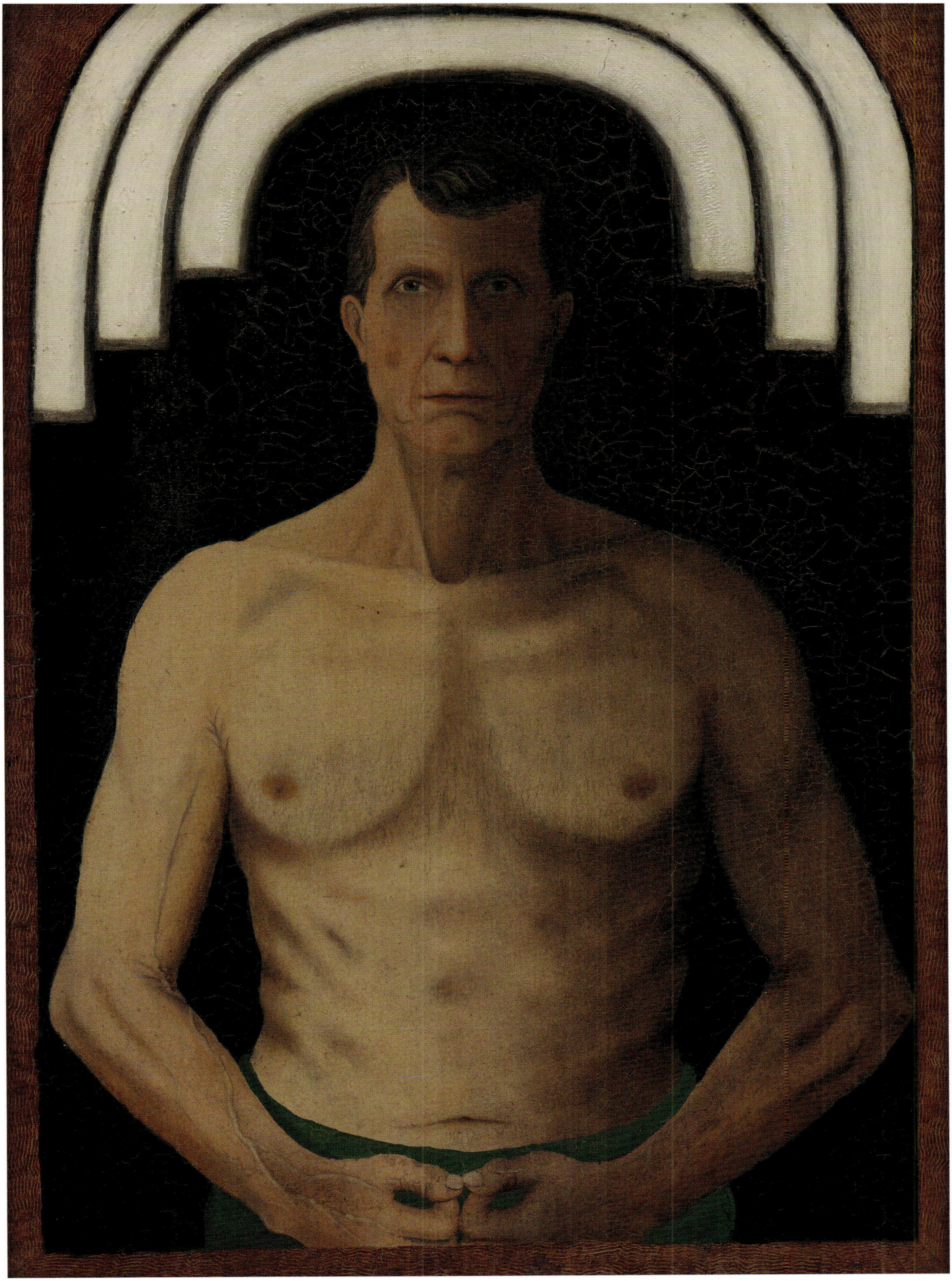

MORRIS HIRSHFIELD

(1872, Western Poland–1946 New York, New York, USA)

At the age of 18, Morris Hirshfield emigrated to America from his native Poland, initially working in a coat factory and eventually owning two fashion manufacturing businesses. Hirshfield's experience in the garment industry heavily influenced his artistic practice, as evident from his patterning process to his surreal detailed textures. He started painting after retirement in 1937 executing with such laborious detail that it took him until 1939 to complete his first two paintings. With the support of Brooklyn museum curator John I.H. Baur, these inaugural paintings—*Angora Cat* and *Beach Girl*—were included in *Contemporary Unknown American Painters* (1939), curated by gallerist Sidney Janis for MoMA's "members' room." His paintings received high acclaim from both artworld critics and the surrealists. After his inclusion in MoMA's *Modern Primitives: Artists of the People* (1941), the museum presented the extensive solo exhibition *The Paintings of Morris Hirshfield* (1943). Though adversely received, its scale and rigor was a landmark for self-taught artists.

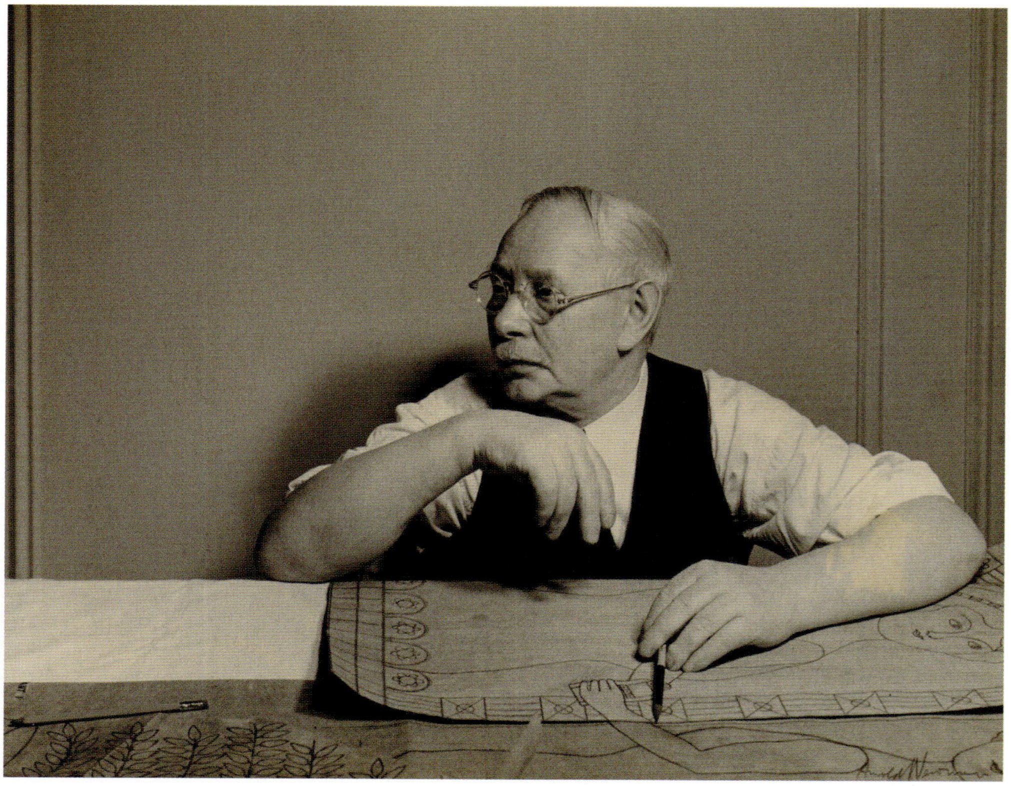

Morris Hirshfield, ca. 1950, photograph by Arnold Newman (American, 1981–2006). This portrait of Hirshfield, with his sketches on the table, demonstrates his process of drafting a composition for a painting first on paper, then tracing it onto the canvas. This patterning-like process was perhaps influenced by his years working in the garment industry.

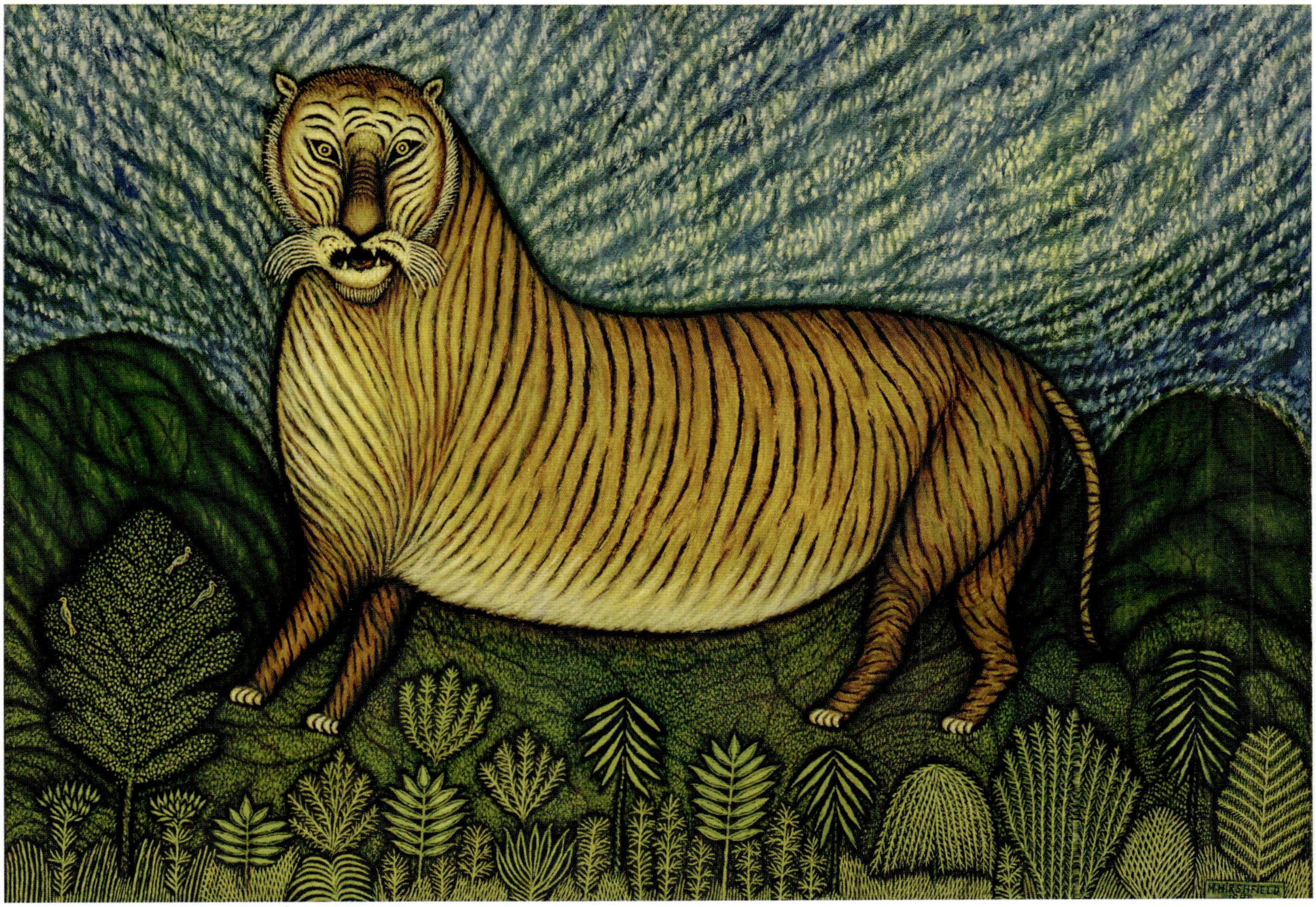

Morris Hirshfield, Tiger, *1940, oil on canvas, 28 × 39⅞ in (71.1 × 101.3 cm). Museum of Modern Art (MoMA), New York.* This painting was included in MoMA's *Modern Primitives: Artists of the People* (1941–1944). With its highly textured surface, perhaps echoing the textiles of Hirshfield's former profession. MoMA's founding director, Alfred H. Barr, Jr. considered *Tiger* to be the most "unforgettable animal picture."

Morris Hirshfield's career in the clothing industry spanned almost 50 years and included ownership of two garment manufacturing companies. The first, co-owned with his brother, fabricated women's suits and coats, while the latter, more successful, business manufactured slippers. The influences of the apparel industry, omnipresent in Hirshfield's oeuvre, resulted in exquisitely executed details.

Mimicking the fashion patterning process, Hirshfield would draft a full-scale composition on paper first, then trace it onto the canvas (the paper drawing was recognized as a tool only and discarded). His highly detailed painting technique also included the rendering of patterns reminiscent of tweed and knit textiles. Unusual and inventive textures featured heavily throughout his canvases, with considerable detail paid to the execution of upholstery, drapes, or fabrics. Emotionally charged, the canvases palpitate specifically from his distinct patterned repetitions and symmetrical techniques.

Hirshfield was unaware of contemporaneous avant-garde movements, yet his cryptically alluring textures aligned with surrealism. Hirshfield's style painted objects as if they were in a near-levitating state and gave them a dreamlike perspective. These conceptual and stylistic choices further affiliated him with the fantastical juxtapositions produced by surrealists' Max Ernst and Salvador Dalí. This alignment led to Hirsfield's inclusion in the New York exhibition *First Papers of Surrealism* (1942), the first official surrealist exhibition in America. It was directed by André Breton, who also published Hirshfield's *American Beauty (Nude with Mirror)* in his 1972 edition of *Surrealism and Painting*.

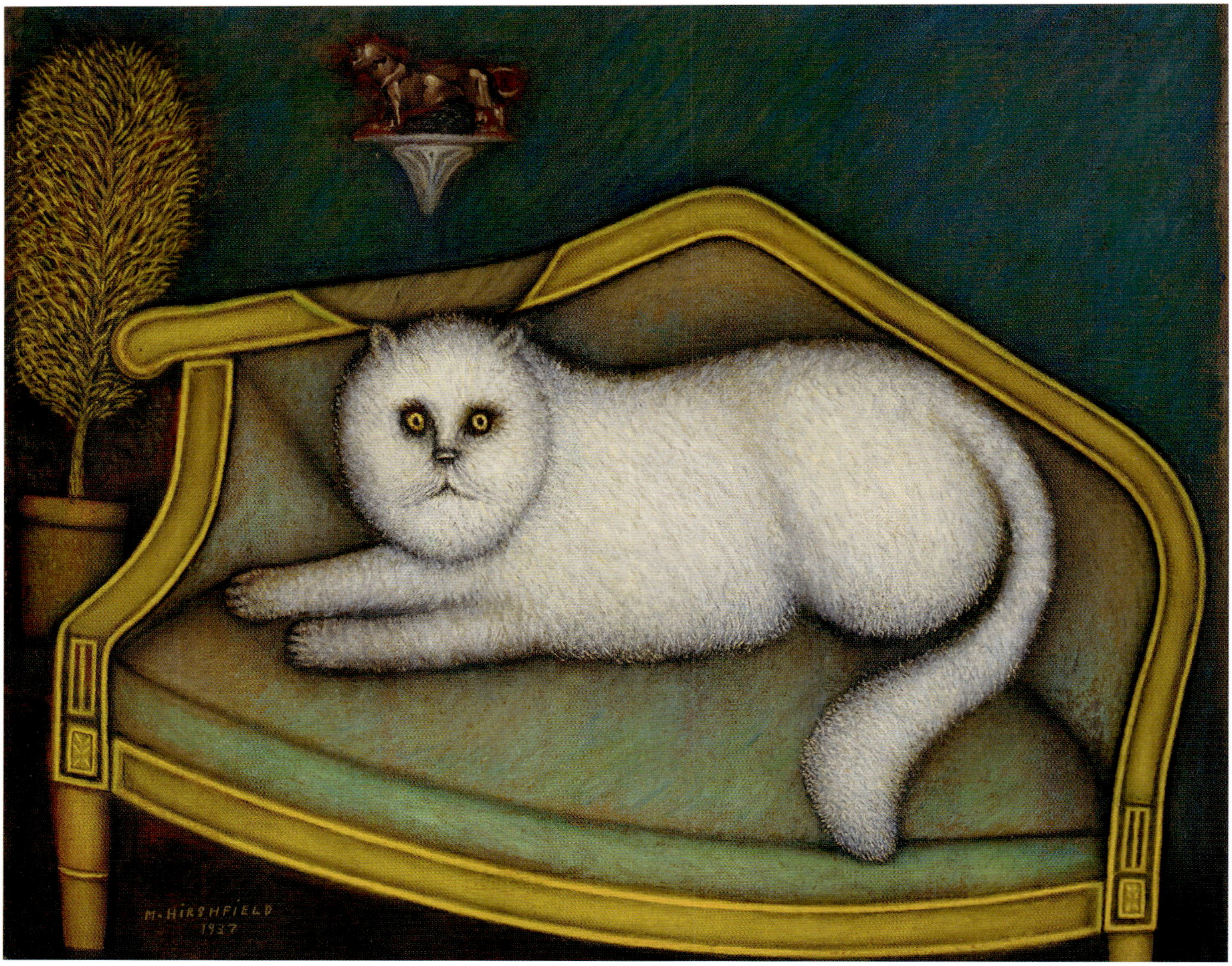

Morris Hirshfield, Angora Cat, *1937–1939 (date on painting 1937), oil on canvas, 22⅛ × 27¼ in (56.1 × 69.1 cm). Museum of Modern Art (MoMA), New York.* The expansive but awkward position of the cat symbolizes Hirshfield's domestic conflict: his wife was unencouraging of him developing an artistic practice. The cat became a dominating feminine symbol, while the small lion on a pedestal behind is representative of masculinity. Strange and mysterious, the bizarre quality of the couch is lauded as giving the painting a sense of humor.

Hirshfield's process was labor-intensive and meticulous, which led him to complete only 74 paintings between 1937 and his death in 1946. His compositions required covering the canvas completely and often centrally focused on a woman or animal. Whether feline or female, Hirshfield's characters' gaze uncannily balances between confident and self-conscious. His women are formally posed and often framed by decorative elements. This construct reconfirms his dedication to eerie interior decoration and sublime ornamentation.

"To Hirshfield the reality is the actual brushstroke, the manipulation of paint and of color." – Sidney Janis (1896–1989), American art dealer, collector, and writer[28]

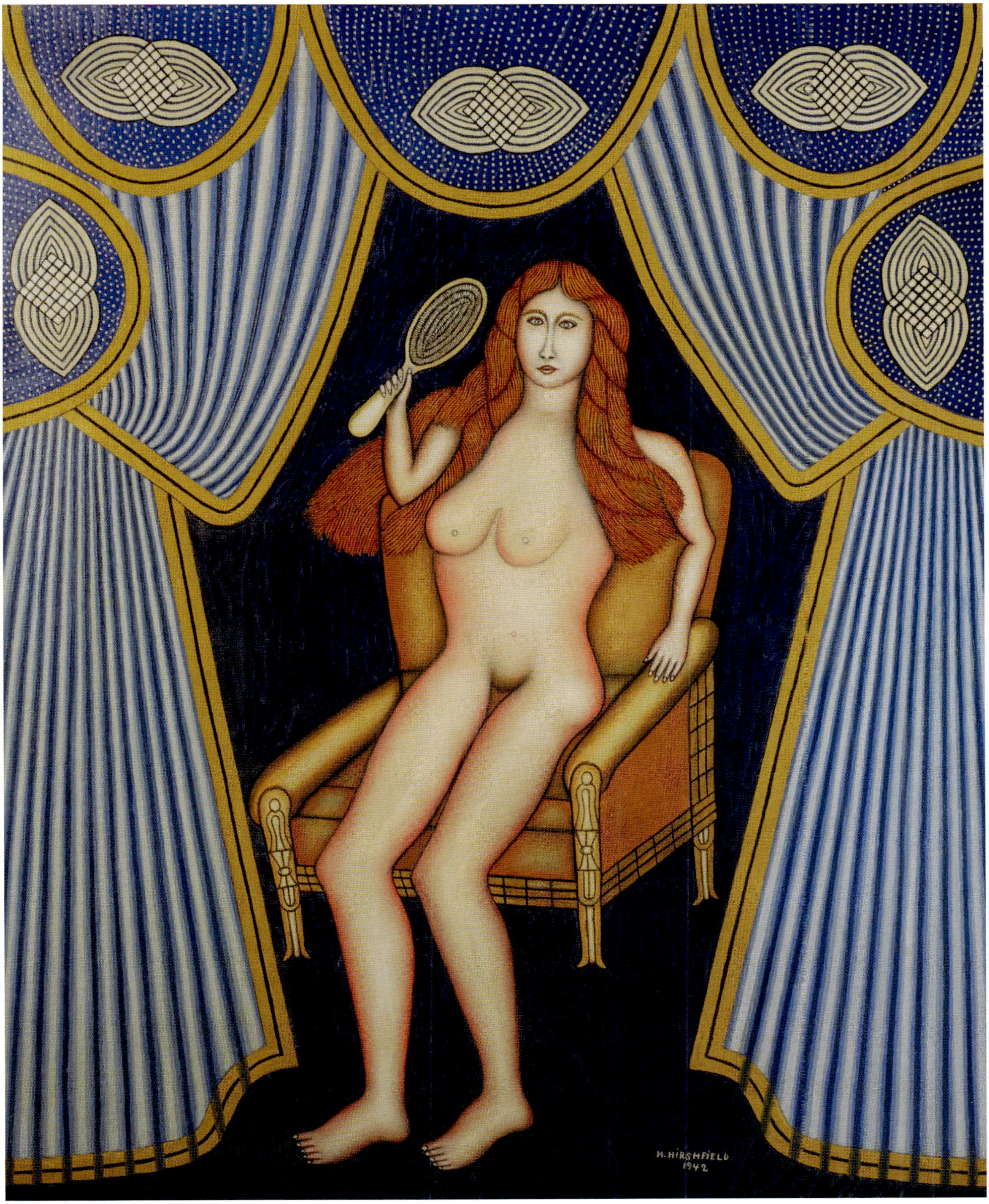

Morris Hirshfield, American Beauty (Nude with Mirror), *1942, oil on canvas, 18¹⁵⁄₁₆ × 15¾ in (48 × 40 cm). Collection Mickey Cartin.* Though Hirshfield did not paint from live models, his interest in the female form can be observed in its detailed execution. The dreamlike qualities, including the ambiguity between floor and background, demonstrate Hirshfield's association with, and appreciation of, the surrealists.

HORACE PIPPIN

(1888–1946, West Chester, Pennsylvania, USA)

Horace Pippin painted recollections of wartime, moments of African American life, interpretations of history, and portraits, registering him as one of the most distinguished African American artists of his generation. Considered an entirely self-taught artist, his paintings are characterized by their bold colors and authentic spatial perspective. His first solo exhibition was held in 1937 at the West Chester Community Center. Despite being held in a segregated venue, his debut received diversely wide acclaim and led to his inclusion as the only African American artist in the exhibition *Masters of Popular Painting: Modern Primitives of Europe and America* at MoMA (1938). Pippin's artistic recognition straddled the complex lines of both race and the validity of self-taught artists. Key advocates of Pippin included art dealer Robert Carlen and scholar Alain Locke. In 1947, Pippin became the first African American artist to be the subject of a monograph, *Horace Pippin, a Negro Painter in America*. Pippin's work was featured in *Outliers and American Vangard Art*, National Gallery of Art, Washington, D.C., (2018) and in *Gatecrashers: The Rise of the Self-Taught Artist in America*, High Museum of Art, Atlanta (2021).

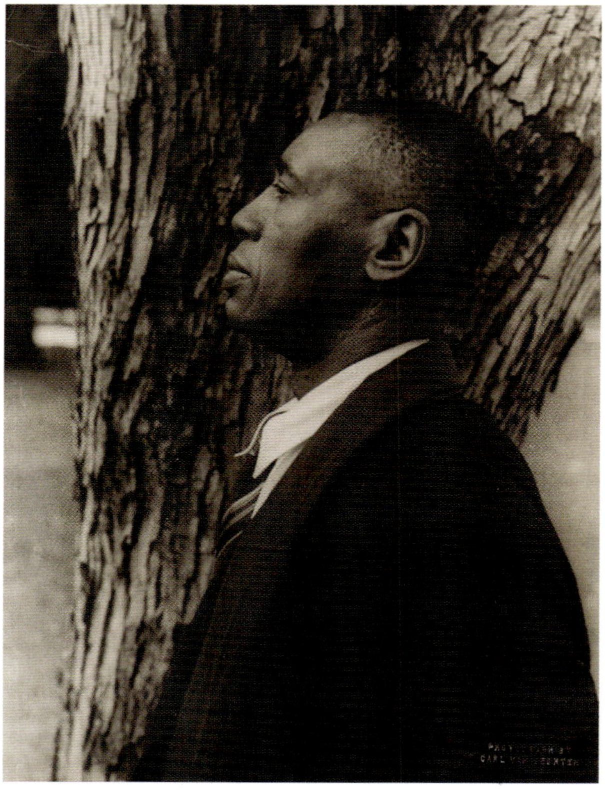

Horace Pippin, 1940, photograph by Carl Van Vechten (American, 1880–1964). Archives of American Art, Smithsonian Institution. This portrait by Van Vechten was taken in the same year as Pippin's solo exhibition at Carlen Galleries, Philadelphia, organized by Albert C. Barnes. Pippin is in front of a tree at the Barnes Foundation, where he was studying at the time.

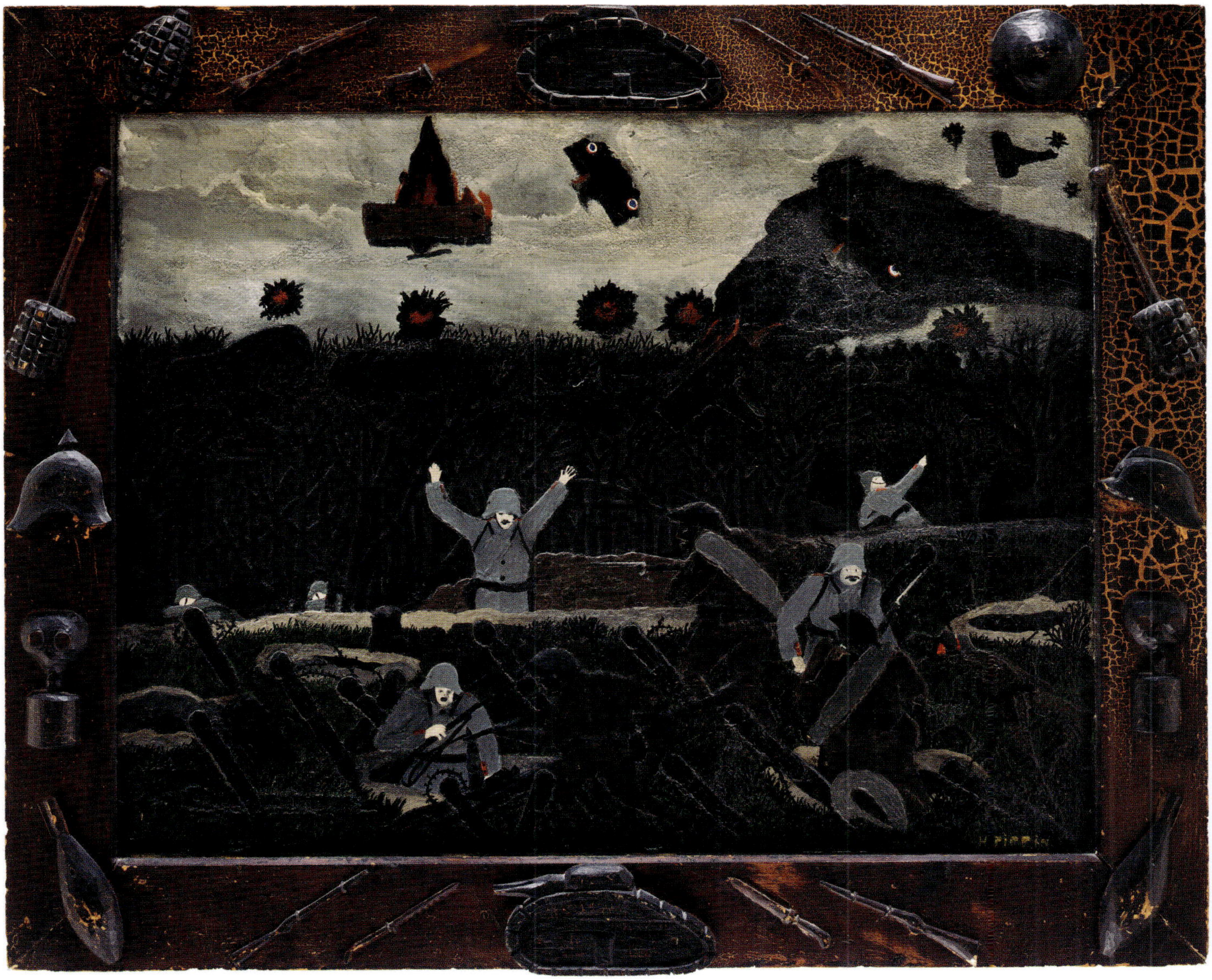

Horace Pippin, The Ending of the War, Starting Home, *1930–1933, oil on canvas, 32 × 39½ × 2 in (81.3 × 100.3 × 5.1 cm) (framed). Philadelphia Museum of Art.* This depiction of wartime is Pippin's most exhibited work. Considered one of his earliest completed oil paintings, it documents the tenacity of the mostly African American 369th infantry amid a German surrender. It was heavily exhibited, in part due to its relevance within Pippin's artistic progression. His first creative attempts, while still rehabilitating his arm, were burning designs into wood panels with a hot poker, as seen in this painting's bespoke frame.

In 1917, Pippin enlisted in the National Guard and served in World War I as part of the predominantly African American 369th Infantry Regiment of the US Army. While overseas, Pippin kept an illustrated journal of his experience. Wounded in battle by a German sniper, he sustained an injury that resulted in near paralysis of his right arm and an honorable discharge in 1918. Pippin's status as a veteran and lasting impairments from his service injury became intrinsically linked to his artistic identity, serving as promotional adjectives for galleries and institutions. His earliest experiments with artmaking were perhaps therapy for his severely impaired right arm and readjustment to civilian life, and by 1928 he had begun oil painting.

Aesthetically, Horace Pippin is credited for his forceful color choice and radicalized perspectives; both of which form an emotional intensity in his paintings. There is also a consideration for graphic design within his compositions. This consideration further influenced Pippin's proportional

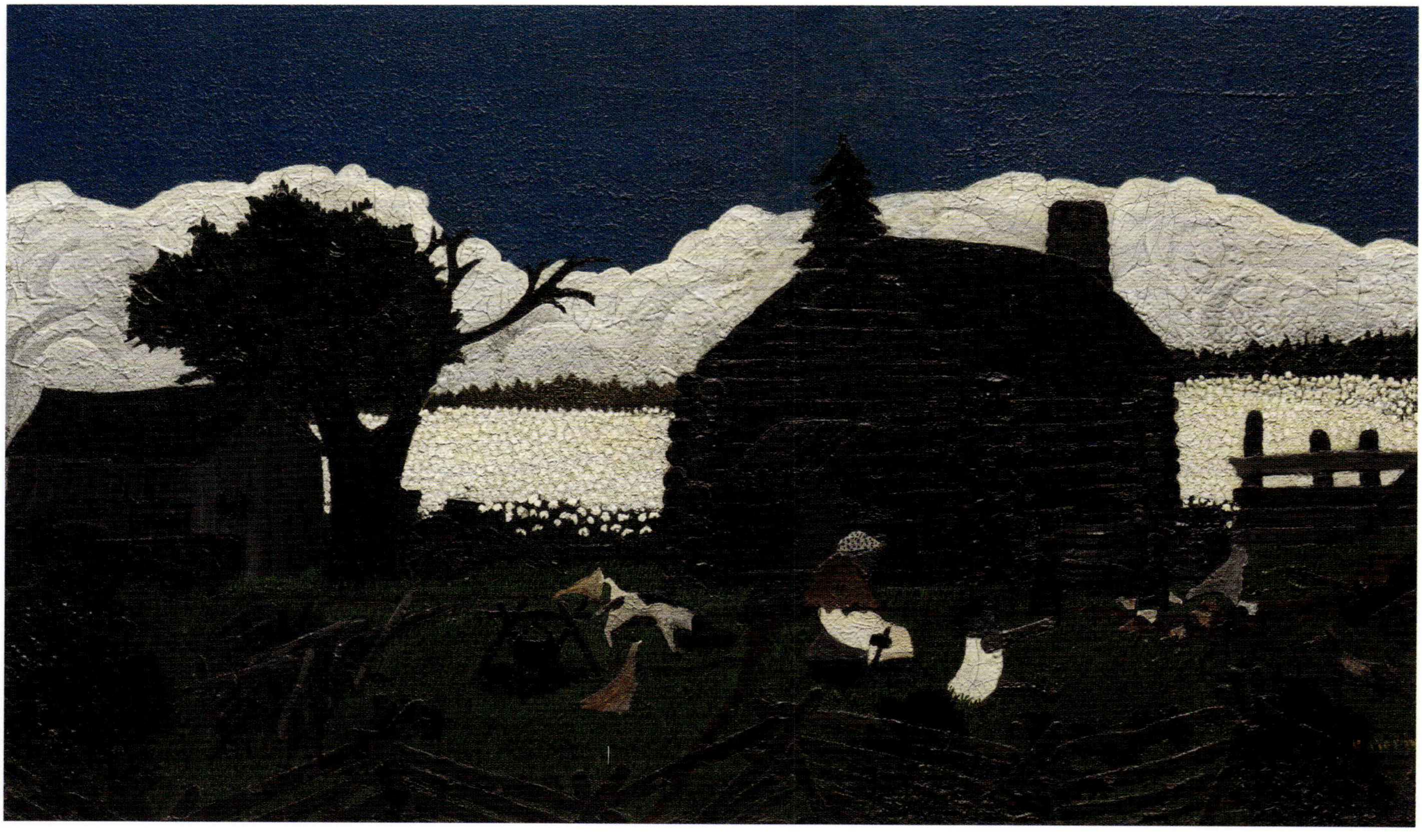

Horace Pippin, Cabin in the Cotton*, 1933–1937, oil on cotton mounted on masonite, 20 × 33½ in (51 × 85 cm). Art Institute of Chicago.* As Pippin was based in Pennsylvania, his depictions of cotton fields likely came from popular culture. Specifically, this painting is compositionally linked to the film *The Cabin in the Cotton* (1932) starring Bette Davis. In 1937, Pippin's *Cabin in the Cotton* was in the window of a shoe repair store in West Chester when it was first seen by art critic Christian Brinton and notable illustrator N.C. Wyeth.

decision making and in particular, persuaded his seemingly decorative details. The outcome became an emotional construct, rather than a physical representation.

Pippin's exposure as an artist straddled racial boundaries through a strong recognition from white patrons, most notably Albert C. Barnes, and placement by philosopher Alain Locke, founder of the "New Negro" movement, within exhibitions focused on elevating African American culture. His artistic identity further hedged the labeling of "self-taught," "folk," or "naive." This was under critical consideration, in particular from his African American peers, who were concerned that identifying with these marginalized positions created a dubious interest from institutions and patrons.

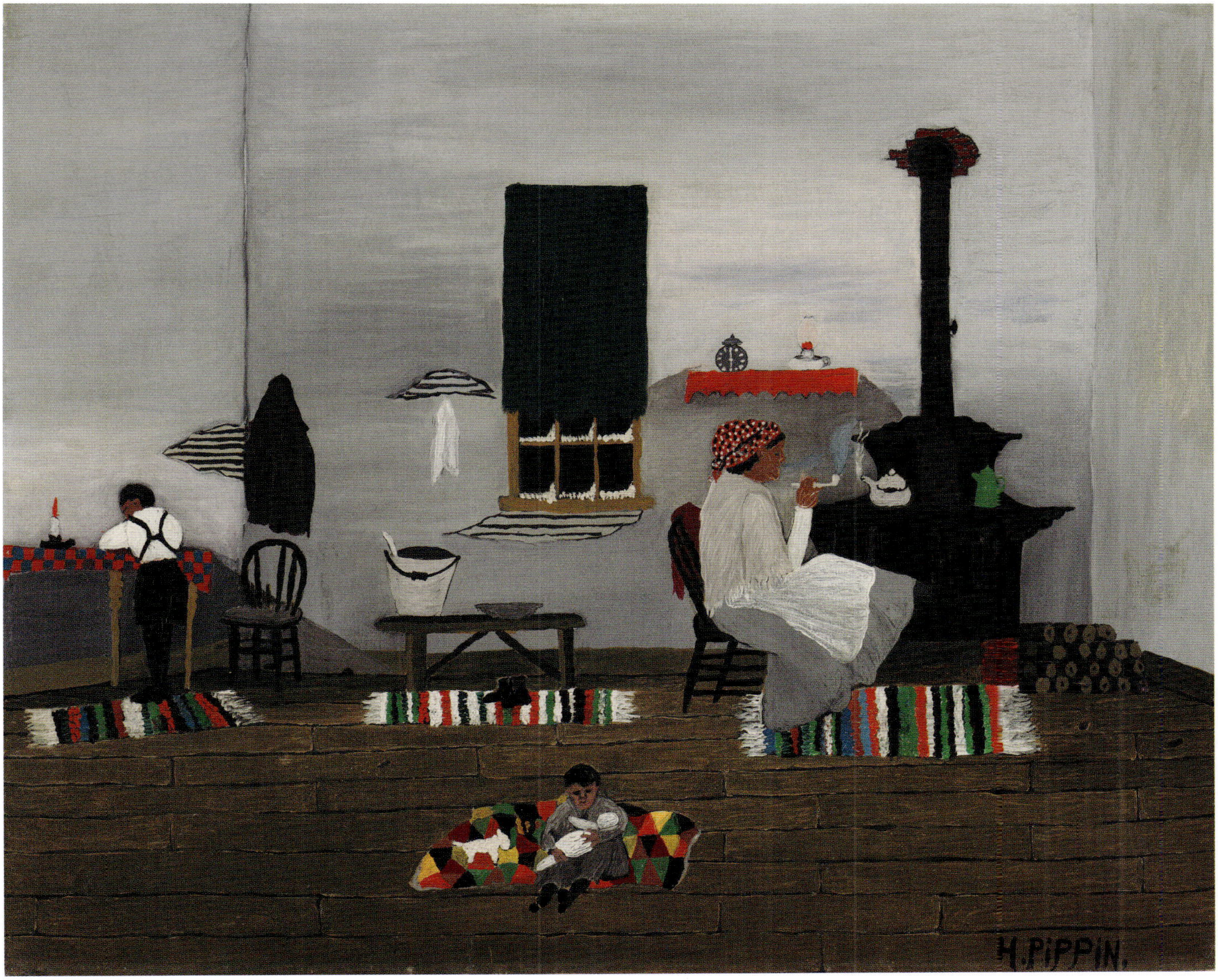

Horace Pippin, School Studies, *1944, oil on canvas, $24\frac{1}{8} \times 30\frac{3}{16} \times \frac{1}{16}$ in (61.2 × 76.6 × 0.2 cm). National Gallery of Art, Washington. School Studies* is part of Pippin's semi-autobiographical oeuvre. This series of domestic interiors often represented African American families engaged in domestic or communal activity. This painting is archetypal for Pippin's idiosyncratic implementation of perspective and flat geometric shapes. The lines in *School Studies* are abundant, forming the cracks in the wall and patterns of three floor rugs.

"Pippin expressed the feelings and experiences of African American life—its peculiar isolation and loneliness, its waste, terrors, beauty, dreams of peace and brotherhood. His scenes from the lives of black people are dominated by reality and filled with dignity and repose as well as the vigor and continuity of life."
– Romare Bearden, American artist and writer[29]

PEDRO LOPEZ CERVÁNTEZ

(1915, Wilcox–1987, Clovis, Arizona, USA)

Born to parents of indigenous Mexican and Spanish heritage, Pedro Lopez Cervántez was one of only two Latino artists to achieve significant recognition during the New Deal art programs (1933–1943) in the United States. Directed by curator Holger Cahill, The Federal Art Project (FAP) was created as a branch of the Works Progress/Projects Administration (WPA) in 1935 under the American New Deal, generating creative work relief to counteract the Great Depression. Cervántez was raised in Texico, New Mexico, where in the 1930s he trained under painter Russell Vernon Hunter. This tutelage led him to assist Hunter on the FAP mural *The Last Frontier* (1934). Following this commission, Cervántez prolifically painted throughout the years of the FAP. Preferring still-lifes and landscapes, he developed an enigmatic style that rendered his prosaic locale extraordinarily. He was included in *Masters of Popular Painting: Modern Primitives of Europe and America* (1938) and *Modern Primitives: Artists of the People* (1941–1944), both by MoMA, New York. Later in his lifetime, Cervántez exhibited at the Whitney Museum of American Art, and throughout the Western United States.

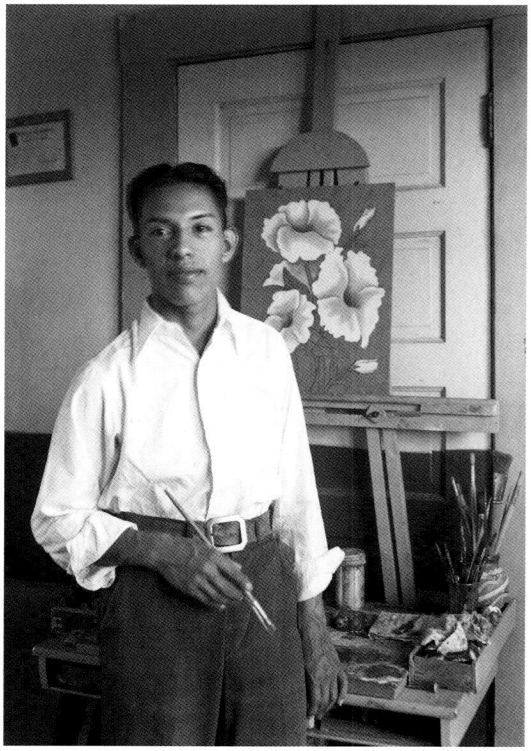

Pedro Lopez Cervántez, 1935–1943, photograph. Courtesy of the Palace of the Governors Photo Archives. Recognized for his talent at a young age, Cervántez was employed by the Federal Art Project (FAP) in the easel painting division. He worked from original sketches that were submitted to the FAP office in Santa Fe for approval before he began painting. Cervántez was only 23 years old when his paintings were exhibited at MoMA, New York.

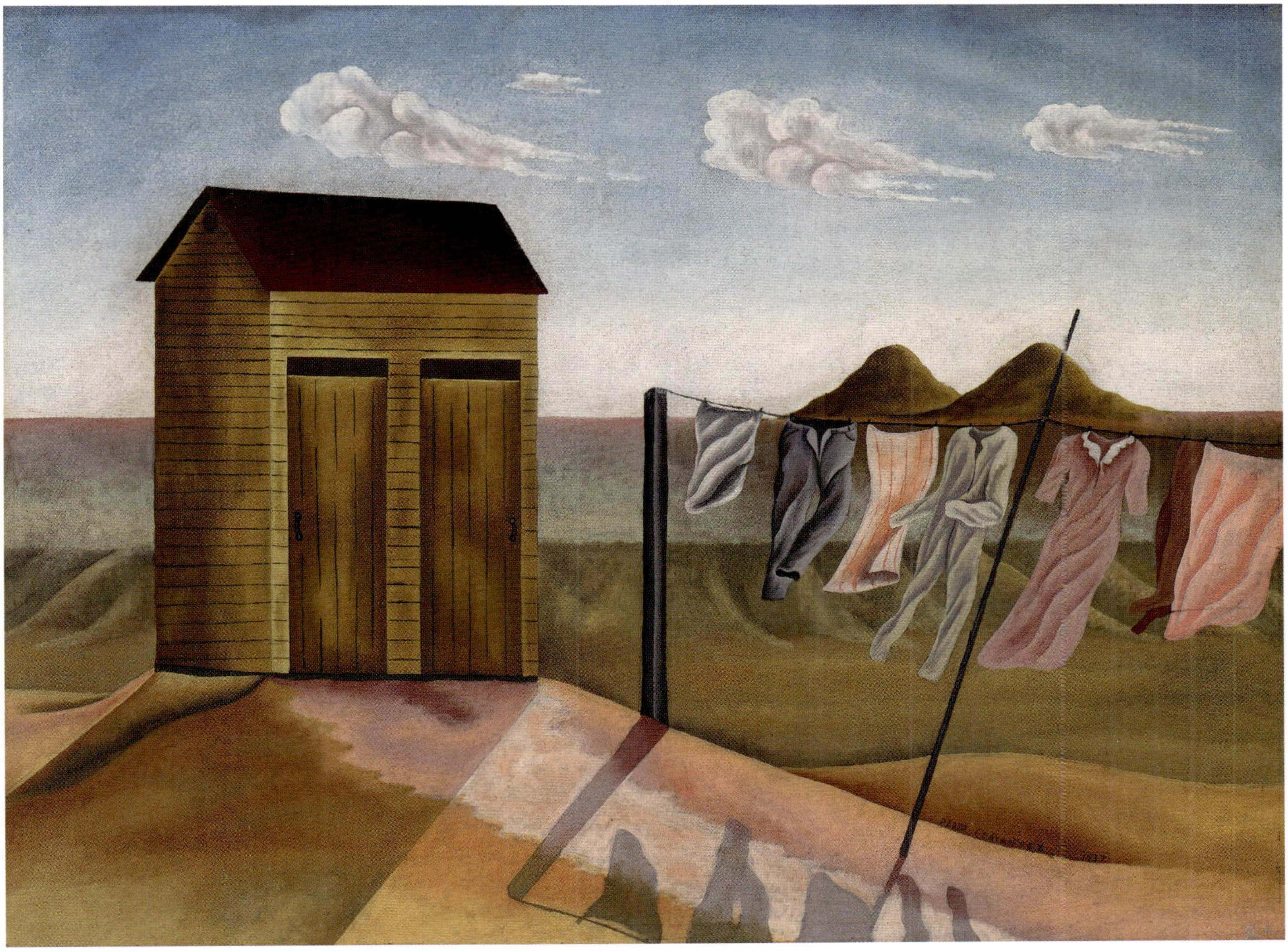

Pedro Lopez Cervántez, Los Privados, *1937, oil on fiberboard, 14¾ × 19¾ in (37.5 × 50.2 cm). Smithsonian American Art Museum.* Included in MoMA's *Masters of Popular Painting: Modern Primitives of Europe and America* (1938), *Los Privados* is typical of Cervántez's late 1930's style, notably his acute attention to detail: treating even the cast shadows of the clothes line on the ground as fundamental. Movement is generated in the painting via the "dancing" clothes in the breeze and rolling clouds.

Despite the co-efforts from Pedro Cervántez, Russell Vernon Hunter is widely credited as the sole contributor to *The Last Frontier* mural at the de Baca County Courthouse in Fort Sumner. Yet there is evidence that demonstrates several segments of the mural were created with more extensive input from Cervántez than previously implied. From both a stylistic and compositional viewpoint, elements of the mural intrinsically resonate with Cervántez's *Bovina Elevators* (1935). Cervántez worked with Hunter for a second commission, and within Hunter's role of state FAP Director for New Mexico, he officially hired Cervántez as an artist for the Project.

The registration of Cervántez's young success during the FAP (1935–1943) was multifaceted. The critical *Masters of Popular Painting: Modern Primitives of Europe and America* (1938) curated by Holger Cahill included ten paintings by Cervántez. He received press and mentions in FAP-published material including *New Mexico: A Guide to the Colorful State* (1940) and *Santa Fe Tourist Guide* (1941). His paintings were also included in national exhibitions related to the WPA; Cahill also featured a slide of Cervántez's work in his official FAP speech.

Compelled to depict his locale, Cervántez featured in his landscapes both the local architecture of Texico but also the natural phenomenon of Llano Estacado—the extraordinary mesa encompassing eastern New Mexico. His depictions of New Mexico and northwest Texas are likened to contemporaneous regionalist painters such as Grant Wood and his representation of Iowa. However, Cervántez's work progressed beyond the concepts of serene countryside to impart a blunt yet sincere realism to the intensity of the desert.

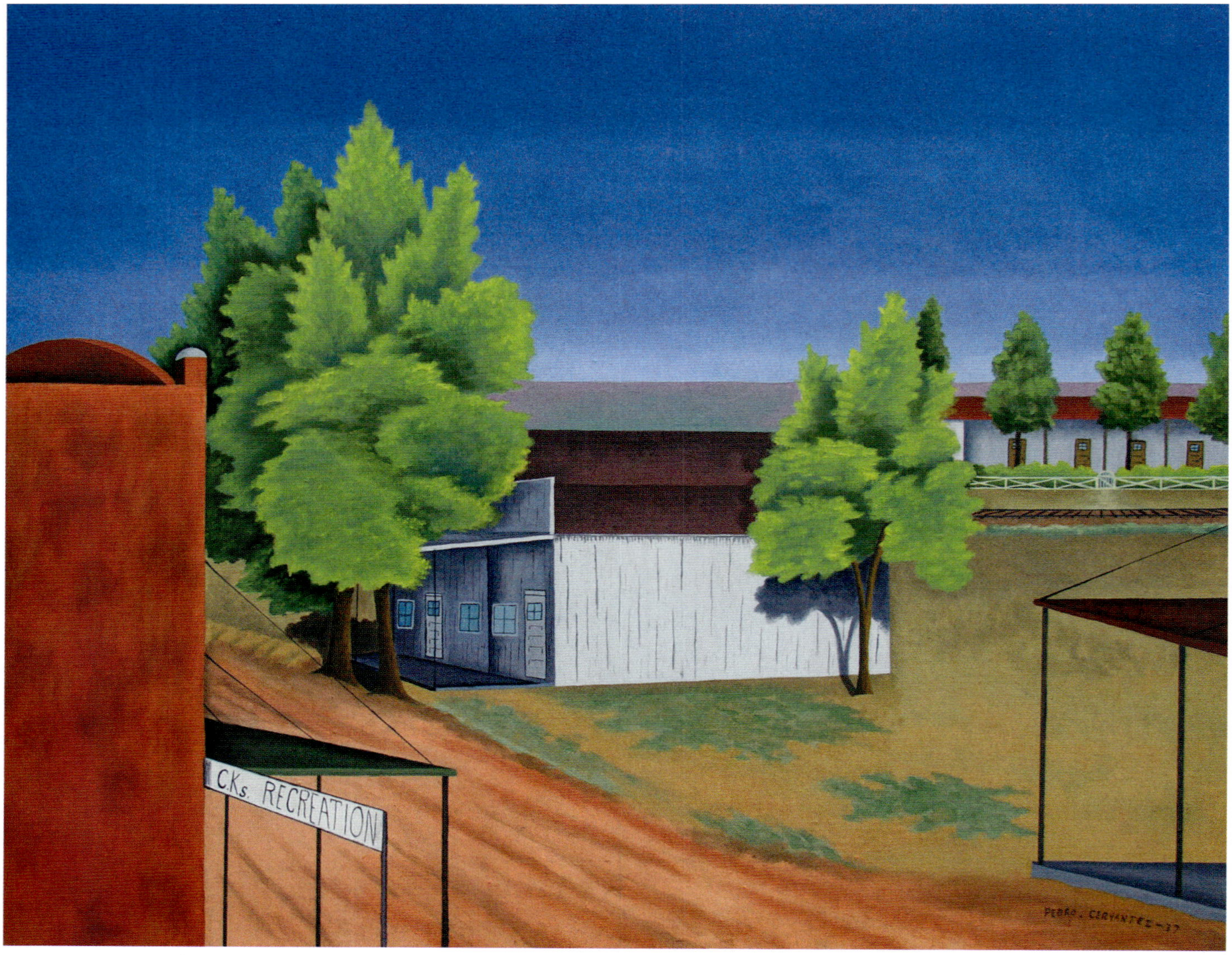

Pedro Lopez Cervántez, Esquina en "Taxco" (Texico) (Streetcorner in Texico), *1937, gouache on masonite, 18½ × 23 in (47 × 58.4 cm). Oklahoma City Museum of Art.* This painting depicts Cervántez's local town Texico, New Mexico. The FAP gave this painting the title *Street Corner in Taxco* (reassigning the scene's locale to Mexico), yet obvious in the painting is the background featuring the Llano plains of New Mexico. It was originally titled by the artist: *Corner Street in Texico, New Mexico.*

"Pedro Cervántez [sic] is one of the most interesting formists in the Southwest. His canvases are units of creative design, and he uses color with exact regard for its function within the creative, overall design. He could be placed with some of the best formists in Europe and stand up under the most exacting comparison."
– Alfred Morang, painter, author, and art critic for the *Santa Fe Tourist Guide* (1941)[30]

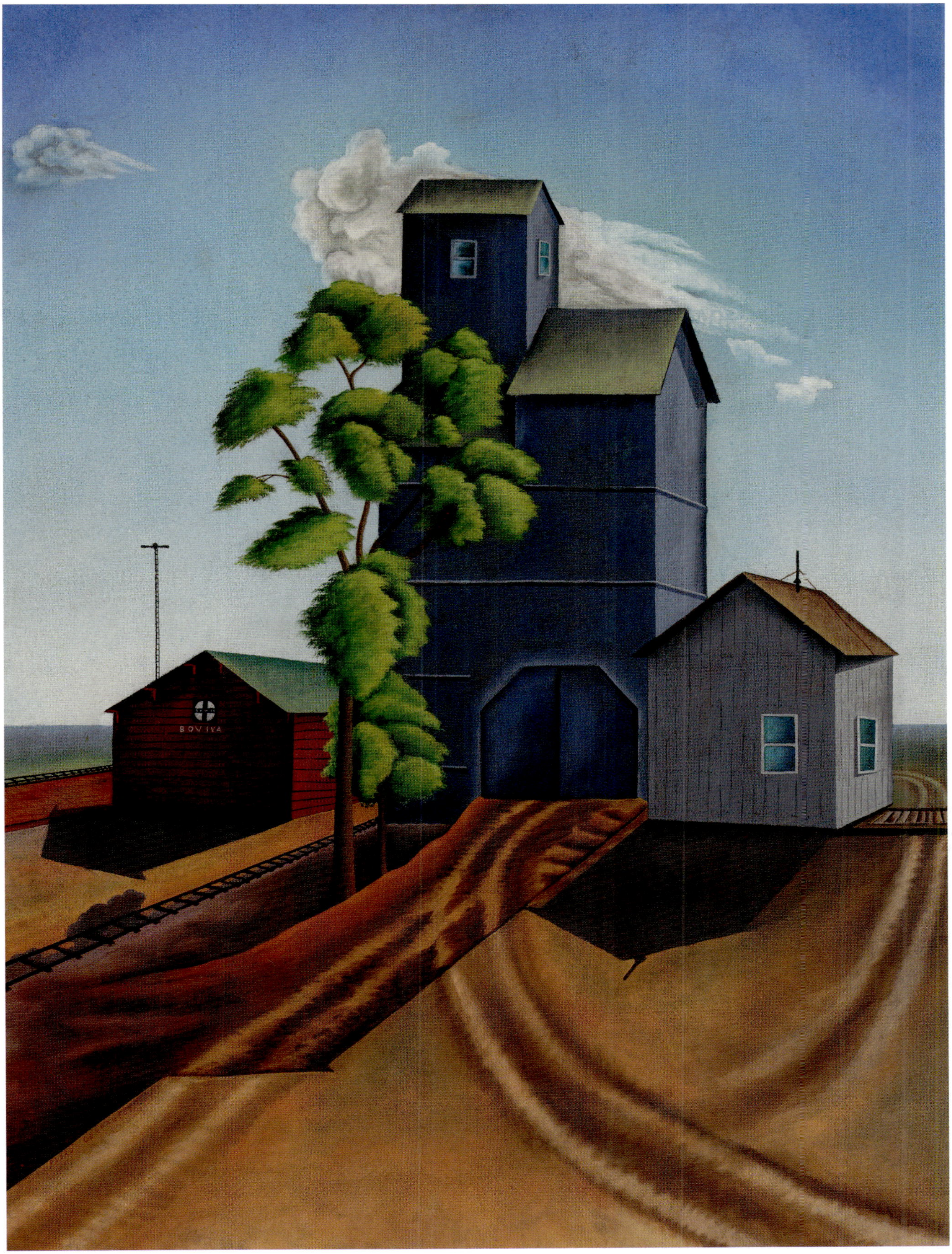

Pedro Lopez Cervántez, Elevadores en Bovina (Bovina Elevators)*, 1937, oil on masonite, 26½ × 20⅜ in (67.3 × 51.8 cm). Sheldon Museum of Art.* The style and details of this painting when compared to Hunter's *The Last Frontier* mural, on which Cervántez assisted—its subtle use of concentric wavy lines, color palette, and shadows—demonstrates similarities suggesting Cervántez's larger involvement in the mural's composition.

CHAPTER 2

L'ART BRUT: DEFINING CREATIVE AGENCY (1942–1966)

THE ORIGINS OF ART BRUT, HISTORY AND LEGACY

Sarah Lombardi

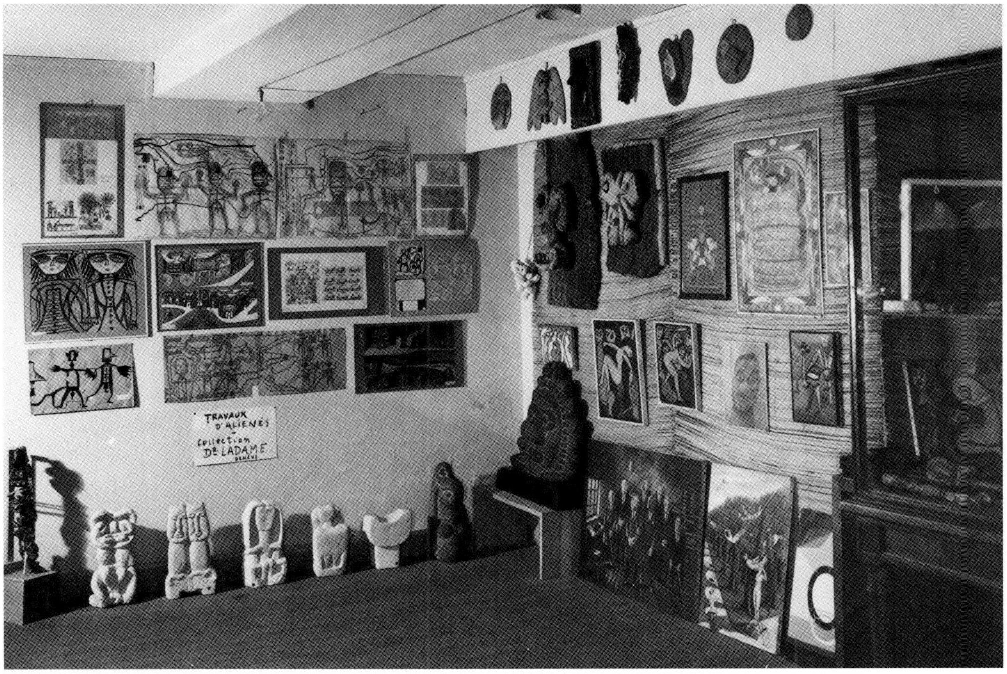

The Foyer de l'Art Brut in the basement of Galerie René Drouin in Paris, February 1948. Collection de l'Art Brut, Lausanne. This installation image shows an early exhibition organized by Jean Dubuffet. Before René Drouin offered his main gallery for the temporary exhibition *L'Art Brut* in 1949 to Dubuffet, he lent to him the gallery's basement to organize art shows. Featured here are drawings by Robert Gie (1869–n.d.) and an anonymous sculpture from a set known as "Le Barbus Müller."

In 1942 the French painter and sculptor Jean Dubuffet began to "question cultural rites and seek an art less controlled by fixed norms."[1] Intent on bringing together work from outside the established art world, Dubuffet took an early interest in graffiti, children's drawings, and popular and naive art, which had in common their creation by artists considered self-taught. It was only later, in around 1945, that he began to collect creative output from asylums, aided by artists, doctors, and psychiatrists whose innovative approach echoed his quest for extra-cultural works.

At the invitation of the Lausanne section of the Swiss Central Tourist Office, then headed by his writer friend Paul Budry, Dubuffet stayed in Switzerland from July 5–22, 1945, accompanied by Jean Paulhan, also a writer, and the architect Le Corbusier. On this occasion, he asked to visit psychiatric hospitals in particular, as well as several collections of art from asylums and prisons. During this trip, Dubuffet met Dr. Walter Morgenthaler, former director of the Waldau psychiatric clinic in Bern. He was also the author of *Ein Geisteskranker als Künster* (1921), published in English as *Madness and Art*, which presented the artwork of his former patient, Adolf Wölfli (see page 64). Senior consultant and director of Waldau until 1933, Morgenthaler was a key figure in the recognition of what was historically referred to as "the art of the insane." Dubuffet went on to develop one of the largest collections of "asylum art" in Europe, only second to that of Dr. Hans Prinzhorn in Heidelberg, Germany, which includes several thousand works by patients diagnosed as schizophrenic.

Dubuffet took the opportunity to visit several asylums and psychiatric clinics, including the Waldau, where he met Dr. Jakob Wyrsch, Morgenthaler's successor. In the attic of Waldau, he found a "small museum" containing numerous works by asylum patients. These were collected by Morgenthaler between 1914 and 1930 and prominently included drawings by Adolf Wölfli.

Dubuffet immediately fell under the spell of this colossal body of work by Wölfli, both because of the sheer output of this Swiss German artist, and the plastic and graphic richness of his compositions. To mark the occasion Wrysch gave Dubuffet an early work by the artist. This first Wölfli drawing was followed by many further additions to the burgeoning collection of the French artist. In the wake of this visit to Switzerland and its many fruitful revelations, Dubuffet, in a letter to his painter friend René Auberjonois in August 1945, used the oxymoron *art brut* ("raw art") to designate the works he was beginning to collect, whose creators were self-taught, non-establishment, and artistically unorthodox. He kept an account of his stay in a diary titled *Trip to Switzerland*, now in the archives of the Lausanne museum, in which, in Paulhan's summary, he speaks of "an immediate, untrained art—an *art brut* whose rudiments [he thought] are to be found among the insane and the imprisoned."[2]

A year later, and once again thanks to a doctor, Dubuffet was exposed to another artist who would become a major figure in the history of Art Brut: Aloïse Corbaz (see page 56) from Lausanne. Dr. Hans Steck, director of the La Rosière psychiatric hospital in Cery (from 1920 to 1960), where Corbaz was a patient, first became fascinated by her work, together with Dr. Jacqueline Porret-Forel, who introduced Dubuffet to the shimmering power of Corbaz's painterly universe[3].

During his explorations in 1945, Dubuffet also visited various French psychiatric hospitals. In Saint-Alban, in the Lozère département, he identified works that were greatly interesting, among them the wooden sculptures of Auguste Forestier (see page 76). The first pieces by Forestier entered Dubuffet's collection in 1948, given by Dr. François Tosquelles, director of Saint-Alban, via Jean Oury, an intern at the hospital. Oury was Dubuffet's main intermediary prior to Dr. Roger Gentil, who helped Dubuffet considerably in his Art Brut enterprise. Oury also sent Dubuffet embroideries made by female patients, including those of Marguerite Sirvins (see page 80). Later, Dr Gentil provided Sirvin's masterpiece, the famous wedding dress made from threads she pulled from bed sheets. In 1963, the dress became part of the Compagnie de l'Art Brut Collection at 137 rue de Sèvres in Paris.

Dubuffet gradually brought together the drawings, paintings, embroideries, writings, and sculptures collected during his research in France, Switzerland, and other European countries, and even beyond, thanks to his expanding network of contacts in psychiatric and other circles. However, from his initial engagement with psychiatric hospitals, which Dubuffet regarded as the creative locus (the furthest removed from the upper-crust, elitist art circles he was so opposed to), he would soon integrate other artists unrelated to the psychiatric field into his collection. He did this by widening his field of investigation, notably to the marginalized and to Spiritualist circles. He added to his collection the paintings of the miner Augustin Lesage (see page 72); those of Fleury-Joseph Crépin (see page 68), whose particularity was working with droplets of paint; Madge Gill's large Indian ink compositions on calico (see page 88), which initially obscured the more extensive oeuvre of which they were a part; and the semi-abstract compositions in blue or black ink by Laure Pigeon, without, however, grouping them under the categorization of Spiritualist art. For Dubuffet, what these artists—men and women from distinctly different backgrounds, producing distinctly different work, but all classified together—had in common beyond the fact of being self-taught was obliviousness of institutional or artistic constraints. As for the works themselves, what fascinated Dubuffet was their utter uniqueness.

These works, acquired either through purchases or donations, were initially grouped together and presented from November 1947 onwards at the Foyer de l'Art Brut. This little-known space was located in the basement of Galerie René Drouin on Place Vendôme in Paris. A friend and the first gallerist to show Dubuffet's own work, Drouin made the space available to him for preserving and exhibiting his growing collection of Art Brut. As a printed leaflet stated, "One of the basement rooms at Galerie René Drouin will be given over to investigations into Art Brut. At the desk manned by art critic Michel Tapié visitors will find all the information they need. Paintings, statuettes, drawings, objects, and various other works can be examined and exhibitions will be held periodically."[4] In this cramped basement, Dubuffet organized numerous monographic and group exhibitions from his collection. On occasion he would borrow works collected by his colleagues from artist or doctor friends to round off presentations on view to a small circle of intimates, artists, and collectors. These exhibitions were often accompanied by modest brochures.

In October 1948, Dubuffet established the founding members of the Compagnie de l'Art Brut, among them André Breton, Jean Paulhan, Michel Tapié, and Charles Ratton. The aim was to provide a structure for the consolidation and development of the collection in the making, paired with research into self-taught artists considered on the fringes of the system. As was previously the case, works would not be for sale. The collection now moved to a house in Paris on loan from the publisher Gaston Gallimard.

In 1949, René Drouin offered Dubuffet not the gallery basement, former home of the collection, but an opportunity to exhibit his collection in the "official" space located on the prestigious Place Vendôme. Curated by Dubuffet, and simply titled *l'Art Brut*, the presentation ran from October to November of that year. The first exhibition to be held outside the headquarters of the Compagnie de l'Art Brut, this was an exceptional event; not only because it brought together 200 works by 63 creators, mainly from the collection of the Compagnie de l'Art Brut, but also because it reinforced and clarified the notion of Art Brut as Dubuffet understood it at the time. Moreover, it represented a radical departure from an exhibition organized in February 1946 at the Hôpital Sainte-Anne in Paris, which was limited exclusively to works by patients from psychiatric hospitals around the world. In fact, while Dubuffet had brought together works by so-called "insane" artists, among them Aloïse Corbaz, Gaston Duf, Auguste Forestier, Robert Gie, Marguerite Sirvins, and Adolf Wölfli, who represented half of the selected participants, the exhibition also included works by "mediumistic" artists such as Fleury-Joseph Crépin and Jeanne Tripier, as well as marginalized artists or others working in parallel to their professions, such as Miguel Hernandez, Henri Salingardes, Joaquim Vincens Gironella, and Pascal-Désir Maisonneuve. The exhibition also included works by 16 anonymous artists, as well as children's drawings and several popular artifacts.

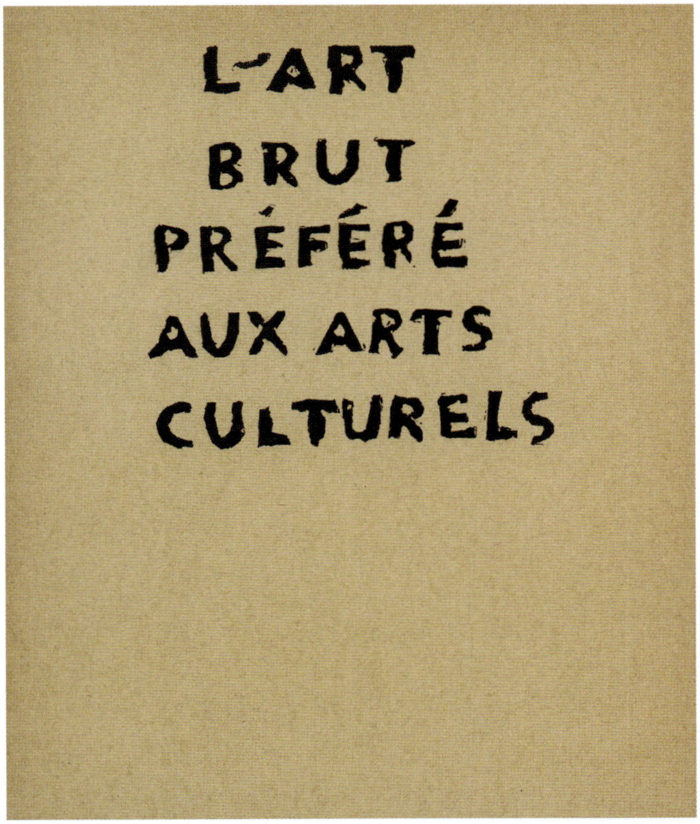

Catalog cover for l'Art Brut *exhibition at Galerie René Drouin, Paris (1949). Collection de l'Art Brut, Lausanne.* This publication served as a catalog for the 1949 exhibition *l'Art Brut* at Galerie René Drouin, asserting Dubuffet's interest in what he considered as "Art Brut" over that of "cultural art."

For Dubuffet, in the fall of 1949, *l'Art Brut* and the accompanying catalog, *L'Art Brut préféré aux arts culturels*, were manifestos. They enabled him, in the wake of the subsequent interest of contemporaneous artists' circles, in particular the Dadaists and surrealists, but also certain psychiatrists, to broaden the conception of art for the artistic community and the public. The exhibition presented self-taught artists, who in external circumstances were considered "madmen," marginalized figures, and mediums, to be recognized as artistic producers in their own right.

A key moment in the history of Art Brut, this exhibition demonstrated Dubuffet's final alignment of works by psychiatric hospital patients, and marginalized and eccentric individuals together with children's drawings, and art categorized as popular or naive art under the concept of Art Brut. All of them, in other words, were deviations from his understanding of the standard art line. It was only after the exhibition at Drouin's that Dubuffet began excluding children's drawings and works of folk and naive art, which he no longer considered under the Art Brut heading.[5] This exclusion became more systematic from 1962 onward, when the collection returned from its 11-year exile in New York following the dissolution of the Compagnie de l'Art Brut in 1951,[6] and was installed in its new—and last—Paris home, on rue de Sèvres.

Today, as the recognition of self-taught artists is becoming normalized, it can be understood that Jean Dubuffet's pursuits were innovative and modern for mid-century Europe. It is significant to now grant recognition to artists who, like those within Art Brut in 1940s, have received no artistic training.

In a way, it was by legitimizing the creators of Art Brut as authentic artists, and by considering their works as equal, if not superior, in value to those of established artists (think Dubuffet's 1949 catalog-manifesto *L'Art Brut préféré aux arts culturels*) that Dubuffet and Art Brut greatly contributed to the legacy of contemporary self-taught artists. Recognizing the gradual acceptance of Art Brut's historical significance by the art world in general, self-taught creatives are gaining traction as legitimate and credible artists regardless of their lack of formal training. In other words, the recognition of Art Brut and its creators has facilitated the acknowledgment of untrained contemporary artists.

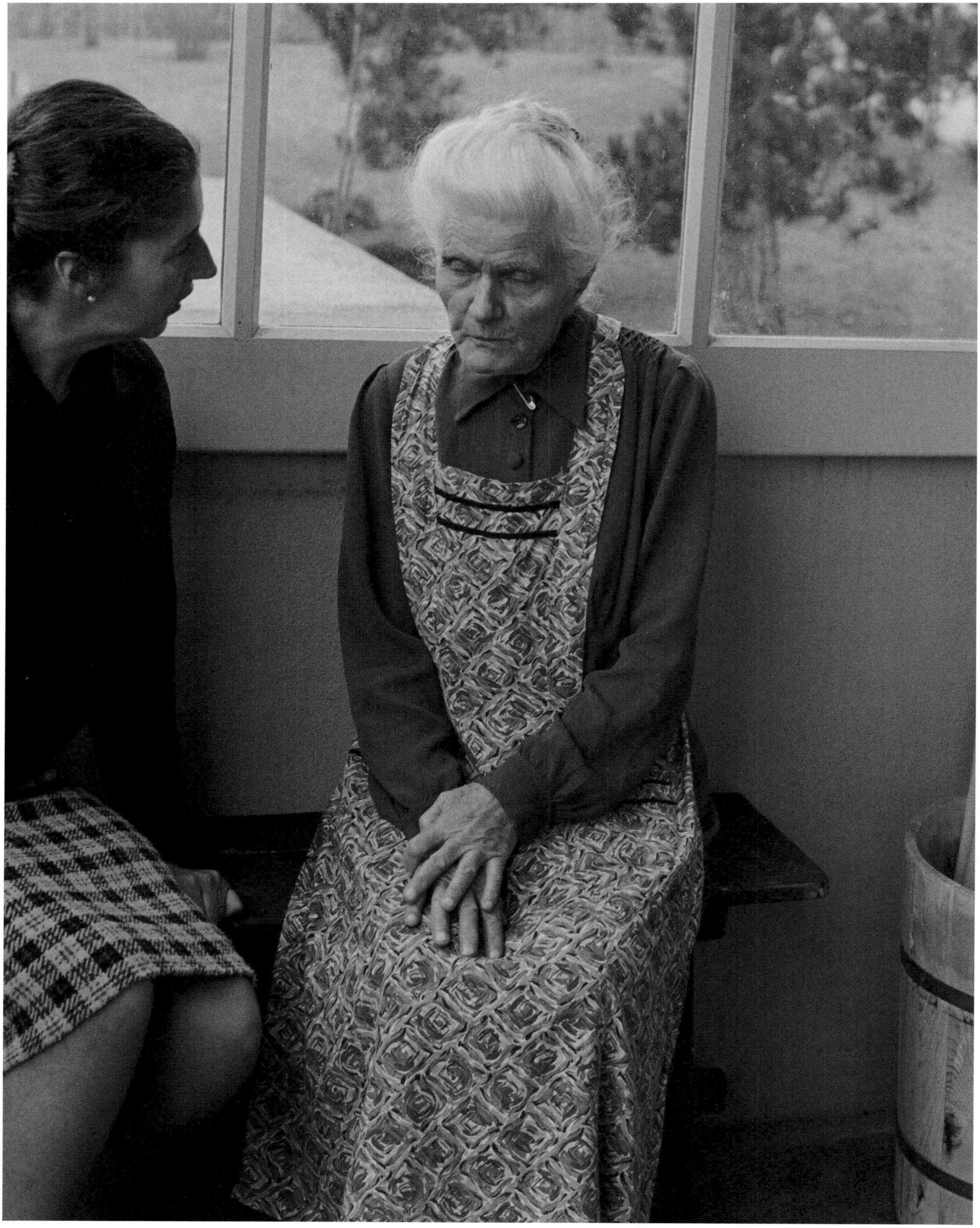

Aloïse Corbaz, 1963, photograph by Henriette Grindat (Swiss, 1923–1986). Swiss Foundation for Photography. This portrait of Corbaz shows her with Jacqueline Porret-Forel (profiled left), who was one of her key advocates. Taken in 1963, a year before Corbaz's death and nearly 20 years after Porret-Forel had learned about Corbaz during a lecture in 1946.

ALOÏSE CORBAZ

(1886, Lausanne–1964, Gimel-sur-Morges, Switzerland)

Aloïse Corbaz was encouraged from a young age to pursue her interests in opera and music—passions profoundly reflected in her later artistic practice. In 1911, Corbaz became a governess within the court of German Emperor Wilhelm II. During this post, she developed an intense, and imaginary, love affair with Wilhelm. These intense thoughts and further irrational behavior led to her committal to a psychiatric hospital in 1918, where she remained under institutional care until her death in 1964. There Corbaz began to draw using found paper and materials, such as rose petals and toothpaste. She worked in secret until 1936, when she was recognized by the hospital director Professor Hans Steck and later by Dr. Jacqueline Porret-Forel—both of whom became her advocates. In 1946, she was introduced to French artist Jean Dubuffet, who became entranced with Corbaz's operatic drawings of lovers and society figures. Corbaz's drawings featured significantly in the exhibitions, publications, and collection of Dubuffet's Foyer and Compagnie de l'Art Brut; and her work has continually exhibited on an international scale into the 21st century.

Aloïse Corbaz referenced the opera, from *Tosca* to *La Traviata*, and societal figures, including Élisabeth de Cerenville, Woodrow Wilson, and Napoleon, and transposed such references into complex visual narratives that explored feminine emotion and influence. Her personal universe deconstructs and reconstructs the sentiment that the *personal is political*, allowing a truly authentic, historic, feminine perspective to be heard. Corbaz has an entangled relationship with the genre of Art Brut, within which she is historically defined. Constituted of artists Jean Dubuffet considered free of cultural conventions, the genre is made further complex by narratives intrinsically linked to mental illness, and thus became the predisposed context for Corbaz. However, her visually operatic compositions articulate far beyond the perimeter of institutional therapy and she cannot be categorized as an individual unaware of her immediate and cultural surroundings. The act of shedding predispositions has the potential to propose a parallel between her life and creativity that provides a permissive, nonrestrictive condition.

Starting in the 1920s, but culminating in the 1940s, Corbaz's artistic explorations were integral to her personal campaign for identity. Corbaz addressed her phrenic transformation by creative expression as becoming a divine light with reflecting powers. Corbaz's involvement in two torrid love affairs, one imaginary but no less intense, appear influential to her gesturally drawn narratives, reflecting passion, romance, and frustration; love and loss. Often erotic and sexual, lovers are a central theme to her work, with women almost exclusively paramount. Her bold but delicate oeuvre of symphonic scenes and socialite scenarios were all created while in a Swiss institution—uncategorically simple, and instead complex explorations into existence via her personal story, the (un)balance of feminine power, restraint, and restriction.

Aloïse Corbaz, often exhibited as simply Aloïse/Aloyse (historically in Europe patients often lost their surname when medically institutionalized), was born in June 1886 in Lausanne, Switzerland, to a relatively large family of six children. Her father was a postal official while her mother passed away when Corbaz was only 13, rendering her older sister Marguerite in charge of the siblings. The Corbaz family had moderate wealth, allowing Aloïse's interest in opera and musical theater to be fostered. Yearning to one day be a famous performer, she received private singing lessons, was introduced to the opera, and began composing religious anthems from a young age. In particular, Corbaz's passion for theater became a preeminent influence on her later conceptual method of sequencing her drawings into acts and scenes of a play. Aesthetically too, the visual grandeur of opera and theater sets informed the exaggerated scenography in Corbaz's work.

There are several significant years marking the biography of Corbaz. From her repetitive choice of erotic lovers to her visual offerings of densely filled pupil-less eyes emoting passion, not restricted to romance; her consequential experiences are reflected in her creative output. The first was in 1911, when she embraced a denounced relationship with a laicized priest studying theology in Lausanne. When her sister Marguerite became aware of this relationship, she sent Corbaz to Germany to terminate the affair. She had previously completed her school degree and thus her duty abroad was to be a governess. Within months Corbaz landed a position in Potsdam within the court of Emperor Wilhelm II. While culturally relevant because of her exposure to great literature, alchemy, and diagrams (reflected in later works), emotionally, this period was also significant because of an intense, but imaginary, love affair formed with Willhelm II. In 1914, the intensity of world war required Corbaz, who was still infatuated with the emperor, to return to Switzerland. Home in Lausanne, her concerning behavior surrounding the projected affair was compounded by extreme religious and pacifist sentiments, and improper erotic conduct.

In February 1918, Corbaz was committed to Cery, a psychiatric hospital associated with the University of Lausanne. She spent two years at Cery, where she was deemed incurable. With this diagnosis in 1920, Corbaz was transferred to La Rosière psychiatric clinic in Gimel-sur-Morges, where she remained until her death in 1964. This first decade in Cery and Gimel-sur-Morges was a particularly turbulent time emotionally and psychologically for Corbaz. In a letter to her father from Cery, she wrote, "*Je ressens une ruine physique lente et sûre, fanatisme de folie amoureuse qui m'a arraché tout du corps.*" ("I feel a slow and sure physical ruin, fanaticism of madness in love which tore everything from my body.")[7]

It was at La Roisèrie that Corbaz began to draw in secret with modest and appropriated materials. Initially, she drew on small scraps of found paper and later stitched together discarded papers to achieve a larger format, drawing on them with toothpaste and crushed rose petals. The act of creating for Corbaz in a myriad of ways paralleled her progression to serenity with existence.

In 1936, the director of the Cery clinic, Professor Hans Steck, took notice of Corbaz's creative production and encouraged her by providing materials, along with preserving and collecting her drawings. Steck also began establishing, within the hospital, an audience for Corbaz by presenting her work in lectures to medical students and staff. Subsequently, a lecture in 1941 established perhaps the most pivotal year for Corbaz with the attendance of Dr. Jacqueline Porret-Forel. With this introduction to her work, Porret-Forel became a seminal figure and advocate for Corbaz. She was devoted to studying all aspects of Corbaz's life; even writing her doctoral thesis on Corbaz, entitled *Aloyse ou la peinture magique d'une schizophrène: contribution a l'étude de l'art psycho-pathologique (Aloyse or the Magical Painting of a Schizophrenic: contribution to the study of psycho-pathological art)*, which was published in 1953. Called "Angel Forel" by Corbaz, she worked extremely closely with her not as a psychiatrist (Porret-Forel was a general practitioner), but as a confidant and champion. The period between 1941 and 1946 was prolific for Corbaz, during which it became apparent that articulating her private universe through artistic creation had a profound impact on her life. Porret-Forel described her progression from completely withdrawn to the emergence of life.[8]

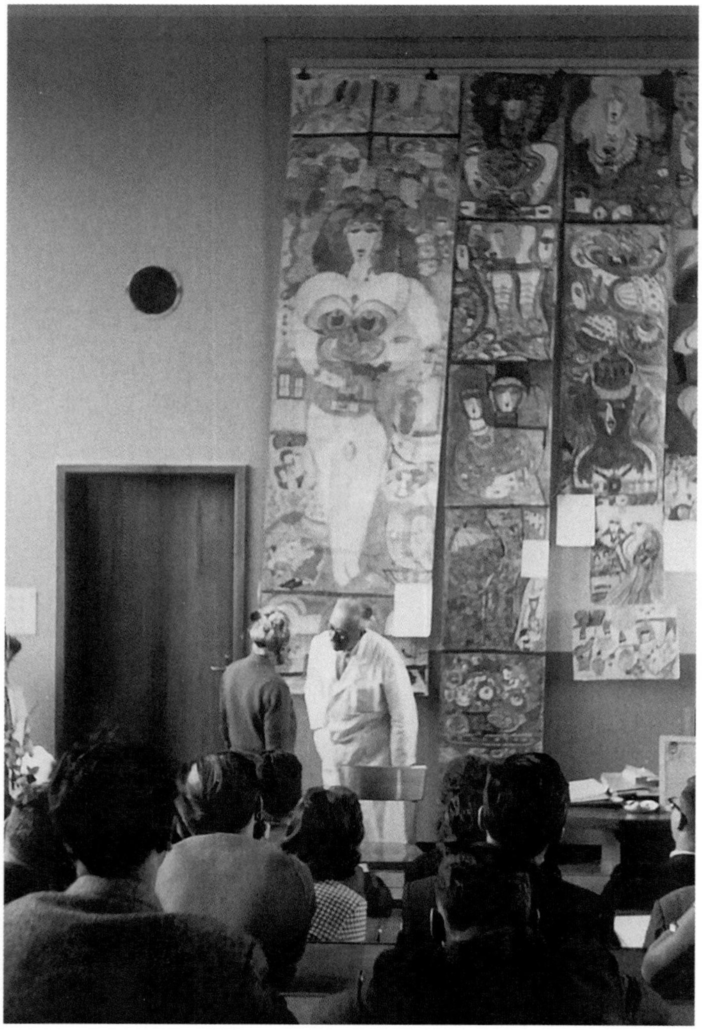

Aloïse Corbaz, 1960, photograph. Archives cantonales vaudoises. This photograph of Corbaz, taken in June 1960 at the Cery psychiatric hospital, shows her with Professor Hans Steck, who first recognized Corbaz's drawings, during her last clinical lesson. The theme of the lesson was "artistic creation for patients" and hanging on the back wall are long scrolls by Corbaz.

In 1946, Porret-Forel introduced Corbaz's work to Jean Dubuffet, who became entranced with its dramatic and delicate femininity and eroticism. In 1948, Dubuffet's Compagnie de l'Art Brut published a solo presentation on Aloïse (Aloyse) with writing by Porret-Forel, and her work was featured in *l'Art Brut* at Galerie René Drouin, Paris (1949), and it's accompanying publication of *L'Art Brut préféré aux arts culturels.* Dubuffet committed to exhibiting and writing about Corbaz's works for decades following his initial introduction to her practice, stating in 1966, "*Je crois que la vaste tapisserie à mille volets d'Aloïse peut être regardée comme la seule manifestation vraiment resplendissante, dans la peinture, de la pulsation proprement féminine.*" ("I believe that Aloïse's vast tapestry with a thousand shutters can be regarded as the only truly resplendent manifestation, in painting, of the truly feminine pulsation.")[9]

From this ongoing support from Steck, Dubuffet, and especially Porret-Forel, Corbaz's output and recognition continued to rise steadily. In 1951, Corbaz completed *Le Cloisonné de théâtre*, considered her most ambitious and compelling work. This monumental 14-meter-long work was composed theatrically as a three-act play. Given by Corbaz

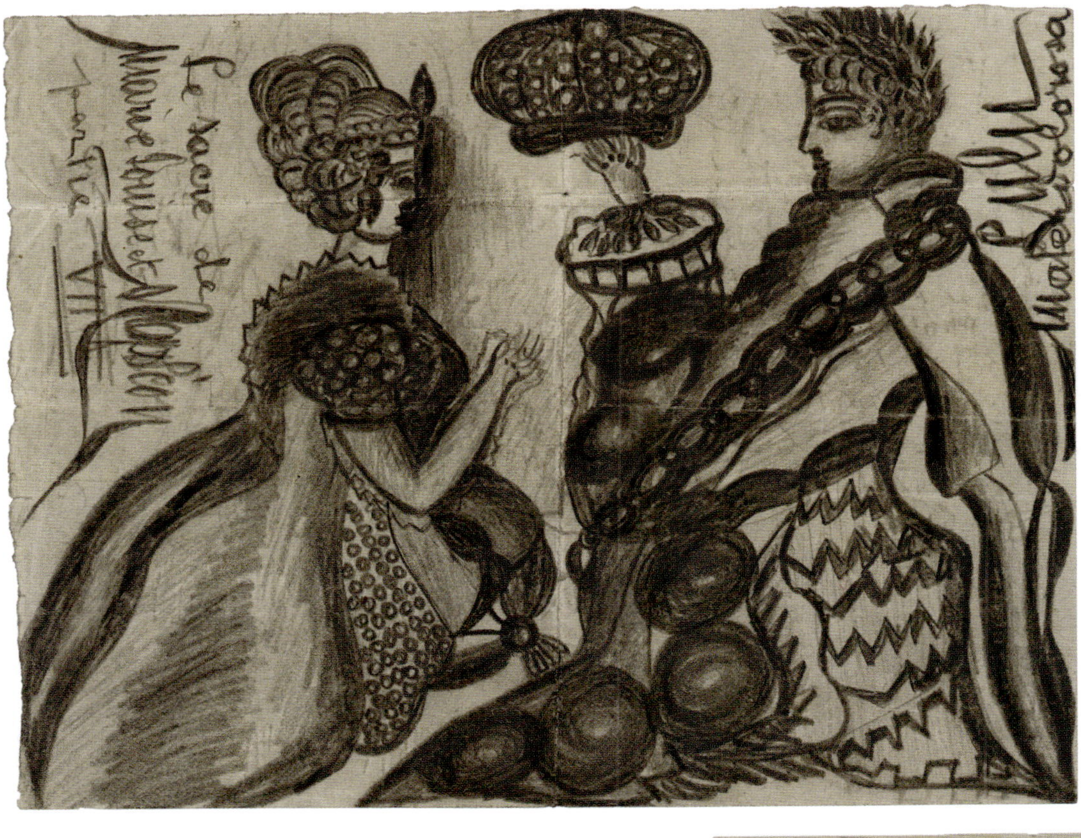

Aloïse Corbaz, Le sacre de Marie-Louise et Napoléon (The Coronation of Marie-Louise and Napoleon), *1922, graphite on recycled paper, 4¾ × 6⅜ in (12 × 16.2 cm). Collection de l'Art Brut, Lausanne.* This is an early example of Corbaz's work, made within the first couple of years at La Rosière. Small in scale and drafted in graphite, it demonstrates the limited materials available to her.

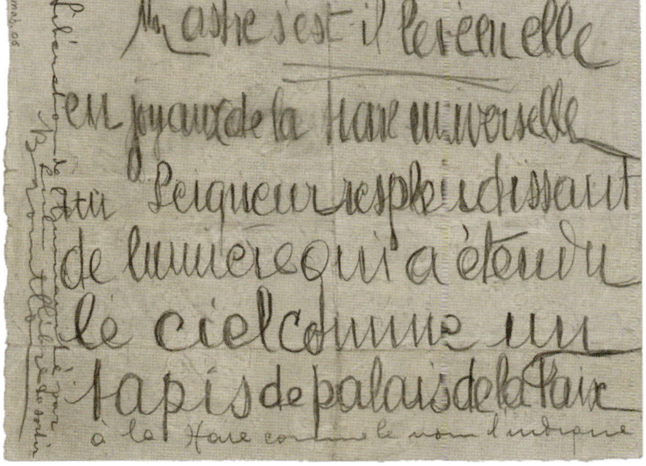

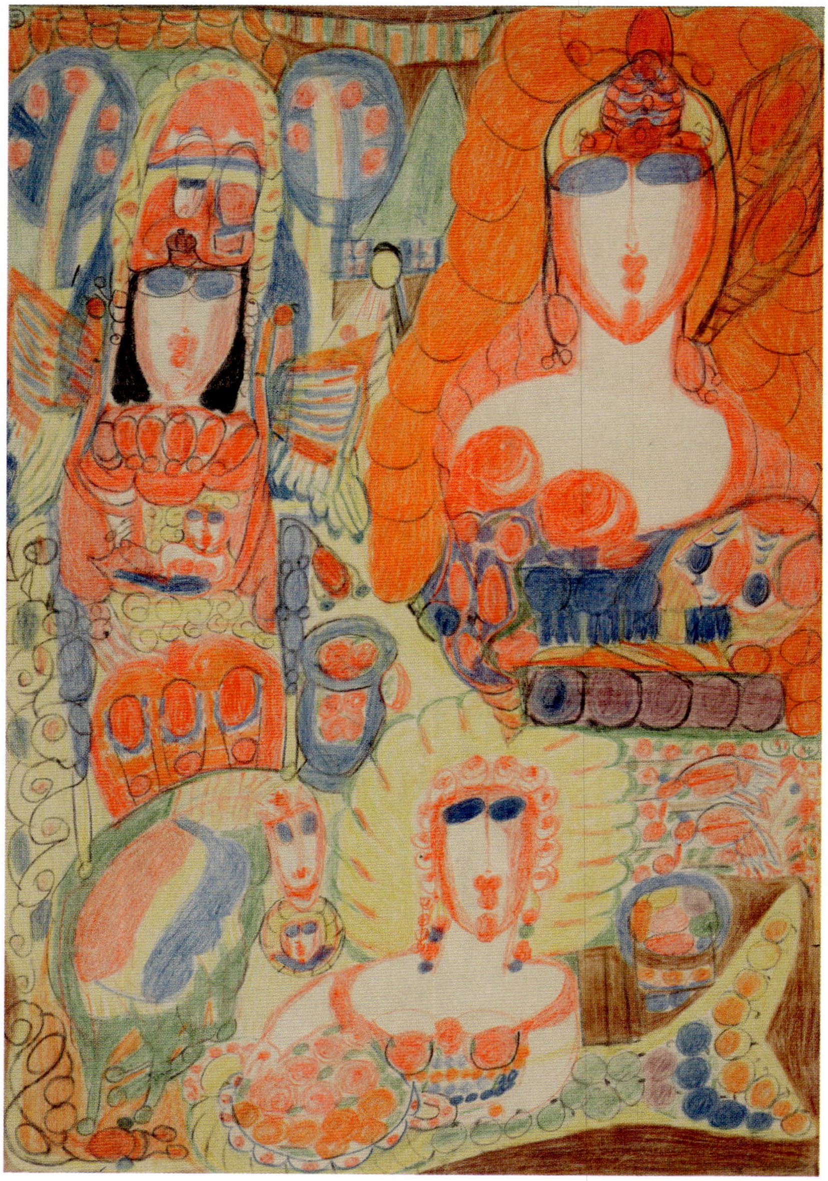

Aloïse Corbaz, Scène de groupe avec pape, sphinx et sirène (Group scene with pope, sphinx, and mermaid), *1946–1947, colored pencil on paper, $22\frac{13}{16} \times 17\frac{3}{4}$ in (58 × 45 cm). Collection de l'Art Brut, Lausanne.* This scene depicts a pope next to an empty throne (left), a sphinx with purple grenades (right), and a blond mermaid with an Easter egg basket near her tail (bottom). This drawing was included in the exhibition *L'Art Brut*, Galerie René Drouin, Paris, (1949) and in Jean Dubuffet's associated publication, *L'Art Brut préféré aux arts culturels*.

Aloïse Corbaz, Un baiser à l'aviateur (A kiss to the pilot), *ca. 1955, colored pencil on paper, $59\frac{1}{16} \times 39\frac{3}{8}$ in (150 × 100 cm). Collection de l'Art Brut, Lausanne.* This work illustrates Corbaz's focus on lovers as a central theme, and her consistent placement of camellia flowers as breasts. More subtle symbolism can be found throughout the composition, including a pilot carrying a Christmas tree. In a state of extreme mental duress, Corbaz referred to herself as an "extinguished Christmas tree."

to Porret-Forel, the opus contains numerous papers stitched together and covered completely by gestural marks. *Le Cloisonné de théâtre* is also a grand paradigm to explore the styles, characters, and symbols significant throughout her practice. With the opening scene featuring Corbaz as a young princess, Porret-Forel described each act as representing Corbaz's "artistic and spiritual evolution."[10] The second act introduces Corbaz's struggles with mental instability, illustrated by the iconography of La Rosière and symbolic camellias as the breasts of the scene's main character. Camellia flowers are a repeated motif within Corbaz's work, representing love, madness, and the physical world. The final act is preceded by a dark depiction of birds emotive of frantic and intense feelings, then leading into a "spiritual resurrection"[11] that features the characters Psyche and Cupid. The finale is both erotic and divine, with them swirling upside-down with uncharacteristically translucent skin. Filled with metaphorical flamboyance and dramatic circumstances, *Le Cloisonné de théâtre* demonstrated a rhapsodic quest for Corbaz to solidify her identity and

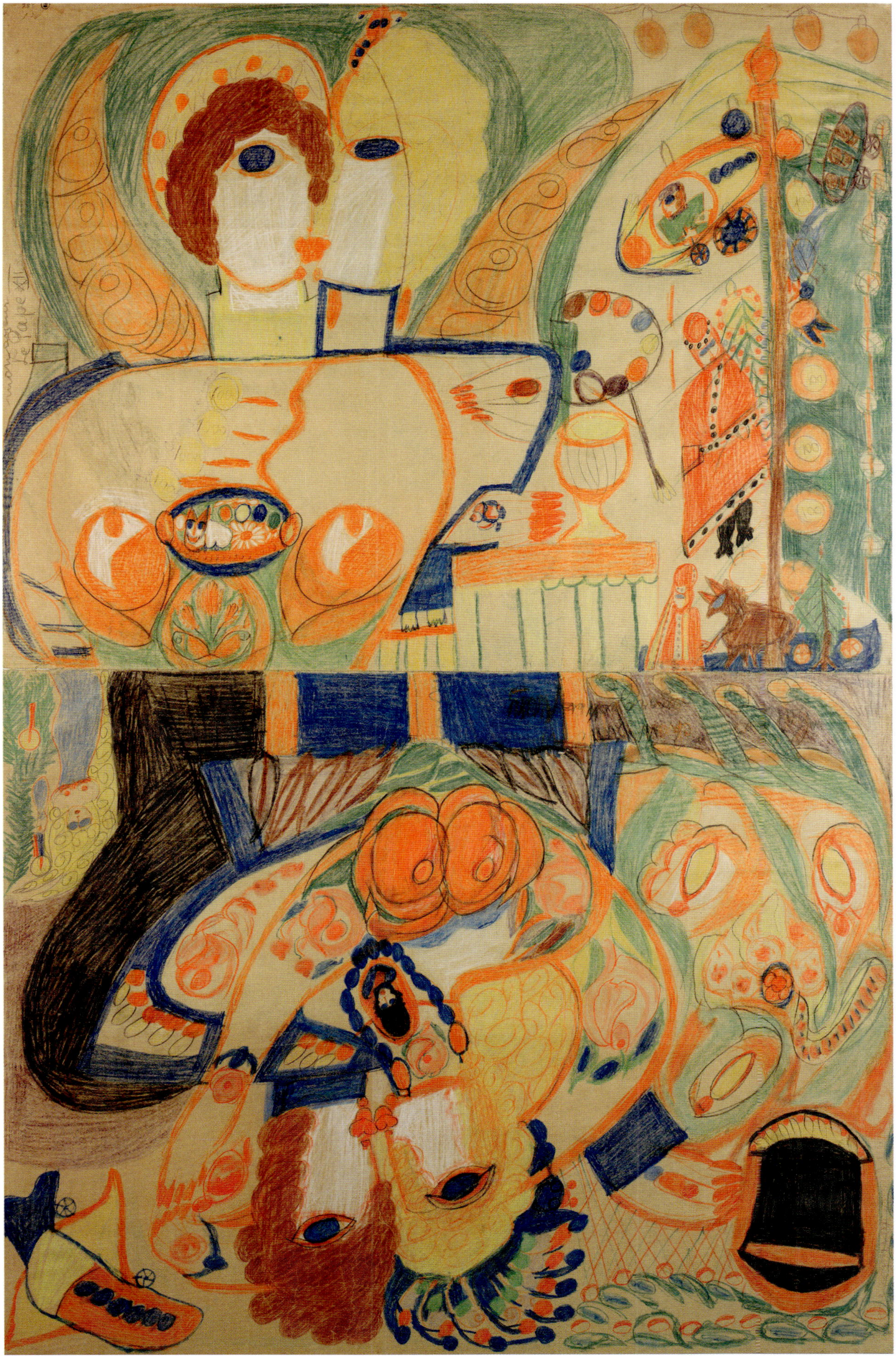

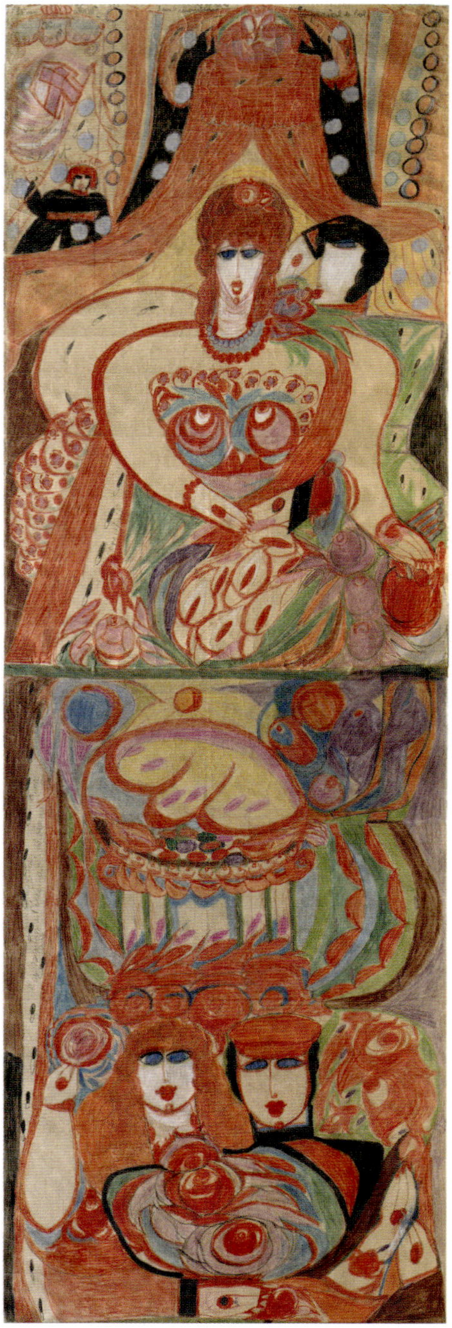

1

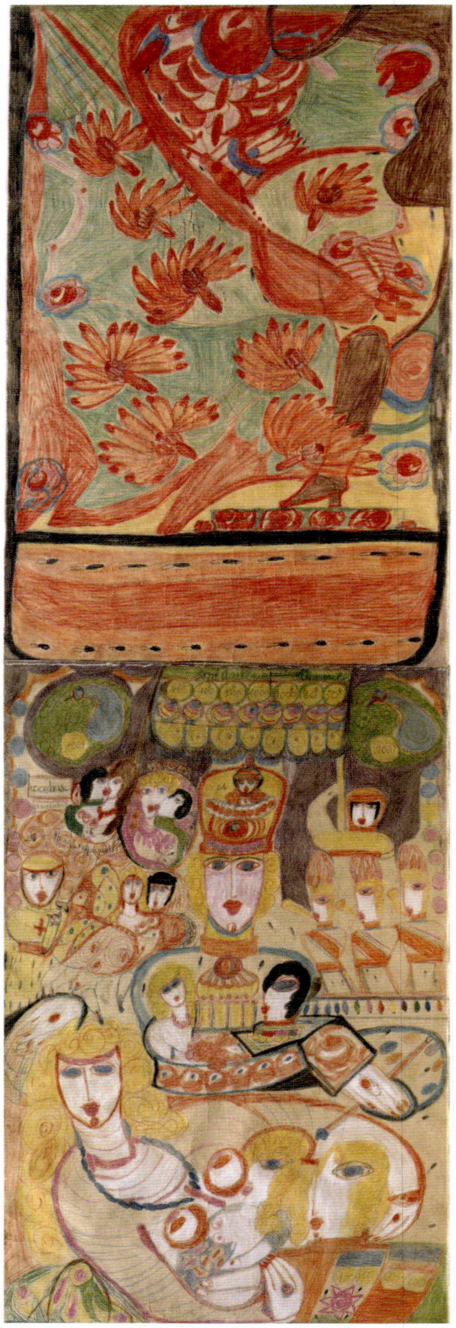

2

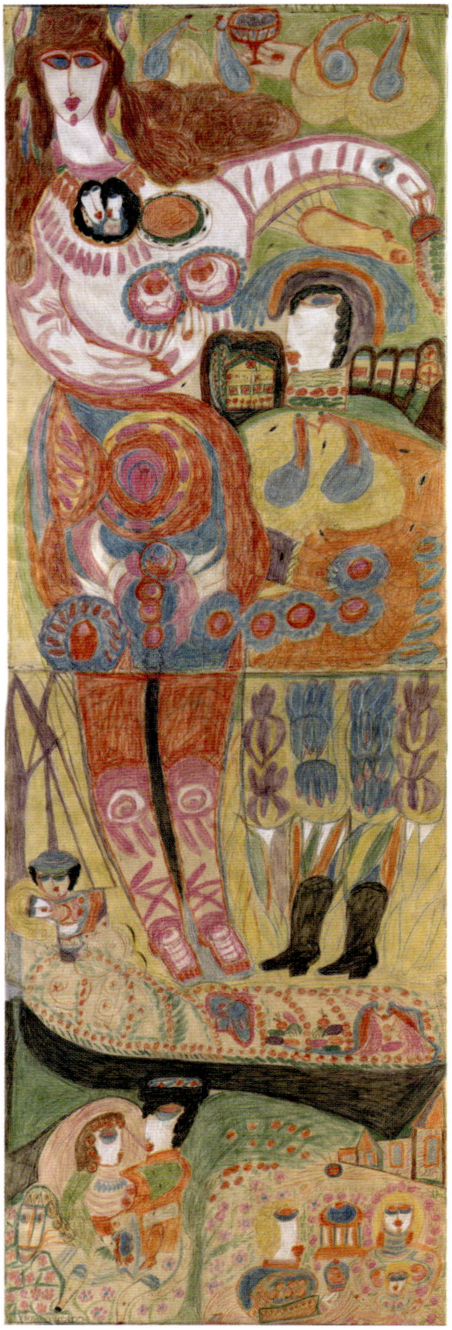

3

Aloïse Corbaz, Le Cloisonné de théâtre (The Cloisonné Theater), *1951, colored and black pencil on paper, 552¾ × 29 in (1404 × 99 cm). LaM, Lille, Collection Christine and Jean David Mermot.* This is considered to be Corbaz's single most significant creation for both its scale and complex dramatic narrative implemented with her symbols and iconography. The long scroll demonstrates her interest in theater divided into three distinct acts of a play. Each act is abruptly separated visually by hulls of ships, and filled with metaphorical representation.

present her narrative, her universe. With a steady supply of materials, the 1950s brought continued productivity to Corbaz. She evolved to working in oil pastels, and in 1960, partly due to failing eyesight, her final works were produced in Neocolor and marker. In 1963, just six months before her death, Corbaz was included in the *Swiss Society of Women Painters, Sculptors and Decorators* at the Cantonal Museum of Fine Arts, Lausanne, which she attended alongside Porret-Forel. She continued making work until three weeks before her death on April 5, 1964. Considered the most acclaimed female artist associated with the emergence of Art Brut, the intimate universe dramatized in her oeuvre is significant beyond the confines of original classification. To balance the bombastic with fragile, the unconscious and calculated, in the style and stories by Corbaz, speaks to a past, present, and future of feminine narratives.

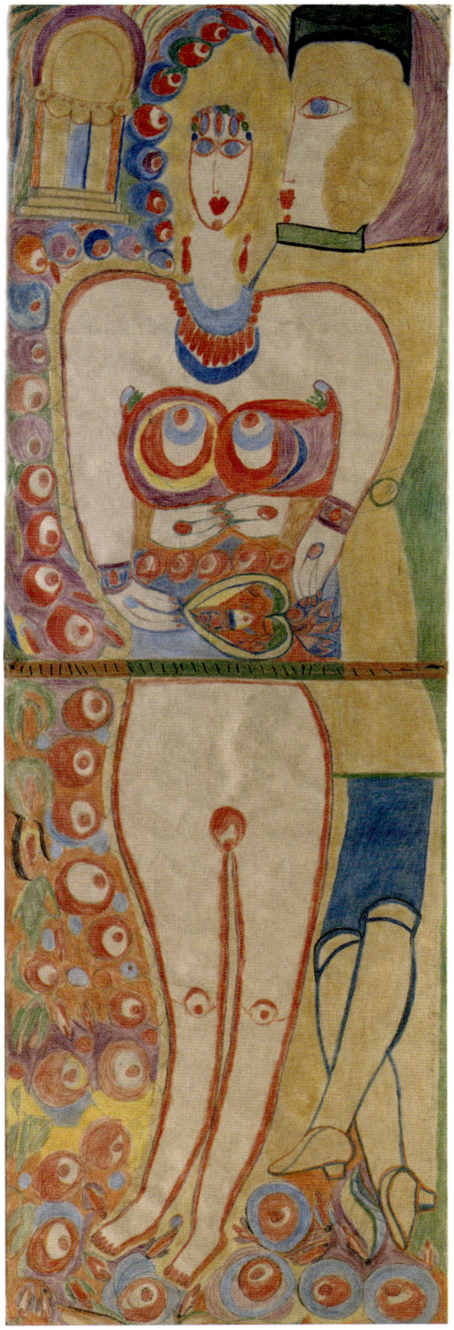

4

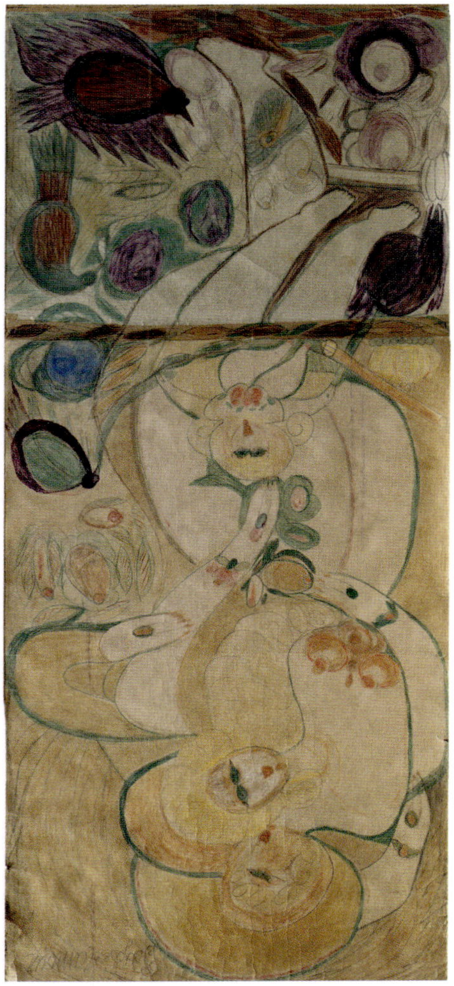

5

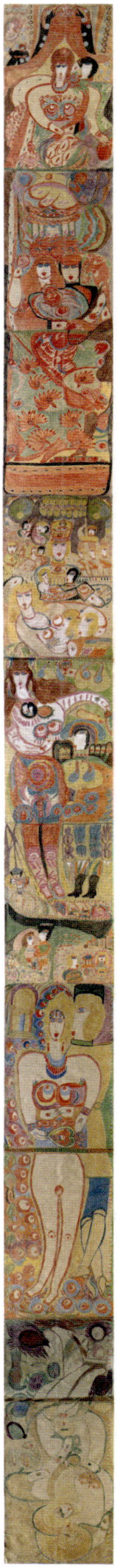

1

2

3

4

5

ADOLF WÖLFLI

(1864–1930 Bern, Switzerland)

Composer, writer, and illustrator, Adolf Wölfli's prolific oeuvre emulates power, beauty, and tension. His creative output of drawings, collages, and musical scores was produced while confined to the Waldau Mental Asylum (now the Psychiatric University Clinic). Wölfli had a tumultuous and impoverished childhood, and following his attempts to commit sexual assault, he was admitted to Waldau in 1895. He was a violent and aggressive patient, but in 1899 his behavioral tendencies were mitigated when he began to draw. Wölfli is widely identified for the meticulous visual sophistication of his drawings. Complex and detailed, their palpable emotive qualities were recognized by Dr. Walter Morgenthaler who studied, preserved, and championed Wölfli's oeuvre. He published the key monograph *Ein Geisteskranker als Künstler (Madness and Art: the Life and Works of Adolf Wölfli)* in 1921. Following a trip to the Waldau Mental Asylum in 1945, French artist Jean Dubuffet was immediately magnetized by the work of Wölfli, who posthumously became one of the most significant artists categorized under Art Brut.

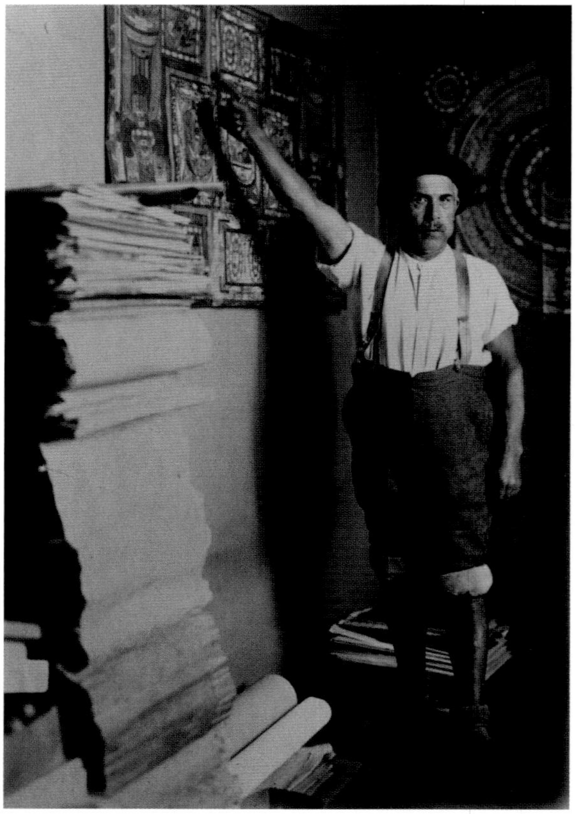

Adolf Wölfli, 1921, photograph. Archives of the Collection de l'Art Brut, Lausanne. This portrait of Wölfli, taken in his room at the Waldau Mental Asylum in Bern, captures his prolific output of both writing and drawing. At the time of this photograph Wölfli was working on his third body of work: *Hefte mit Liedern und Tänzen* (*Books with Songs and Dances*, 1917–1922).

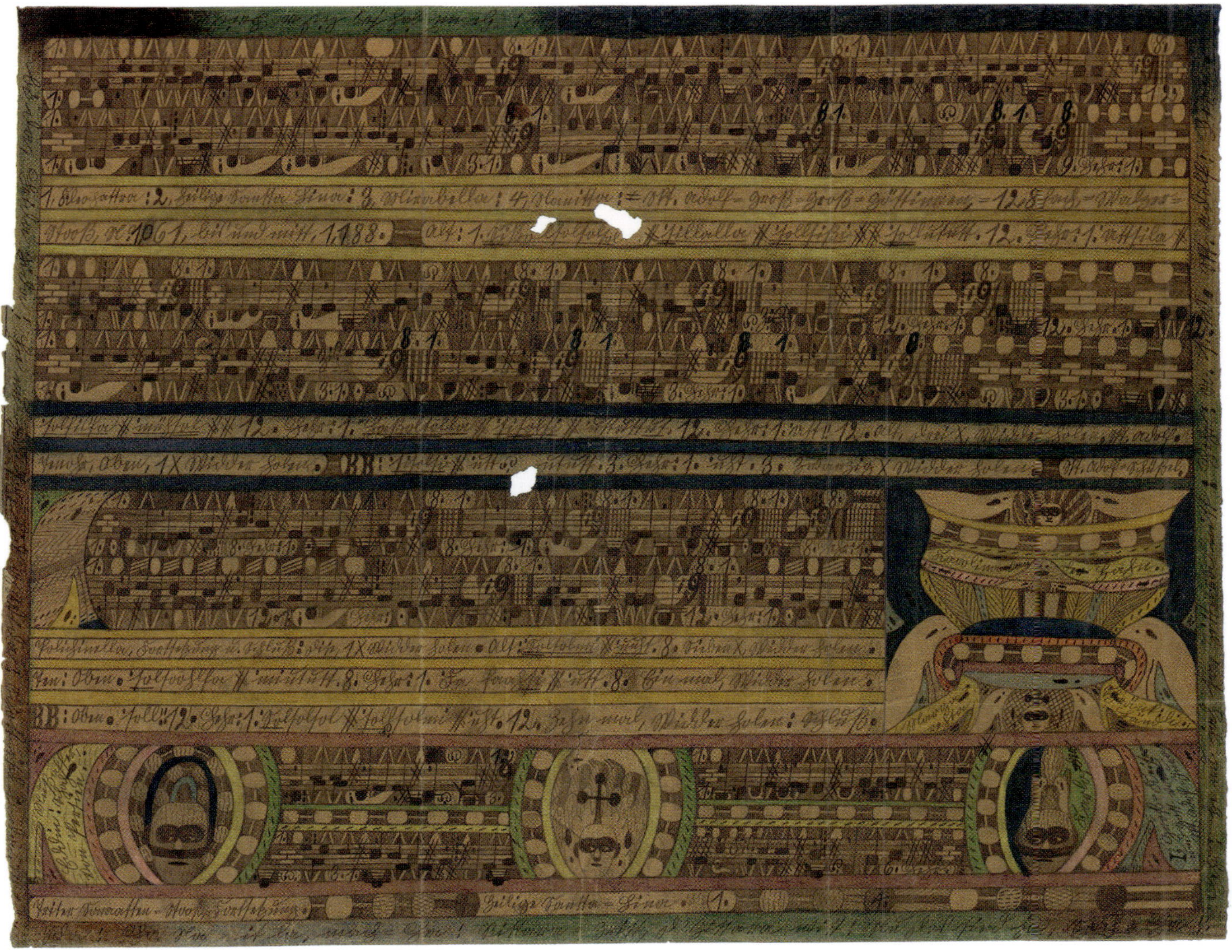

Adolf Wölfli, Sonate en clef de Saint Adolf (Sonata in key of Saint Adolf), *1916, graphite and colored pencil on paper, $27\frac{9}{16} \times 35\frac{13}{16}$ in (70 × 91 cm). Collection de l'Art Brut, Lausanne.* This sonata from 1916, part of Wölfli's second work *Geografisch und Algebraische Hefte* (*Geographic and Algebraic Books*, 1912–1916), is significant for the genesis of *Skt. Adolf-Riesen-Schöpfung* (*St. Adolf Giant Creation*), creating/canonizing his authored ego, "St. Adolf II," in July of 1916.

Admitted to the Waldau Mental Asylum at age 31, Adolf Wölfli spent more of his life under the confines of institutionalization than not. Prior to his incarceration, Wölfli was both the victim and culprit of several abhorrent circumstances. Born into an impoverished family, he was abandoned by his father around 1870, followed by the death of his mother a few years later. Orphaned, he faced neglect and abuse as an indentured child laborer. From 1880, Wölfli was a transient farmhand for various properties and suffered an immense heartbreak concerning a forbidden romance with a farmer's daughter. Between 1890 and 1895, he was arrested twice for attempts of sexual assault on young girls resulting in the examination of his mental state. After being committed to Waldau Mental Asylum, Wölfli remained there for 35 years until his death in 1930.

Wölfli's narrative oeuvre—developed from 1908 until his death—is his magnus opus. Consisting of five extensive works, it totals 25,000 pages of illustrated prose, drawings, collages, and musical scores. Fictional but partly auto-biographical, Wölfli's creative production provided a self-reflective space within the narrative. In his first work *Von der Wiege bis zum Graab* (*From the Cradle to the Grave*, 1908–1922) Wölfli introduces his alter ego "Doufi." Positioned as a travelogue, it references his early lived experiences, set specifically while his mother was still alive, with fictional elements prominently observable, such as the story's opening with Doufi's family immigrating to America. The second work, *Geografisch und Algebraische Hefte* (*Geographic and Algebraic Books*, 1912–1916) proposes the development of *Saint Adolf-Giant-Creation,* expanding

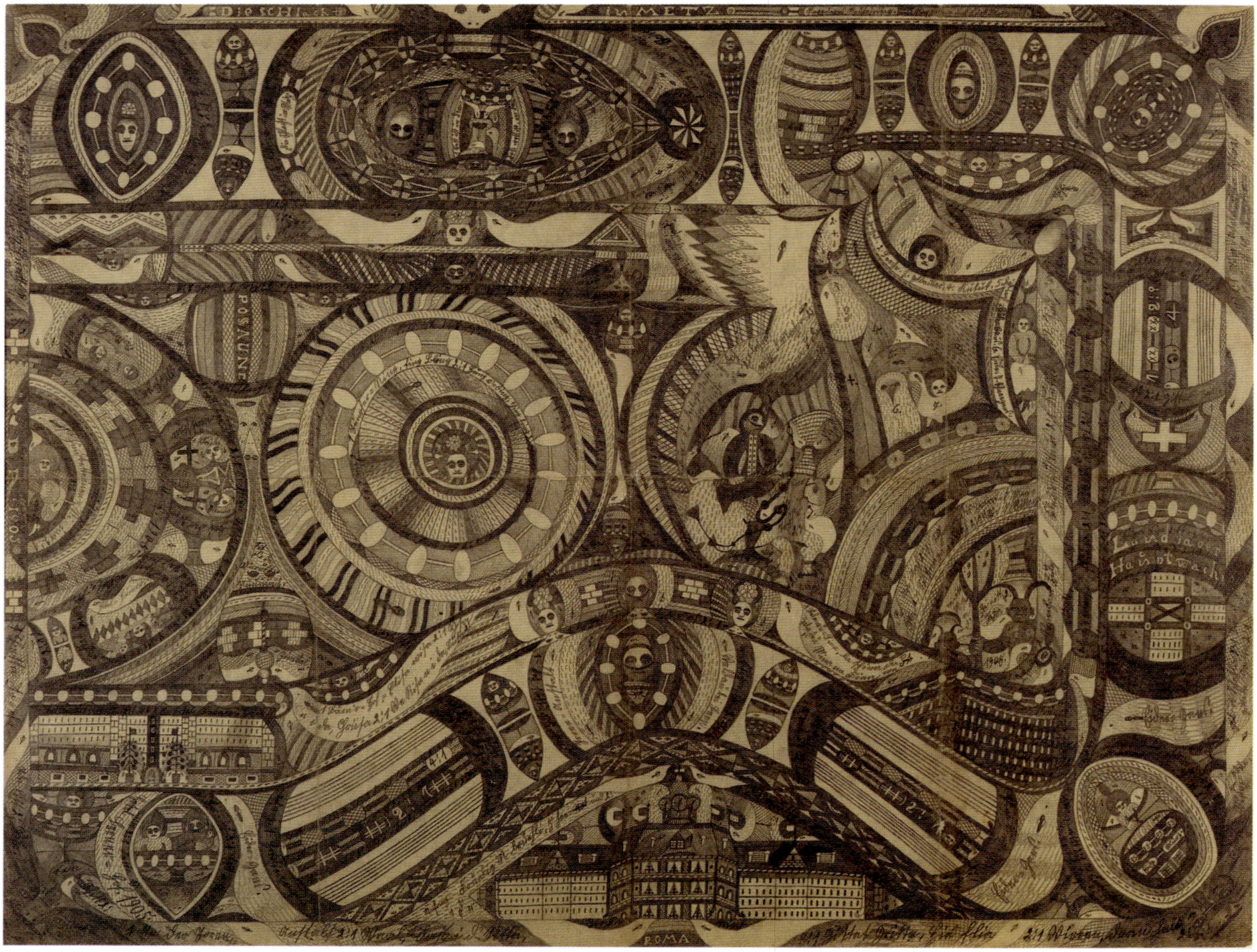

Adolf Wölfli, Hotel Berner-Hof, *1905, graphite pencil on newspaper, 29 11/16 × 39 3/16 in (75.4 × 99.6 cm). LaM, Lille Métropole musée d'art moderne d'art contemporain et d'art brut.* An example of a rare early work by Wölfli and part of several surviving drawings. Records indicate that Wölfli may have been drawing as early as 1899, and these initial works are monochromatic. A couple of years after this drawing, in around 1907, he switched to working in color, perhaps prompted by the arrival of Walter Morganthaler.

from worldly to intergalactic travel, and in 1916 Wölfli also proclaimed himself "St. Adolf II." Wölfli introduces an invented numerical set and compelling visuals that calculate Doufi's fortune. In the subsequent works *Hefte mit Liedern und Tänzen* (*Books with Songs and Dances*, 1917–1922), *Album-Hefte mit Tänzen und Märschen (Album Books with Dances and Marches*, 1924–28) and *Trauer-Marsch* (*Funeral March*, 1928–1930) the narrative continues to evolve from autobiographical to mythic to fantastical via texts, illustrations, collage, and music.

"Would you, kind reader, like to stage with me a majestic voyage, as far as or to the very farthest heavenly bodies in the realm of the divine Universe: So kindly accompany me by ship, vehicle, and railway, to the gigantic God-Father-Heaven Island, in the Southern part of the immense, almost endless, Great-East Sea. Ha, ha, ha."
– Adolf Wölfli, excerpt from *Geographic and Algebraic Book* 11, (1913)[12]

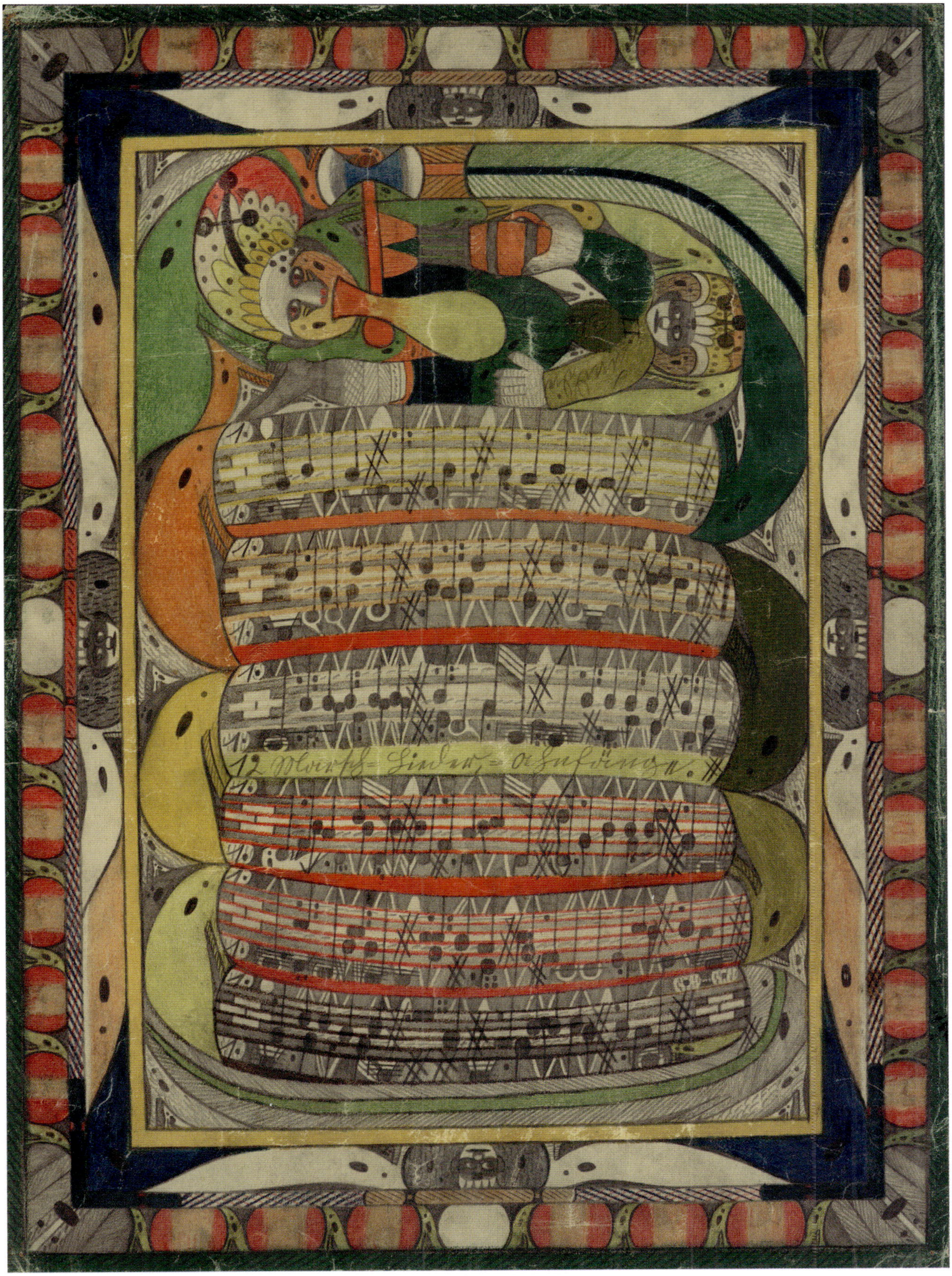

Adolf Wölfli, Saint Adolf mordu à la jambe par le serpent (Saint Adolf bitten in the leg by a snake), *1921, graphite and colored pencil on paper, 26¾ × 20¹⁄₁₆ in (68 × 51 cm). Collection de l'Art Brut, Lausanne.* A part of *Hefte mit Liedern und Tänzen* (*Books with Songs and Dances*), which features marches, polkas, and mazurkas and was exhibited in the 1949 *l'Art Brut* exhibition at Galerie René Drouin, Paris. The top of this drawing illustrates St. Adolf being bitten by a snake and performing oral sex. The snake's coiled body is covered with musical notes and inscriptions.

FLEURY-JOSEPH CRÉPIN

(1875, Hénin-Liétard–1948, Montigny-en-Gohelle, France)

Fleury-Joseph Crépin was initiated into Spiritualism[13] in 1930 and became a respected healer within the French Spiritualist circle in Arras. Crépin was born and raised in northern France and eventually ran an ironmonger business. In 1938, while transcribing music, Crépin declared guardian angels guided him to start drawing. Initially, the creative markings were only sketches or designs confined within a notebook. Lead by spirits, in 1939, Crépin began reinterpreting each "sketch" into a painting. The greater number of his paintings depict temples seen by him in dreams, while the details also feature abstracted figures and animals. The totality of his oeuvre is based on the principle of symmetry. Crépin's painting technique is considered unique to him—the application of small drops of paint as the final layer to give dimensionality. Artist Jean Dubuffet had a particular interest in mediumistic makers within his pursuits of l'Art Brut, and he featured Crépin in his seminal exhibition *l'Art Brut* at Galerie René Drouin, Paris (1949). Crépin was also influential to avant-garde artists, including André Breton, who collected and referenced Crépin's work within surrealism.

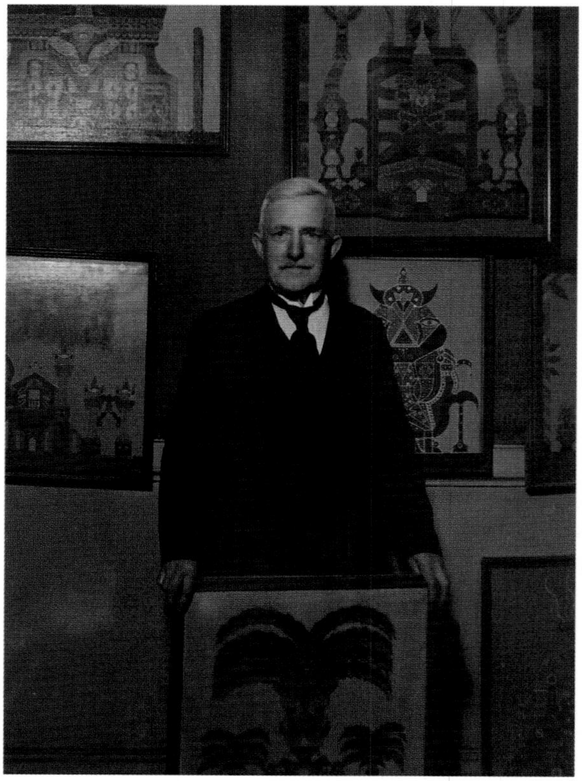

Fleury-Joseph Crépin, 1946, photograph by Marton Ervin (Hungarian, 1912–1968). LaM, Lille Métropole musée d'art moderne d'art contemporain et d'art brut. A portrait of Mediumstic Crépin, taken at a French Spiritualist exhibition. Art defined as "mediumistic" implies the work was created by a power or spirit beyond the earthly realms and the artist, the medium, is merely a vessel.

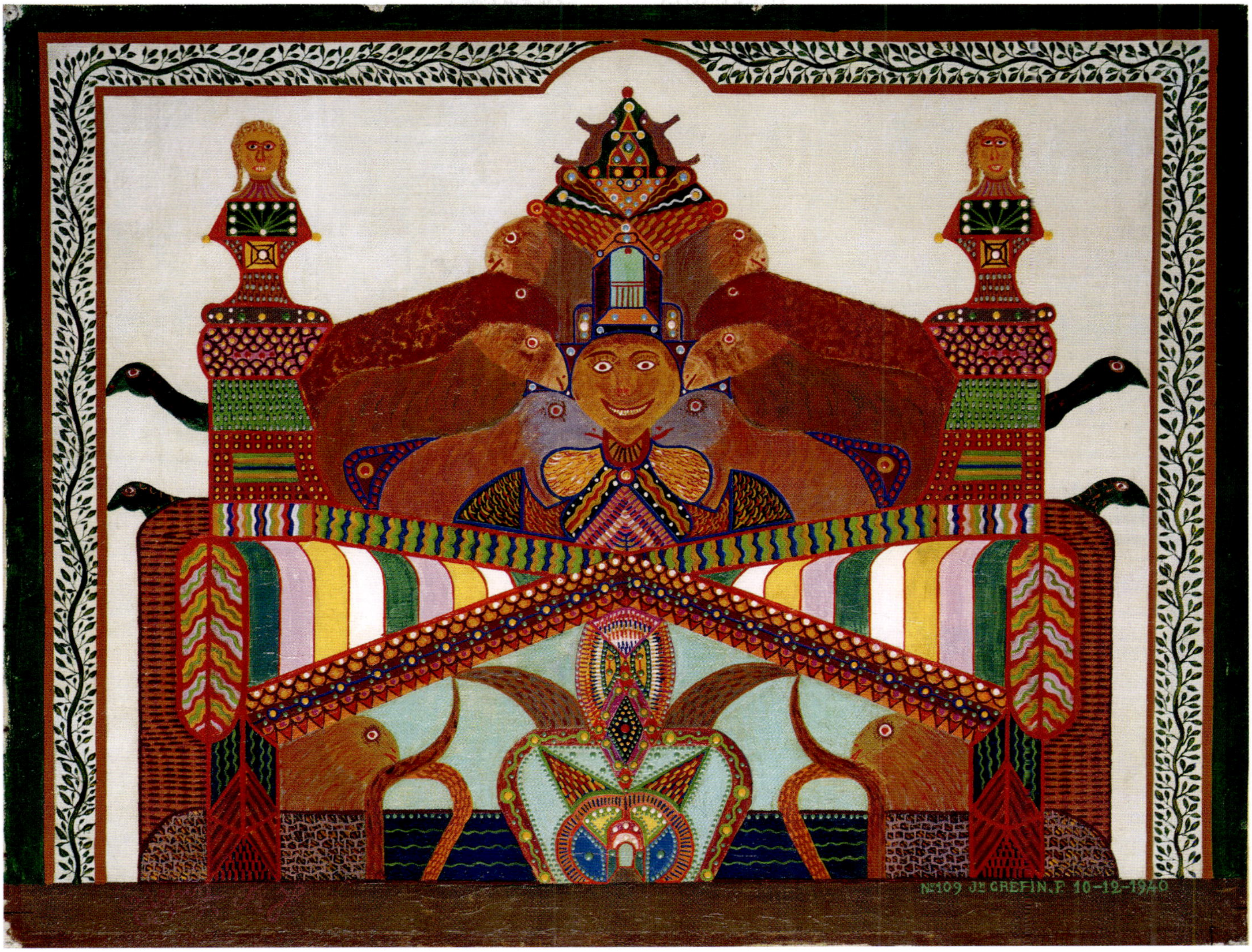

Fleury-Joseph Crépin, Composition no. 109, *1940, oil on canvas, 22 13/16 × 29 3/4 × 1 3/8 in (58 × 75.5 × 3.5 cm). Collection de l'Art Brut, Lausanne.* Number 109 of Crépin's first 300 compositions; each element is painted in a flat manner with minute details and semi-abstract animals amid the temple. It was included in the exhibition *l'Art Brut*, Galerie René Drouin, Paris (1949), and Jean Dubuffet's associated publication *L'Art Brut préféré aux arts culturels*.

Fleury-Joseph Crépin's mediumistic practice employed a precise symmetry, resulting in a divine quality. His geometric depictions of flora and fauna emote a place beyond our natural environment. In 1930, at 56 years of age, Crépin became a spiritual healer. He joined the Spiritualist circle of Arras, France, alongside Victor Brauner and Augustin Lesage, who both later became defined as mediumistic artists. Crépin was well respected for his healing work, for which he used his hands and a watch as a pendulum. He had no artistic output until he was directed by an initial voice from guardian angels.

The connection between Crépin and World War II raises uncanny circumstances of either spiritual intervention or sublime coincidence. In 1943, after the death of his wife, Crépin was living with his daughter and would paint at night. One evening while painting in solitude, Crépin heard a voice instructing him that upon completion of his 300th painting, the war would come to an end. This premonition manifested as true. Part of Crépin's process was to number and date each painting composed from his initial notebook sketch. The work cataloged by Crépin as 300 is dated May 7, 1945. Similarly, a historic study on him notes that homes with Crépin paintings were spared bombardment during World War II when most of the region was demolished.[14]

The voice from 1943 also informed Crépin that after this 300th painting he would complete a further 45 paintings collectively defined as *tableaux merveilleux* (marvelous pictures). This term relates to his technique of

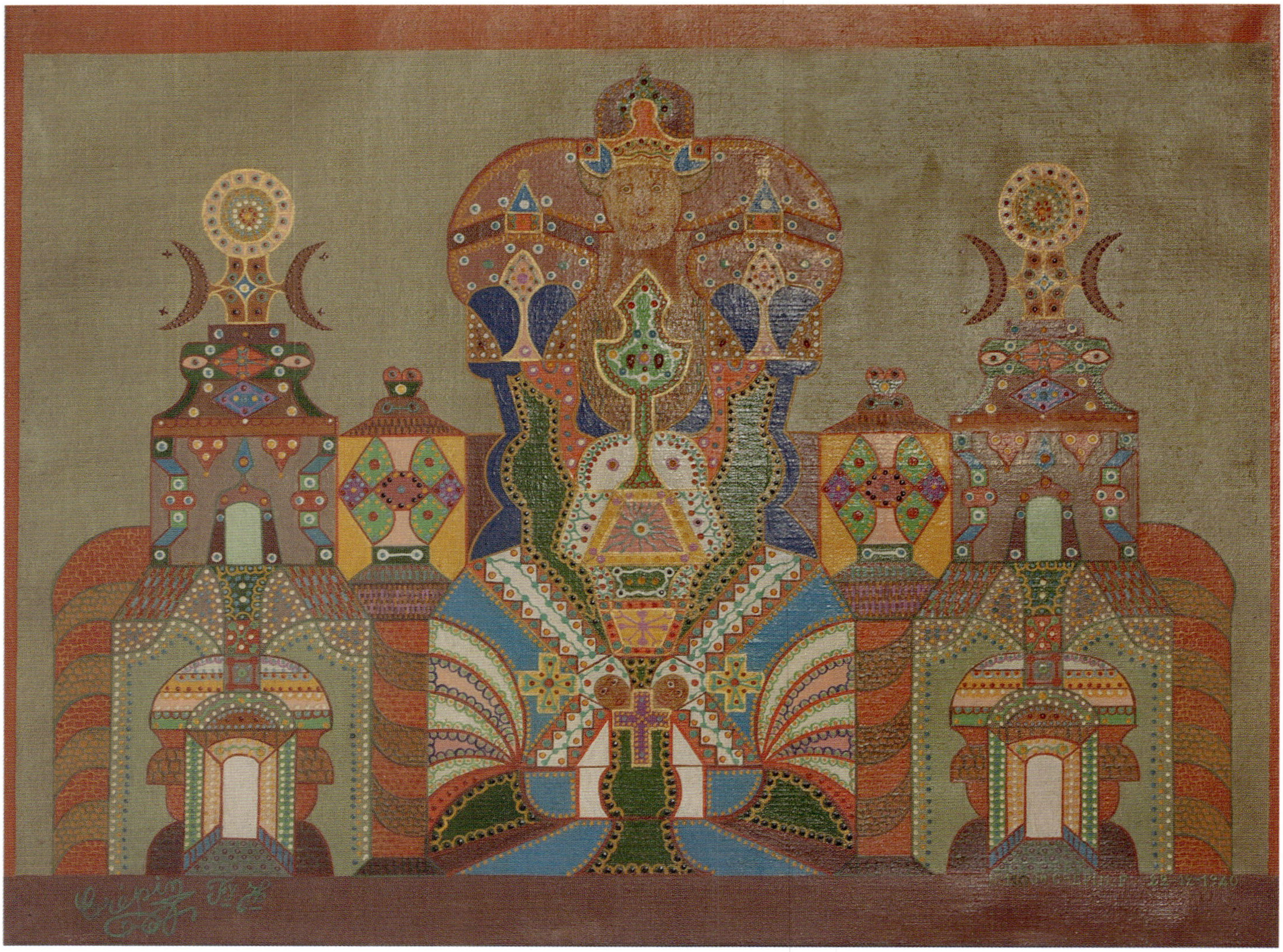

Fleury-Joseph Crépin, Composition no. 110, *1940, oil on canvas, 22⅛ × 29 in (56 × 73.5 cm). The Museum + Gallery of Everything.* This dynamic example of a temple painting by Crépin was number 110 of his first 300. Historically significant, surrealism cofounder André Breton bought the painting at one of Dubuffet's earliest l'Art Brut presentations, Foyer de l'Art Brut in 1947.

three-dimensional paint application, an organized pointillistic system that gives the painting depth and relief, and is still considered unique to Crépin. The spiritual premonition deemed that world peace would be incited with the completion of the 45 tableaux. Crépin commenced work on all 45 paintings, but the 43rd was the last tableaux to be completed.[15]

"His method is as follows: he limits himself to transferring to canvas the drawings in his notebooks, enlarging them as necessary. He is convinced that he is not responsible for the choice or distribution of colors; it is as if he were guided to place this or that color in this or that spot. Because of this, he never hesitates and suffers no regrets: this also means, as he himself has observed, that he has never 'botched a painting'." – André Breton (1896–1966), cofounder of the surrealist movement[16]

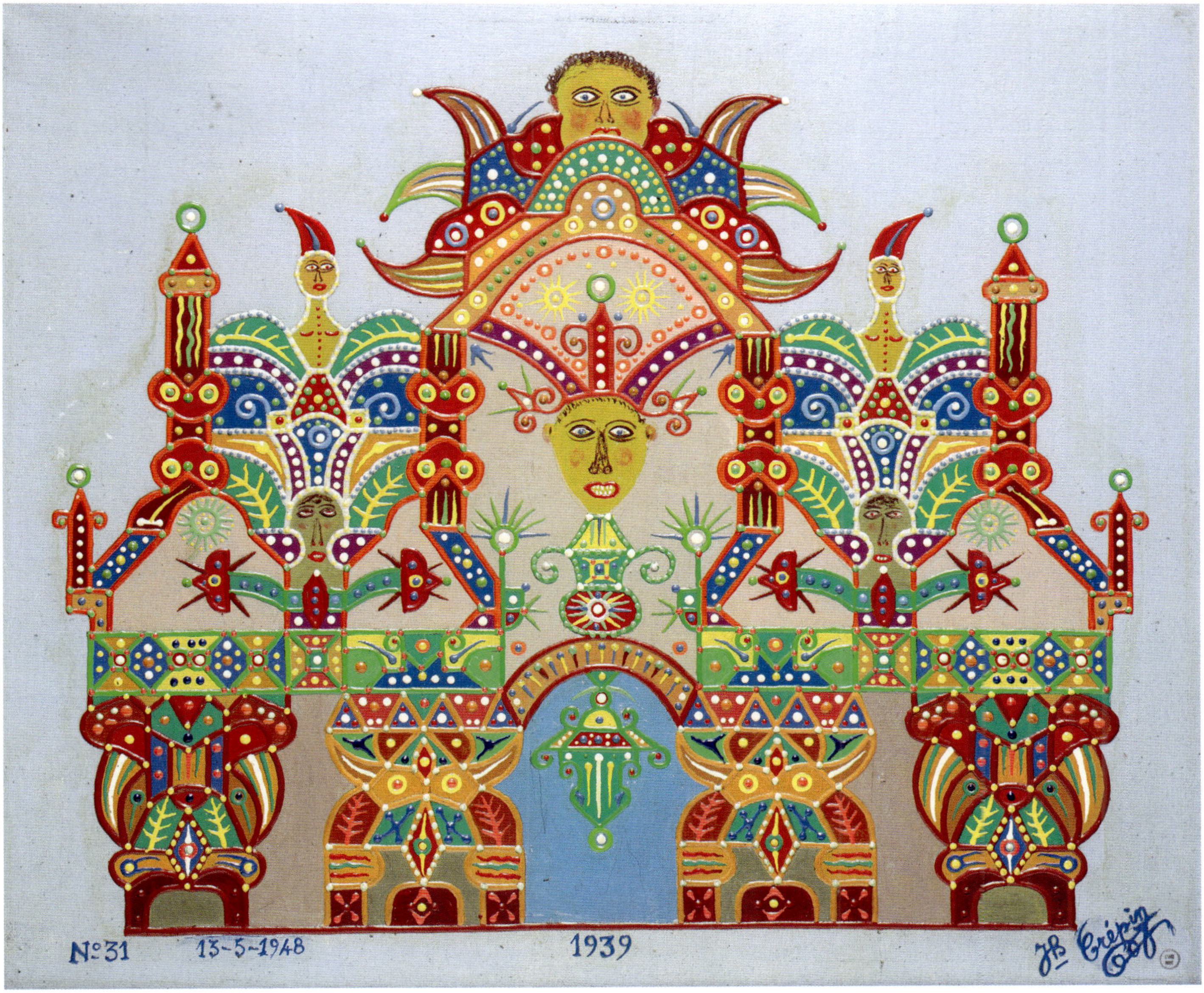

Fleury-Joseph Crépin, Composition no. 31, *1948, oil on canvas, 20½ × 24$\frac{7}{16}$ in (52 × 62 cm). Collection de l'Art Brut, Lausanne.* This painting was Crépin's 31st of his last 45 paintings, considered to be a *tableau merveilleu* (marvelous picture) characterized by its raised pointillistic texture. This temple conveys Crépin's skill in symmetry, and specific to this painting is his implementation of several faces and figures amid the architecture.

AUGUSTIN LESAGE

(1876–1954 Saint-Pierre-les-Auchel, France)

The channels and agency that informed the paintings of Augustin Lesage varied during his mediumistic production, yet his distinct, ornamentally complex oeuvre was consistent throughout. Lesage was in his mid-30s and working as a coal miner when he heard an unknown voice predicting he would be a painter. This premonition propelled his immersion into Spiritualist circles and, in 1912, claiming to be guided by spirits, Lesage began to draw and paint. Prolific in his lifetime, Lesage created over 800 paintings with his distinguishable aesthetic of architectural symmetry laden with patterned motifs and mythical symbolism. In the 1920s, his paintings were exhibited within a Spiritualist context, followed by interest from the surrealists. In 1933, André Breton featured Lesage in his essay *Le Message Automatique,* for the surrealist publication *Minotaure*. Artist Jean Dubuffet included Lesage in his third issue of *l'Art Brut* (1965) where Lesage's position as a medium contributed to Dubuffet's expanded perimeters of his category l'Art Brut beyond its initial focus on mental illness. Significant to his legacy, Lesage was included in *Outsiders* at the Hayward Gallery, Southbank Centre, London (1979), and *The Encyclopedic Palace*, 55th Venice Biennale (2013).

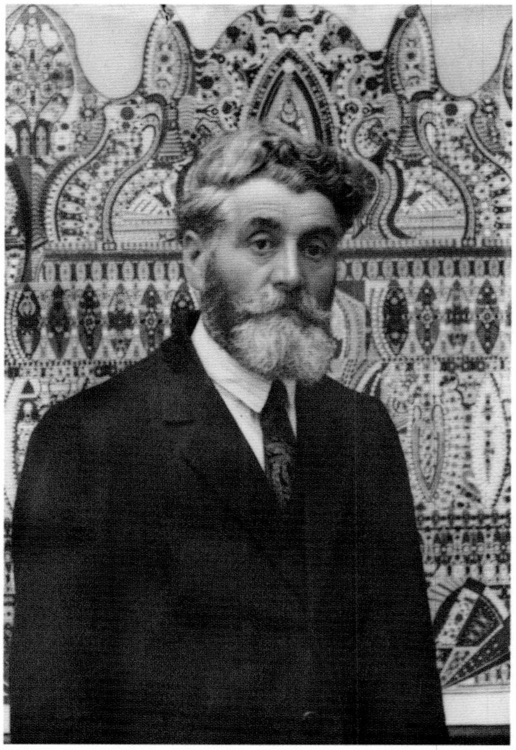

Augustin Lesage, ca. 1927, photograph by Nicolas Dewitte. LaM, Lille Métropole musée d'art moderne d'art contemporain et d'art brut. This portrait was taken in the same year that Lesage was formally legitimized as a medium, following an examined observation by the president of Institut Métapsychique, Dr. Eugène Osty.

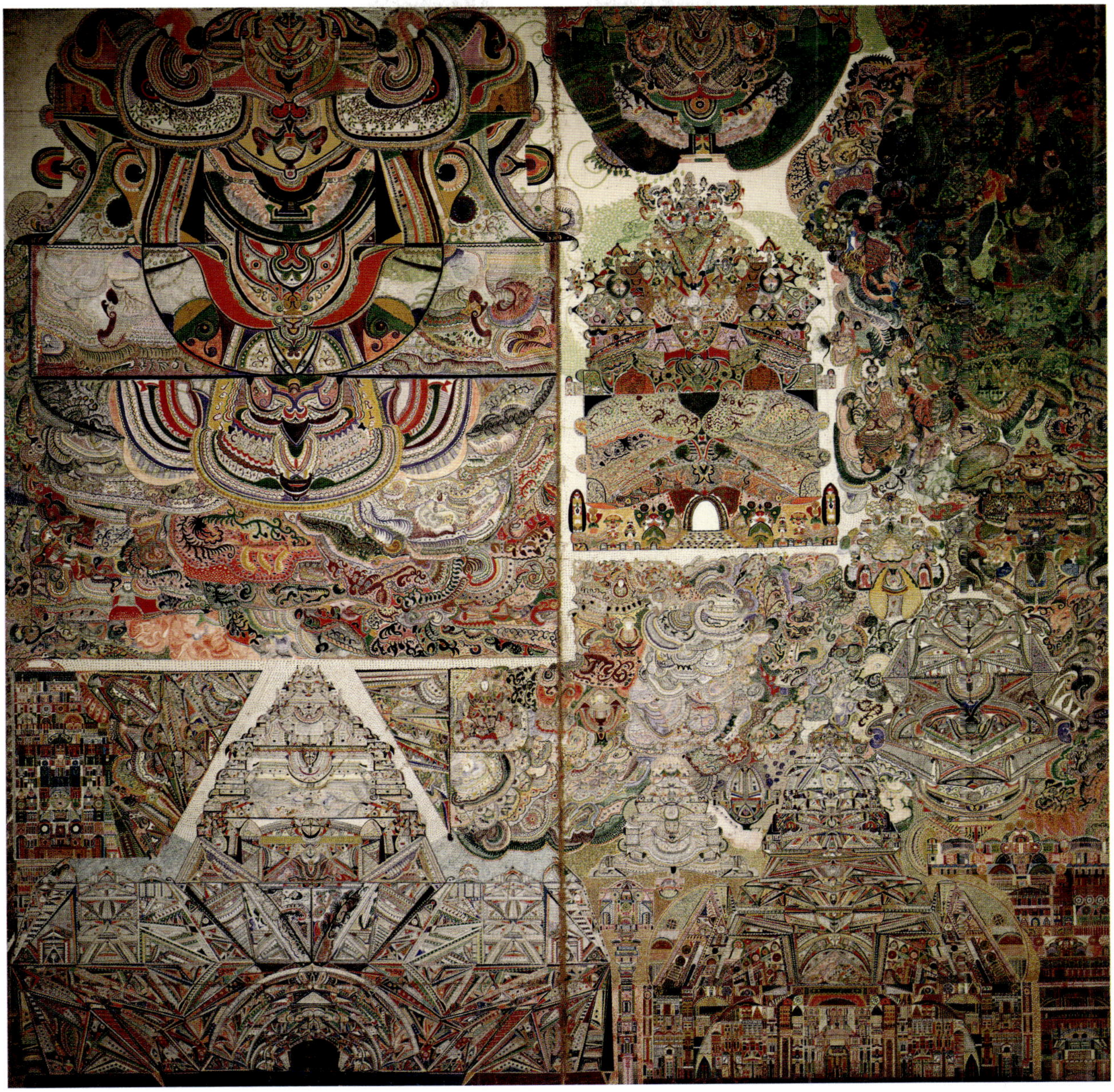

Augustin Lesage, untitled, *1912–1913, oil on canvas, 118⅛ × 118⅛ in (300 × 300 cm). Collection de l'Art Brut, Lausanne.* This monumental painting was the first composition on canvas completed by Lesage. Initiated in 1912, spirits informed him not to cut down the expansive textile into more modest canvases. Compositionally, it appears Lesage divided the work into sections exploring both symmetrical and more organic constructions.

Augustin Lesage's earliest works in 1912 were abstract drawings, created before he began his first painting. He intended to paint on a modest scale; however, when his painting materials arrived, the canvas was considerably larger than he anticipated. Lesage only had a set of small paintbrushes, but disclosed that the spirits instructed him not to cut down the tremendous canvas (118 × 118 in/ 300 × 300cm). With the affirmation that his aesthetic direction was led by spirits and his hand automated through otherworldly influence, he began in the top-right corner to meticulously populate the canvas with pattern, color, and emblematic ornamentation. This extremely detailed and monumental composition took over a year to complete and established a predominant use of large-format canvas in his oeuvre. According to Lesage, the driver of his mediumistic practice evolved throughout his artistic output. His early automatic practice was said to be guided by his deceased sister, Marie (who had died at the age of three); but in around 1925, the authorship transposed to Leonardo da Vinci. Further transpositions were to a guide Lesage called "Marius de Tyane" and to Lesage himself, reincarnated as a preeminent artist of the distant past. Certain later works signed simply "Augustin Lesage" indicated an agency free from mediumism. The non-fixed relationship to authorship perhaps related to an internal struggle of ownership and authenticity.

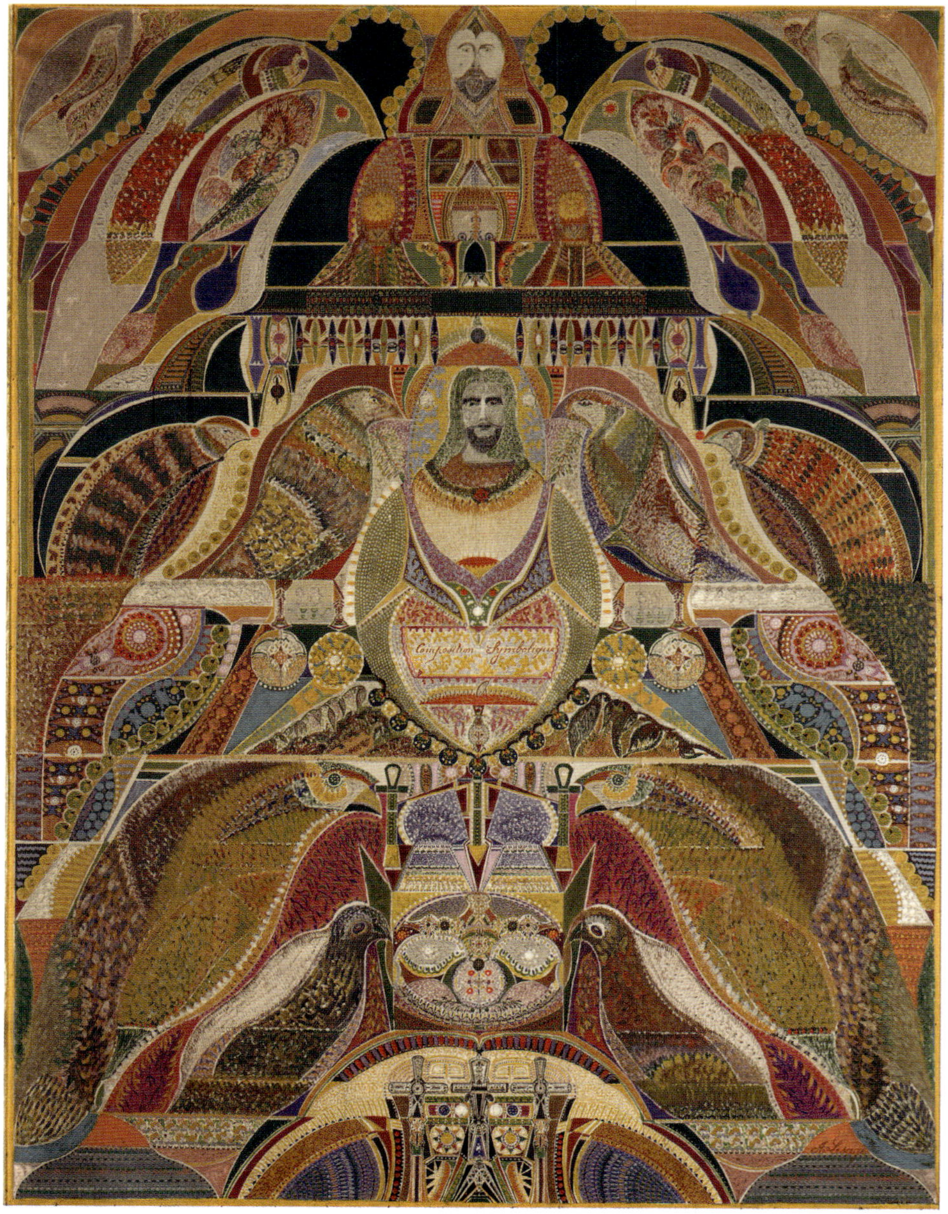

Augustin Lesage, Composition symbolique (Symbolic Composition), *1928, oil on canvas, 55½ × 42¹⁵⁄₁₆ in (141 × 109 cm). LaM, Lille Métropole musée d'art moderne d'art contemporain et d'art brut.* This looser painting by Lesage is more representational than his oeuvre of architectural and strict geometric compositions. Symmetrical profiles of birds are positioned vertically, while two male faces are centered on the middle line. This painting was reproduced in André Breton's *Le Message Automatique*, published in *Minotaure* (1933).

Augustin Lesage, untitled, *1925, oil on canvas, 83⁷⁄₁₆ × 56¹¹⁄₁₆ in (212 × 144 cm). LaM, Lille Métropole musée d'art moderne d'art contemporain et d'art brut.* This painting is an exquisite example of the symmetry and meticulous detail implemented by Lesage. Complex symmetrical axes are applied throughout the composition with ornamental details and repetitive patterns. The selective areas painted in a flat, muted, light color provide a dynamic silhouette and increased dimension.

Despite speculative criticism of Lesage's changing narrative of spiritual authors, his definitive and sophisticated aesthetic emerged without formal artistic or cultural education. Architectural forms, symmetry, and decorative and allegorical ornamental motifs developed almost spontaneously, visually directed by only a few horizontal and vertical penciled lines on the canvas. Produced in a rhythmic but machinelike process, the paintings of Lesage are distinguishable for their microscopic details that constitute a macroscopic composition.

"A picture comes into existence detail by detail, and nothing about it enters my mind beforehand. My guides have told me: 'Do not try and find out what you are doing'." – Augustin Lesage[17]

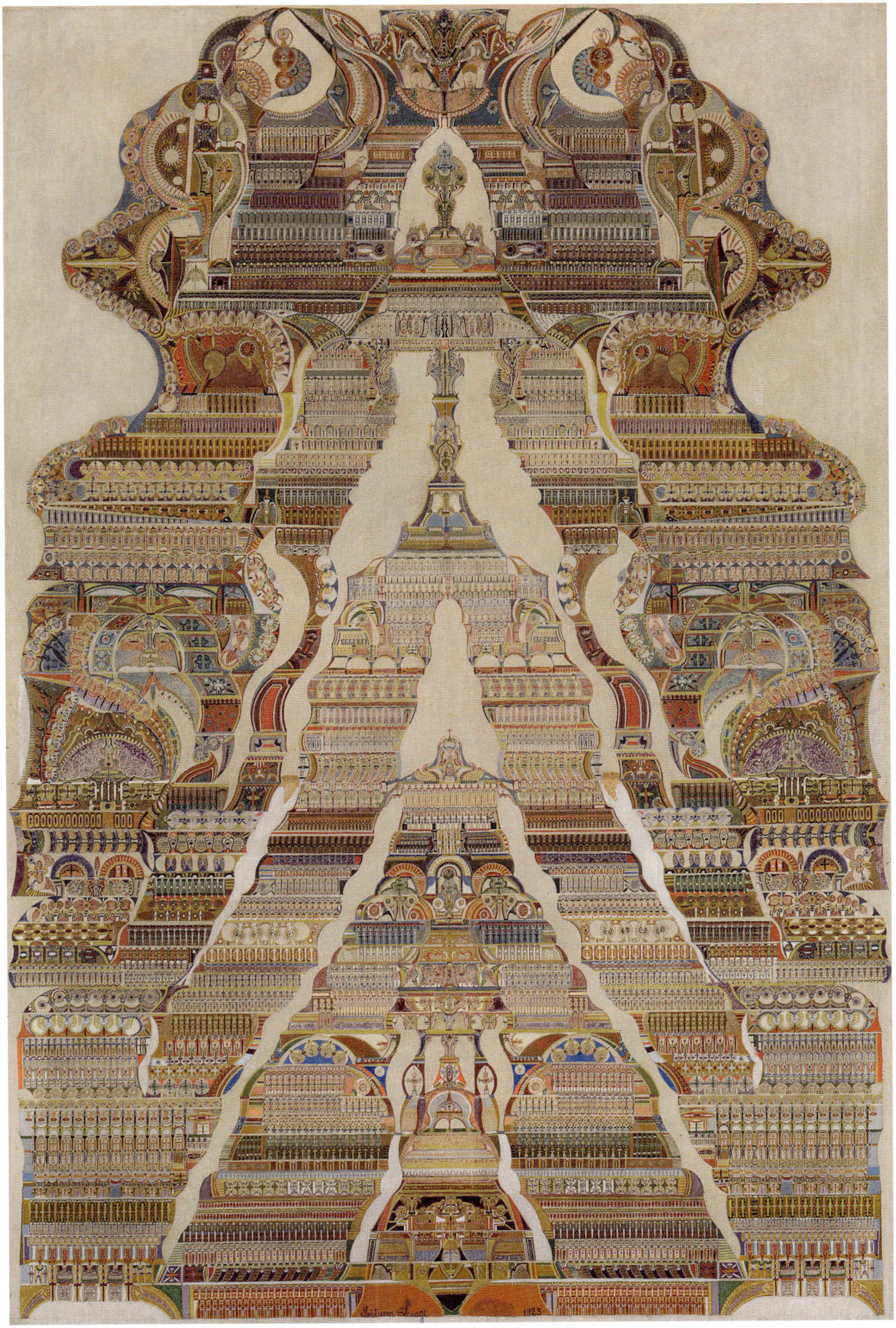

AUGUSTE FORESTIER

(1887 Lozère–1958 Saint-Alban-sur-Limagnole, France)

The desire to be transported seems integral to the life and artistic practice of Auguste Forestier. Raised in rural France, he felt compelled to run away several times during his youth; often these attempts were by boarding a train without a ticket. In 1914, with a developing interest in railroads, curiosity led Forestier to pile rocks onto a railroad track. Catastrophically, the result was not the power of a locomotive crushing the debris as he assumed, but a derailment of the convoy. Consequently, he was admitted to the psychiatric hospital at Saint-Alban-sur-Limagnole. Forestier served purposes in the hospital: working in the store and kitchen and, sometimes using materials from his workplaces, he began to draw and, more profoundly, sculpt. Through carving wood and butcher's bone with a shoemaker's knife, his intimate oeuvre consisted of figures, animals, boats, and medals (which he wore proudly). His creative output was accessible to view and engage with for staff, attendants, and visitors in the hospital. Following a visit to the hospital by French artist Jean Dubuffet in 1945, Forestier's sculptures were first collected by Jean Dubuffet in 1948 and included in the *l'Art Brut* exhibition at Galerie René Drouin, Paris (1949).

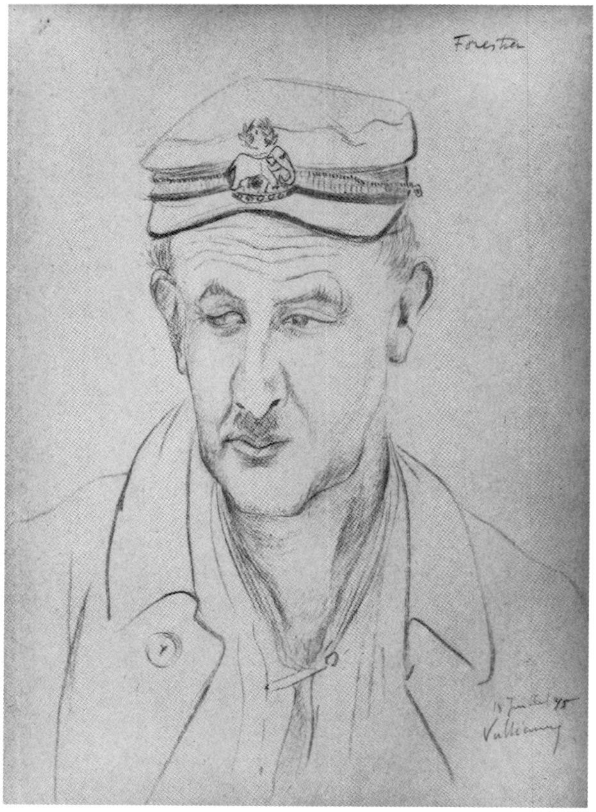

Auguste Forestier, portrait drawn by Gérard Vulliamy (French, 1909–2005), 1945. Collection de l'Art Brut, Lausanne. Although a photograph of Forestier does not exist, surrealist painter Vulliamy drew a portrait of him while spending time at Saint-Alban-sur-Limagnole in the 1940s.

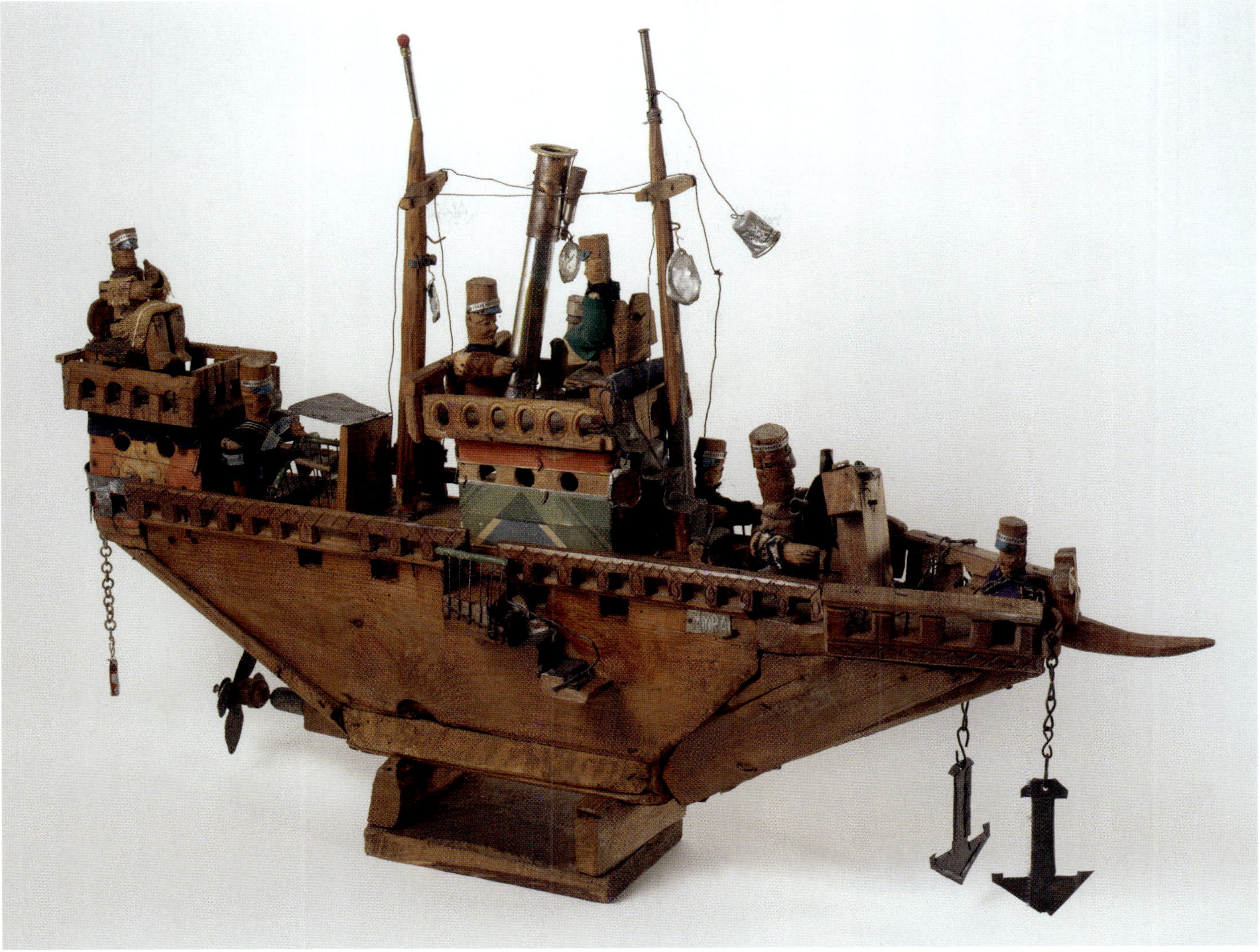

August Forestier, Bateau (Boat)*, 1935–1949, wood, metal, wire, glass, fabric, cardboard, paper, coated canvas, leather, dye, paint, varnish, 32¼ × 47¼ × 9¹³⁄₁₆ in (82 × 120 × 25 cm). LaM, Lille Métropole musée d'art moderne d'art contemporain et d'art brut.* Forestier's sculptures included objects related to transportation—this boat is constructed with immense detail, including metal anchors dangling from chains, ornamental detail carved into the upper deck's railing, and several seaman outfitted in bespoke uniforms. Forestier reused objects found at the hospital—the bell dangling from the top of the boat is a sewing thimble.

Born the seventh child of a farming family, Auguste Forestier's childhood attempts to flee by illegal train journeys were efforts to transport himself from his immediate environment. Following his detainment at the age of 27, Forestier's desire to be liberated from his circumstances remained; between 1914 and 1923 he attempted to escape the hospital numerous times. A psychiatrist at Saint-Alban, Jean Oury, suggested that by establishing himself in the role of creator, Forestier aided his acceptance of his environment, thus subsiding his urgency for physical transformation. The physicality of a need to escape turned into the concept of escapism, allowing the characters and objects made by Forestier to be the transport.

The personal iconography of Forestier's sculptural forms were initially simple, or toylike, figures and animals, then developed into complex boats, soldiers, horsemen, and even monstrous characters. He had a predilection for medals, attributing the carved medallions he wore as laurels bestowed upon him from the railroad company, and adorned his characters with smaller versions. Feathers, fabric, found teeth, and even carved bones (sourced from the hospital kitchen), are a selection of the material and multifaceted elements incorporated into his wooden sculptures.

While the concept of Forestier's oeuvre was personal, inferring a private escapism, his process and practice were outwardly public (within the confines of the hospital). He set up his studio/workshop in the corridor of the institution. When more established in his practice, Forestier relished in sharing his work with those who could leave the hospital—perhaps a metaphorical escape from this environment via the transportation of his carvings to the world beyond.

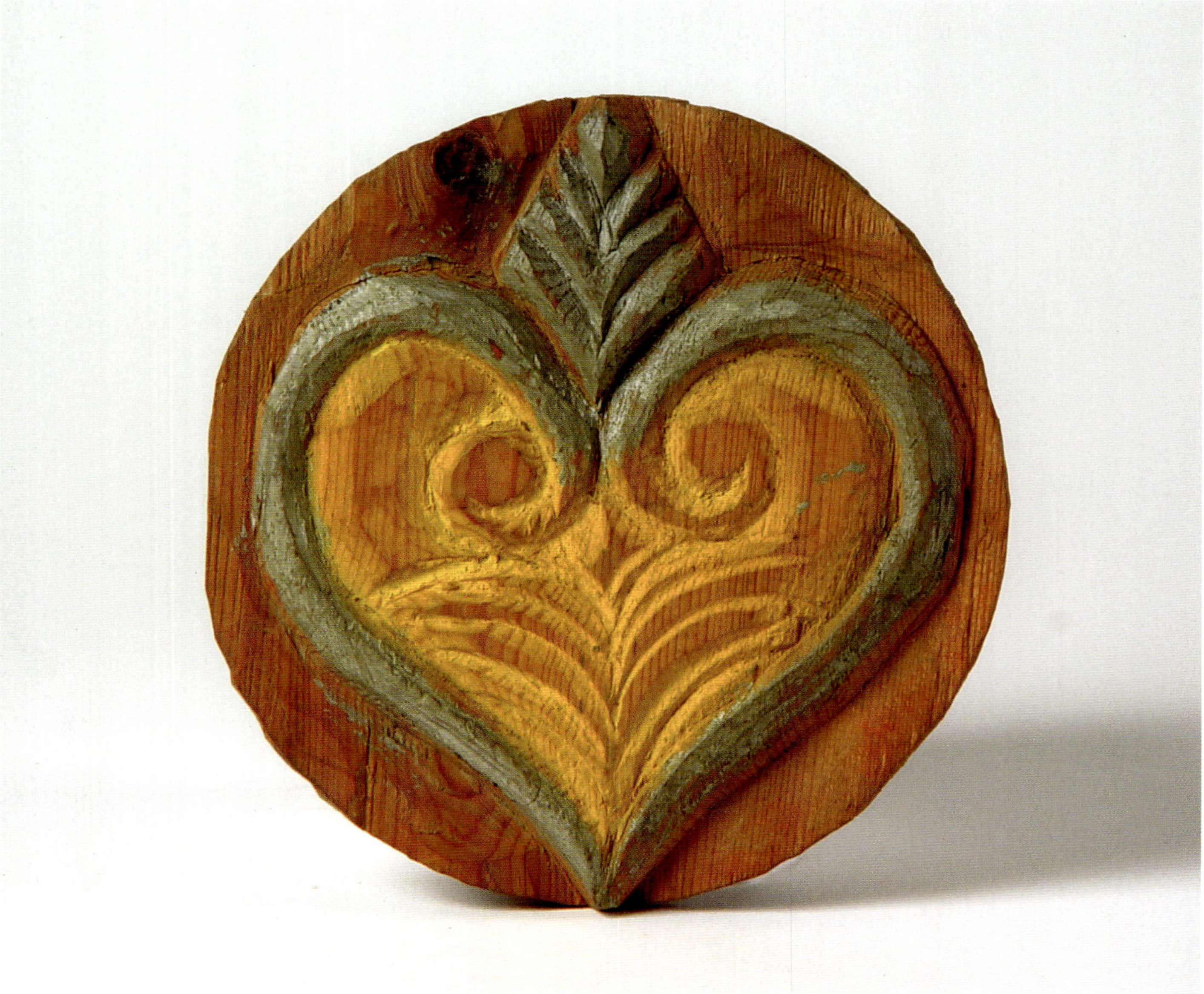

August Forestier, Médaillon orné d'un coeur (Medallion decorated with a heart)*, 1935–1949, wood and paint, 6 5⁄16 in (16 cm) diameter, 1 in (2.5 cm) depth. LaM, Lille Métropole musée d'art moderne d'art contemporain et d'art brut.* Forestier's practice included constructing medallions, which he used to adorn his carved figures (see opposite). The scale of this wooden medal indicated Forestier likely would have worn it himself as a proclaimed accolade from the railroad company.

August Forestier, untitled*, 1935–1949, assembly of carved wood and other materials, 20 3⁄16 × 7 3⁄8 × 9 7⁄16 in (51.3 × 18.7 × 24 cm). Collection de l'Art Brut, Lausanne.* This carved figure with a bird's head was included in the exhibition *l'Art Brut*, Galerie René Drouin, Paris (1949). It demonstrates Forestier's penchant for adorning his carvings with diverse materials, in this case using what appears to be a zipper for detailing the cap and neck, as well as fringed fabric draping at the chest.

"This transformation from a nomad into a sedentary man can only be the logical result of the transformation of a traveler into a producer. But Forestier's work will always bear traces of the ideal of the traveler." – Psychiatrist, Jean Oury (1924–2014)[18]

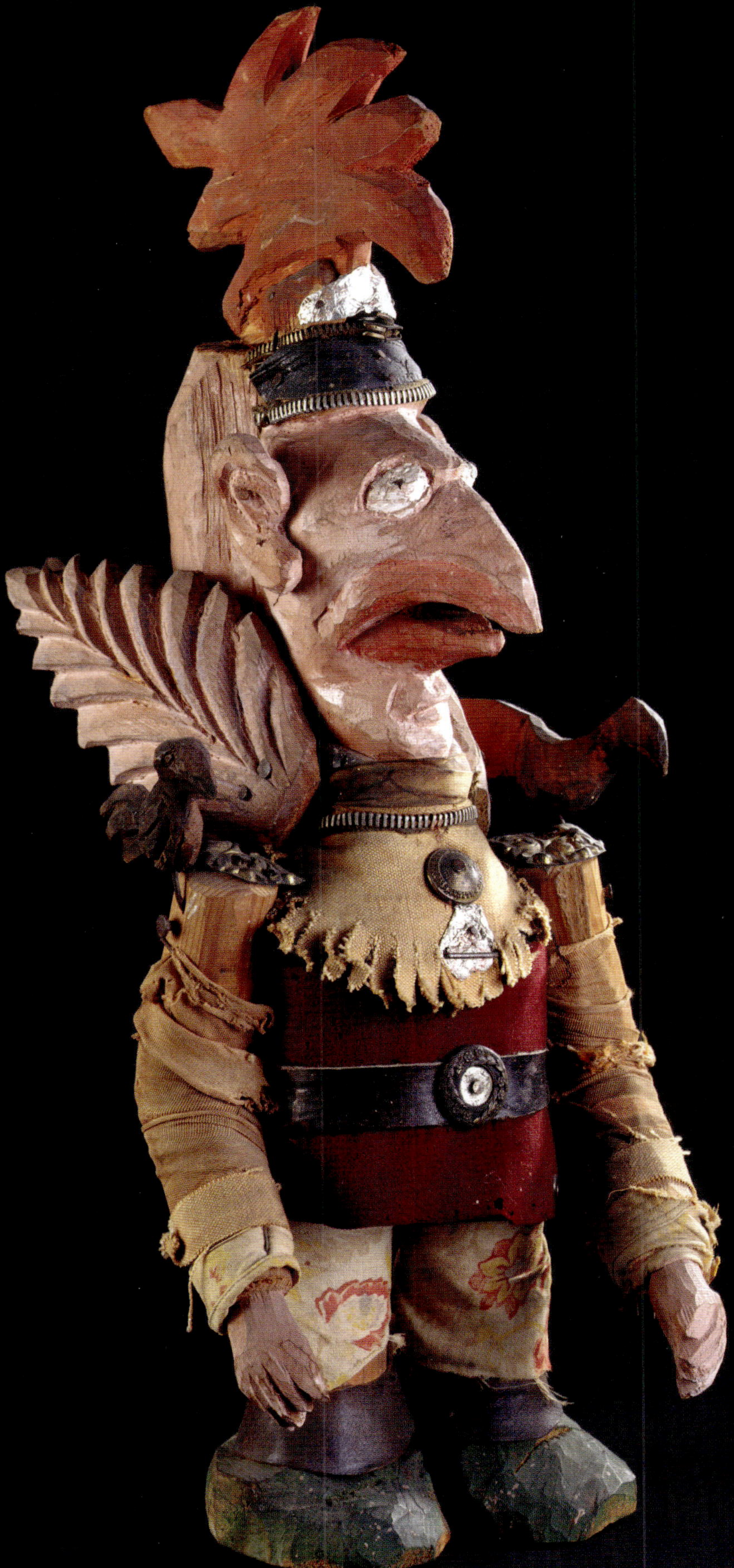

MARGUERITE SIRVINS

(1890–1957 Lozère, France)

Living in Paris from 1925, Marguerite Sirvins was excelling in her millinery studies when, in 1930, subsequent to her sister's marriage, she suffered severe depression. Following several suicide attempts and a return to her place of birth, Lozère, Sirvins was admitted to Font d'Aurelle hospital in Montpellier. After a year she was transferred to the psychiatric hospital at Saint-Alban-sur-Limagnole, where she would remain until her death. In 1944, she began to draw and embroider with techniques influenced by her millinery training. Sirvins' creative endeavors relieved aspects of her mental instability. Artist Jean Dubuffet's intrigue in art from psychiatric institutions propelled a correspondence with Saint-Alban, and Sirvins was included in Dubuffet's *l'Art Brut* exhibition at Galerie René Drouin, Paris (1949). Her most ambitious textile, however, would not be produced until the last two years of her life. From 1955, she commenced the construction of her final work—an intricately embroidered wedding dress executed without a sketch or pattern. Due to experiencing intensified delusions, Sirvins believed the exquisite bridal gown was for her forthcoming, though only existent in her imaginary realm, wedding.

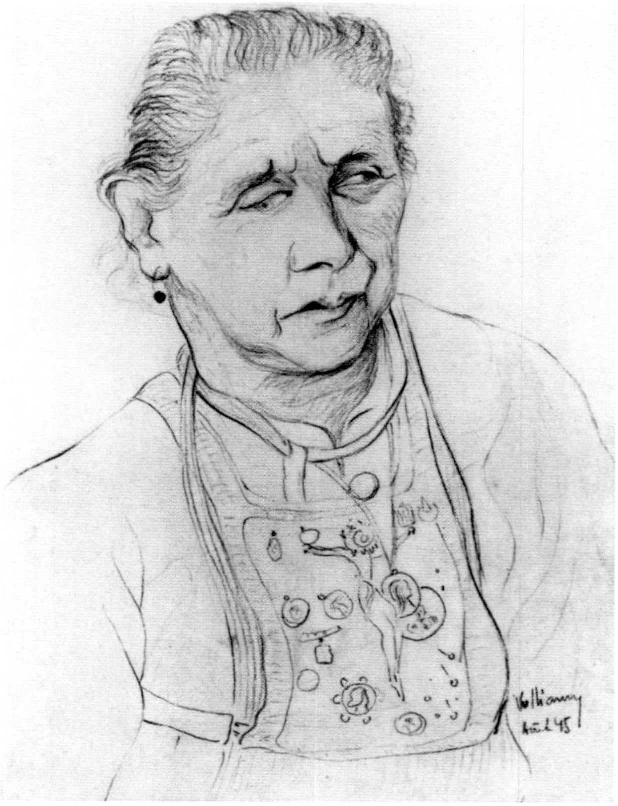

Marguerite Sirvins, portrait drawn by Gérard Vulliamy (French, 1909–2005), 1945. Succession Gérard Vulliamy. Although a photograph of Sirvins does not exist, surrealist painter Vulliamy drew a portrait of her while spending time at Saint-Alban-sur-Limagnole.

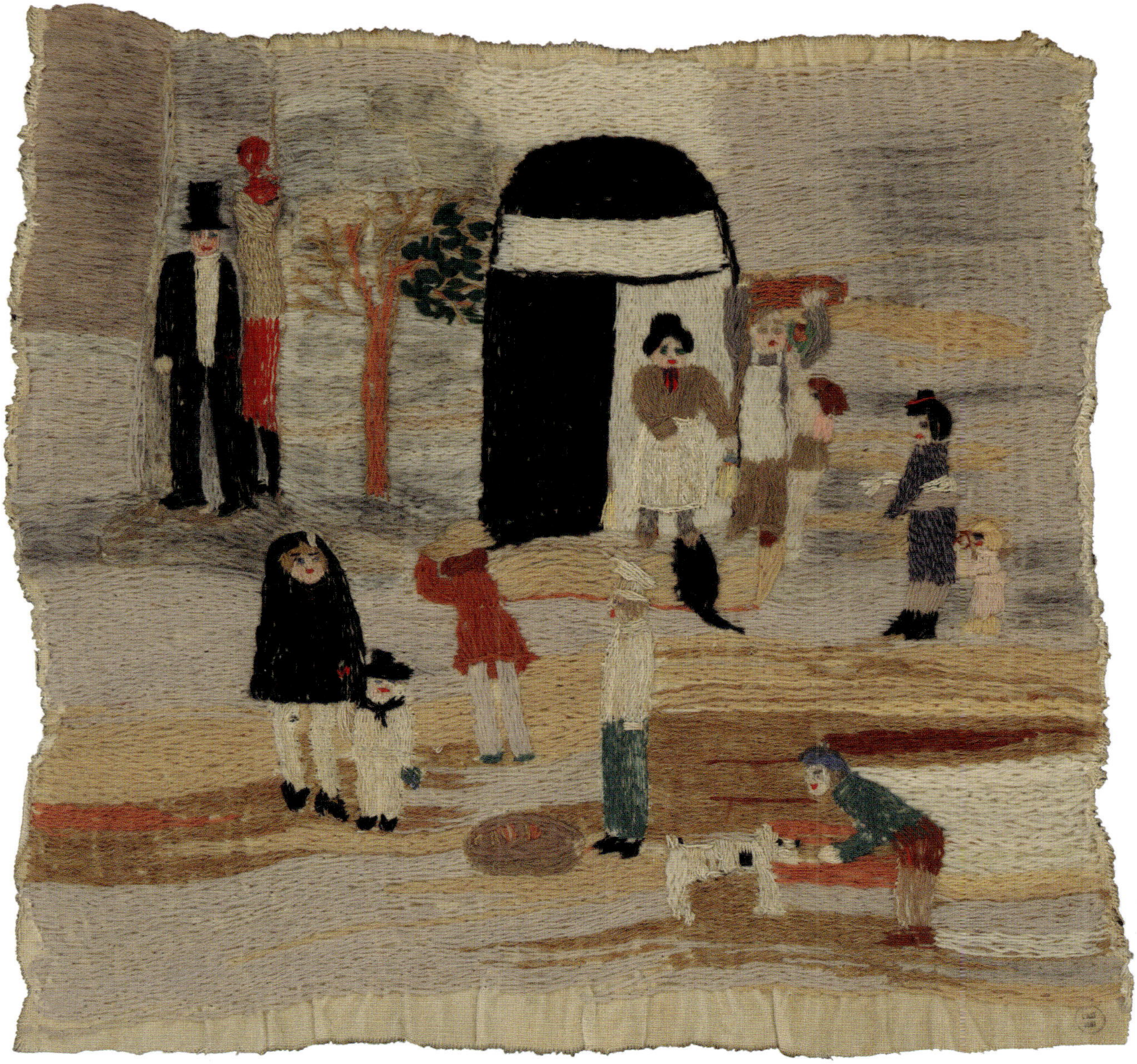

Marguerite Sirvins, untitled, *1944–1957, embroidery on canvas, 13⅜ × 14³⁄₁₆ in (34 × 36 cm). Collection de l'Art Brut, Lausanne.* Under the name Marguerite Sir, this work was included in the exhibition *l'Art Brut*, Galerie René Drouin, Paris (1949) and Jean Dubuffet's associated publication *l'Art Brut préféré aux arts culturels*. This was the first textile to be included in the Compagnie de l'Art Brut and features a pastoral scene with a man in a top hat.

Marguerite Sirvins was under psychiatric care for almost 13 years before her creative practice emerged. As explained by Dr. Roger Gentis of Saint-Alban in 1944, during a hospital-led event, Sirvins started cutting a piece of paper with scissors to reveal a well-executed capeline. This representation of a wide brim hat related to her previous millinery skills and introduced her ability to construct textiles or accessories without a pattern. Sirvins experienced symptoms of personality disorder which manifested in paranoid delusions and aggressive behavior.

With the encouragement of nurses to continue producing creatively, her aggression was mitigated through embroidering and drawing. Sirvins' embroidery process was extremely detail-oriented, from the preparation of materials to execution. The preparation included unraveling discarded rags to repurpose individual threads into sophisticated textile techniques. Compositionally, Sirvins produced pastoral scenes and landscape through her early drawings and embroideries, perhaps as recollections of her early childhood. Though creativity alleviated Sirvins' hostility, by

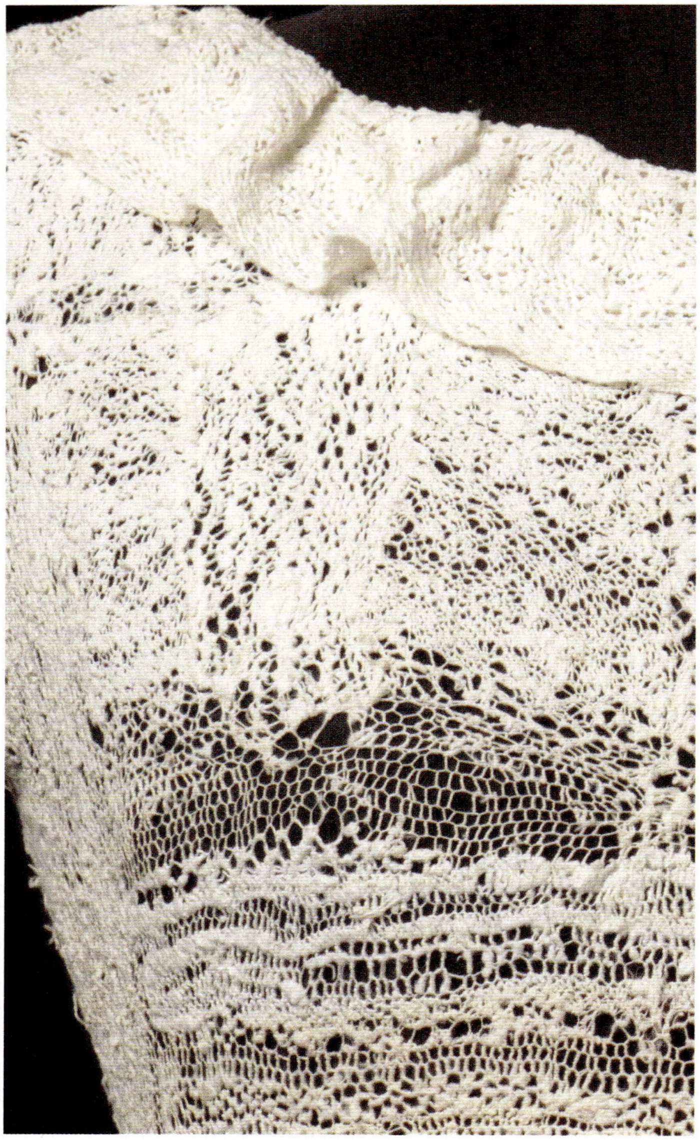

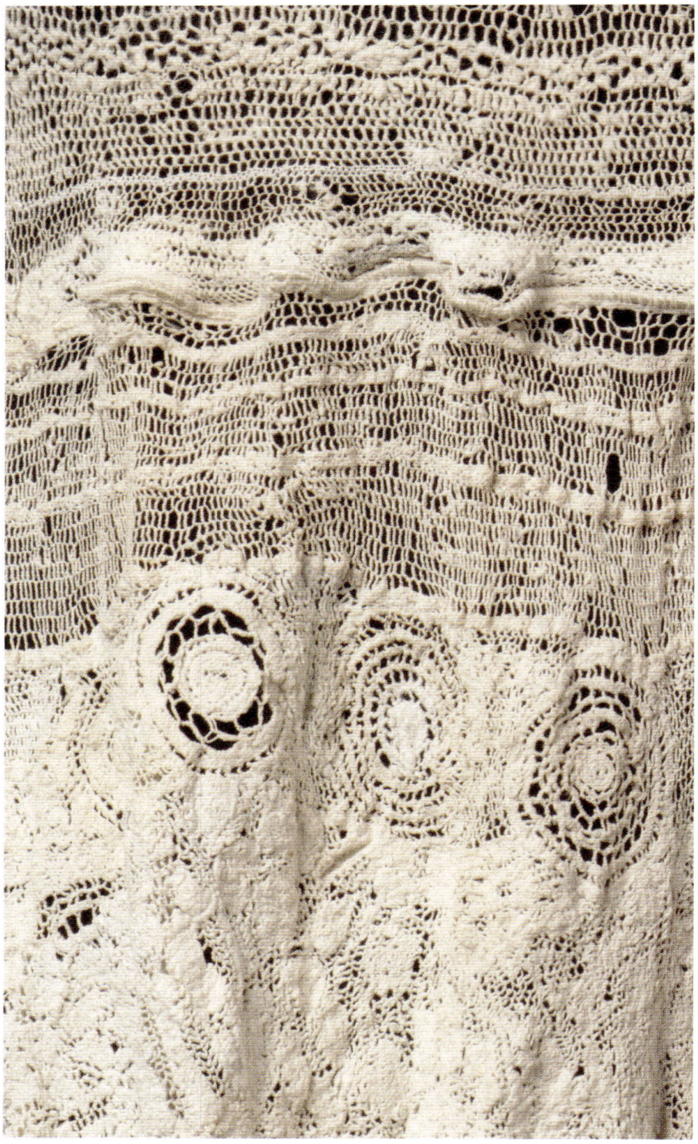

Marguerite Sirvins, untitled, *1944–1955, lace sewn from used sheets, 38⁹⁄₁₆ × 13⅜ × 10⅝ in (98 × 34 × 27 cm). Collection de l'Art Brut, Lausanne.* After the wedding dress became part of the Collection de l'Art Brut, it was featured in *Art Brut Fascicle No. 6* (1966), a publication launched by Jean Dubuffet in 1964, which featured monographs of the creatives he considered to be Art Brut.

1955 her condition had declined into advanced delusions and dementia. Sirvins believed she was 18 years old when she initiated work on her bridal gown, though she was actually 64. Sirvins' initial mental instability had coincided with her sister's wedding in 1930, and in this later disturbed emotional state, she expressed looking forward to her own wedding day, and subsequent roles of wife and mother. The garment, solely consuming the final years of her life, was constructed without patterns, sketches, or machinery. The complexity of the various methods and applications—needle sewing, crochet, embroidery, and knitting—resulted in remarkable levels of textile opacity. Despite limitations on materials, Sirvins produced her own lace by secretly removing single threads from her own hospital bedding. The wedding dress was preserved by Dr. Roger Gentis after Sirvins' death in 1957. Gentis' long-term correspondence with Dubuffet contributed to the eventual inclusion of Sirvins' wedding dress into the Collection de l'Art Brut in 1963.

"Je suis un peu dédoublée; quelqu-un profite de mes doubles." ("I am a little split; someone takes advantage of my doubles.") – Marguerite Sirvins[19]

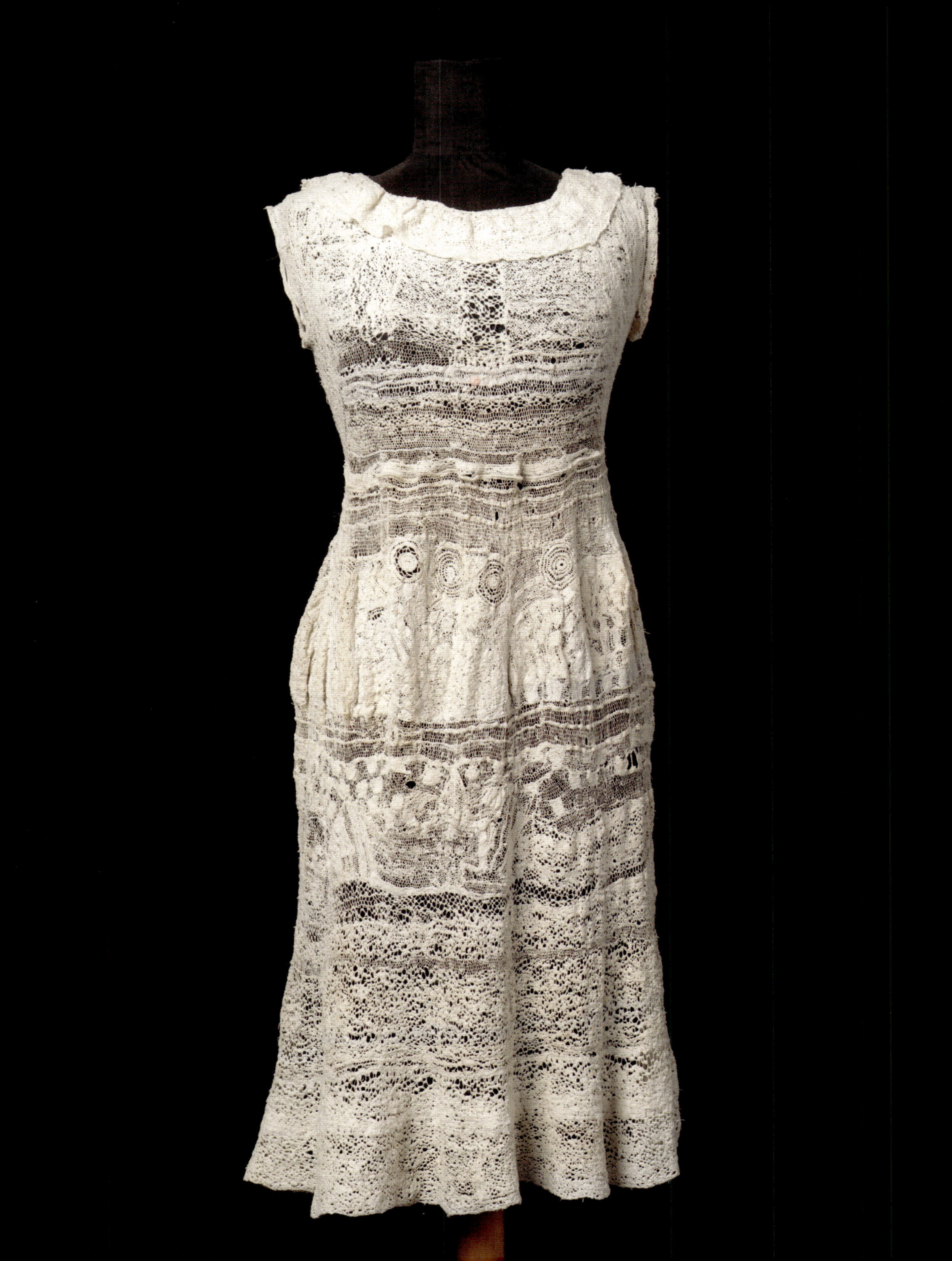

CHAPTER 3

OUTSIDER ART: THE TITLE THAT SHAPES A GENRE (1972–1979)

ROGER CARDINAL, THE ART OF THE ARTLESS

John Maizels

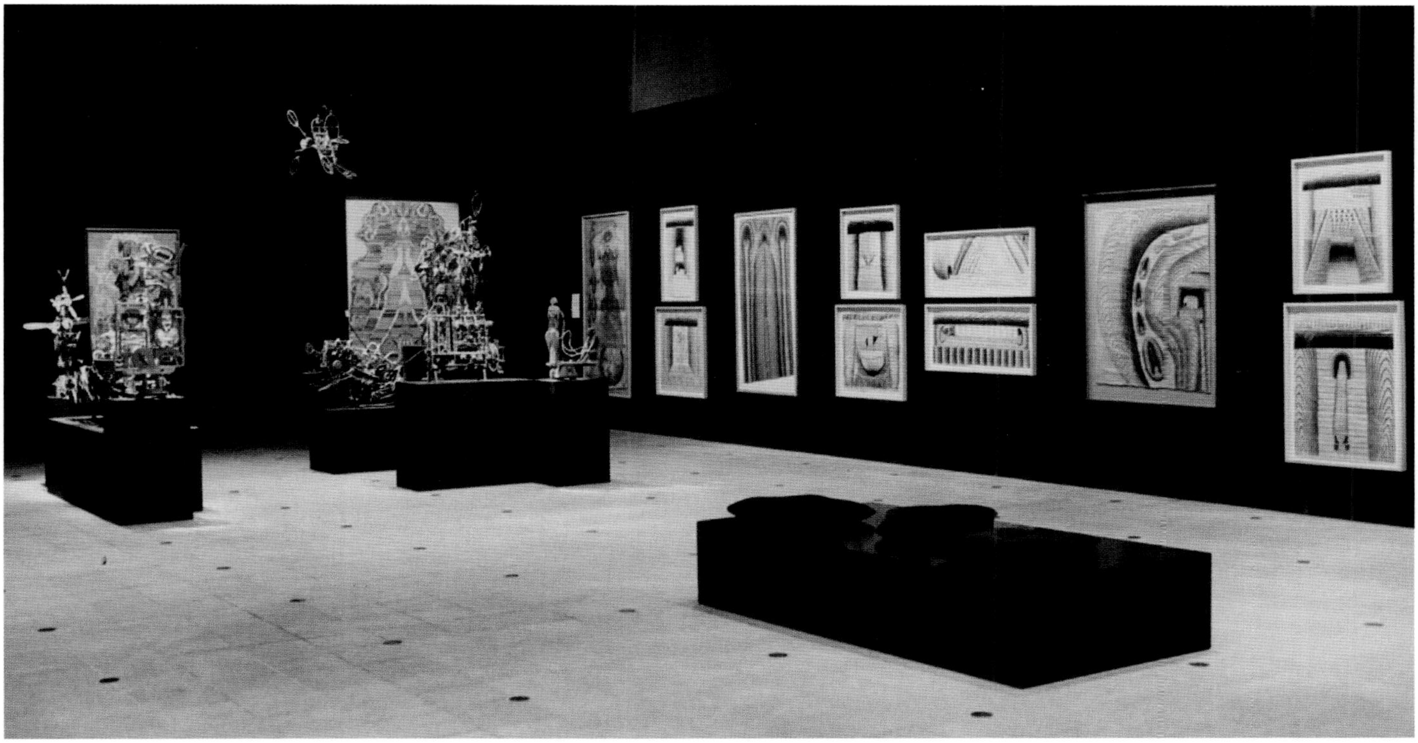

Installation view of Outsiders: An Art Without Precedent or Tradition, *Hayward Gallery, London (1979). Courtesy of the Hayward Gallery.* This exhibition detail features paintings by Augustin Lesage (left), drawings by Martín Ramírez (right), and sculptures by François Monchatre (central). *Outsiders* also exhibited work by Madge Gill, Johann Hauser, Friedrich Schröder-Sonnenstern, August Walla, Scottie Wilson, and Anna Zemánková.

Roger Cardinal (1940–2019) was a British poet and lecturer of French at the University of Kent when, in 1967, he traveled to Paris with Robert Short in order to carry out research for their book *Surrealism: Permanent Revelation* (1970). During this and subsequent trips they met with André Breton and other important players in the surrealist movement, and it was here that Cardinal was first shown the almost secret collection of unknown works still being amassed by French painter Jean Dubuffet.

During Cardinal's 1967 visits, Dubuffet's Collection de l'Art Brut was not open to the public, even though it was housed in a spacious building in the rue des Sèvres in central Paris. Dubuffet only allowed admittance to serious scholars or enthusiasts. Cardinal was one of the first British writers to be allowed to experience this covert collection of unique creations. He was able to meet with Dubuffet who introduced him to works by some of the great stars of the collection such as Adolf Wölfli (see page 64), Aloïse Corbaz (see page 56), and Augustin Lesage (see page 72).

Cardinal proposed to the publisher of his book on surrealism, Studio Vista, that he should publish the first text in English on the phenomenon of Art Brut, as then defined by Dubuffet. After several further visits to the collection in Paris and the awareness of architectural creations such as the *Watts Towers* built by itinerant worker Simon Rodia in Los Angeles, and the Facteur Cheval's *Palais Idéal* in France, Cardinal was able to put together his revolutionary book. He had fully absorbed Dubuffet's theories and the important anti-cultural position that he took. Cardinal could see that the art he would be championing to the English-speaking world was in stark contrast to the accepted art of high culture, where even Dada and surrealism were a part of cultural and intellectual discourse. His first title, *Art of the Artless*, was rejected as was *Art Brut*, but Cardinal eventually allowed the publisher's name of *Outsider Art* to be used, even though he only gave it a mark of 7 out of 10 at the time. Under this ambivalent title, *Outsider Art* was published in 1972. Little did they know how this term would become a worldwide definition into the future.

The art that appeared in Cardinal's book had never been publicly seen outside of the European mainland. It was considered a secretive and subversive art that threw into doubt all the claims of cultural and art movements over the years. Here, farmers, laborers, prison inmates, hospital patients, and people claiming to be mediums and instruments of God were producing work that had never before been considered as art and yet, under this new framework it was now affirmed to be a higher and purer form of visual expression.

In *Outsider Art*, Cardinal considered Dubuffet's position that *art culturel* was "a pampered racehorse that compares highly unfavorably with the teeming variety of all the other species."[1] Developing from Dubuffet's *Asphyxiante Culture* (1968), Cardinal asserted the art featured was a more honest and direct form of expression, which until then had been ignored and overlooked. He examined how cultural conditioning had a strong hold on our mentality:

"The sense of a glorious continuum, of a 'history of art' in which man has progressed triumphantly from mastering the technique of painting on the walls of caves to that of producing silk-screen prints, ignores the fact that true art history is in fact a succession of revolts and heresies. Over all dissension, though, an academic standard has tended to prevail, whereby all that purported to be art had to conform to certain fundamental principles."[2]

Although *Outsider Art* was a revolutionary and visionary book in its own right, when released it was generally ignored by the conservative British literary reviews and newspapers. In fact, its sales were so poor that it became remaindered and Cardinal tried to buy up the last copies for himself. Fortunately, it was better respected in America when it was published the following year in paperback, but it soon ran out of print. Even though it did not take long for the book to develop iconic status and great influence, the volume has never been reprinted.

Victor Musgrave was the owner of the London Gallery One and the only English member of Dubuffet's Compagnie de l'Art Brut. Through his connections with the government-sponsored Arts Council, he was able to persuade the Hayward Gallery to present one of the most audacious exhibitions ever held in London, the 1979 exhibition *Outsiders: An Art Without Precedent or Tradition*. Planning for the exhibition started years earlier and in July 1977, with Musgrave close to persuading the Arts Council to commit to his proposal, he asked Cardinal to act as co-organizer.[3]

Dubuffet's expansive collection had, by this time, been installed as the Collection de l'Art Brut in Lausanne, with a policy of no loans, leaving Musgrave and Cardinal to search for their material from a variety of private sources, collectors, and galleries. Dr. Leo Navratil at the Gugging hospital in Austria loaned works by artists such as Johann Hauser (see page 108) and August Walla (see page 112). Navratil also brought Hauser on a rare visit to London to see the show. French impresario collector Alain Bourbonnais owned a large holding of younger French self-taught artists such as Michel Nedjar and Pascal Verbena. Although Bourbonnais contributed many works from his collection, he insisted that the exhibition included his own creations, *Les Turbulents*, even though they were not works of "Outsider Art." This move understandably brought criticism to the exhibition.

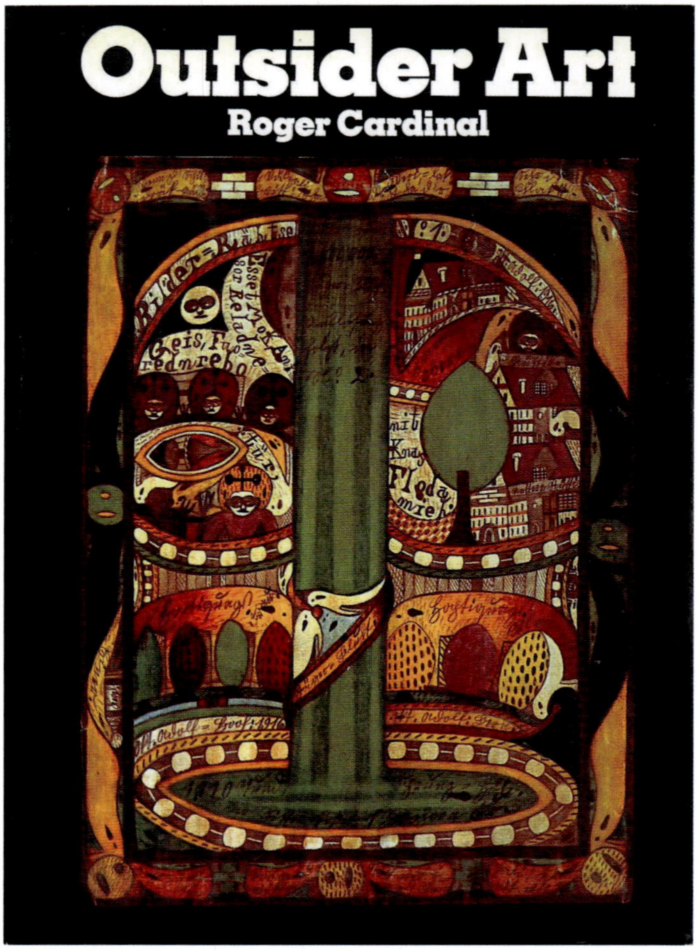

The cover of Roger Cardinal's 1972 book, *Outsider Art*. Since the book has never been reprinted, acquiring a copy in the 21st century is a challenge.

Revolutionary for its time, *Outsiders* featured 42 artists and their 400 works. Inspired by the presentation at Dubuffet's newly opened "anti-museum" in Lausanne, the walls of the Hayward Gallery were black with the works dramatically spot lit. For the first time the great masters of Outsider Art could be seen together in London including stunning displays of works by Adolf Wölfli (see page 64), Madge Gill (see page 88), Henry Darger (see page 156), Anna Zemánková (see page 104), Martín Ramírez (see page 336), Friedrich Schröder-Sonnenstern (see page 100), Scottie Wilson (see page 96), and many others. The exhibition was a huge success in terms of attendance, breaking all records, but was mainly met with bemusement by London's art critics, most of whom had never even heard of Art Brut. Although some had an idea of the motives behind the show and praised its revelation, for others, it was an outrage. The Arts Council even published a disclaimer on the show in the introduction to the catalog in direct response to Musgrave and Cardinal's claims that Outsider Art was equal to cultural art of the time[4]. The exhibition truly let the concept of "Outsider Art" out of its box and into the world.

For some critics the experience was just too much and they were too disturbed or angry to accept it. Such critical responses included a review from *The Spectator*: "The most lasting impression of outsider art, mad art, or whatever else you call it, is of boring repetition."[5] The BBC reported: "if you are interested in the sophisticated and intelligent expression of culture, you will find this unbelievably depressing—it is filled with quite dreadful and horrible and disturbing things, and it has brought, for me, the lunatic into the city square"[6]; and the *Daily Telegraph* stated: "the objects in the exhibition are the works of lunatics. As such they are of interest to those concerned with mental medicine, and information of use to sociologists."[7]

Other critics further addressed derogatorily the oeuvres of artists that today are internationally acclaimed. Wölfli's work was described in the *Observer* as "relentless psychotic drizzle" and Gill's drawings as "cosmic Paisley scribble," and the exhibition as a whole as "a catalog of frustrations and losses."[8]

So, although the exhibition excited many and pioneered a whole new way of thinking about art and creativity, it also began years of discrimination and condescension in Britain toward self-taught artists categorized under Outsider Art. This discrimination is still evident today with Britain being the only important cultural center without a museum dedicated to this form of art. The collections of the national art museums, such as Tate Britain, London, do not include even a single tiny Madge Gill postcard in their storage, let alone on public view.

Cardinal was initially downhearted by the lack of acknowledgment of the artists featured in his work and his introduction of new creativity pushing the boundaries of what was considered art, but his influence and legacy was major. *Outsider Art* became a bible to many who went on to make their own journeys of expanding their perceptions of art. The exhibition inspired a whole generation of art followers to see there was another art beyond the "cultural citadel" where the "weeds" grew at the edges of the cultivated garden.[9]

In the decades following the exhibition and into the 21st century, Cardinal's term "Outsider Art" has become ubiquitous, yet uncontrolled, with many people using it as a label for anything unusual or self-taught. It is also criticized for being pejorative to artists who may already be outsiders in their society. Although it was originally intended to be just an anglicized version of Art Brut[10], Outsider Art has been used so fluidly that it means various things to different people and has become an all-enveloping umbrella term. Even so, it established itself as the international standard term for work in this field, replacing such labels as "folk art," "visionary art," and "vernacular art," which were previously in common usage in America. The use of the term in the title of New York's *Outsider Art Fair* (founded in 1993) further emphasized its place as the prime commercial, as well as cultural, definition. The validity of art considered in the remit of Outsider Art was strengthened even more by the 1989 founding of *Raw Vision* in London with Cardinal as one of the founding writers. This international journal dedicated to the subject is still in print today with over 100 issues.

Over time Cardinal's own position has become cemented as one of the great founding trinity of Outsider Art—Prinzhorn, Dubuffet, Cardinal.[11] His influence has been immense and unprecedented. His visionary writings inspired hundreds of large museum exhibitions, scholarly books, and thousands of gallery exhibitions all around the world. Apart from Britain, where the cultural scene very much reflects the hierarchy of society generally, the art and artists considered within Outsider Art are now accepted in museum collections and revered as something special to be treasured.

Cardinal in his closing essay "Aberrant Paths" in *Outsider Art* concluded: "An alternative art exists. It need not be geographically remote, nor need it have a single location."[12]

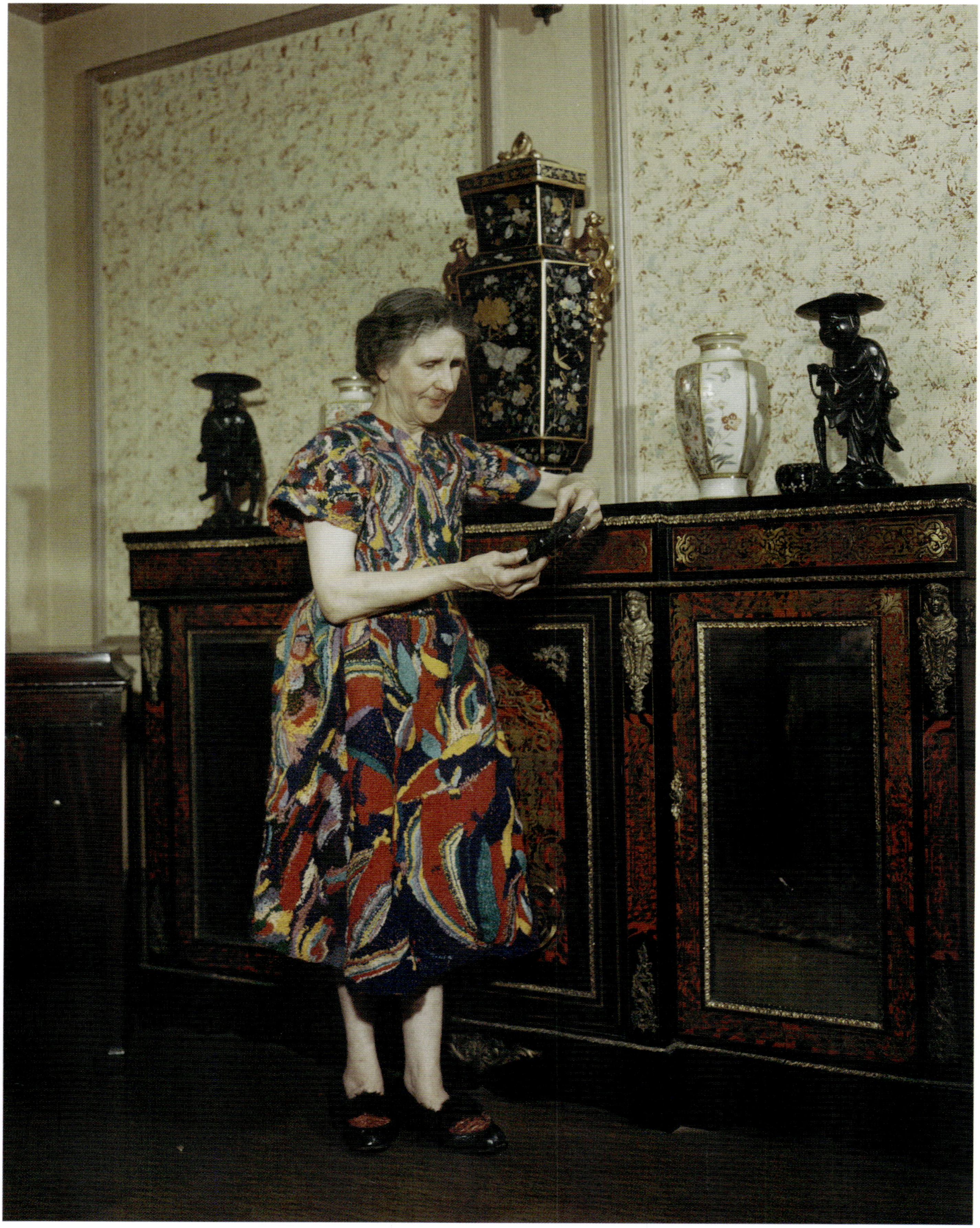

Madge Gill, 1947, photograph. This portrait of Madge Gill was taken at her East London home in the neighborhood of Plashet Grove, East Ham. Gill also worked creatively, embroidering wool and is wearing a dress of her own embroidered textile.

MADGE GILL

(1882–1961, London, England)

Madge Gill's evenings were dedicated to her automatic practice for decades. In 1920, her son described witnessing her creative awakening and connection to her spirit guide, Myrninerest. Subsequent accounts recalled variations of her sudden artistic urges under Myrninerest's influence. Gill's output was prolific. Under the guidance of Myrninerest, she wrote, embroidered, dictated other languages, and drew with intricate detail. Born out of wedlock in 1882, Gill's life was undoubtedly filled with turmoil—from time spent in orphanages to extreme illness, but her greatest emotional and physical strain occurred in 1921, when her only daughter was stillborn. Gill's creative output supported her recovery through her continued mediumistic relationship with Myrninerest, she produced a diverse oeuvre including significant drawings of sublimely ink-drawn stylistic faces surrounded by a vortex of architecturally rendered ectoplasm. Making work until 1958, Gill was promoted through Spiritualist events, press, and art exhibitions, however, it is posthumously that Gill has become most widely recognized, including her feature in Roger Cardinal's influential book *Outsider Art* (1972) and the exhibition *Outsiders* at the Hayward Gallery, London (1979).

Madge Gill's creativity brought resilience and recovery to her many traumatic experiences, but she encountered her mediumistic relationship[13] to her spirit guide as an involuntary responsibility, and at times burdensome. To understand Myrninerest, interpreted to mean "my inner rest self," is to explore this spirit guide's shifting roles and influence on Gill.[14]

The Spiritualist concept of a medium is one of oscillation and paradox, dealing between public and private, celestial and mortal. Within Gill's biography, the accounts of her spirit guide, Myrninerest, are fluid and at times contradictory, but objectively they do not seem to be discrepancies within an invented narrative. Instead, these varying accounts provide exposure to the complexity of Gill's experience. Distinctly, the inextricable link between Gill's mediumship and her creative output poses a particular negation surrounding the authorship of her oeuvre. To understand Madge Gill is to contextualize the process and output of her mediumistic practice within her lived experiences of trauma and mental illness.

Spiritualism's popularity in the United Kingdom developed from the mid-19th century. It provided a sense of direct spiritual connection and an alternative to established religions and was often embraced by working-class communities. Following World War I and the influenza pandemic of 1918, Spiritualism seemed to offer grief-stricken Britons a means to have transcendental communication with their recently deceased and to experience an escape from their struggles, via the occult. Gill's Aunt Kate was a Spiritualist; her Uncle Bert studied astrology and her son Laurie joined the Theosophical Society in 1924. For years Gill lived with Laurie, Kate, and Bert, which provided an encouraging environment for her creative endeavors but also a communal context to foster the family's shared esoteric interests. From their East London home, their activities included seances and astrological readings. While her family had wider involvement with spiritual studies and beliefs, the role of a medium was unique to Gill.

Born Maude Ethel Eades in London in 1882, Madge Gill was born illegitimately and kept publicly hidden for the first years of her life. Her extended family was unable to provide the necessary care and, in 1891, she was placed in an orphanage. This placement within the British orphanage system led to her migration to Canada, where she remained until she was 18.

By 1901, she had returned to the United Kingdom, found work as a nurse, and was living with her aunt in London's East End. Gill began a relationship with her cousin, Tom Gill, and they married in 1907. Though a troubled marriage, which led to a later estrangement, Gill gave birth to four children. Laurence (Laurie) was her first-born child in 1906, followed by her second son Reginald in 1910; who at age eight passed away from influenza complications. Following this tragedy, Gill experienced considerable emotional distress. In 1920, adjacent to her creative spiritual awakening, she underwent two serious health operations: the removal of her left eye due to a cancerous tumor and the extraction of her teeth as a result of gum poisoning. However, the most devastating event for Gill was in February 1921, when her highly anticipated only daughter was stillborn. The severe emotional and physical trauma brought on by the miscarriage and erratic behavior associated with her creativity led her husband to admit Gill to Lady Chichester Hospital in Hove in January 1922, a highly progressive clinic for women and children. Gill spent four months at the hospital under the care of its founder, Dr. Helen Boyle.

Prior to Gill's entry to Lady Chichester Hospital, Myrninerest—a parallel spiritual form—had communicated with her in March of 1920. This encounter was reported by Boyle in her medical records[15]. Gill described a sudden and intense influx of inspiration followed by uncontrollable singing. Boyle's report continued that Gill led her sons outside while claiming to witness "the clouds part and see Christ on the Cross and angels in the sky."[16] This distinct encounter was described in a broadsheet written by Laurie in 1926, titled *MYRNINEREST – The Spheres*. He wrote that he similarly recalled his mother's first instance with her spirit

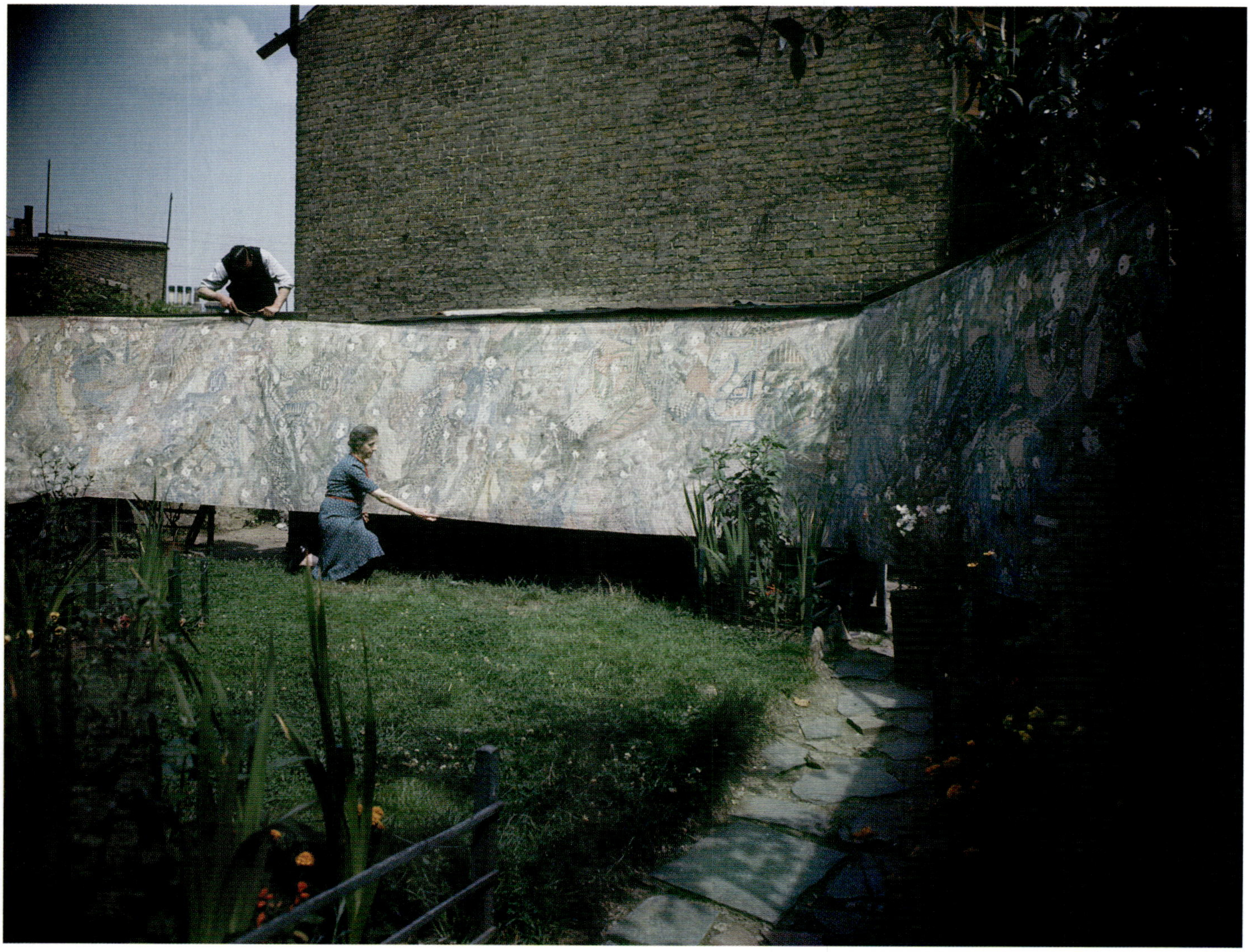

Madge Gill, 1947, photograph. Gill's son Laurie was an advocate for her creative practice from a young age and supported her in a variety of ways. This included constructing different rigs and furniture to assist the production of her large calico drawings, such as this outdoor rig allowing Gill to view the expansive work in its entirety.

guide: "It was on March 3rd, 1920 when the now medium was taken in a trance and controlled by a very progressed Spirit, whom we now know as Myrninerest her Guide. All that day the medium was in a trance . . . from that day until the present time the Inspiration has been one true reality . . ."[17]

Gill's son Laurie was an integral supporter of her art practice and it seemed he understood Myrninerest as a very active participant in her production. For nearly four decades, Gill was compelled to work prolifically late into the evenings by dim candlelight. This compulsion was said to be inspired, or perhaps demanded by her spirit guide. Her sons worried about her health in these manic states and the visual of her standing up, working into the night, reinforces the implications that the interventions of Myrninerest could have been a burden. Gill later even mentioned in a letter to a friend in 1952: "Dear Louise, I wish I could be normal."[18]

From 1922, Gill began to be recognized as a mediumistic artist in the Spiritualist community. This included interviews concerning her mediumship and in 1923 (the first record of Gill exhibiting), her drawings were included in an exhibition for the International Congress of Spiritualists in Liège, Belgium. Gill's practice continued to be exposed within esoteric circles, and in the 1930s her scope expanded to participation in Whitechapel Gallery's annual East End Academy exhibition between 1932 and 1947. She also exhibited alongside Henry Moore at an exhibition at Hertford House, London in 1942.

Gill's work was materially diverse and prolific: automatic writing[19], including what could appear to be invented or ancient languages; embroidery; and, perhaps best-known, drawing executed on both a grand and intimate scale. These drawings, almost exclusively

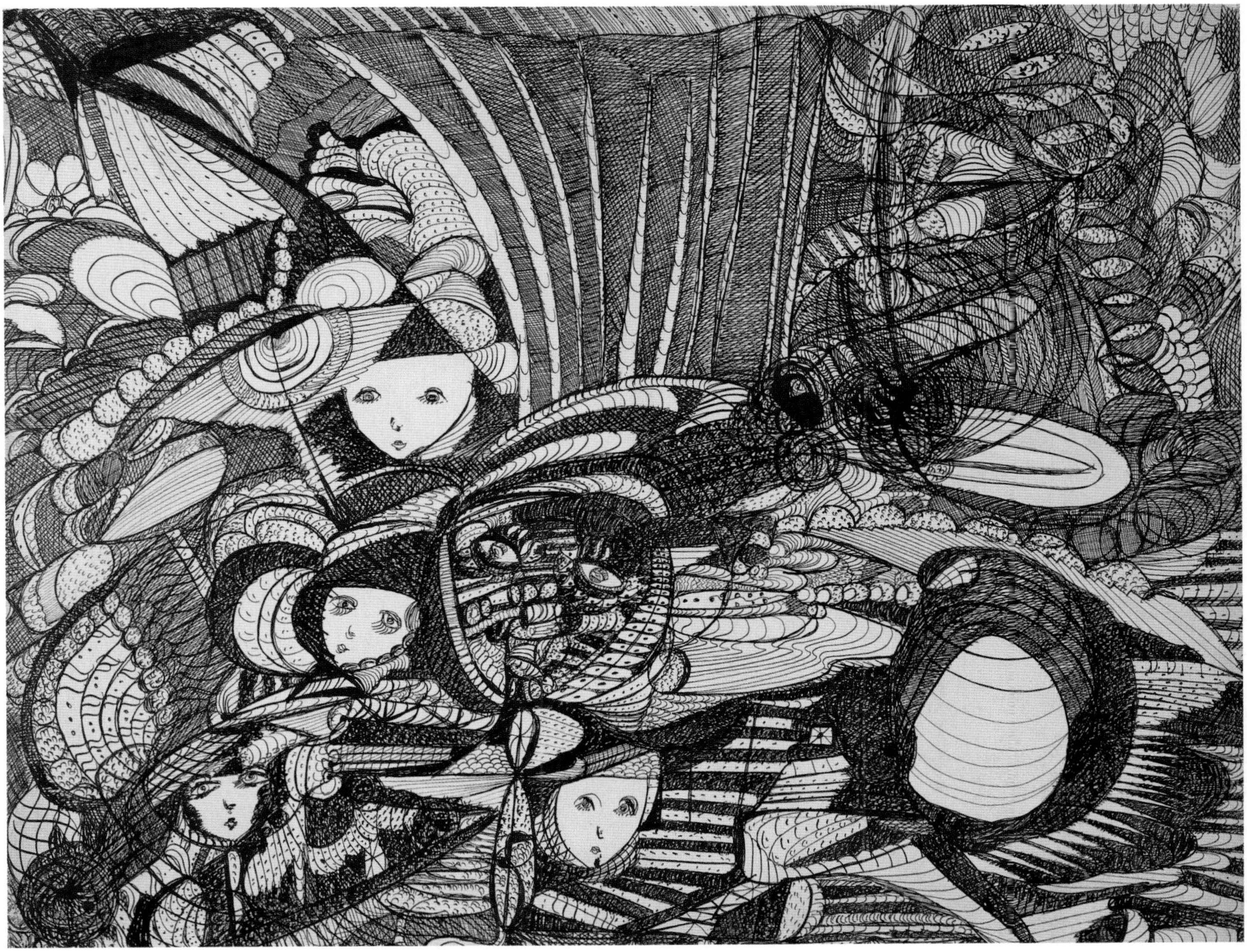

Madge Gill, Faces, *1920–1960, ink drawing on paper, 21⅞ × 24¹³⁄₁₆ in (55.5 × 63 cm). London Borough of Newham Heritage Service.* This is an archetypal drawing of faces among vortex-like patterning by Gill. Four gestural feminine faces appear with long eyelashes and petite lips. Their transparent faces without bodies emerge among Gill's dense patterns of loops and lines.

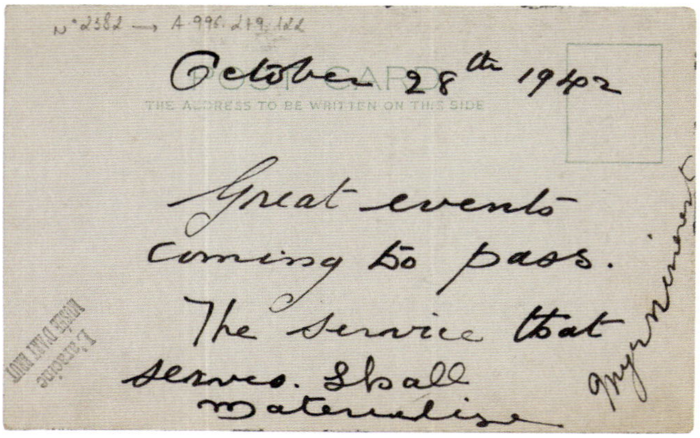

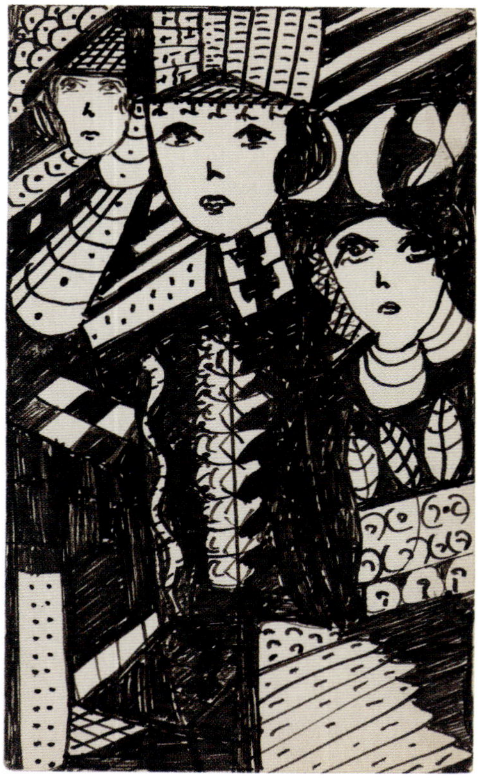

Madge Gill, Great events coming to pass. The service that serves shall materialize. Myrninerest, *October 28, 1942, Chinese ink on reverse of a postcard, $5\frac{7}{16} \times 3\frac{3}{8}$ in (13.8 × 8.5 cm). LaM, Lille Métropole musée d'art moderne d'art contemporain et d'art brut.* Gill would sometimes complete up to a dozen postcards while drawing through the night. This one shows three feminine faces amid architectural decoration insinuating various planes. It was also signed by her spirit guide.

Madge Gill, Architectural Fantasy, *October 27, 1951, Chinese ink on paper, $25\frac{3}{16} \times 20\frac{1}{16}$ in (64 × 51 cm). Collection de l'Art Brut, Lausanne.* An example of Gill's abstract architectural illustrations void of figures, this drawing presents a suggestion of a cityscape while checkered patterns, set on various planes, provide an unset perspective. *Architectural Fantasy* has specific significance because of its inscription on the reverse in reference to the devastating death of Gill's son Reginald:
October 27 51
Reggie passed away 1918 October 27
Born 27 April 1910

drafted with a limited palette of India ink, are considered Gill's most significant output and offer rich consideration into the relationship between her and Myrninerest. The large-scale drawings on calico were laboriously executed in isolated sections on a custom rig built by Laurie. On a more modest scale, she composed multitudes of drawn postcards; completing up to a dozen in one evening. Very few uncompleted works by Gill exist, suggesting her process would have been predetermined rather than improvisational. Given the lived trauma experienced by Gill, it seems undeniable that her creative practice and intervention of Myrninerest provided an objective space for Gill's own emotional and spiritual self.

Female characters juxtapositioned against a vortex of semi-abstracted staircases and repeated forms—checkered, wavy, circular—comprise Gill's drawn oeuvre. The feminine faces are translucent compared to the geometric ectoplasm that surrounds them, suggesting a celestial emergence from another dimension. Their faces indicate a connection to a body, but the emphasis is undeniably facial. Compositionally, heads emerge among fields of ornamental abstraction and flowy garments. The uniformity of the feminine faces suggests they are potentially a representation of a set character. Taking Gill's personal narrative into account, her absent mother or stillborn daughter could be conceptually inferred. Also, it is widely considered that the drawn figures represent the spirit guide itself. This conceptual framework, and faithful absence of a recognizable male figure, further suggest that Myrninerest was a female spirit.

Contrary to that binary gender assumption, an interview by Gill in 1922 for the *Sunday Express* detailed her guide as a masculine spirit. In this account she said, "The spirit who comes to me is that of a high priest... He lived in ancient Babylon." This sets forth a reading of Gill's work under the influence of a male guide who sends her messages. This written record also suggests there was an earlier emergence of Myrninerest, as Gill continued. "He first visited me three years ago, and since then has spoken to me continually." This reference to the relationship with her spirit guide initiating in 1919, differs from the accounts told to Boyle or recalled by Laurie. Years later, in 1937, for an interview in *Prediction Magazine*, Gill again recollected, "It was in 1919 when I first started my work. I then had inspiration to take up my pen and do all kinds of work of an artistic type. I felt that I had an artistic faculty seeking expression... All the time I was in quite a normal state of mind and there was no suggestion of a 'spirit' standing beside me. I simply felt inspired... But I felt I was definitely guided by an unseen force, though I could not say what its actual nature was."

In this interview, Gill presented her creative practice as fundamentally innate, de-emphasizing the impact of her spirit guide. With the majority of her works signed "Myrninerest," this perhaps echoed a tension felt by Gill to

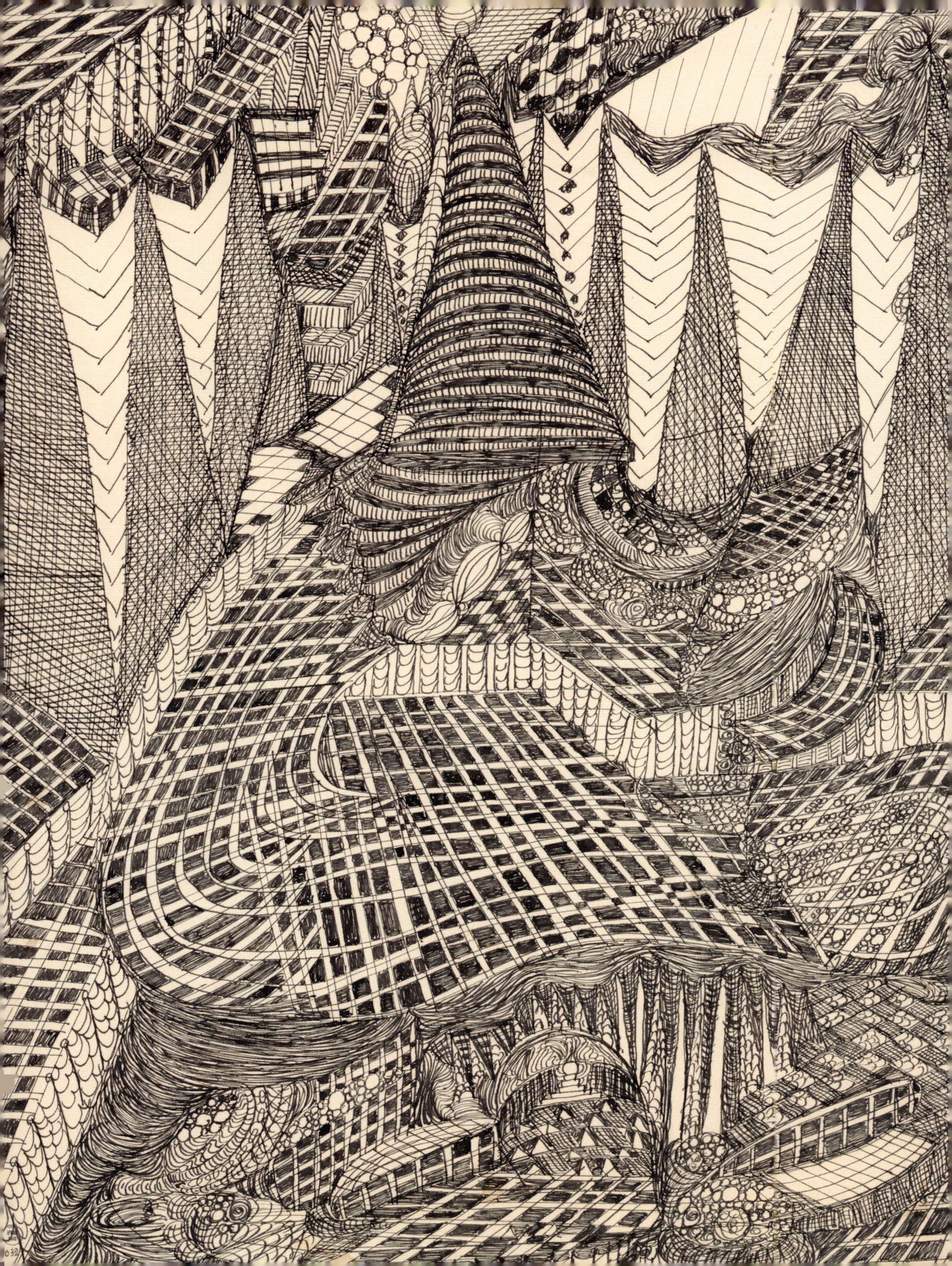

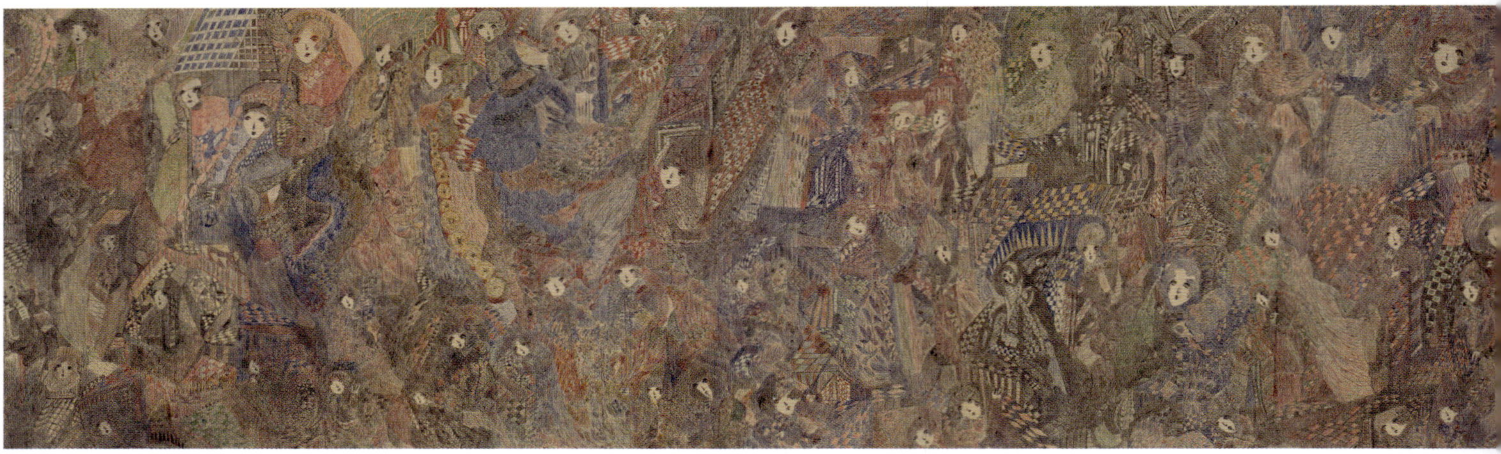

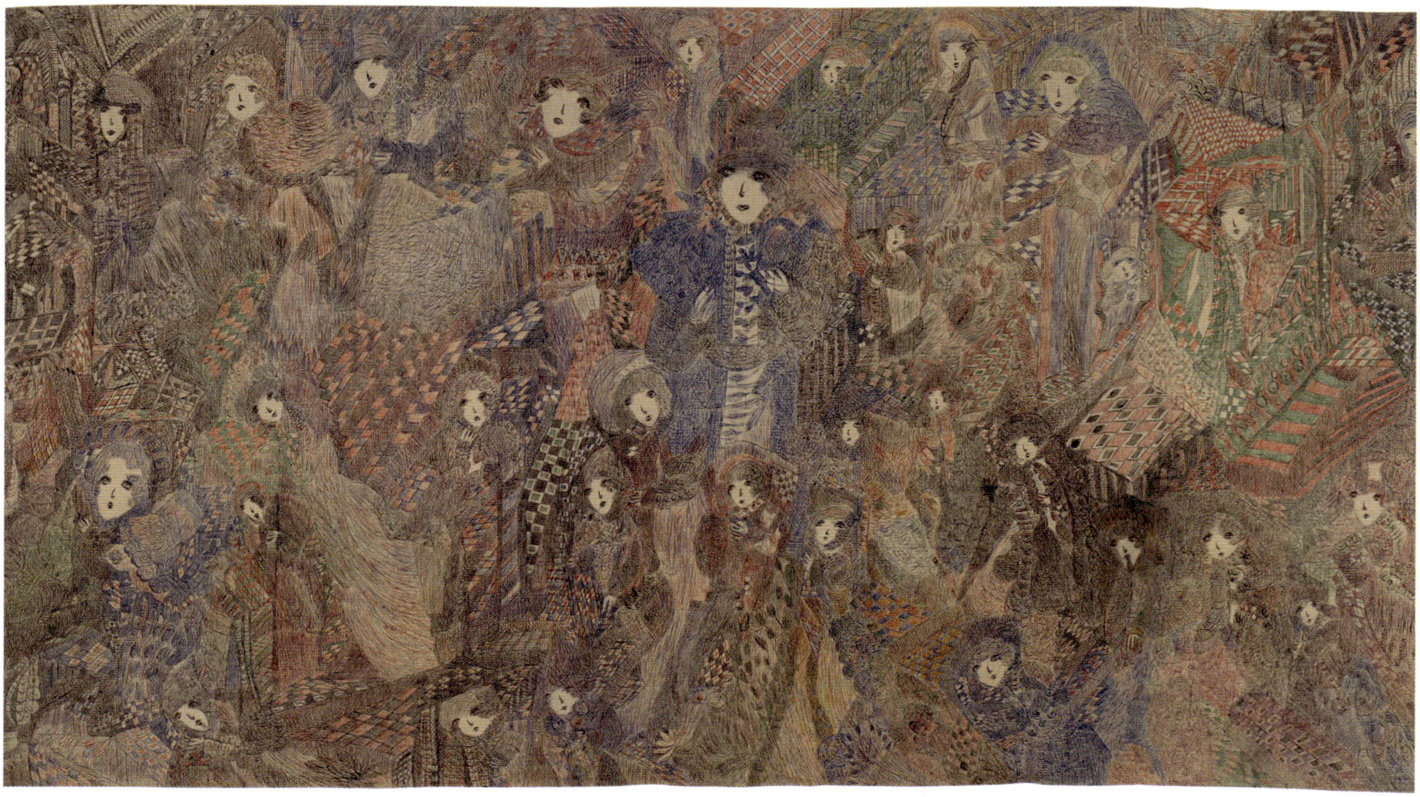

Madge Gill, Crucifixion of the Soul, *1934, drawing on textile, 58 × 418 in (147.3 × 1062 cm). London Borough of Newham Heritage Service.* The cohesiveness of this monumental drawing is stunning, considering that Gill never saw the totality of the composition while working on it. Her largest calico, *Crucifixion of the Soul*, was posthumously exhibited in *Outsiders: An Art Without Precedent or Tradition*, Hayward Gallery, London (1979).

her particular paradox regarding the authorship of the work. Research, including that of Roger Cardinal for *Outsider Art*, demonstrated Gill's reluctance to sell her works because they belonged to her spirit guide. Potentially, modesty at being the medium, not the creator, further led to Gill refusing exhibition opportunities, but in contrast, Gill's expressed hopes for a solo exhibition also have been documented.[20] This paradoxical tension doesn't pertain to the validity of historical accounts, but exemplifies the inner turmoil of Gill's role as a medium.

Gill continued her prolific output into her seventies and passed away in 1961. Upon her death, she left behind thousands of pieces of work in her home, which Laurie donated to their local London council. Her first solo show came to fruition posthumously in 1968 at Grosvenor Gallery, London. Since Gill's death, her narrative and mediumistic practice have gained considerable interest within the emerging discourse of nontraditional artists. Roger Cardinal's research and inclusion of Gill in *Outsider Art* (1972) were paramount to her recognition. The placement of her work in the groundbreaking *Outsiders* exhibition at the Hayward Gallery, London (1979), was also significant.

Within Myrninerest, there is a palpable paradox of the influence and fluid form of this spirit that guided Madge

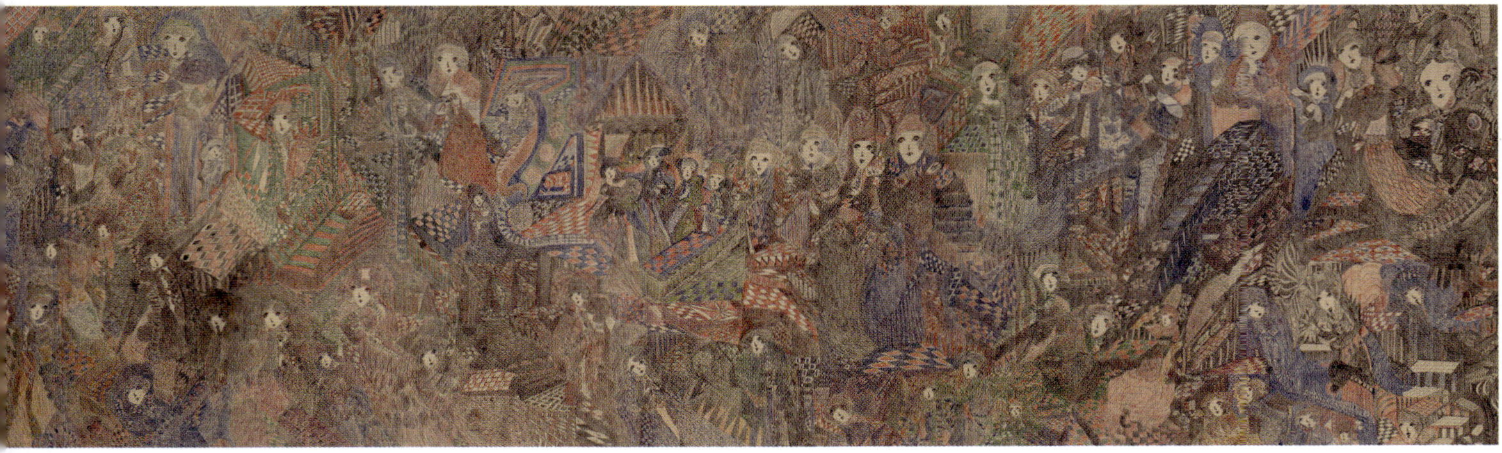

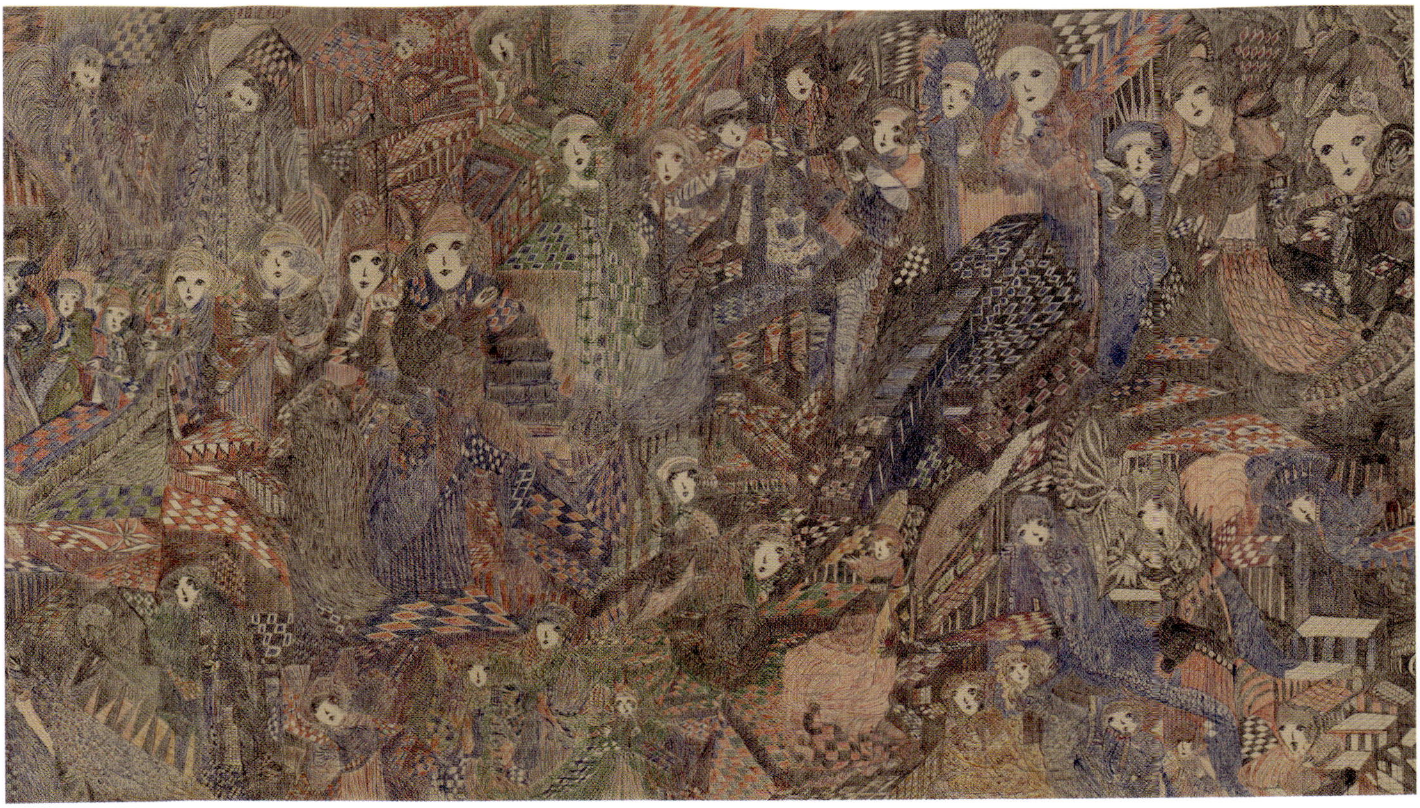

Gill. Like the multifaceted characteristics we find on Earth, Myrninerest takes on shifting personas and significance in Gill's life. As a medium, Gill was embraced by both the mortal and spiritual world, but such a position would render isolation and hardship. As an artist, Gill's life experiences, mental health, and circumstances also undeniably shaped, whether consciously or subconsciously, her creative production.

"The space projected in these drawings is mimetic of the mental trajectory that the artist followed: no longer more than a perfunctory acknowledgment of external space, it may be considered in quite literal terms as the delineation of a private world, a realm of subjective fantasy rendered concrete in the act of figuration."
– Roger Cardinal, *Outsider Art*[21]

SCOTTIE WILSON

(1891, Glasgow, Scotland–1972, London, England)

The balance between real and imaginary found within the repetitive lines of Scottie Wilson's drawings was revered by the surrealists. Born Louis Freeman into a working-class immigrant family, he left school at the age of nine to sell goods on the street with his brother. Aged 16 he joined the army, serving in India, South Africa, and later in World War I. After the war, Wilson returned to Britain and later emigrated to Canada. It was in 1931, in Toronto, that Wilson—compelled by an "unnamed agency"—began to draw. This creative action developed and by the age of 44, he was drawing daily, his signature doodle-aesthetic abundant with creatures. After returning to England in 1945 and identifying as Scottie Wilson, his portfolio of drawings was well received by London galleries. Following his inclusion in *Exposition Internationale du Surréalisme*, Galerie Maeght, Paris (1947), he continued to exhibit internationally, including in New York and Basel. His practice was of interest to Jean Dubuffet, who featured his work in *l'Art Brut* at Galerie René Drouin, Paris (1949), before his feature in Roger Cardinal's influential book, *Outsider Art* (1972). Wilson's drawings are now in the collections of the Museum of Modern Art, New York, and Musée de l'Art Moderne, Paris.

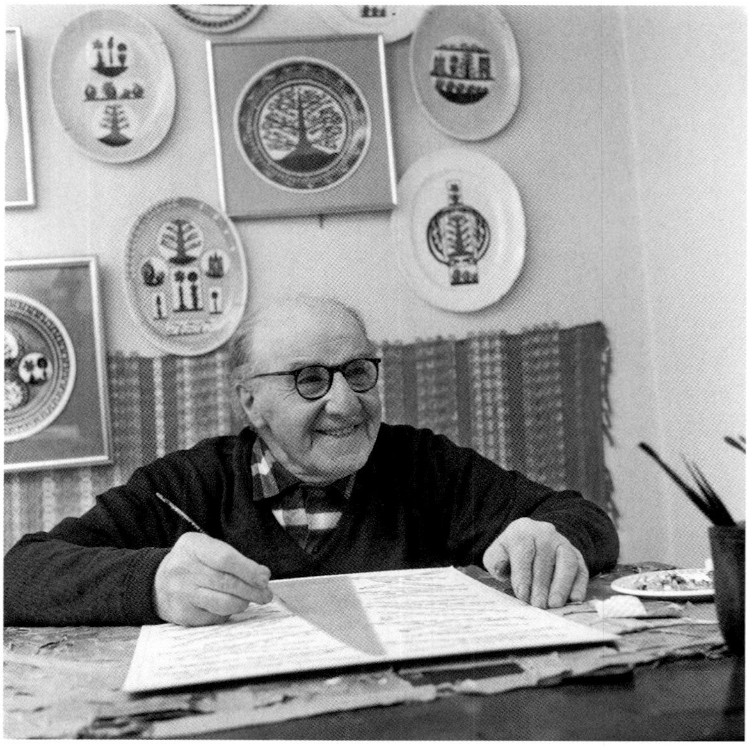

Scottie Wilson, 1967, photograph. Taken late in life, Wilson is 76 years old in this photograph and still doodling. His artwork adorns the back wall of his Kilburn flat in northwest London, including his painted earthenware, which he developed for an English porcelain company.

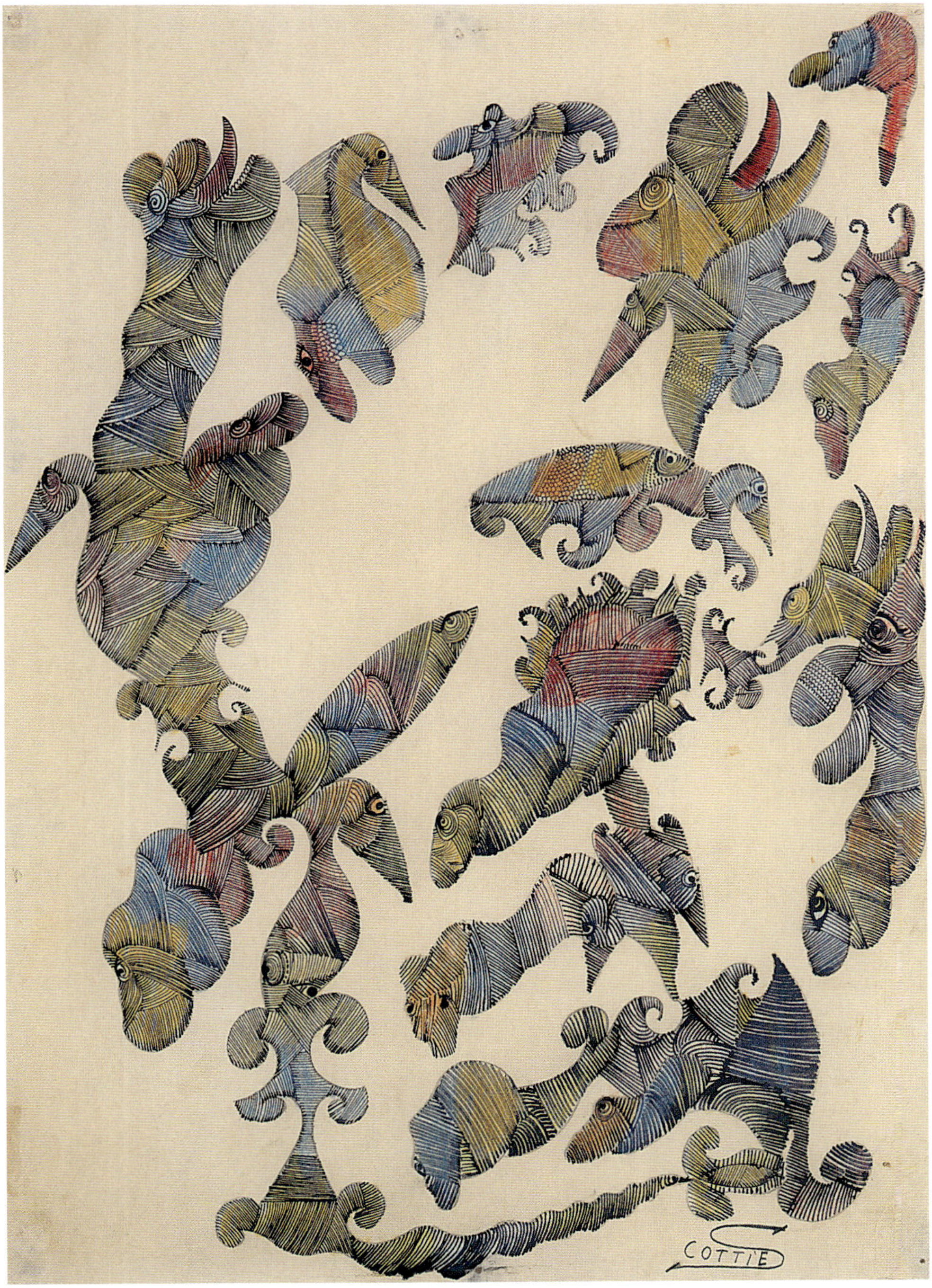

Scottie Wilson, Herd of Greedies, *1929–1942, pencil, colored pencil, and ink on paper, 15 × 11 in (38.1 × 27.94 cm). Milwaukee Art Museum.* This drawing by Wilson introduces his characters, "Greedies," named as the grotesque and sinister representations of evil. *Herd of Greedies* may appear fluid and abstract upon first view, but the "Greedies" can be identified by locating their staring eye(s) within Wilson's colorful crosshatching.

In the early 1930s, while residing in Toronto, Scottie Wilson[22] was dismantling fountain pens to resell their gold nibs for money. Fortuitously during this process, he was confronted with a pen that he considered too extraordinary to disassemble. With this attraction and an innate spontaneity, Wilson dipped the pen into ink and began doodling. He drew for two days until the covering of his tabletop was enveloped with intricate designs.

"I paint when the mood comes on me. The ideas come to me in dreams: sometimes I get an original idea from something I see in the bus, say, a chimney in the distance, then in my mind's eye I do the rest by elaborating on the chimney with fields, people, houses, and so on." – Scottie Wilson[23]

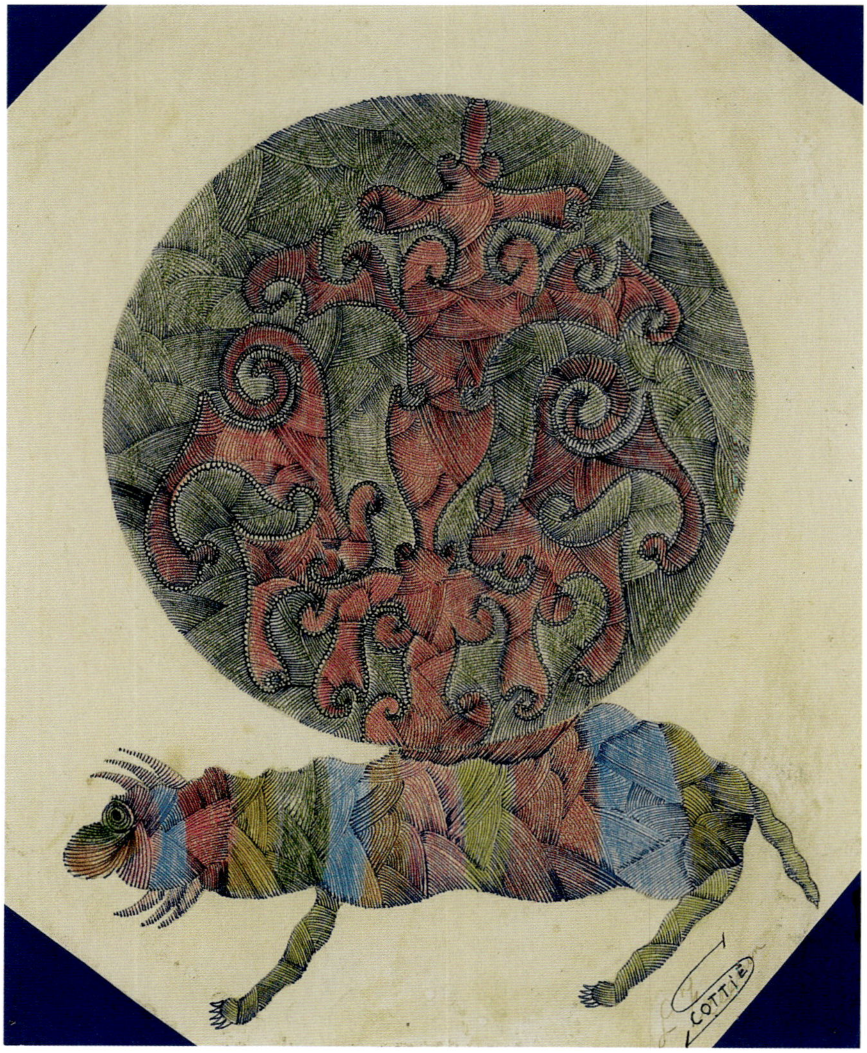

Scottie Wilson, Animal and Globe, *ca. 1935–1940, ink and crayon on paper, 13 × 10½ in (33 × 26.7 cm). Milwaukee Art Museum.* This work was included in the exhibition *Outsiders: An Art Without Precedent or Tradition*, Hayward Gallery, London (1979) and illustrated in the associated catalog, which notes of Wilson's style: "His intense early images portray in stylized form the struggle between destructive and creative forces."

When Wilson relocated to Vancouver, he was drawing daily with continuous motivation and even covered the walls of his room with his doodles. This period in Vancouver established consistent motifs and styles for Wilson's oeuvre. His burgeoning aesthetic involved shapes filled with countless lines drafted in pen. His characters—referred to as "Greedies" and "Meanies"—were introduced as representing evil forces. In contrast, his drawings from the 1950s developed a more utopian style, with the "Greedies" replaced by benevolent "Clowns." Compositionally, this Canadian era also embraced totemic shapes seemingly influenced by the totems of Northwest native cultures visible in Vancouver.

Wilson's drawings portray varying levels of abstraction, but he provided ample semiotics that allowed his subject matter to be recognized. His subjects of phantasmagorical faces, birds, fish, and frogs often look toward the viewer (or at Wilson himself) with a stoic meditative gaze. When asked about his work, Wilson often addressed his process rather than the intentions behind it. Intense repetition and spontaneity were characteristics of this process. His practice has been deciphered as a meta-doodle,[24] implemented without a preconceived plan and improvisational. Regardless of intent or categorization, Wilson's drawings present a definite sense of activity and traces of movement.

"If the main characteristic of the naïf is his earnest indebtedness to reality, if materiality and the Great Real experience their rediscovery in the art of the naïf, Scottie Wilson has severed the umbilical cord that links him with the visible things of this world." – Oto Bihalji-Merin, art historian and critic in 1959[25]

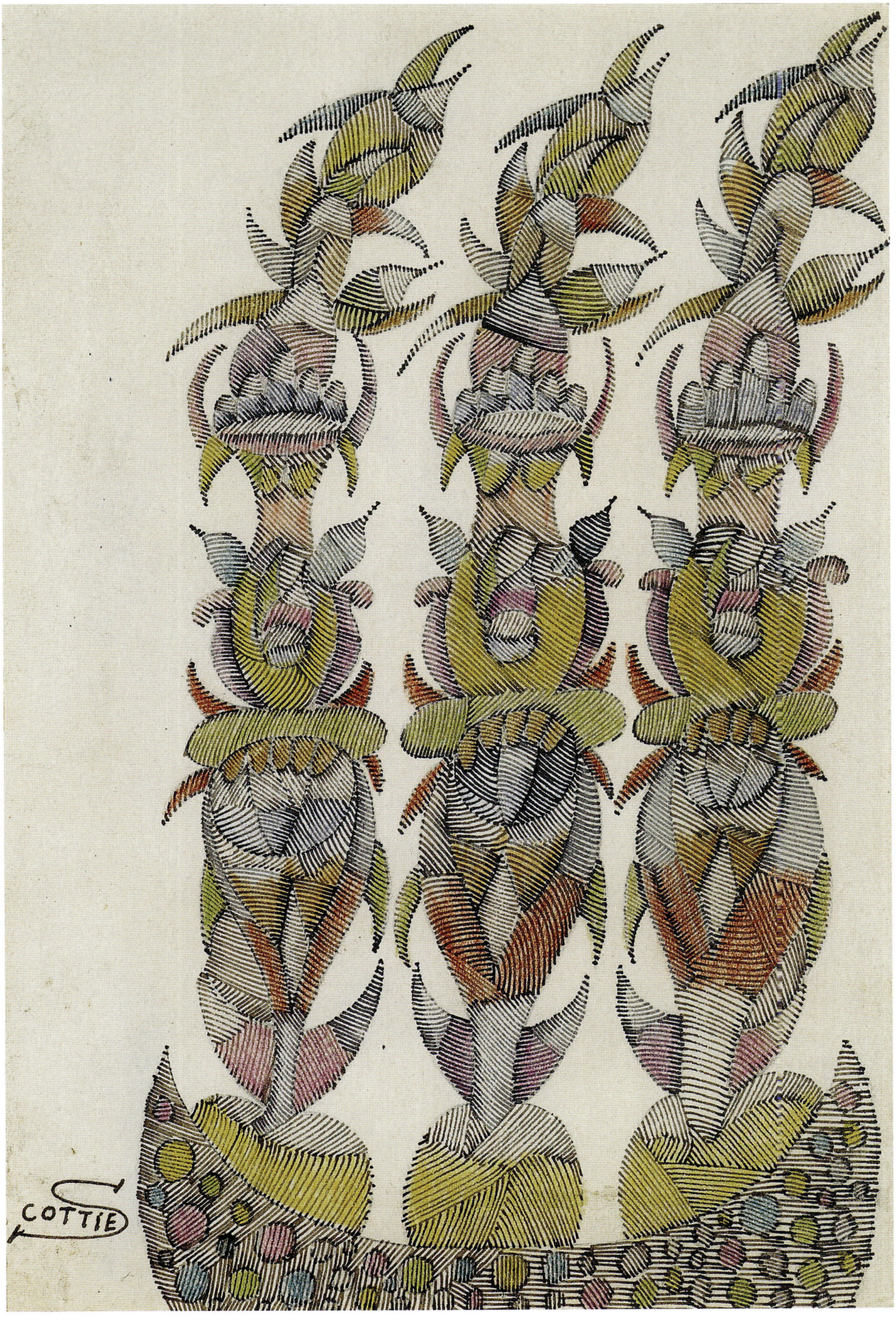

Scottie Wilson, Sailing Totems, *1929–1942, pencil, colored pencil, and ink on paper, 11 × 7½ in (27.9 × 19.1 cm). Milwaukee Art Museum.* This work was included in the exhibition *Outsiders: An Art Without Precedent or Tradition,* Hayward Gallery, London (1979) and illustrated in the associated catalog. It indicates the possible influence of the Stanley Park totem poles in Vancouver, Canada, on Wilson's compositions.

FRIEDRICH SCHRÖDER-SONNENSTERN

(1892, Kaukehmen, East Prussia [now Russia]–1982, Berlin, Germany)

Friedrich Schröder-Sonnenstern's oeuvre is a collision of the erotic and grotesque, utopian and dystopian, vibrantly formed through the lens of an anti-establishment agenda. Schröder-Sonnenstern didn't become an artist until 1949. His life prior to this and his identity as an artist within the postwar European art world were polemic. He had a difficult childhood: admitted to medical and correctional institutions from the age of 14, and, in 1918, admitted to a sanatorium under a diagnosis akin to adolescent schizophrenia. Released a year later, Schröder-Sonnenstern reinvented himself, fraudulently posing as a naturopath in Berlin. The 1930s brought further admittance to mental hospitals and incarceration for fraud. Remerging at age 57, he began to draw regularly and actively situated himself within Germany's current art scene. He was embraced by artists, in particular the surrealists, and was notably included in *l'Exposition Internationale du Surréalisme*, organized by André Breton and Marcel Duchamp, in Paris (1959). However, the shifting dialogue of his drawings' relationship with Schröder-Sonnenstern's previous mental instability acted as both an accelerator and restriction.

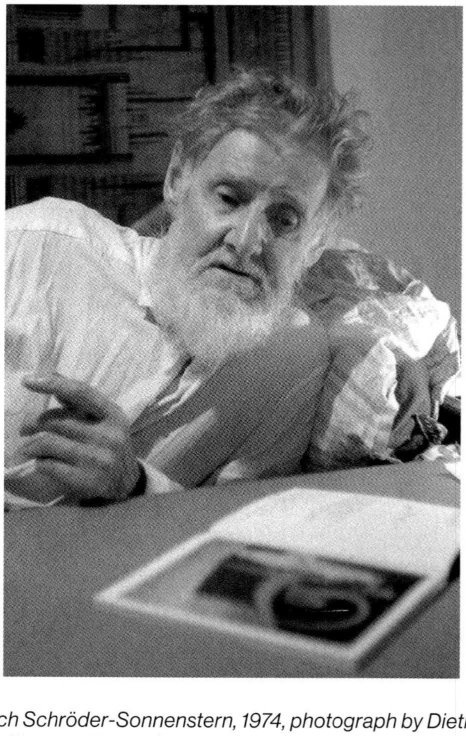

Friedrich Schröder-Sonnenstern, 1974, photograph by Dietmar Bührer (German, b. 1947). This portrait shows Schröder-Sonnenstern later in life, posed while looking through a catalog featuring his drawings.

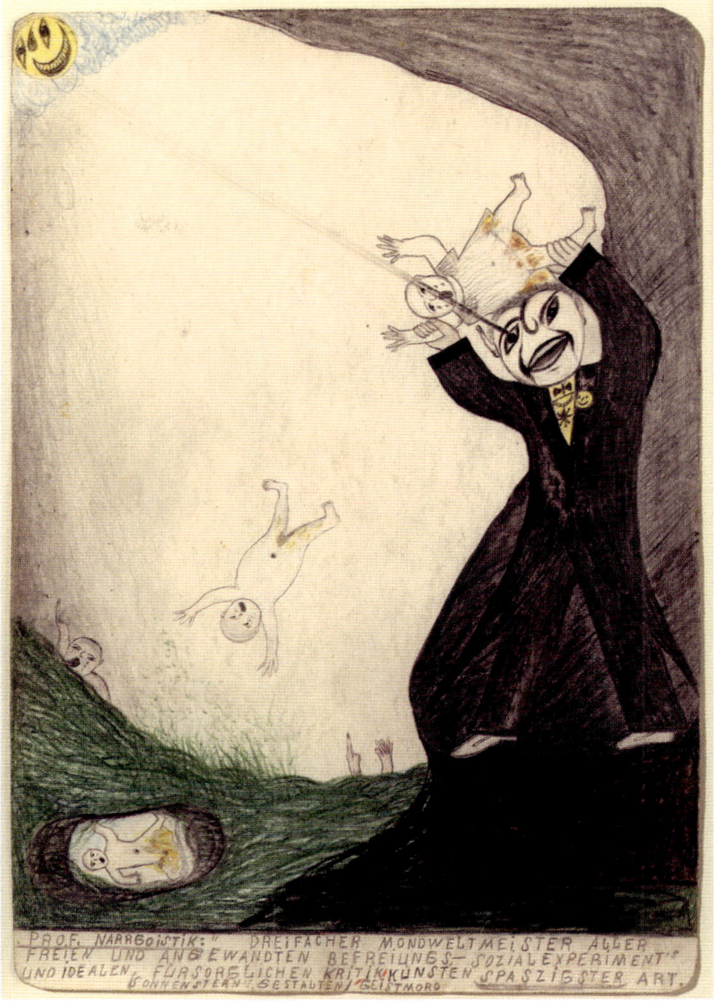

Friedrich Schröder-Sonnenstern, Prof. Narrgoistik, *1950–1952, pencil and colored pencil on paper, 12¼ × 8½ in (31 × 22 cm). Courtesy Galerie Brockstedt.* This is one of Schröder-Sonnenstern's first drawings with demonical undertones. It features a professor with a diabolical grin throwing infants to their deaths. He produced a series of "professors," often titling them with cryptic names. His invented name for this character, Narrgoistik, combines elements of the German wording suggesting both fool (narr) and selfishness (egoistik).

Friedrich Schröder-Sonnenstern's character was dualistic: a complicated trait that appears transferrable to dialectical tension in his drawings. In contrast to his diagnosis in 1918, he was later released from a state mental institution in 1933, deemed completely "sound of mind." Concurrently, in the 1920s, under the name Professor Dr. Eliot Gnass von Sonnenstern, he was a charlatan naturopath/healer. He dubiously performed fraudulent healings and fortune-telling, yet he donated his earnings to hospitals and poor children.

A further paradox existed between Schröder-Sonnenstern's innate mental health issues and potentially self-enhanced psychopathic character. Struggling to secure his place in the German art scene of the 1950s, he variably attempted to elevate his position or intrigue as an artist by referring to his previous identities as a schizophrenic and as a spiritual healer. This may have been strategic, as he was aware that the surrealists and expressionists embraced art made by "psychotics" and "mediums." In a letter to gallerist Rudolf Springer, he wrote "I am a harmless lunatic" and in his *Autobiographie* he stated, "I threw myself into a state, up until then unknown to me." Among the early discourse around Schröder-Sonnenstern's practice were problematic pushes and pulls relating his aesthetic to his mental state.

The abundance of contradictions is poetically present in Schröder-Sonnenstern's oeuvre. His drawings have lyrical phrenic energy executed with sophistication. Fantastical and grotesque beings present parables of biblical, mythical, and literary amalgamation.

"Schröder-Sonnenstern's art is one of scandal and derisive caricature that assaults the social prejudices and sexual taboos that are the props of civilized man."
– Roger Cardinal, *Outsider Art*[26]

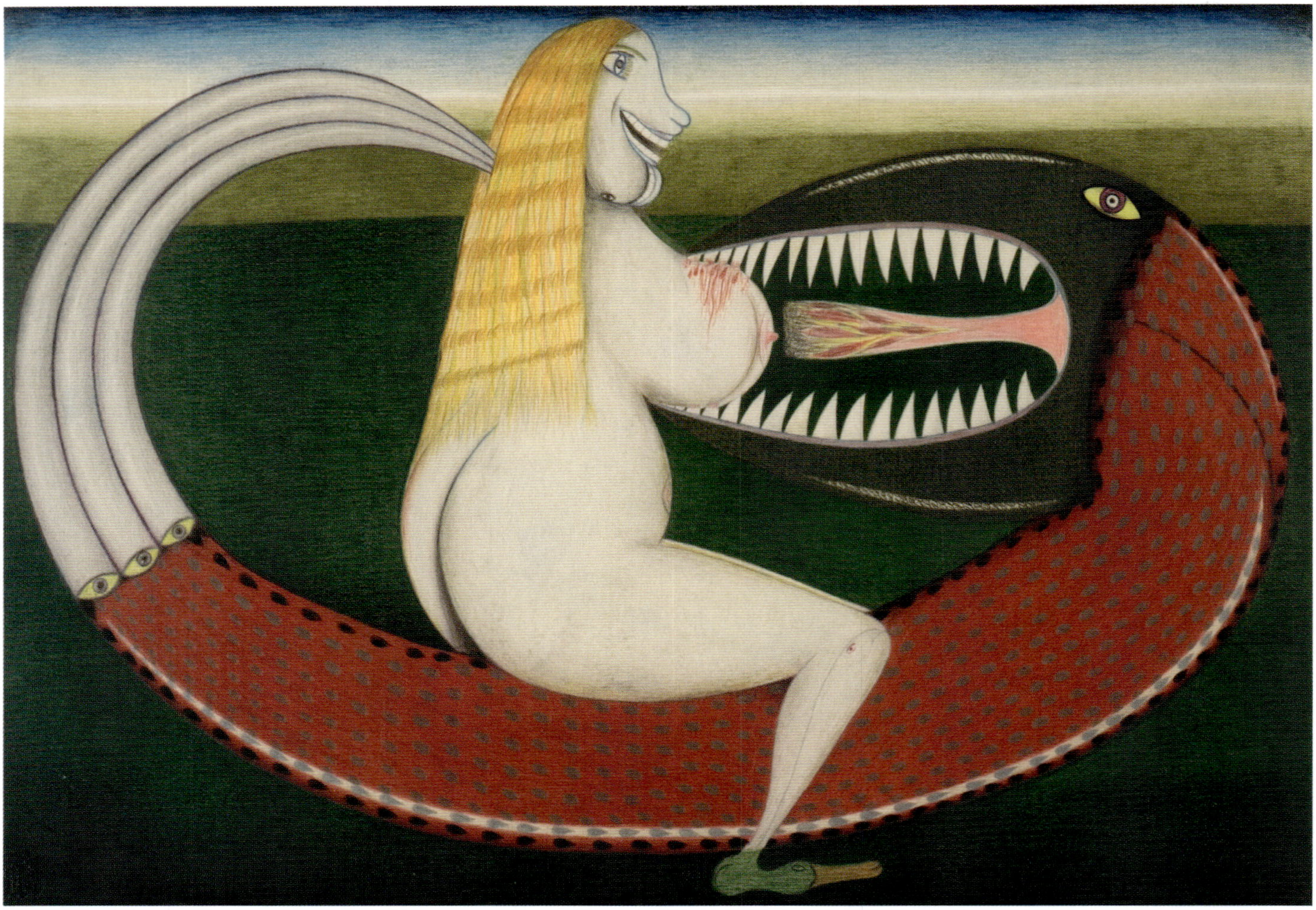

Friedrich Schröder-Sonnenstern, The Jealous Tragedy, *ca. 1956, colored pencil on cardboard, 20 × 28¾ in (51 × 73 cm). Courtesy Galerie Brockstedt.* Exhibited in *Outsiders: An Art Without Precedent or Tradition*, Hayward Gallery, London (1979), it was described in the catalog as a lunar-mooral fancy bird. Erotic in nature it features a voluptuous blond woman on top of a creature who is biting her breast.

Friedrich Schröder-Sonnenstern, The People's Joyful Miraculous Shirt, *1955, colored pencil on cardboard, 28¾ × 20 in (73 × 51 cm). Courtesy Galerie Brockstedt.* Also referred to as the *Moralistic Scarecrow*, it is suggested the moralistic tone of this work was in response to Germany's "call for wholeness." Symmetry implemented by Schröder-Sonnenstern renders a sense of authority with this drawing where a personified cloak hangs on a crosslike structure, above a dubious character with horns.

"You shattered my hope, muzzled my spirit, tormented my soul, and now you stinking brats want me to vote for you—I vote for myself." – Friedrich Schröder-Sonnenstern[27]

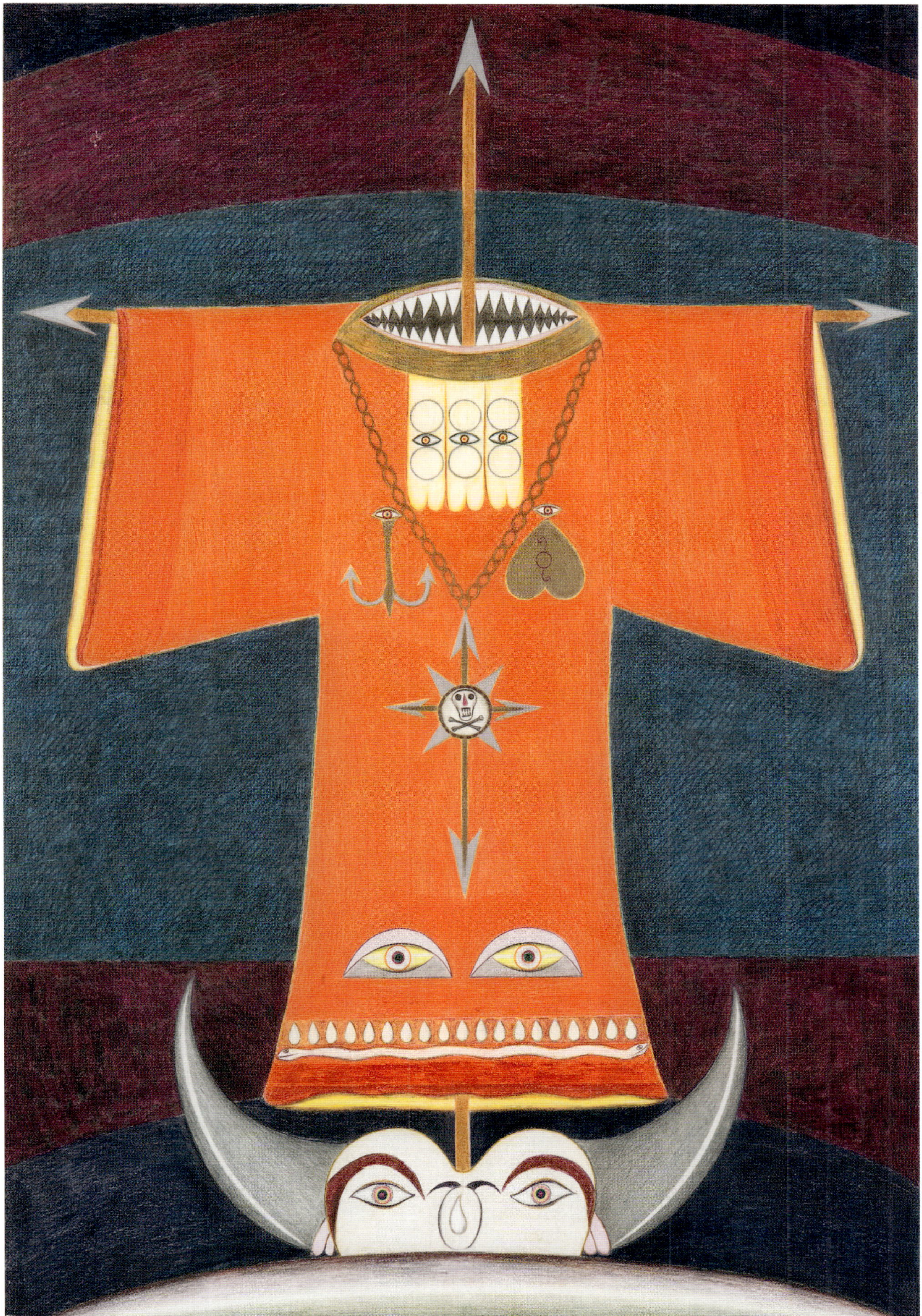

ANNA ZEMÁNKOVÁ

(1908 Moravia [now Olomouc]–1986 Prague, Czech Republic)

The compositions by Anna Zemánková of otherworldly botanicals are abundant with imaginative transformations. From their amphibious qualities to suggestions of sexual eroticism, her drawings are transportive. She was interested in art from a young age, but was discouraged by her family to pursue it professionally. Czechoslovakia gained its independence during her youth, in 1918, and a national resurgence of tradition and craft emerged, becoming influential to her later practice. In the mid-1950s, after marrying and raising a family in Prague, Zemánková experienced emotional duress and insecurities. Her sons encouraged her to begin drawing again to mitigate her suffering, and after some trepidation, she began to draw floral compositions. Reminiscent of automatic Spiritualist practices, Zemánková developed a creative early morning routine of drawing in a state considered between sleep/dream and consciousness. In 1964, she first presented her oeuvre in her home, titled *The Open House Day*. This led to several significant exhibitions in her lifetime, notably *Outsiders*, at the Hayward Gallery, London (1979). Posthumously, Zemánková has continuously been shown internationally including the *Encyclopedic Palace*, 55th Venice Biennale (2013) and *The Museum of Everything #6*, Kunsthal Rotterdam (2016).

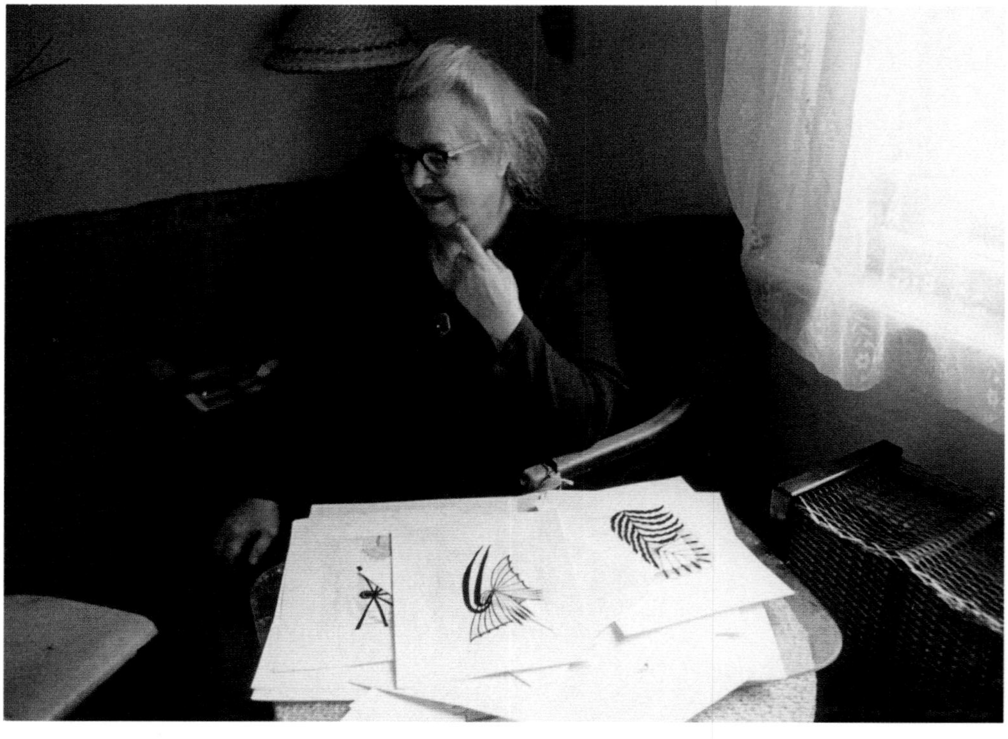

Anna Zemánková, ca. 1980, photograph by Jan Reich (Czech, 1942–2009). Courtesy of Anna Zemánková & Cavin-Morris Gallery. Taken a year after her inclusion in *Outsiders: An Art Without Precedent or Tradition*, Hayward Gallery, London (1979), Zemánková is seen here with her drawings at her apartment in Prague.

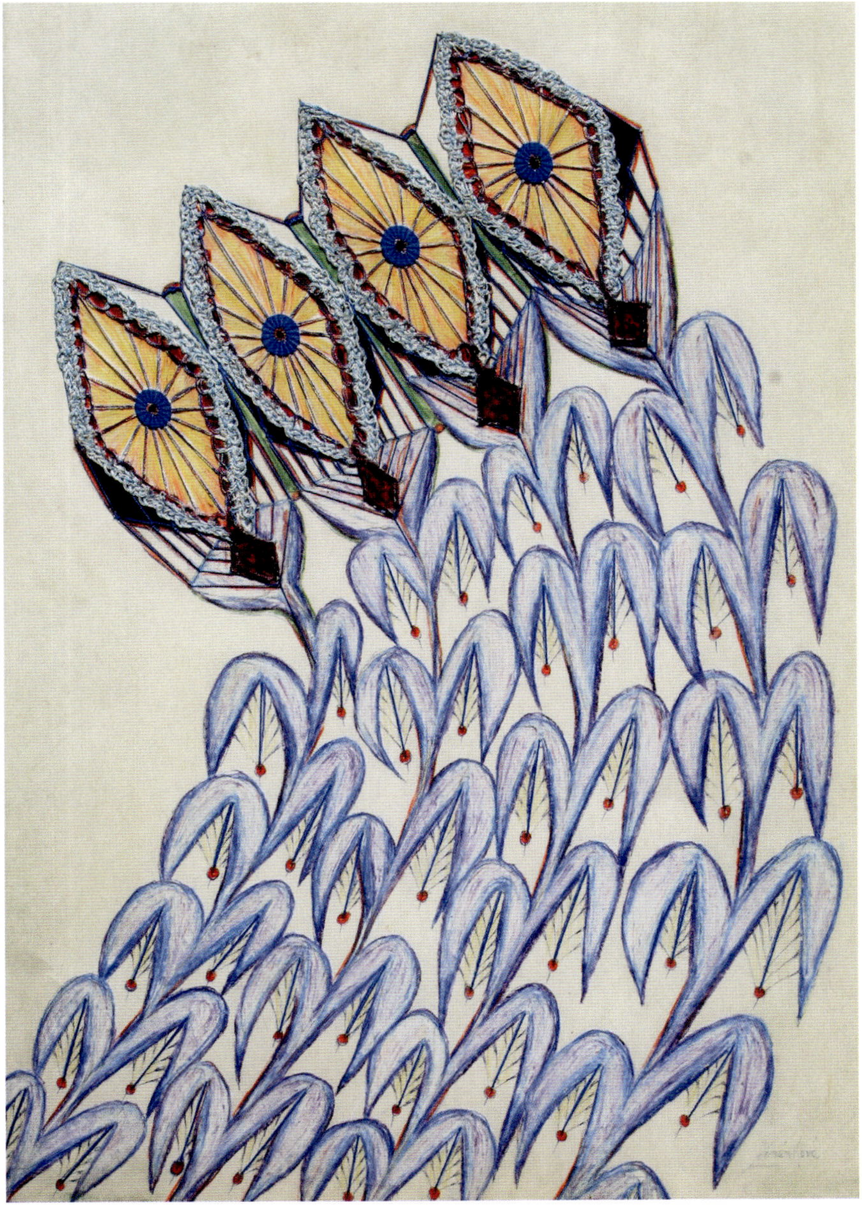

Anna Zemánková, untitled, *ca. 1970, pastel, ink, and thread on paper, 24⅝ × 17¾ in (62.5 × 45 cm). The Museum + The Gallery of Everything.* This botanical composition by Zemánková plays with geometric abstraction that feels kaleidoscopic. The sharp geometric pastel lines are mitigated and made intimate with her application of detailed embroidery.

As a mother, Anna Zemánková wholly dedicated herself to her children, using her tenacious creativity to foster their development and enrich their experience. According to her granddaughter, Terezie Zemánková, "motherhood for her became a higher mythical mission." Therefore, her children establishing independence as they matured likely contributed to her declining mental health in the mid-1950s. Marriage difficulties and arduous menopause were also contributing factors. With her powerful identity as a mother weaning, Zemánková circumvented her creative force into her drawing.

Rudimentarily and consistently botanical in subject matter, Zemánková's aesthetic evolved from realistic to fantastical. Her creative practice commenced very early in the morning while her family was still asleep. Her almost trancelike state at dawn, still wakening herself from her dreams, allowed for creative spontaneity. She often continued her practice in the afternoon when she was alone in the house and drew up to eight hours a day. Transcending ordinary references—music, Moravian embroidery, and the landscape of her Prague neighborhood—into extraordinary blooms, her environment served as direct and indirect influences on her practice.

Over the course of her practice, Zemánková's materials advanced, as did her compositions. However, her subconscious spirit continually and constantly reverberated in the work. Initially rendered in tempera, her depictions of botanical shapes were in a representational aesthetic.

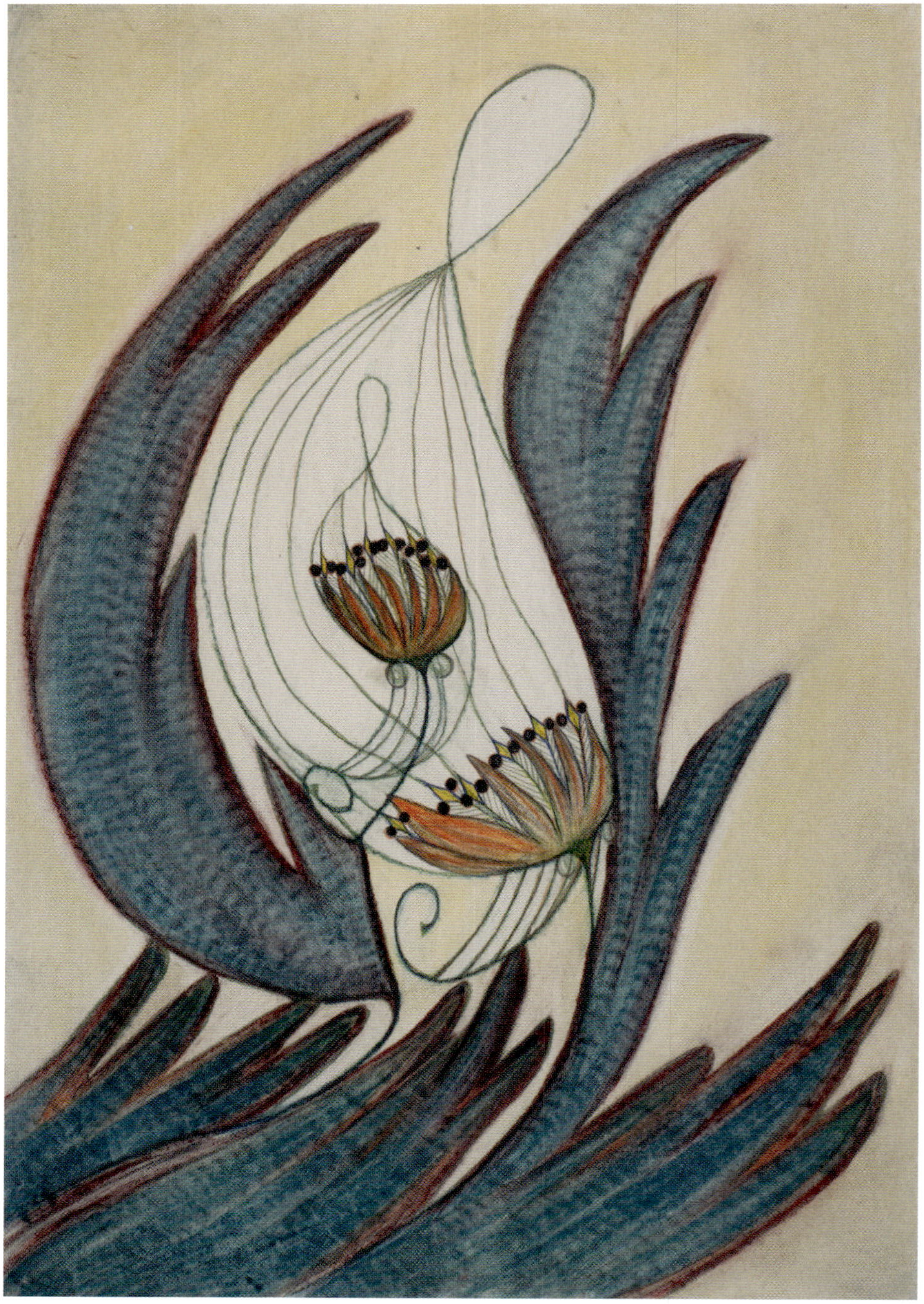

Anna Zemánková, untitled, *ca. 1960, pastel on paper, 24 × 17 in (61 × 43 cm). Courtesy Cavin-Morris Gallery.* An earlier work from the 1960s demonstrates the aquatic-like execution of flora in only pastel. The organic curves and voluptuous center bud have womblike qualities, perhaps evoking Zemánková's love of motherhood.

Anna Zemánková, untitled, *n.d., pastel, ink, and embroidery on paper, 24⅝ × 17¾ in (62.5 × 45 cm). The Museum + The Gallery of Everything.* The technique and aesthetic of Moravian textile adornment is evident in this pastel and embroidery work. A highly botanical and geometric composition, it features two floral blooms of minute stitching details with pearl-like beads.

Later, her practice evolved into elaborate forms executed in pastel and incorporated tactile elements, such as perforation, embroidery, and collage.

Zemánková's semi-abstracted invented botanicals are kaleidoscopic and sublime; sensual and organic. Echoing her creative drive and dedication in her role as a mother, the ornamental detail and phytogeographical geometry of her oeuvre infer Zemánková's artistic desire for beauty and radiance.

"I am growing flowers that are not grown anywhere else."
– Anna Zemánková[28]

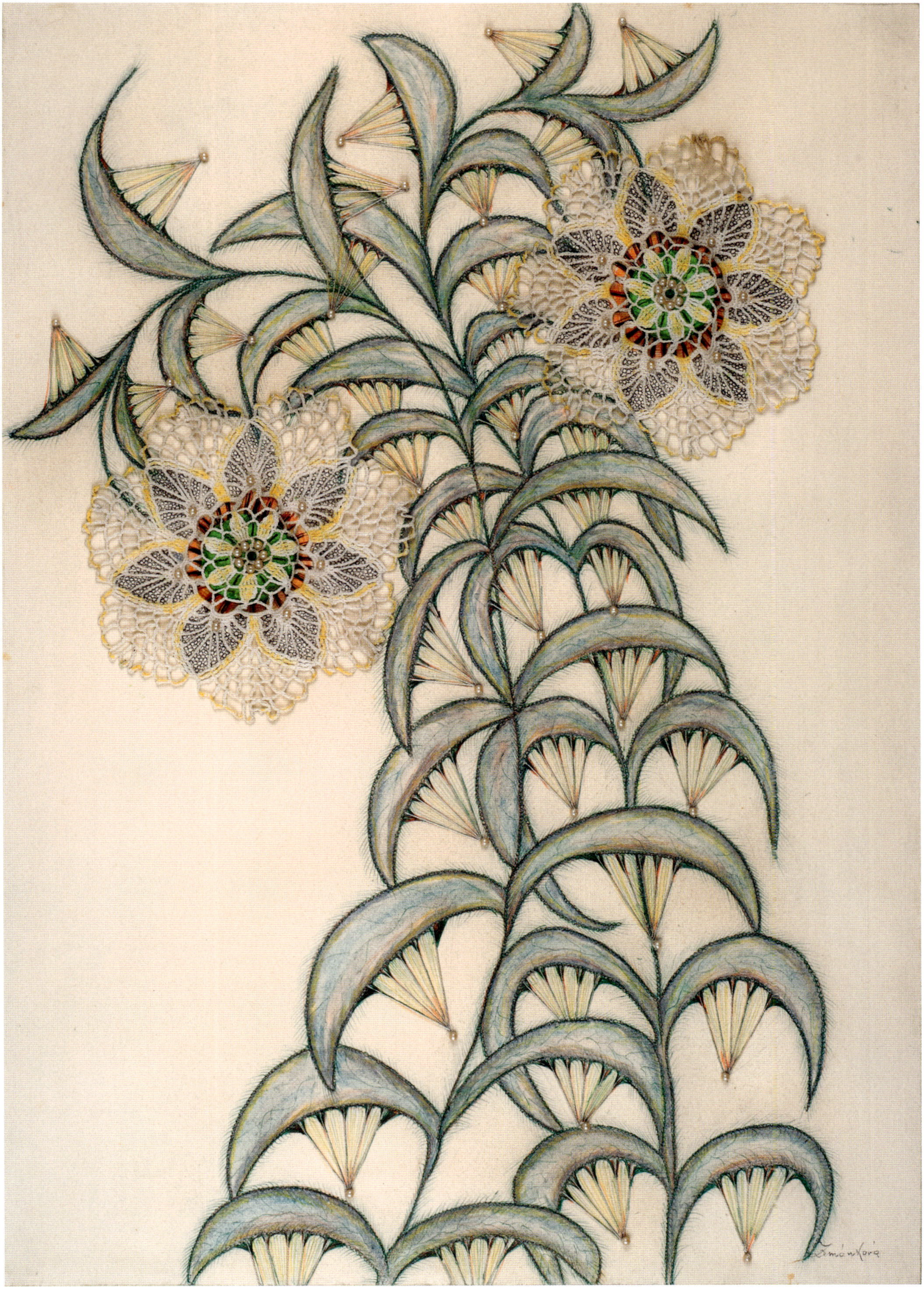
Zemánková

JOHANN HAUSER

(1926, Bratislava, Slovakia–1996, Klosterneuburg, Austria)

Johann Hauser was one of the original members of the artist-patient program at the Maria Gugging Psychiatric Clinic. As a refugee, Hauser moved with his family to Austria during World War II, where they lived in a resettlement camp until 1946. Hauser was born with an intellectual disability and encountered mental health issues early in life; he was institutionalized at 22 years old. He began to draw in 1959 under the encouragement of Dr. Leo Navratil, who later formalized a center at Gugging for artists (see page 112). Hauser's drawing oeuvre is most widely recognizable by his portraits of females, which are simultaneously sexual and rudimentary. The intensity of his aesthetic—color and stroke—was often related to his emotional state. His work was championed by avant-garde artists of the 1960s, and by the late 1970s his drawings were being curated into museum exhibitions, including at Cologne Kunsthalle and the Museum of Modern Art Vienna. Hauser was one of several artists from Gugging exhibited as part of the *Outsiders* exhibition at the Hayward Gallery, London (1979).

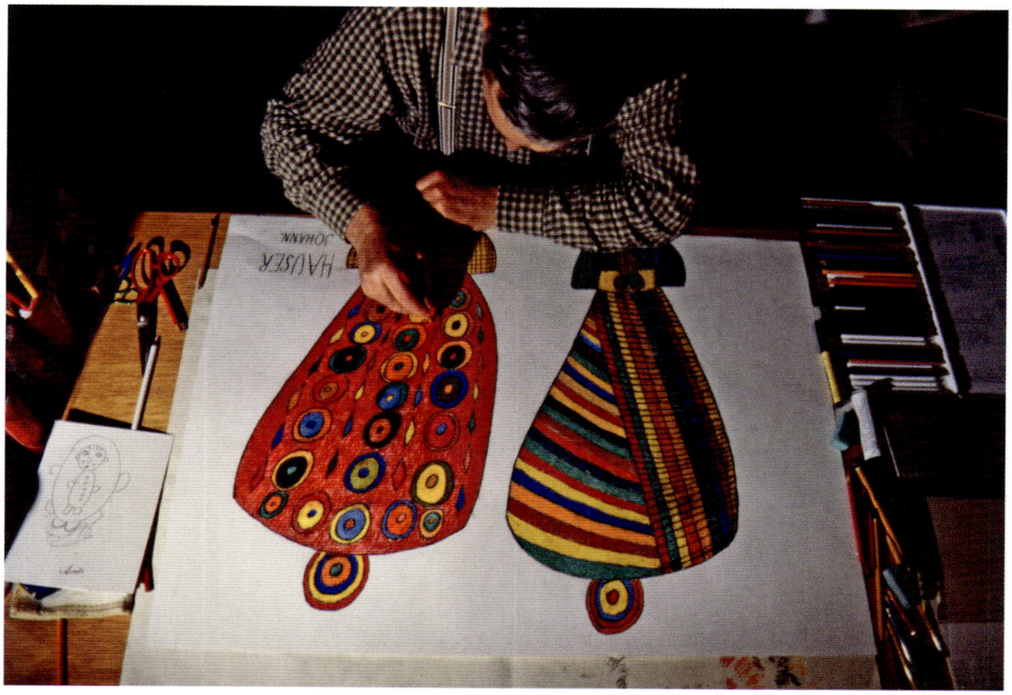

Johann Hauser, 1989, photograph by Johann Feilacher (Austrian, b. 1954). Private Foundation—Artists of Gugging. This portrait shows Hauser in the studio at Gugging while working on the drawing *Tethered Balloons*.

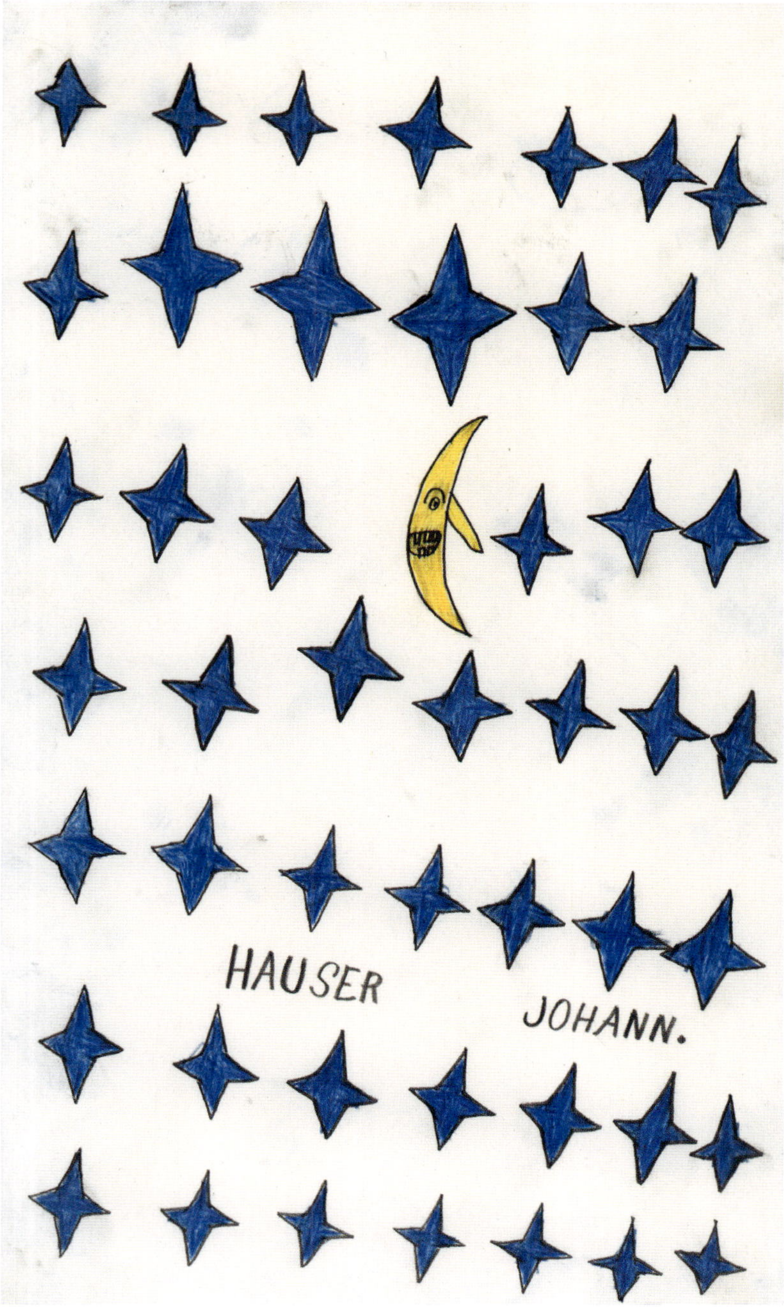

Johann Hauser, Stars, *n.d., pencil and colored pencils, 15⅜ × 9¼ in (39 × 23.5 cm). Private Foundation—Artists of Gugging.* The four-pointed blue star is an important emblem for Hauser. It is considered to be his invention and has become an icon for the artists of Gugging.

From a cultural-historical point of view, Johann Hauser's position as a refugee with an intellectual disability and mental health issues in Austria amid the Nazi regime of World War II is relevant. Systemically, individuals within Hauser's circumstances would have been neglected by the state and mistreated in their early encounters with institutions. Therefore, Hauser's ability to not only survive, but thrive, creatively in his relational condition is in itself exceptional.

Hauser was formally diagnosed as bipolar. Navratil, who conducted a clinical study on Hauser in 1978, proposed his drawings can be identified as, or influenced by, his emotional state, an opinion that historians have expanded upon. The compositions made while Hauser was considered to be in a manic state are more flamboyant and bold. Contradictorily, works made while he was in a depressive state appear more melancholic, with simple geometrical patterns. It is considered that Hauser had a consistent and deliberate practice from its inception, but it was the 1980s that marked the most significant years for his output.

While Hauser's female portraits are at the center of his practice, his oeuvre does include series of planes and scenery inferred to relate to his childhood amid the war.

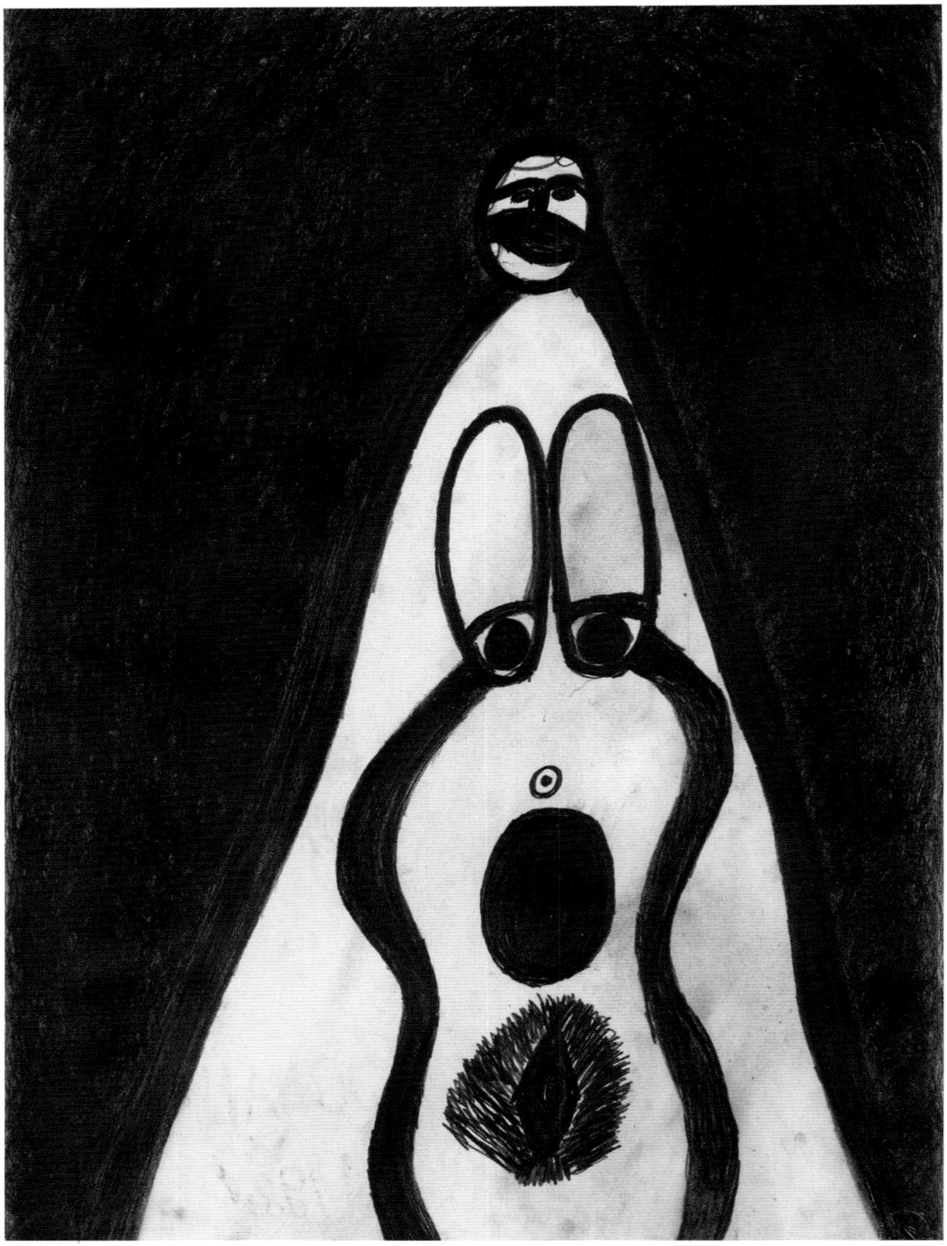

Johann Hauser, Female Nude, *1985, pencil and colored pencils, 24 7/16 × 17 5/16 in (62 × 44 cm). Private Foundation—Artists of Gugging.* A somber monochromatic female portrait, *Female Nude* places emphasis on the breasts and genitals. Hauser's positioning of the erotic body parts and overall commitment to symmetry presents the form in totem-like manner.

Johann Hauser, Frau (Woman), *1966, pencil and colored pencils, 17 5/16 × 12 3/16 in (44 × 31 cm). Galerie im Lenbachhaus, Munich.* With the subject of women integral to his practice, this female portrait is one of Hauser's most iconic. Considering Navratil's study of Hauser's emotional state related to his drawings, this could be considered a manic illustration. *Woman* was exhibited in *Outsiders: An Art Without Precedent or Tradition*, Hayward Gallery, London (1979).

Yet, his compositions of women undoubtedly draw the most intrigue. These feminine figures were drawn oblately without a notion of volume or attempt to mimic three-dimensionality. Breasts and vaginas take on various geometric and organic shapes but are often depicted as the most important among Hauser's figurative semiotics. Often naked and positioned in an upright position, the stacking of hair, eyes, mouth, breasts, navel, genitals equates to a totemic female figure.

"I think it simplistic to reduce them to symptoms of a single, ubiquitous lustfulness. Rather, the serial visualization of erotic signs allows the viewer to lose track of the cliché and to drift into private reverie, a form of indiscriminate musing." – Roger Cardinal, art historian, on Hauser's female portraits[29]

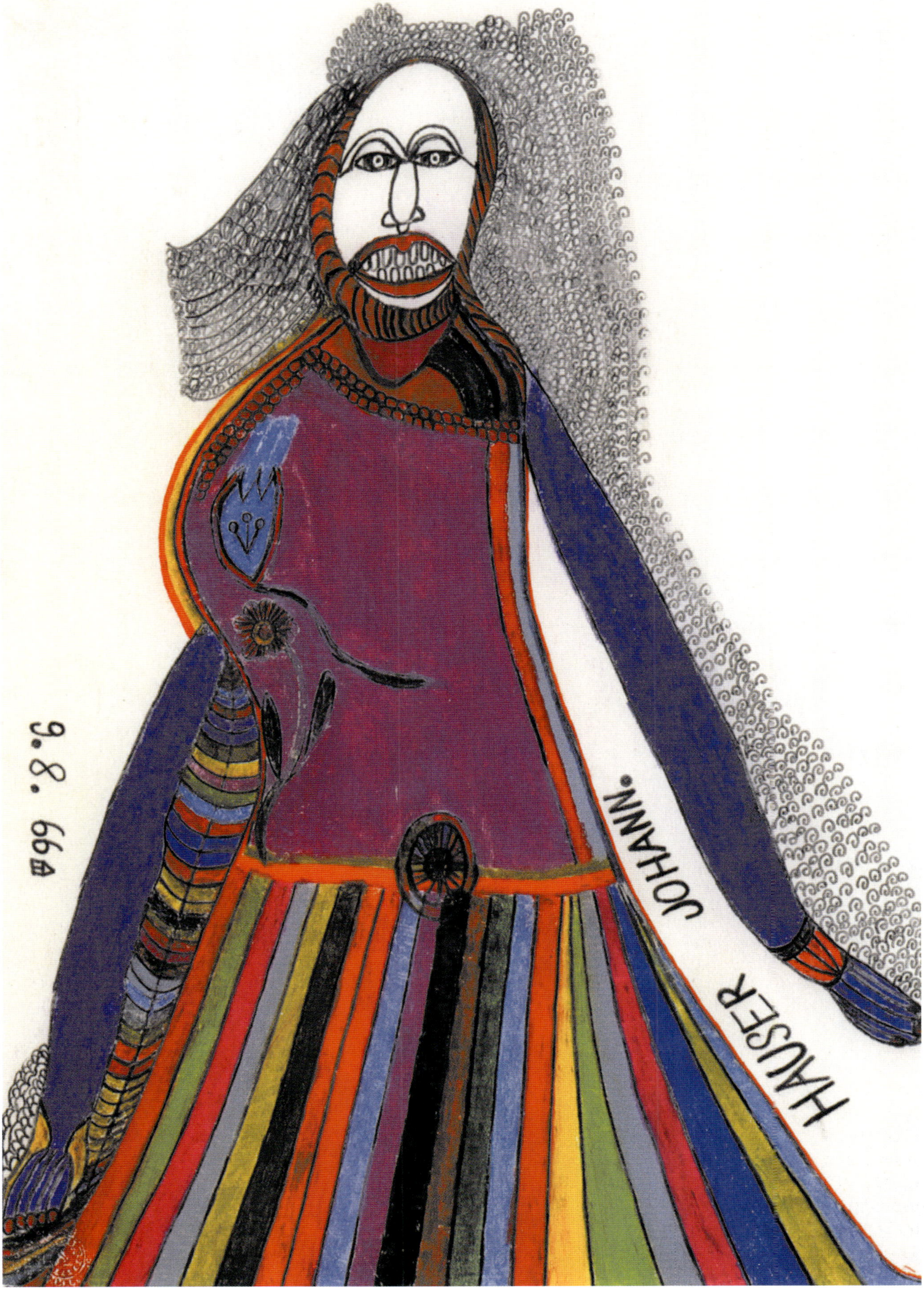
HAUSER JOHANN.
9.8.66

AUGUST WALLA

(1936, Klosterneuburg–2001, Vienna, Austria)

August Walla communicated by writing on objects. From trees in his allotment to his bedroom walls, and more traditionally on paper and canvas, his devised language "Welltallendefremdsprache" expressed his personal universe and private mythology. Raised by a single mother in Klosterneuburg, Walla was intermittently institutionalized for mental health concerns from when he was young into adulthood. In 1970, while at the Maria Gugging Psychiatric Clinic in Austria, his drawing practice was first observed by psychiatrist Dr. Leo Navratil. Navratil not only fostered Walla's creativity, but also formed a center at Gugging for artists and later the House of Artists[30]—a residence where Walla and his mother lived from 1983 until their respective deaths. Within Walla's language-led practice he often explored themes of sexual identity, religion, politics, and eternity. He was one of several artists from Gugging exhibited as part of the *Outsiders* at the Hayward Gallery, London (1979). Walla is most recognized for the creative transformation of his bedroom, in which he scribed personal vocabulary from floor to ceiling. In 1984, he also painted an exterior mural on the facade of the House of Artists.

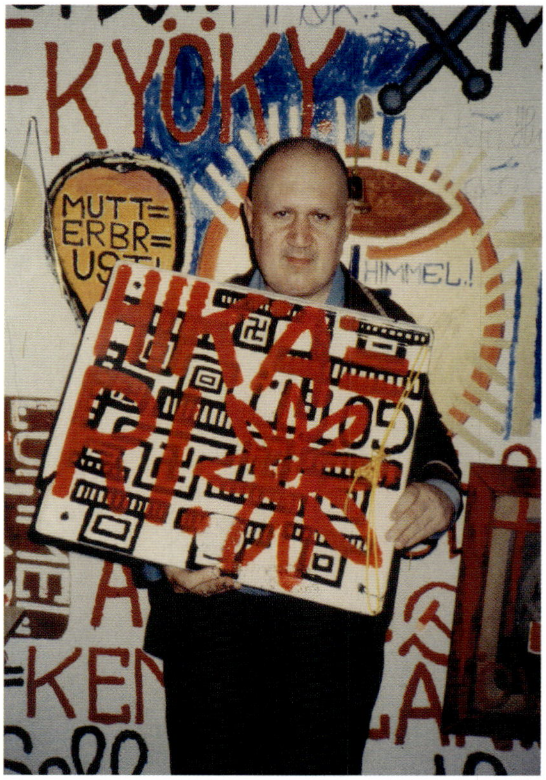

August Walla, ca. 1980s, photograph. Art Brut KG. Walla's penchant for expressing himself visually to communicate is demonstrated by the signboard he holds of his invented language "Welltallendefremdsprache," as well as the wall behind, inscribed with further language and designs.

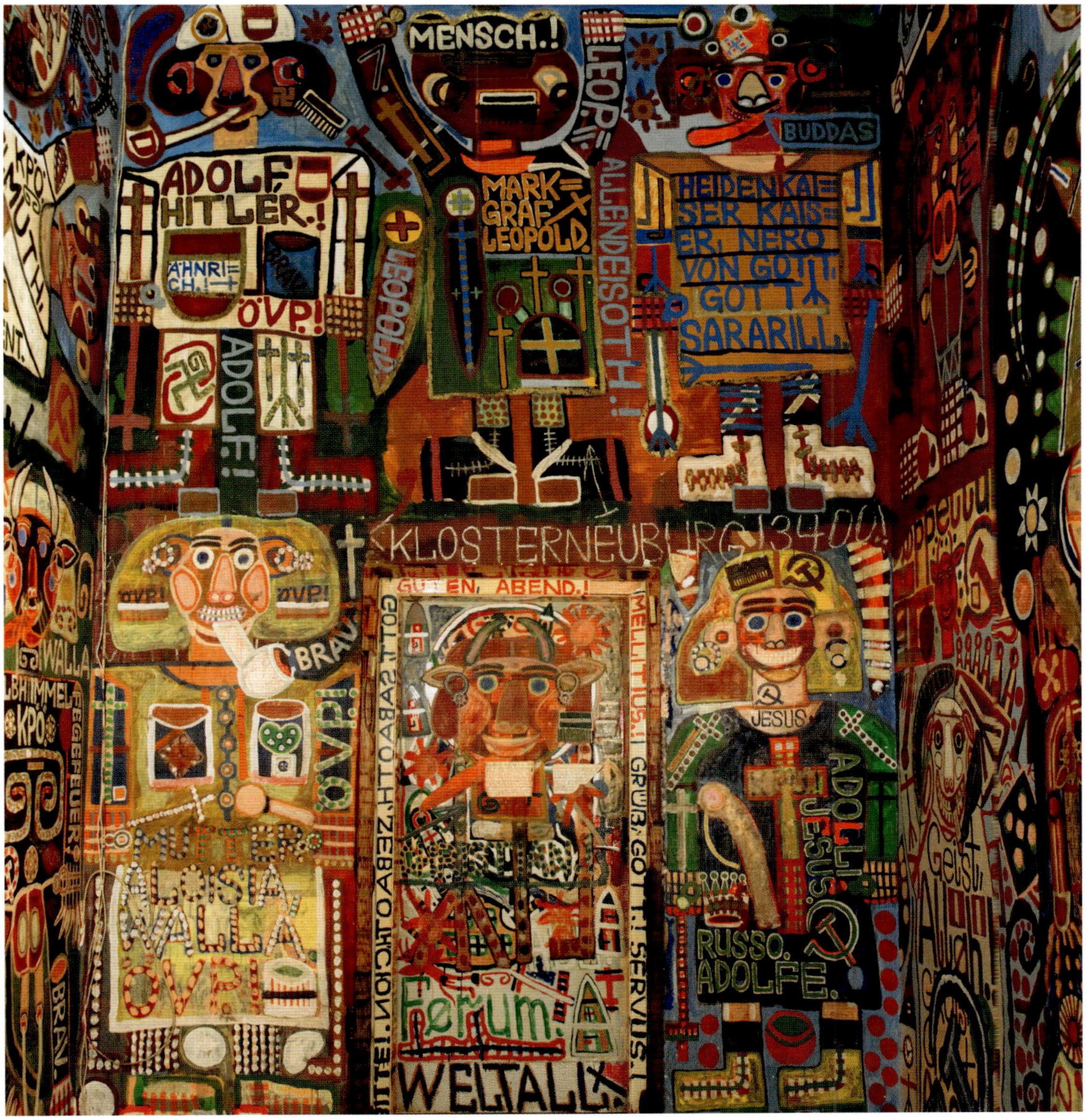

August Walla, photographic detail of Walla's room, 2001. When Walla was almost 50 years old, he moved to Gugging's Haus der Künstler, where he stayed until his death. He painted the walls and ceiling with vibrant but cryptic symbols and language, making evident his aesthetic alignment with graffiti. The top-left of the main wall juxtaposes a figure labeled "Adolf Hitler.!" next to a character labeled "Mensch.!"

It was rare for August Walla to communicate verbally with anyone but his mother, so his creative transcriptions were integral to his personal expression. His spiritual concerns were with the concept of post-eternity, referred to, and explored within, his idiosyncratic language "Welltallendefremdsprache"—translated as "Universe-End-Foreign-Language." Visually adjacent to graffiti, he established his own set of typeface and principles of punctuation. His vocabulary implemented various languages—among them Russian, Hebrew, and Indonesian. Further to the alphabet, he employed symbolic characters and figures to convey his intimate messages.

An example of his symbolism was Walla's use of political emblems the swastika and hammer and sickle. Walla's mother had been distressed amid World War II that her son would be drafted into the military, and consequently raised him as a girl so that he would be disguised. His theoretical recollection of this period was that he was born female until Russian occupants transformed him into a male. As a result, Walla uses the symbol of a swastika to represent femininity and the hammer and sickle for masculinity.

Following the *Outsiders* exhibition at the Hayward Gallery, the 1980s brought collaborations and opportunities to Walla in the wider contemporary art world. This included a project with Austrian artist André Heller, Keith Haring, and Georg Baselitz, among other contributors. In 1990, he received the Oskar Kokoschka Prize, the most prestigious art award in Austria.

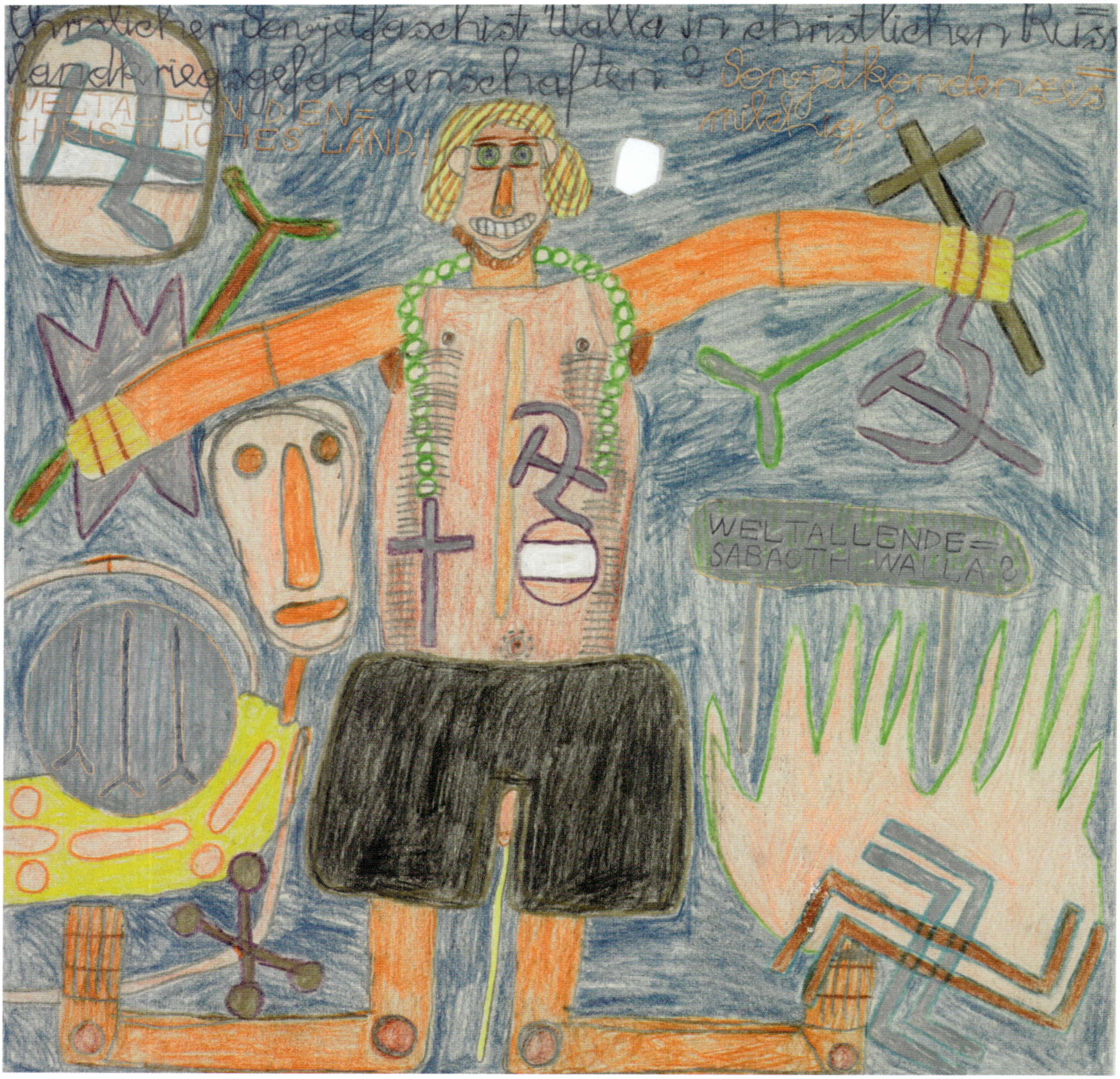

August Walla, Weltallendechristliches Land (End of Universe Christian Country!), *n.d., pencil, colored pencil and ballpoint pen on paper, $11\frac{13}{16} \times 12\frac{3}{16}$ in (30 × 31 cm). Art Brut KG.* This drawing demonstrates Walla's personal symbolism with the iconic hammer and sickle (masculinity) and swastika (femininity). As suggested by the title, it also introduced crosses, likely a reference to Christianity—all in relation to his concept of Universe-End-Land.

"His art works overflow with words, emblems, and symbols. They often centered on his self-made polytheistic philosophy: a mysterious world populated with spirits, with the prospect of a faraway 'Universe-End-Land' that may be the realm of the dead, paradise, limbo, or the great nothingness. The Universe-End-Land marks the transition to that successive cosmos."
– Johann Feilacher, artistic director and curator of Museum Gugging[31]

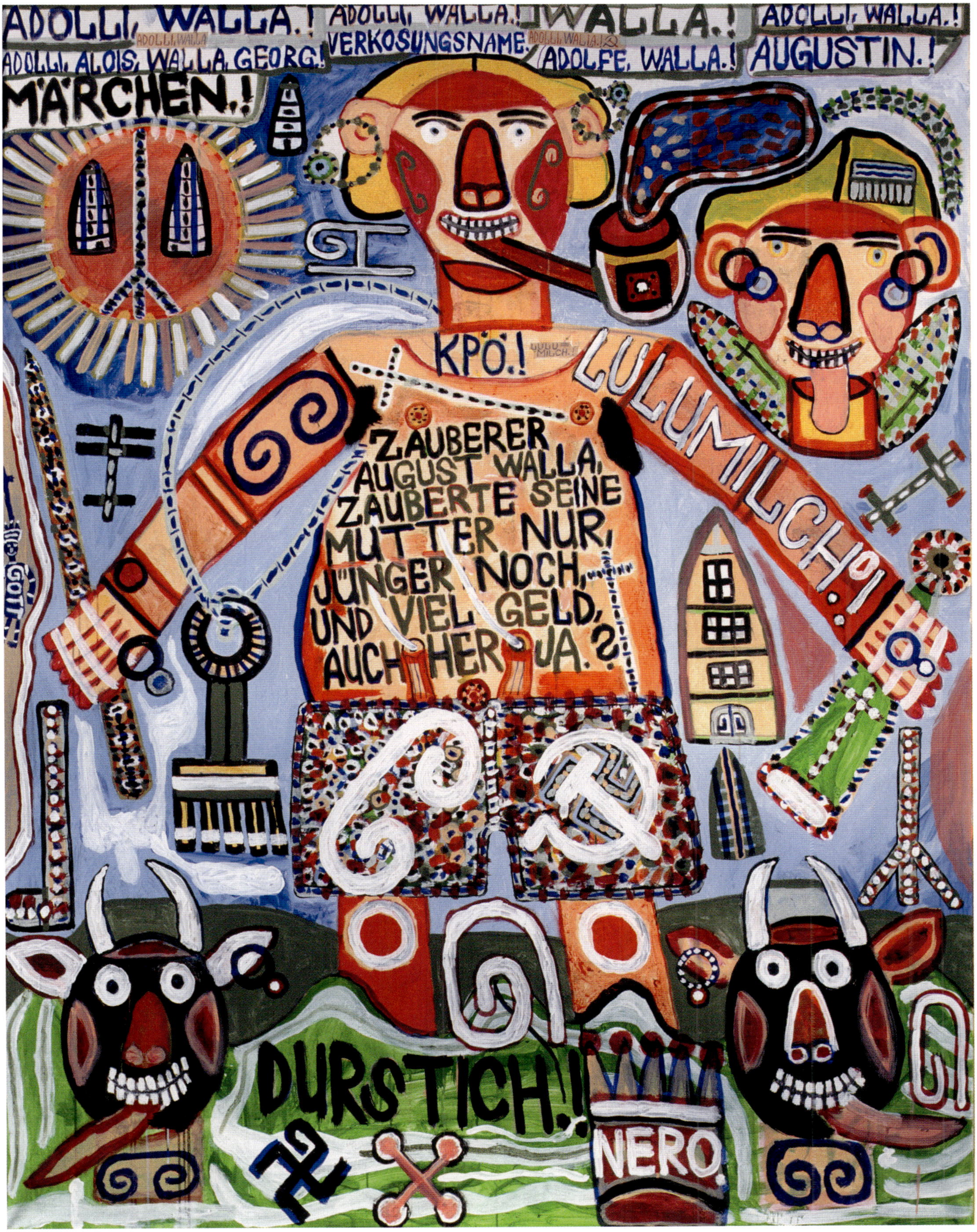

August Walla, Märchen.! (Fairy Tale.!), *1989, acrylic on canvas, 78¹¹⁄₁₆ × 63 in (200 × 160 cm). Art Brut KG.* In this vibrant painting Walla identifies himself as a wizard with exuberant iconography throughout. His use of language and cultural references can be observed with such inscriptions as: NERO. (Roman emperor) over a crown, and M*A*RCHEN (fairy tale). Presumably a self-portrait, Walla stands proud in the center smoking a pipe.

CHAPTER 4

BLACK FOLK ART: PRESENTING SELF-TAUGHT AFRICAN AMERICAN ARTISTS (1976–1982)

WHAT IT WAS, BLACK FOLK ART IN AMERICA

Cheryl Finley, Ph.D.

Black Folk Art in America, 1930–1980, curated by Jane Livingston and John Beardsley for the Corcoran Museum of Art in Washington, D.C. (1982), opened amid the brewing "culture wars" just steps from the National Mall. A little over a decade prior, Black artists, curators, cultural workers, and their allies protested the controversial blockbuster, *Harlem on My Mind* (1969), at the Metropolitan Museum of Art, noting the exclusionary practices of mainstream art museums and galleries in New York, which rarely showed or collected Black artists or employed Black professionals in leadership positions. That pivotal flashpoint of the Black Arts Movement (1965–1975) had rippling effects around the country, igniting allied protests in major cities for greater access to exhibitions, institutions, collections, and jobs for Black professionals and others from underrepresented groups, including women. Their efforts resulted in the founding of a number of cultural institutions advocating for Black arts and communities, notably the Studio Museum in Harlem (1968) and the Cinque Gallery (1969) in New York.

Two predecessors to *Black Folk Art in America* worth noting are *Missing Pieces: Georgia Folk Art 1770–1976*, Atlanta Historical Society, Atlanta (1976), organized by Anna Wadsworth Murray, and *Two Centuries of Black American Art*, Los Angeles County Museum of Art (1976), curated by Dr. David C. Driskell, both mounted on the occasion of the Bicentennial of the United States.[1] The former brought together painting, sculpture, textiles, and environmental works by little-known, rural Georgia folk artists and included the work of Nellie Mae Rowe (see page 138) for the first time in an exhibition. *Two Centuries of Black American Art* featured more than 200 works by 63 primarily male, academically trained painters and sculptors, objects of material culture and decorative arts, including furniture by Thomas Day and pottery by David Drake, and work by the self-taught artists Minnie Evans (see page 338), Clementine Hunter, Horace Pippin (see page 44), and William Edmondson (see page 24). Demonstrating the long tradition of African American art on this seminal national anniversary, *Two Centuries* also featured the work of recognized, professionally trained artists ranging from portraitists Joshua Johnson and Archibald Motley to landscape painters Edward M. Bannister and Robert S. Duncanson, to established 20th-century painters Henry Ossawa Tanner, Aaron Douglas, Jacob Lawrence, Löis Mailou Jones, and Charles White. Driskell selected works from major public and private collections around the country to propose a network of collecting as he lay the groundwork for the first comprehensive survey of African American art from 1750 to 1950. The national tour of *Two Centuries of Black American Art* whet the country's appetite for Black art in America following the advances of the Black Arts Movement. Together with *Missing Pieces*, these critically acclaimed shows set the stage for *Black Folk Art in America* in the years to come.

Black Folk Art in America is undeniably one of the defining exhibitions in the history of African American folk, vernacular, and self-taught art. The original Corcoran installation included nearly 400 works by 20 artists, notably Southern artists Bill Traylor (see page 120), Sister Gertrude Morgan (see page 134), Sam Doyle (see page 142), and Nellie Mae Rowe, as well as Elijah Pierce (see page 130)

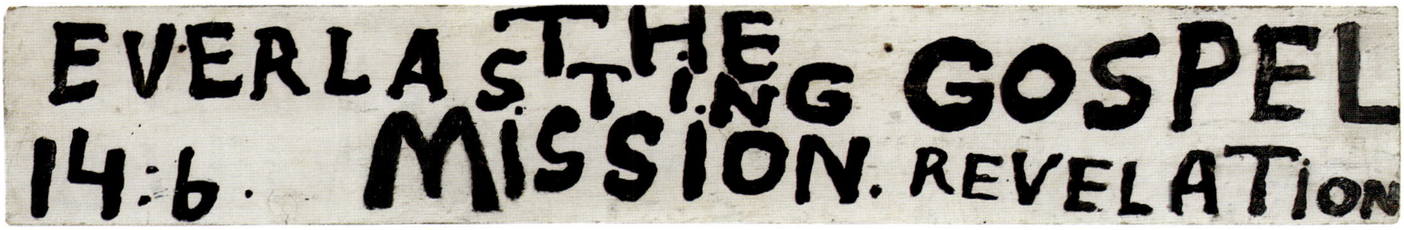

Sister Gertrude Morgan, THE EVERLASTiNG GOSPEL MiSSiON REVELATiON 14:6, *ca. 1970, acrylic on board, 7⅜ × 48⅛ × ¾ in (18.8 × 122 × 1.8 cm). The Museum + The Gallery of Everything.* Exhibited as part of *Black Folk Art in America, 1930–1980*, Corcoran Gallery, Washington, D.C., in 1982, this was signage for Morgan's home, which also served as her place of ministry.

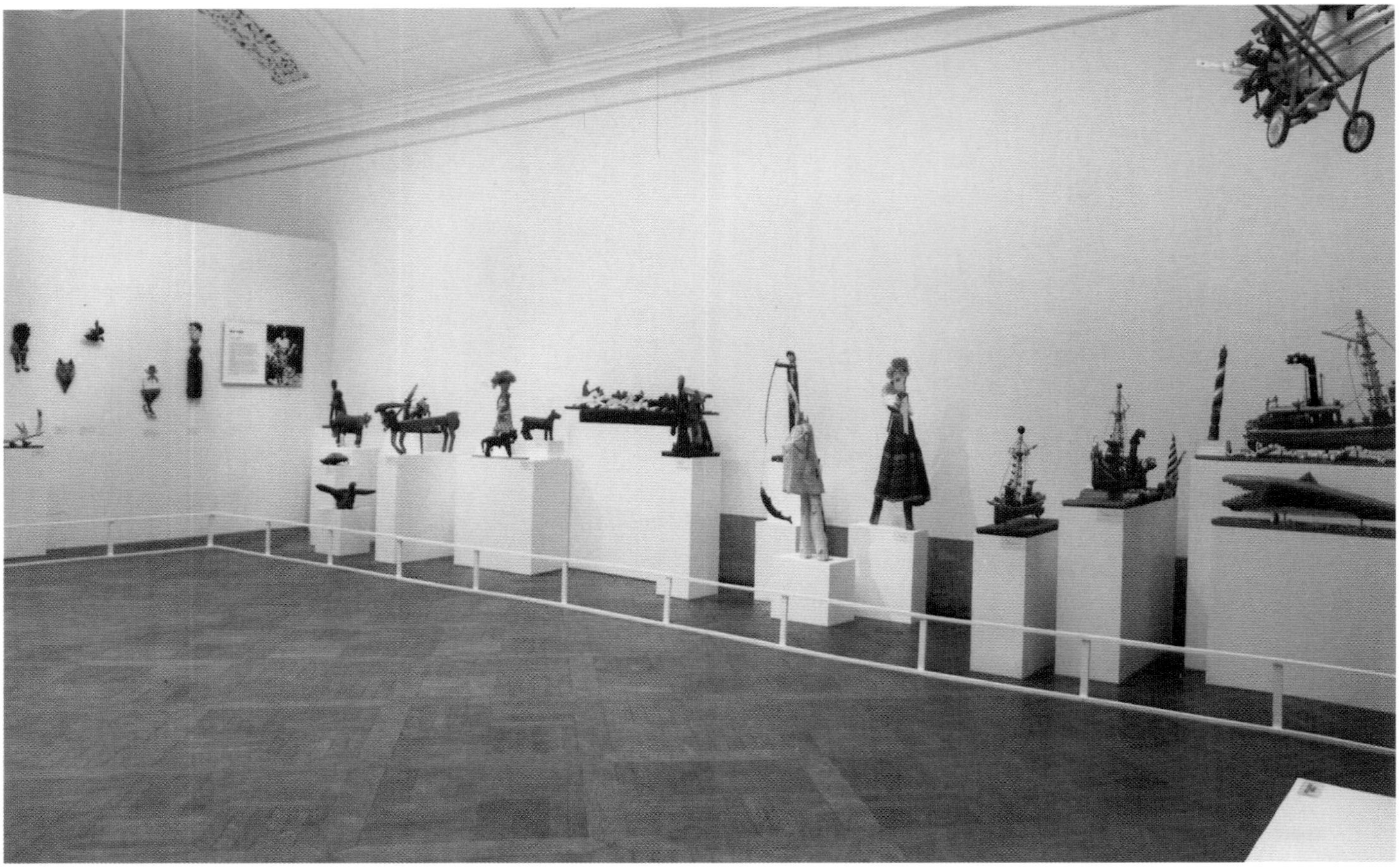

Installation view of the exhibition Black Folk Art in America 1930–1980, *Corcoran Gallery, Washington, D.C., 1982. Corcoran Gallery of Art.* With each of the 20 artists exhibited in singular presentations, this shows the work of Virginian artist Steve Ashby (1904–1980).

and Joseph E. Yoakum (see page 126), two of the few artists who hailed from northern states. Arranged by artist, the installation set out to showcase the individual contributions, talents, and practices of a cadre of little-known, mostly Southern, artists working in wood, metal, stone, painting, drawing, and installation, as well as with found objects, and distinguished them as the baseline of a newly "discovered" genre. Hugely popular in Washington and throughout the subsequent 15-month national tour, *Black Folk Art* both sought to define the terms of an artistic genre and to establish a demand for it within the mainstream art market.[2]

The exhibition was accompanied by an expansive illustrated catalog, numbering nearly 200 pages, including essays defining the category of Black folk art, extensive bibliographical and donor data, and intimate profiles of each of the 20 artists. The cover featured the work of Bill Traylor in a posthumous tribute to the prolific artist, presciently affirming his place within the history of art as well as in the emerging marketplace for Black folk art. Jane Livingston's essay, "What it is," grapples with naming the category of Black folk art and lays out the overall aims of the exhibition in codifying the genre. Proscriptive in tone, she explains, "The artists working in this aesthetic territory are generally untutored, yet masterfully adept . . . tend to have begun making art at a relatively mature age," and have suffered significant hardship.[3] Livingston's essay is complemented by an art historical analysis by Dr. Regenia A. Perry connecting the artists to a 400-year African American creative practice with far-reaching ties to Africa and its diaspora. The artists' profiles feature black-and-white photographic portraits, examples of work, and biographical sketches connecting each artist to the others through purported "affinities," stemming from their (shared) Southern upbringings within a frequently impoverished, working-class setting alongside spiritual, religious, or revelatory visions that called the artists into service, often later in life. The Black Church, sacred and blues music, African influences, and Christian iconography were popular themes in works by Sister Gertrude Morgan, Sam Doyle, and Elijah Pierce, ranging from painting and sculpture to assemblage, collage, and installation art.

The curators' tendency to situate the artists as "outsiders" and unique in ways that separate them from their local Black communities, or their contemporary artistic counterparts was quickly rejected by critics. Dr. Mary Schmidt Campbell, then executive director of the Studio Museum in Harlem, warned, "Taken together, the essays and biographical material present a compelling argument. It is an argument, however, that has a recurrent theme that is disturbing: an emphasis upon isolation, uniqueness, and individuality of each artist and of these artists as a group."[4] In his review, Eugene W. Metcalf offered an overview of African American art history through a reading of Driskell's *Two Centuries of Black American Art*, noting how Black folk art often was omitted from the African American canon. *Black Folk Art's* concept seemed like a step toward rectifying this wrong. However, ultimately, Metcalf concluded that the exhibition and corresponding catalog presented more contradictions and confusion than answers. "In defining the art in *Black Folk Art in America*, there is an attempt to assert a communal tradition as well as the idea of strikingly individual artistic expression. The result is a confusion of context, with the organizers of the exhibition claiming that the works fully respond both to the long history and tradition of Black folk art and to overpowering and unprecedented individual artistic visions."[5] Campbell and Metcalf were among a number of prominent critics who condemned the mixed messaging of *Black Folk Art*, calling attention to the binaries of high/low, folk/professional that the curators proffered, and noting the overlooked value of these artists' ability to maintain cultural practices and traditions.

Criticism of *Black Folk Art* voiced by curator and art historian Kinshasha Holman Conwill exposed some of the contradictions of the art market. Speaking at the symposium *Cult, Culture, and Consumers: Collecting Self-Taught Art in Twentieth Century America* (National Museum of American Art in Washington, D.C., 1990), Conwill asked, "Is it mere coincidence that so many of the artists are Southern, poor, Black, and without formal training and that those who collect their work are often white, educated, and affluent?"[6] Calling out the stereotype of the "modernist primitive," Conwill pressed further, "Why are some of these same individual collectors and institutions apparently less interested in the work of trained Black artists, such as Maren Hassinger, Melvin Edwards, and Howardena Pindell?"[7] Campbell had asked a similar question in her 1982 review of *Black Folk Art*, "Is there any relationship between Elijah Pierce and modern literary painters like Jacob Lawrence and Romare Bearden, who both have Southern roots," driving home once more the danger of binaries used to classify Black art producers (folk/modern, Northern/Southern, and so on).[8]

Concurrent with the national tour of *Black Folk Art in America*, the Studio Museum in Harlem reopened on June 15, 1982 in New York City with three critically-acclaimed exhibitions, the largest among them, *Ritual and Myth: A Survey of African American Art*, curated by Dr. Leslie King Hammond, with over 70 works by 45 artists from Africa, the Caribbean, and the US.[9] Spanning two centuries, *Ritual and Myth* defined the African diaspora well before it was in vogue and demonstrated stylistic, thematic, and material connections across geographies and time from self-taught to academic and modern to contemporary. In many ways, *Ritual and Myth* responded to, if not revealed, the shortcomings of *Black Folk Art*, by offering a dynamic, thematic installation of work by Black self-taught artists that built bridges to their African heritage and their contemporary African American successors. As art historian Dr. Kellie Jones recalled, "The impressive overview, *Ritual and Myth: A Survey of African American Art* (1982), highlighted the Black visual tradition . . . through paired visions of the fantastic and the sacred."[10] The other exhibitions on view at the Studio Museum, including *Images of Dignity: A Retrospective of the Works of Charles White* (1982) and *Harlem Heyday: The Photography of James VanDerZee* (1982–1983), further amplified the broader, narrative Black artistic traditions of which the self-taught artists were a part.[11] In contrast, *Black Folk Art* shied away from providing a comprehensive historical or cultural context for individual artists in the show, one that would have situated them within a trajectory of sustaining, practicing, and innovating Black artistic and cultural traditions.

That curators, critics, and art historians continued to discuss the merits of *Black Folk Art* shows its lasting impact on the art market, art history, and curatorial practice. Dr. Regenia A. Perry writing in the *International Review of African American Art* more than a decade after the opening concurred, calling the show the "catalyst that inaugurated an unparalleled vogue for this 'modern primitive' category of art whose momentum continues to the present."[12] That year, in 1993, the first Outsider Art Fair was held in downtown New York, a commercial enterprise that continues to this day, and Julie Dash's groundbreaking Black feminist film, *Daughters of the Dust*, opened to critical acclaim, foregrounding long preserved and maintained Black and African diasporic folk traditions of the Georgia Sea Islands.[13] Despite its shortcomings, an underlying aim of *Black Folk Art in America* in the impending era of multiculturalism was to attract the attention and support of Black Washingtonians and to fuel dialogue about access, opportunity, and strategies for combatting longstanding institutional marginalization of Black artists.[14]

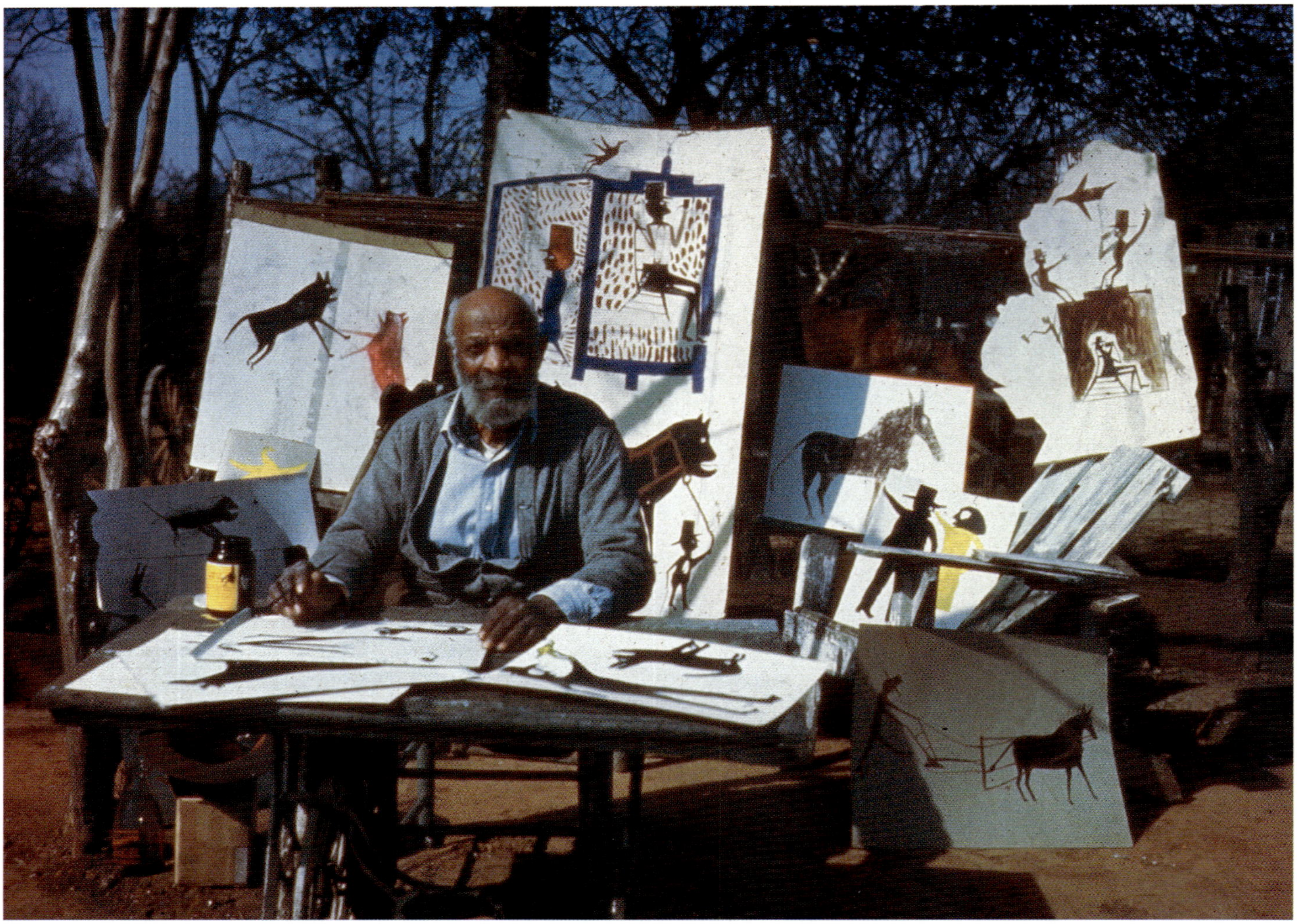

Bill Traylor, 1946, photograph by Horace Perry. Alabama State Council on the Arts. This is a posed portrait of Traylor taken following a decline in his health after he had moved in with his daughter. This non-candid photograph was staged for a photoshoot for *Collier's* magazine for the feature: "*He Lost 10,000 Years*" in June 1946.

BILL TRAYLOR

(ca. 1853, Dallas County–1949, Montgomery, Alabama, USA)

Being born into slavery and spending over 50 years working on plantations in rural Alabama, Bill Traylor only began to draw at 86 years old. In 1939, when Traylor was regularly drawing outside a shop in his Montgomery neighborhood, Charles Shannon became an early supporter of his work. Shannon was part of New South, a local cultural coalition that went on to present Traylor's first solo exhibition in 1940. His allegorical tableaux and symbolic subjects were often drawn on found paper and cardboard. His pared-back compositions were full of emblematic qualities, often inferring power and fear of Southern racial oppression. Traylor died in 1949, having only exhibited twice within his lifetime. Posthumously, his inclusion in the exhibition *Black Folk Art in America, 1930–1980* at the Corcoran Gallery, Washington, D.C., provided national recognition for his work. Now considered one of the most important American artists of the 20th century, Traylor has been the subject of numerous retrospectives, including *Between Worlds: The Art of Bill Traylor* at the Smithsonian American Art Museum (2018).

Bill Traylor's practice, a modest but steadfast production by a reserved individual, almost belied the radical agency found in his drawings. Nearly a century on, his modernist yet allegorical oeuvre is as pertinent as ever. There are few direct references or documented accounts of Traylor discussing his work. Yet, his drawing's innate aesthetic (and extensive 21st-century research by historians and curators) lends to a considered allegorical reading, where Traylor's inclination as a storyteller is undeniable. His singular vision is relevant to the history of the postbellum South, and his open-ended symbolic narratives examining racial tension, power, and fear still resonate deeply. Through Traylor's conceptual edits, his drawings present the essential emotions and metaphorical characters devoid of superfluous content.

Traylor's identity, interpreted into drawings, presented a personal social history of the American South—an intimate reflection of a man who was born enslaved and became a first-generation African American US citizen. Traylor's own environmental journey was a poignant dualistic circumstance. Though he lived predominantly within the state lines of Alabama, the contrast between nearly 50 years on the plantations of John G. and George H. Traylor (the white owners whose last name he bears) to the buzzing streets of Montgomery's Black Business District bears consideration.

An accurate biography of Traylor has been difficult given his position born into slavery and existence shortly after emancipation. Biographical details of such circumstances are difficult to substantiate because of the subpar record-keeping for African Americans at the turn of the century. Oral accounts, facts, and assertions by researchers, most notably by Leslie Umberger inform Traylor's accounts here within.[15]

William (Bill) Traylor was born around 1853 on the John Getson Traylor (J.G.) plantation in Dallas County, Alabama. In 1863, President Abraham Lincoln set forth the Emancipation Proclamation which, dependent on a Union (North) war victory, would end slavery. With the end of the Civil War, the freedom of slaves was ratified through the 13th Amendment in 1865. The effects of this monumental act, however, were slow to immediately impact African Americans. As such, a young Traylor and his family remained on the George Hartwell Traylor (G.T.) plantation in Lowndes County as farm laborers. Traylor spent over 50 years on the plantations of J.G. and his brother, G.T., marrying twice and having at least nine children.[16] In 1908, he moved to Montgomery County and married for the third time a year later. Following the death of his third wife and with his children grown (most of whom relocated north with the Great Migration), Traylor moved alone to the city of Montgomery in 1927. In stark contrast to rural Alabama, the Black Business District of heavily segregated Montgomery was a thriving microcosm of African American business, thought, and creativity.

At 86 years old, drawing from his prior life experiences, which undoubtedly informed his art practice, Traylor entered the preeminent years for his creative legacy. Given his age, Traylor's health was fragile and in decline. He was walking with two canes and was without a permanent residence. Research indicates Traylor likely started drawing in 1938. However, it is between 1939 and 1942 that Traylor was drawing regularly, marking his most prolific years. The majority of works still in existence are from this period. Initially sketching in only pencil and more simply in form, his style and complexity developed with acceleration.

His usual drawing locale was outside of the blacksmith shop, which was where he met Charles Shannon and John Lapsley, members of the New South: a new coalition of white creatives aiming to form an arts community in Montgomery. The members of New South, most notably Charles Shannon, became key advocates for recognizing Traylor's ability, but perhaps more critical was their initial collecting of Traylor's drawings, which served as a future archive. Shannon also introduced support in several ways: providing art materials (though Traylor often preferred the character of found paper); purchasing his drawings (forming future collections); and facilitating archival processes, such as writing descriptions on the back of drawings if Traylor described them. In this period, Traylor seemed to identify with and commit to being an artist with perpetration. In 1940, he had his first exhibition at New South's eponymous Montgomery gallery. *Bill Traylor: People's Artist* (1940) featured almost 100 works and was the only instance in which Traylor saw his work in a formal setting.

From 1940 to 1942 in particular, Traylor's materials expanded to colored pencils and paints. This included a penchant for an ultramarine blue recognizable in many of his works. He also developed a unique drafting process that mirrored anatomy by first drawing skeletal lines then overlaying them with organic fuller shapes. Referred to as the Florescence period[17], these years set forth exemplary drawings to examine Traylor's allegorical and symbolic narratives. Specific animals provide a paradigm for such examinations. Traylor composed various animals in varying circumstances and with a dual purpose. Depending on the composition, they seem either candidly animal or metaphorically human.

For example, his draftsmanship of rabbits has an almost hybrid quality, further suggesting their role as a human metaphor. They have elongated, almost human-like, legs and appear to be a character fearfully pursued.[18] To build upon the allegory, Traylor's symbolism of dogs has a complex, non-fixed dimensionality. His metaphorical language for animals appears to be diagrammatically explained in *untitled (Chase Scene)* (ca. 1940). This drawing depicts a dog chasing a rabbit, while below, as almost a fraction, is a figure chasing a black man. In this equation, the symbolism of dogs is to be considered: animals that could be companions, but also physical enforcers of superiority and obedience. Further in Traylor's series of fighting dogs, this oscillating presence of canines in plantation life seems evident. These drawings evoke fear and violence. While in *Man and Large Dog* (ca. 1939–1942), Traylor's use of scale fluidity elevates the potential storyline. In this drawing, a large black dog is leashed and bound to an undersized white man. This narrative implies the dog has an unfixed symbolism and has shifted from the oppressor to the oppressed. These are but a few examples of the multi-representational readings into Traylor's animalistic allegories. They exemplify Traylor's symbolic potential of enigmatically examining slavery. As considered in the historical context—Traylor's social circumstance as a postbellum Black man in Alabama—overtly depicting scenarios of racial tension would have been problematic, even dangerous.

Further allegories in Traylor's oeuvre included more open-ended narratives often presented on semi-abstracted architectural forms. These reinstate the fluidity of his symbolism and subject. Leslie Umberger said, "Traylor's manner of using structures to stage his dramas vary in consequence but should be carefully considered and never presumed neutral."[19] His choice of constructed stage was perhaps another narrative arcane device implemented by Traylor to explore race.

There are multitudes of symbolic and allegorical examples within the totality of Traylor's oeuvre. Those not explored here include domestic structures, tree scenes (lynching), portraiture (both of his local community and self), and religious symbolism of both Christianity and Conjure. What is evident throughout Traylor's work is his extraordinary ability of reduction, presenting the essential essence of each character or object as poetically raw.

In 1942, Traylor had the second and last exhibition of his lifetime, *Bill Traylor: American Primitive (Work of an Old Negro)* at the Ethical Culture Fieldston School in Riverdale, New York. MoMA Director Alfred Barr, Jr. expressed interest in Traylor's work but this opportunity was not pursued to its

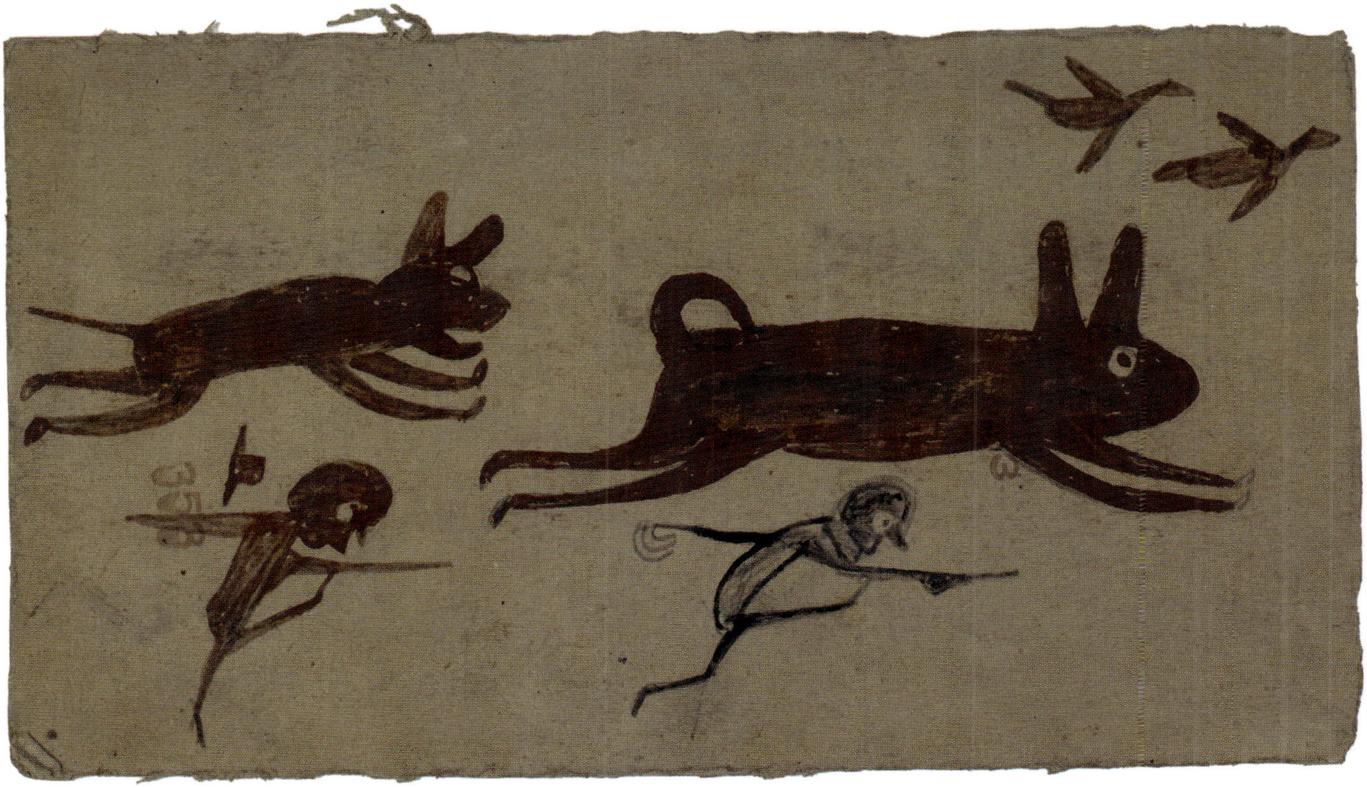

Bill Traylor, untitled (Chase Scene)*, ca. 1940, pencil and opaque watercolor on paperboard, 7 × 13¼ in (17.8 × 33.7 cm). Smithsonian American Art Museum, Washington, D.C.* In *Chase Scene*, Traylor subtly equates the African American man to a rabbit being chased ferociously by a dog. Traylor's selective choice in his drawings to elongate the limbs of animals suggests further assimilation to reading them as human.

conclusion by Shannon, who was akin to a representative.[20] After a short period with one of his daughters in Detroit, in 1945 Traylor was back in Montgomery living under the care of his daughter Sarah. These final years were mired with discontent for Traylor who was discouraged by his living arrangement and had several surgeries due to diabetes complications. He was still drawing but these works were not saved. Traylor passed away on October 23, 1949, still relatively unknown as an artist but a significant amount of works were well preserved by Shannon and other (mostly New South artists) who had collected his work.

Posthumously, a pivotal moment for Traylor was his inclusion in *Black Folk Art in America, 1930–1980* at the Corcoran Gallery in Washington, D.C. (1982). Curated by Jane Livingston and John Beardsley, the exhibition traveled nationally and featured 36 of Traylor's works, including *Snake* (ca. 1939–1942), which was also the catalog's cover image. Despite oppressive obstacles and restrictive opportunities within his lifetime, the rigor and poetic resonance of Traylor's work has led to it becoming internationally appreciated in the 21st century.

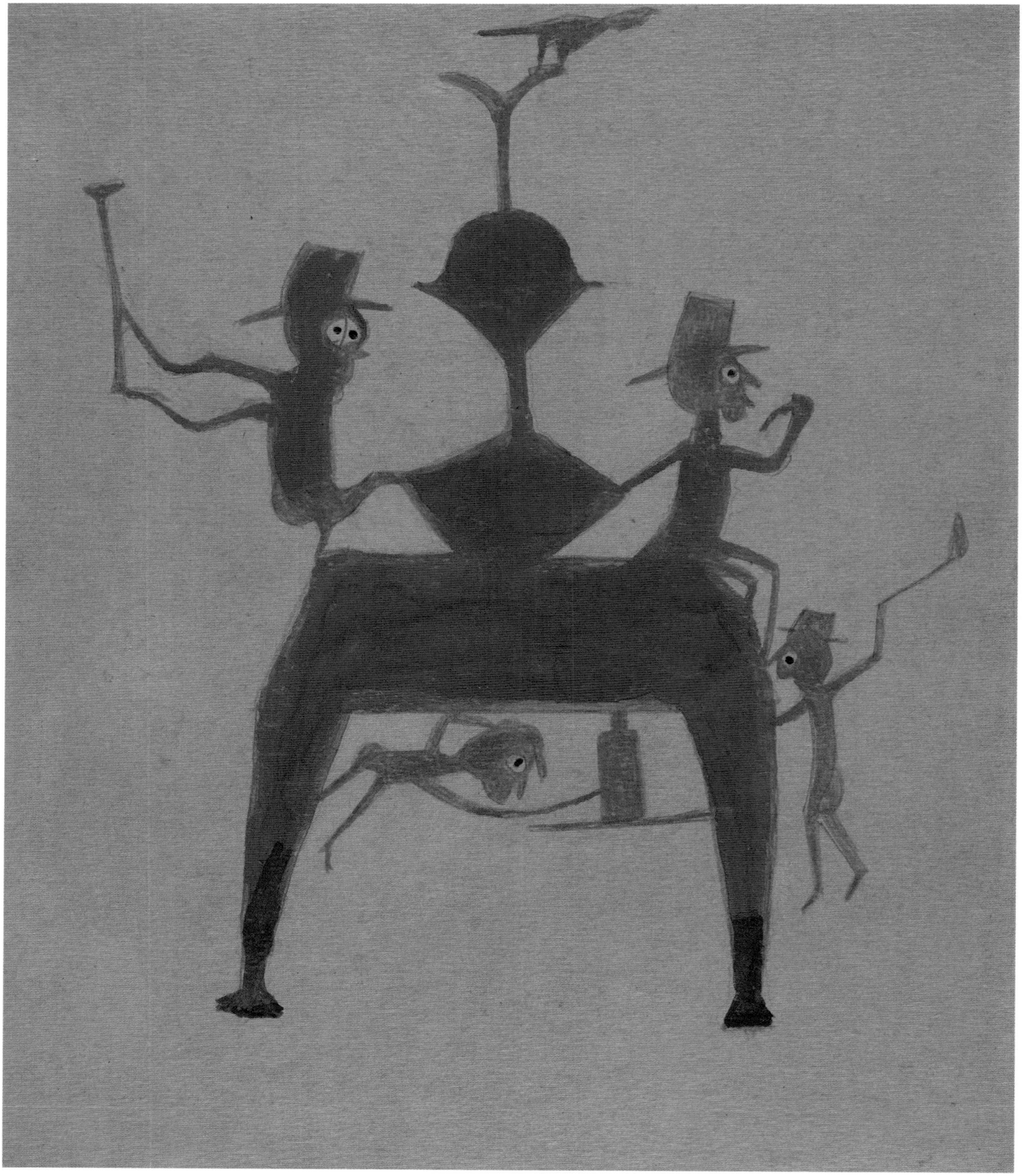

Bill Traylor, Figures on Blue Construction, *ca. 1939–1942, gouache and pencil on cardboard, 14 ⅞ × 13 ¼ in (37.8 × 33.6 cm). Museum of Modern Art (MoMA), New York.* This is a dynamic example of Traylor's "exciting events" and exemplifies his compositions of more open-ended narratives.

Architecturally, Traylor seemed inspired by his local surroundings with the central object evocative of both a public monument and domestic object. *Figures on Blue Construction* also presents Traylor's reuse of materials for canvas and his affinity for ultramarine blue.

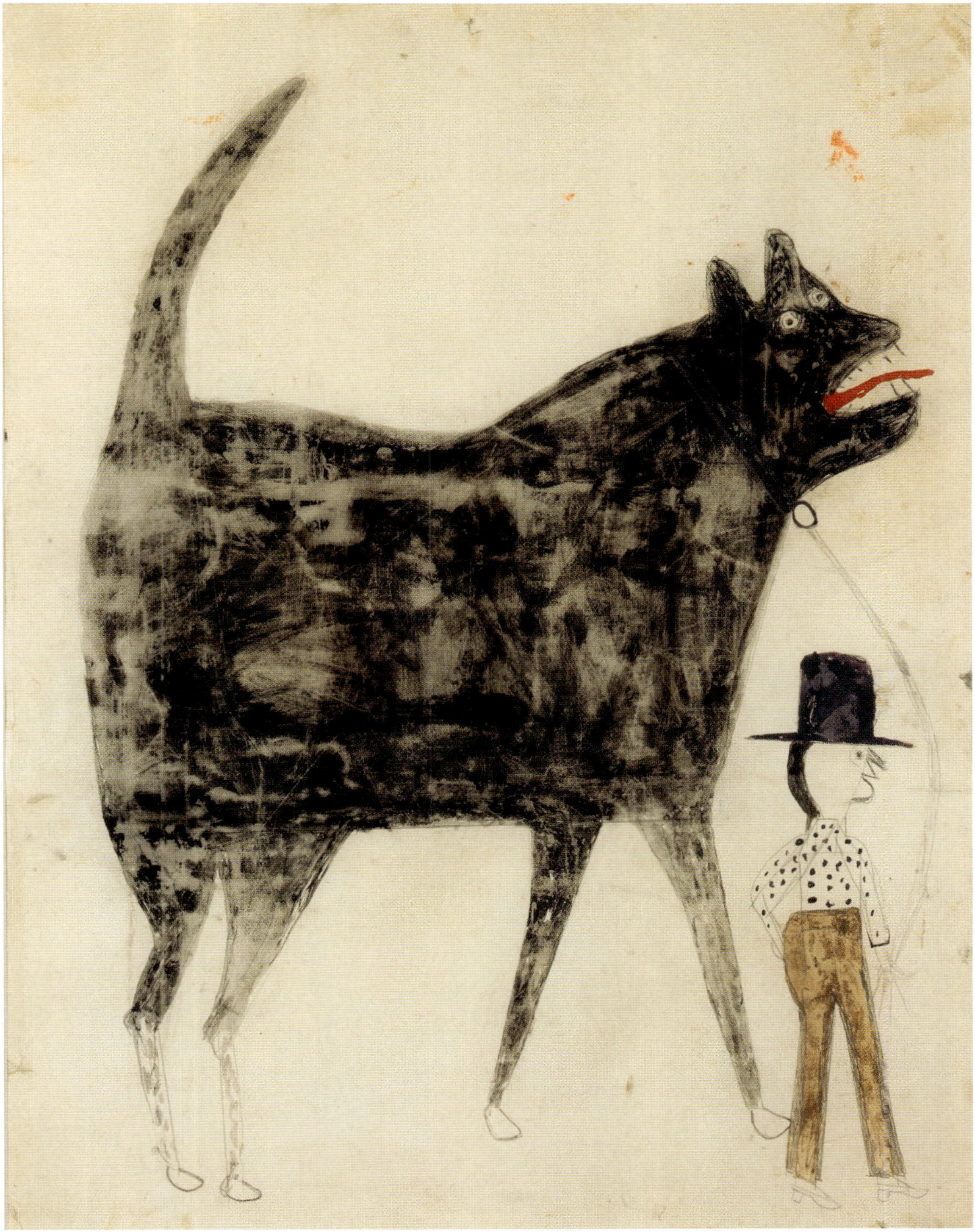

Bill Traylor, Man and Large Dog, *ca. 1939–1942, poster paint, pencil on cardboard, 28 x 22 in (71 x 56 cm). Private Collection.* Exhibited as part of *Black Folk Art in America, 1930–1980*, Corcoran Gallery, Washington, D.C., *Man and Large Dog* illustrates the allegorical potential of addressing race through scale and animal symbolism.

JOSEPH E. YOAKUM

(1890, Ash Grove, Missouri–1972, Chicago, Illinois, USA)

Joseph E. Yoakum's skillful and dreamy anthropomorphic landscapes came to fruition on paper late in life, drawn from what deeply religious Yoakum called "spiritual unfoldments." The designated scenes recollect his earlier excursions and accounts thereof. Born in Missouri to parents of Cherokee and African American descent, from the age of ten, Yoakum traveled around the United States with touring circuses. World War I found him stationed in Europe, and postwar he spent the 1920s roaming nationally and internationally. Loitering sceneries became the key conceptual thread to his illustrative practice that commenced once he had retired and was living on the South Side of Chicago. Following an exhibition in 1967 at a local church coffee shop, he gained advocates and collectors of this work, including the Chicago Imagists who exhibited his work at the Museum of Contemporary Art Chicago in 1969. Yoakum was recognized with a solo show at the Whitney Museum of Art in 1972, the year he passed away. Posthumously, he was included in the significant exhibition *Black Folk Art in America*, 1930–1980, at the Corcoran Gallery in Washington, D.C.(1982). In 2021, the retrospective *Joseph Yoakum: What I Saw* opened at The Art Institute of Chicago and traveled to MoMA, New York and the Menil Collection, Houston.

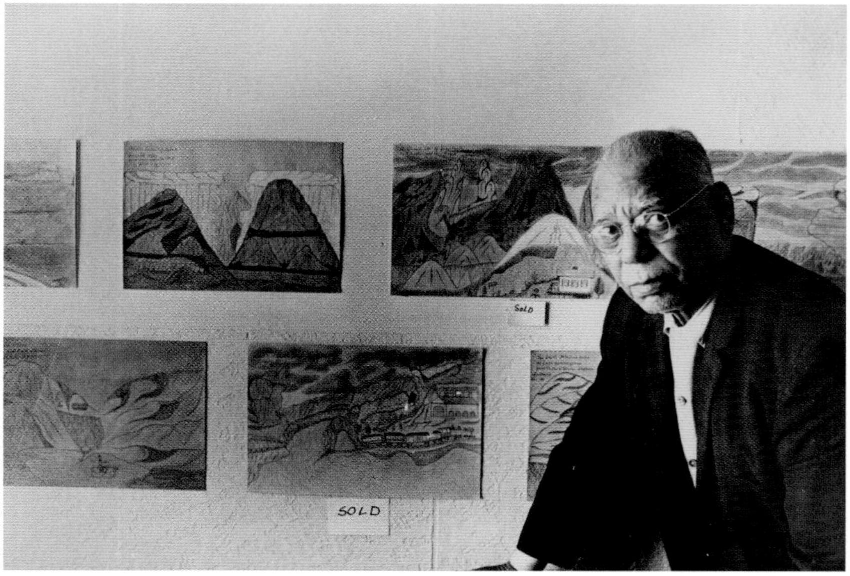

Joseph E. Yoakum at "The Whole" Cafe in Chicago, 1967, photograph. Smithsonian Institution. Within a year of this humble first show, Yoakum received a solo show at the Edward Sherbeyn Gallery in 1968. Whitney Halstead, a professor at the School of the Art Institute of Chicago (SAIC), attended the show and subsequently became a life-long advocate and advisor for Yoakum.

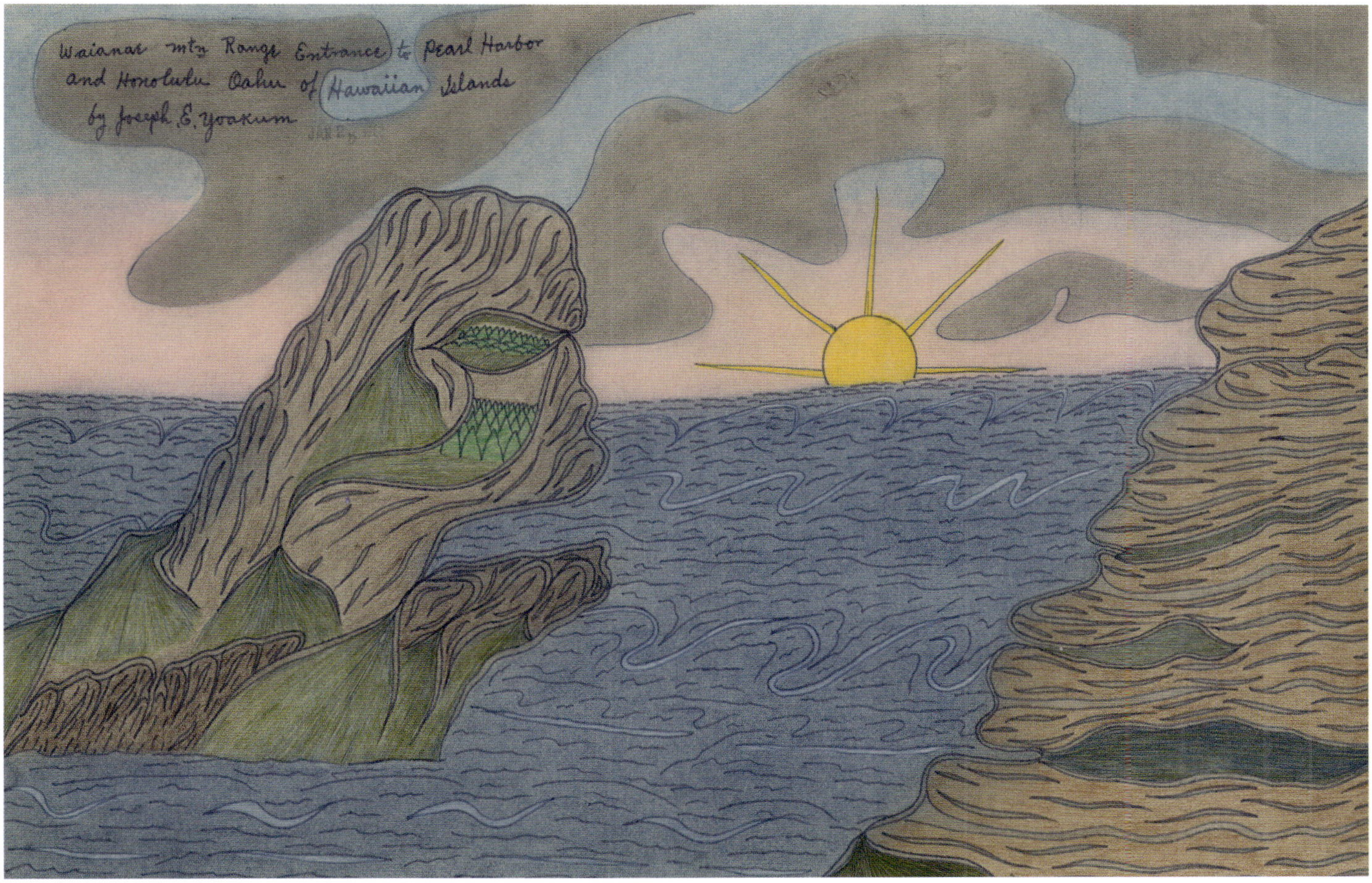

Joseph E. Yoakum, Waianae Mtn Range Entrance to Pearl Harbor and Honolulu Oahu of Hawaiian Islands, *1968, blue felt-tip pen, blue ballpoint pen, pastel, and colored pencil on paper, 12 × 19 1/16 in (30.5 × 48.4 cm). Collection of Christina Ramberg and Philip Hanson.* Exhibited as part of *Black Folk Art in America, 1930–1980*, Corcoran Gallery, Washington, D.C., in 1982, this drawing takes on anthropomorphic qualities with the stylized island emerging from the water appearing as a facial profile. The image infers an open mouth to the sea, while an open eye is filled with small patterned trees.

Accounts from Joseph E. Yoakum, and research by historian Derrel B. DePasse, suggest he joined the Great Wallace Circus as a horse handler in 1900 and later toured with Buffalo Cody's Wild West and Ringling Brothers. Questions surround the precise details of Yoakum's travels, but because he labeled each drawing with a specific location, hundreds can be linked to exact (and even remote) circus routes of the 1900s.

Yoakum's military travel also served as inspiration in his work. In the summer of 1918, Yoakum was drafted into the Headquarters Company of the 805th Pioneer Infantry, an all-African American infantry deployed to France. Similar to his depictions of the circus routes, Yoakum's illustrations follow the route of the 805th, including their initial encampment in Kansas, the course of the ship on which they sailed to Europe, and Clermont-en-Argonne, France, where the infantry spent a lengthy encampment. After the war, Yoakum did not return to his wife and family, instead he traveled around the United States, doing a variety of jobs including a railroad inspector, farmworker, and miner. Reportedly, a stint as a seaman allowed him to once again travel abroad, including to Australia and Asia.

"Joseph Yoakum in the subtlety and lyricism of his landscape compositions can hardly be termed 'primitive' in any sense." – Jane Livingston, co-curator, *Black Folk Art in America, 1930–1980*[22]

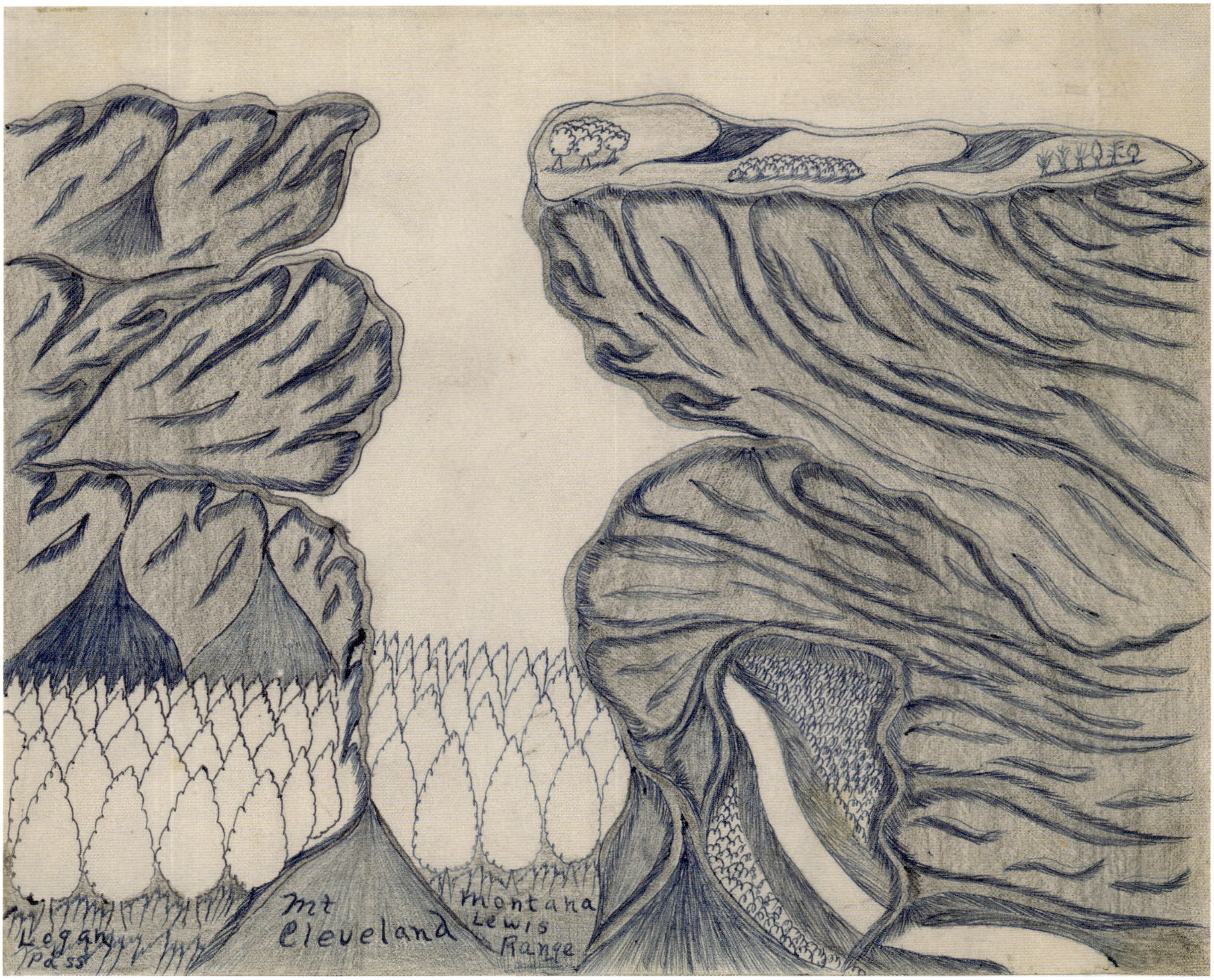

Joseph E. Yoakum, Logan Pass Mt. Cleveland Montana Lewis Range, *1963–1965, blue ballpoint pen and graphite pencil on cream wove paper, 8 × 10 in (20.3 × 25.4 cm). Art Institute of Chicago.* This Montana mountain range likely refers to Yoakum's travel with the circus as a young man. The monochromatic, stylized patterning of trees and textured depth of the mountain evoke the tribal motifs of Yoakum's Native American heritage.

By his own account, around 1962, Yoakum had a dream which motivated him to begin drawing. Already devoutly Christian, he described his creative production as "spiritual unfoldment": a borrowed term from Christian Science. His process of spiritual unfoldment was defined by intuitively beginning a drawing without a predetermined subject and allowing it to be revealed to him while he drew. Yoakum's aesthetic style is abundant with nods to various visual cultures; from graphic elements in railroad signs to Native American tribal motifs, his cross-cultural renderings speak to his heritage and life experiences, reading visually as surreal topographical maps.

"I had it in my mind that I wanted to go to different places at different times. Wherever my mind led me, I would go. I've been all over this world four times."
– Joseph E. Yoakum[21]

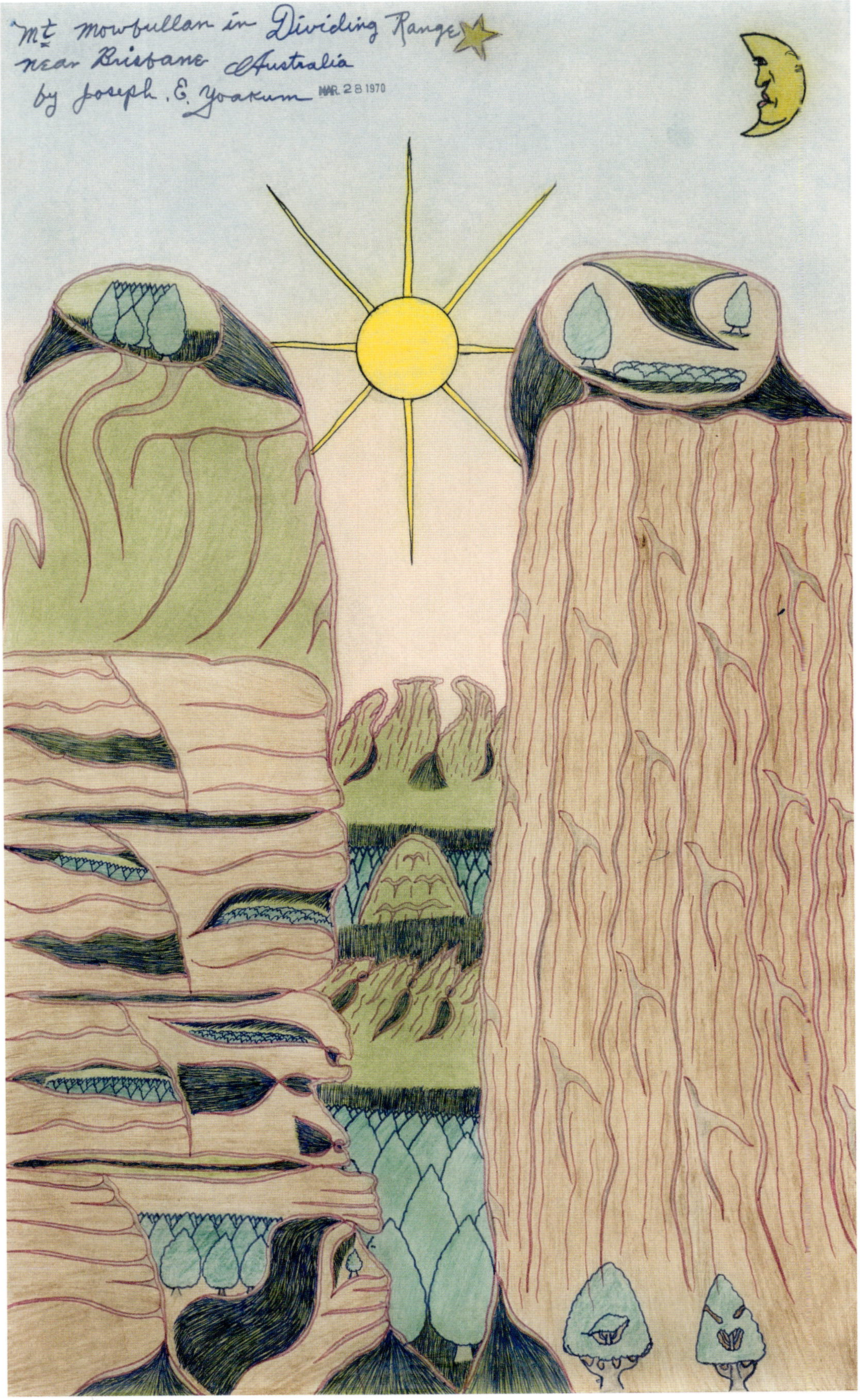

Joseph E. Yoakum, Mt. Mowbullan in Dividing Range near Brisbane Australia, *1970, red felt-tip pen and blue ballpoint pen and colored pencils, with colored chalks and smudging, dated with rubber ink stamp, on off-white wove paper, 19 × 11¹³⁄₁₆ in (48.3 × 30 cm). Smithsonian Design Museum.* This Australian landscape likely refers to Yoakum's international travel after his service during World War II. His graphic sensibility is evident in this drawing, particularly in the upper mountain tops, where smaller landscapes appear as isolated graphic emblems.

ELIJAH PIERCE

(1892, Baldwyn, Mississippi–1984, Columbus, Ohio, USA)

The emotionally carved tableaux of Elijah Pierce were both an extension of his ministry and a platform to examine the complexities of race, through investigations into political events and autobiographical experiences. The son of formerly enslaved parents, Pierce grew up in rural Mississippi and began carving wood when he was eight years old. In 1920, following the death of his first wife, Pierce was certified as a preacher and departed from Baldwyn as part of the Great Migration. He eventually settled in Columbus, Ohio, in 1923 and began carving again shortly thereafter. In Ohio, Pierce established a synthesis between his trade as a barber, his calling to preach, and his passion for sculpting. He opened his own barbershop in 1951 with a sculpting studio that also served as a local gathering hub. In the 1970s, Pierce began receiving attention for his sculptures beyond his local community. Following his inclusion in the exhibition *Black Folk Art in America, 1930–1980* at the Corcoran Gallery in Washington, D.C. (1982), he was awarded a National Endowment for the Arts National Heritage fellowship.

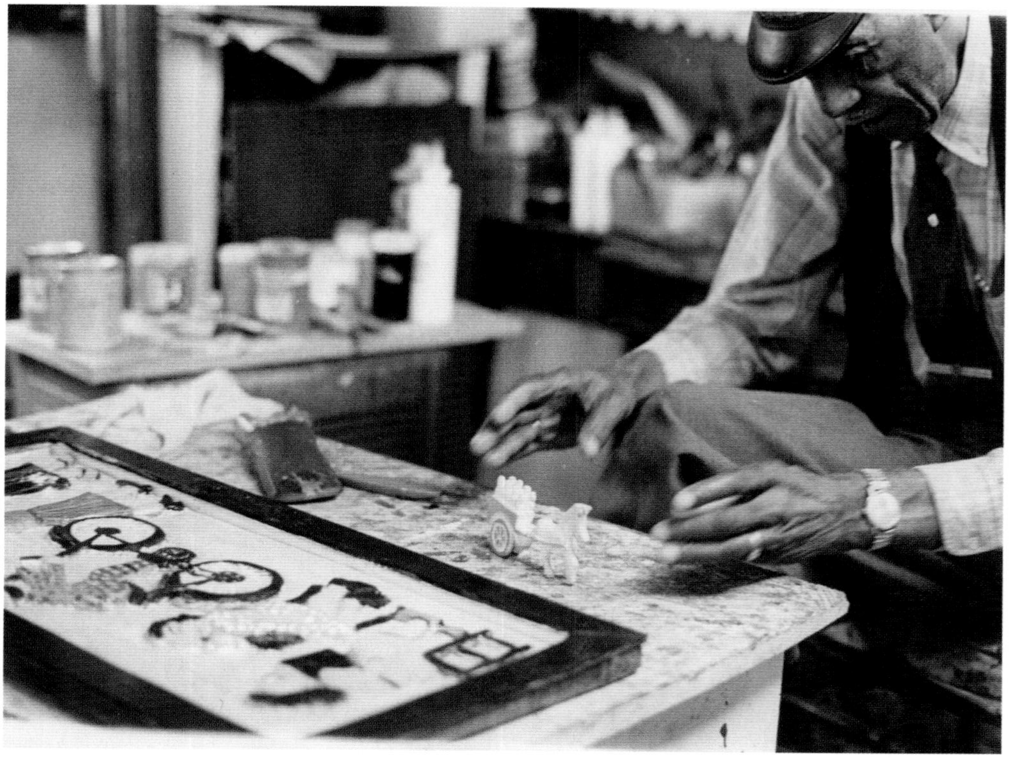

Elijah Pierce, ca. 1982, photograph by Kojo Kamau (American, 1939–2016). Columbus Museum of Art, Ohio. Pierce is shown working on a small wood carving of a horse-drawn carriage in his barbershop studio, Columbus, Ohio.

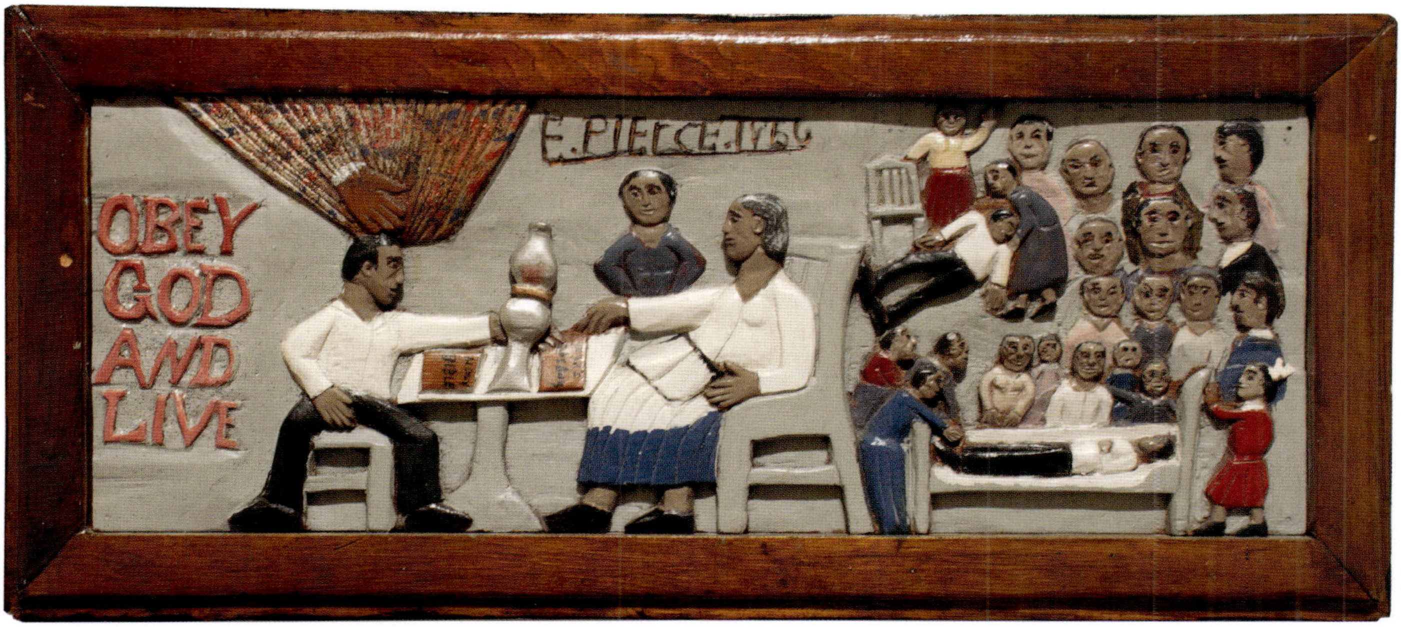

Elijah Pierce, Obey God and Live, *1956, carved and painted wood relief with glitter and marking-pen ink, $12\frac{7}{8} \times 29\frac{5}{16}$ in (32.7 × 74.5 cm). Columbus Museum of Art, Ohio.* This autobiographical carving and parable, tells the story of Pierce being struck by God for choosing to read the Sears Roebuck catalog instead of the Bible, demonstrating the results of unfaithful decisions. "OBEY GOD AND LIVE" and the carved hand of God present the didactic symbolism.

From a young age, Elijah Pierce had been called a preacher and had an innate desire to carve wood. While he denied his religious calling as an adolescent, his creative craft was fostered by his uncle Lewis Wallace. Once he embraced his calling to be a preacher in Columbus, Pierce established an interconnected environment for his pursuits, allowing his barbershop to be a communal congregation for his religious messages and his studio for developing and sharing his sculptural pieces.

A significant work by Pierce that addressed his devotion to religion is *Obey God and Live* (1956), in which he depicted an autobiographical parable of a young Pierce reaching for a Sears Roebuck catalog instead of the Bible. He recounted the aftermath of this wrong decision by being struck by God and thought for dead.

Also autobiographical was *The Mob* (ca. 1950), a carefully illustrated escape scene recounting when Pierce was falsely accused of murdering a white man. Race and slavery were consistent concepts explored by Pierce through his larger messaging and with reference to his contemporaneous political and cultural context.

There is a dynamic quality in the carvings of Pierce, echoing his belief that his creative practice was an extension of ministry, and used specifically as a medium to communicate stories. While his sermons were memorialized in the woodworkings, his performance-like practice—carving wood with a pocket knife between haircuts at the barbershop and while hosting the community—further activated this dynamic characteristic.

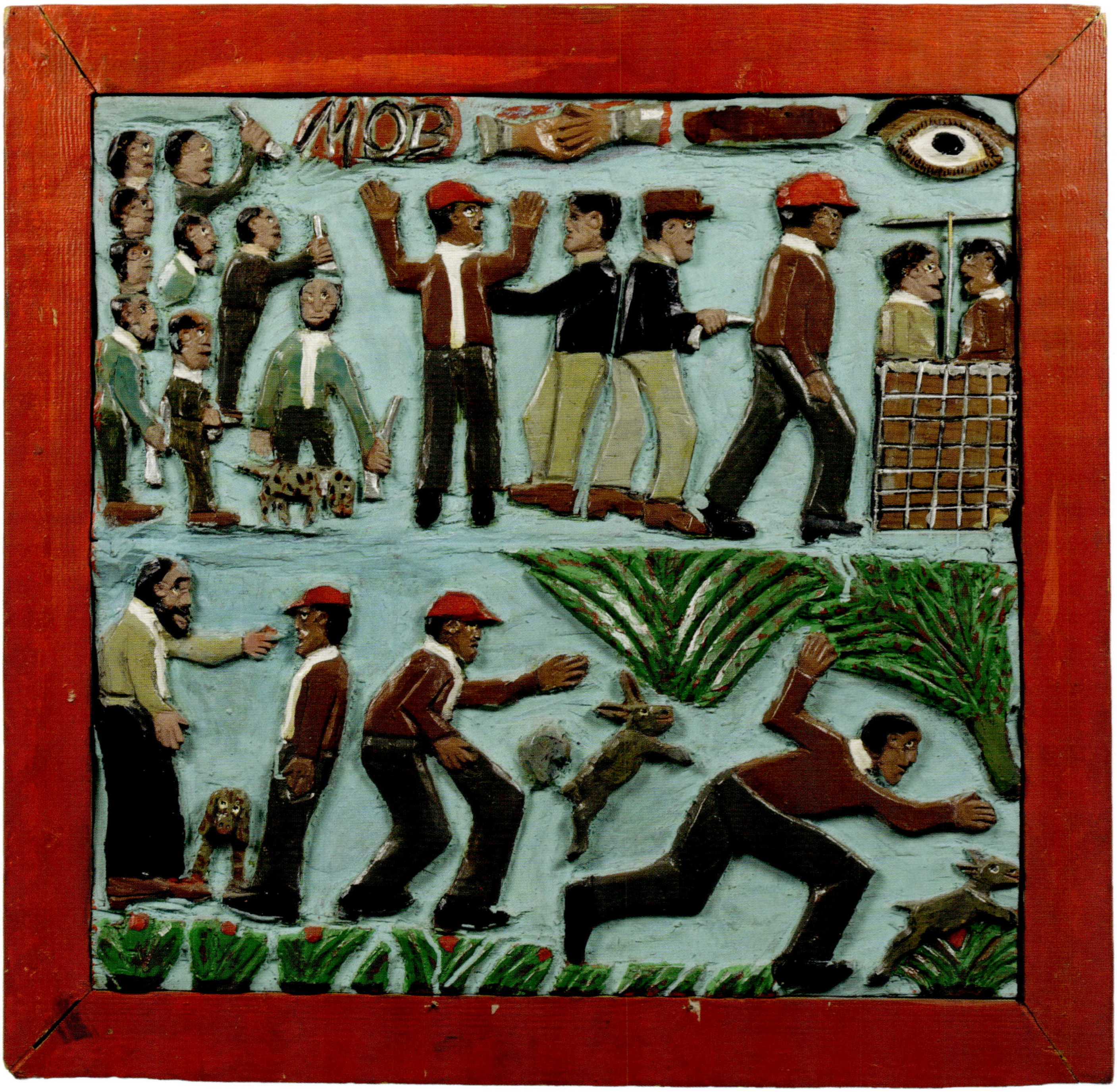

Elijah Pierce, Elijah Escapes the Mob, *1950s, carved and painted wood relief, 27½ × 28⅜ × 1 in (69.9 × 72.1 × 2.5 cm). Columbus Museum of Art, Ohio.* This epically detailed carving documents Pierce being wrongly accused of murdering a white man. It illustrates a violent accusing mob and chase scene.

"Pierce's strength is based on his religion and his concept of the importance of the individual . . . He reduces what he wants to say to the simplest forms and compositions. They are decorative, direct, bold, and amusing. He uses glitter and all kinds of devices to make his message clear. It gives his work an immediacy that's very appealing." – Thomas N. Armstrong, curator at the Whitney Museum of American Art[23]

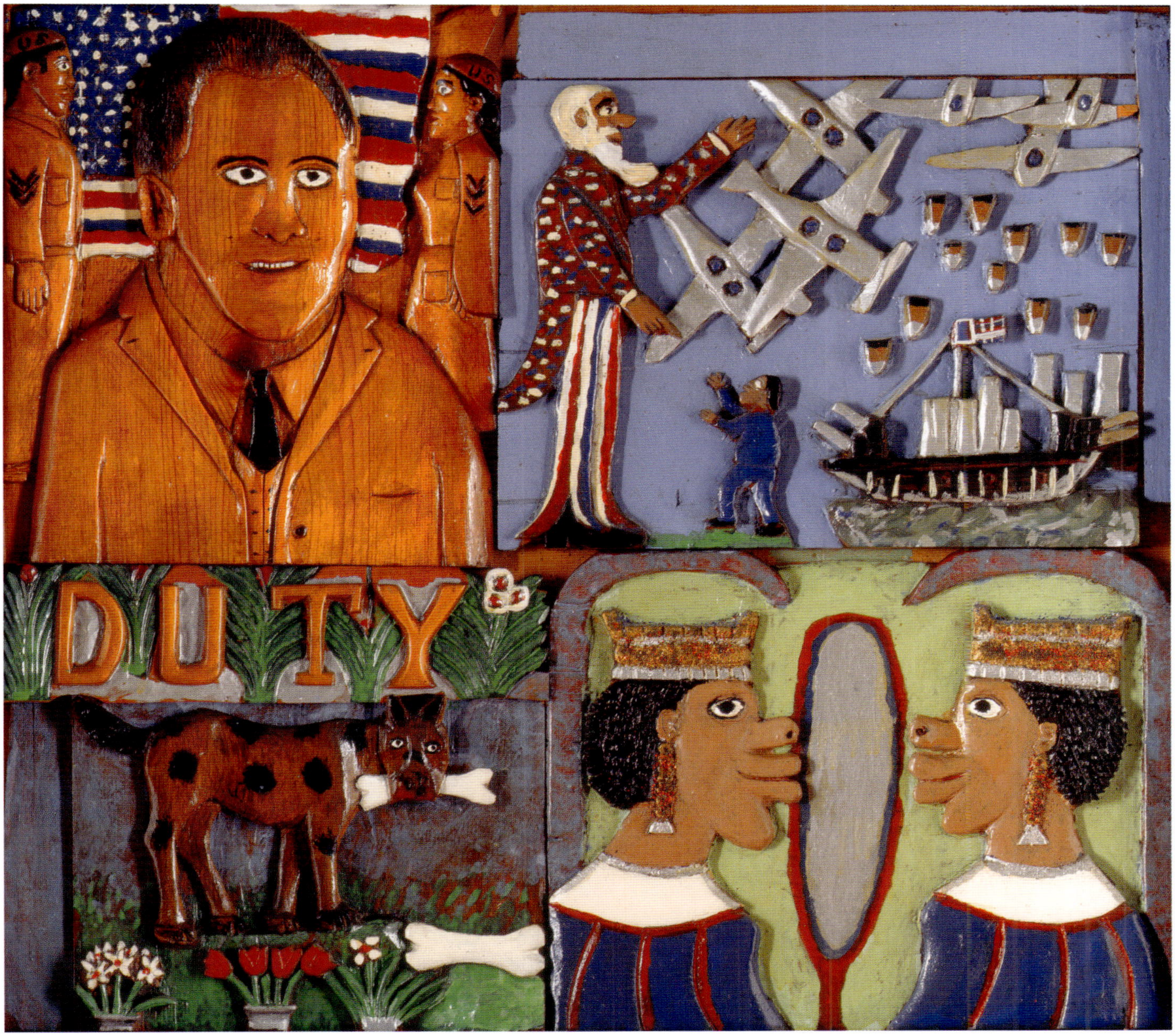

Elijah Pierce, Pearl Harbor and the African Queen*, ca. 1941, carved, assembled and painted wood with glitter, 23¼ × 27 × 1½ in (59.1 × 68.6 × 3.8 cm). Milwaukee Art Museum.* Exhibited as part of *Black Folk Art in America, 1930–1980*, Corcoran Gallery, Washington, D.C., in 1982, *Pearl Harbor and the African Queen* shows Pierce's interest in having his carvings serve as a social commentary to examine political events and cultural juxtapositions.

"Every piece of work I got carved is a message, a sermon, you might say." – Elijah Pierce[24]

SISTER GERTRUDE MORGAN

(1900, LaFayette, Alabama–1980, New Orleans, Louisiana, USA)

Shaped by lyricism and charisma, there was remarkable direction in the creative practice of Sister Gertrude Morgan. Religious from her late teens, on December 30, 1934, Morgan received her first direct calling to evangelize. In 1939, she settled in New Orleans and became an active preacher within the African American Baptist Holiness-Pentecostal missionary. A further transformative event occurred in 1957 when she had the divine revelation that she was the Bride of Christ, a role she took very seriously and resulted in her wearing exclusively white to signify the union. For Morgan, her paintings, performance, and music did not singularly function or exist as art; rather, they were didactic tools to support her missionary pursuits. Initially inspired directly from the Bible and maturing to include autobiographical depictions, from the 1960s she was regularly painting her bold message-led compositions. Her multidimensional practice penetrated the cultural scene of the South and in 1970 she was included in three significant national exhibitions. Posthumously, Morgan was the most heavily featured artist in *Black Folk Art in America, 1930–1980*, at the Corcoran Gallery in Washington, D.C., (1982). More recently, her work has been included in *The Museum of Everything #7*, The Museum of Old and New Art, Hobart (2017) and *Outliers and American Vangard Art*, National Gallery of Art, Washington, D.C. (2018).

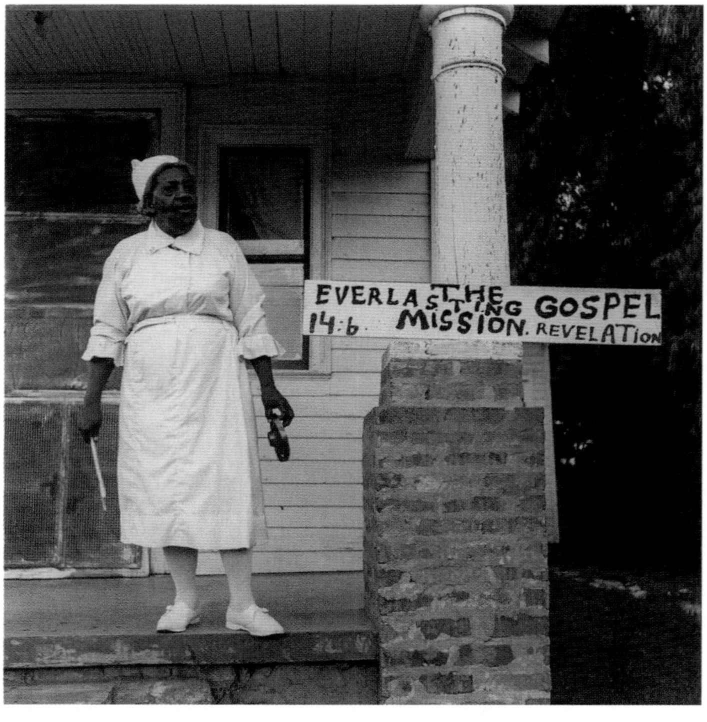

Sister Gertrude Morgan, 1973, photograph by Guy Mendes (American, b. 1948). This portrait shows Morgan donned in her all-white (bridal) uniform on her front porch, which she called "Front Gallery" and used to showcase her work. She called her home, which she also ministered from, Everlasting Gospel Mission.

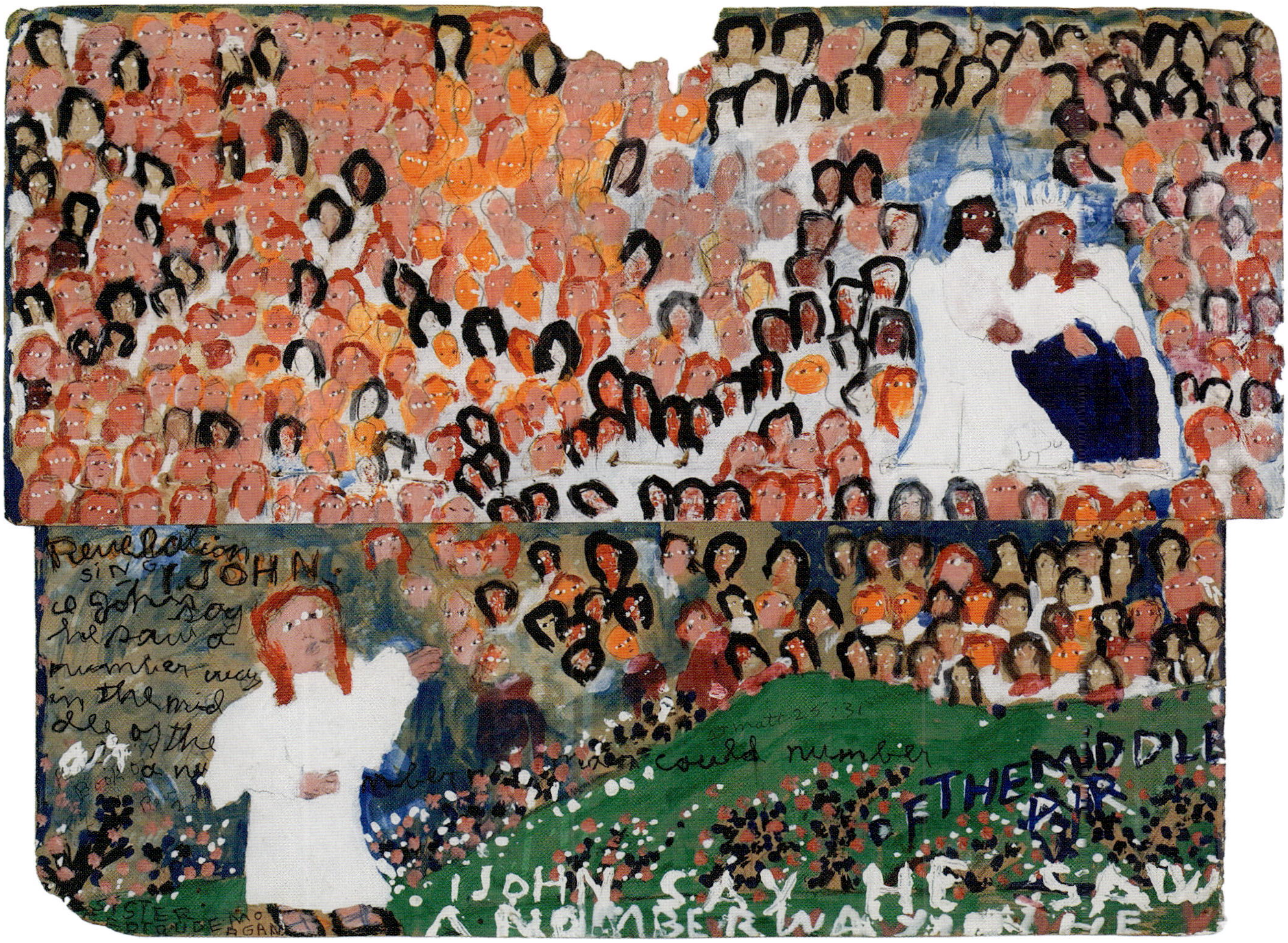

Sister Gertrude Morgan, untitled (Revelation/JOHN), *n.d., acrylic, pencil, ink on two cardboard panels, 21⅞ × 30 in (55.6 × 76.2 cm). The Museum + The Gallery of Everything.* Painted on found material, this composition illustrates Morgan wearing all white in her marriage union with Jesus Christ. Surrounded by a multiracial crowd, she is situated on the upper right while St. John is speaking from the bottom left.

Sister Gertrude Morgan was an exuberant preacher, musician, poet, and painter who harnessed her charisma and creativity to support her religious messages. She forewent traditional art supplies such as canvas, instead often implementing materials she had available: notebook pages, cardboard, styrofoam packaging, lampshades; drawing and painting on them with acrylic, tempera, watercolor, wax crayons, pen ink, and pencil. Aesthetically musical and improvisational, her iconographic gestures of visual culture and faith vocabulary seemed intrinsically informed by her Pentecostal traditions.

A divine message instructing her to seek a new method of pronouncing the Gospel led Morgan to paint and draw. The initial exposure to her creative practice (including performance and music) to the wider cultural scene of New Orleans was supported by Morgan's longtime advocate, property owner and art dealer Larry Borenstein; later art historian Regenia A. Perry emerged as another key advocate nationally. Marked as a pivotal year, 1970 saw Morgan's paintings featured in three important national exhibitions, including *Dimensions of Black* at the La Jolla Museum of Art in California, while musically, she performed at the New Orleans Jazz & Heritage Festival, alongside Duke Ellington and Mahalia Jackson.

The development of Morgan's oeuvre can be broadly categorized into three periods. Thematically, her earliest works were stringently biblical and executed predominantly in crayon. Compositionally these often featured a central subject spatially anchored by a horizon line. These early compositions feature less text than her later periods. Principally, her inscriptions gained prominence and purport as her work evolved. In her middle period, Morgan's style turned more expressive through her experimentation with brushstrokes, and conceptually she expanded to autobiographical content inclusive of self-portraits. The later period is recognized for its dominance and commitment to text, though she may have continued with painterly works concurrently. In 1974, Morgan's visual creative production ceased abruptly, following a message from her Lord telling her to cease painting.

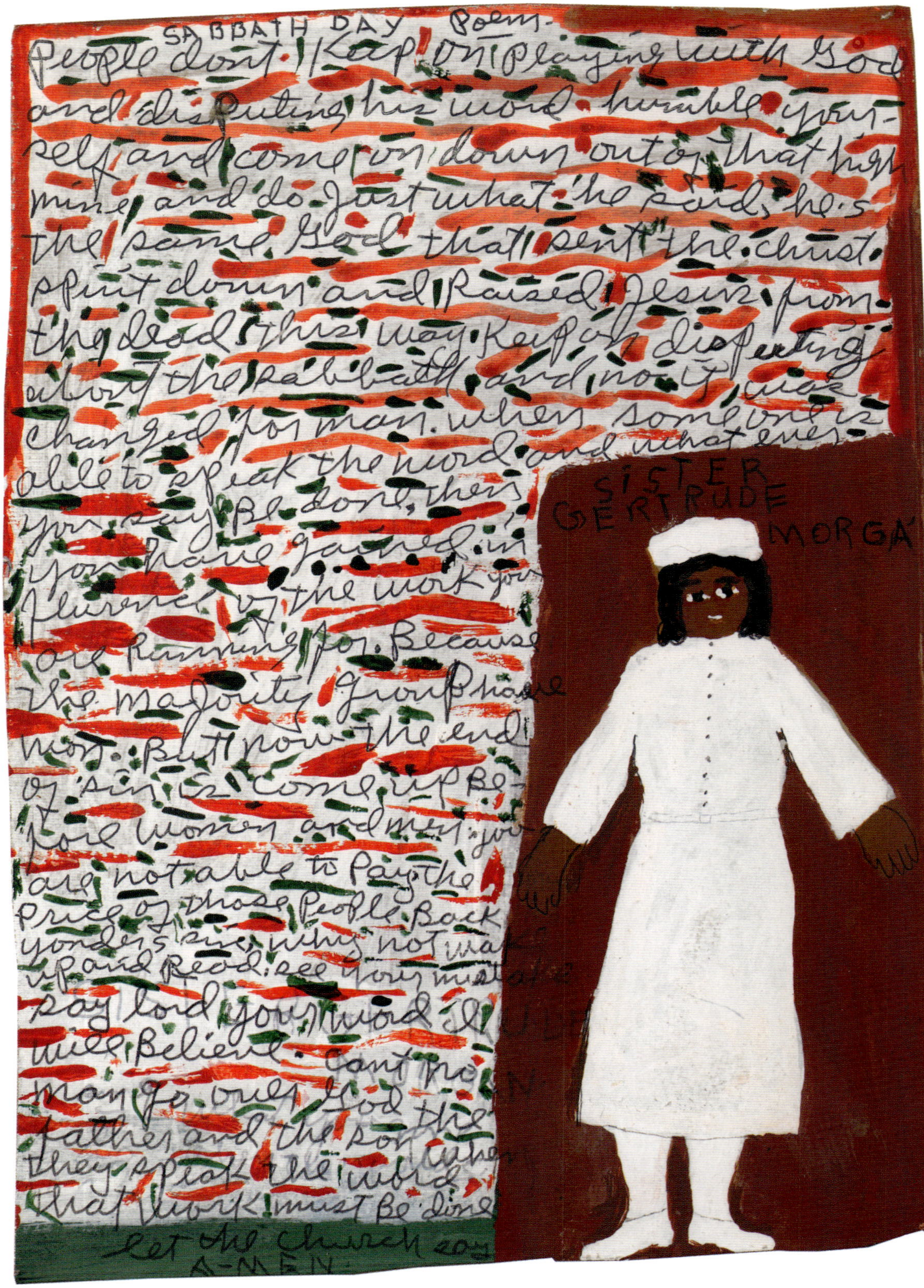

Sister Gertrude Morgan, untitled (SABBATH DAY Poem), *n.d., paint on card, 12⅛ × 8⅝ in (30.5 × 22 cm). The Museum + The Gallery of Everything.* This painting on card exemplifies Morgan's development of self-portraits within her oeuvre. The dominance of text—her "SABBATH DAY Poem" and closing with "let the church say A-MEN"—is consistent with her later work.

"Just be sure and credit Jesus for what I do. He's the one that deserves all the praise. He's the one that made me do it." – Sister Gertrude Morgan[25]

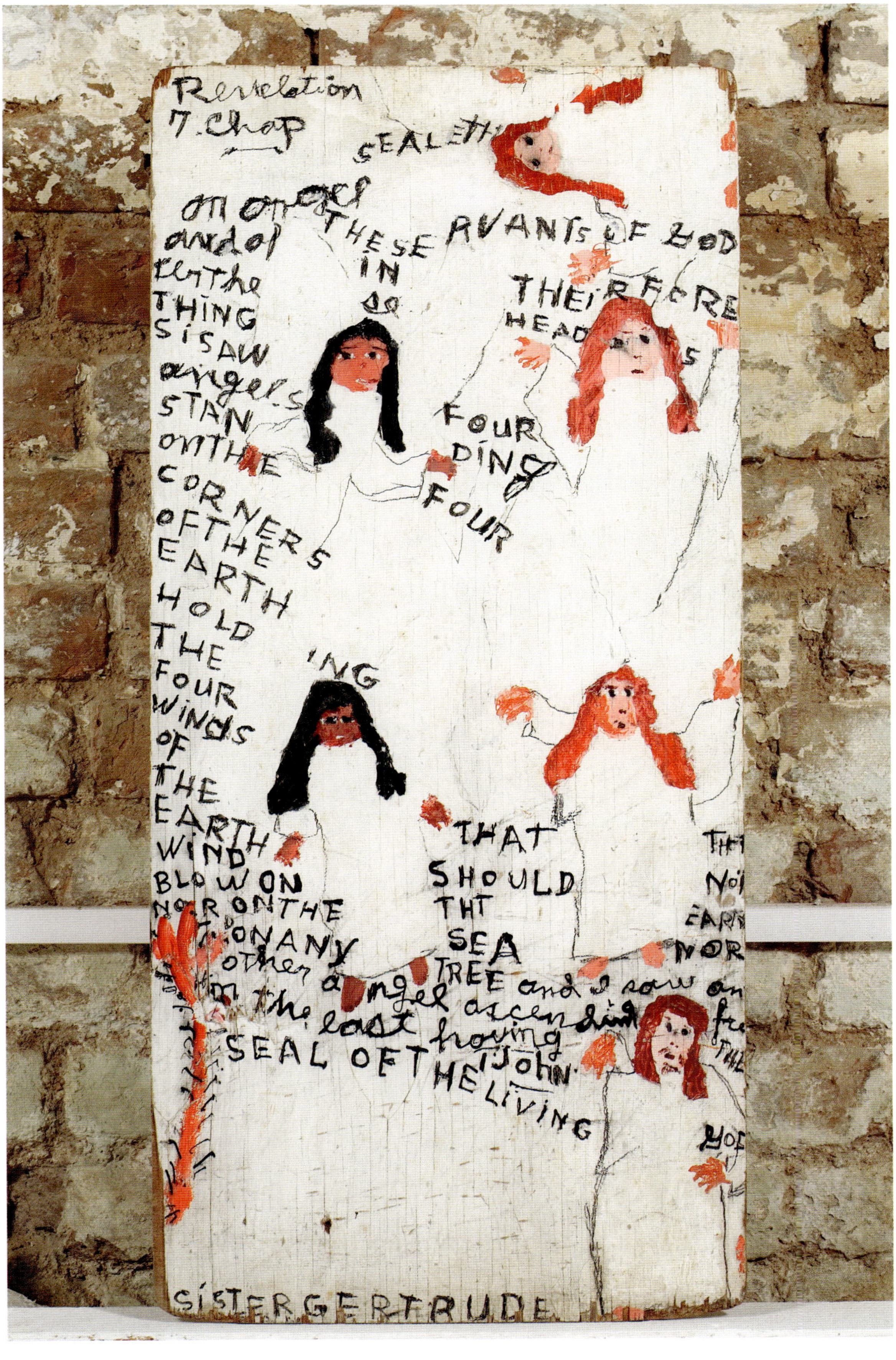

Sister Gertrude Morgan, untitled (Revelation 7. chap), *n.d., acrylic, watercolor, and ink on card, 32¼ × 15⅜ in (82 × 39 cm). The Museum + The Gallery of Everything.* Exhibited as part of *Black Folk Art in America, 1930–1980*, Corcoran Gallery, Washington, D.C., in 1982, this piece presents biblical text and figures expressively floating throughout the composition. Their weightlessness and multidirectional placement suggest they are celestial beings.

NELLIE MAE ROWE

(1900, Fayette County–1982, Vinings, Georgia, USA)

"I ain't fooling around no more" were the words of Nellie Mae Rowe in 1948, following the death of her second husband. In this moment of independence, Rowe prepared to explore her own identity and embrace the imagination of her childhood. Auspiciously born on the July 4, 1900, she was raised picking cotton with her family in rural Georgia. Her parents encouraged Rowe to be creative; however, marrying at 16 rendered little time for artistic pursuits until she was widowed. At 48, her creativity surged: first, she adorned her yard with ornamentation and populated it with large artist-made dolls, followed by drawings in the 1960s. Rowe's most complex works were produced from 1981, when she was diagnosed with terminal cancer. In these late drawings, she poetically attempted to comprehend her own mortality through personal symbolism. Rowe was one of only three female artists featured in the exhibition *Black Folk Art in America, 1930–1980*, at the Corcoran Gallery in Washington, D.C. (1982). In 2021, she was the subject of *Really Free: The Radical Art of Nellie Mae Rowe*, High Museum of Art, Atlanta.

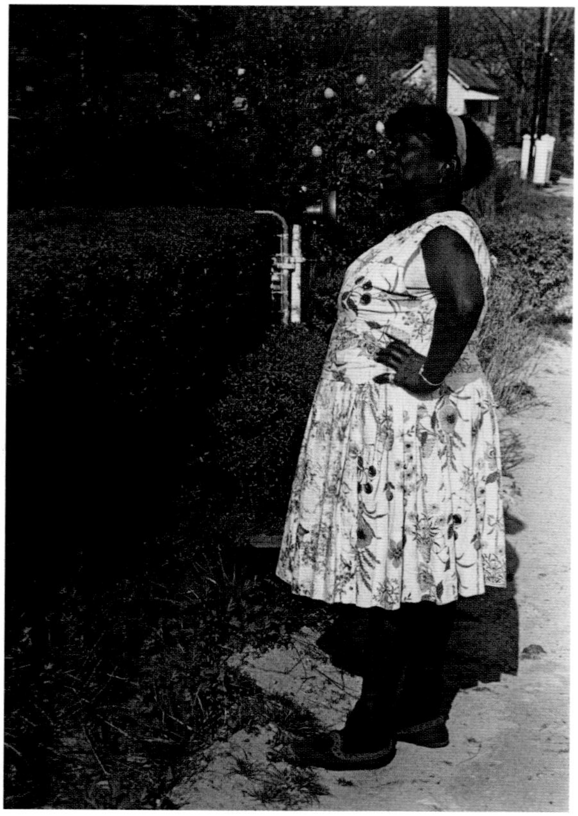

Nellie Mae Rowe, 1971, photograph by Judith Alexander Augustine (American, b. 1949). The Judith Alexander Foundation. This portrait of Nellie Mae Rowe at her garden gate was taken by Judith Alexander Augustine when she was a photojournalism student at Boston University.

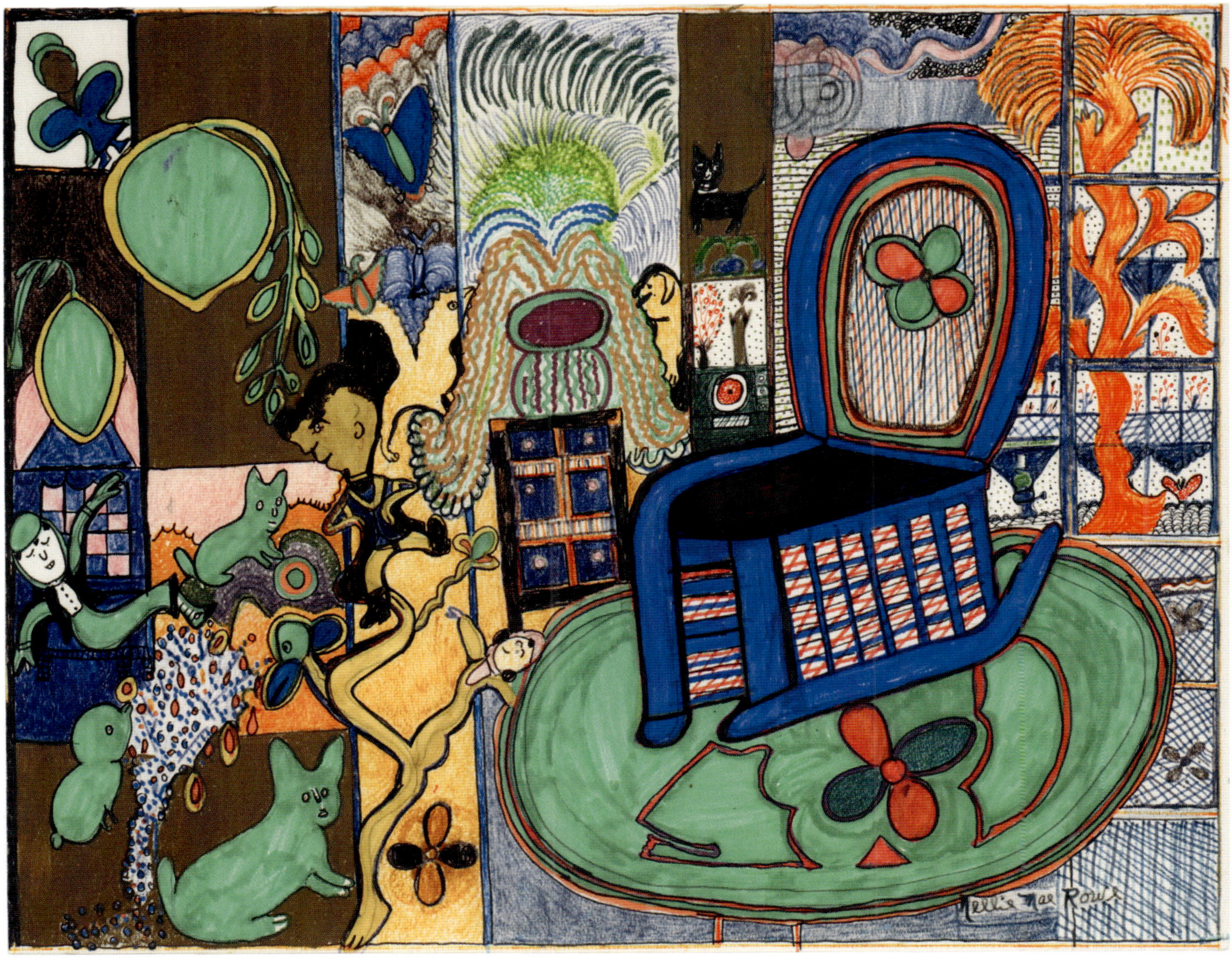

Nellie Mae Rowe, Rocking Chair, *1981, crayon, felt-tip pen, and pencil on paper, 18¾ × 24 in (47.6 × 61 cm). Souls Grown Deep Foundation.* There is a longstanding art historical tradition of using domestic objects as metaphors for death—these objects are often referred to as a *memento mori*. After being diagnosed with terminal cancer, the rocking chair was one of Rowe's first symbols of death.

In 1948, Nellie Mae Rowe was twice-widowed and living in a modest home in Vinings, Georgia. With the independence of being without a husband, she embraced a return to her youth in terms of artistic freedom. Her initial pursuits involved decorating her front yard with various ornamental found and donated objects, as well as life-size dolls constructed from stuffed stockings. Rowe's home-turned-self-proclaimed "playhouse" on the outskirts of Atlanta was situated in an area of racial divide on a major residential road. With its high-visibility, her early installations were met with harassment, such as her dolls being stolen and rocks thrown at her window. Eventually, Rowe's public oeuvre gained positive attention, devoted visitors, and demonstrated her artistic integrity to her early art enthusiasts.

Rowe's early drawings and sculptures are considerably more simple than her later work, and the scope of her stylistic and conceptual intricacy profoundly developed from the late 70s. It was in 1981, after being diagnosed with terminal cancer, that Rowe created her most significant drawings. This emblematic body of work teeters between literal and allusive, abundant with the symbolism of Rowe's narrative of comprehending her own fatality. She adapted complex pictorial metaphors for death to address her imminent challenges of understanding mortality and subjects included a rocking chair, an angel, dying plants, butterflies, and a black dog. A number of works from the last year of her life also featured personal inscriptions. Though Rowe was steadfast in her intention of returning

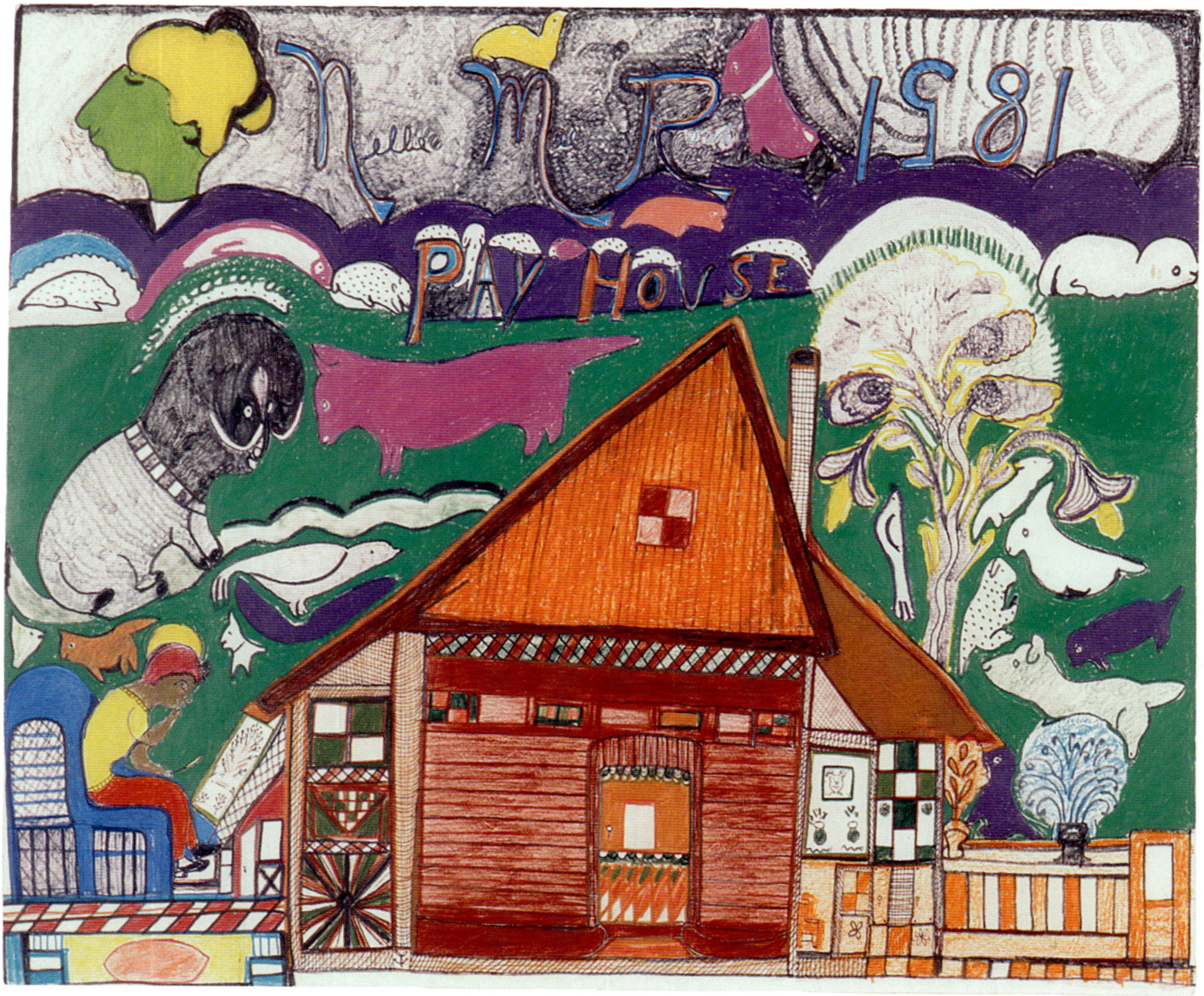

Nellie Mae Rowe, Playhouse, *1981, crayon, ink, and graphite on cardboard, 24¾ × 29½ in (62.9 × 74.9 cm). High Museum of Art, Atlanta.* Rowe referred to her home as liberating and considered it her playhouse stating, "Now I'm going to get back to when I was a little gal playing in the yard, playing in my playhouse." Here, quilt-making is referenced pictorially and through graphical composition.

to childhood through her artistic practice, her drawings have compositional sophistication and highly developed symbolic representations.

Rowe's first exhibition was an inclusion in a folk art presentation with the Atlanta Historical Society in 1976, where art dealer Judith Alexander first encountered her work. Alexander presented Rowe's first solo exhibition in 1978 and continued to advocate for Rowe, by exposing her practice to a wider audience. This advocacy included a significant donation in 2004 of Rowe's work to the High Museum of Art, Atlanta resulting in Rowe's work remaining on permanent public display at the museum.

"Meeting artists like . . . Nellie Mae Rowe, one is struck by a radiant force of will, a palpable sense of courage, and self-knowledge." – Jane Livingston, co-curator, *Black Folk Art in America, 1930–1980*[26]

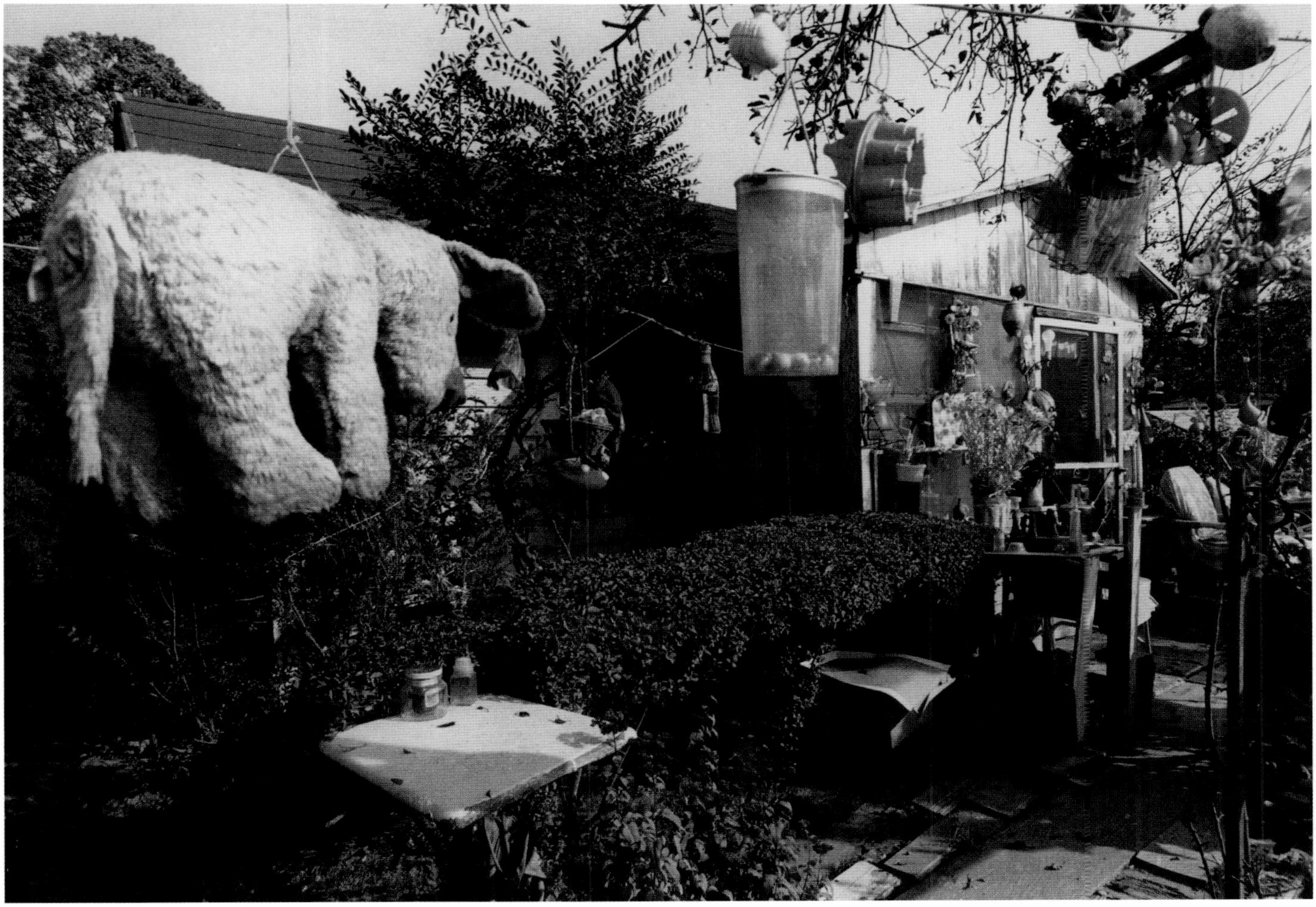

Nellie Mae Rowe, 1971, photograph by Lucinda Bunnen. Souls Grown Deep Foundation. Rowe's home, which she referred to as her "playhouse", was torn down posthumously but this photograph from 1971 exemplifies her process and whimsy of adorning the exterior of her home and yard.

I Will See You Later Bird
Lost Lost Dog
Sleepy Girl
I Have a Ride at Last
I Will Be Back When the Weather Gets Cool
Going Home
– Nellie Mae Rowe, inscriptions from her final year[27]

SAM DOYLE

(1906 Saint Helena Island–1985 Beaufort, South Carolina, USA)

Through his creative practice Sam Doyle held the responsibility of chronicler and documentarian for his community. Doyle was born in 1906 on Saint Helena Island, where he was immersed in Gullah culture. His local community received limited information on national current events and culture from elsewhere. Young Doyle was encouraged to develop his artistic talent while attending the island's Penn School, but left after the ninth grade. He likely began painting around 1944 and dedicated himself to his art in the 1970s, following his retirement. His bold and colorful paintings were regularly composed on repurposed roofing tin using enamel paint. Regaling the local gossip pictorially, commemorating local achievements, and presenting national African American events to Saint Helena, Doyle placed his compositions throughout his yard and facades of his home and studio. His audience grew beyond his local community due to the exposure of his evolving public displays. Doyle's first exhibition leading to his eventual national prominence was the seminal *Black Folk Art in America, 1930–1980*, at the Corcoran Gallery in Washington, D.C. (1982).

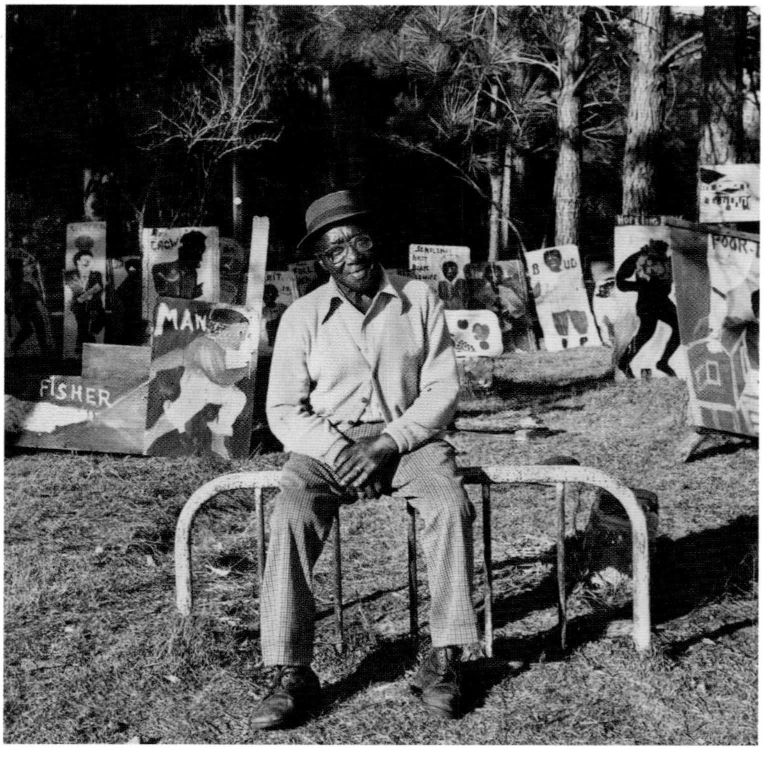

Sam Doyle, 1983, photograph by Roger Manley (American, b. 1952). Roger Manley Archive. This portrait from the 1980s shows Doyle seated with his many paintings displayed in a crowd-like manner in the background. He often painted on roofing tin and sheets of wood, which stand erect in the outdoor environment.

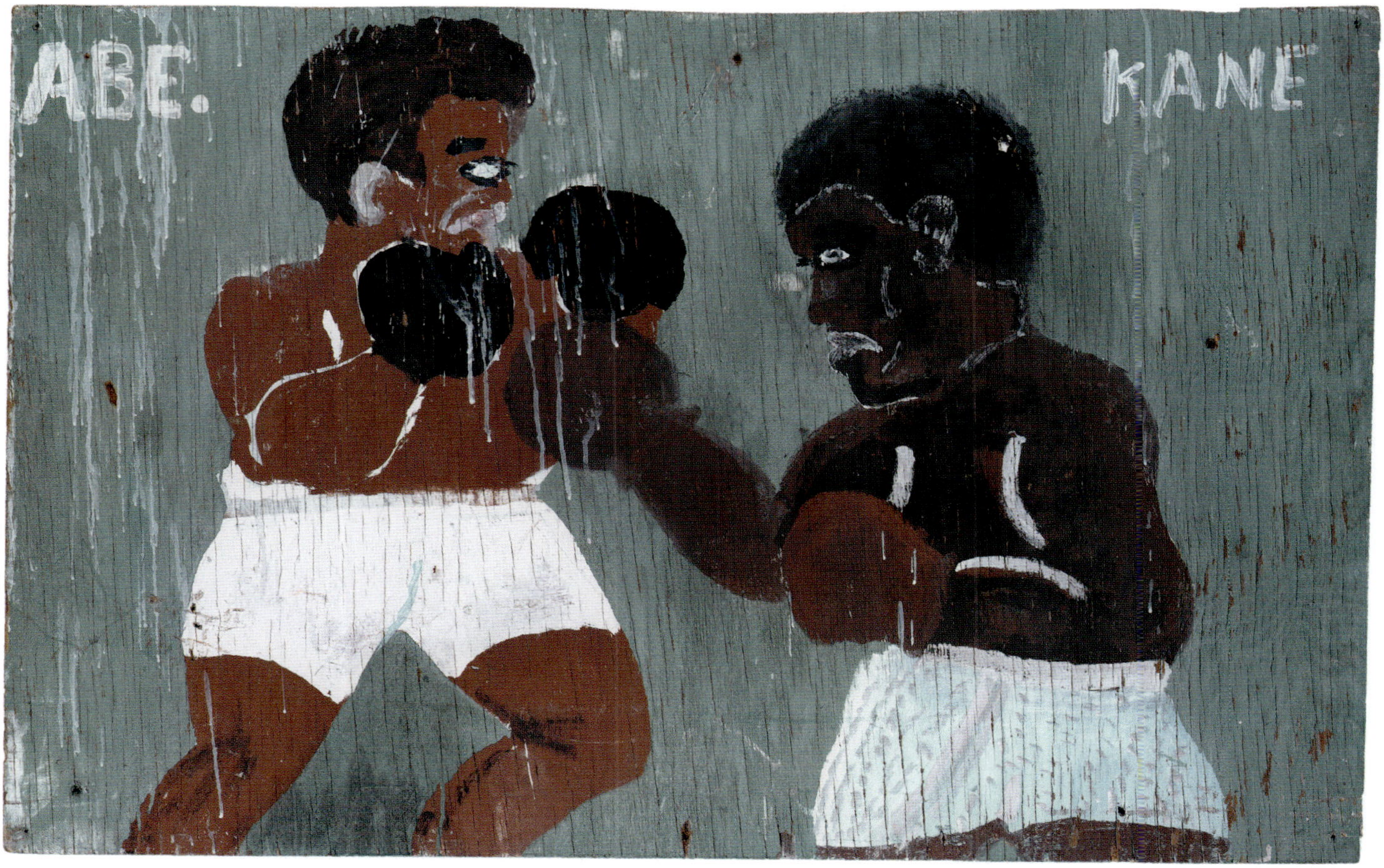

Sam Doyle, ABE. KANE, *ca. 1970s, house paint on plywood, 30 × 48 × ½ in (76.2 × 121.9 × 1.3 cm). American Folk Art Museum.* Exhibited as part of *Black Folk Art in America, 1930–1980*, Corcoran Gallery, Washington, D.C., in 1982, this painting poses dual narratives. It presents Doyle's interest in depicting national African American culture with a scene of boxers Abe Attell and Peter Kane, yet his abbreviation of their names suggests a link to the biblical parable of Cain and Abel.

Saint Helena Island has a compelling history that informs the context of Sam Doyle's artmaking. The South Carolinian island was predominantly populated by descendants of enslaved African people. Given its geographical isolation and cultural concentration, it became a focal point for Gullah culture. As a cultural community, Gullah preserved their African cultural heritage and cultivated distinctive traditions and language. It also became one of the first emancipated territories of the American South during the Civil War in 1861. In 1865, the Penn School was founded by Quakers as the first educational institution in the South for the formerly enslaved. In 1906, Sam Doyle was born into the Gullah community of Wallah on Saint Helena Island, which at the time was still primarily inhabited by Black Americans and had limited sources for the flow of national information to its public.

Doyle's public-facing practice presented the history of the island, community gossip, and profiles of local luminaries. In an example, Doyle dedicated a series to commemorating, via portraiture, the moments when members from the Saint Helena community became the first to take a professional position. With text outlining "First Black" or "First Woman," the series included an undertaker, midwife, and barber. Doyle's practice was committed to keeping his community informed of African American accomplishments in wider American mainstream culture, with specific subjects such as boxer Joe Louis and Martin Luther King, Jr., as well as Abraham Lincoln. Mythical lore and the island's connection to Southern healing traditions of Conjure are also featured in his conceptual remits. Doyle had an overarching interest in commenting on the changing social race relations on the island and in America.

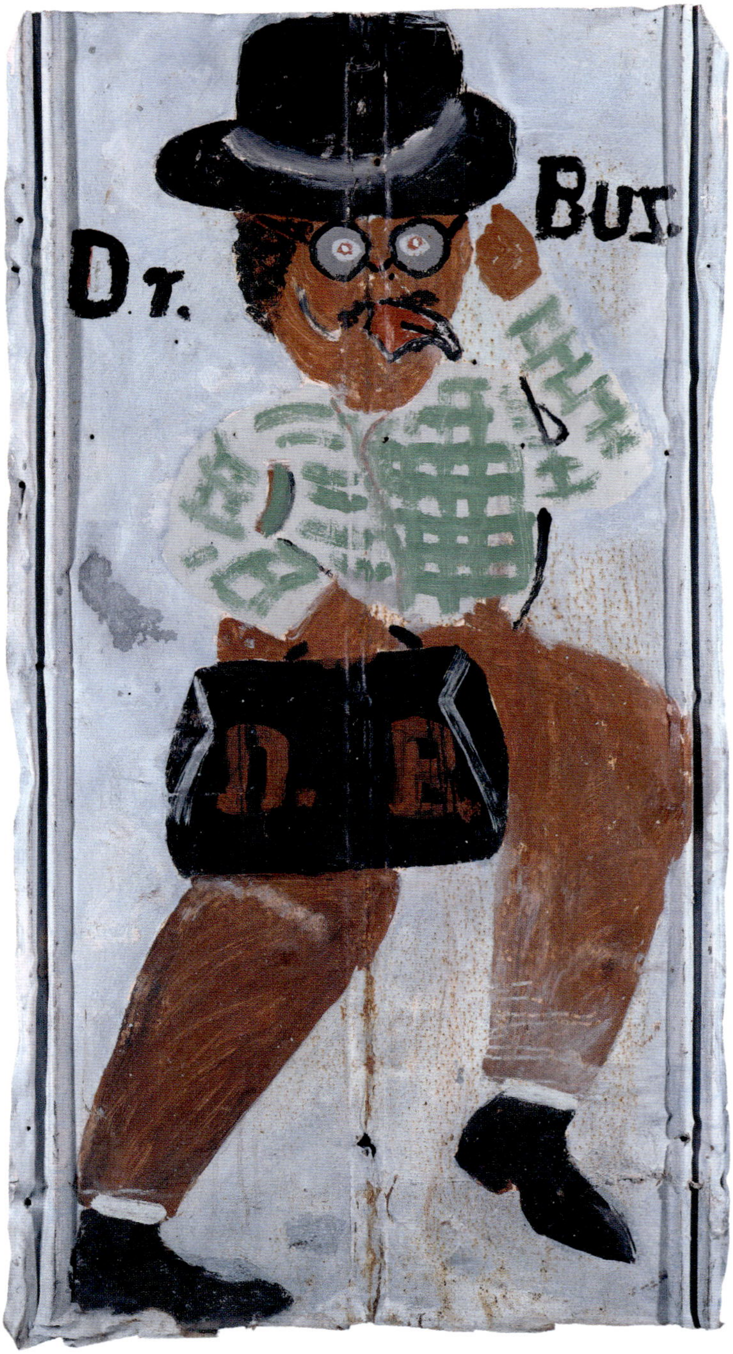

Sam Doyle, Dr. Buz, *n.d., oil on sheet metal, 49½ × 26½ in (125.7 × 67.3 cm). American Folk Art Museum.* Exhibited as part of *Black Folk Art in America, 1930–1980*, Corcoran Gallery, Washington, D.C., in 1982, this work fits within Doyle's remit of depicting local culture, which included nontraditional medicine doctors, most notably Dr. Buzzard.

Sam Doyle, untitled (St. First Woman under taker HELEna), *ca. 1970–1985, enamel on tin, 10¼ × 26 in (26 × 66 cm). The Museum + The Gallery of Everything.* This work shows Doyle's commitment to documenting his community's professional firsts—in this case commemorating a woman's first role as an undertaker.

Aesthetically, Doyle's paintings appear simple at first, possibly even rudimentary, but are encoded with complex social commentary. Cryptic suggestive undertones are communicated via facial expressions and compositional decisions. His choices in grammar and capitalization are further important to consider when understanding his conceptual layering. Emotive, complex, bold, and colorful, Doyle's output became revered by contemporary artists, including Ed Ruscha and Jean-Michel Basquiat, following his debut in *Black Folk Art in America, 1930–1980* (1982).

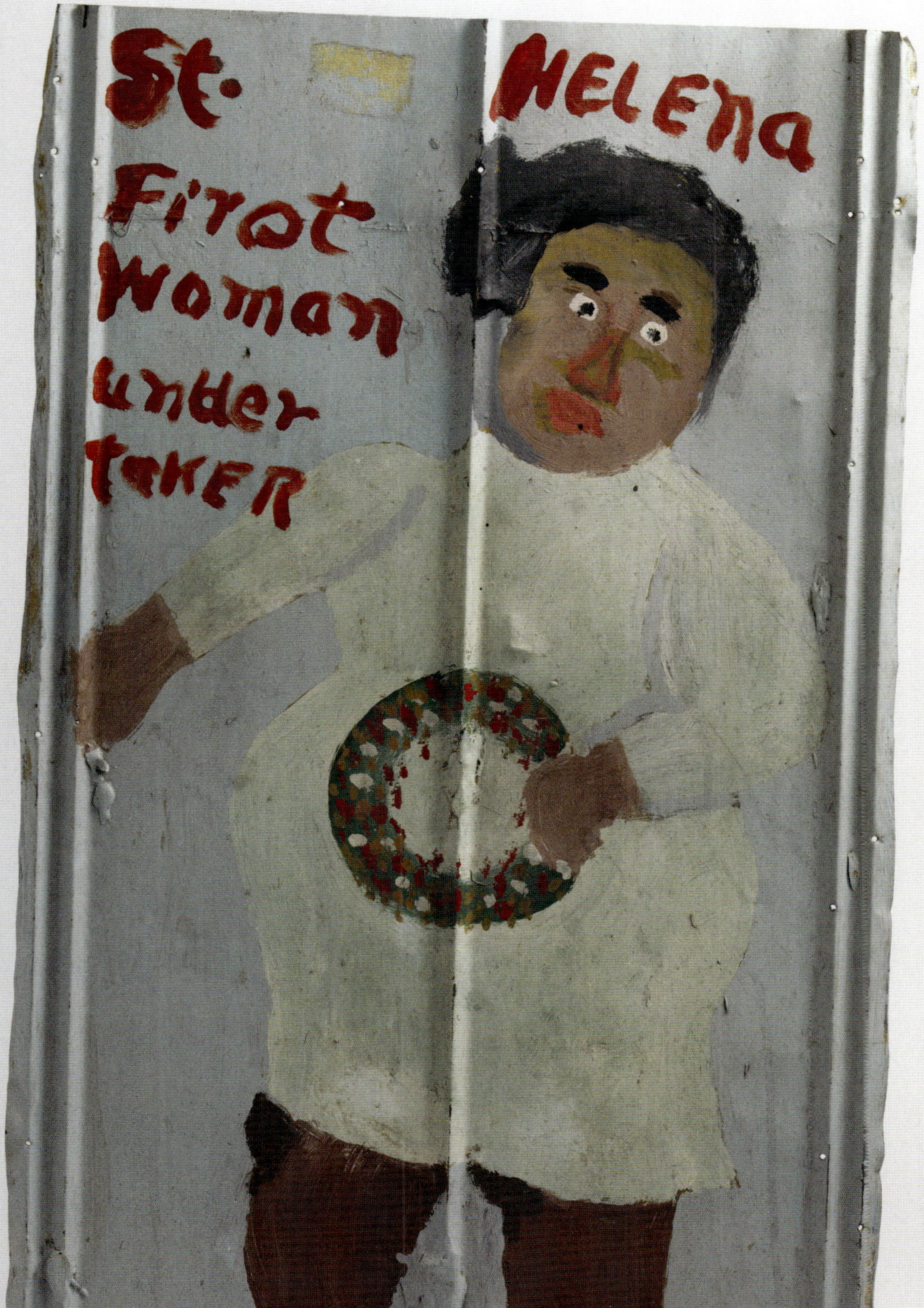
St. HELEna
First Woman under taker
S.D.

PART 2: DISPARATE BOUNDARIES

Disparate Boundaries explores four concepts of creative practice to demonstrate the ambiguity of the current perimeters of self-taught. To illustrate its nebulous nature, each chapter is in deliberate opposition to the others. *Clandestine* examines creativity that thrived in circumstances of privacy and intimacy, juxtaposed with *Renegades*, which focuses on artists and their relationship to messaging and communal awareness. *Environment* demonstrates the concept of an artist as a builder or architect developing a singular vision. The last chapter, *Ability*, explores the development and role of studios that foster artistic development for artists with disabilities.

Each chapter is prefaced by a curator or specialist, followed by a focus on a seminal artist archetypal of the concept. Thoughtful presentations of Henry Darger, Lee Godie, Nek Chand, and Judith Scott are followed by exemplary artists within each chapter. *Disparate Boundaries* also introduces artists both working internationally and into the 21st century.

CHAPTER 5

CLANDESTINE: EXPLORING PRIVACY, INTIMACY, AND ISOLATION IN CREATIVITY

PORTALS OF THE IMAGINATION

Michael Bonesteel

The primary Imagination I hold to be the living Power and prime Agent of all human Perception, and as a repetition in the finite mind of the eternal act of creation in the infinite I AM. The secondary [Imagination] I consider as an echo of the former . . .
— Samuel Taylor Coleridge (*Biographia Literaria*)

Searching for the origins of an artist's creative practice is easy: just go back to childhood where it all starts. The imaginations of children between the ages of three and five are generally erupting with incandescent energy, but by the time they reach kindergarten and first grade, their sense of wonder has become dampened by the surrounding culture. Nevertheless, some individuals manage to maintain access to that secret state of unadulterated creativity into adulthood. Regardless of whether they go into artmaking professionally or keep it private, they tend to favor their own homegrown methods rather than emulating the pedagogical techniques taught in art schools. Of course, we know now that there is no such thing as pure innocence, we are all exposed to some level of cultural influence, but this does not dispel the fact that the invented methods and expressions of some artists remain paramount to the secondary impact of the surrounding environment.

When autodidactic author/artist Henry Darger (see page 154) was four years old, his mother died. This traumatic event, occurring at the optimum stage of young Henry's development, must have made a lasting imprint, not only emotionally, but creatively. Sensitized to human loss and death at this impressionable age, he later imagined an entire world of orphans subjected to the vicissitudes and cruelties of uncaring adults. Unwilling to master the scholarly procedures[1] required to render his art in a traditional fashion, the epic world builder turned to appropriating what he needed to construct his *Realms of the Unreal* by using a montage approach to both verbal and visual materials.

Darger's use of artistic and literary collage began with the writing of his 15,000-page magnum opus, *The Story of the Vivian Girls in What is Known as the Realms of the Unreal, of the Glandeco-Angelinian War Storm Caused by the Child Slave Rebellion,* between 1910 and 1912. This was about the same period that Picasso and Braque began their first experiments in cubist collage, although it is highly unlikely that Darger was aware of their work. However, collage was not an entirely unknown medium at this period. British artist Kate Edith Gough (1856–1948) put together her Gough Album of watercolor and albumen silver print collages in the late 1870s. It is equally unlikely that Darger was aware of Gough's album, although her hybrid images of human-headed waterfowl bear a striking resemblance to the human-headed creatures Darger dubbed Blengiglomenean Serpents (also referred to as "Blengins"). Darger's eminent contemporary, T.S. Eliot, was using extensive literary appropriation in his 1922 poem *The Wasteland*, although plagiarism among lettered writers goes back at least as far as Shakespeare's *Othello*. Again, it is more likely than not that Darger's practice of borrowing material from other sources was original to him.[2]

The highly personal perspectives of an artist like Darger are shared by many innovative nonconformists. Reminiscent of Darger's approach, James Castle (see page 162) fabricated his artworks from found materials upon which he drew with a sharpened stick dipped in a mixture of soot and saliva. Unlike Darger, however, Castle enjoyed showing his work to family members and then squirreled them away in secret locations, carefully tied up in bundles. In order to safeguard his privacy, Darger sequestered himself in his boarding-house room where he could construct his imaginary universe. Castle also had his own small cottage on the family's property where he could ensconce himself. The latter's deafness and limited verbal communication were other barriers that contributed to his isolation, possibly playing a similar role in Castle's life as Darger's misanthropic behavior played in his. For both artists, the individuality of their processes is perfectly reflected in the meticulously idiosyncratic nature of their artistic products. As a result, their personal expressions stand out in marked contrast to those mirroring (as in Coleridge's "secondary Imagination") the tired trends of the mainstream artworld.

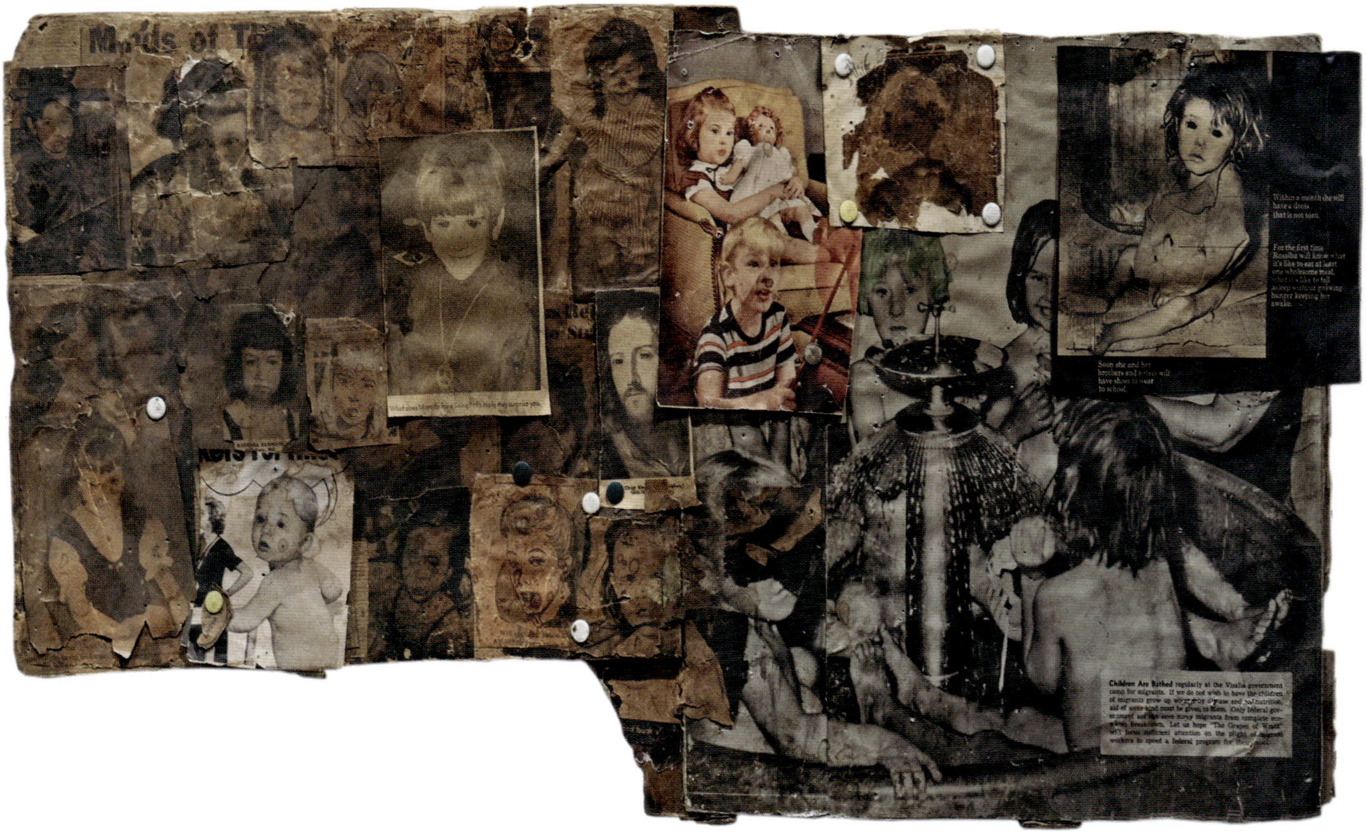

Henry Darger, untitled (collage with comics of Little Annie Rooney and misc. other children, women, Jesus, etc.), *n.d., newspaper and magazine clippings on board with tacks, 14 × 28½ in (35.6 × 72.4 cm). The Center for Intuitive and Outsider Art.* Darger's use of collage was both for reference and creative implementation. Likely unaware of contemporaneous artists experimenting with collage, his influence of available printed and visual culture transpired into his imaginary world in the *Realms of the Unreal.*

The voluminous artistic output of Charles A.A. Dellschau (see page 166), can be effectively compared to Castle's and Darger's prolific bodies of work. Dellschau's watercolor drawings of flying machines were originally assembled into 12 (possibly more that have since gone missing) handbound books, just as Darger's writings and artwork were initially sewn into numerous volumes and portfolios. Castle sometimes collected his drawings into books as well, and like the compilations of Dellschau and Darger, a number of these were later dismantled and sold off piecemeal. Dellschau clipped articles on early aeronautical developments from newspapers and magazines, and collaged them into many of his compositions, just as Castle commandeered alphabet letters, and Darger repurposed figures from coloring books, newspapers, comics, and fashion advertisements. Yet, the way all three artists adapted and transformed their source materials made their work singularly memorable. Perhaps it is not serendipitous that the profuse practices of all three seem to connect to their inordinately determined and driven personalities.

Diagnosed as a schizophrenic, Melvin Way (see page 170) makes work that confronts and defies the viewer's understanding. His production began as a private examination keeping his intimate compositions reserved and protected in his pockets. As for Way's artistic, often clandestine, process he has said: "All my works have to go through emissions, baptisms, and transmigrations before I release them into the stratosphere. I carry five hundred drawings at a time in my raincoat, and they go through rain, sleet, and snow, sometimes staying in my pocket for six months at a time."[3] He utilizes mathematical equations, chemical formulas, and mechanical diagrams as the building blocks of his compositions in much the same way as other artists use figurative or abstract forms. These elements are combined to create perplexing configurations that seem to push science into a realm of what could be termed "quantum metaphysics" or pure alchemy. When Way's handling of science becomes art, a third thing is born that is the creative essence of both art and science, yet points beyond them to the realm of the transcendent. By nature, such a realm is mysterious and ineffable, and thus his works are redolent of that which cannot be known or explained.

Investigating Way's processes, one cannot entirely dismiss the connection between creativity and mental health challenges, even though the use of art as a diagnostic tool in the manner in which psychiatrists from Cesare Lombroso (*Genius and Madness*, 1864) to Leo Navratil (*Schizophrenia and Art*, 1965) employed it may no longer be viable[4]. By today's academic standards any correlation between art and mental illness is to be considered a dangerous romanticization[5]. Nevertheless, it is by no means coincidental that the core artists of Jean Dubuffet's initial *l'art brut* (raw art) circle were composed entirely of psychiatric patients (for example, Adolf Wölfli (see page 64), Heinrich Anton Müller, Louis Soutter, Aloïse Corbaz (see page 56), Auguste Forestier (see page 76), and Guillaume Pujolle). Dubuffet subsequently added to his select group a number of other artists who were mediumistic visionaries, as well as those deemed social eccentrics or outcasts. Regardless of their backgrounds, it was always the unorthodox mental perspectives of its practitioners that defined this field.

As disparate as the psychologies of Darger, Castle, Dellschau, and Way may be, they share a portal to their secluded imagination that remains free of cognitive impairments or inhibitions. The mediumistic visionary Guo Fengyi (see page 174) also found a fruitful path to a rich wellspring of creative possibilities when she sought relief from the impediments that stalled her life. A painful arthritic condition forced her to seek help through the meditative disciplines of Qigong which, in turn, led to experiencing inner visions that found expression in her monumental drawings. These works often started with an anatomical form that expanded and morphed into landscapes and semi-abstract energy fields.

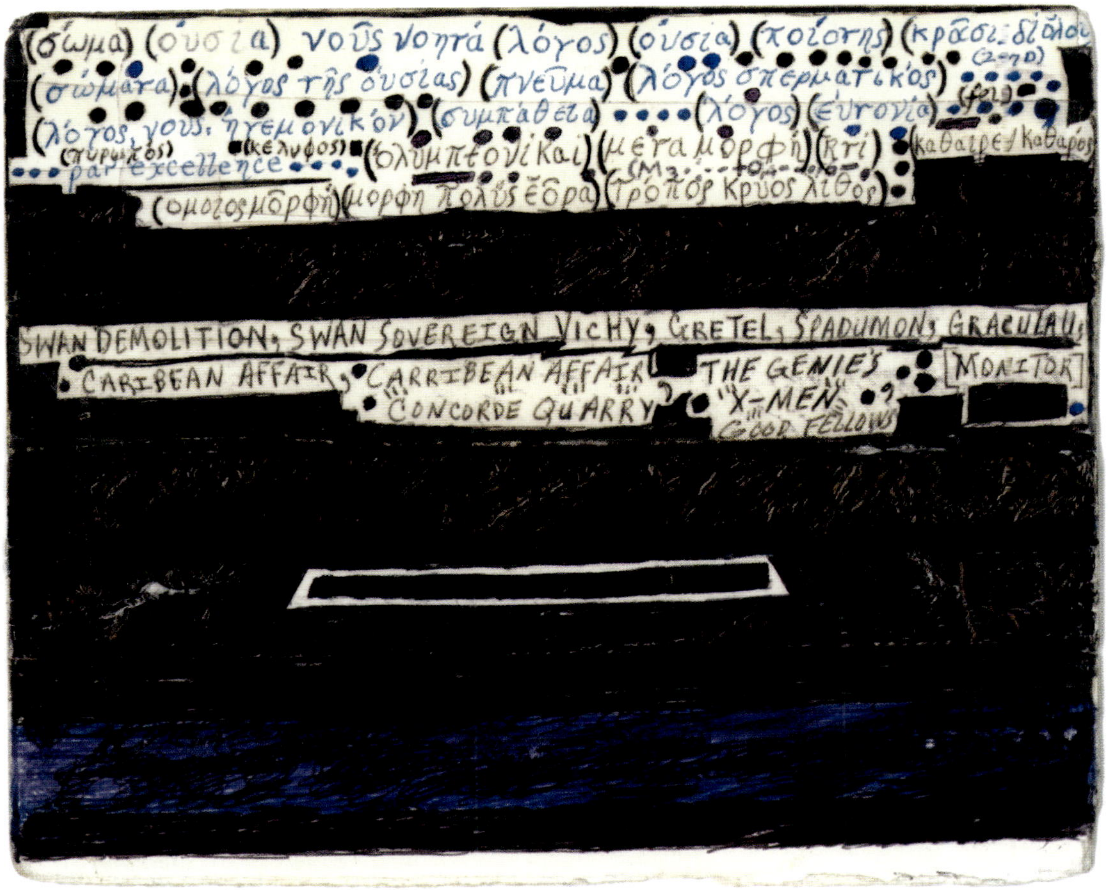

Melvin Way, Spellbound ft. Washington Armory Haven Kiosk, *ca. 1989, ballpoint pen on paper with Scotch tape, 5½ × 7 in (14 × 17.8 cm). Courtesy the Artist and Bullet Space.* This intimate drawing by Way is mostly hidden by deep markings of blue and black pen. Of the text displayed, the upper portion appears to be a foreign or invented language, while segments of the English reveal statements including "par excellence," "SWAN SOVEREIGN," and "CARIBEAN AFFAIR."

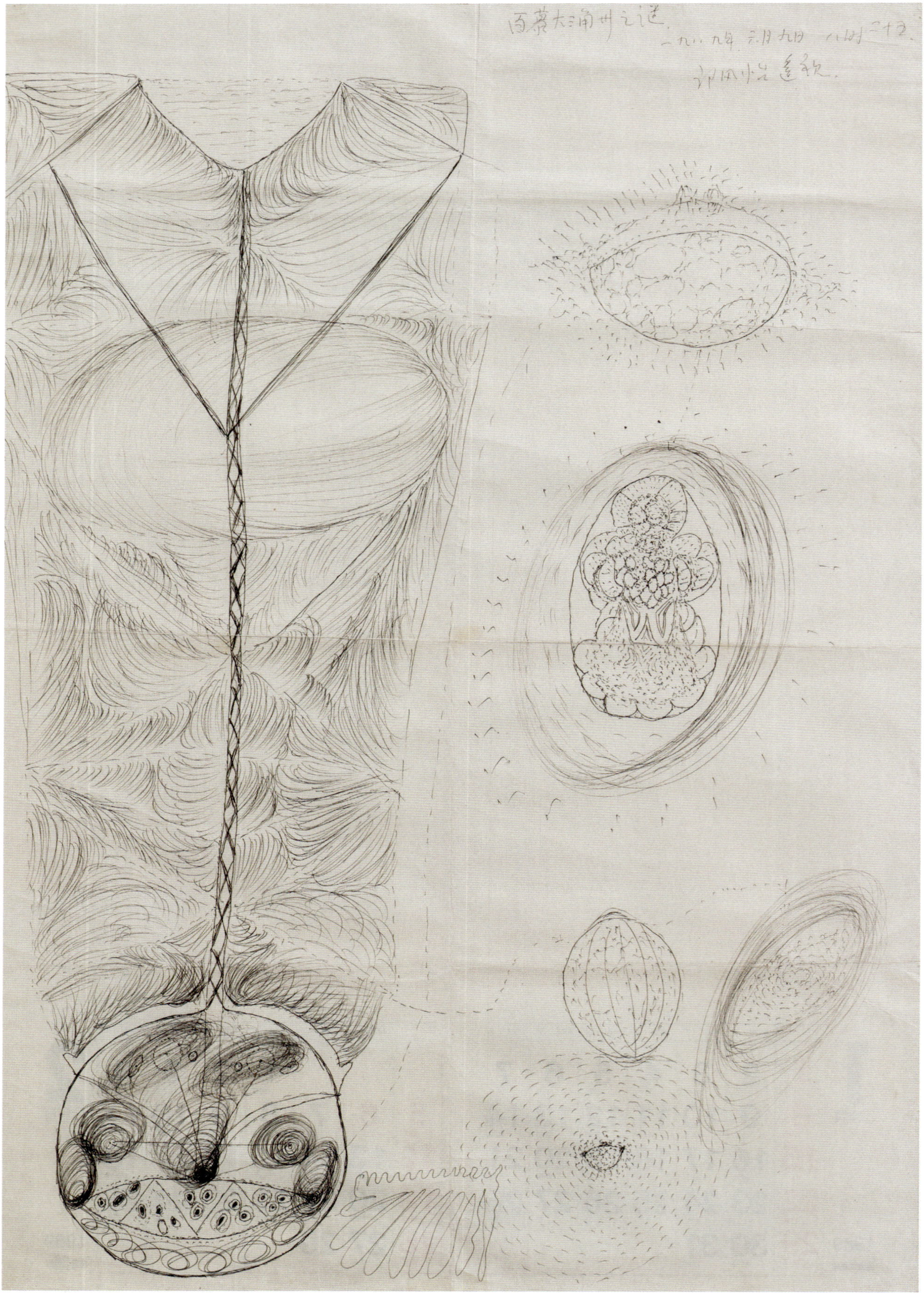

Guo Fengyi, Mystery of the Bermuda Triangle, *1989, ink on glazed printing paper, 27⁹⁄₁₆ × 19⅞ in (70 × 50.5 cm). Long March Space.* This diagrammatic drawing was Fengyi's first completed outside of her notebook analyzing this mysterious phenomenon and introduces her interest in exploring the energy of distant places.

Like Fengyi, creative Emery Blagdon (see page 178) endeavored to cure his physical ailment through intuitive innovation. From 1950 to the end of his life, Blagdon—attempting to stave off the cancer that had ravaged his family—constructed an enormous collection of some 400 exotic mixed media contraptions comprised of copper wire and other conductive materials that were connected to live electrical currents. Suspended like elaborate chandeliers from the ceiling and walls of a crude wooden shed in his backyard, he considered the entire assembled environment, in effect, as one all encompassing "Healing Machine." His work displays indisputable beauty, but making art was probably the last thing on Blagdon's mind. The goal was far more practical. And yet it was imagination that provided the key, if not the answer, to his quest.

In his book about the history of the imagination, author Patrick Harpur wrote: "In Renaissance Florence, and again, among the German and English Romantics three hundred years later, imagination was exalted not only as the most important human faculty, but as the very ground of reality."[6] In the late 19th century, Sigmund Freud's discovery of the personal subconscious, and, probing deeper still in the 20th century, Carl Jung's identification of a collective archetypal unconscious, laid the groundwork for Dubuffet's field of Art Brut—a species of art with psychological, mythological, and metaphysical underpinnings—to be recognized, and ultimately respected and appreciated. Now that Art Brut, or Outsider Art as it tends to be known in English-speaking countries, has become an acknowledged presence in the 21st century, the work in establishing it as a legitimate classification may be done. But with the ever broadening of this group to include self-taught African American vernacular artists within its ranks (which has consequently spurred ongoing debates about the usefulness or appropriateness of an umbrella term like Outsider Art), maybe it's time to allow all of these artists to stand on their own, without an overriding catchall label to qualify, define, or confine them. By any other name, individually or collectively, the unique creative practices and productions, whether private or public, of nonconformist artists will always serve as portals to a paradise of the "primary Imagination."

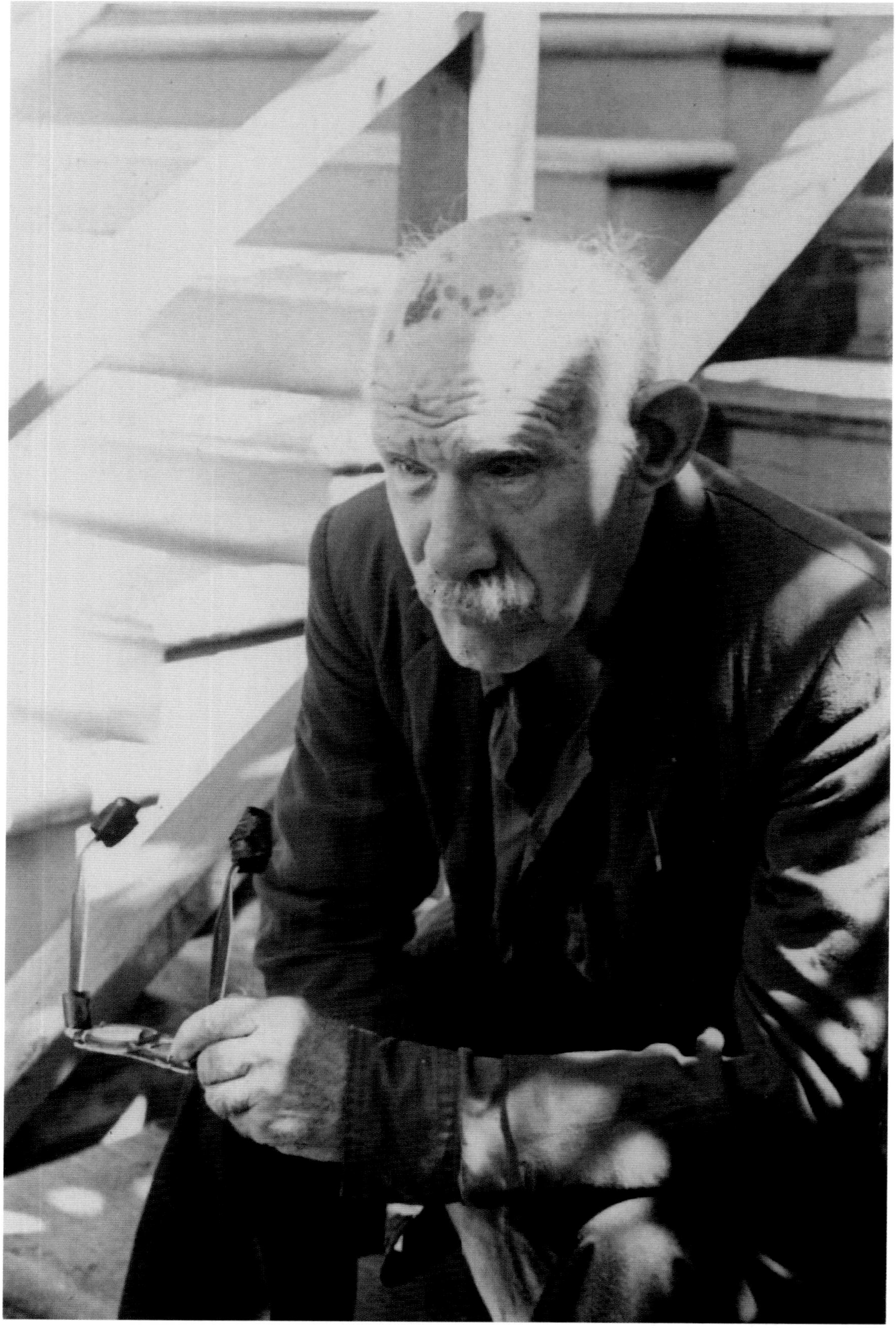

Henry Darger, ca. 1970, photograph by David Berglund. Musée d'Art Moderne de la Ville de Paris Archive. This is one of the few photographs of Henry Darger that exist. It was captured late in life by Berglund, who lived in Darger's building on the north side of Chicago and, along with Nathan Lerner, subsequently found Darger's oeuvre.

HENRY DARGER

(1892–1973, Chicago, Illinois, USA)

The extraordinary chronicles of the virtuous Vivian Girls, by Henry Darger were only disclosed following his death after being found by his landlord, Nathan Lerner. His visual and written prose tells the harrowing otherworldly tale of seven young sisters fighting to end child slavery. Full of fantasy, it also contains graphic violence and an ambiguous sexual tone. Researchers have revealed evidence of traumatic events in Darger's life and accounts of his behavior that support the presence of mental health issues. At a young age, Darger lost his mother, was separated from his sister, and soon after orphaned. In 1904, he was admitted to an asylum for "feeble-minded" children in Lincoln, Illinois. By the age of 17, he had escaped back to Chicago and spent the next 50 years working for Catholic hospitals. Aside from his job and attending mass multiple times a day, Darger lived an extremely private and reclusive life. In around 1912, he began his masterwork *The Realms of the Unreal*—a 15,000-word manuscript accompanied by fantastical scrolling illustrations. Posthumously, his drawn and collaged pastiches of historical references, popular culture, and news events have become an art world phenomenon

"Unlike most children, I hated to see the day come when I will be grown up"[7]

Opinions vary on the type of person that Henry Darger was—his characteristics, intentions, and mental health—and often predetermine an understanding of his oeuvre. There has been extensive research regarding the psychological state of Darger that facilitates a reading of his work contextualized by his inferred emotional state. This essay serves as an introduction to Darger's artistic legacy that presents his biographical details as inherently influential to his prolific creativity. It also specifies the potential complexities of his state of mind, not for formal analysis, but in consideration to his artistic practice. There are no interviews with Darger discussing the motivations and intentions behind his work. In his autobiography, *The History of My Life,* written toward the end of his life, he only made a single reference to being an artist. His autobiography is the source of the following Darger citations.

"To make matters worse, now I'm an artist, been one for years."[8]

The start of Darger's traumatic experiences began at the age of four, when his mother died and his newborn sister was put up for adoption. He lived with his elderly father until around 1900, when he was placed in a Catholic boys' home. During these few years with his father, select pivotal behavioral characteristics that informed Darger's later creativity emerged: avid reading and a keen observation of severe weather.

"I was very interested in summer thunderstorms (still am, old as I am) and during winter (cold) I could and would stand by the window all day, watching it snow, especially if there was a great big blizzard raging."[9]

While living at the boys' home, Darger was accused of aggressive and disruptive behavior, including violent encounters with other children. In 1904 he was admitted to the Illinois Asylum for Feeble-Minded Children in Lincoln. The research of Michael Bonesteel indicates that Darger experienced physical, emotional, and "very possibly, sexual abuse" while at the asylum[10]. Darger's autobiography presents a more banal, even affectionate, assessment of the asylum. Regardless, he attempted to run away from the asylum several times, the first following the traumatic news of his father's death.[11]

"I got the bad news that my father has died at St. Augustine home. I did not cry or weep however. I had that kind of deep sorrow that, bad as you feel, I could not."[12]

At aged 17, Darger successfully escaped and resettled in Chicago. From 1909 to 1963 he worked between three Catholic hospitals in positions that included dishwasher, janitor, and later prepping bandage wraps. While presenting his life in this period, before introducing his concurrent private creative practice, it is also worth noting that Darger was a devout Catholic who attended mass multiple times each day. He formed a complicated relationship with God, which was inquisitive and argumentative[13]. In 1917, Darger was drafted into the army, but was discharged due to eye trouble and never deployed. He only had one friend as an adult: William Schloeder. It is believed Darger never had a romantic or sexual relationship of any kind. He was also very fond of the concept of children, especially young girls, with a preoccupation with their safety. Darger always kept obsessively busy and informed, but isolated. He would read every newspaper; meticulously track the weather, even copy the Bible and wrap balls of twine to steadfastly stay active.

"I also believed that I had read in the Holy Bible that children, especially all good and innocent ones, were more important to God than grownups . . . if harming a child, to have a millstone (not feather) to be tied around his neck and be drowned in the depth of the sea."[14]

In around 1912 Darger began writing *The Story of the Vivian Girls, in What Is Known as the Realms of the Unreal, of the Glandeco-Angelinian War Storm, Caused by the Child Slave Rebellion*. It developed, in over 15,000 type-written pages and 15 volumes, into the longest work of fiction ever written.[15] Its narrative also served as the basis for Darger's illustrative drawings and collage for which he is most recognized. Set in another world, *Realms* is a pastiche of good and evil, regaling the story of the Vivian Girls and their plight to end child slavery against the empire of Glandelinia. From the Catholic nation of Abbieannia, the protagonistic Vivian sisters (Violet, Joice, Jennie, Angeline, Daisy, Hettie, and Catherine) are the virtuous and saintlike daughters of the emperor. They are supported by Blengiglomeneans, human-creature hybrids helping to protect the children. Their opposition is the

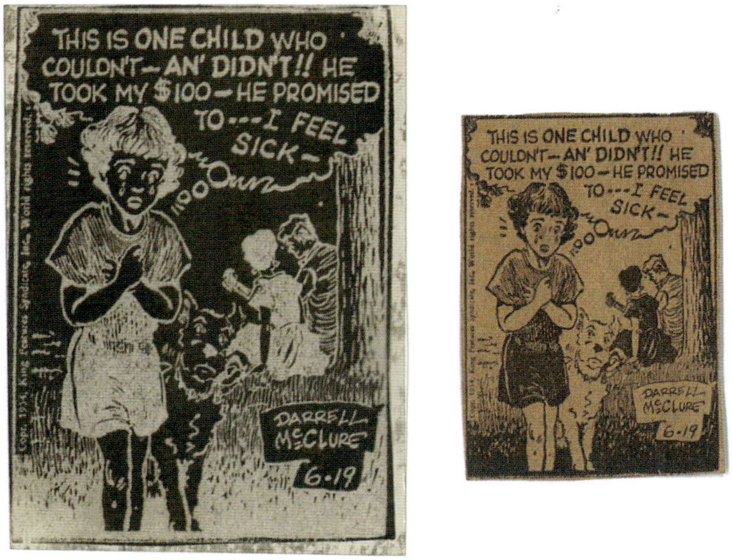

Comic and negative of Little Annie Rooney, *1954, newspaper, 2¼ × 1½ in (5.7 × 3.8 cm) and negative, 3¼ × 2¼ in (8.3 × 5.7 cm). The Center for Intuitive and Outsider Art.* Darger referenced the comic character Little Annie Rooney in his illustrations. This clipping and negative demonstrate the photographic enlargement process implemented by Darger from around 1945, which gave him greater range and diversity in his drawing technique.

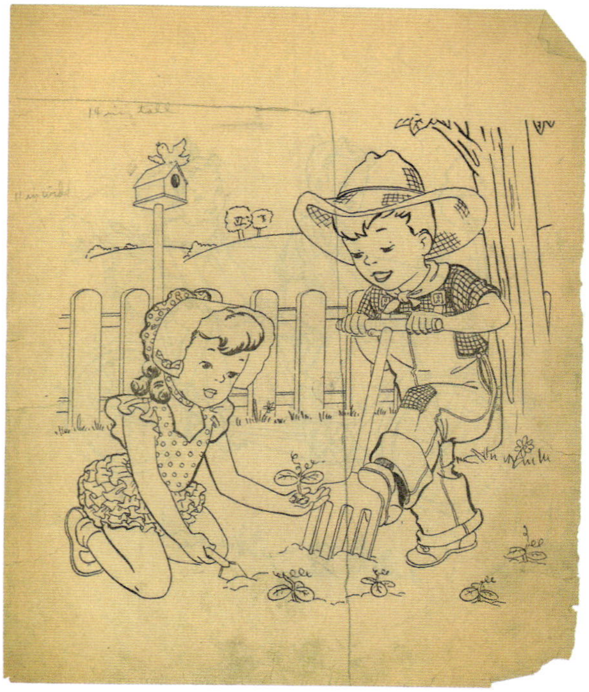

Untitled coloring book page (little girl and boy digging), *n.d., paper, 13 × 10½ in (33 × 26.7 cm). The Center for Intuitive and Outsider Art.* A coloring page found among Darger's collection of source materials. The picket fence and birdhouse can be seen referenced throughout his oeuvre.

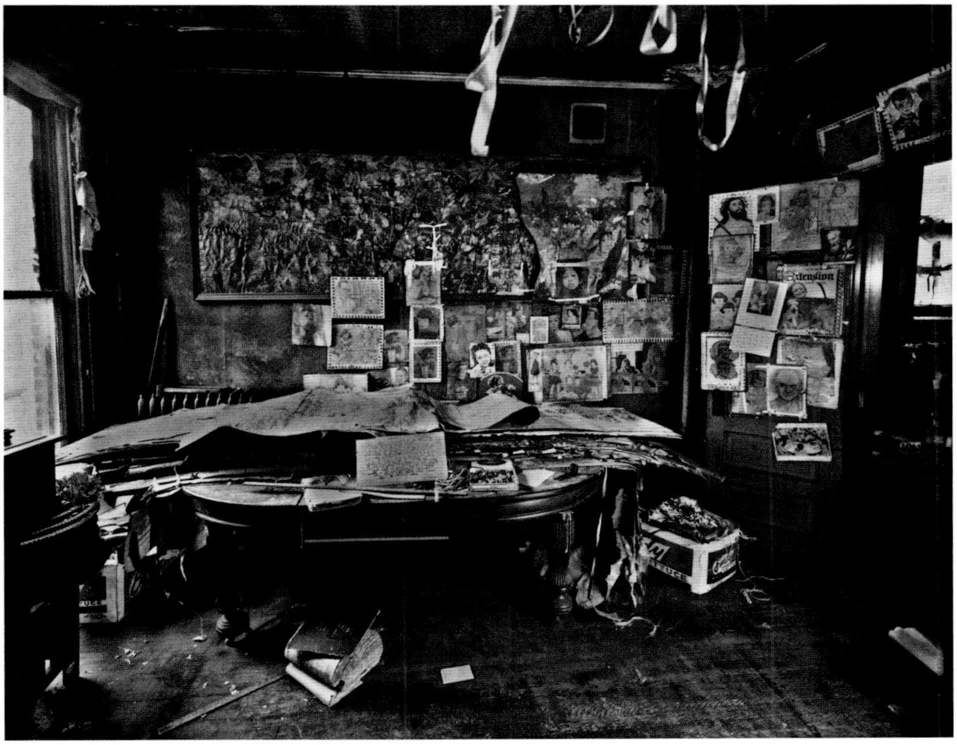

Henry Darger's work table at 851 Webster Ave., Chicago, *n.d., photograph. Musée d'Art Moderne de la Ville de Paris Archive.* A photograph of Henry Darger's room and work table in the building on Webster Avenue in Chicago. His drawings, writings, references, and sources can be seen throughout.

adversarial Glandelinians. It is believed that Darger spent 20 years on the manuscript, more than 50 years illustrating it, and never considered it complete.

Darger's earliest visual creations were likely from around 1915 and involved introductory collage methods. An astute collector and archivist of visual material, he started with collage and developed his signature style of implementing existing imagery as a key tool for his image-making. His experimentations with tracing likely followed, and in the 1920s he started to paint with watercolors. Building scenes from references, memory, and imagination, Darger later began developing diptychs and triptychs. At this stage, his characters were traced from coloring books, newspapers, and advertisements and then enhanced. From around 1945[16], he began using photographic processes, ordering enlargements of imagery[17]. This allowed Darger to experiment with scale, depth, and perspective, which he was previously unable to do. Visually, his compositions reverberate with violence juxtaposed against both cuteness and nature. Dismemberment, strangulation, and crucifixions of charming children are placed within acutely detailed flora and fauna. The criticality of weather, especially clouds, storms, and tornadoes, is given pictorial importance and substantiated by illustrative notes. Darger's process of copying figures presents a repetitive army-like feel and compositions that are cinematic in quality.

Due to Darger's reliance on references, his oeuvre is completely imaginary, yet inherently echoes his contemporaneous American zeitgeist. Exploring the pastiche in Darger's practice demonstrates, regardless of isolation, his engagement with history and culture. It also suggests that validating certain references in the domain of popular culture could mitigate their appearance in *Realms.* Darger's mainstream pictorial references were via his extensive visual catalog of thousands of collected images. The majority of these images were of girls: photographic, illustrated, but also newspaper clippings of lost, murdered, and kidnapped children. While Darger's transferred and repeated versions of the Little Annie Rooney and others, including generic girls from children's coloring books, can introduce dubious interpretations in terms of his portrayal of young girls, it is important to confirm that these visuals were readily accessible and marketed as acceptable within his time. This accessibility could also inform his depictions of

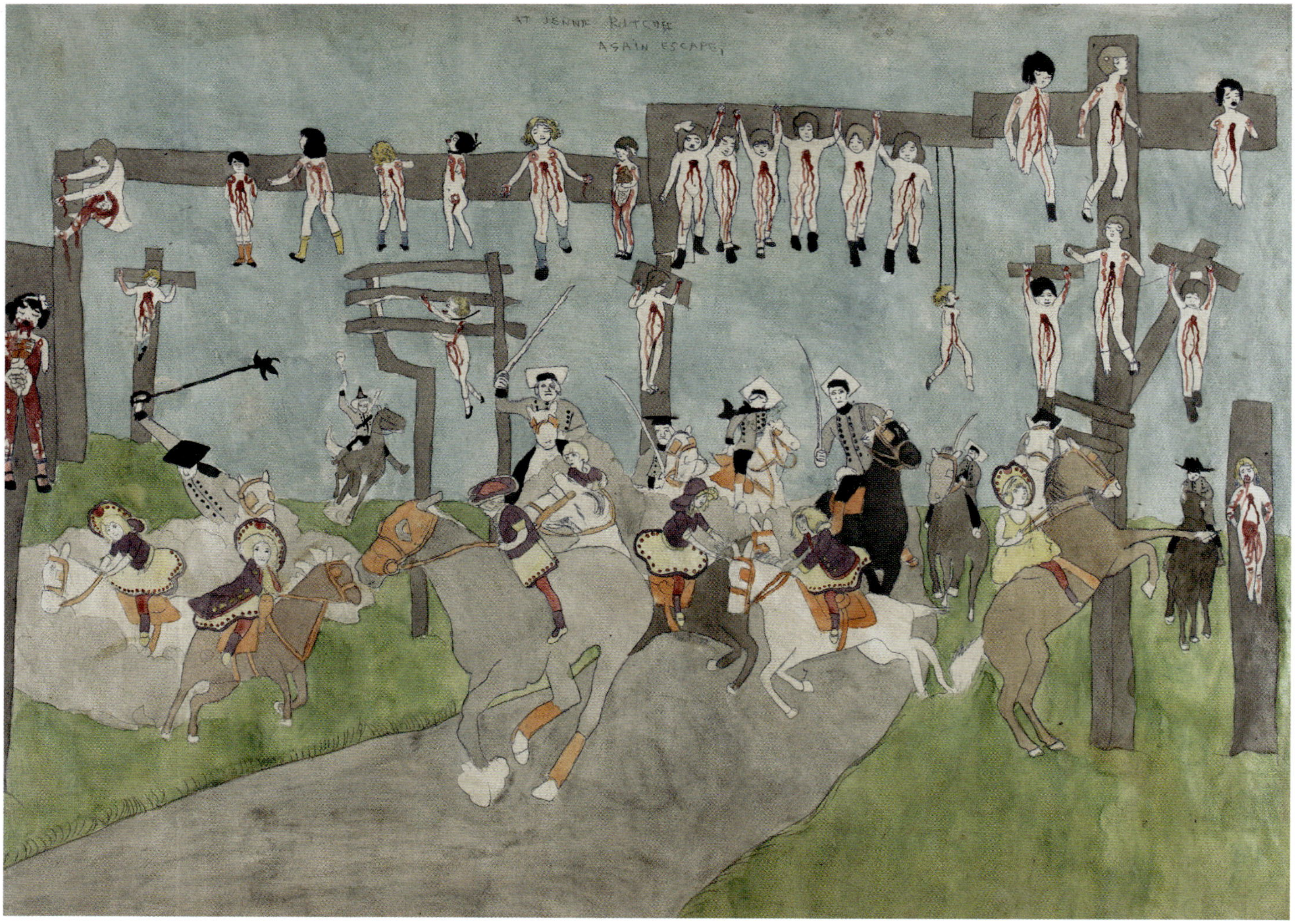

Henry Darger, At Jennie Richie, Vivian Girls escape with booty but in crossing river nudded are captured by Claverinean boy scouts who mistake them for Glandelinian girl scouts, *(this detail, verso, central panel,* At Jennie Richee, again escape*), 1930–1940, graphite pencil, watercolor, gouache, black ink, and varnish on three sheets of vellum paper, 22 1/16 × 88 3/8 in (56 × 224.5 cm). Musée d'Art Moderne de la Ville de Paris.* This composition by Darger embodies his penchant for violence, battle scenes, and (as an extremely devout Catholic) his implementation and emblematic consequence of crucifixion, as demonstrated in the upper right corner.

children being crucified. For Darger—who was consistently surrounded by Catholic imagery—the visual of crucifixion may have felt normalized and been implemented for its symbolic use.

Further to exploring violence in *Realms*, many battle scenes are referenced from the media's depiction of the two world wars. Darger was extremely interested in how history documented war, noting from a young age that victory was dependent on who was recording it. He also had an interest in the American Civil War, allocating Confederate uniforms to the evil Glandelinian army. Further evident is Darger's understanding of the history of slavery in America—*Realms* is a war epic about abolishing child slavery. Darger also borrowed from Harriet Beecher Stowe's *Uncle Tom's Cabin*, with characters from her book having cameos. Subsequent influences of mostly children's literature included: Lewis Carroll books; Booth Tarkington's *Penrod*; the illustrated version of *The Swiss Family Robinson*; and aptly *Heidi (*a young orphaned girl protagonist) by Johanna Spyri.

Perhaps the most significant literary influence on Darger were *The Oz* books by L. Frank Baum, which also introduced several key concepts of *Realms* and contextualizing thereof. *Realms* cited many locations after characters in *Oz* such as Munchkin Town and Gnome King Town. While *The Wonderful Wizard of Oz* likely set the stage of an alternate universe, *Realms* departed from it with its violence. *Oz* aided his development of weather as powerful and having a transformative quality. Darger's thought process seemed primarily based on Catholic virtue and repercussion, therefore, he also used weather as a tool to imply God's wrath and salvation. Describing extreme (violent) weather allowed Darger a mode of expression and experience[18]. His autobiography also aligns severe weather to violence.

"They sure were handing each other a perfect storm or 'cyclone' of fist blows."[19]

Placing *Realms* in parallel to *Oz* also proposes a potential context for what is often considered the most striking element in Darger's visual work—the female children are mostly depicted with penises. *Oz* could have set the precedent for the gender fluidity of Darger's characters. Similar to *Realms, Oz* features an army of girls, and in its second volume presents a boy named Tip who later reveals himself as a woman[20]. Darger's illustrations are rife with nude children that seem to undulate between innocent oblivious nakedness and nudity with violent undertones. Whether ignorance, Catholic piety, or other, there are no references to sexual acts, pregnancy, or birth in *Realms*. The drawn male genitalia don't appear to be exaggerated or emphasized and are only featured in the illustrations, not addressed in Darger's writing.

Perhaps in response to his own struggles with good and evil, in *Realms* Darger presents cameos of himself in both benevolent and malevolent roles. He also wrote a scene where the Vivian Girls discover the book *Realms of the Unreal* authored by Darger from a faraway Chicago. This sets up the paradigm of fluctuations between Darger's reality and fiction. In *Realms,* the head of the opposition, General John Manley, is named after a childhood foe, while Schloeder, Darger's only adult friend, co-serves as the head of Gemini child protective services. The most intense of these oscillations is the link between Elsie Paroubeck and Annie Aronburg. Elsie Paroubeck was a young Chicago girl, whose brutal murder was featured in the *Chicago Daily News* on May 9, 1911. It appears Darger intended to base the *Realms* character, Annie Aronburg, on Paroubeck's newspaper clipping. Aronburg was a Joan of Arc-like character and leader of the slave rebellion. Darger misplaced this clipping and its loss was repeatedly incorporated into the narrative as having great consequence. From *The Realms* vol, one: "July 12: Picture of Annie Aronburg gone! Mysteriously Missing!"[21] The misplacement of this photograph prolonged the great war in *Realms* and caused an intense inner struggle for Darger with God. The physical loss of Darger's clipping/photograph of Elsie Paroubeck became in *Realms,* the "Aronburg Mystery."

The above is a limited introduction to the life and work of Henry Darger. What does seem inherent in his copious creative output is the polarity between comfort and conflict, serenity and violence, good and evil. While Darger's personal life—from traumatic childhood to reclusive tendencies—has often defined his artistic standing, his evident knowledge of American history and references to his contemporaneous cultural zeitgeist present a dialectical juxtaposition to his classification as an "outsider." In 1973, Darger passed away in a home for the elderly, which he had moved to the previous year with the assistance of his landlord Nathan Lerner [22] and fellow tenant David Berglund. It was while clearing out his vacated apartment that Berglund identified the magnificent opus of Darger. Prior to his death, Berglund visited Darger to inform him of the findings of his creative output, to which Darger simply responded "Too late now"

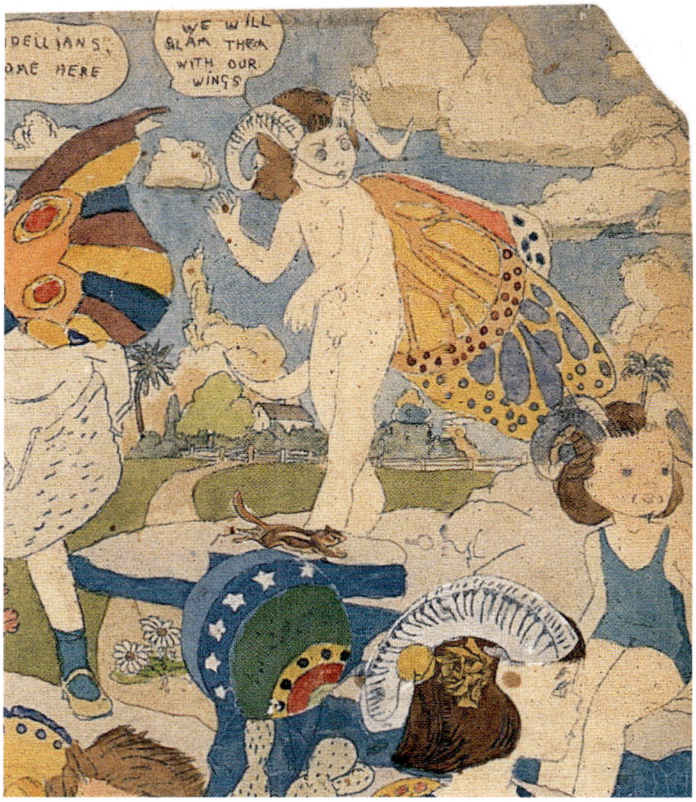

Henry Darger, I see Glandellians, if they come here I'll . . . We will slam them with our wings, *(detail), n.d., watercolor, pencil, carbon tracing, and collage on pieced paper, 24 × 106½ in (61 × 270.5 cm). American Folk Art Museum.* Centrally compelling to Darger's oeuvre are his depictions of female characters with penises. In this detail, the young female with male genitalia is a character belonging to Darger's Blengiglomeneans; benevolent creatures supporting the plight of the Vivian Girls.

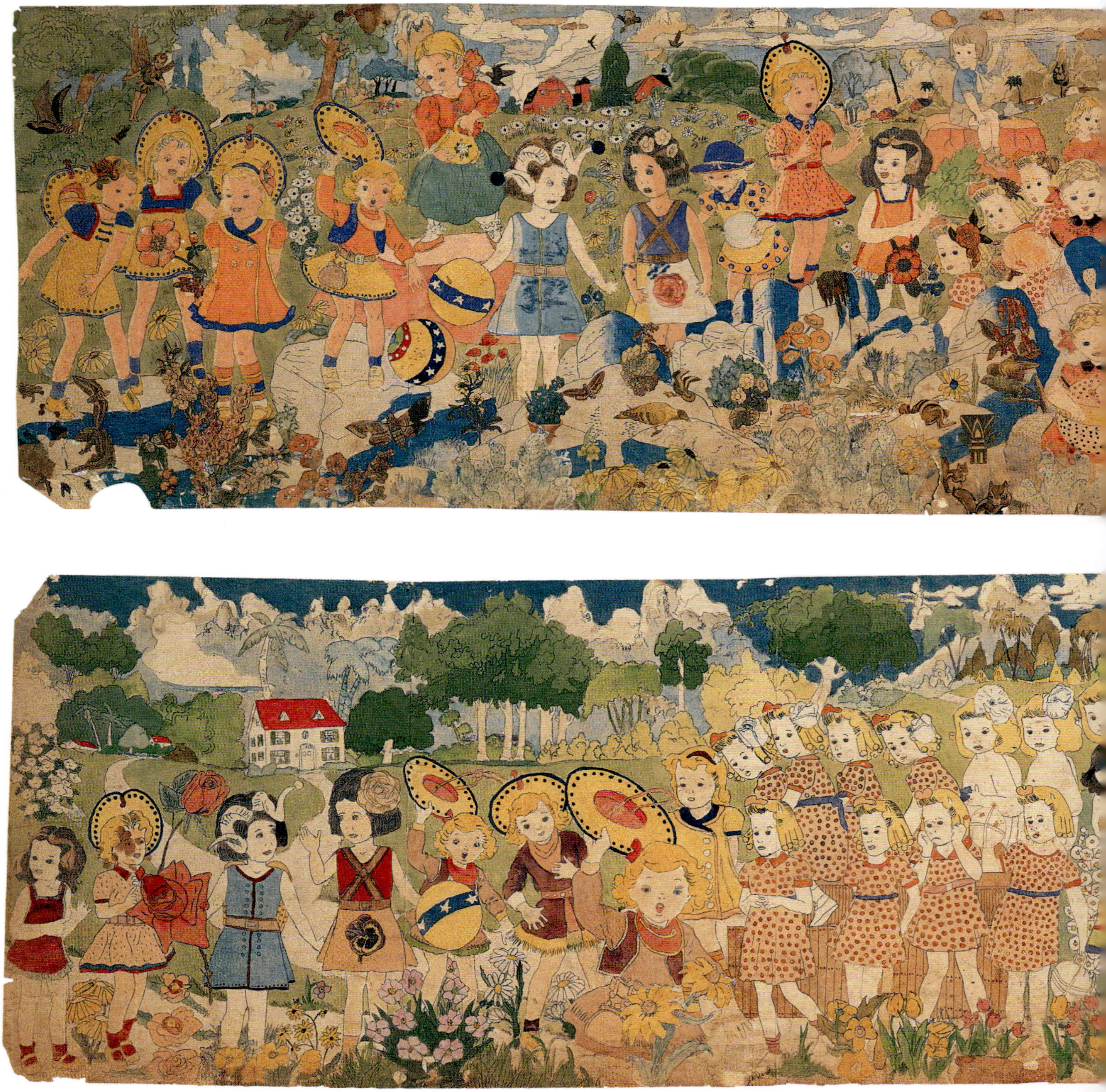

Henry Darger, I see Glandellians, if they come here I'll . . . We will slam them with our wings, *n.d., watercolor, pencil, carbon tracing, and collage on pieced paper, 24 × 106½ in (61 × 270.5 cm). American Folk Art Museum.* This epic, double-sided illustration by Darger is emblematic of his process. It demonstrates his effective use of tracing repeating characters, including (seen in bottom panel) his ability to scale his characters using a photo enlargement process. Collaged elements are also present, which demonstrate his interest in depicting flora and weather.

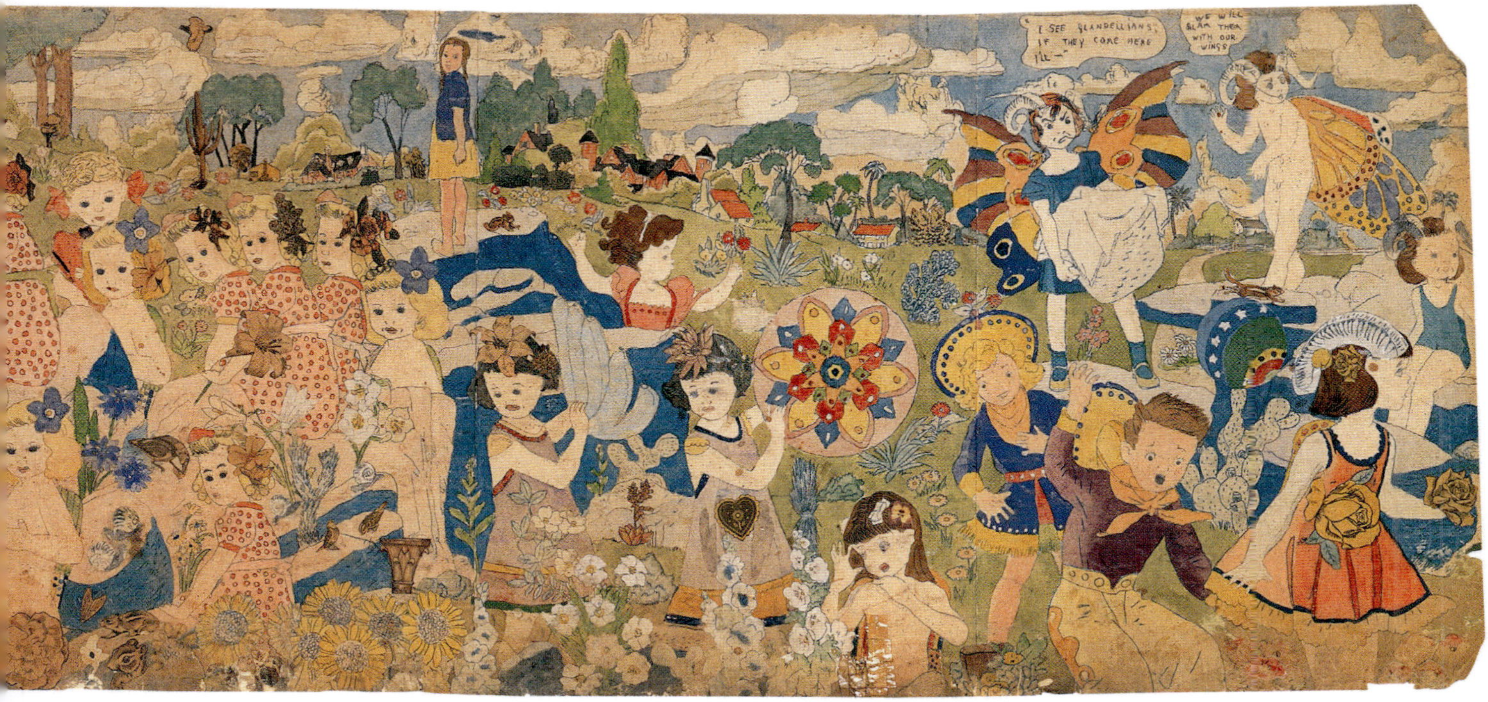
"I SEE GLANDELINIANS; IF THEY COME HERE I'LL—"
WE WILL SLAM THEM WITH OUR WINGS

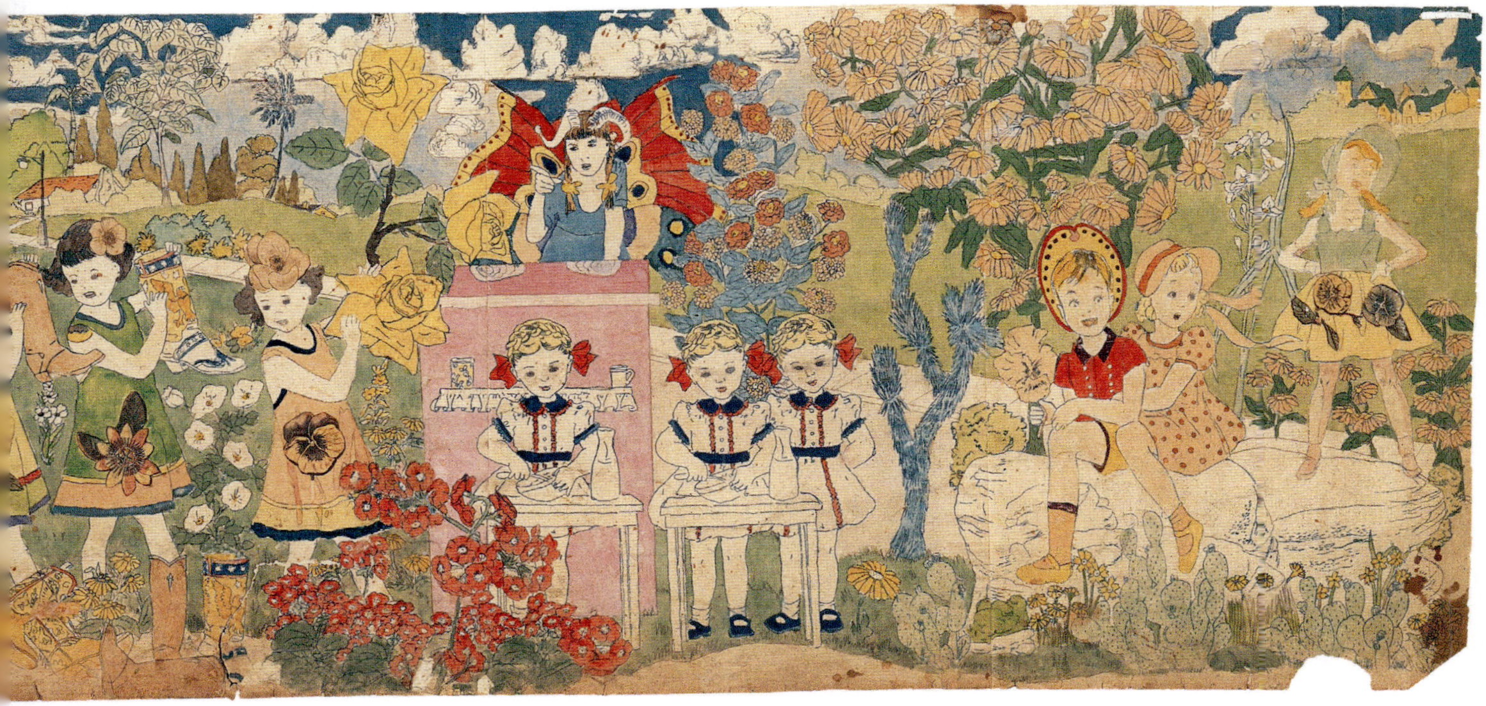

JAMES CASTLE

(1899, Garden Valley–1977, Boise, Idaho, USA)

James Castle began drawing at age six and dedicated almost seven decades exclusively to his art practice. His intense focus may have been provoked, in part, by his rather reclusive and solitary position. Castle was born deaf in a small mountain community in Idaho, and while he had limited schooling, he never learned to read, write, or sign. Dependent on his family, Castle began living with his sister after losing both of his parents by 1948. Working in solitude and meticulous about archiving his own work, he developed a profound body of work consisting of delicate drawings, handmade books, and constructions from a range of locally and domestically found materials. Around 1950, his work was heralded by his nephew Robert Beach, an art student in Portland, who began showing Castle's work to his college art professors. This exposure led to his first of many solo exhibitions beyond the university at Image Gallery, Portland (1962). Castle is now part of major museum collections and received his first comprehensive museum retrospective in 2008 at the Philadelphia Museum of Art.

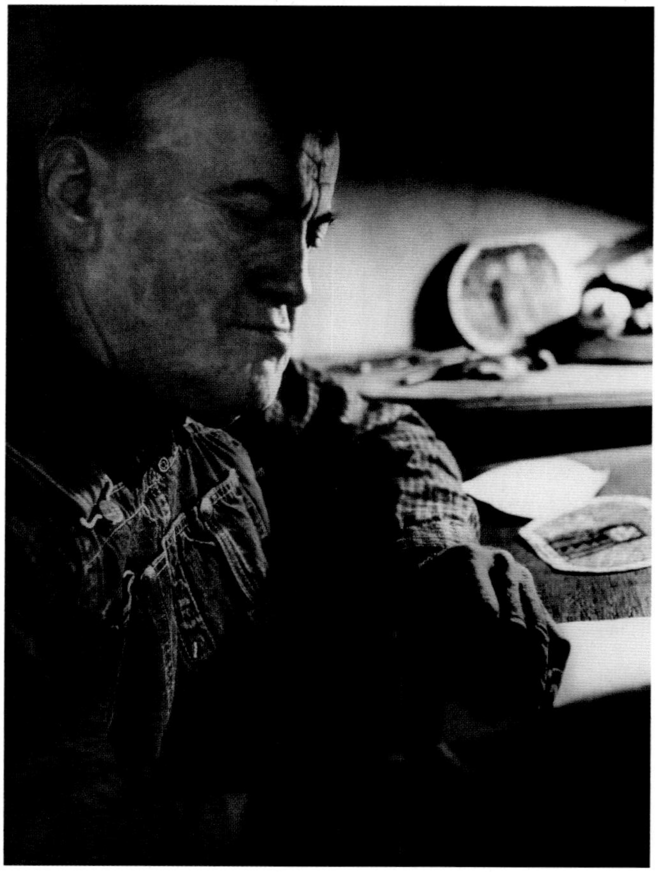

James Castle, ca. 1961, photograph. James Castle Collection and Archive. James Castle at his desk in Boise, Idaho.

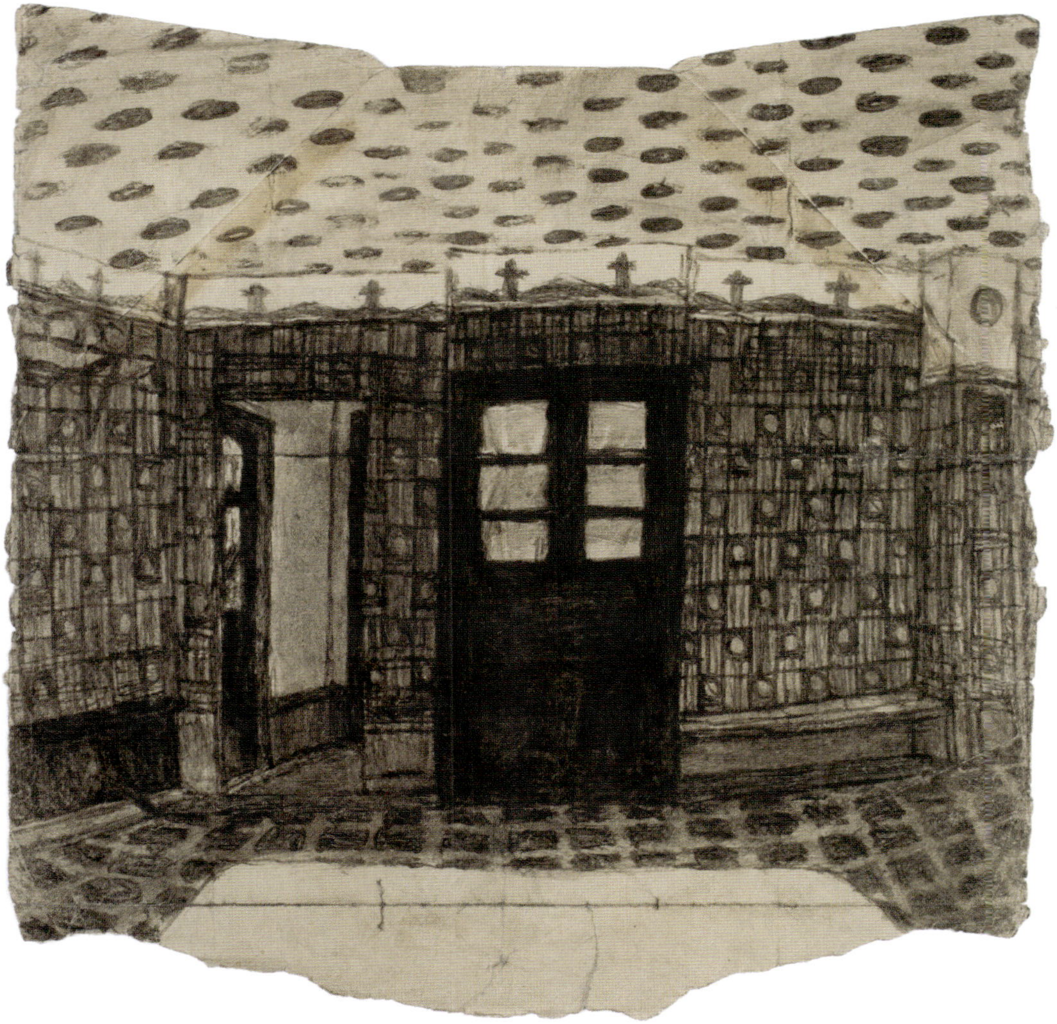

James Castle, untitled (interior with hutch), *n.d., found paper and soot, 9½ × 10½ in (24.1 × 26.7 cm). James Castle Collection and Archive.* This interior drawing by Castle demonstrates his penchant for representing interior spaces. His implementation of graphic pattern to demark the various dimensional planes creates a room that suggests it exists between real and unreal.

There are no interviews with James Castle, and he never recorded details about his creative process, thus limiting an artist-led discourse regarding his relationship with, and agency to, artmaking. Castle also didn't title or date any of his creations, thereby denying outsiders the opportunity to study the evolution of his practice. However, he was fastidious about preserving and storing his portfolio of works. He packed handcrafted cases for similarly sized drawings and constructed custom-sized boxes for other works. The archive boxes were wrapped with twine and stored safely in inconspicuous spots, from high up in the roof rafters to inside a chicken coop.

While Castle chose to work in privacy and solitude along with discreetly storing his work, it is necessary to note that he was neither keeping his practice nor his art a secret. On the contrary, Castle would present his drawings to family and visitors. Furthermore, Castle conveyed an understanding of his responsibility as an artist to investigate his surroundings on both a physical and subconscious level. His remarkably considered oeuvre strikes whimsy and tenderness.

The most prolific body of Castle's work is a series of drawings that are primarily executed by combining saliva with soot from a wood-burning stove. His drawn compositions seem the most dedicated to a recollection of his visual and mental environment.

The family ranch, local farmhouse, and native landscape appear as inferred and confirmed spaces: a signifier that his immediate surroundings were influential. His draftsman technique was fluid but deliberate, oscillating between an act of recording and aspirational proposals. Stylistically, Castle transposed from "real" to representational within a single work, morphing an object from a realistic depiction to simple geometry. His technique also included the insertion of abstract aura-like shapes among an otherwise representational landscape.

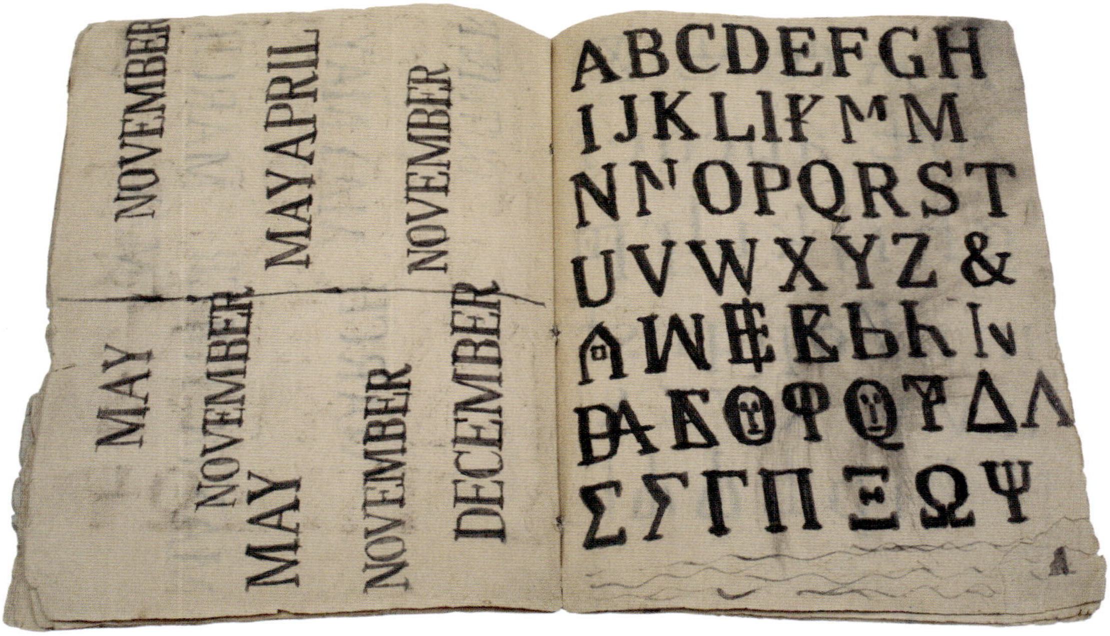

James Castle, untitled (BON-TON)*, n.d., 24 pp, found paper, soot, and string, 8½ × 6¾ in (21.6 × 17.2 cm). James Castle Collection and Archive.* Pages of Castle's books are composed with variations of his own language. A semiotic approach included a series of horizontal wavy lines—an inference to text. Other books, as seen here, present hieroglyphics amalgamated from Roman and Cyrillic alphabets, as well as Castle's own typographic inventions. These textual interpretations were accompanied by illustrations appropriated from magazines, products, and memory.

"Perhaps the most intriguing and puzzling thing about this work is its relation to contemporary art. It fits no current category. It is not naive nor primitive; it is not traditional or modern art; but it is certainly art."
– Jack McLarty, Director of Image Gallery speaking to press about Castle's 1962 exhibition, *A Voice of Silence: Drawings by James Castle*[23]

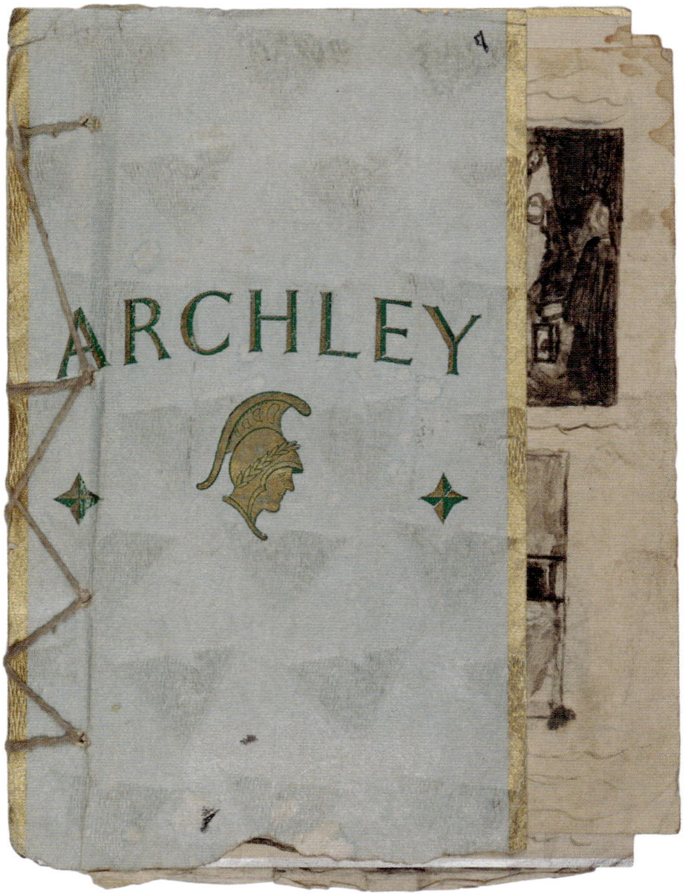

James Castle, untitled (ARCHLEY)*, n.d., 22 pp, found paper, soot, and string, 8¼ × 6⅜ in (21 × 16.2 cm). James Castle Collection and Archive.* Assembling books was a significant output for Castle. Though he was illiterate, his respectful process of production (meticulously crafted, stitched, and bound) and preservation thereafter, implies he understood the function and integrity of books.

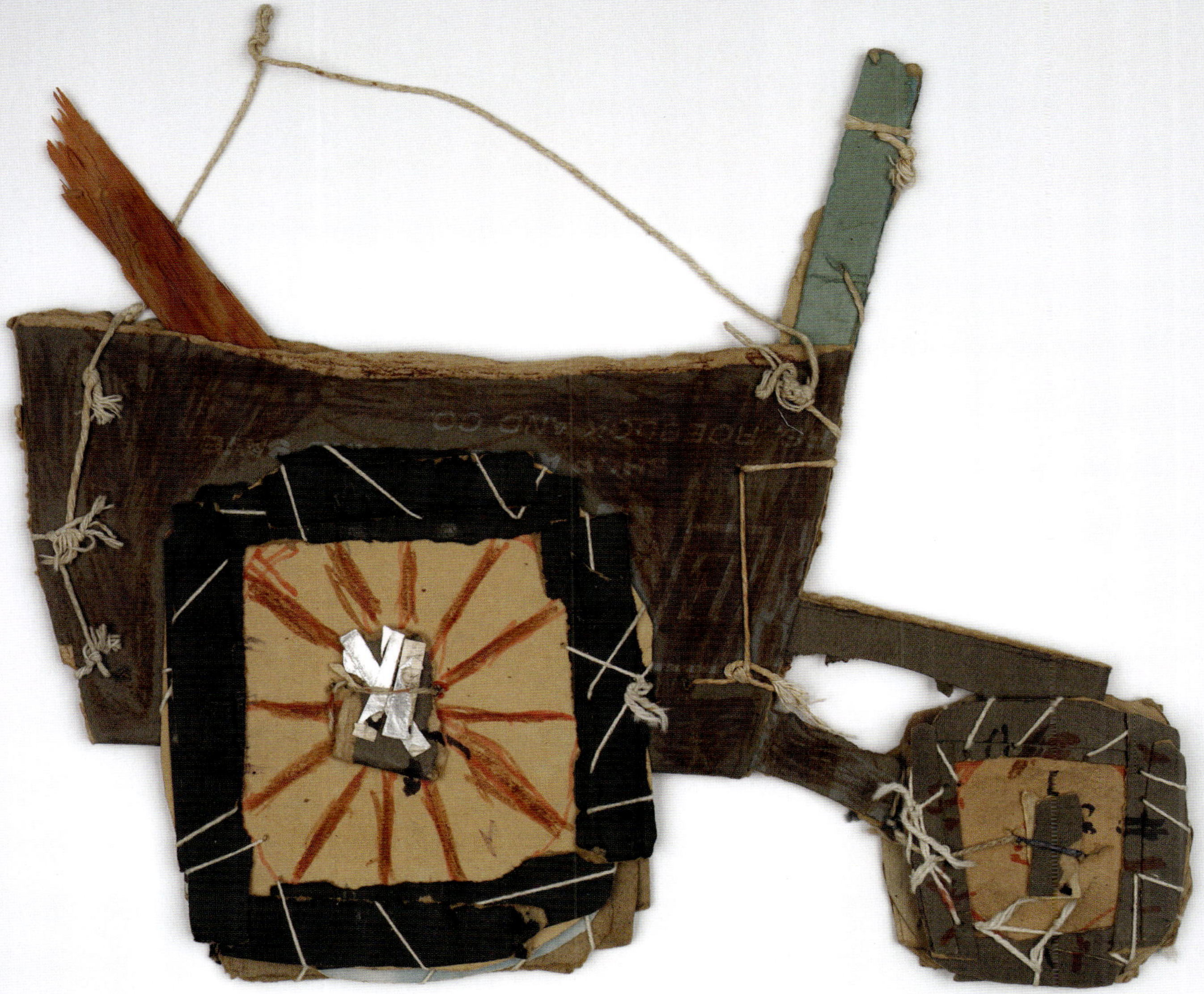

James Castle, untitled (wheelbarrow construction)*, n.d., found paper, color, and string, 14 × 18 in (35.6 × 45.7 cm). James Castle Collection and Archive.* Built from brochures, invoices, discarded envelopes, ice-cream cartons, even his siblings' homework, Castle's constructions, like this wheelbarrow, convey the diversity of found materials he used, adding external cultural reference points to the work.

CHARLES A.A. DELLSCHAU

(1830 Prussia–1923 Houston, Texas, USA)

The *Sonora Aero Club* was a mid-19th century secret society that invented state-of-the-art flying machines; such was the detailed narrative conceived by and illustrated by Charles A.A. Dellschau. Born in Prussia, he emigrated to America in 1849 and settled in Texas. In 1861, Dellschau married and started his own family, predestinately the following decades are marked by the tragic deaths of his family. Toward the end of the 1890s, he was living with his surviving widowed step-daughter and her children in Houston, where his reclusiveness was increasing. Around 1889, Dellschau began recording the story of the *Sonora Aero Club*, and in 1908 he commenced on his voluminous creative oeuvre of exquisitely drawn flying machines detailed with collage and calligraphic detail. At the age of 93, Dellschau passed away and his epic oeuvre, bound together into a series of large notebooks, were left unnoticed for generations. It was only in 1967 that an antique dealer recognized the large notebooks amid a garbage disposal site, after being discarded by the family 40 years after Dellschau's death.

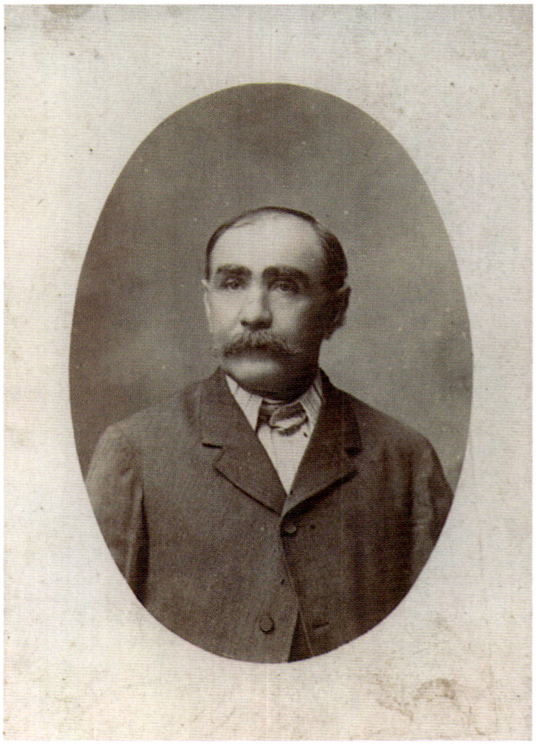

Charles A.A. Dellschau, ca. 1895, photograph. The Menil Collection, Houston. Segments of Dellschau's life are unaccounted for, but it is likely that prior to 1860 he spent time in California, which at the time was a draw for many in the gold rush era. Certainly, that would have served as inspiration for his California-set narrative of the *Sonora Aero Club*.

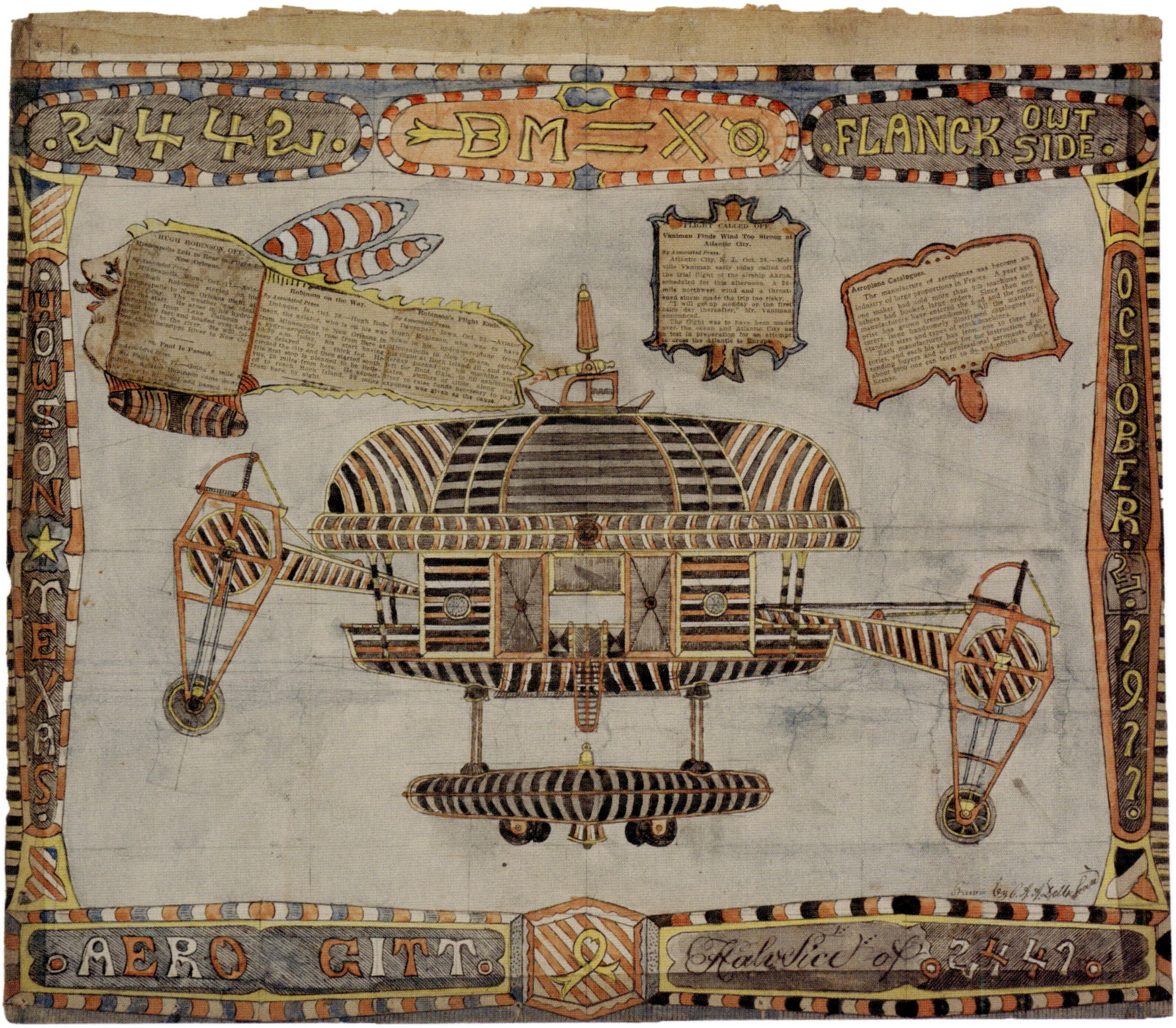

Charles A.A Dellschau, Aero Gitt, Flank Outside, *October 27, 1911, watercolor, gouache, graphite, and ink with newspaper on paper, 15¾ × 19⅛ in (40 × 48.6 cm). The Menil Collection, Houston.* With his flying machine, AERO GITT central, Dellschau included three current event collages, or "press blooms" above. The news items captured here are related to flight, including an article on "Aeroplane Catalogues" and a hydro-aeroplane in Iowa.

Arriving at the Port of Galveston from Europe, Charles A.A. Dellschau likely spent some time in California before settling back in Texas, where he worked as a butcher and started a family. Between 1877 and 1893, Dellschau tragically encountered the death of both his first and second wife, and three of his children. In 1893, Dellschau moved to Houston with his widowed step-daughter, Elizabeth Stelzig. He spent the next 30 years in the family home until his death. It was here, in the solitude of a private room, that he chronicled the accounts of the *Sonora Aero Club* and the illustrated volumes of the club's invented flying machines (referred to as *aeros*). Written as three memoirs, Dellschau started the narrative of the *Sonora Aero Club* around retirement in 1898. These initial texts addressed the purported inner workings of the club and Dellschau's participation within. They were comprised of key analysis of the secret society inclusive of member profiles: designers, engineers, builders; diagrams and descriptions of specific *aeros*; and their formula for *Supe*, the clandestine gas that set the flying machines afloat. Subsequently, his multimedia collaged pictorials were made between 1908 and 1921. With the concept of *aeros* central, these were double-sided and bound by shoestrings into large notebooks. Focusing on the various flying models, the polychromatic renderings featured a distinct ribboning of lines acting as borders to multiple elements of each composition. Calligraphic details were written in English,

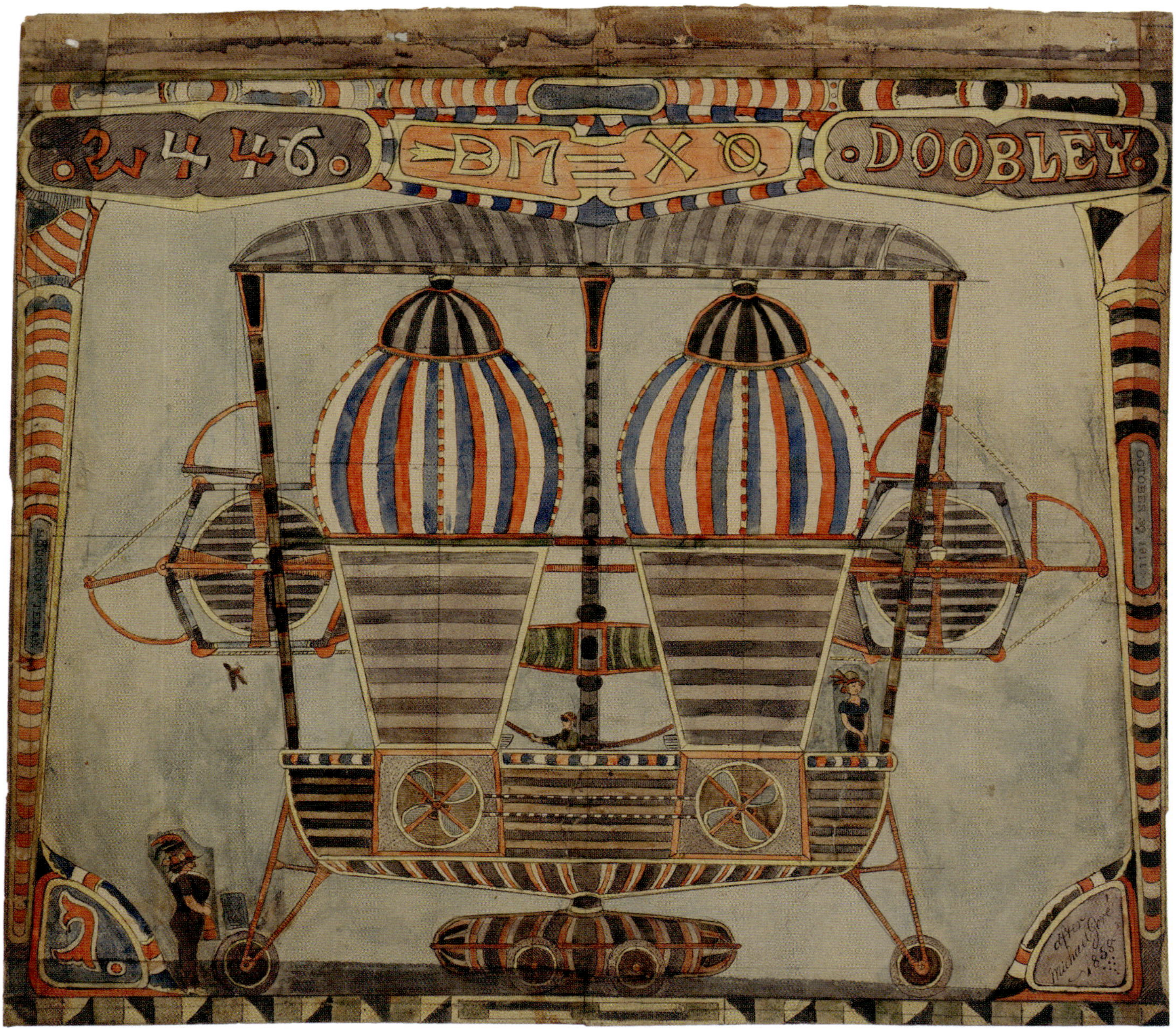

Charles A.A. Dellschau, Doobley, *October 30, 1911, watercolor, gouache, graphite, and ink on paper, 16½ × 19 in (41.9 × 48.3 cm). The Menil Collection, Houston. Doobley* uses the principles of symmetry in both the construction of the machine and overall composition. The ribboning motif used, serves as both an ornamental framing device, but also fits within structural components of the Doobley.

Prussian, and arcane code. Dellschau also often inserted press clippings/current events that he called "Press Blooms" as a contextual layer.

After second-hand dealer Fred Washington found Dellschau's notebooks, which the Stelzig family had discarded, he showed them to art history student, Mary Jane Victor, in 1968. Encouraged by Washington, she showed them to Texan benefactor and art patron Mrs. de Menil, who acquired four of the notebooks. In 1969, Peter Navarro viewed Dellschau's notebooks as part of the exhibition *The Sky is the Limit*, University of St Thomas. Navarro went on to acquire the remaining eight books and his pursuits commenced the research into a more complete understanding of the oeuvre of Dellschau. Into the 21st century, Dellschau's collaged drawings are in many significant private and institutional collections.

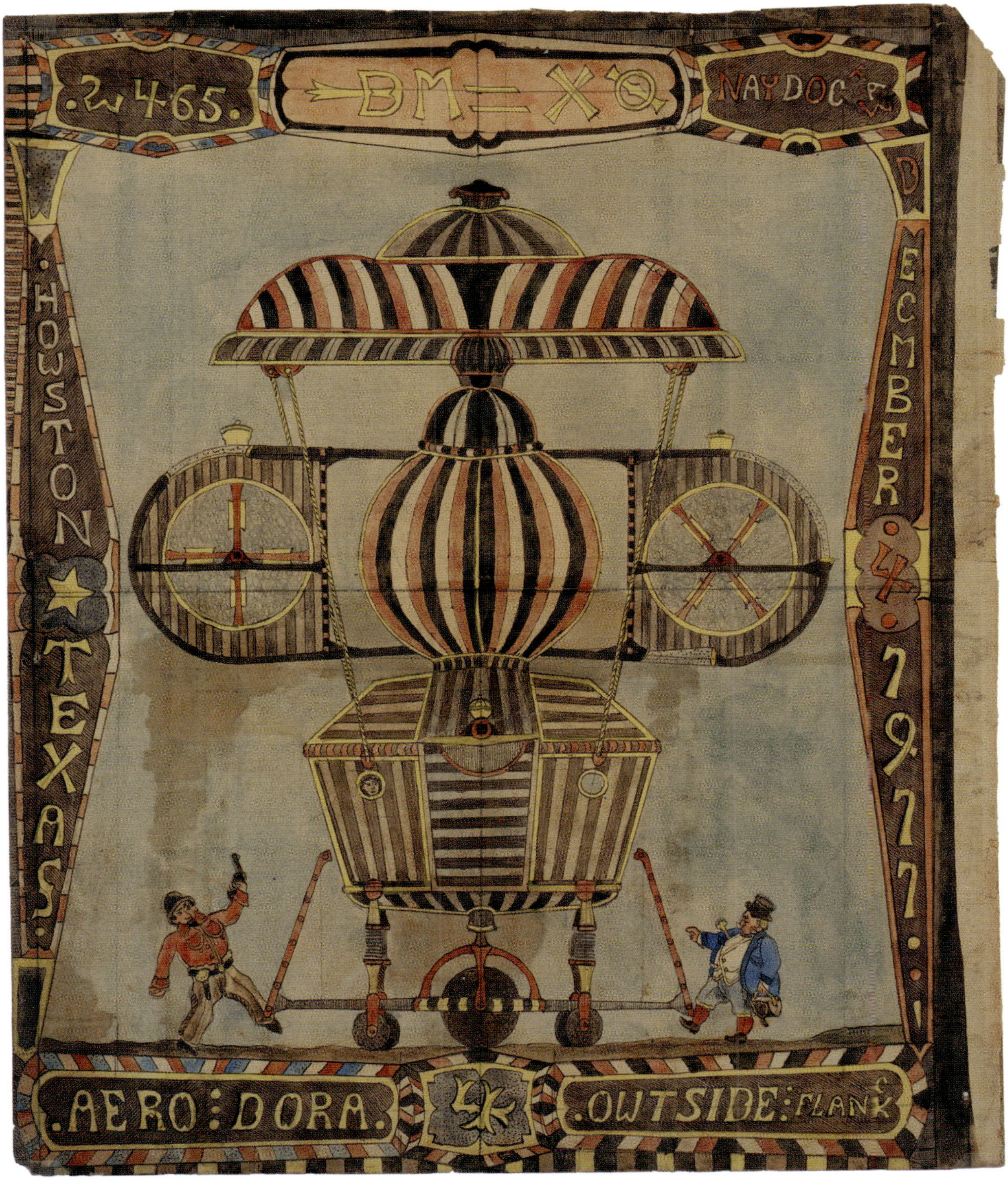

Charles A.A Dellschau, Aero: Dora 4. Outside: Flanck, *December 4, 1911, watercolor, gouache, graphite, and ink on paper, 19¼ × 16½ in (48.9 × 41.9 cm). The Menil Collection, Houston.* One of the bespoke machines of the *Sonora Aero Club*. Dellschau's oeuvre documenting specific flying machines often state the time and place, in this work stating "HOWSTON TEXAS" and "DECEMBER 4 1911," but it also includes more cryptic or foreign writing such as "NAYDOCTAW" in the upper right.

"Who was Peter Mennis? A California Miner, a German up in the fourthies, a plain yes a rough Man, whit as kind a hearth as to be found in verry few living beengs. a genius in getting Up useful contrivances, but adicted to strong drink, and for ever out of Means, "Flat brocke" as the wordgoes. Now to astonnish his Friends and Neighbours he was tinkering for some time on some contraption, borrowing nails, Screws, Wire and other articles to fix his Airostant Goose," – Dellschau describing Sonora Aero Club protagonist, Peter Mennis[24]

MELVIN WAY

(b. 1954, Ruffin, South Carolina, USA)

Melvin Way's personal account of his life fluidly superimposes himself throughout the past, present, and future. His experiences inform his evocative and complex drawings of equations and diagrams. Way was born in South Carolina and raised primarily in Brooklyn by extended family. Perpetual interest in science and music led Way, as a teenager, to study for a technical degree and play multiple instruments. However, by the mid-1970s, his mental and environmental stability deteriorated, and he eventually encountered homelessness. While staying at a shelter in 1989, Way disclosed to an artist, Andrew Castrucci, the intimate diagrammatic drawings that he had been producing in private. Castrucci was leading art workshops by Hospital Audience Inc. (H.A.I.). Both H.A.I. and Castrucci emerged as long-term affiliates for Way. Since the mid-2000s, Way's cryptogrammatic drawings that richochet between art and science are receiving international recognition and are now represented in the collections of the Smithsonian American Art Museum, Washington, D.C., and the Museum of Modern Art, New York.

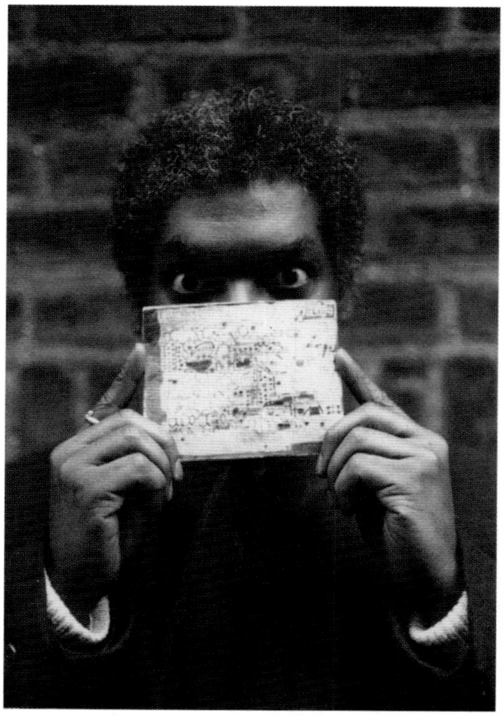

Melvin Way, early 1990s, photograph by Andrew Castrucci (American, b. 1961). Way first disclosed his drawings to Castrucci when the latter was leading reintegration creative workshops for the homeless on Wards Island, an area of New York that was defined by drugs and violence in the 1980s.

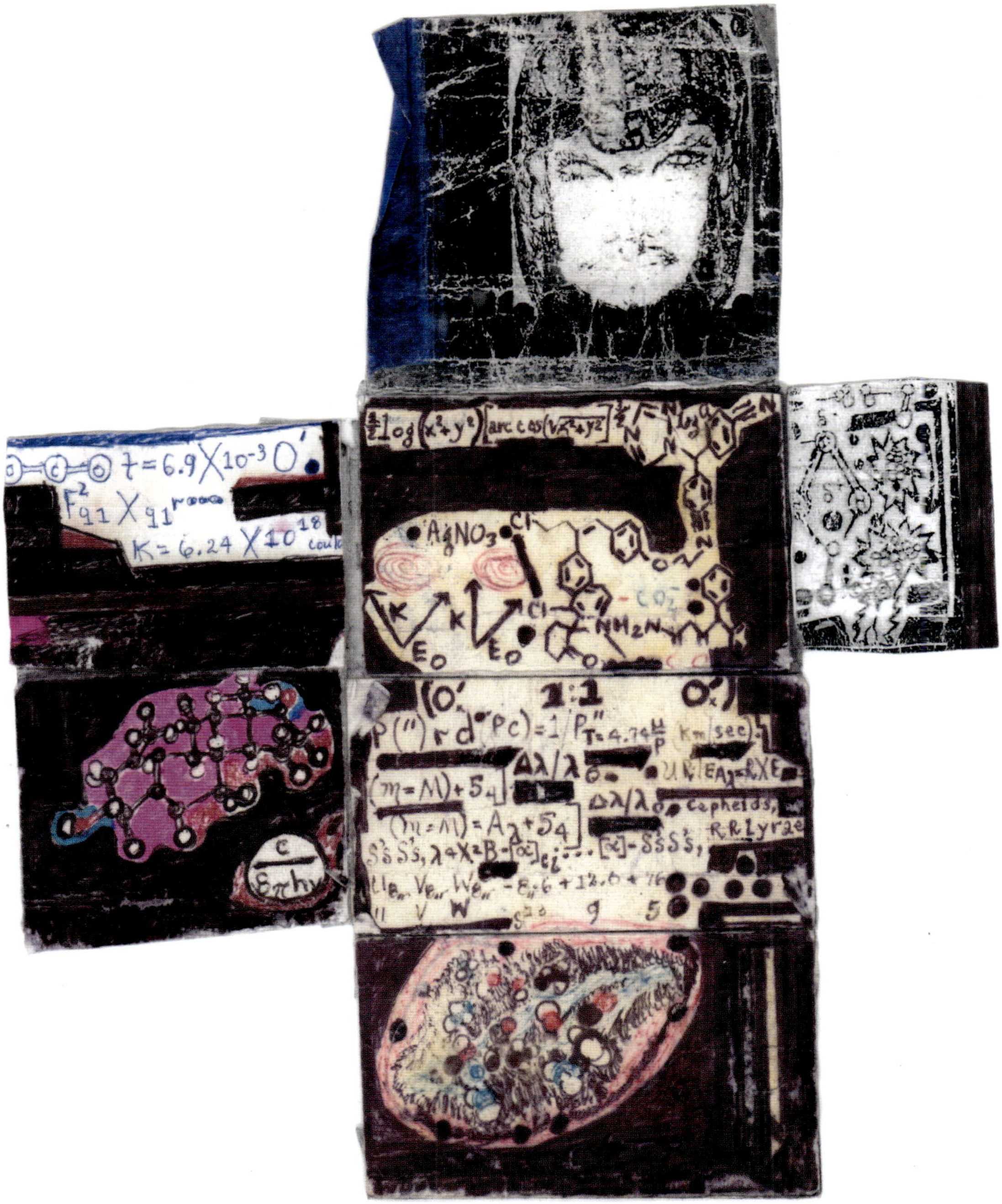

Melvin Way, AgN03, 2015, ballpoint pen on paper with Scotch tape, 8½ × 7 in (21.6 × 17.8 cm). Courtesy the Artist and Bullet Space. This collaged drawing shows Way's process of taping together various pieces of paper to form a single composition. The creasing and wear of the drawing is inherent to his practice, which often involved carrying the works folded up in his pocket for periods of time.

The framework in which Melvin Way defines himself is integral to his artistic output. Understanding the powerful and transposable position Way places on himself leads to a more considered entry point to his work. In a particular scenario, Way is a trinity of three variants of famous names: Vandeprint (American businessman, Cornelius Vanderbilt), Abulwefer (Persian mathematician and astronomer, Abu al-Wafa' Buzjani), and Dracula. Informed by his superimpositions and elastic understanding of time, Way refers to having been several United States presidents and playing multiple instruments for the band Funkadelic on a single stage.[25]

Way's drawn constructions, often interpreted as talismans, can take from weeks to a year to complete. His intuitive practice emerged through the use of materials that could be sourced within Way's previously limiting circumstance of homelessness. As a result, most of his drawings, especially early works, are on small pieces of

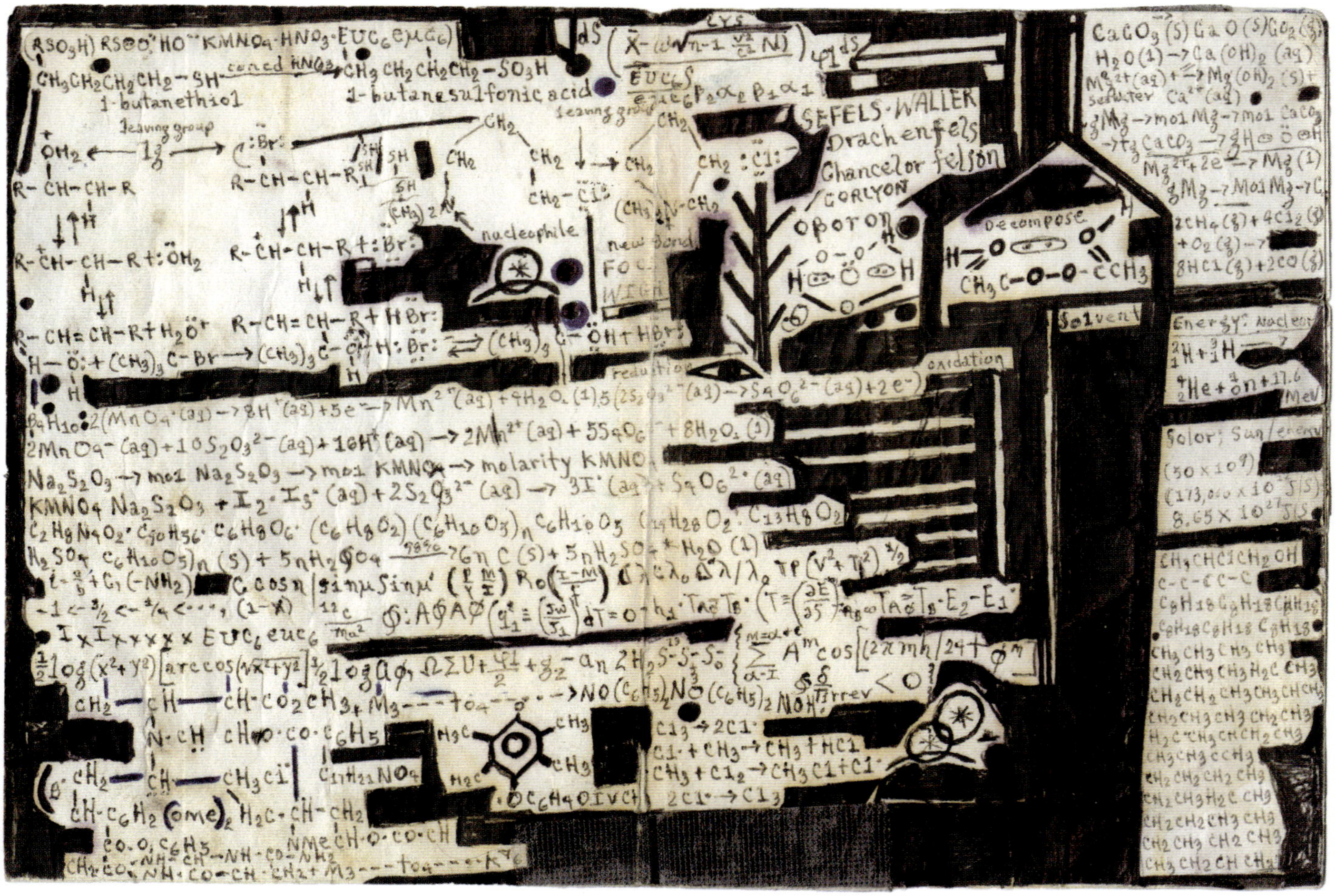

Melvin Way, Pluton, *2003–2004, ballpoint pen on paper, 6 × 9 in (15.2 × 22.9 cm). Courtesy the Artist and Bullet Space.* The word "decompose" is written within a house-like structure with a chemical compound below, near the upper right of this drawing. Way's use of dark lines emotes an aesthetic akin to puzzles and mazes. With chemical equations filling the voids, his graphic ink lines also depict an eye and tree branch.

paper, such as discarded stationery and found scraps. Way keeps initiated works folded up in his pocket or stored between pages of a book, a habit relational to circumstance that allows a continuous evolvement of his drawing process. His profound and often intimate work is also concise with materials, often scribed in blue and black ballpoint pen then covered and sealed with translucent tape.

Way's metaphysical compositions are comprised of words, equations, and chemical compounds, perhaps presenting solutions via a merged language from his inspired disciplines. The words range from cryptic phrases and invented portmanteaus to specific signifiers like "innerdirected." His mathematical equations enter the realms of calligraphy and musical scores. His chemical and molecular compounds become the visual graphic design, giving his works movement and a maze-like quality, suggesting Way's understanding of the flexibility between the dimensions of time and space. Way's works deal in transcendent alchemy, through figurative, literal, and compositional density.

"Dots, dashes, parentheses, letters, or ellipses turn out to be his aesthetic version of deep sequencing, and add up to someone exploring the spaces between what is known and unknown, imagined, wished for, impossible, and written in visual language." – Jerry Saltz, art critic[26]

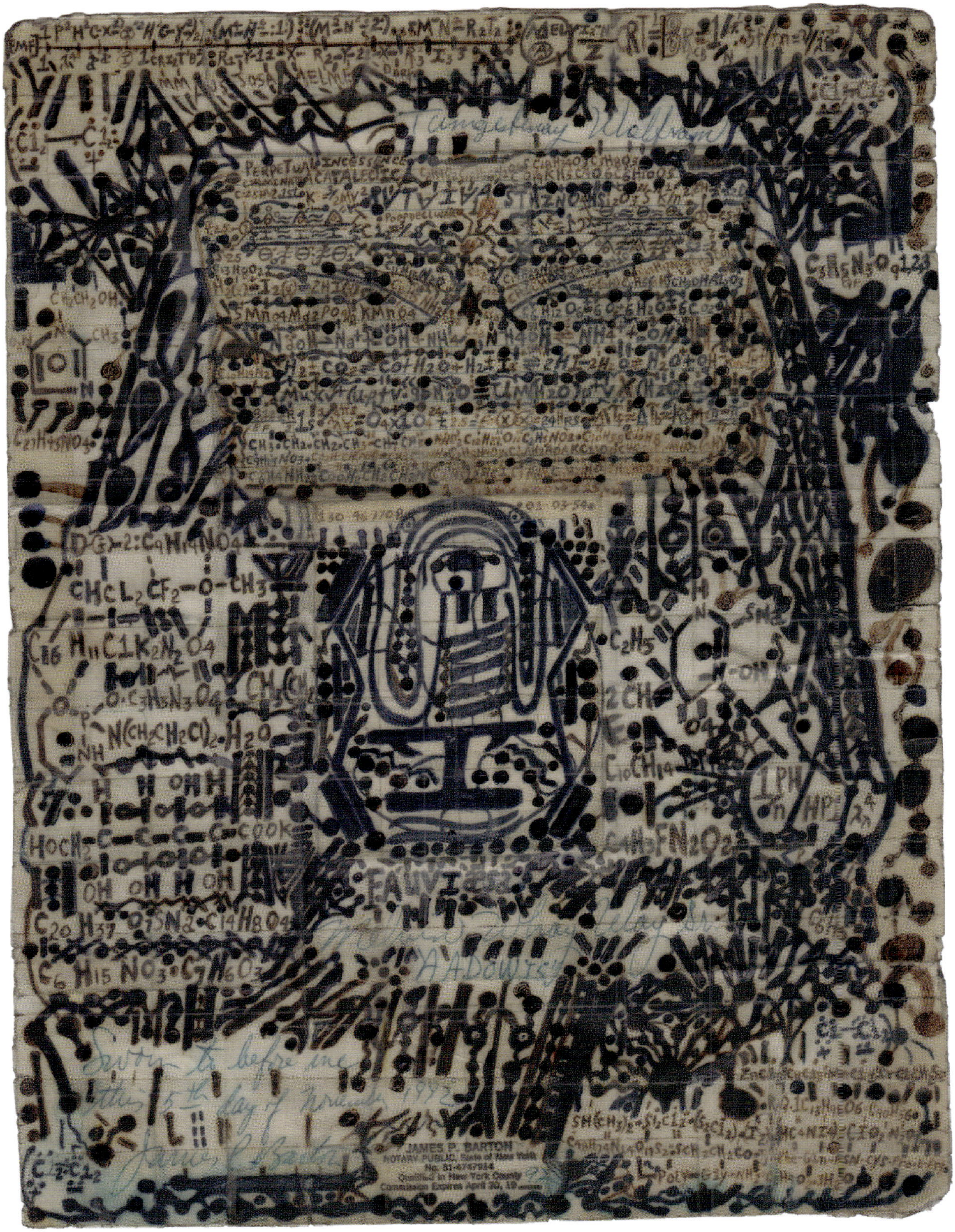

Melvin Way, untitled, *1989–1992, ballpoint pen on paper with Scotch tape, 10⅞ × 8⅜ in (27.6 × 21.3 cm). Courtesy the Artist and Bullet Space.* This semi-symmetrical drawing on reused paper from a New York public notary demonstrates Way's complex combinations of information. Written and diagrammed chemical compounds along with more graphic elements form the overall composition, but snippets of language are also featured, including "Melvin Whay Way Sr" to the more cryptic "PERPETUAL INCESSENCE."

"I'm 58 at this time, but next year I'll be about 470."
– Melvin Way[27]

GUO FENGYI

(1942–2010, Xi'an, Shaanxi Province, China)

After working at a chemical fertilizer plant in Xi'an for 18 years, Guo Fengyi took early retirement at the age of 39 due to acute rheumatoid arthritis. She began to practice the traditional Chinese martial art of Qigong to improve her declining health. Qigong combines physical movements with meditation and as Fengyi refined this practice, strong visuals emerged during her meditations. In 1989, she began an intuitively led drawing process to reveal her universal visions. Privately over the next two decades, Fengyi developed an interwoven creative and spiritual practice of emotionally intricate ink-drawing. Her subject matter consisted of diagrammatic references to ancient culture and definitive but enigmatic portraits. Curator Lu Jie became aware of her practice and included Fengyi as part of the 2002 *Long March Project: A Walking Visual Display* in Lijiang, China. Fengyi continued to produce her transcendent drawings full of concentric lines and circles until her death, aged 86. Despite her unsettled position as a self-taught female artist within the scope of Chinese contemporary art, in 2010 she received the first of many international accolades with her inclusion in the 8th Gwangju Biennale in South Korea.

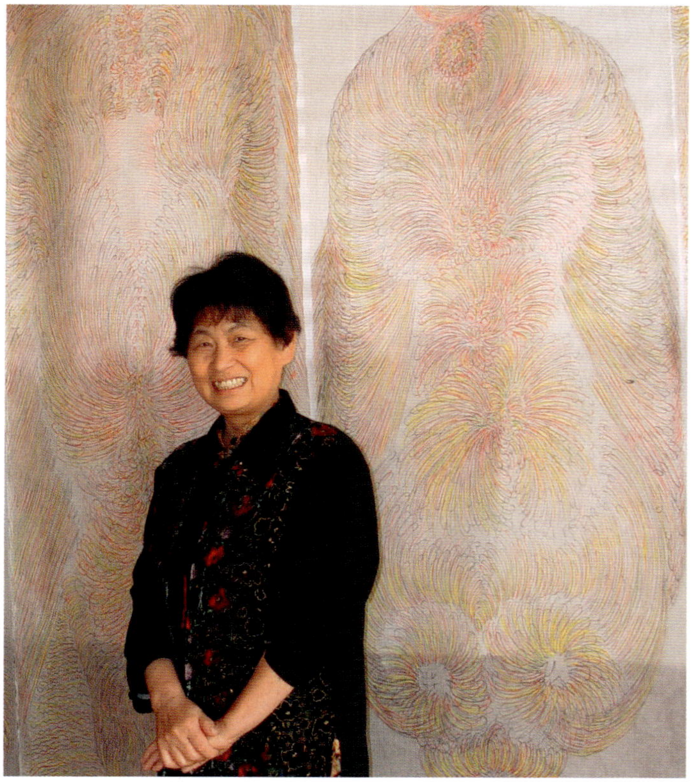

Guo Fengyi, n.d., photograph. Long March Space. The practice of Qigong combining movement and meditation was, for Fengyi, a quest for physical healing and spiritual alignment. Qigong is to be practiced at specific times to absorb the correct amount of Qi. Her ink drawings are consistently labeled with time and date of commencement and completion, aligning with this concept of cosmic rhythm and order of time.

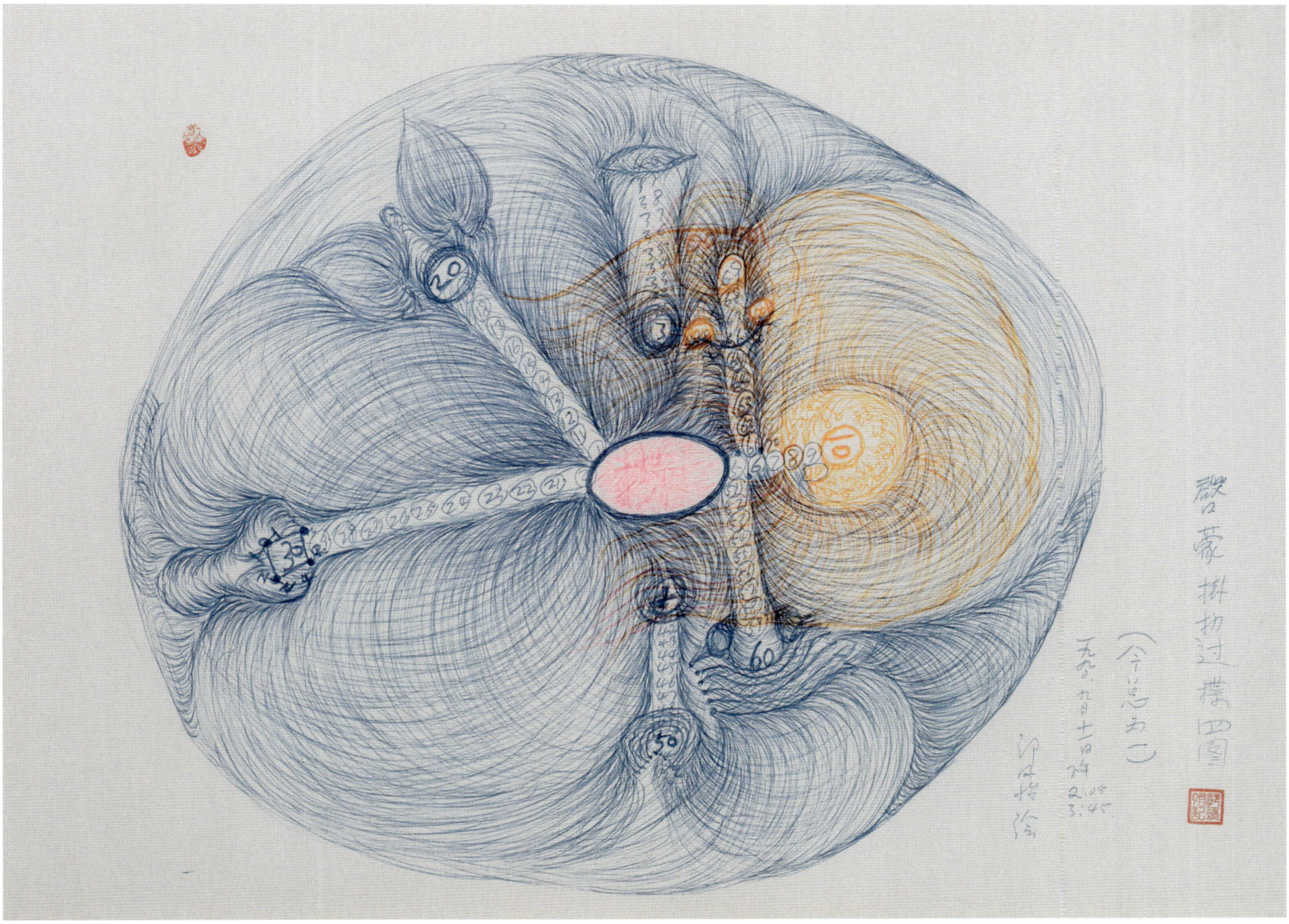

Guo Fengyi, Four Diagrams of the Divination Procedures in Zhu Xi's The Basics of I Ching, *1990, colored ink on rice paper, 48 × 35 1/16 in (122 × 89 cm). Long March Space.* With the ancient divination text, *Book of Changes (I Ching)*, influential to her creative practice, in this early drawing Fengyi examined the text in relation to neo-Confucian philosopher Zhu Xi (1130–1200).

When Guo Fengyi first witnessed bold colors, shapes, and figures while meditating, she began a journal to describe these visions. Her first journal entry was on March 12, 1989, describing an apparition of a yellow Buddha. Later that year, drawn figures materialized within Fengyi's written accounts, leading her to execute meditative drawings beyond the journal. Considered meditation, not art, her frequent early drawings were on the backs of calendars or other repurposed materials.

One of Fengyi's earliest self-contained drawings was of the Bermuda Triangle. Subject matter for her drawings also included the Eiffel Tower and the Statue of Liberty, demonstrating Fengyi's interest in evaluating the energy of unattainable international sites. This interest introduces a compelling duality in Fengyi's work: whereas her drawings were indisputably led by visions, she still maintained a level of agency over the subject matter. Binary influences were also evident in Fengyi's diagrammatic content, which was informed by both meditation and research, including her studies of the *Book of Changes* (*I Ching*), an ancient Chinese divination text.

Often composed on rice paper up to 30 ft (9 m) in length, the long vertical quality of the scrolls gives her figurative drawings cosmic weightlessness and an atmospheric element. The esoteric figurative works by Fengyi exemplify her ability to represent and alter the aura of her subjects—from a god to a politician, her characters fluctuate between spirit, humanoid, animal, and plant.

In a private metaphysical state, Fengyi produced over 500 drawings between 1989 and her death in 2010. They all have detailed calligraphic similarities and are distinguishable by their radiating concentric lines, created with ink. The process and outcome of Fengyi's drawings helped her understand what she did not know. Qigong and drawing substantiated Fengyi's quest for development and understanding of the boundaries and limitlessness between the physical and spiritual realm.

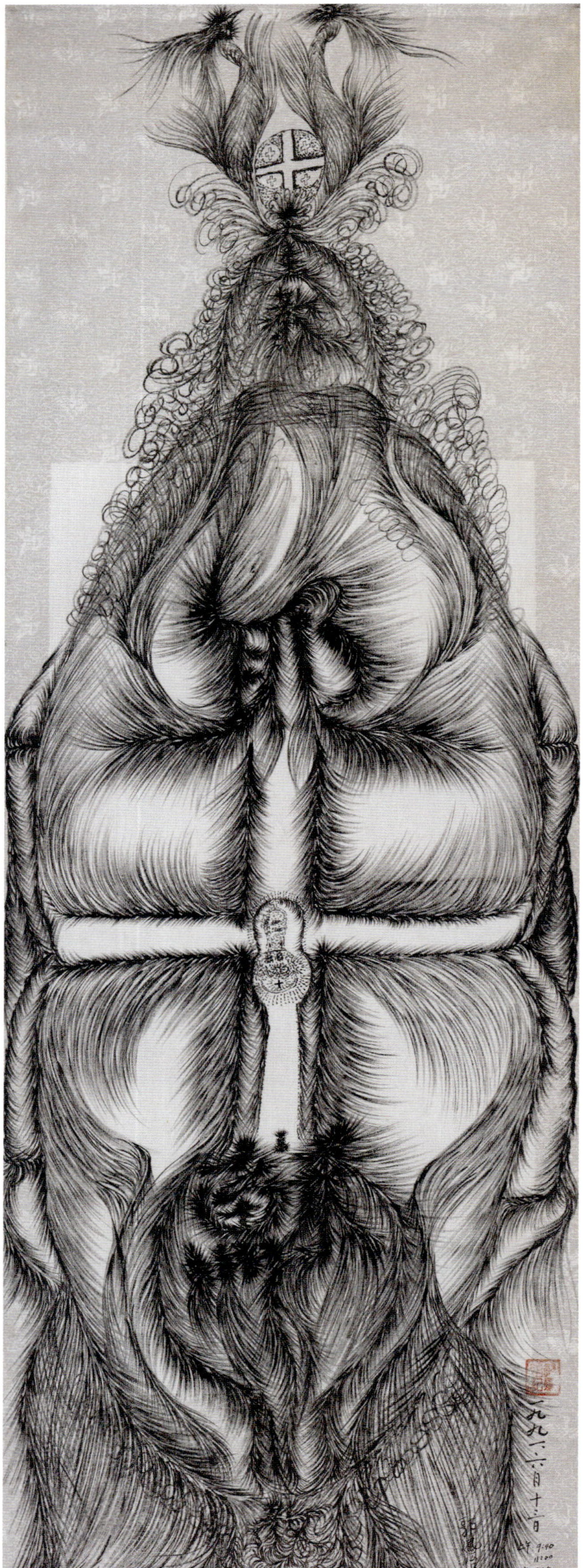

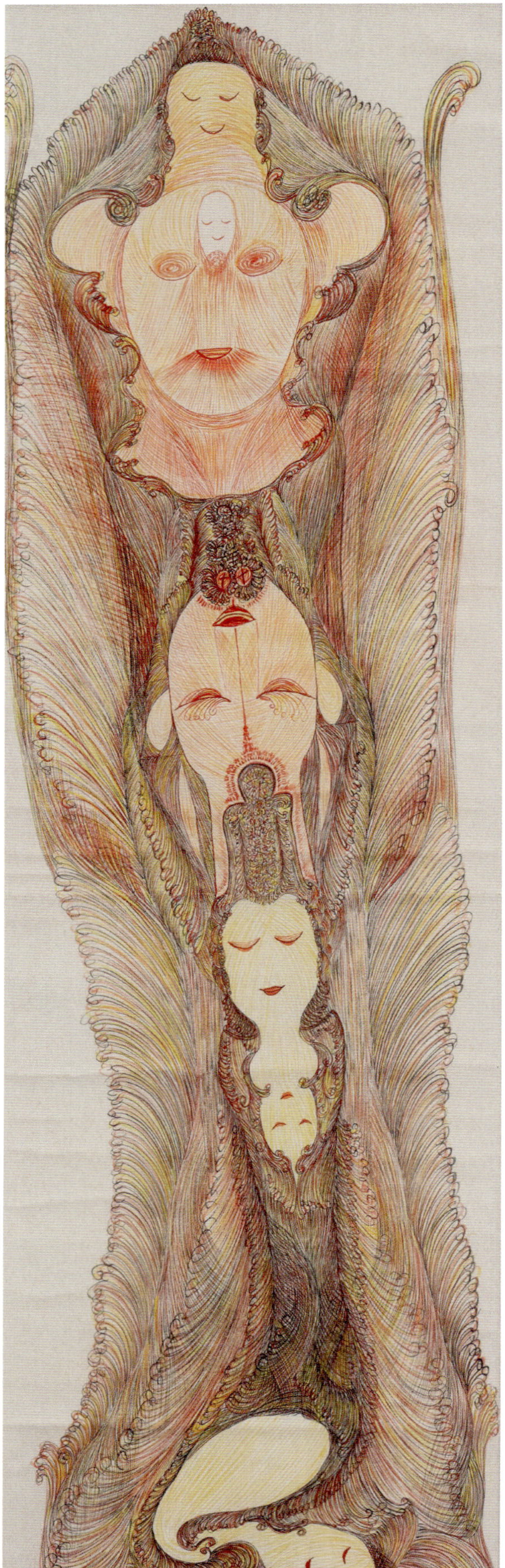

"I'm different from you guys . . . you people paint after you understood, and yet, I understand only after I paint."
– Guo Fengyi speaking to contemporary Chinese artist Xu Tan[28]

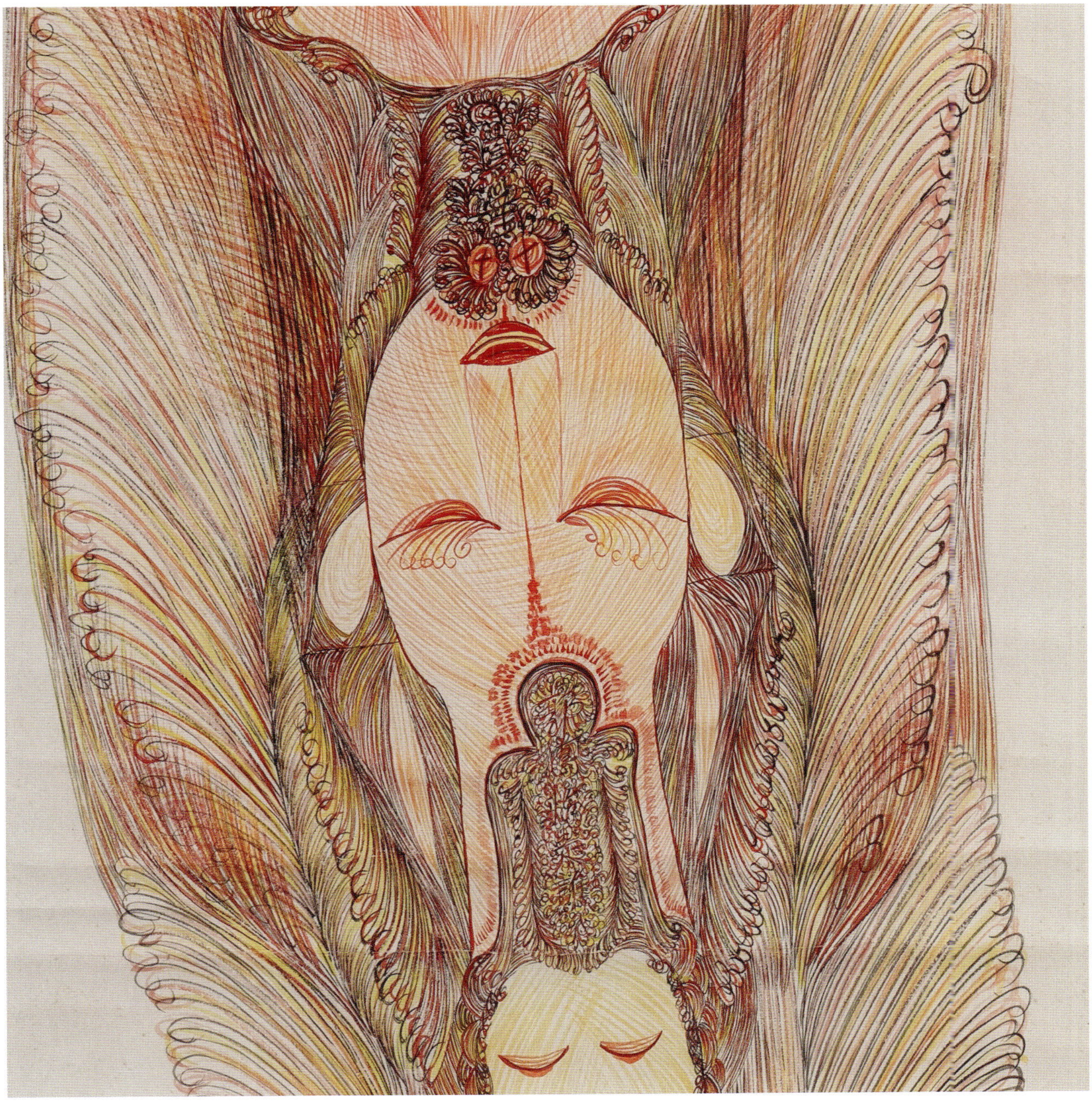

Guo Fengyi, Jesus, *1991, ink on cloth, original hanging scroll, $64\frac{15}{16} \times 22\frac{3}{8}$ in (165 × 56.8 cm). Long March Space.* Exploring spirituality via different religions, this drawing examines the Christian figure, Jesus. Fengyi's ink markings here appear more textured, like hair or fur, then concentric. The representation of a cross is central to the composition, and the cross motif is repeated within smaller details at both the top and bottom.

Guo Fengyi, Who is Guo Fengyi, *1993, ink on cloth, original hanging scroll, $60\frac{5}{8} \times 16\frac{15}{16}$ in (154 × 43 cm). Long March Space.* Totemic and atmospheric, Fengyi's self-reflective title presents her own inquiries explored through her spiritually led practice. The vertical scroll features serene faces, most with obvious smiles, both upright and inverted, and merging together. Concentric lines radiate from the various figures creating the sense of a single being.

EMERY BLAGDON

(1907–1986 Callaway, Nebraska, USA)

Emery Blagdon spent nearly three decades intimately and ardently focused on his endeavor to channel healing energy. Through this personal quest of implementing the power of electricity, alchemy, and the Earth, he created the Healing Machine—an intensely compelling installation of more than 500 components. Housed in a shed on his property, it was a cacophony of intricate sculptures, electric wiring, lighting components, and strategically arranged paintings, all with the intention of alleviating the pain of those who entered. Born the oldest of six children to a family of farmers, young Blagdon was considered sensitive, imaginative, but noted for his lack of interest in pursuing education or farming. He traveled the American West for a number of years but returned home to Callaway in around 1935 due to his mother's terminal illness. Witnessing her suffering and death, followed by that of his father in 1951, had a profound effect on Blagdon. Until his own death in 1986, he was focused on expanding, calibrating, and developing the curative potential of channeling the Earth's energy into the Healing Machine.

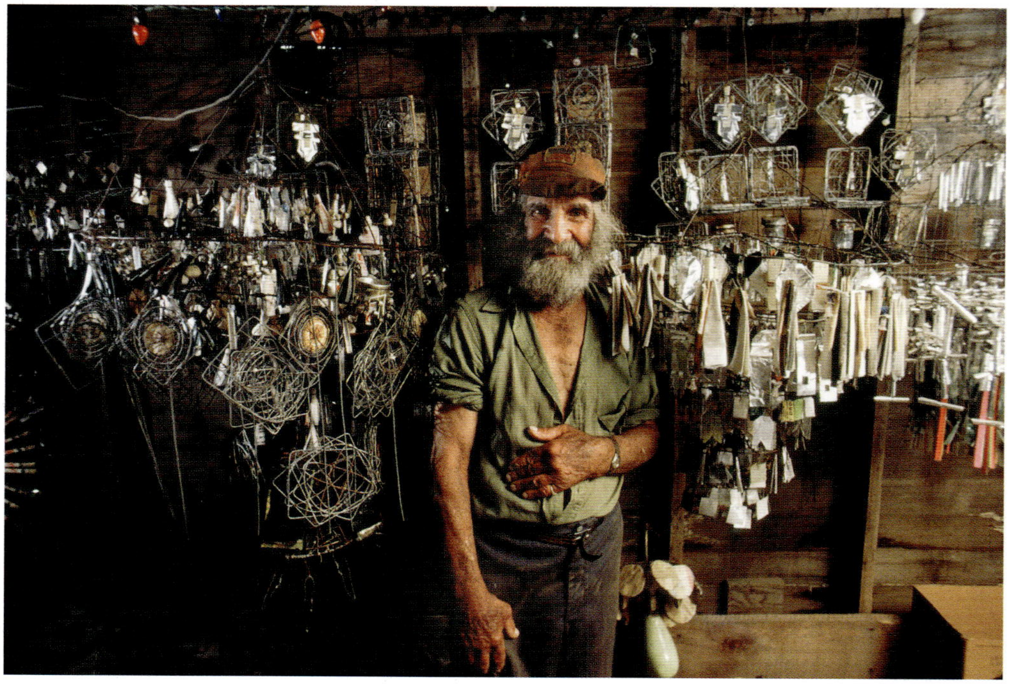

Emery Blagdon, 1979, photograph by Richard Greenhill. Blagdon is pictured here, surrounded by elaborate components of his Healing Machine. The chandelier-like compositions featured on his left and right demonstrate his inclination toward symmetry and visual balance.

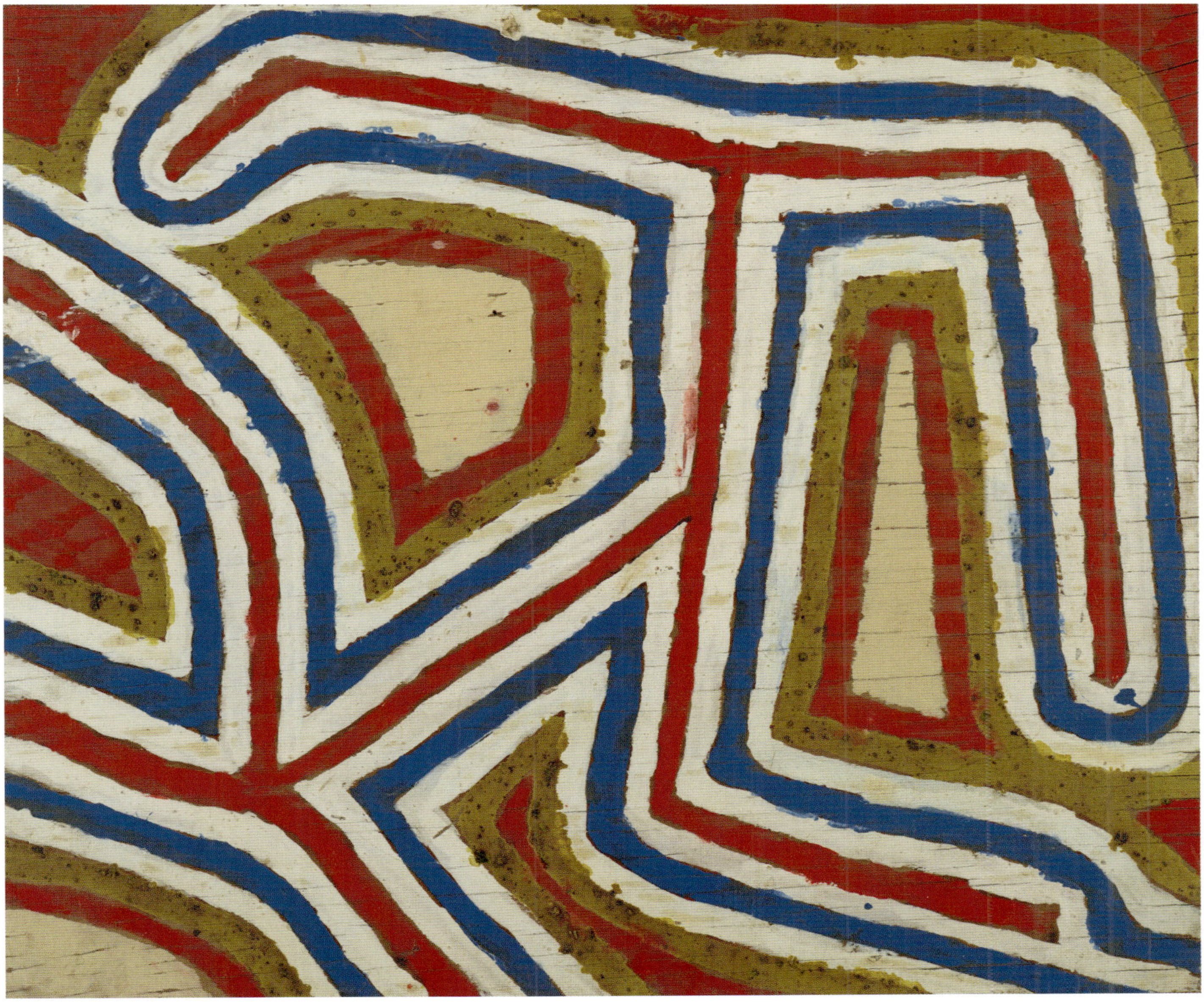

Emery Blagdon, untitled, *1955–1986, acrylic on wood, 13⅛ × 15¾ in (33.3 × 40 cm). Philadelphia Museum of Art.* Archetypal of Blagdon's paintings, this geometrically abstract composition on wood features energetic mazelike concentric lines of red, white, blue, and brown.

Observing the immense pain and distress of both of his parents dying of cancer, and his own suffering from arthritis, set forth for Emery Blagdon a heightened interest in pain mitigation and the concept of healing. He began constructing metal sculptures in the 1950s. Referred to as "pretties," they were small constructions combining materials such as copper, foil, wire, and jars that developed elaborately in scale, composition, and materials. Blagdon's interest in the remedial potential of electricity and magnetic fields continued and he progressed to making the sculptures active as conductors to harness energy.

At the start of the 20th century, the practice of electropathy (the implementation of high-frequency currents to alleviate various ailments) was popular in America and likely contributed to Blagdon's interests/concerns. Further to this, mid-century Americans were propagating an enthusiasm for electricity's varying potential in improving the quality (or ease) of life. Blagdon was also likely informed by the 1962 textbook given to him by a Callaway schoolteacher, *Matter and Energy: A Survey of Physical Sciences*. His practice seemed to converge electricity, the Earth's energy, and divination (not as an organized religion, but as an unknown/untapped power). In the 1960s Blagdon conceptualized a central space to hold and harness his experiments of healing. His personal understanding of healing and his relationship to energy was also intensifying;

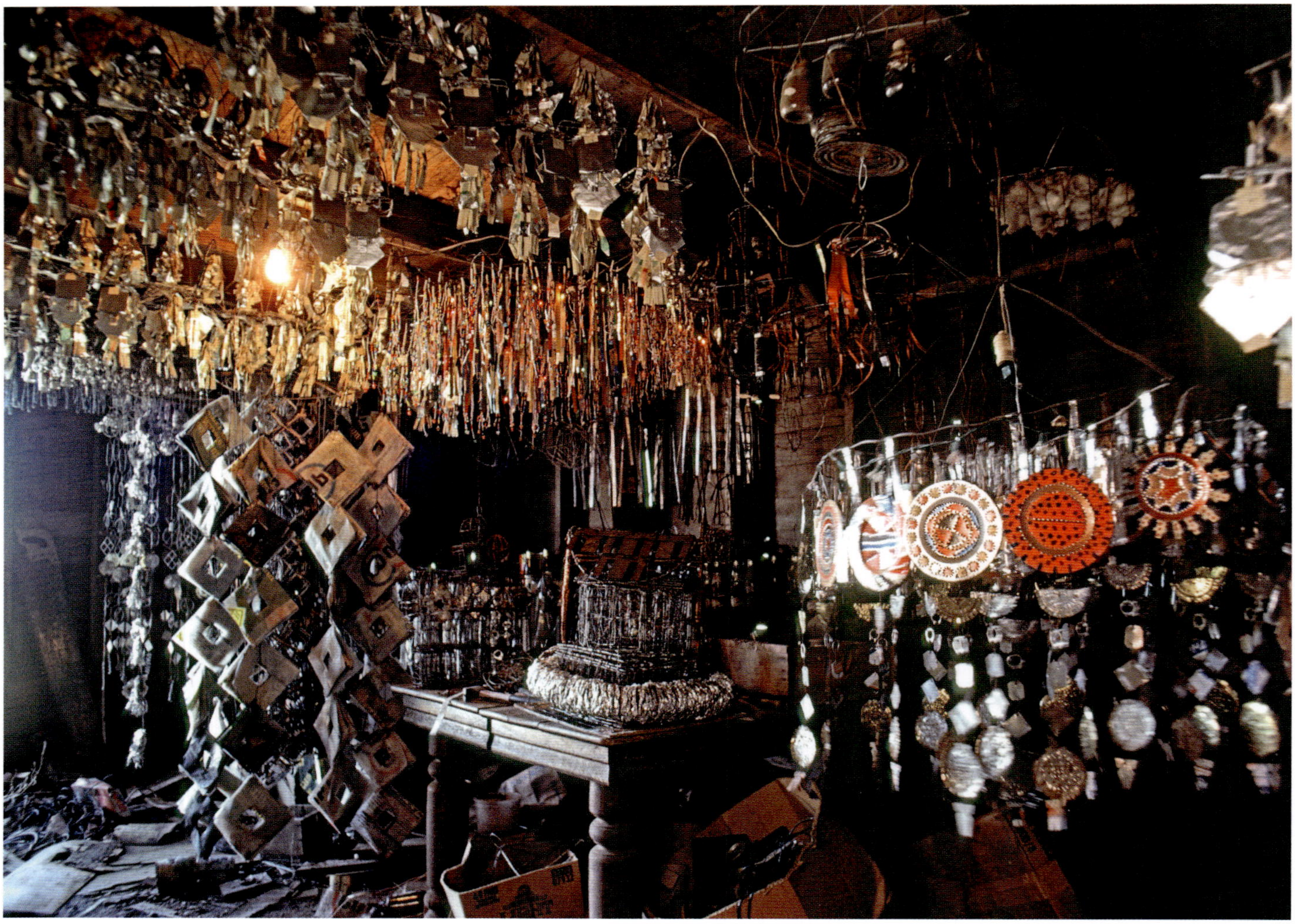

Emery Blagdon, 1979, photograph by Richard Greenhill. This view shows the intricacy and all-encompassing nature of Blagdon's Healing Machine. He was dedicated to continually developing the machine's potential for harnessing healing power, and cardboard boxes of electric components and other debris demonstrate the space as an ongoing experiment.

documented in his decision to stop cutting his hair as he believed it would reduce his power. Following the roof caving in on the barn that was housing his experiments, he repurposed the wood for a purpose-built space. It was rudimentary but had two adjacent rooms, one for his studio and one for what he then identified as the Healing Machine. It was also constructed with no foundation so that Blagdon could be directly connected to the Earth. His paintings, mostly enamel on wood, were largely abstract geometric designs frequently stacked like conductors. In the decades that followed, the Healing Machine became more complex and elaborate. A relationship between aesthetics and energy also seemed to exist within it, connecting a cohesive or balanced visual flow to the flow of energy.

Blagdon was noted for his solitude but was close with his family, a few select friends, and built a relationship with Dan Dryden[29] in 1975, who was integral to the preservation of the Healing Machine. Fully dedicated and with the Healing Machine in flux, Blagdon worked day and night like a scientist constantly experimenting and testing various elements. He maintained that being in its presence alleviated suffering. Doctors believe that Blagdon was likely living with cancer for ten years before his death in 1986, with his only treatment being his Healing Machine.

"He opened this door and reached around the corner, threw on a couple of switches. All the Christmas tree lights came on. Some stayed on. Some were blinking on and off, reflecting off hundreds and thousands of pieces of copper wire, tin foil, painted tin can lids. It hit me all at once." – Dan Dryden, on his first visit to the Healing Machine[30]

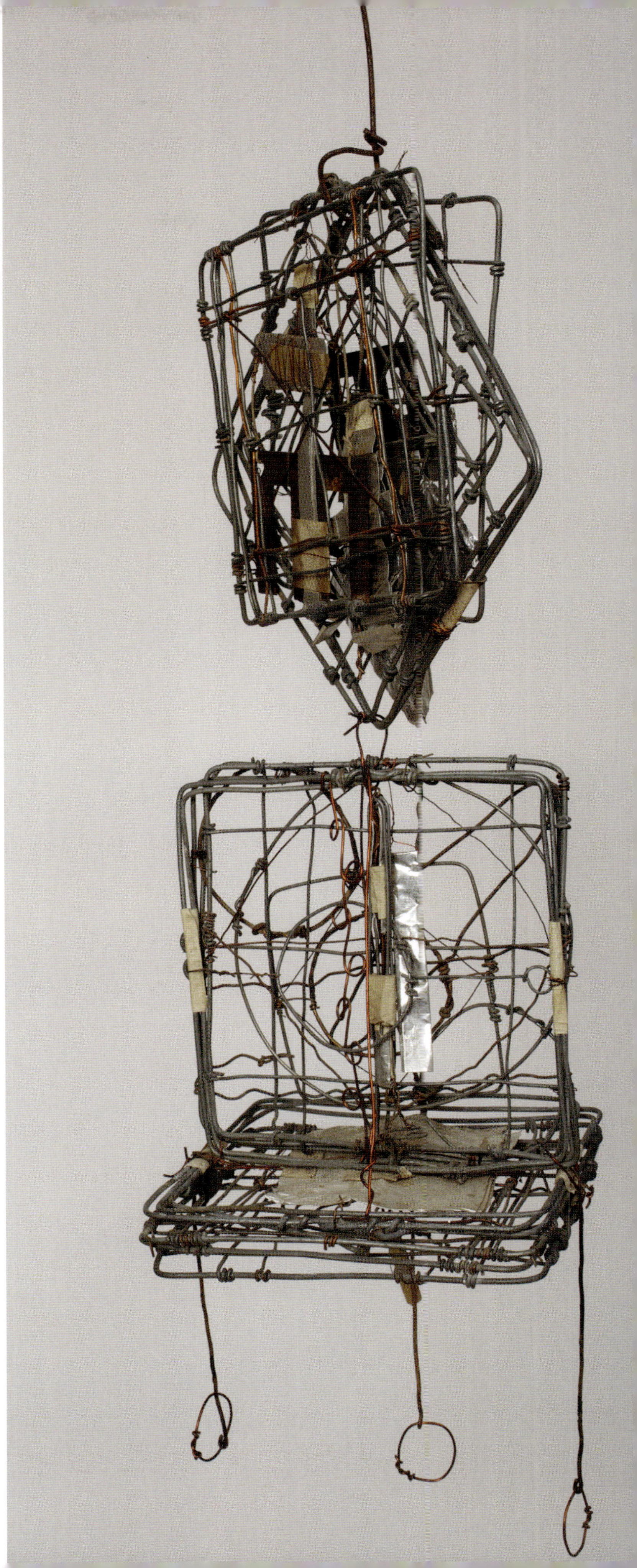

Emery Blagdon, Balance (section of the Healing Machine), *1955–1986, mixed materials, 54 × 18½ × 8 in (137.2 × 47 × 20.3 cm). Philadelphia Museum of Art.* This extracted element of the Healing Machine, especially when seen against a white background, allows the intricate detail of Blagdon's work to be observed. This symmetrical suspended composition is made of various metals, wires, and sheets. This individual component would have contributed to the overall Healing Machine housed by Blagdon.

CHAPTER 6

RENEGADES: PERSONA AND MESSAGING IN ART PRACTICE

THE ORIGINAL RENEGADE(S)

Phillip March Jones

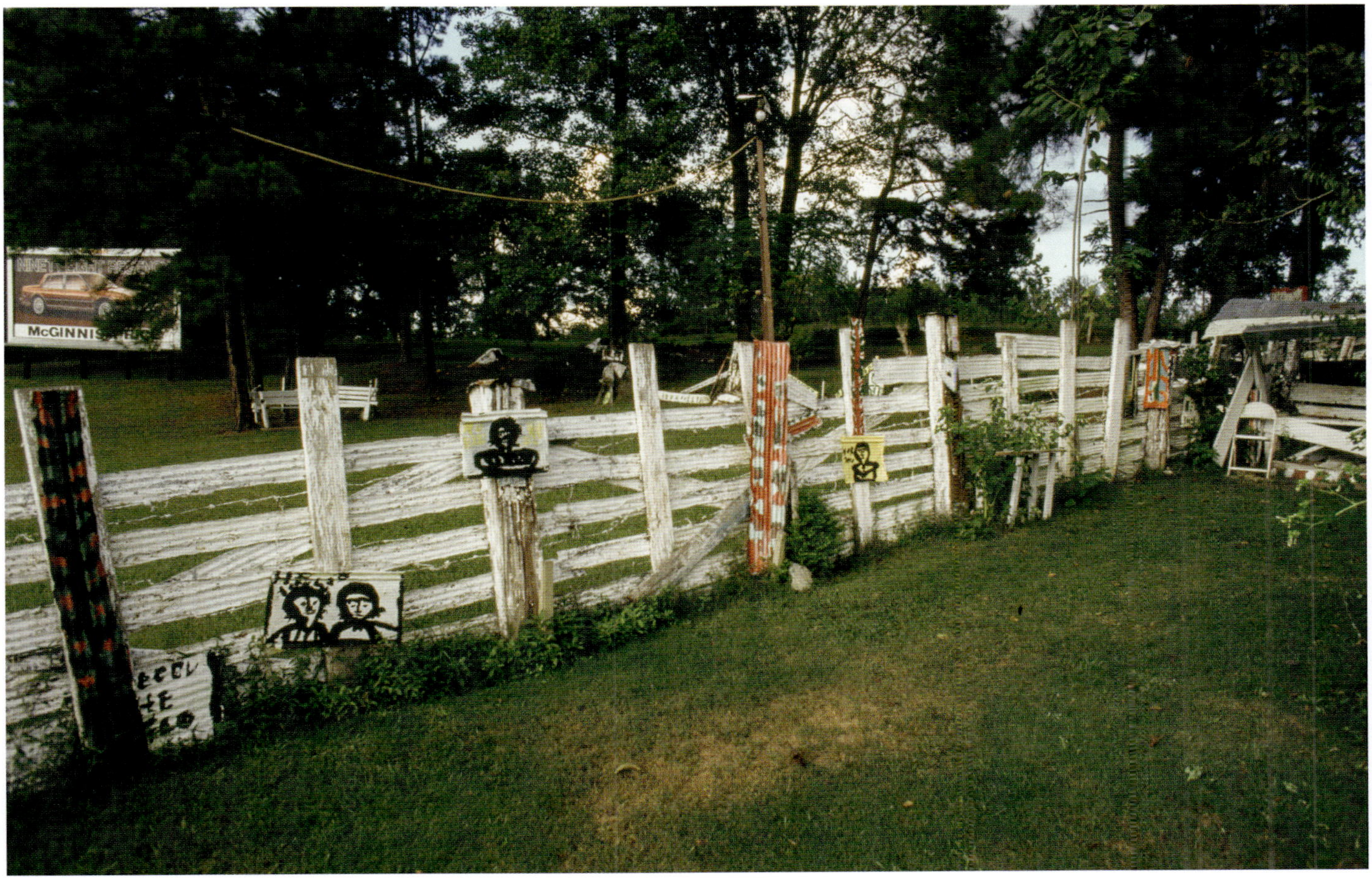

Mary T. Smith's Mississippi property, October 1986, photograph. Souls Grown Deep Foundation. This view of Smith's yard from the 1980s shows her use of a built fence as her own gallery wall, exhibiting for her local public. The juxtaposition of the billboard in the background to Smith's yard embodies her understanding of the power of messaging.

On September 25, 2019, Jalaiah Harmon, a 14-year-old girl from the suburbs of Atlanta, uploaded a video to Instagram of herself and her friend Kaliyah Davis performing the now famous Renegade dance to K-Camp's *Lottery*. Harmon had choreographed the complex dance, incorporating original and viral moves, and soon thereafter, Tik-Tok celebrities such as Charli D'Amelio began popularizing the routine to their massive audiences. It became a viral sensation with celebrities, families, and seemingly everyone with an iPhone creating their own version. Harmon's reaction was simple: "I was happy when I saw my dance all over," she said. "But I wanted credit for it."

Harmon's role as creator of the dance would have been lost to history had the *New York Times* not published *The Original Renegade*, an article explaining the genesis of it all. The celebrities and audience for Harmon's dance were not, for the most part, malevolent in their lack of crediting the young girl's creation; they simply didn't think it was necessary, an attitude that has plagued entire swaths of the creative world since time immemorial.

So it goes.

Crediting, messaging, authenticity, and audience all play important roles in cultural exchange and in the art world. In particular, these concepts resonate with, and at times contradict the assumptions about, artists considered self-taught—where flimsy categorical presumptions often include isolation and creating without a preconceived position. In creativity, such opposition to expectation exists. This individual dissidence is not necessarily political or drastic, but necessary for personal expression. Renegades, a label likely coveted by many contemporary artists, speaks to rebellion and unconventionality in creative practices. Defying both the conventions of the art world, and preconceived notions of "self-taught," artists have used display, documentation, and performance to convey their message—each an *Original Renegade*.

Artist Lonnie Holley (see page 196), who is still active in nearly every aspect of the creative process (drawing, painting, sculpture, music, film, installation) was responsible for the creation of an ambitious environment in Birmingham, Alabama—a refuge for conveying his complex ideas and physically articulating his intersecting philosophies. Condemned by the city for the proposed expansion of the Birmingham International Airport in 1997, Holley's home and yard were ultimately destroyed but that in no way put an end to the artist's work and career. Instead, he has continued to make unabashedly political artworks in an ever-evolving riff on the human condition. Holley thrives on all-encompassing engagement with materials, technology, and other humans—as he almost always refers to people.

Holley sums up his eternally optimistic and learned approach to both his work and humanity: "I'm an African American artist, and ultimately we all can teach, we can teach all the teachers, all the professors, all of the high-minded, all the skilled-minded. We can help them to help the little minds grow. I would prefer to see them try, than to see a child die without ever having got access to information."[1]

Holley may be among the most rebellious of the bunch, possessing dangerous and timely ideas to address inequality, hunger, environmental degradation, racism, and other problems threatening humanity. He also possesses, thanks to the proliferation of his music, a platform to share those ideas far and wide, through both recordings and live performances across the globe.

Prominent 19th-century African American educator and reformer Booker T. Washington in his autobiography described an area of America known as the Black Belt: "a part of the country which was distinguished by the color of the soil. The part of the country possessing this thick, dark, and naturally rich soil was, of course, the part of the South where the slaves were most profitable, and consequently they were taken there in the largest numbers. Later, and especially since the war, the term seems to be used wholly in a political sense—that is, to designate the counties where the black people outnumber the white."[2]

The region was home to hundreds of artists with unique practices, "who made their art, sang their songs, and lived and died in obscurity."[3] In the years immediately following the assassination of Martin Luther King, Jr. (1929–1968), a flowering of creativity proliferated across the Southern United States as African American artists for the first time in their collective history began to express themselves publicly, in the same way they had done so privately. Artworks that would have traditionally been created and displayed in cemeteries, parlors, and backyards were instead displayed in the front yard as elements of artistic environments or yard shows. Within this cultural cultivation of yard shows, creative renegades utilized their public-facing property as means of commentary. Holley's dedication to his Birmingham property is an archetype for those who created sophisticated yard shows, despite the inherent risk of alienation, ridicule, or worse.

In the Southern state of Mississippi, Mary T. Smith (see page 200) was born in 1904, the daughter of sharecroppers, and lived beneath two large billboards advertising all manner of products and services to passersby on State Highway 51. In the late 1970s, she began to paint, ultimately creating an environment that functioned as a counter-advertisement to the more worldly and adjacent offers of banks, car dealers, and fast-food chains. Smith understood the power of those images above her property and borrowed their formula of pairing images with text to great effect. The resulting paintings were bold, confident depictions of family, friends, visitors to her home, and devotional works. Their content was almost completely apolitical and certainly reverent. Smith, after all, was a church-going lady and painted numerous works depicting Jesus or other images referencing her Christian faith. Her protest was less overt than fundamental—a sprawling proclamation rendered in paint, word, and form: "Here I am. Don't you see me?"

Royal Robertson (see page 204) similarly understood the power of advertising and mass communication and applied it to creative messaging. Trained as a sign painter, the artist embellished his home and yard in Baldwin, Louisiana, with bold, painted panels that warned would-be trespassers to stay away with threats, biblical verses, or outlandish claims about his ex-wife's licentious behavior. The effect of Robertson's yard was the complete opposite of Smith's, a brightly painted deterrent to anyone who might have the wrong intentions. Unlike Smith, Robertson was completely unrepentant and remained steadfast in his devotion to both his visions of worlds beyond and his earthly struggle with the imagined infidelities of his ex-wife.

Despite his training in hand-painted sign making, Robertson's aesthetic perhaps owes a greater debt to

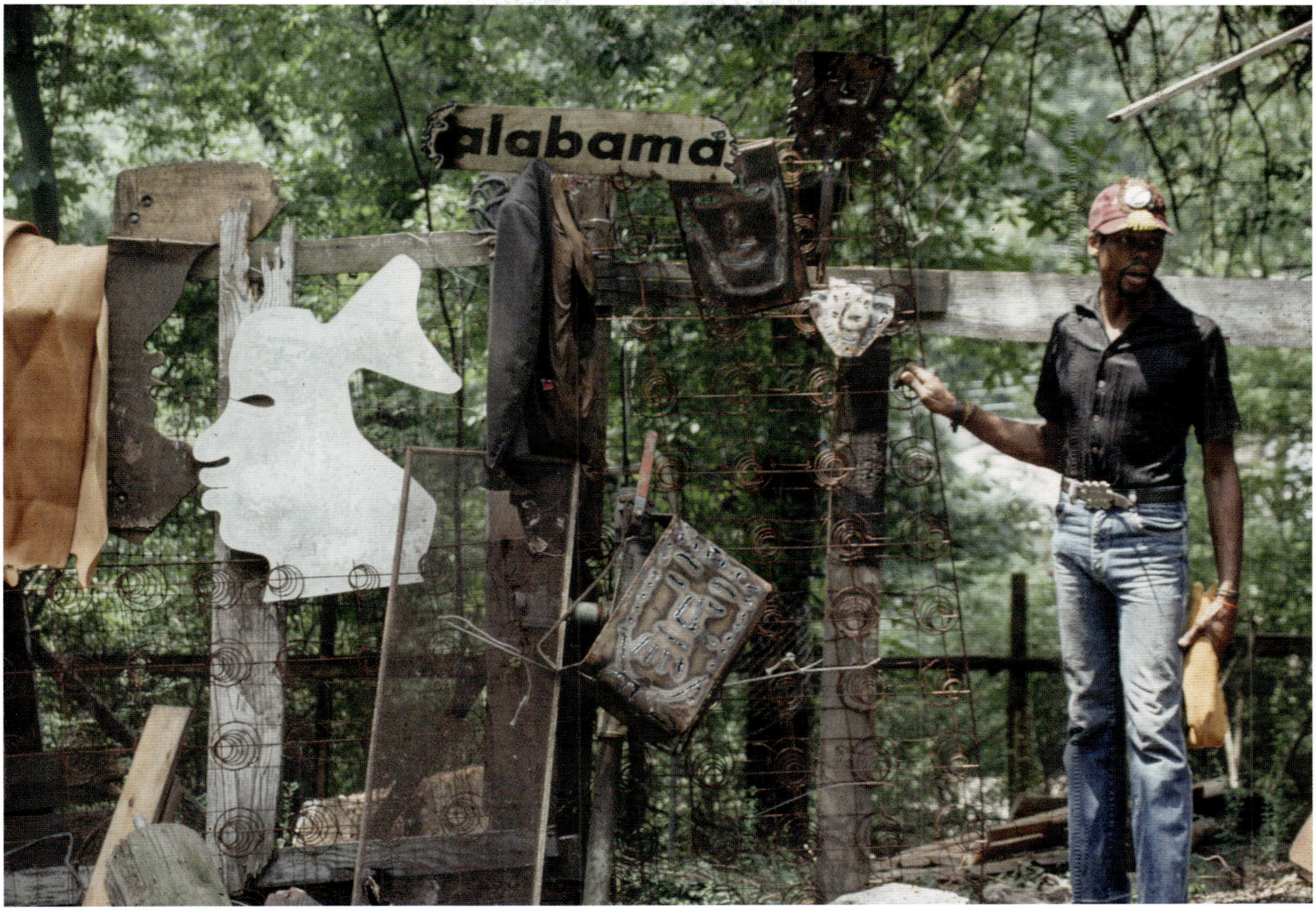

Lonnie Holley, ca. 1980–1990s, photograph. Souls Grown Deep Foundation. Here, Holley stands with his artwork in his yard. He created a complex environment on his property in Birmingham, Alabama, until it was destroyed by the authorities in 1997.

a more modern communication device, the television. In form, his drawings and paintings are almost always surrounded by perfectly outlined borders that mimic early television screens. It is, of course, possible that Robertson experienced his visions, in sleep or waking hours, much like one views a show or movie, and may have found these drawings to be the most direct method to broadcast his messages to the world.

In Kumasi, Ghana, trained in a similar manner as Robertson, Kwame Akoto (see page 208) implements the skills and aesthetic of sign painting and advertising to carry out his messages. Akoto is the proprietor of the *Almighty God Art Works*, an open-air studio and sign shop with its facade covered, almost constructed, from his paintings. For a fee, the studio under Akoto's direction produces any number of signs or hand-rendered marketing materials for local businesses but perhaps his most significant contribution is the paintings Akoto makes to express his personal convictions and faith. In addition to being a professional commercial artist, Akoto is a preacher and healer with membership in the House of Faith Ministries, a Pentecostal sect. This aspect of his life flavors his personal work: visual sermons that take a distinctly Christian trajectory with wholesale condemnation of societal ills like drinking, prostitution, and smoking. While many of Akoto's works might feel menacing, especially to sinners or non-believers, there are also moments of utopian belief or transcendence in his work, including the recurring theme of a post-racial world featuring images of split-race figures accompanied by the phrase "Black and White Are One." In juxtaposition to painted signs, advertising aesthetics, and private property as conveyors, for a radical Lee Godie (see page 186), the establishment and communication of her persona seemed as important, perhaps more so, than

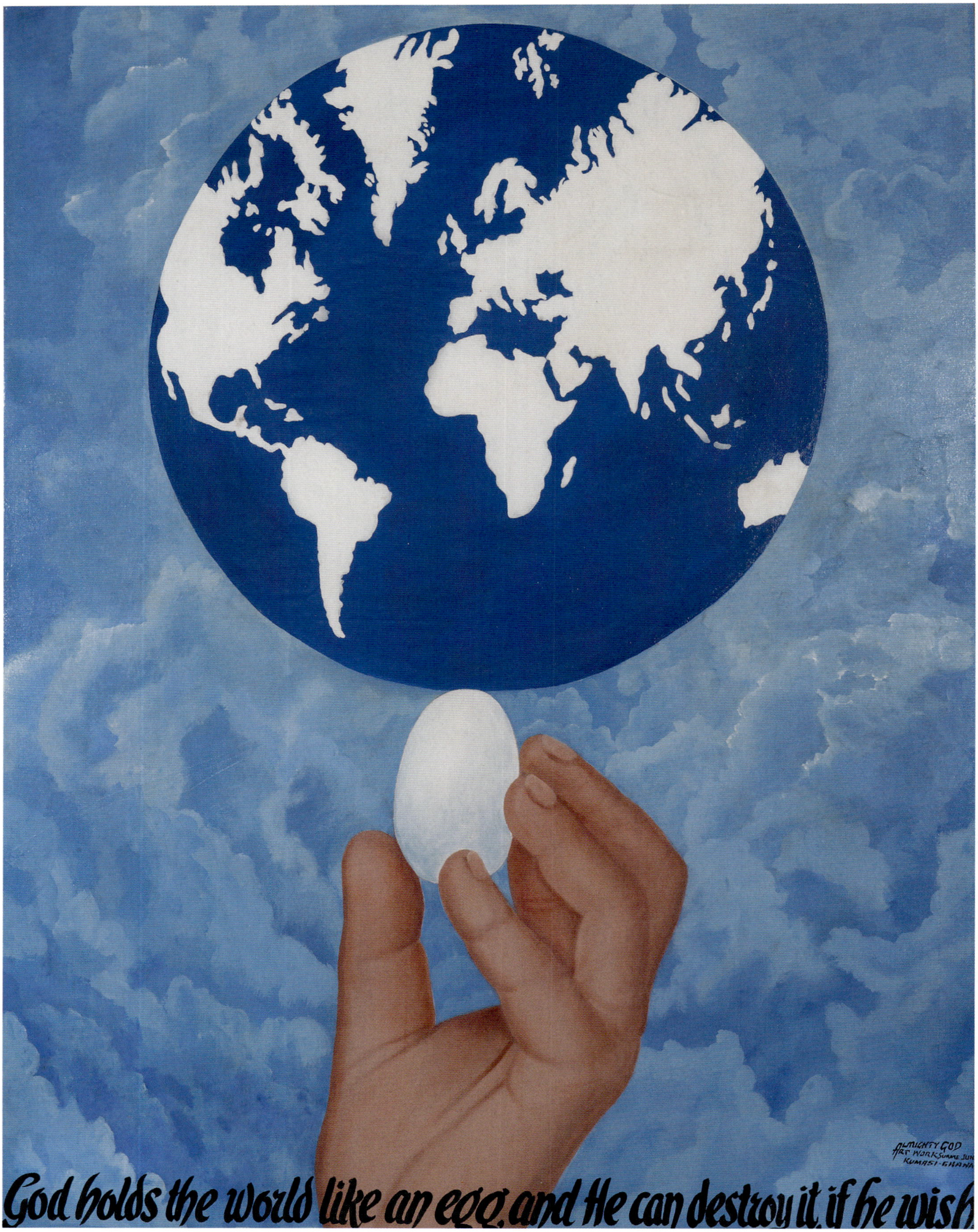

Akoto Kwame, GOD HOLDS THE WORLD LIKE AN EGG, *2017, oil on canvas, $56\frac{5}{16} \times 45\frac{1}{4}$ in (143 × 115 cm). Courtesy Françoise Adamsbaum.* This enigmatic painting of the world and a hand holding a single egg is archetypal of Akoto's moral-driven paintings. In black calligraphy along the bottom of the painting, he proclaims the delicacy of God's power comparing the fragility of the earth to an egg.

then her drawings and paintings. In 1968, in Chicago, a self-proclaimed French impressionist named Lee Godie began selling her paintings on the steps of the Art Institute of Chicago, a bold declaration of confidence and statement of her intention to be recognized among the greatest artists known in the modern world. Throughout the city, she created and hawked her paintings of figures, birds, hands, and flowers, with dance, performance, and gusto. Indeed, the act of buying a work was part of the thrill and she would not sell to just anyone.

Godie lived and worked on the street and slept outdoors or in cheap hotels. Her lifestyle seems to have been, at least in part, a choice based on preference and not resources as she made decent money selling her work. An important part of Godie's process of authenticating her persona was a series of self-portraits taken at the Chicago bus station photo booth, which served as documentation of her position. By posing with various props (a paint set or a handful of cash), Godie created a legacy of herself as a famous artist, as successful—constructing her own identity.

As realized with Godie, the act of documentation is a powerful tool that is also evident in the work of Horst Ademeit (see page 212). Akin to the inherent power of pairing images with text found in the yard shows of the American South, for Ademeit it was a technique that allowed him to document and perhaps confront his ultimate fear: the omnipresent invisible radiation that permeated his home and world. Beginning sometime in the late 1980s, Ademeit used a Polaroid camera to document his surroundings including newspapers, bicycles, plumbing fixtures, parked cars, abandoned lots, his feet, and anything else within his field of view. The basic content of the writing on Ademeit's photographs was meticulously gathered using thermometers, clocks, compasses, rulers, and other measuring devices but, the intangible was also recorded: sensory experiences, smells, feelings, musings, and other emotive realities. Ademeit's intent was not as an artmaker, but as a documentarian of "cold rays," as he referred to them, which were perhaps a metaphor for other unknown forces at work. Regardless, for Ademeit, nothing was coincidental and all worth noticing—and notice he did.

The relative size of our world grows smaller with each passing day, a result of new technologies and points of connection. This reality drives artists, curators, critics, and others to seek out pockets of resistance to the status quo in our ever-homogenizing global society. It is within this context that many of the aforementioned artists have come to our attention—a result of the efforts of those seeking some light in the darkness or a glimmer of universal truth among the monotony of the 24-hour news cycle and endless scrolling of social media networks. This search further drives us to ask more fundamental questions. What is the true nature of art? Does it exist to critique or judge? Or is it meant to affirm? To simply document the existence of a particular reality? Or to imagine an alternative? To whom is it addressed? The immediately local? Or the universal? And does the latter exist? As for me, I will look to the Harmons and the Holleys, the Ademeits and the Godies, the Akotos and the Robertsons. And the Smiths—bright stars in a dark night. Renegades in a modern world.

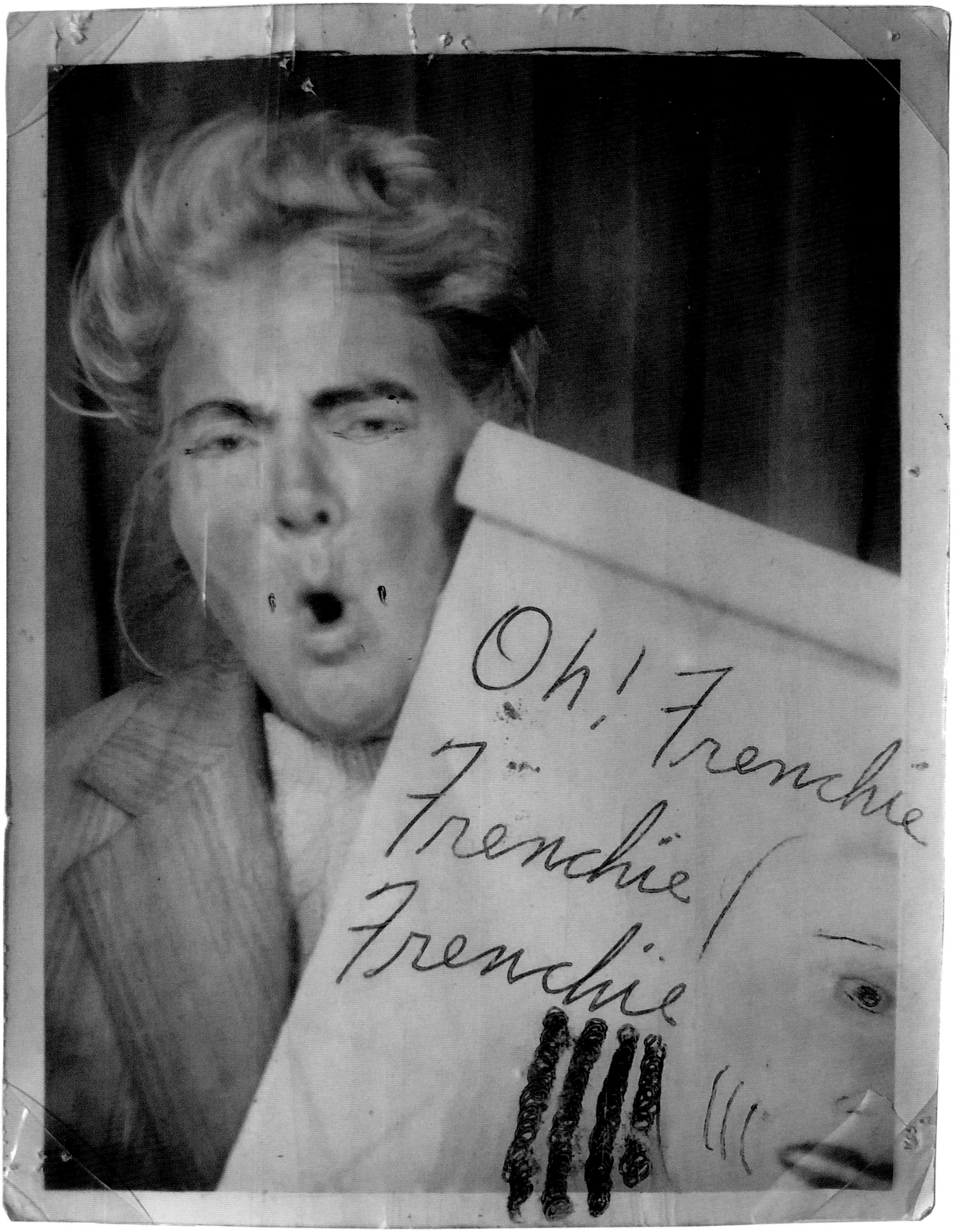

Lee Godie, Oh! Frenchie Frenchie, *n.d., photo booth photo, 5 × 3¾ in (12.7 × 9.5 cm). Courtesy Carl Hammer Gallery.* This photo booth self-portrait confirms Godie's identity (and self-proclamation) as a French impressionist. Her process of often enhancing her photographs can be seen here with the writing of the song lyrics, "Oh! Frenchie Frenchie Frenchie." Fond of dimples, Godie drew them onto her face along with added definition to her eyes and eyebrows.

LEE GODIE

(1908, Chicago–1994, Plato Center, Illinois, USA)

In 1968, Lee Godie emerged onto the steps of the Art Institute of Chicago, self-reinvented as a modern-day "French impressionist," where she sold her paintings and theatrically constructed her narrative to a constantly growing audience. From holding soirées in the park to keeping her belongings in department store lockers, Godie turned downtown Chicago into her home, gallery, and studio. Godie was extremely private regarding the first 60 years of her life. During that time, Godie lived through the highs and lows of two marriages, gave birth to four children, and struggled with suspected substance abuse. Her paintings strike a sublime balance between intensity and glamour. This tension reflects active inquiries into the aesthetics of glamour. Her drawn portraits reference feminine ideals, while in photographic self-portraits she performed characters that framed her as a socialite and femme fatale. By 1975, she was included in a Hyde Park Art Center exhibition. Further, her collector base was broadening, registering her as a notable cultural figure in the wider Chicago art scene. Life and art were inseparable for Godie. After spending over 20 years in the public eye, she passed away in 1994. Godie is still known as Chicago's most collected artist.

A renegade: an individual who rejects conventional behavior; having rejected convention; untraditional. This defining trait can be applied to, and perhaps widely substantiated by, a myriad of artists in history, and certainly aligns with multifaceted creative practices. A true renegade to perception, Lee Godie rebelliously dissolved the boundaries between art and life, public and private, narrative and experience. From 1968 to 1990, she spent most nights sleeping outside in parks or beaches, checking into hotels only when the weather required. However, she emulated a woman—an artist—of glamour, beauty, and culture, unaware that she could be perceived as a person living on the streets. Often wearing a fur coat and sipping Lipton tea from a silver goblet, Godie would romance art students and curators alike, persuading them to buy her paintings and participate in her ritual-like exchanges. Lee Godie—a renegade to her past, present, and future—undeniably constructed, performed, and controlled her discourse.

Godie was extremely private about her early years. Researchers, friends, and family members have formed a cohesive history that provides potential context and circumstance about her life. Jamot Emily Godee was born in 1908, the sixth of eleven children to Swedish–American parents in Chicago, Illinois. Godie was first married in 1933 to a man on his third marriage. He was previously incarcerated and accused of domestic abuse. Godie gave birth to three children in this relationship, but only the youngest, Bonnie, lived beyond 1943. Godie finalized the divorce of her first marriage in 1948, losing custody of Bonnie in the process. Later that year she entered into her second marriage and gave birth to her fourth child. There are indications of substance abuse and mental instability around this time for Godie[4]. In 1950, Godie relocated with her family to her husband's hometown of Tacoma, Washington, but within a couple of years, she abandoned her family and left the West Coast. [5]

Godie's limited mentions of her past were fluid with references to her childhood "homestead" and nearby "prairie." She discussed her dreams of becoming a nightclub singer and trips to Europe foiled by love interests. Godie very rarely acknowledged being a wife or mother, only occasionally mentioning a deceased daughter who was "as beautiful as Shirley Temple."[6] Her impetus to create came from a red bird telling her to paint.[7] Her version of her life, told through enhanced or edited memories, seemed not to be a delusion of grandeur but a presentation of how she wanted to be viewed.

Ultimately, in 1968, Godie appeared on the front steps of the Art Institute of Chicago, selling her paintings. She had reinvented herself as a *modern-day French impressionist*: a narrative she developed and achieved by implementing the city of Chicago as her theatrical backdrop and the public as both audience and actors. She was a woman with steady self-confidence who consistently cultivated her identity. She was complex and paradoxical in nature. Despite her flamboyant and persistent public persona, Godie kept a level of reservation. She could be temperamental and had strong preferences on her acquaintances. For over 20 years, until 1990, the steps of the Art Institute were her gallery; Grant Park was her venue for hosting soirées and meetings; and all of Chicago her stage and inspiration—blurring the lines between art, persona, and public.

Godie's art was particularly admirable and elaborate. The transaction of selling a painting was driven as much by performance as it was by commerce. She would evaluate each potential customer to consider her selling price. Art students would recall acquiring a painting for $5.00 in the 1970s, while in contrast, a curator from the Art Institute would have paid $100.00 contemporaneously. She would approach potential buyers with romantic openers such as "Don't you think she has a lovely smile?" (in reference to the woman in the painting). To confirm a sale, she would include promotional items such as brooches, tins of sardines, and teabags. She even introduced a rental scheme for her paintings. While her early works were typically sold for between $5.00 and $20.00, by the mid-80s she was consistently selling pieces for between $50.00 and $200.00. She would also write her appraisal prices on the back of canvases, with notes like "value $3,500.00."

An essential symbol of sophistication for Godie's identity as an artist was placement within a French context. In part, this construct was informed by her proximity to the Art Institute, which holds one of the strongest collections of late 19th-century French art. She fittingly aligned herself specifically with impressionism and its primary appreciation of visual aesthetics. This allowed Godie to validate her own priority of conventional beauty. Her self-assigned title and mantra of "modern-day French impressionist" was vital to her conversations and even included in her artist signature. Her photographs were also adorned with song lyrics, "Oh! Frenchie, Frenchie, Frenchie." She also chose a French pronunciation regarding her last name—declaring it "Go-day." After reading Renoir's biography, Godie steadfastly adopted his motto: *I can make my living with my brushes*.

Further to Godie's penchant for traditional beauty and glamour, idealistic femininity was at the forefront of her persona, performance, and practice. Godie never wore trousers, claiming it was unladylike. Instead, she would construct dresses by wrapping remnants of fabric from the ends of bolts. In her practice, Godie's hyper-feminine portrait paintings exaggerated stereotypical gender traits and overt traditional beauty. Her renderings of intensified and melodramatic eyelashes are a key trait of this technique. Though Godie's primary emphasis in her portraits was to achieve images of beauty, the facial features, if examined closely, offer a glimpse into Godie's emotional ferocity. In particular, the palpability in Godie's execution of penetrating stares and taut toothy grins articulated the intensity of personal lived experiences.

Godie had specific muses that were paramount to her depiction and emulation of beauty, including silver screen icons Mary Pickford, Joan Crawford, Clara Bow, the original "it" girl, and femme fatale Theda Bara. She was also inspired by the Gibson Girl, an Edwardian fashion plate by American artist Charles Dana Gibson. Godie was a serial artist, producing many copies and variations on a theme. Throughout this process, these muses served as pinnacle archetypes; most notably the Gibson Girl and Joan Crawford. She was told once by a friend that she looked like Crawford, and this prototype is distinguishable in Godie's portraits of women who feature a headband and scalloped

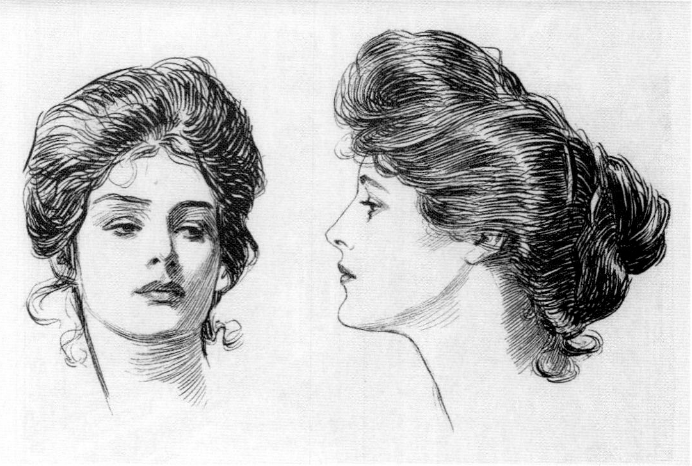

Charles Dana Gibson, untitled*, n.d., ink on paper.* The "Gibson Girl" became the term to define the women drawn by Charles Dana Gibson (1867–1944). His drawings of women became influential to the development of feminine style in American society around the turn of the century; and later as influential to Godie's feminine oeuvre.

Would you like to buy some canvases? I'm much better than Cezanne. – Lee Godie[8]

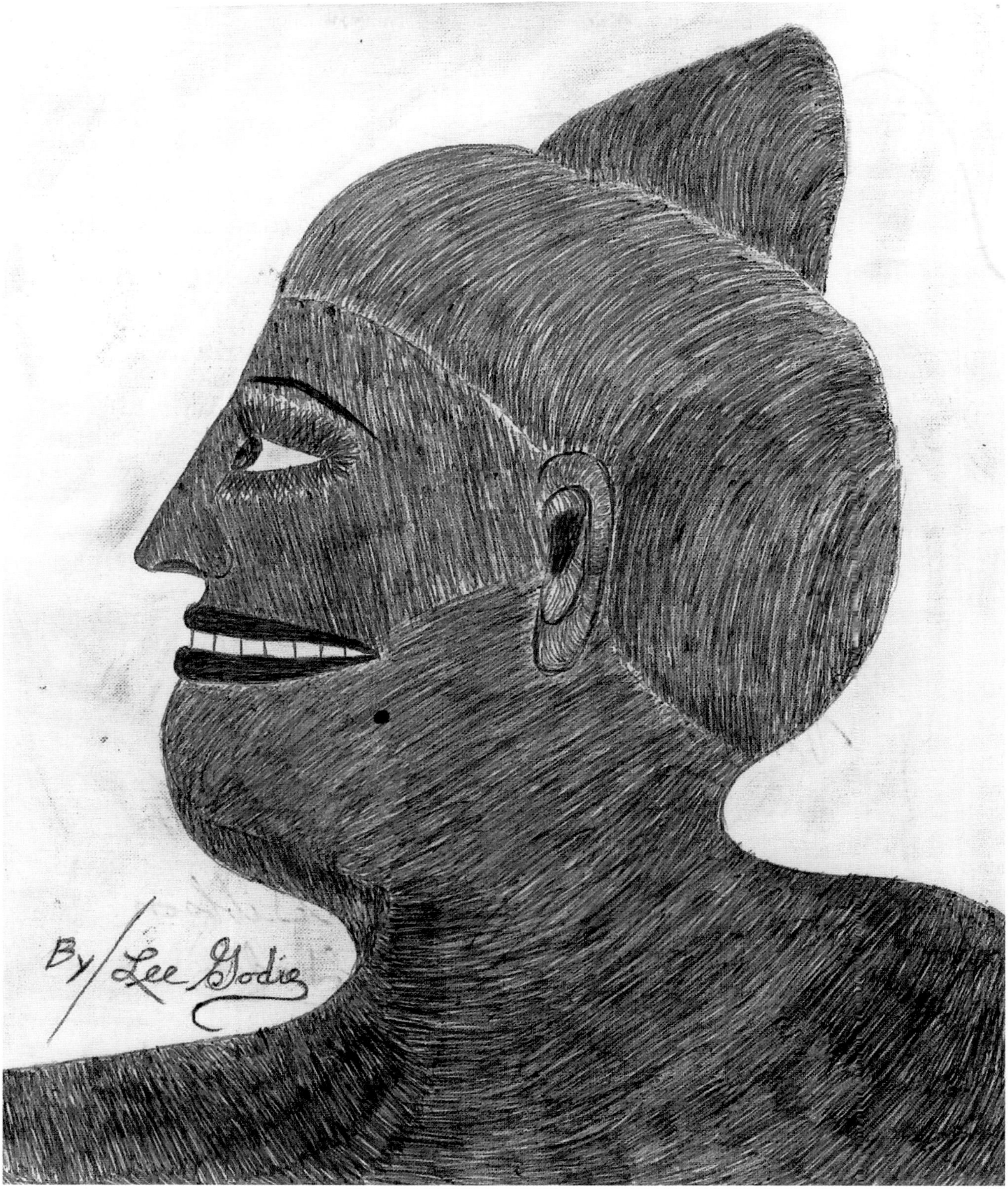

Lee Godie, Miss Gibbson, *n.d., ballpoint pen on canvas, 7 1/16 × 6 3/16 in (18 × 15.75 cm).* Godie's selective references for her portraits of sublime femininity included an Edwardian fashion plate, known as the "Gibson Girl." This influence on Godie's oeuvre can be seen in profile portraits with hair worn in an up-do. The rhythmic ballpoint markings on canvas display one of Godie's few monochromatic works.

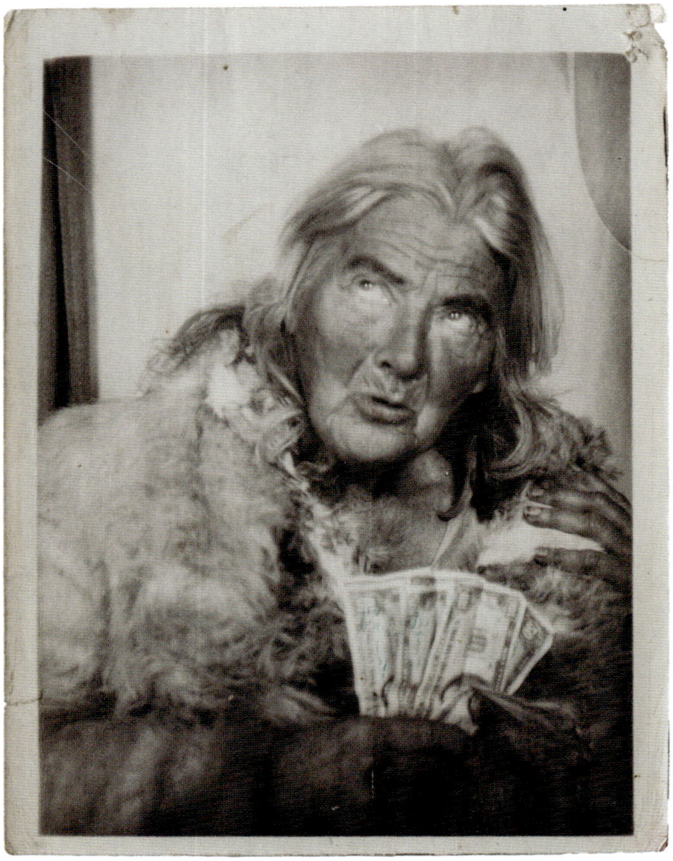

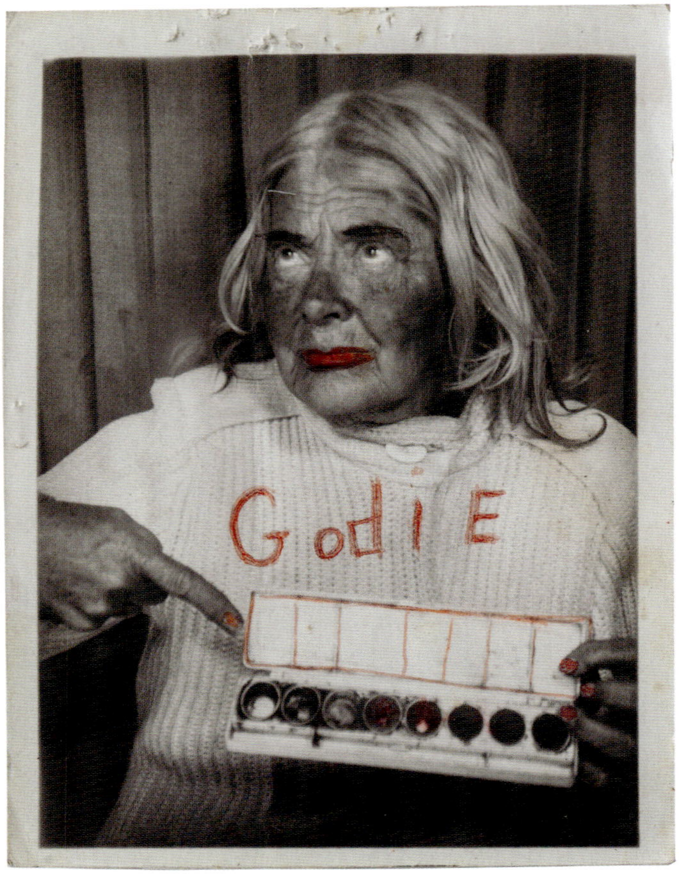

Lee Godie, untitled (photo booth self-portraits), *n.d., gelatin silver print and ink, 4¾ × 3 in (12.1 × 7.6 cm). Collection of Orren Davis Jordan and Robert Parker.* Godie's stylized self-portraits taken in a Chicago station photo booth documented personas and characteristics that were important or necessary for her. Here, Godie poses in a fur coat with a handful of cash to demonstrate wealth and status, accentuated by her overlay of green marker on the money in her hand. In her self-portrait with brightly colored red lips and nails, and with "Godie" written across her chest, Godie establishes her role as an artist while she holds and points to a set of watercolor paints. In the third photograph, she takes on the key characteristic that she associated with glamour and sophistication—being French—illustrated through wearing a beret and the writing on the reverse of the portrait, which reads, "Miss Godie the French Muralists."

trim neckline. The Gibson Girl prototype appears in portraits with a side profile and the hairstyle swept up in a bun. Godie preferred to draw women but had a few male archetypes. These usually had similar feminine facial features to her portraits of women, with redefined hair and clothing. Two of these male archetypes are most prominent: "The Waiter," distinguishable with black sideburns and a moustache, and Prince Charming (originally based on a portrait of Picasso from the museum bookstore), often defined by a sharp widow's peak.

The role of muses or characters also played significantly into Godie's photographic self-portraits. These narrative explorations, led by conceptual personas, resulted in an image that was still undeniably Godie: feminine but ultra-powerful. The intent was not to be a photograph of Theda Bara played by Godie, but rather Lee Godie the femme-fatale, Lee Godie the socialite, Lee Godie the famous artist (among other personas). These characters were all documented in a public photo booth at a Chicago bus station and enhanced with physical props. Afterward, Godie would use a pen or marker on top of the photograph. The markings heightened Godie's physical appearance by mimicking cosmetics and she used a green marker to highlight the importance of dollar bills. Intimate and intense, her photographs inferred documentation of her constructed world of beauty and extravagance. In contrast, Godie did not like her photograph to be taken by others and few exist beyond her self-portraits. She once said, "There's only one thing wrong with photographs: people can still see you after you're dead."

Godie had a prolific practice, executing thousands of drawings and paintings on a variety of materials, from cardboard to window shades. Her photographs, postcards, and brooches were affixed to paintings, further developing a

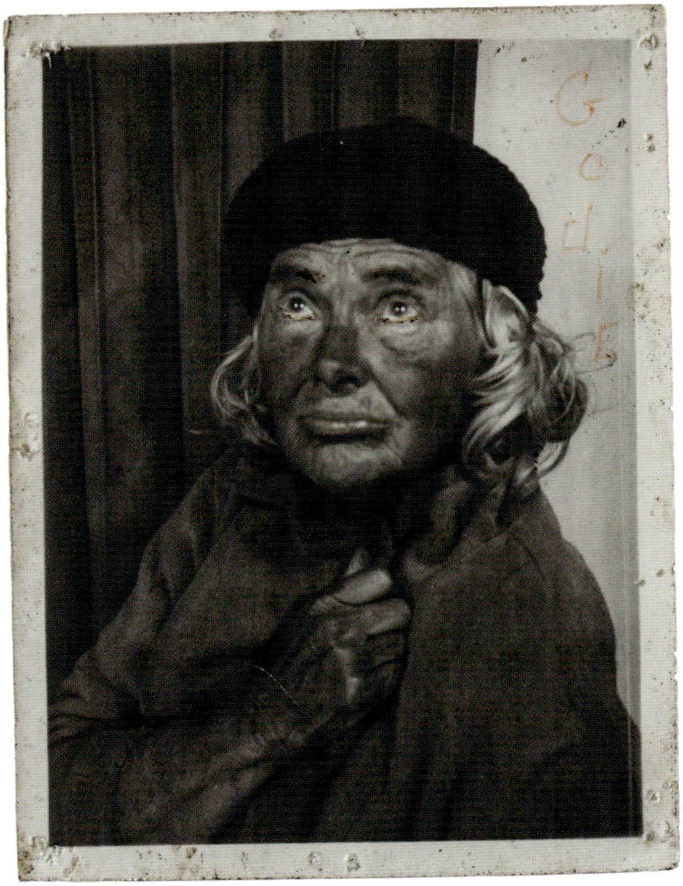

fascinating body of collage. While her first enthusiasts were art students working at the museum bookshop, including Alex Wald, Laren Wilks, Barbara Stafford, and Michael Thompson, by 1975, Godie's performative persona was becoming an established fixture in the Chicago cultural scene. She was included in an exhibition at the Hyde Park Art Center that February, and by April 1975 her work was being collected by Ruth Horwich and Chicago Imagist Roger Brown.

Godie chose to maintain her lifestyle on the streets of Chicago, despite her artistic success and assumed available means. In 1988 she was reunited with her daughter Bonnie who offered assistance to get her mother off the streets, but Godie still embraced her alternative position until an accident at age 82. A year before her death, in 1993, Godie received her first retrospective at the Chicago Cultural Center. A misleading assumption is to view Lee Godie's drawings as jejune, not recognizing their authenticity and the uncanny expressive quality that makes them exquisite. Michael Bonesteel, curator of the retrospective and esteemed historian of Godie, succinctly stated that her "oeuvre is spiritually naked and psychologically honest." Her unconventional and rebellious approach was intertwined with the Chicago cityscape and dependent on public interaction for development and sustainability. Everything for Godie had a theatrical presence, but it was through Godie's own choice of lens.

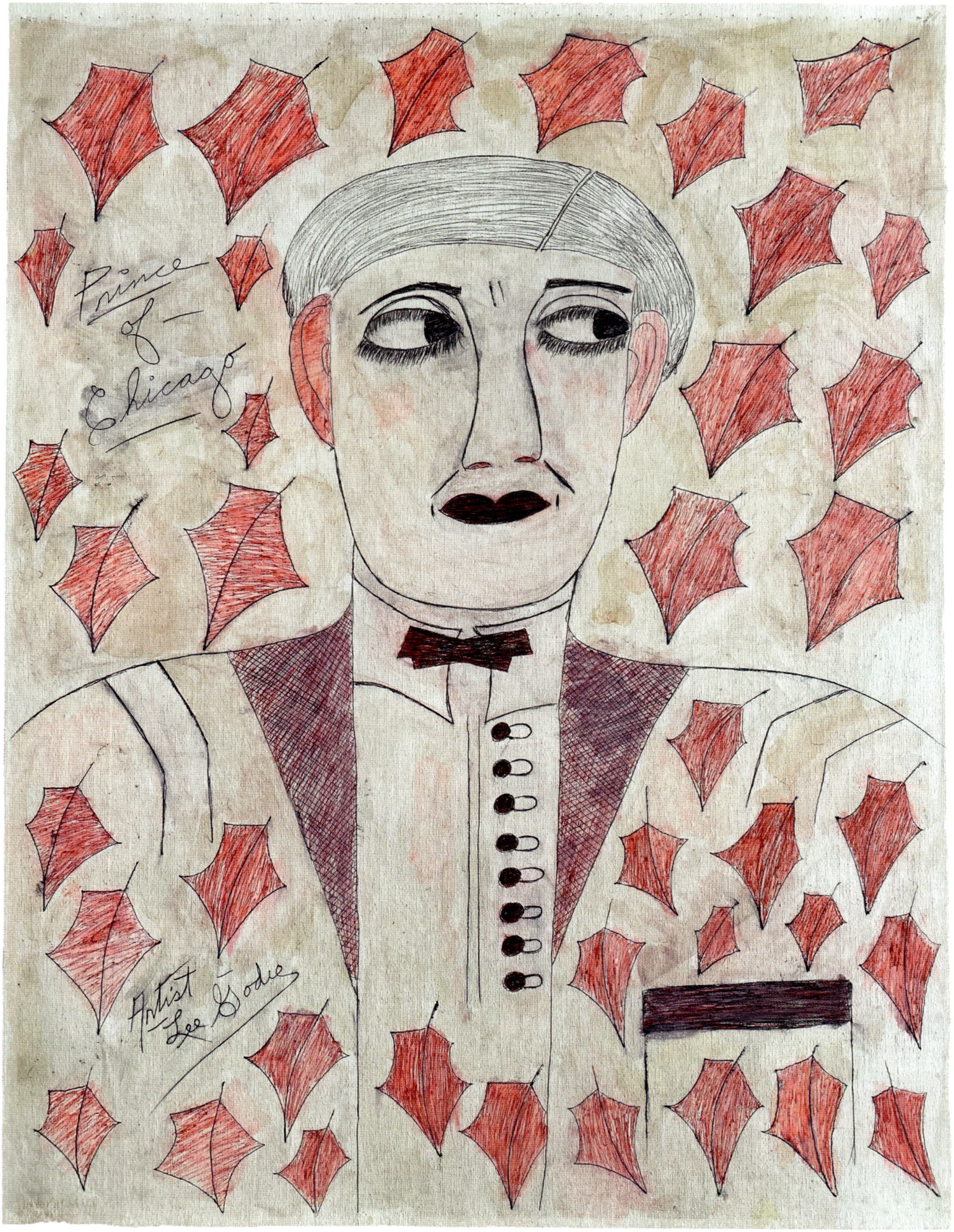

Lee Godie, The Prince of Chicago, *ca. 1970, pen and watercolor on window shade, 25 × 20 in (63.5 × 51 cm). Collection of Laura Wehrman.* This exuberant drawing by Godie takes influence from a Pablo Picasso postcard from the Art Institute of Chicago. While the portrait is male, the facial features still feel very feminine. Conceptually, Godie plays with perceptions through her rendering of pink leaves as both the background and the pattern on the prince's suit.

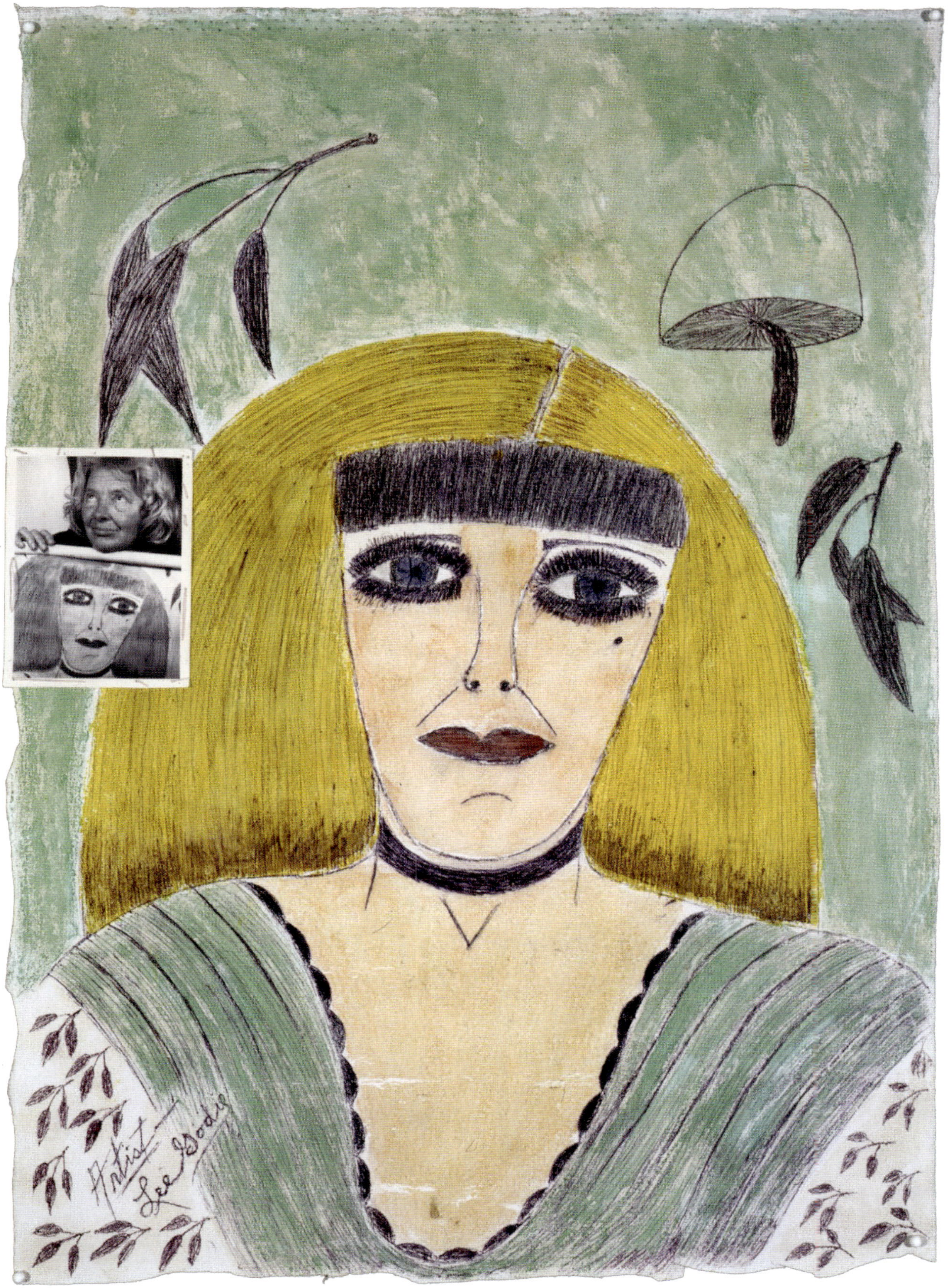

Lee Godie, Irish Rose, *ca. 1980, mixed media and gelatin silver print on canvas, 26¼ × 19½ in (66.7 × 49.5 cm). Collection of Robert Alter and Sherry Siegel.* This portrait by Godie exemplifies her prototype of Joan Crawford, with the blond woman wearing both a headband and scalloped neckline. Facing the viewer straight on, tension is exuded by the exaggerated eyelashes. The collaged self-portrait adorned to the left, shows Godie posing with the main artwork, inserting a visual provenance.

LONNIE HOLLEY

(b. 1950, Birmingham, Alabama, USA)

Lonnie Holley is a profound artist, educator, and visionary. His diverse practice spanning over four decades encompasses sculpture, assemblage, and music. After a tumultuous and difficult youth, Holley began sculpting in 1979, in response to a family tragedy. Reflections upon memories, African American tradition, and the intimate history of materials emerged as key concepts to his practice. The result is a profoundly personal oeuvre of juxtapositioned found objects in poignant dialogue with one another. In 1981, he was included as an emerging artist in *More Than Land and Sky: Art from Appalachia*, at the Smithsonian Museum of American Art, Washington, D.C. Internationally, Holley was included in *We Will Walk—Art and Resistance in the American South*, at the Turner Contemporary gallery, Margate, UK (2020). Holley lives and works in Atlanta and has become a prominent artist of the American South and revered musician with the release of his first album in 2012. His works are in the collections of the Whitney Museum of American Art, New York, and the Metropolitan Museum of Art, New York.

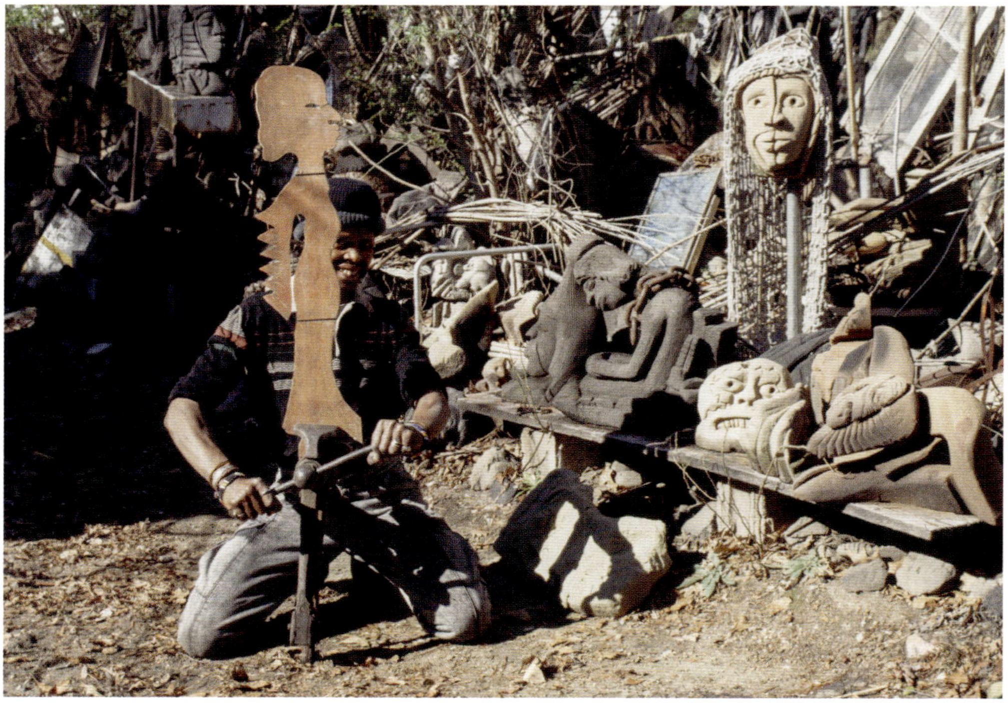

Lonnie Holley, ca. 1980–1990s, photograph. Souls Grown Deep Foundation. Holley's diverse and multifaceted practice is illustrated here, showing his use of carving and assembling from repurposed materials. While this image was captured in around 1990, Holley's practice further evolved to encompass music and more complex assembled installations.

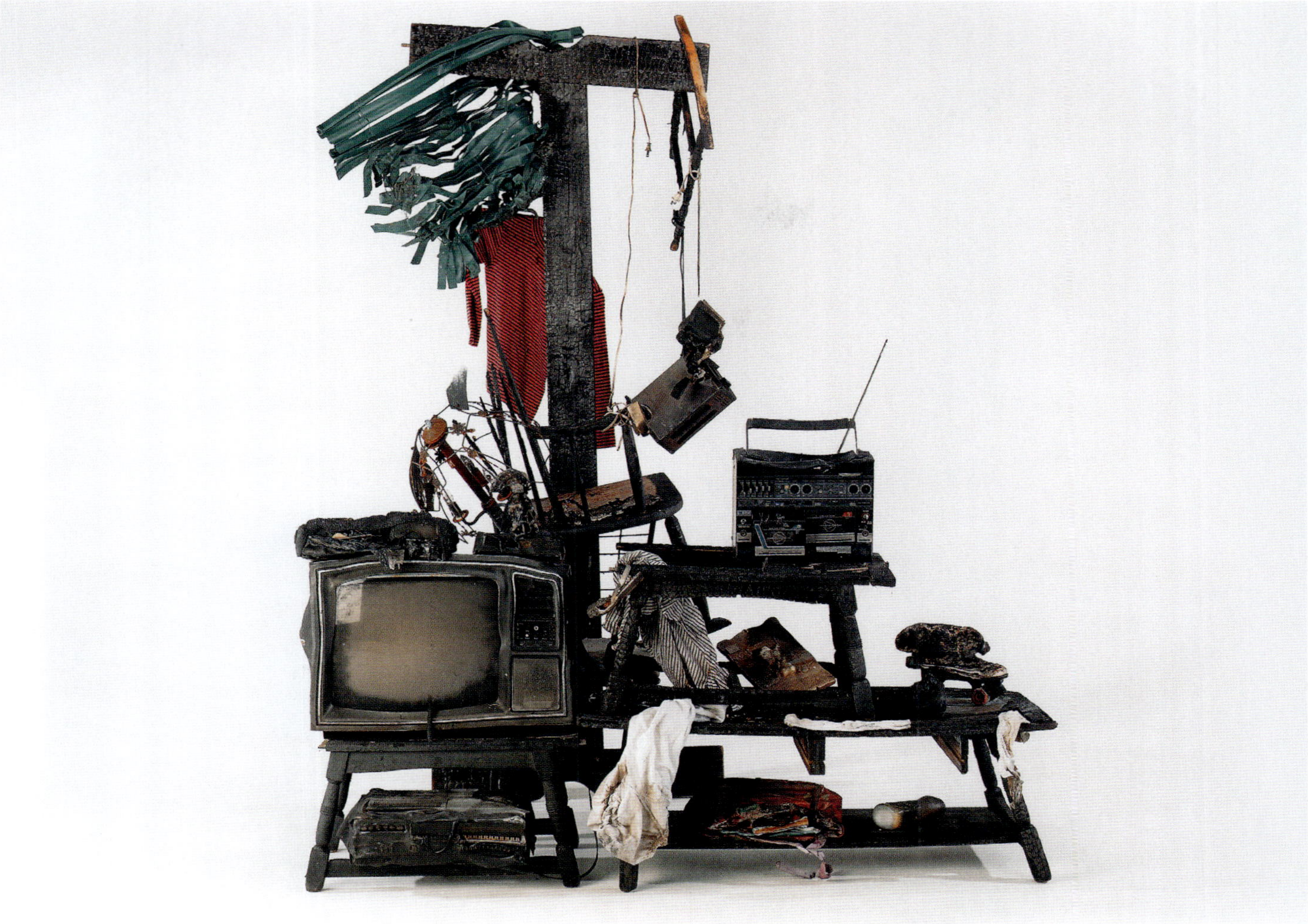

Lonnie Holley, The Fifth Child Burning, *1994, found materials from a burned house: wood table, book bag, detergent bottle, shoe, wall plaque, glass bowl, child's clothes, metal chair, wooden rocking chair, electrical cord, table lamp, window blinds, television, toaster oven, radios, cable box, electric can opener videocassette recorder, roller skate, bed parts, and other materials, 87 × 72 × 60 in (220.1 × 182.9 × 152.4 cm). Baltimore Museum of Art.* This assemblage of burned household items is Holley's representation of a child's sorrow and notion of unexpected tragedy. The title is in reference to the Birmingham church bombing that killed four children, placing the sculpture's subject within a specific tragic context significant to the Civil Rights Movement.

Lonnie Holley has dedicated his life to his creative practice since he was 29, when he carved sculptures of tombstones for his deceased nieces whom he had lost in a fire. Equally, a great number of Holley's works are in response to his personal experience and reflections on his traumatic childhood. The memory of accompanying his grandmother to a landfill to source materials to sell at flea markets seems to resonate with his artistic practice in regards to the sentiment of giving used objects a secondary existence.

The 1990s marked a significant situation for Holley, who had dedicated years to constructing site-specific sculptures and assemblages throughout his property. With plans for the Birmingham Airport to claim his property as part of an expansion, he entered into a long dispute with the airport authority. Threats by the authorities resulted in environmental sculptures being destroyed. In his creative activism, he constructed new assemblages from the remnants of destroyed sculptures. Holley's understanding of his creative constructions' temporal existence sets forth powerful freedom in his lack of need for permanence. He eventually lost the dispute and in 1997 his environment was destroyed and Holley was relocated by the authorities to Shelby County, Alabama.

The history of found objects, from broken appliances to thrift remnants, are important to Holley. Conjuring up their domestic, industrial, and private pasts to configure ritual-like objects speaks to Afro-Atlantic cultural history and the African American tradition of yard shows. The actions

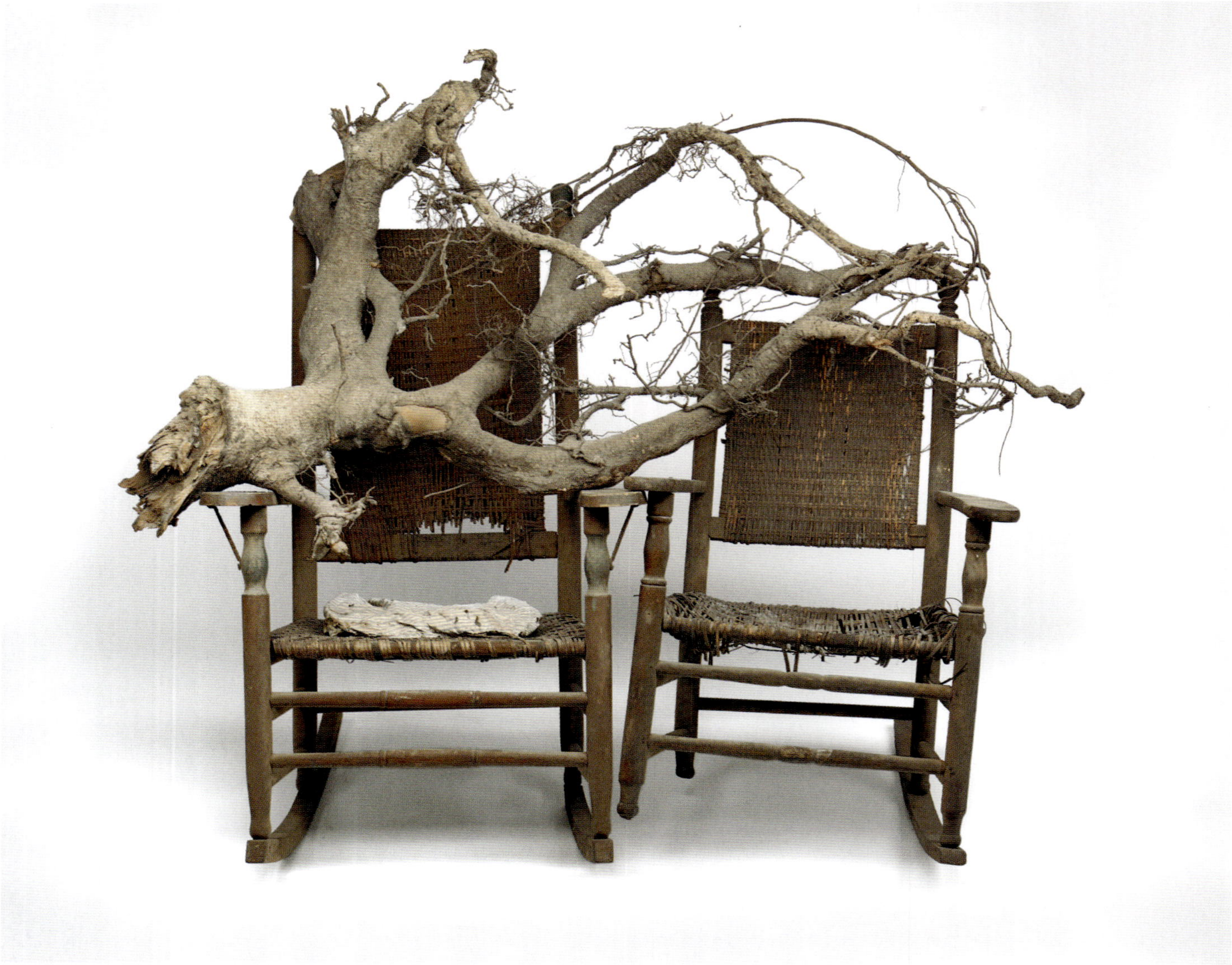

Lonnie Holley, Him and Her Hold the Root, *1994, rocking chairs, pillow, and root, 45½ × 73 × 30½ in (115.6 × 185.4 × 77.5 cm). Fine Arts Museums of San Francisco.* This enigmatic sculpture uses the metaphorical power of roots. The large root is placed across two rocking chairs, reminiscent of the positioning on a front porch, to powerfully suggest, or perhaps remind, the connectivity of family. Holley said "I am the root. All my relatives is part of that root, and their spirit supports it."

of assembling and improvisation are evident in Holley's assemblages within his synthesis of cast-off materials and found objects. Often binding and embellishing with twine, rope, or wire, the combinations of materials speak to spiritual insight—a past, present, and future. In *Him and Her Hold the Root* (1994), Holley's synthesis of two worn rocking chairs side by side with a large root stretched across them invokes the ancestral and spiritual concepts of connection.

"I'm always interested in learning, in seeing what else is available. A lot of times I may pick up something and it may take a year or six months before I even put my thought to it or find the other components to go with it. My grandchildren say Grandaddy is a hoarder but, in these days where young people see things as trash, I'm trying to get them to understand they should identify additional uses for them, use them to expand their mind." – Lonnie Holley[9]

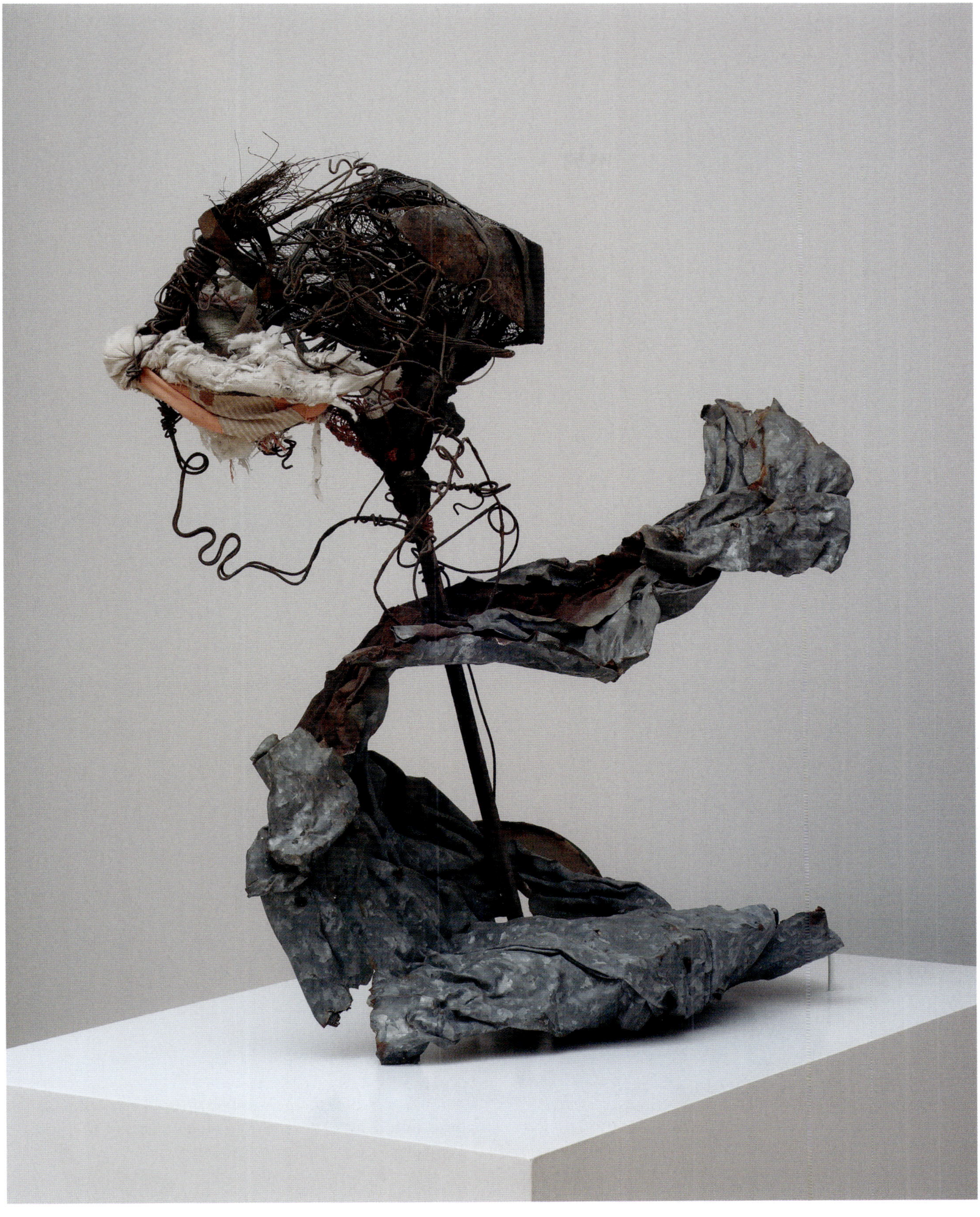

Lonnie Holley, Finally Getting Wings for the Forty-First Floor, *1996, found metal, plastic, and cloth, 32 × 31 × 16½ in (81.3 × 78.7 × 41.9 cm). High Museum of Art, Atlanta.* This sculpture with wire profile is in memoriam of Holley's friend of Jewish heritage. Holley connected with her and her ancestors' experience with loss and trauma. She had lived on the 44th floor, so when Holley learned of her passing, his intention was to give her wings to ascend to her apartment.

MARY T. SMITH

(1905, Copiah County–1995, Hazlehurst, Mississippi, USA)

The concepts of communication and having a voice became key themes of Mary Tillman Smith's visionary installations. From an early age, it was apparent that Smith had a severe hearing impairment, which made it difficult for her to communicate. While her family recognized her astute intellectual abilities, Smith was often dismissed by others. It was not until the 1970s, when Smith was retired, that she began producing bold creative expressions in her yard. Smith created a remarkable visual language across her property—a discourse of signs, paintings, and sculptures, full of audacity and ingenuity—by using found materials and disposed components from a nearby refuse depot. Smith passed away in 1995, before her work became known by a larger audience. With great posthumous appreciation of her improvisational aesthetic, her work is now held in the collections of the Metropolitan Museum of Fine Art, New York, and the Smithsonian Museum of American Art, Washington, D.C.

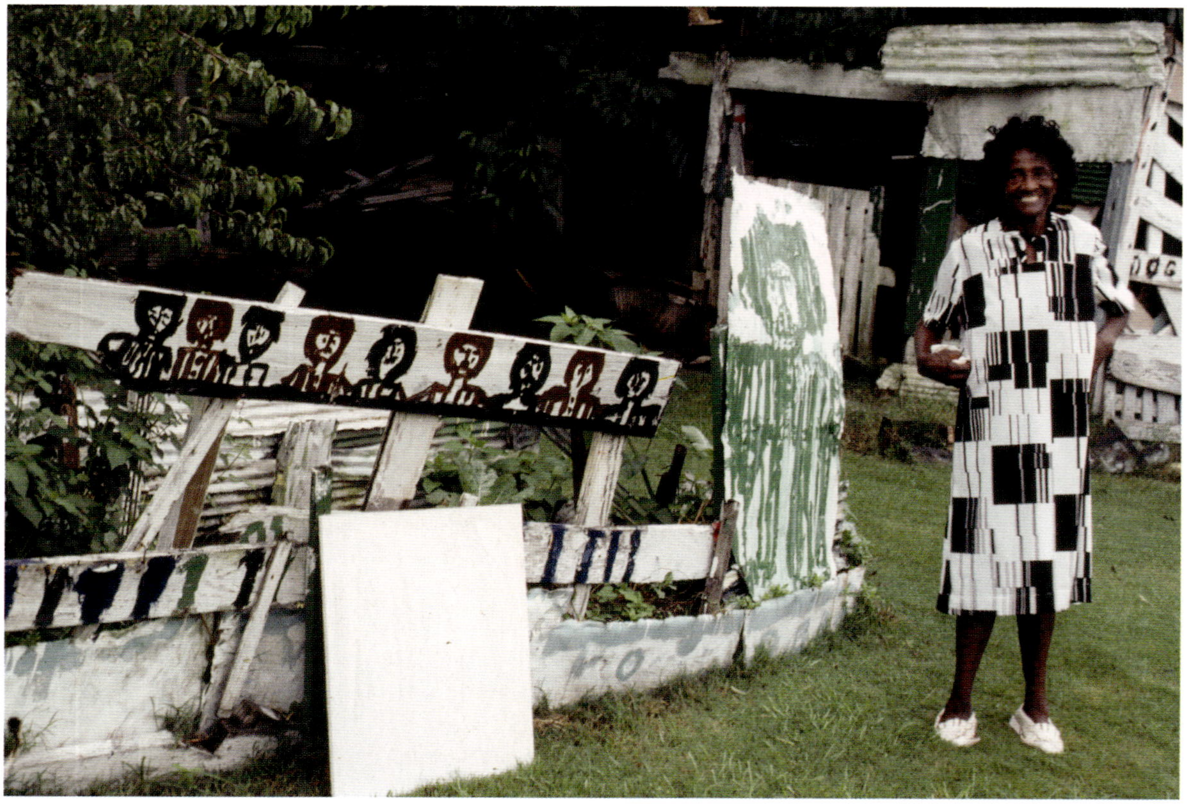

Mary T. Smith, August 1987, photograph. Souls Grown Deep Foundation. This portrait of Smith in her yard also illustrates her creative interpretation through fashion. Smith had an extensive wardrobe, and she used her personal style for further expressive takes and conveying of thought.

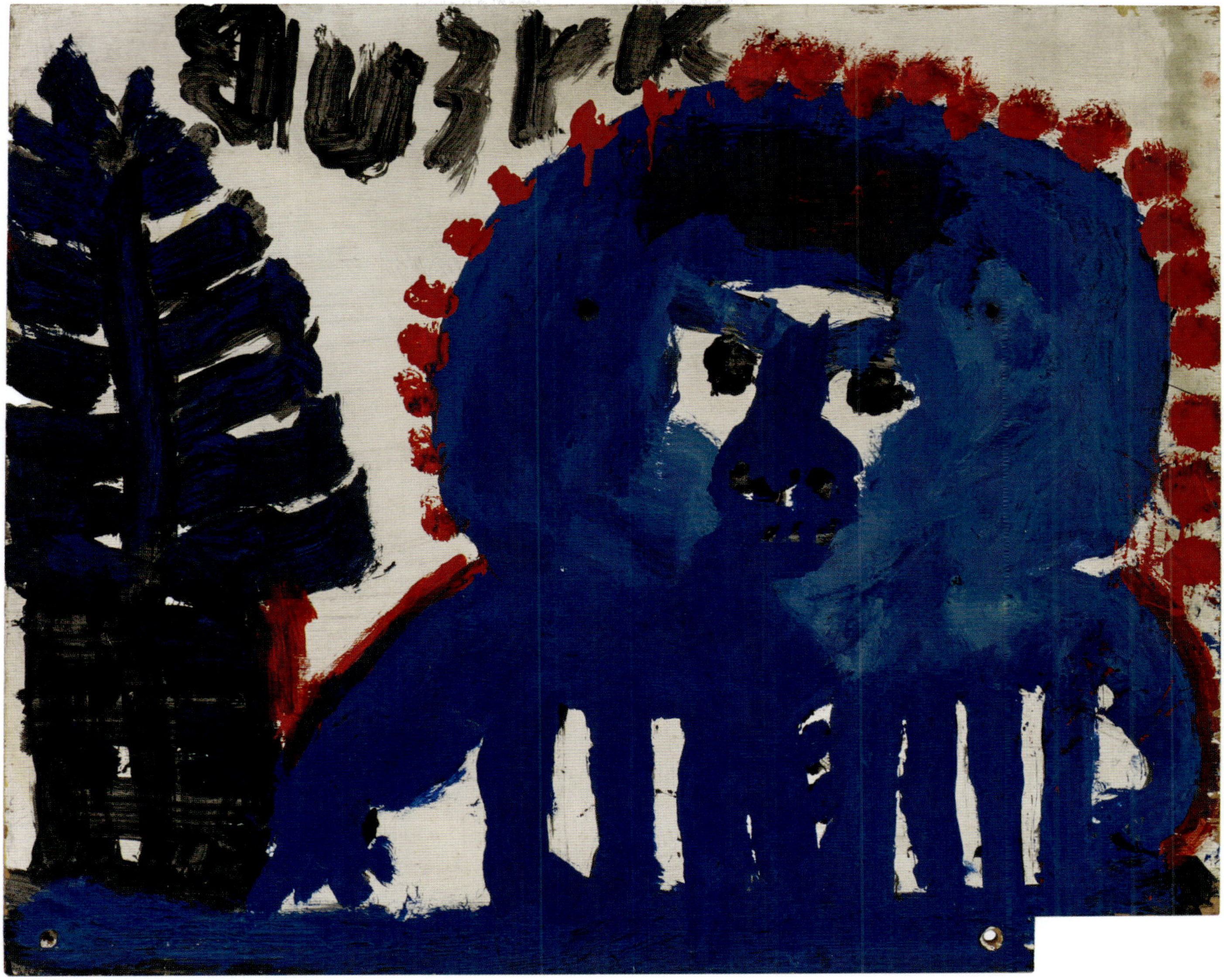

Mary T. Smith, Jesus, *1987, paint on wood, 21¾ × 27¾ in (55.3 × 70.5 cm). Souls Grown Deep Foundation.* Jesus was an important and consistent theme for Smith. In this painting, Jesus is rendered in a strong blue surrounded by red painted dots, emulating an aura. With her implementation of intentful cryptic language, Jesus is referred to as "Buzyk."

Mary T. Smith's output is an embodiment of "yard shows," a significant Southern tradition of African Americans emerging from the 1960s. This critical cultural phenomenon enacted the decorations on properties to convey messages not otherwise heard. Smith's house was on an acre of land on the main road heading into Hazelhurst, Mississippi. The primary material for early works was corrugated tin sourced from a nearby garbage depot. Her initial pursuits involved dragging individual remnants of tin back to her yard and building a corrugated fence around her property that acted as an initial exhibition space. Smith's home was adjacent to two vast billboards that mirrored, and perhaps informed, Smith's communication style, which is reminiscent of advertising in its striking but simple iconography and succinct slogans.

Smith's yard universe allowed her to directly convey her messages, perhaps as a way to transcend her communication challenges. Provocative, expressive, and direct, Smith cultivated her own personal painting vocabulary, which consisted of portraits, texts, and patterns. The iconography of Jesus appears abundantly in her work as figurative, abstract forms, and with specific biblical references to the holy trinity. Text in Smith's work is an intriguing component to her installations because she was literate but implemented invented language, known

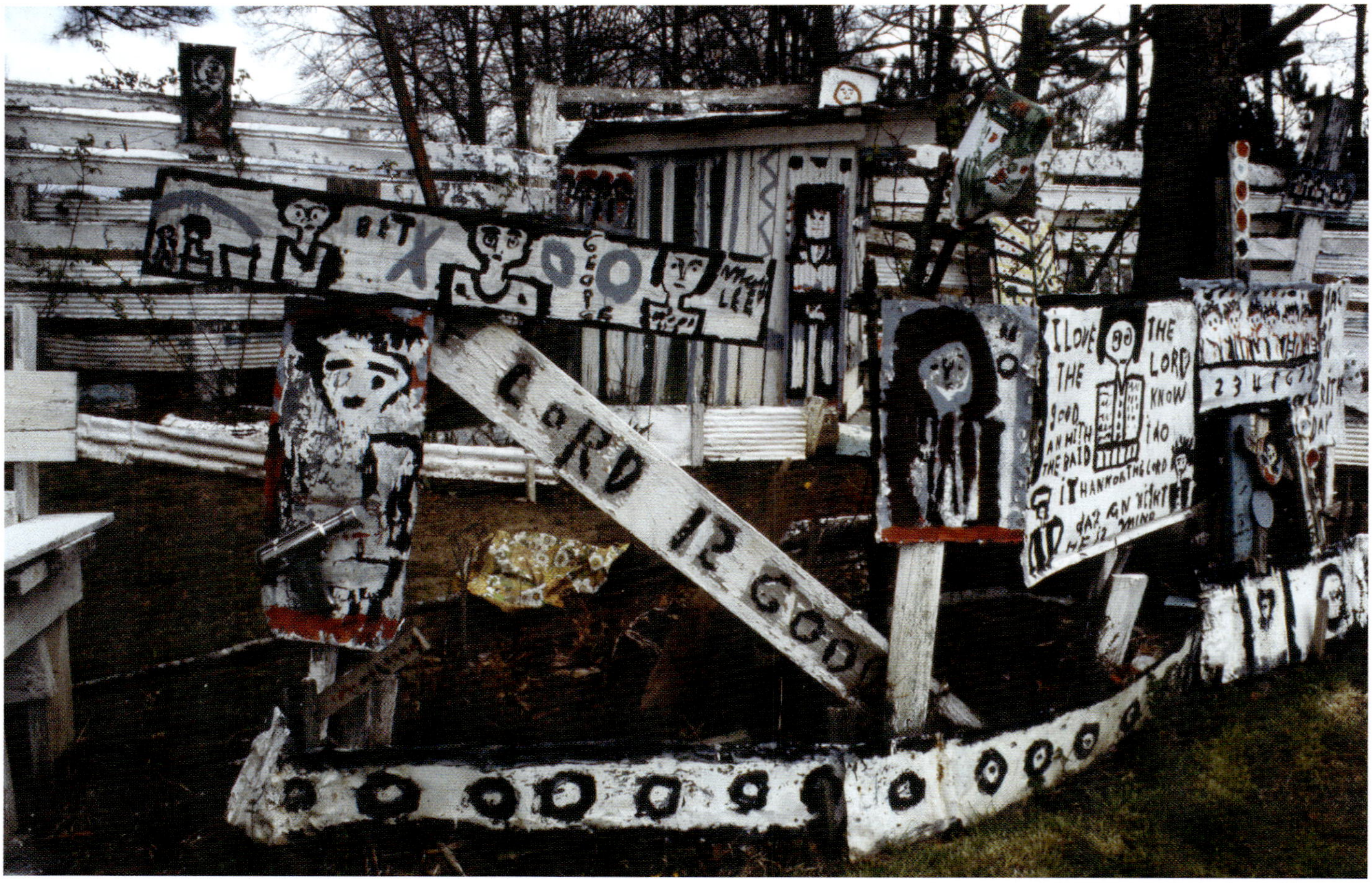

Mary T. Smith's Mississippi property, n.d., photograph by Willem Volkersz. SPACES. This view shows Smith's commitment to material and messaging. Painted on wood and corrugated metal, her figures and statements were displayed at multiple heights, directions, and planes. A painted face peers over the shed roof, while a diagonal plank stating "... E LORD IS GOOD" is joined by a low row of painted circles on reused material.

misspellings, and anagrams alongside conventionally written slogans. The use of circles as a repeated motif and pattern is evident, yet also enigmatic, throughout her practice. Personal graphic symbolism and the presentation of alternative language were overt decisions by Smith, cryptically leaving public clues to her visual prose.

Smith's work can be categorized into two eras, early (1975–1985) and late (1985–). The early works appear more explicit, often with white backgrounds and almost cartoonlike outlines of figures and characters. The later works have a noticeable complexity that is developed with colored backgrounds.

"When the rest of us were doing hopscotch, Mary would get on the ground somewhere else and draw pictures in the dirt and write funny things by the pictures."
– Elizabeth Alexander, Mary T. Smith's sister[10]

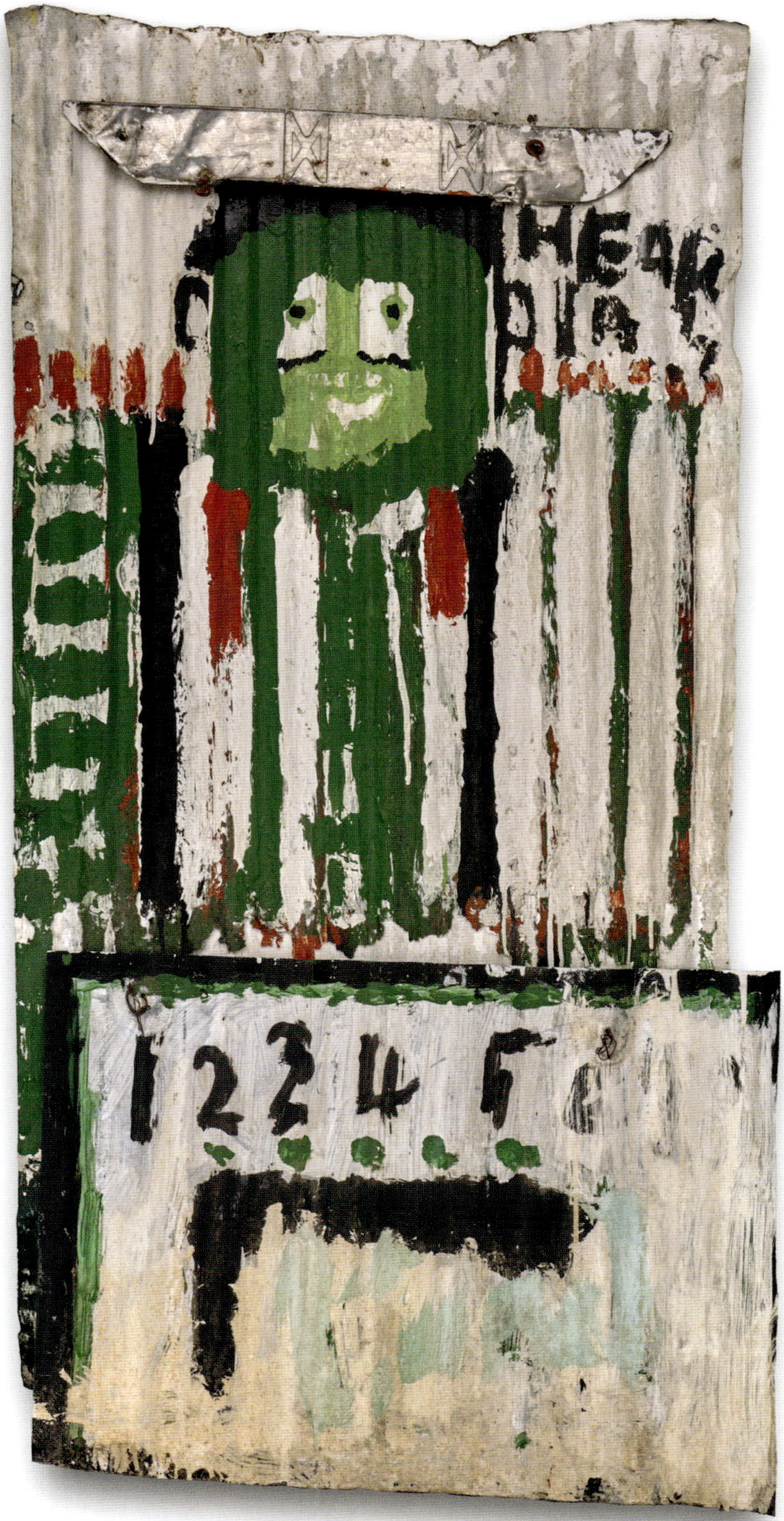

Mary T. Smith, Here I Am 12345, *1985, paint and chrome on tin, 49 × 27 in (124.5 × 68.6 cm). Souls Grown Deep Foundation.* This painting on tin shows Smith's use of wordplay and intentional misspelling. Here, she makes the statement "HEAR I AM" instead of "HERE I AM," very possibly referring to her own former struggles with communication due to her impairment.

PROPHET ROYAL ROBERTSON

(1936, St. Helena Parish–1997, Baldwin, Louisiana, USA)

A self-proclaimed prophet, Royal Robertson's creative output was composed of his visions and informed by a trinity of powerful sources: biblical scripture, science fiction, and his own autobiography. Living the majority of his life in Louisiana, Robertson was married to Adell Brent from 1955 until 1975. Their marriage ended, and with mental health issues already present for him, the devastation of divorce further pulled Robertson from reality. Residing alone, he began to transpose his visions into drawings and progressed into displaying sign-like graphics on the facade of his house. Adell was the central character in the narrative of his work, portrayed as the archetype of adultery and symbol of the apocalypse. Robertson's radical production was from the perspective of a prophet, forecasting a future both privately and publicly. Despite his home and yard being destroyed by Hurricane Andrew in 1992, Robertson's surviving work began appearing in exhibitions from 1997, the same year as his death. In 2011, he was the subject of the solo exhibition NO PROUD BASTARDS with White Columns, New York, and his work has been acquired into the collections of the African American Museum, Dallas, and the Smithsonian Museum of American Art, Washington, D.C.

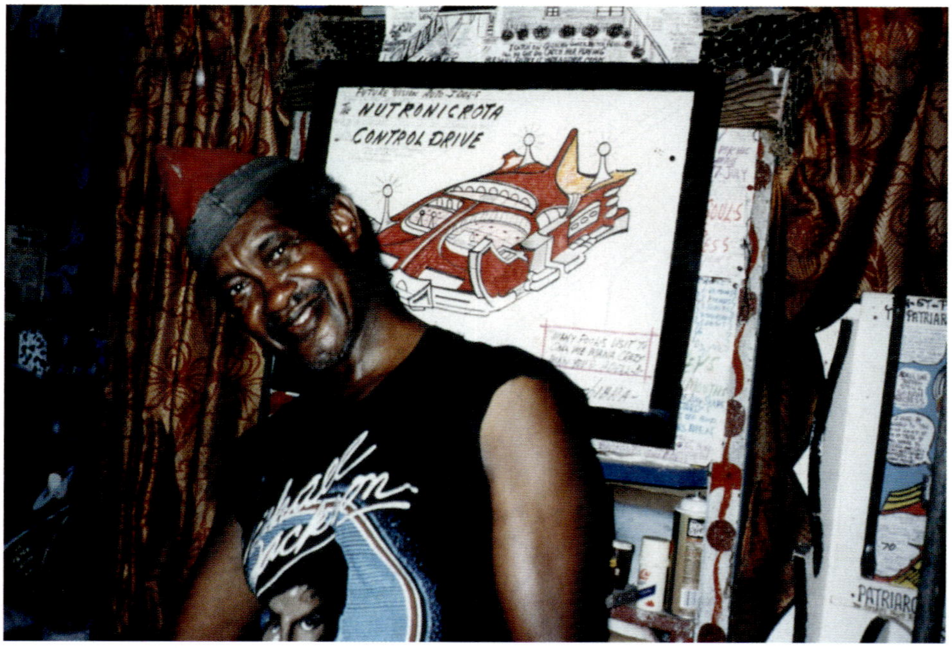

Prophet Royal Robertson, n.d., photograph. The Orange Show Center for Visionary Art, Houston. Here, Robertson is posed for the camera inside his Baldwin home. His drawings, which he created parallel to his sign and public-facing practice, are on view behind him.

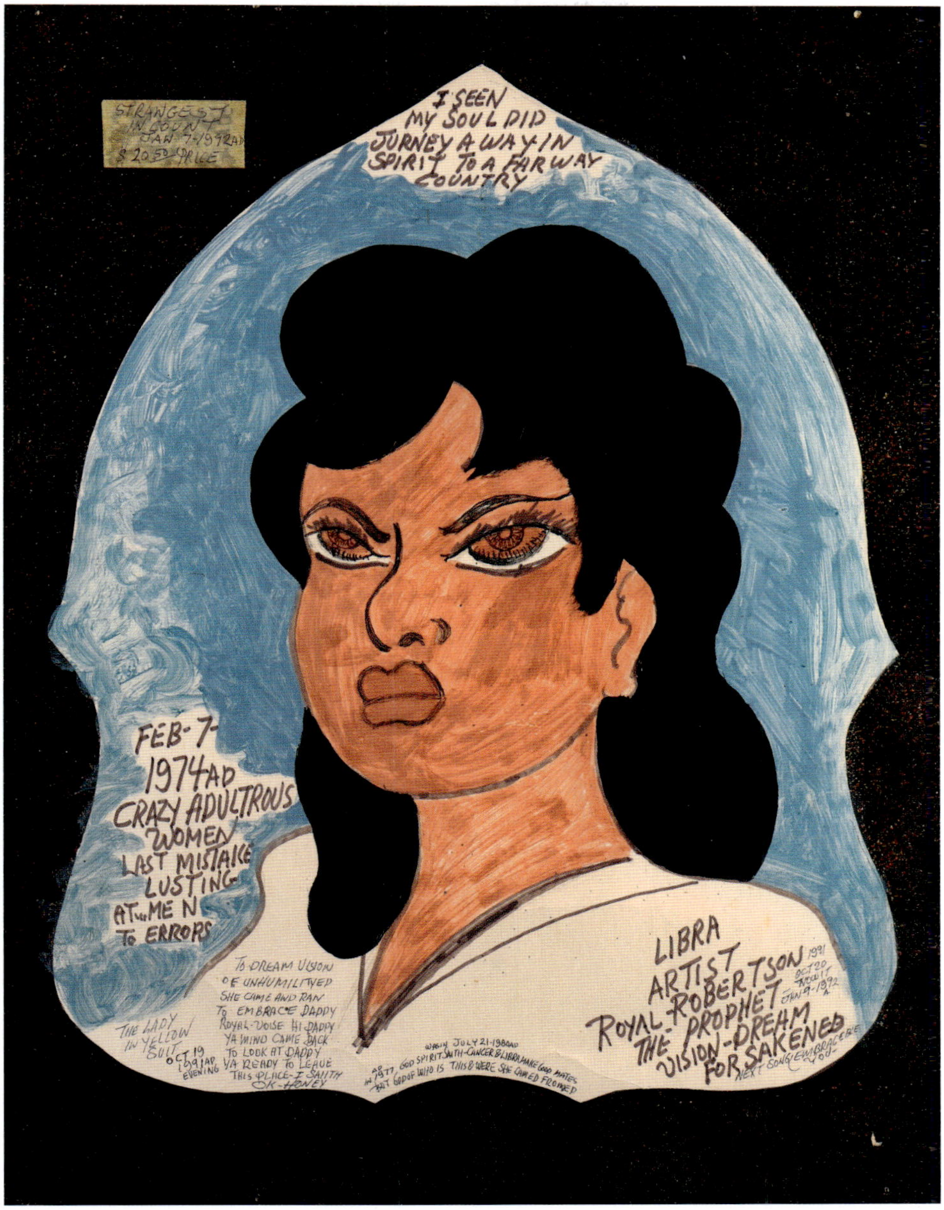

Prophet Royal Robertson, I Seen My Soul Did Journey Away, *1991, ink on paper, 28 × 22⅛ in (71 × 56 cm). The Museum + The Gallery of Everything.* The use of his ex-wife as a symbol of sexual adultery was at the core of Robertson's principle explorations into the dichotomy of the apocalypse and utopia, and the judgment between good and evil.

Prophet Royal Robertson's drawings and signs have a clear aesthetic attributed to science fiction and evangelism. Magazine advertisements and television commercials from the 80s and early 90s also influenced him stylistically. Without context, the subjectivity of Robertson's work is sporadic, even random, yet when his references and experience are elucidated, the concept becomes cohesive.

At the forefront of his oeuvre, Robertson's ex-wife Adell was employed as the ultimate symbol of sexual adultery. The couple were together for almost 20 years before she left, moving to Texas with their 11 children. Robertson had previously struggled with mental health, but the effects of his wife leaving him caused lasting trauma on his psyche. Adell became the paradigm for unfaithfulness and adultery. An updated Jezebel, "Adell," "prostitute," and "whore" became interchangeable and heavily featured throughout his work. Through his visions, Robertson further equated Adell to the apocalypse, substantiated by Bible verses from Leviticus. His autobiographical heartbreak and betrayal became an allegory that combined Christianity and intergalactic theory, filtered through hallucinatory visions. His domestic public installations displayed signs including: "SATAN CLAIMED SILLY ADELL" and "KEEP OUT HERE CRAZY BASTARDS WHOREMONGERS."

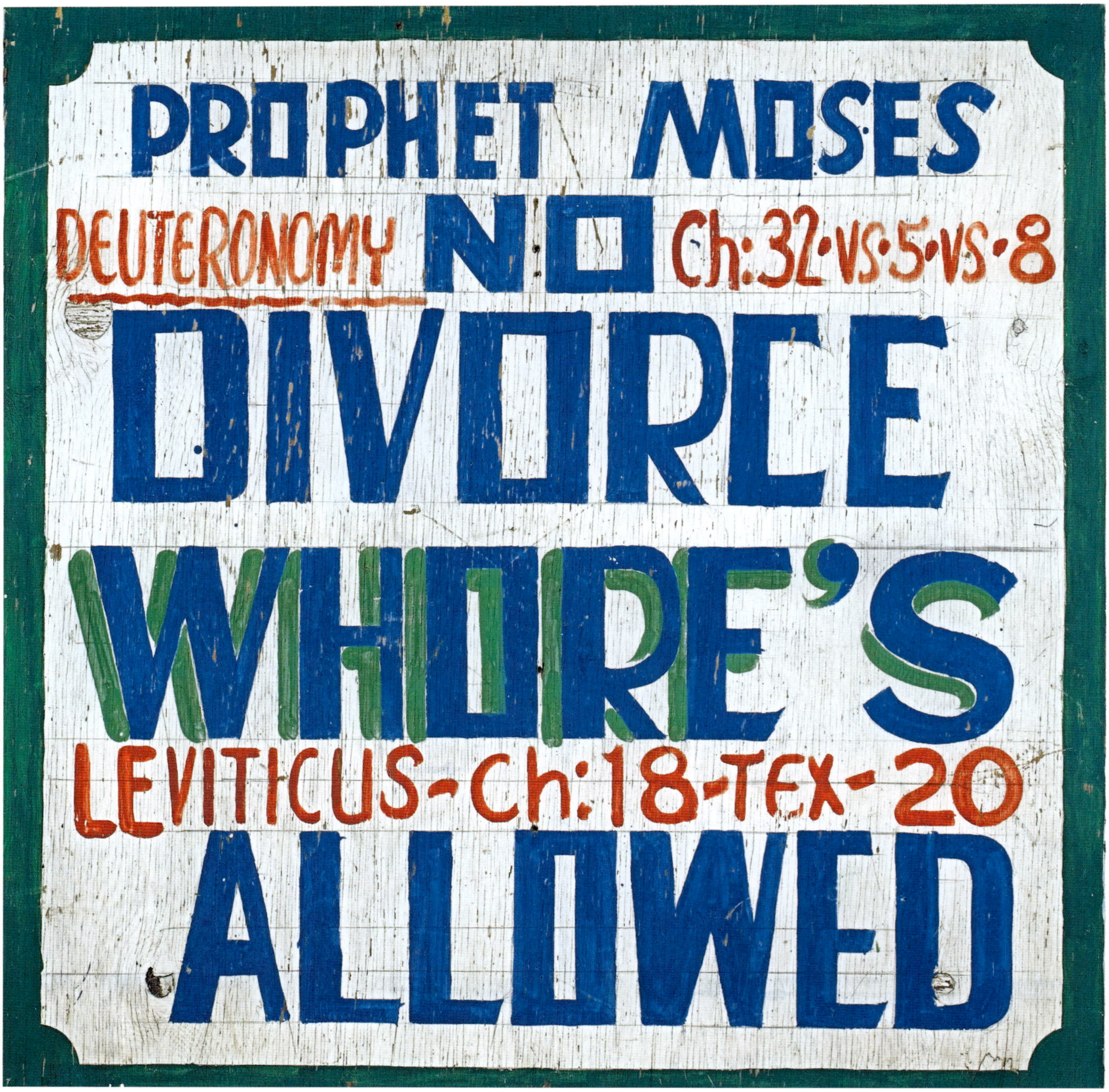

Prophet Royal Robertson, untitled (NO DIVORCE WHORE'S ALLOWED), *ca. 1980, paint on wood, 47⅝ × 48⅛ in (121 × 122 cm). The Museum + The Gallery of Everything.* This iconic sign painting, previously displayed outside of his home, encapsulates Robertson's drive to broadcast his intense messages, both biblical and addressing his unfaithful ex-wife. Aesthetically, it also demonstrates his training as an apprentice to a sign painter.

Robertson's "visions"—trances, hallucinations, and dreams—were steadfastly transcribed, providing the framework for his creative messaging. Robertson applied skills he learned working as an apprentice to a sign painter when he was younger to broadcast his visionary premonitions. On a prophetic mission, he populated his home's facade and front yard with bold polychromatic signs to spread his message to his immediate public. Robertson's more private practice of drawing included purely cosmic elements alongside Adell, as well as apocalyptic ponderings, calendars, and architecture that ranged from utopian proposals to apocalyptic shelters.

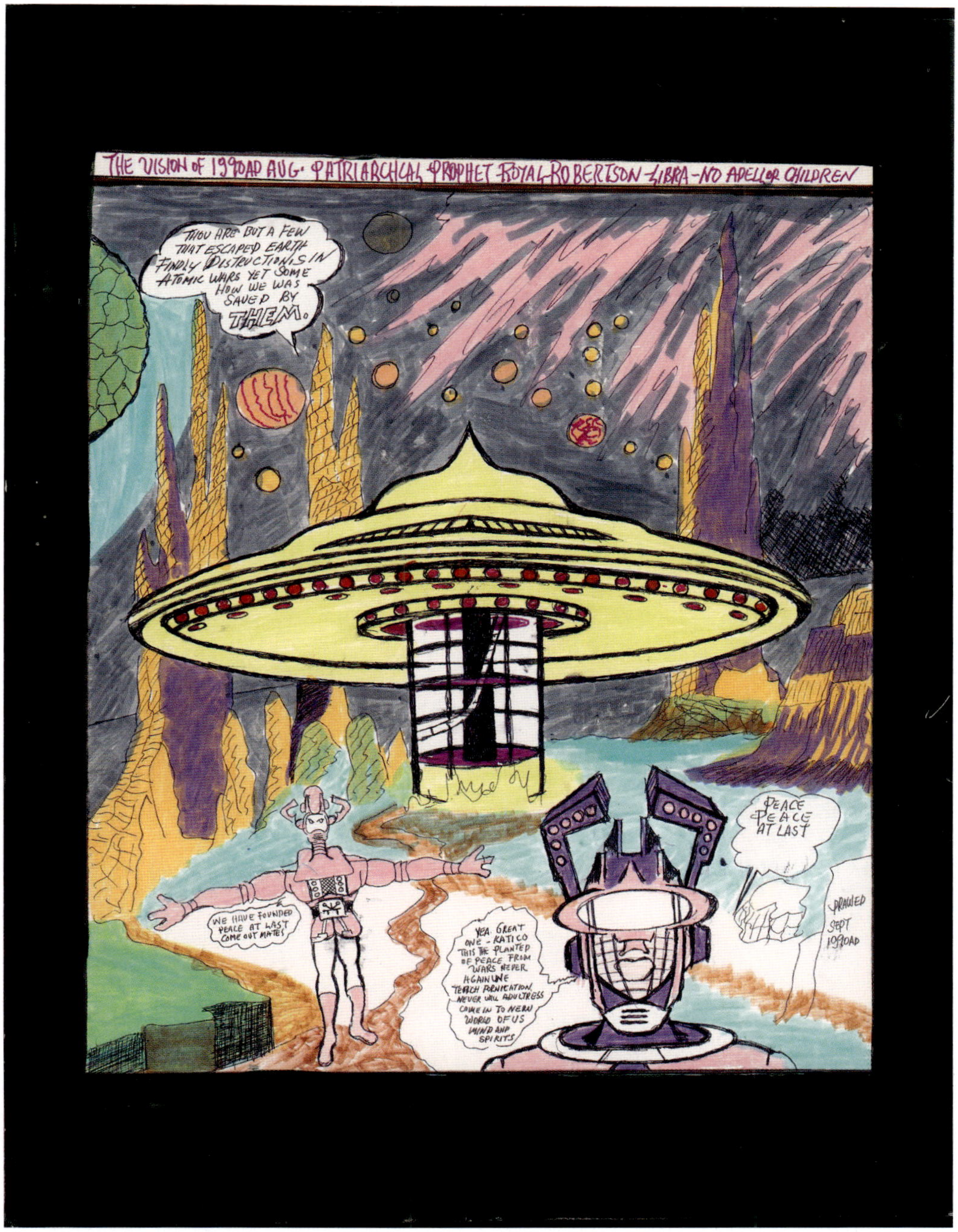

Prophet Royal Robertson, The Vision of 1990 AD Aug.. Thou are But a Few that Escaped Earth, *1990, mixed media on posterboard, 27⅞ × 22 in (70.8 × 56 cm). Smithsonian American Art Museum, Washington, D.C.* In this cosmic personal drawing, Robertson's vision teeters between the apocalypse and utopia with the arrival to another planet where the text bubble in upper left affirms "THOU ARE BUT A FEW THAT ESCAPED EARTH FINDLY DESTRUCTION. SIN ATOMIC WARS YET SOME HOW WE WAS SAVED BY THEM."

"[H]is work adds logically to the Revelation of Saint John. It represents an ultimate and revised contemporary version of the Apocalypse, it is a final warning, as controversial as it is sincere." – Frédéric Allamel, PhD, sociologist and anthropologist[11]

KWAME AKOTO

(b. 1950, Kumasi, Ghana)

The prolific creative practice of Kwame Akoto combines his profound faith with the aesthetics of graphic advertising, producing unique didactic surrealism. Trained as a sign painter in his native Kumasi, Akoto apprenticed with billboard masters before opening his own sign business in 1972. Following a religious conversion to Christianity in the early 1990s, he re-established his studio as *Almighty God Art Works* (accordingly, the name often identifying him artistically). His vivid paintings heavily feature contemporary Ghanaian culture and Christianity to examine the moral paradigms of vice, morality, and consequence. Often incorporating text, Akoto's paintings are direct, not esoteric. Stylistically aligned with his professional business and sign-painting experience, Akoto often works from references—magazines, celebrity images, and self-portrait photographs. He was included in Susan Vogel's *Africa Explores,* published by the Center of African Art, New York (1991), and exhibited with *The Museum of Everything #7* at the Museum of New and Old Art, Hobart (2017). His paintings are in the collection of the British Museum, London, and Quai Branly Museum, Paris.

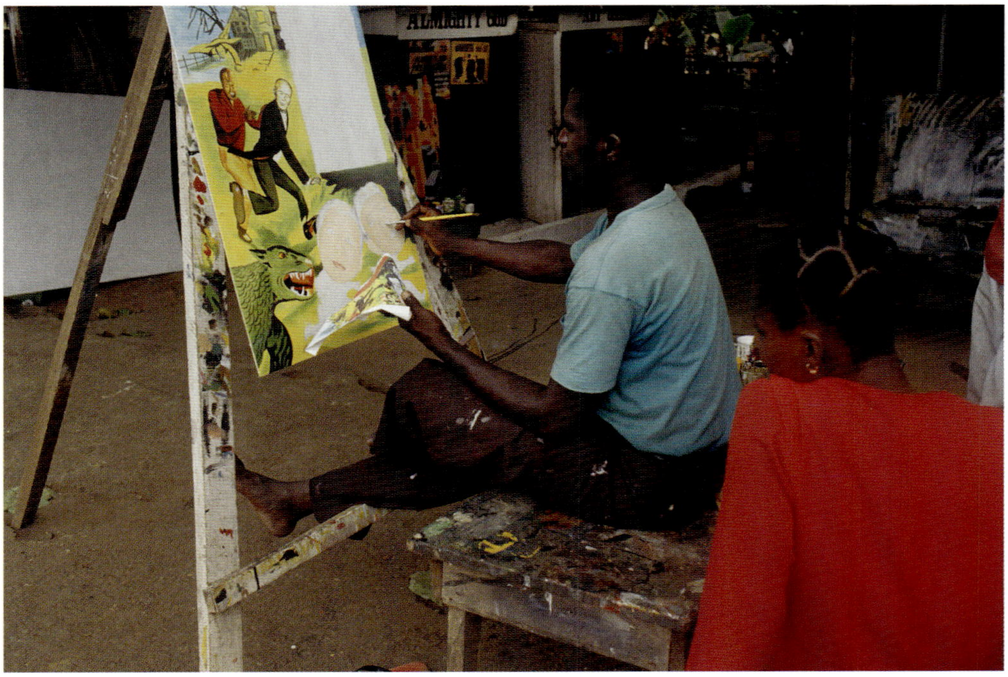

Kwame Akoto, n.d., photograph by Pierre Schwartz. Courtesy Françoise Adamsbaum. Working from his open-air studio in Kumasi, Akoto is painting what appears to be an allegorical composition. Often working with students and apprentices, the photograph features an observer of his work in progress.

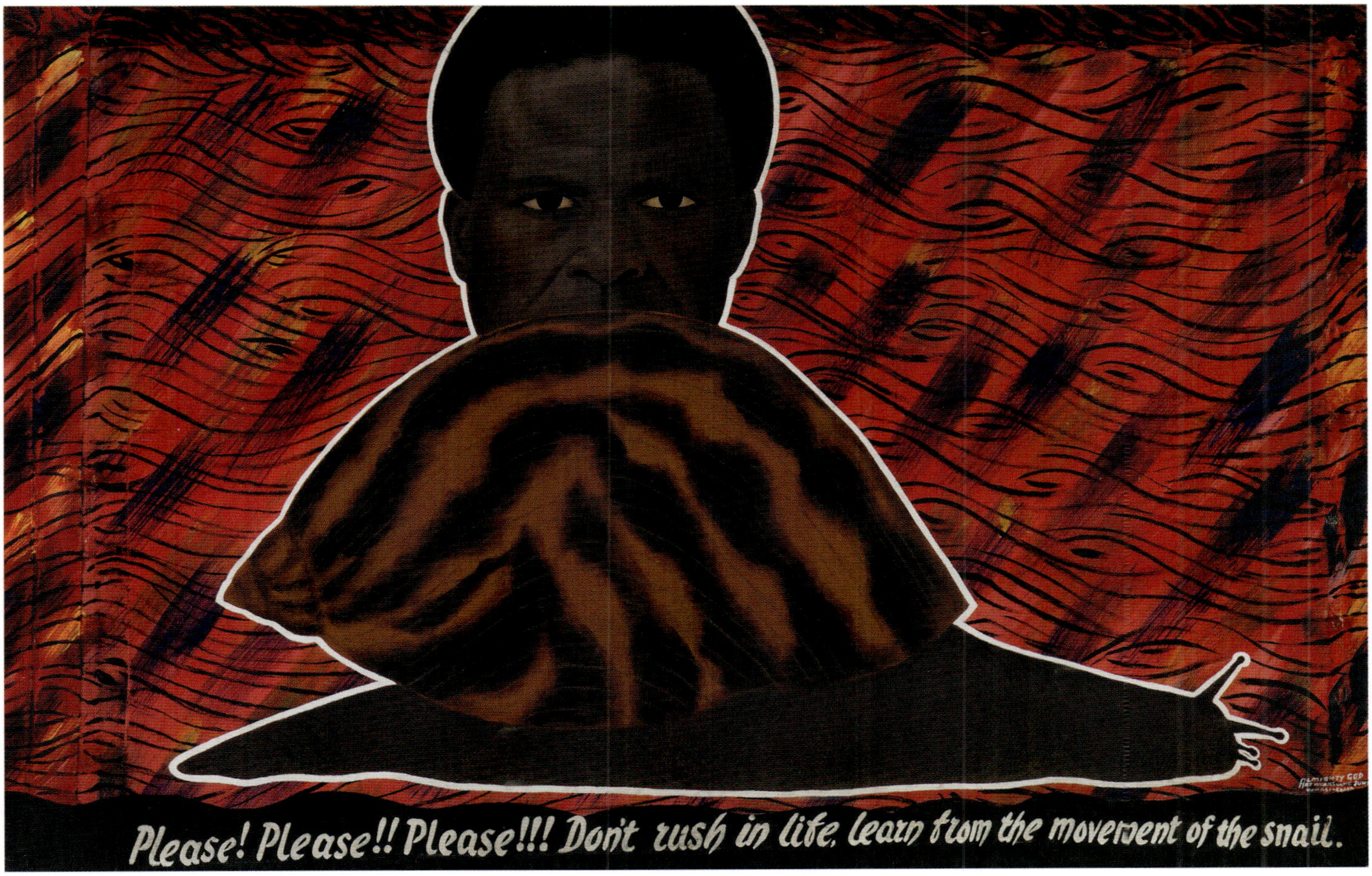

Kwame Akoto, Don't Rush in Life, *n.d., oil on canvas, 34¼ × 53⁹⁄₁₆ in (87 × 136 cm). Courtesy Françoise Adamsbaum.* Set against a densely patterned background, in this allegorical painting Kwame appears from behind a snail shell. The message along the bottom reads: Please! Please!! Please!!! Don't rush in life, learn from the movement of the snail

Kwame Akoto was still in his teens when he began studying under two leading billboard painters in Kumasi, Kwasi Addaï and Kobia Amafi. Subsequent to an extensive apprenticeship, Akoto opened his own shop/studio, initially called *Anthony Artworks*. With a penchant for graphic text, his early focus was custom calligraphy for automobiles and trucks, as well as advertising poster commissions.

When Akoto became a devout Christian in 1991, religion became greatly influential, infiltrating many aspects of his life. As a member of the Pentecostal House of Faith Ministries for decades, he has established himself as a renowned preacher and healer, adjacent to his creative messaging. His visual creative practice has become an extension of his ministry, influenced by his autobiographical accounts, community interaction, biblical narratives, and popular culture.

The studio and sign shop *Almighty God Art Works* is an expansive space in Kumasi. Hervé Di Rosa, French artist and early proponent, recalled his residency with the artist from 1993, where Akoto sat at an easel with a dozen or so assistants, students, and trainees. The open-air studio is resourceful and materially conservative. Di Rosa recollected Akoto's ability to present a spectrum of colors by mixing yellow, red, blue, black, and white from a limit of five pots of color, using repurposed wood as a palette. The local library is used to source reference images and Akoto's paintings often reveal elements of photographic reproduction.

Akoto's implementation of calligraphy is synonymous with established advertising signage and therefore registers a sense of recognition to the viewer. This aesthetic familiarity provides the allure and effectiveness of advertising to his messages. As visionary messages, his parabolic compositions of vices and virtues include quitting smoking, abusing alcohol, and his personal tribulations of divorce. Self-portraits are also significant in his "Creativity art", which allow Akoto to reflect on his personal, communal, and spiritual positioning. His rebellious act is through the subtle tool of turning his trained aesthetics of advertising into his personal messaging.

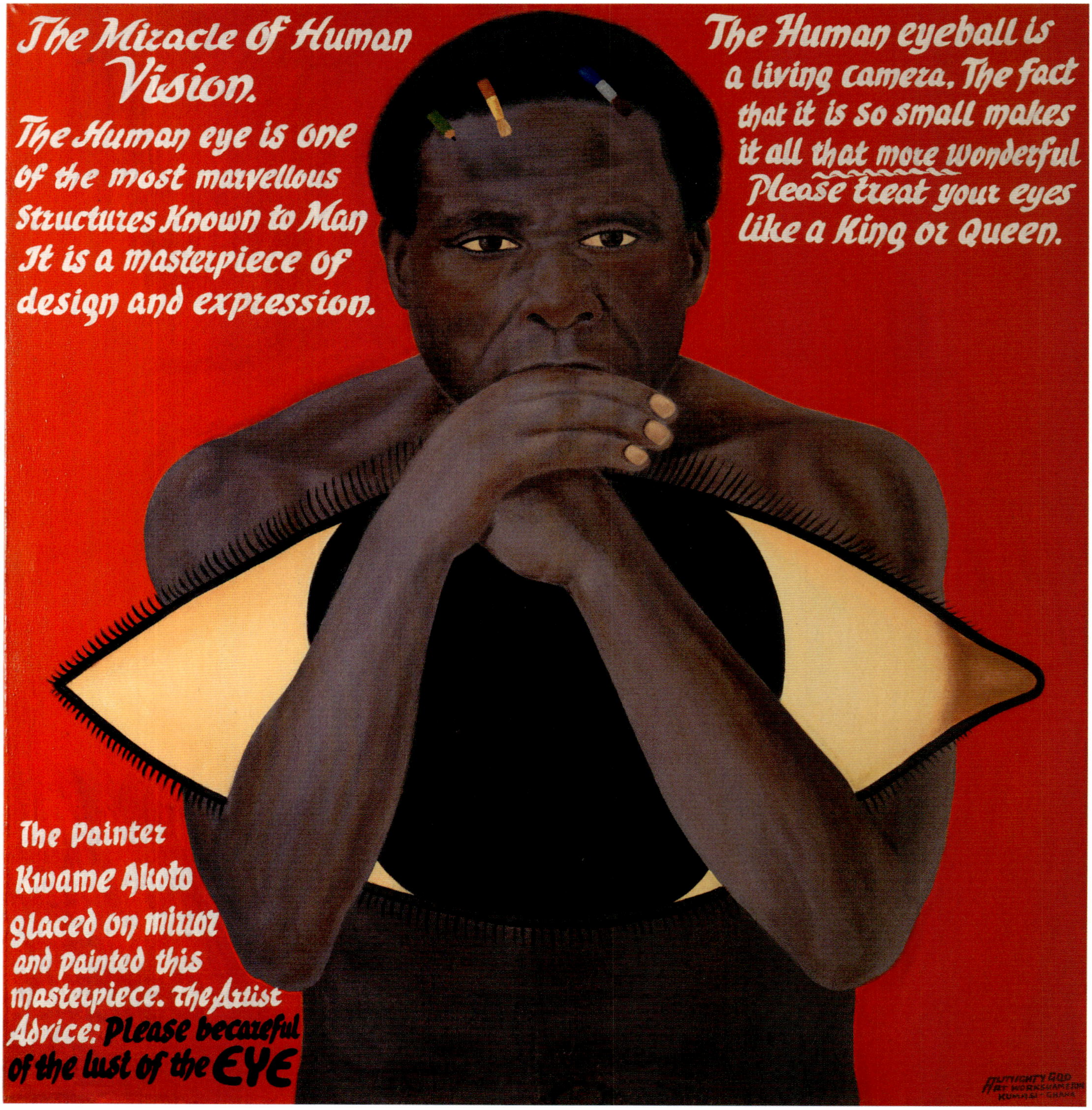

Akoto Kwame, untitled (The Miracle of Human Vision)*, 2016, oil on canvas, 47¼ × 47¼ in (120 × 120 cm). The Museum + The Gallery of Everything.* A self-portrait, Akoto looks at the viewer with a contemplative stare embracing a large eye. With paintbrushes in his hair, he seemingly also aims to establish himself as the artist. His style, influenced by advertisement, relies on imagery juxtapositioned with text.

"What I love most is to be a witness of Jesus Christ, create art, sing, and get physical exercise." – Kwame "Almighty God" Akoto[12]

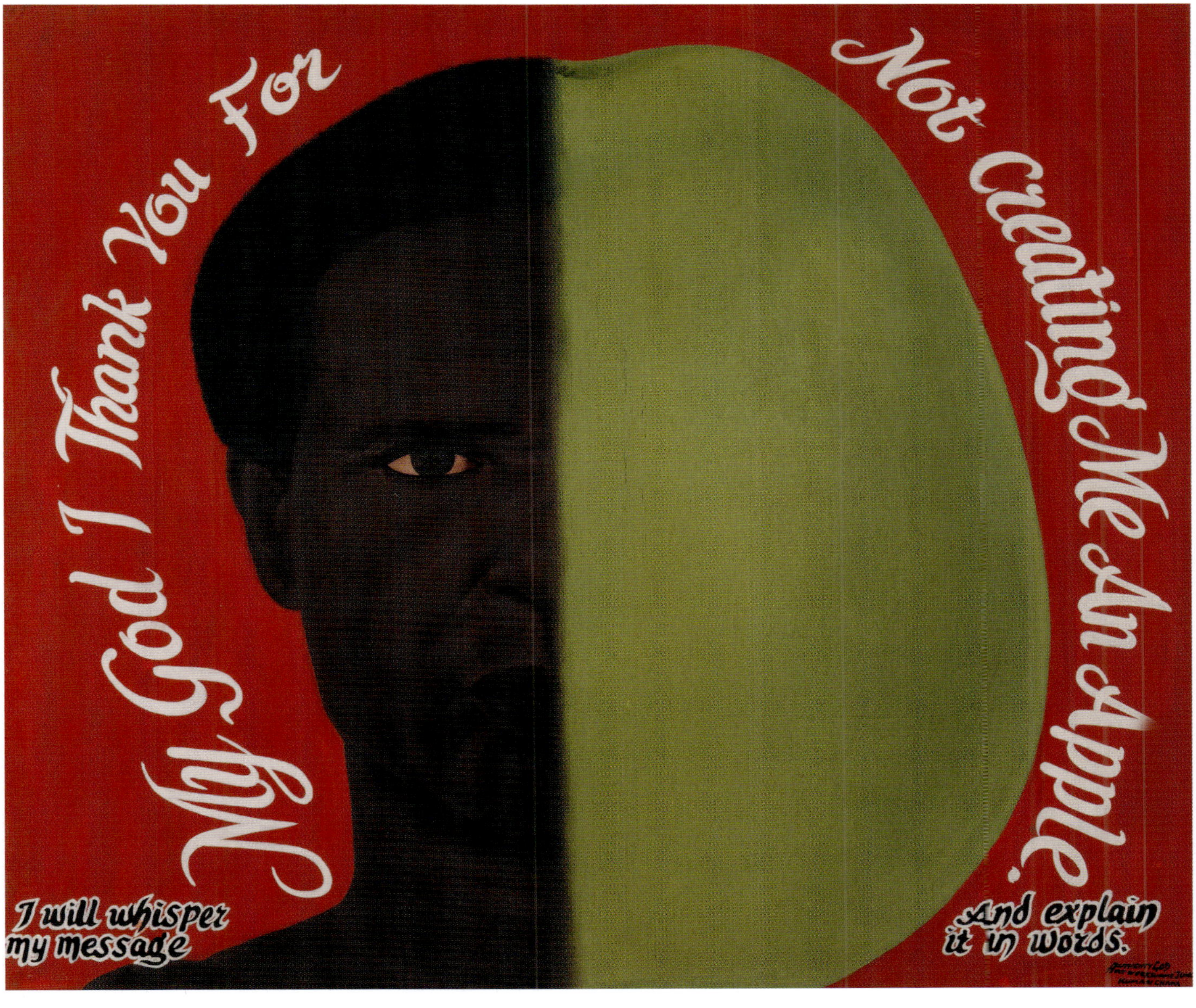

Kwame Akoto, My God Apple, *n.d., oil on canvas, 55 15/16 × 46 7/16 in (142 × 118 cm). Courtesy Françoise Adamsbaum.* The composition of the graphic and conceptual elements of *My God Apple* exemplifies Akoto's text aesthetic developed from sign-painting, with the confidence to make conceptual decisions such as the surreal amalgamation of his face with an apple.

HORST ADEMEIT

(1937, Cologne–2010, Düsseldorf, Germany)

Horst Ademeit initiated an arduous daily practice in 1990 that photographically documented his private and public surroundings. Each photograph is accompanied by meticulous notes that addressed his perceived invisible threats. Lowered body temperature, faulty appliances, and moldy bread were among the initial observations of "cold rays" by Ademeit. He went on to systematically examine these dubious imperceptible radiations, producing over 6,000 polaroids of his immediate and local environment in the process. Ademeit, born out of wedlock in 1937, grew up between orphanages in Cologne and foster care in Thuringia when German cities were under threat during World War II. In 1964 he received a degree in textile design and following his graduation he studied fine art for a semester at Kunstakademie Düsseldorf under the derogatory tutelage of Joseph Beuys who dismissed Ademeit's art as merely decorative. However, his now distinguished collection of polaroids were not conducted as conceptual art, but as a documentary science experiment. Through a circuitous route, Ademeit's polaroids were only first exhibited in 2009 with Galerie Susanne Zander, Cologne. Though he never intended his studies of "cold rays" to be art, Ademeit was content about his recognition, as it shared his concern and analysis of imperceptible radial waves to a wider audience.

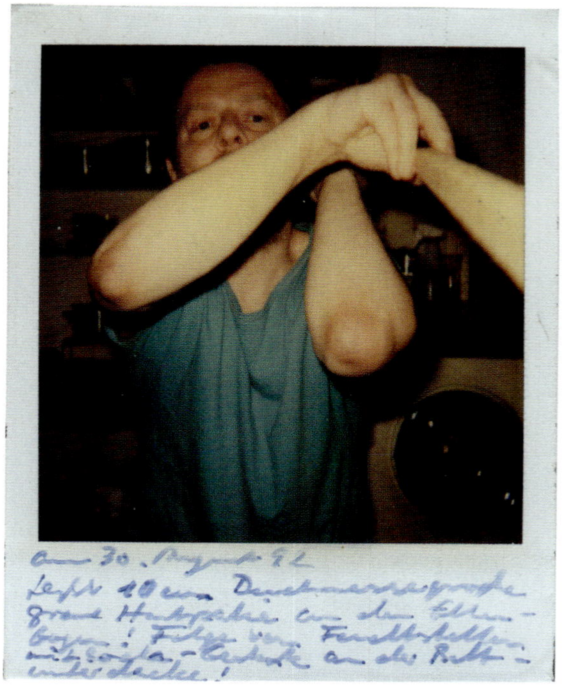

Horst Ademeit, untitled, *August 30, 1992, inscribed polaroid,* $4\frac{5}{16} \times 3\frac{9}{16}$ *in (11 × 9 cm). Delmes & Zander Gallery, Cologne.* This self-portrait, dated August 30, 1992, was recorded as part of Ademeit's daily documentation of "cold rays." With his arms toward the camera his inscription cites "*fast 10 cm Durchmessergroße graue Hautpatie an den Ellenbogen! Folge von Feuchtstellen mit Soda-Gestank an der Bettunterdecke!*" ("almost 10 cm in diameter gray skin patch on the elbow! Result of damp spots with a soda stink on the bedspread!")

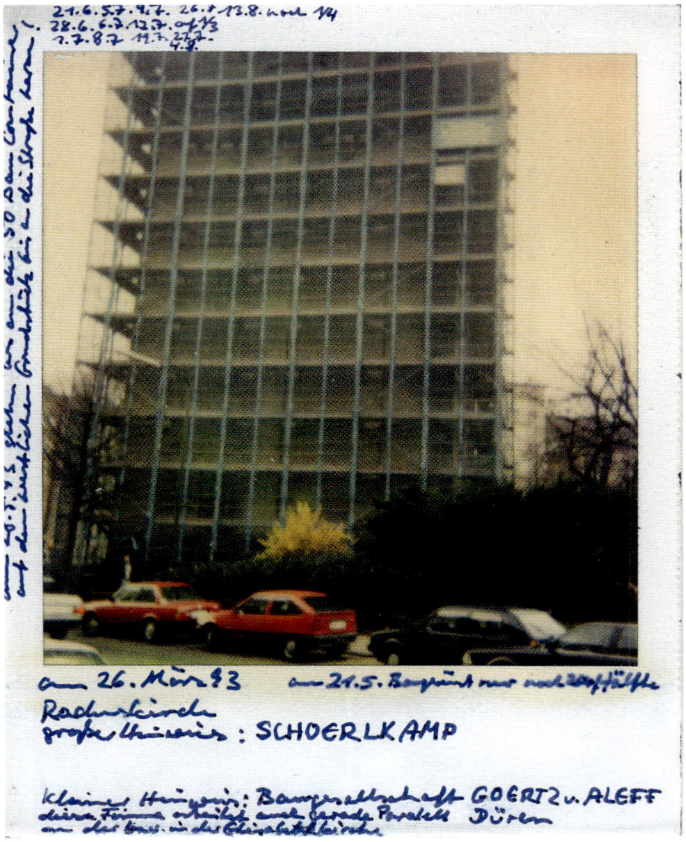

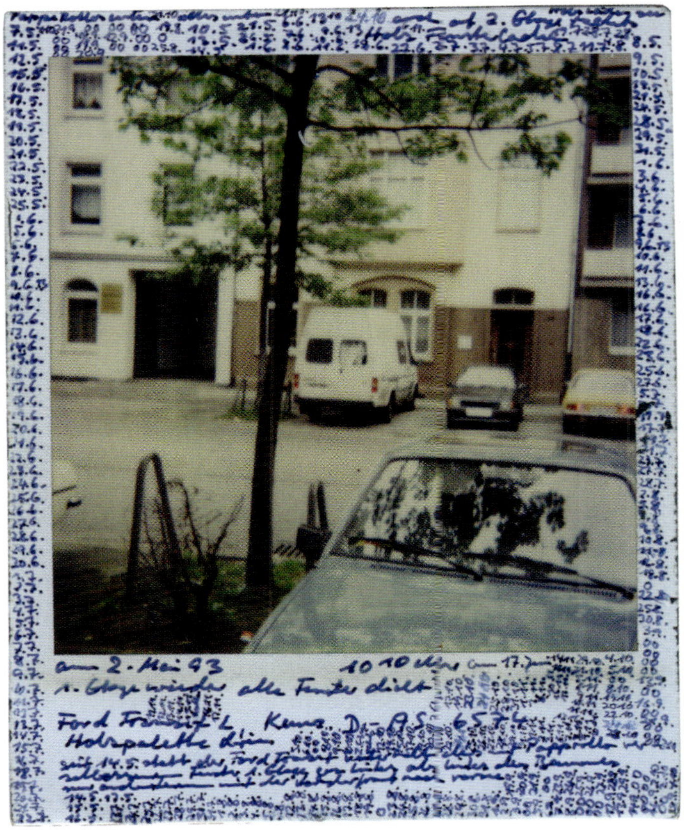

Horst Ademeit, untitled, *March 26, 1993, inscribed polaroid, 4⁵⁄₁₆ × 3⁹⁄₁₆ in (11 × 9 cm). Delmes & Zander Gallery, Cologne.* On this 1993 polaroid taken of temporary scaffolding, Ademeit's notes spanned a period of time: March 23, May 21, and May 28. His reporting includes the number of construction containers on a nearby property, the progression of the scaffolding erected and the construction company, GOERTZ and ALEFF.

Horst Ademeit, untitled, *May 2, 1993, inscribed polaroid, 4⁵⁄₁₆ × 3⁹⁄₁₆ in (11 × 9 cm). Delmes & Zander Gallery, Cologne.* Dated May 2, 1993, this polaroid features what could be considered a very ordinary scene of Ademeit's local neighborhood. However, the accompanying inscription, with hundreds of decimal numbers, implies that Ademeit saw something we cannot.

Horst Ademeit moved into a welfare apartment in Düsseldorf in 1987, and it was in this apartment that he first perceived the effects of what he identified as "cold rays." Ademeit became preoccupied with an idea of invisible radiation that was omnipresent. He was suspicious of the perceived effects he encountered, including electrical appliances suddenly becoming defective, and a lowered body temperature. Motivated by his concerns, he began experiments that extended beyond his theories of cold rays, and into greater considerations of electromagnetic waves that have the potential to encompass X-rays and powerlines.

Two factors for this experimentation process were critical: the immediacy of visual documentation and the functionality of keeping notations inseparable from the image. Pragmatically, in 1990, Ademeit acquired a Polaroid camera which, in addition to its instant processing feature, had the white border, larger at the bottom, that allocated space for his text-based studies. The written transcriptions became denser over time and presented an idiosyncratic framework, including personal observations of smells or sounds, reference to the history of objects in the neighborhood, conjointly with headlines from Germany's local tabloid paper.Through a journey that would last decades, Ademeit's act of documenting daily radiations formed an aesthetic chronology going from personal to public and public to personal.

Part of Ademeit's daily experiments consisted of intimate compositions from inside his apartment and walking through his neighborhood setting his environment as a subject for his studies. Monitoring his locale, he cited seemingly innocuous public elements, such as scaffolding, to be amplifiers of harmful radiation. In addition to his photographic observations, he conducted various conditional measurements from thermometers, light meters, and readings from a plethora of his own constructed devices.

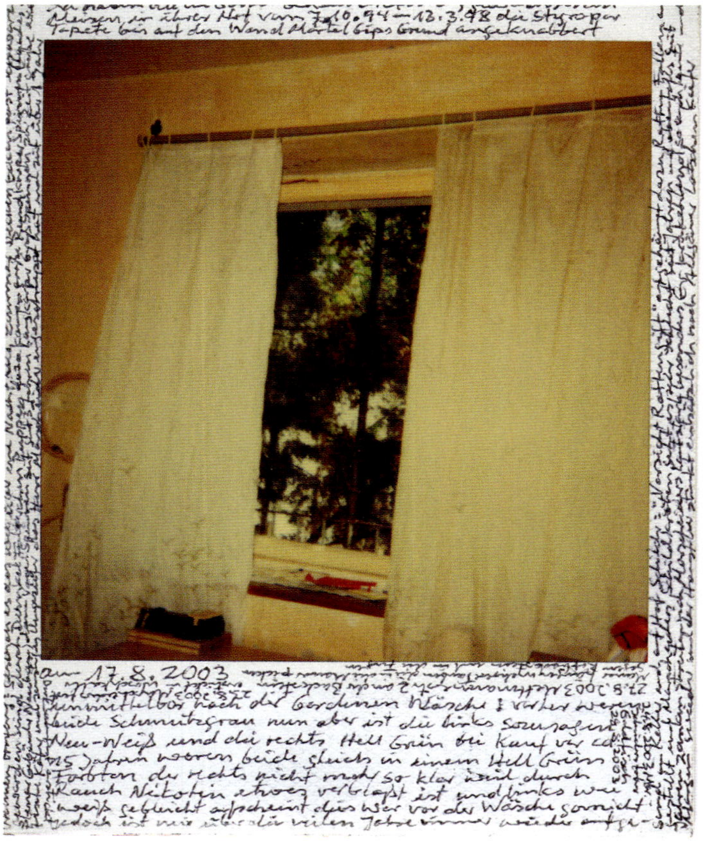

Horst Ademeit, untitled, *August 17, 2003, inscribed polaroid, 4 5/16 × 3 9/16 in (11 × 9 cm). Delmes & Zander Gallery, Cologne.* Dated July 17, 2003, this interior photograph is likely taken in Ademeit's apartment. With its window to the outside world, it acts as a metaphor to his larger concerns and pursuits of harmful "cold rays." For Ademeit, the source of these, beyond the inanimate objects, was both personal and local to his environment. He suspected various specific adversaries throughout his practice.

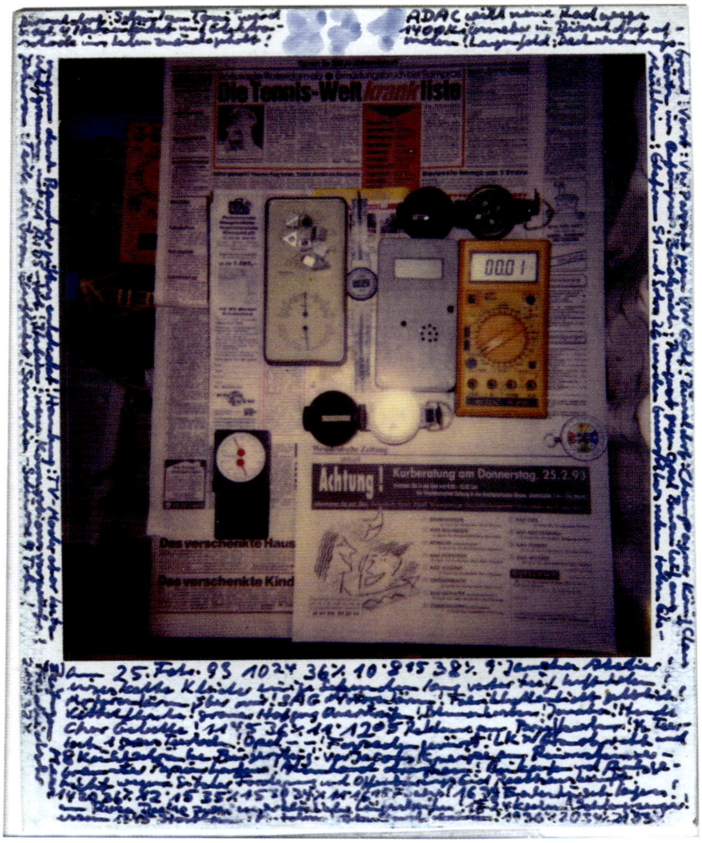

Horst Ademeit, 0871, *February 25, 1993, inscribed polaroid, 4 5/16 × 3 9/16 in (11 × 9 cm). Delmes & Zander Gallery, Cologne.* Part of Ademeit's documentary practice involved setting up compositions of objects inside his apartment. Various measuring devices are carefully positioned on top of layers of newspaper. The upper left is the sports section from a Düsseldorf newspaper, while a newspaper page on the lower left provides documentation of the date, February 25, 1993.

"It's only a question of time, before I'll have caught you in the act." – Horst Ademeit[29]

Horst Ademeit, 4518, *July 29, 2001, inscribed polaroid, 4⁵⁄₁₆ × 3⁹⁄₁₆ in (11 × 9 cm). Delmes & Zander Gallery, Cologne.* This visually abstract polaroid from 2001 demonstrates Ademeit's increasing implementation of inscriptions to accompany his photographs. The compact and small words and numbers become likely indecipherable to anyone but Ademeit.

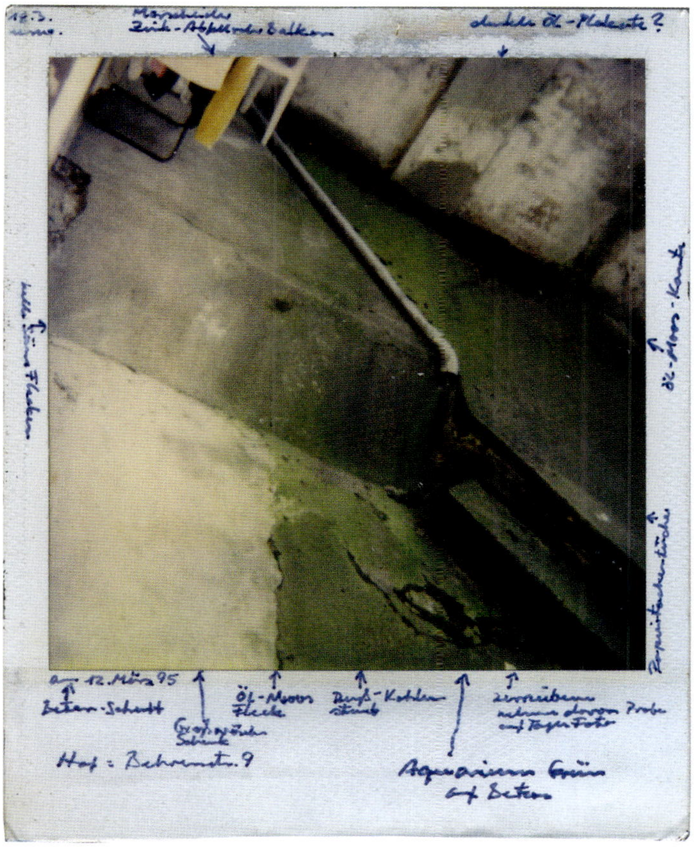

Horst Ademeit, untitled, *March 12, 1995, inscribed polaroid, 4⁵⁄₁₆ × 3⁹⁄₁₆ in (11 × 9 cm). Delmes & Zander Gallery, Cologne.* The relationship between visual and text in this polaroid has a diagrammatic quality. Ademeit used text sparingly, accompanied by drawn arrows for analysis. Such descriptions include "*M. Zink-Abfallrohr Balkon*" ("zinc waste-pipe balcony") and "*helle Säure Flecken*" ("bright acid spots").

CHAPTER 7

ENVIRONMENTS: CHANGING PERSONAL AND PUBLIC SURROUNDINGS

SINGULAR SPACES/ AUTHENTIC VISIONS

Jo Farb Hernández

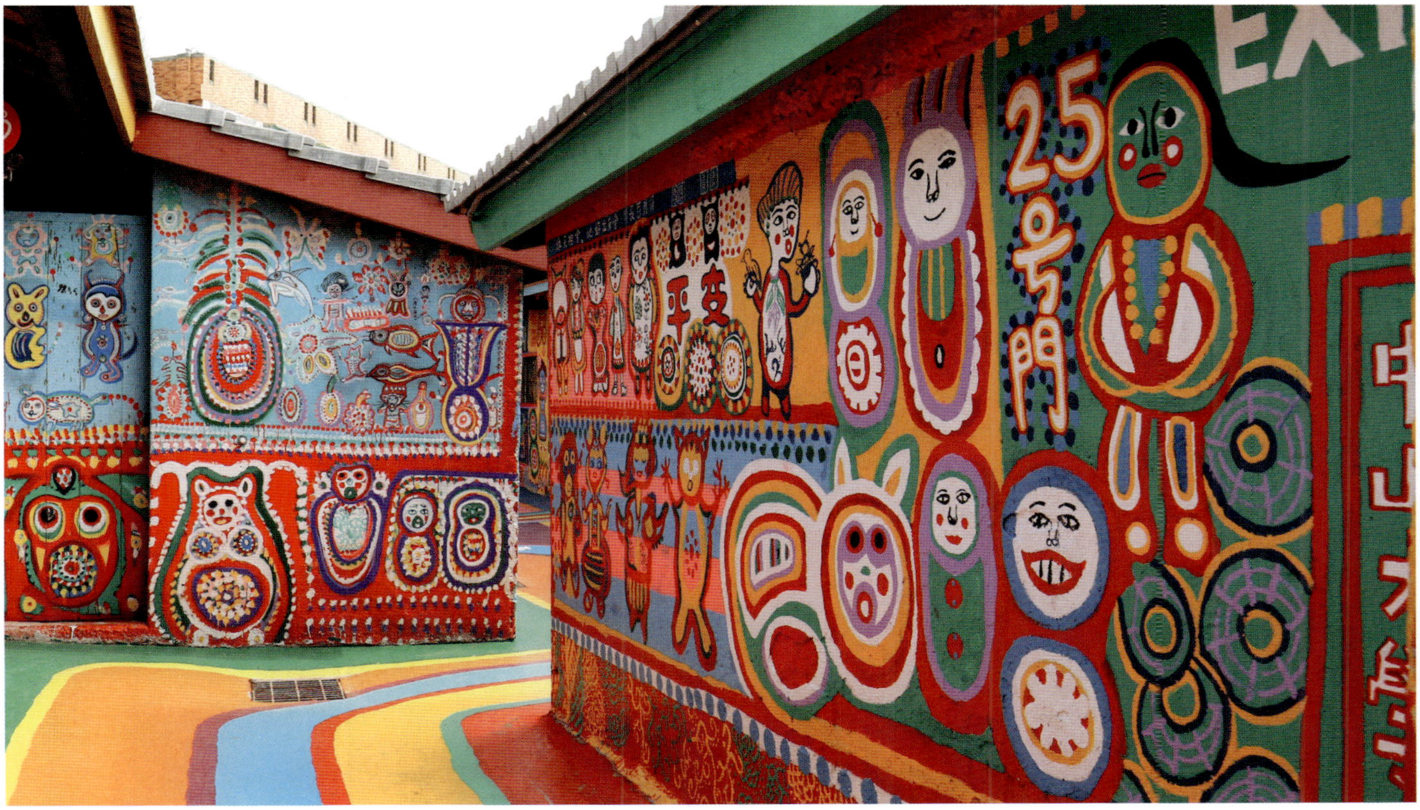

Huang Yong-Fu, Rainbow Village, *Taichung, photograph, n.d. Rainbow CreativeCo., Ltd. Rainbow Village's* alleyways, abundant with Huang's creations, are considered by visitors as a temple to the god of happiness. Some even consider it a pilgrimage, having adopted the ritual of writing their hopes and wishes on small pieces of paper, which are then hung inside the building's caves.

Art environments created by self-taught artists—elaborate site-specific installations constructed on the builder's own property or on a site that holds particular meaning—straddle genres, media, technique, content, and intent perhaps more than most other categories of art. These material "happenings," somewhat less performative than the original spectacles from the 1960s, yet equally linked to review by, and participation from, an often anonymous public, are complex on numerous levels, despite the avowal by past casual researchers of the "spontaneous" nature of their creation. While on rare occasions an art environment builder might envision a grand idea and work toward the realization of that goal, it is more common for these monumental sites to grow organically, expanding accretively to conceptual and physical heights that even amaze its author. "If someone had told me I would make something this big/elaborate/complicated, I never would have believed it," has been the proudly surprised observation made to me by more than one maker. When this happens, the creator-builder's personal identity becomes entwined with a new and previously unanticipated public and socially-defined persona.

I use the term "creator-builder" consciously, as the majority of these makers do not start out considering themselves to be artists, although many do, finally, come

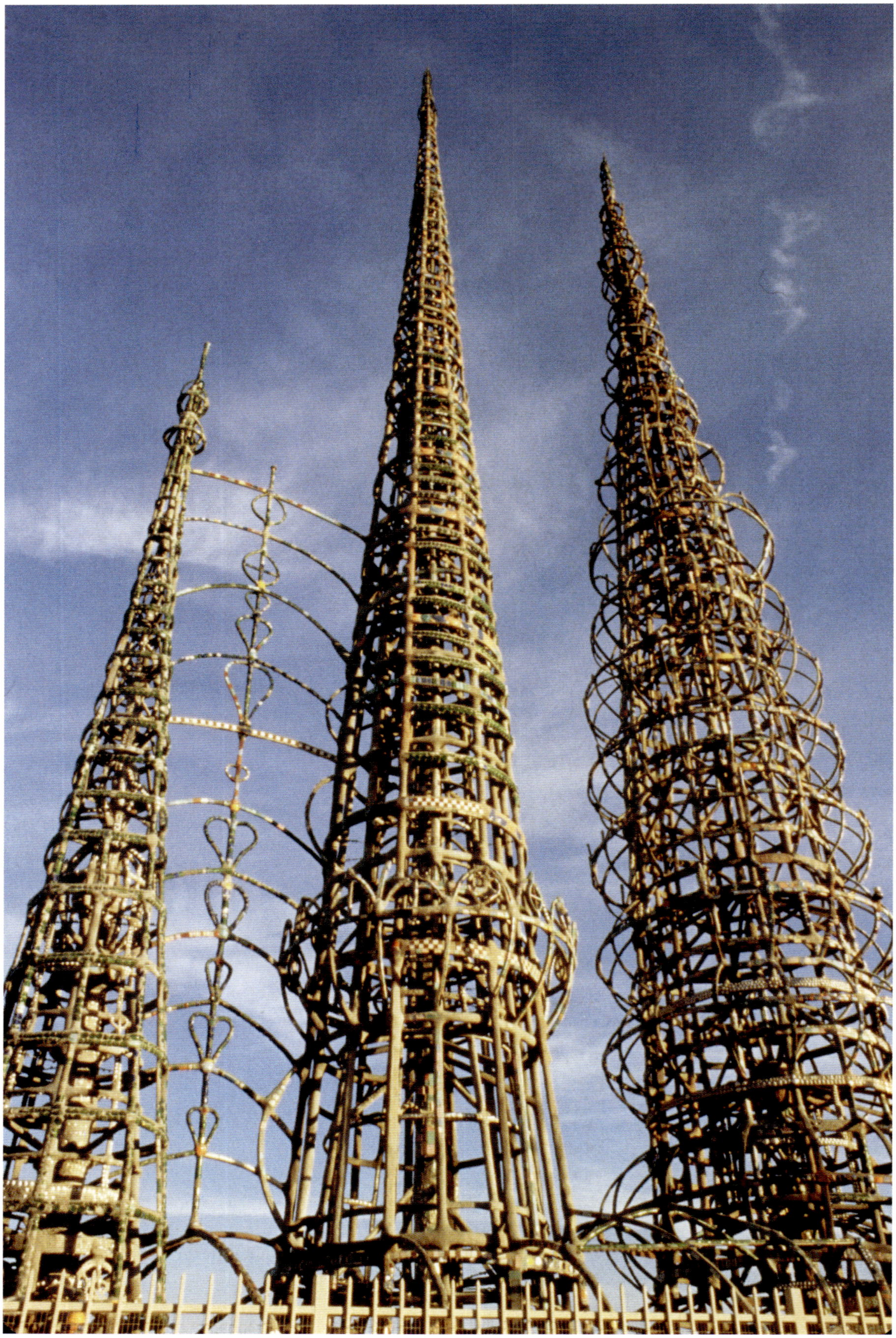

Sabato "Simon" Rodia (1879, Italy–1965, USA), Watts Towers, *Los Angeles, photograph by Jo Farb Hernández, 2002.* Emigrating from Italy, Rodia settled in California and at the age of 43. He began transforming a vacant suburban lot into an extraordinary environment of towers and mosaiced facades. Rodia constructed *Watts Towers* between 1921 and 1956. Nearly 100 years later, his singular vision has been preserved and has gained international recognition.

around to understanding that the most appropriate description of what they have spent years assembling is best defined as art. They may begin with the desire for a bit of home improvement (as was the motivation for Helen Martins, see page 230), or to propound their political philosophies or religious beliefs (Prophet Isaiah Robertson's work is a stellar example of this latter category, see page 234), advocate for a cause (such as Huang Yong-Fu's efforts to save his village from demolition, see page 238), or even just to entertain themselves with an inexpensive and absorbing hobby in their hours of free time (as was the intention of Josep Pujiula i Vila,see page 242). But in all these circumstances, for these first tentative steps at creative expression to evolve into an art environment, a consistent and thoughtful, if not dogged, focus is required, demonstrating a commitment that far outstrips the work ethic of all but the most dedicated of mainstream artists.

This results from, again, a complex set of factors. Primary is that the builder is channeling only his or her unique voice, so there is no compunction before the typical art production fears of beginning self-taught hobbyists such as "I can't even draw a straight line." There is neither playbook nor model for what an art environment "should" look like, and typically these builders have little, if any, knowledge that other such sites exist and, even more, that such a genre has been described and defined. "If I had learned from someone else, I could make a mistake," one artist earnestly told me, "but since I taught myself, I can't make any mistakes." This confidence, then, conjoined with their continuing pleasure at the results of their labors, leads them not only to experience complete freedom as they build, but also to make extravagant proclamations about how nothing like this has ever been seen before.

And, of course, they are right.

With the thousands of art environments that we have documented all over the world, only an infinitesimally small number reveal any communication with, or connection to, any other builder and, therefore, no reference to another's production. It is more likely for inspiration to be personally and uniquely driven, with construction buoyed by skills carried over from the maker's working life or learned through a process of trial-and-error. Making something for nothing may be a recurrent theme, as they navigate family concerns or the realities of an economic life that may be based more on barter than on cash, but it tends to be subservient to the creativity inherent in making use of available resources in innovative and imaginative ways: making something *out of* nothing. And the very human response to success in doing anything is to do more of it, so successfully thinking and collecting and fabricating and building motivates further thinking, further collecting, further fabricating, and further building.

One reason that art environments are so difficult to characterize is that their physical manifestations range from the monumental to the miniature, encompass every known medium, and reveal a wide breadth in aesthetic, technique, goals, intent, genre, and every other marker that might serve as an aide to classification. And without preconceived plans or the constraints of restricting themselves to only architecture, or only painting, or only sculpture, or only landscaping, the maker can branch off in any or multiple directions as ideas change, skills improve, resources become available or, conversely, are used up: the only other limitations are those of the artist's own health, dedication, and energy. And as the totality evolves, distinct components become linked to each other such that they lose their individuality in the eyes of the creator: even if they may describe or identify different elements separately, they meld into a single work such that it is their interaction that defines the whole, and it is as a whole that the artist wants the site to be experienced. From the spectators' viewpoint, however, this complexity is not always understandable with one quick stop: these sites require multiple visits from multiple perspectives, such that first impressions of disorder and disarray will evolve into an understanding of their rhythms and connections, their patterns and textures.

While Nek Chand (see page 222) and Josep Pujiula i Vila are two of the very few art environment creators who erected their masterpieces on land that was not their own, their efforts are as equally bound to—and bound by—the parameters of the site itself as the works of those creators who adorned their personal homes or farms or gardens. The sites on which they all build serve less to frame their artworks than to become an inexorable component that fuels and guides creation, an inseparable ingredient in the stew that melds locale with action to become part of the artwork itself. It is this personal connection to the setting of the artwork that simultaneously underwrites the artists' themes, thanks to their intimate familiarity with the location and the unfurling of the myriad of layers of histories that have contributed to that awareness. It concomitantly drives the intensity of their labors, as they pass by or through the sites daily—or, if they live within, such as Niki de Saint Phalle (see page 246) and her *Empress*, innumerable times daily—giving them the opportunity to continuously view, and review, their works, making adjustments, additions, and deletions with each pass. This is why art environments are best studied not only with reference to visual arts practices, but also to time-based methodologies: unlike traditional art media that are studied on the basis of the finished product, as long as the artist is alive and working, his or her art environment is constantly evolving at the same time that it is constantly complete.

When these activities attain a certain monumentality, the individual identity of the creator begins to evolve into a more socially prominent identity, and becomes subject to previously unforeseen and unimagined characterizations. "Artist" is often a surprising identification they had not

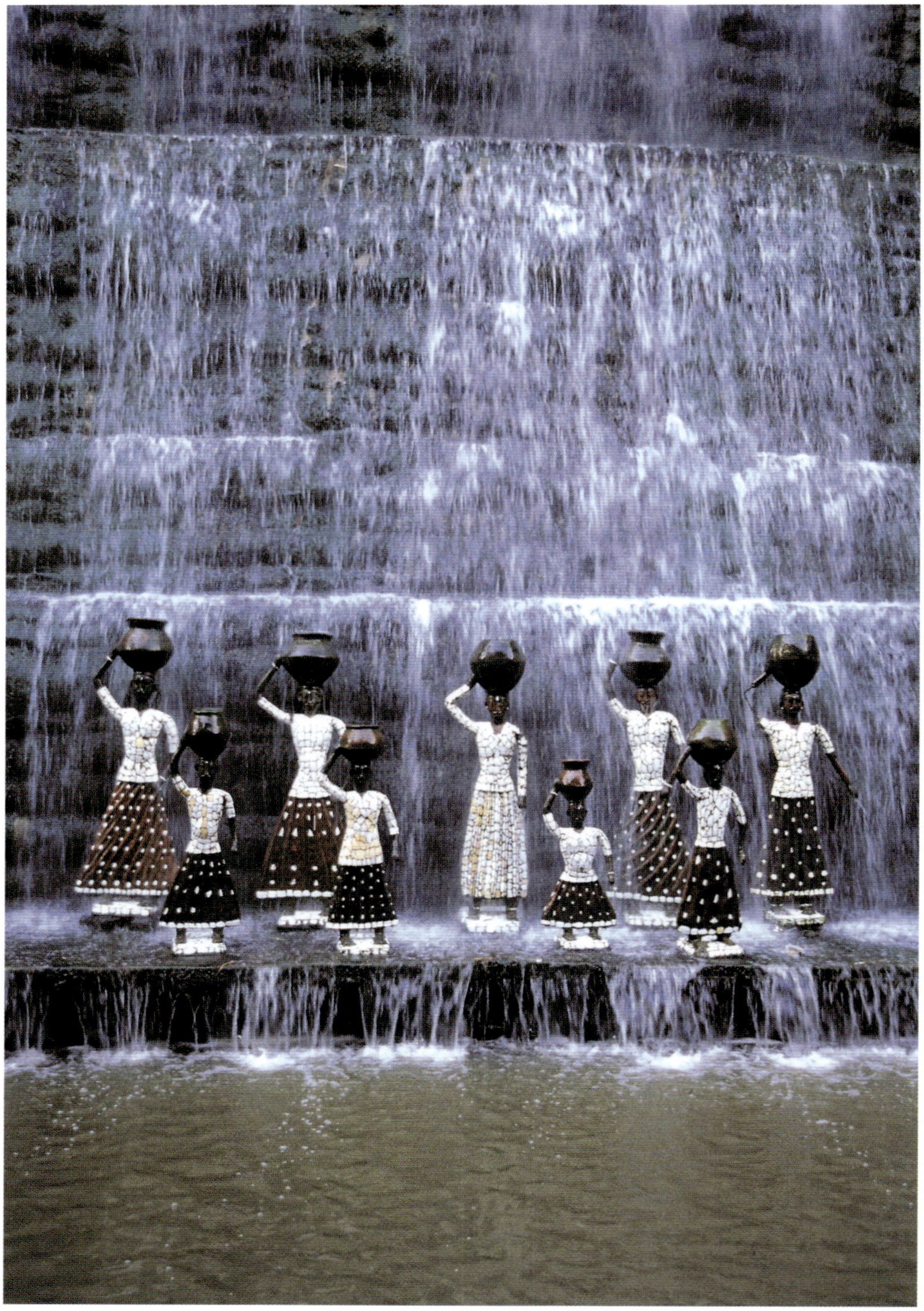

Nek Chand, Rock Garden, *Chandigarh, photograph, n.d. The Nek Chand Foundation.* Built as part of the Second Phase of the *Rock Garden*, this dynamic view of a large waterfall features a series of mosaiced female figures collecting the falling water into pots held above their heads.

contemplated before, but other, less gracious terms are also thrown about: "crazy," "garbage collector," "lawbreaker." This typically takes place as the force of the visual impact of the growing site creates tensions in which an individual's right to structure and adorn their own living spaces (and, sometimes, their final resting places as well) collides with society's right to a certain aesthetic order and consensus. Thus, these environments, although usually not birthed in controversy, may, as they grow, be tagged with this marker, and the creator's response to this changing social identity may affect the rest of their days.

As their identity evolves, so does, often, their intent. Chand and Pujiula both started their labors secretively, making do with easily available materials and seeking primarily to entertain themselves in their free time. Yet as their work attained greater public visibility—gradually, in the case of Pujiula, and more abruptly with Chand—taking that public interest into account began to influence not only the physical form of their work, but also their conceptual approach to next steps and their perception as to why it was important. In both cases they sought to improve the visitor experience—Chand by adding areas for relaxation and entertainment, Pujiula by devising ways to tease or startle visitors with elaborate means of orienting their passages through the site or through humorous visual gags. The resulting increased public visitation fueled their passions and inspired even more obsessive and expansive construction. The fact that both sites were confronted at various stages of their life cycles with casual vandalism as well as governmental decrees mandating demolition, which were clearly significant, if not existential, interim challenges, only served to harden the resolve of the artists and the communities: these art environments became so identified with Chandigarh and Argelaguer that laws, planning codes, and construction regulations were, at long last, ultimately modified or circumvented in order to ensure their survival.

These cases are unusual in the field, however; it is more likely that, even if engagement with the site by out-of-town visitors increases, along with their positive response and enhanced visibility, local response does not often keep pace. In some cases, family and community members might make their peace with the works as long as the artist is alive, whereas in other instances the maker may spend almost as many years and as much energy fighting for the right to continue construction as actually building. Unlike other examples of public art, the legacy of these singular spaces is not generally guaranteed: if the art environment is not "adopted" by a local government, school, or cultural organization, or is not maintained by family members (and it is rare that an heir shares the same skills, interest, and drive as the creator), their survival beyond the life of that creator is rare indeed, particularly if the assemblage includes ephemeral natural materials or found objects. Nevertheless, most creator-builders avoid the discussion about what will happen to their monumental artworks following their passing, assuming, for the most part, that everything will work out fine.

Yet, usually, it doesn't.

Without maintenance and conservation resulting from familial devotion or institutional focus on tourist, cultural, or educational programming, art environments tend to slip toward extinction. The weather takes its toll—directly, through precipitation or blinding sun or freezing temperatures; or indirectly, as heat differentials, for example, may cause concrete to asymmetrically expand, opening up infrastructural metal frameworks to contact with moisture, which produces rust and hastens further deterioration. But equally important are the quality and appropriate use of the chosen materials, the skill set of the builder, and the potential impact of vandalism. And so the legacy of the creator is, more often than not, reduced to reminiscences from an ever-declining number of people who once visited the site, or to visual documentation, underscoring the importance of our work in the field.

This research documenting the global breadth of art environments reveals that although each is distinctive and unique, they are not isolated phenomena. Nevertheless, works in this genre have not yet been recognized at levels commensurate with their quality, their innovation, and their expansiveness, nor have they been treated as such. A large majority of them continue to confront the danger of loss, destruction, and disappearance. It seems increasingly absurd for these works to be exempt from the moral rights applied to most artworks, as the artificial boundaries that isolate this genre from others become ever more permeable. By better acknowledging the fluidity between art historical genres, perhaps we can develop a more generous definition of art itself, and better protect and conserve these often startlingly innovative works of public art, treating them with the recognition and respect they so well deserve.

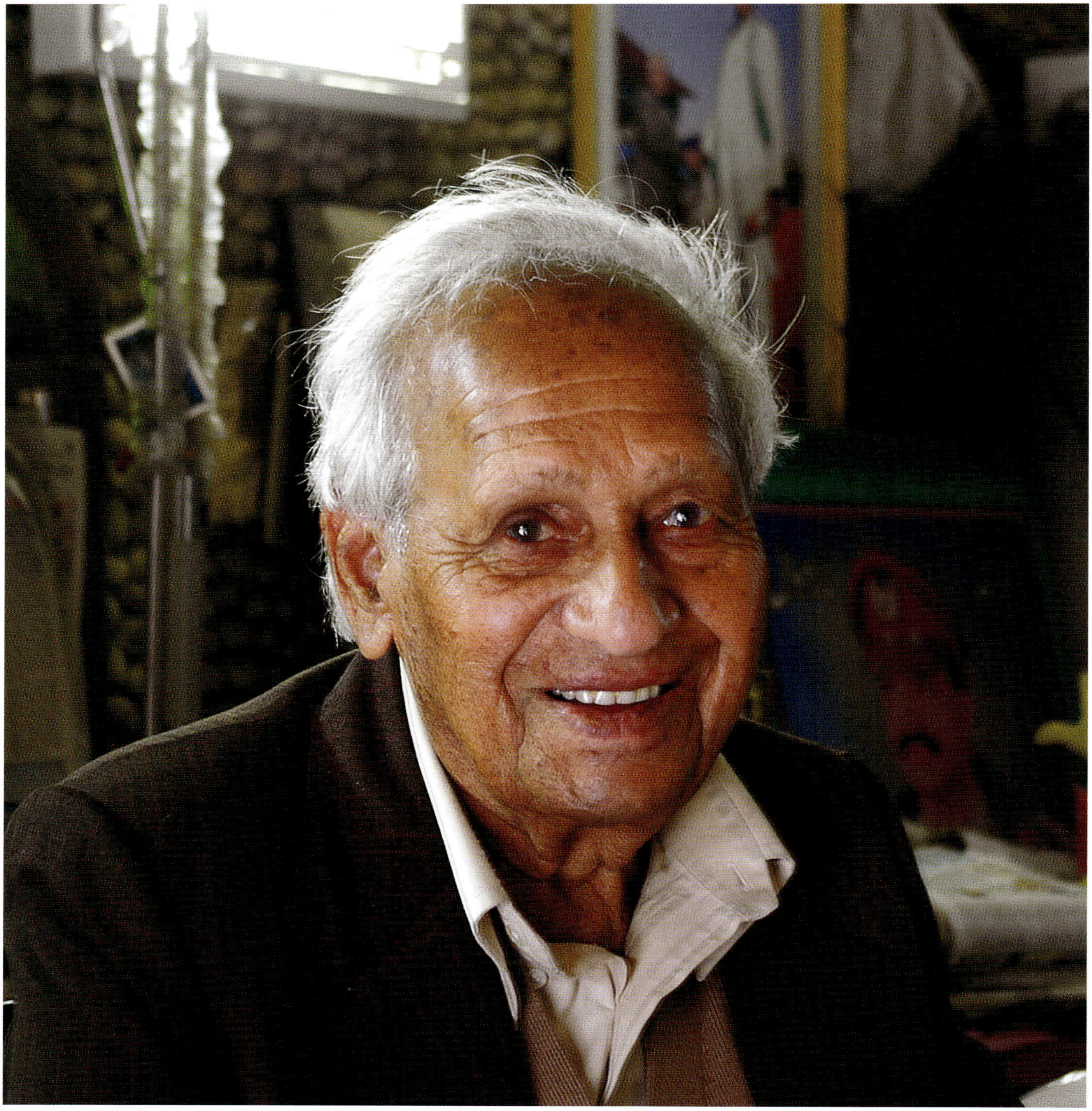

Nek Chand, 2012, photograph. The Nek Chand Foundation. In his late 80s in this portrait, Chand dedicated decades to creating a vision that developed into the incredible and monumental *Rock Garden*.

NEK CHAND

(1924, Barian Kalan [now Pakistan]–2015, Chandigarh, India)
***Rock Garden*, Chandigarh, India**

Featuring natural anthropomorphic stones, waterfalls, and fields of mosaiced figures and animals, Nek Chand's *Rock Garden* has become one of the most visited sites in India, second only to the Taj Mahal. In 1947, India's independence and subsequent turmoil of the Partition rendered Chand a refugee in newly established Pakistan. Following a successful migration back into Indian territory, in 1951 Chand secured employment with the Public Works Department (PWD) and relocated to Chandigarh—a new city capital in redevelopment by architect Le Corbusier. Around 1960, Chand began gathering found stones and local debris on a secluded plot of land on the edge of the city, where he eventually began assembling his creations. Over time, the local authorities identified the emergence of his creative environment. Illegal, but recognized for its artistic merit and popular potential, Chand's sculptural endeavors were encouraged by the city. In 1976, the *Rock Garden* officially opened to the public. The decades that followed brought extensive development via the creative direction of Chand, with support of a community of international and local advocates.

Nek Chand's *Rock Garden* is an extraordinary site among the modernist city of Chandigarh, existing in opposition, harmony, and dialectic symbiosis with the surrounding city. The relationship between the *Rock Garden* and Chandigarh is of visual and cultural significance, while it also intrinsically relates to interpretation of Chand's narrative, influences, and creative process. Research and accounts still seemingly vary in regard to certain historical specifics, but two key concepts are worth exploring when profiling Nek Chand and the *Rock Garden*. The first is the consideration of the support and communal efforts for Chand's environment. Chand has often been presented with isolated-visionary mythos.[1] However, the *Rock Garden* is linked to profound community spirit, which was led by Chand, and was developed with select governmental support (though not without bureaucratic issues and corruption). Its history is one of communal construction and its present and future rely on collective preservation. The second consideration is that of material activism, in equal measure with the inspirational dreams and childhood tales of Chand, which allows the poeticism of his action and reuse of material to be a conceptual point of departure.

In August 1947, India gained independence from Great Britain, which resulted in the Partition of India to establish the independent states of India and Pakistan. This divide affected heavily the regions of Bengal and Punjab, whose districts were suddenly residing in either a Muslim-majority Pakistan or non-Muslim India. This Partition caused great violence and displacement of refugees in the massive border migration. Born to a Hindu family in the Punjabi village of Barian Kalan, Nek Chand Saini, as he is also known was one of the millions displaced post-Partition as he found himself in the newly sectored Islamic area of Pakistan. Despite the turmoil and violence, Chand and his family successfully relocated to the Punjab region in India. In 1951, through an initiative to assist the employment of Partition refugees, Chand found employment through the PWD, which relocated him to the northern city of Chandigarh.

A further result of the Partition was that India's Punjab region lost its capital Lahore to Pakistan. Chandigarh was planned for the region's new capital. India's first prime minister, Jawaharlal Nehru viewed urban planning as a government tool and set to develop its new capital city as a post-colonial modern model. French-Swiss architect Le Corbusier was appointed to lead the design of the city. There was mass demolition to prepare for the city to be erected in its modern image. As a roads inspector for the PWD, Chand directly witnessed the design and vision of Le Corbusier being erected around him. Among the construction, Chand was also taking notice of debris on Chandigarh's newly built roads. With villages destroyed amid the progress of the city, remnants of community—from fragmented crockery to broken jewelry—were part of this visual landscape of modernization.

As early as 1958[2], Chand began collecting stones with a particular interest in unusual shapes and forms that appeared morphed by nature (erosion or water). This was followed by gathering community debris that he observed during his day job. This act of collecting gradually broadened beyond village debris to include materials found from hospitals and factories. Chand started transporting stones and found materials by bicycle to a discreet plot of public land on the outskirts of the city in Sector 1, near Sukhna Lake. Spending evenings and weekends on-site into the 1960s, he cleared an area of land, cultivated various plants, and eventually, embarked on building and assembling from the gathered components.

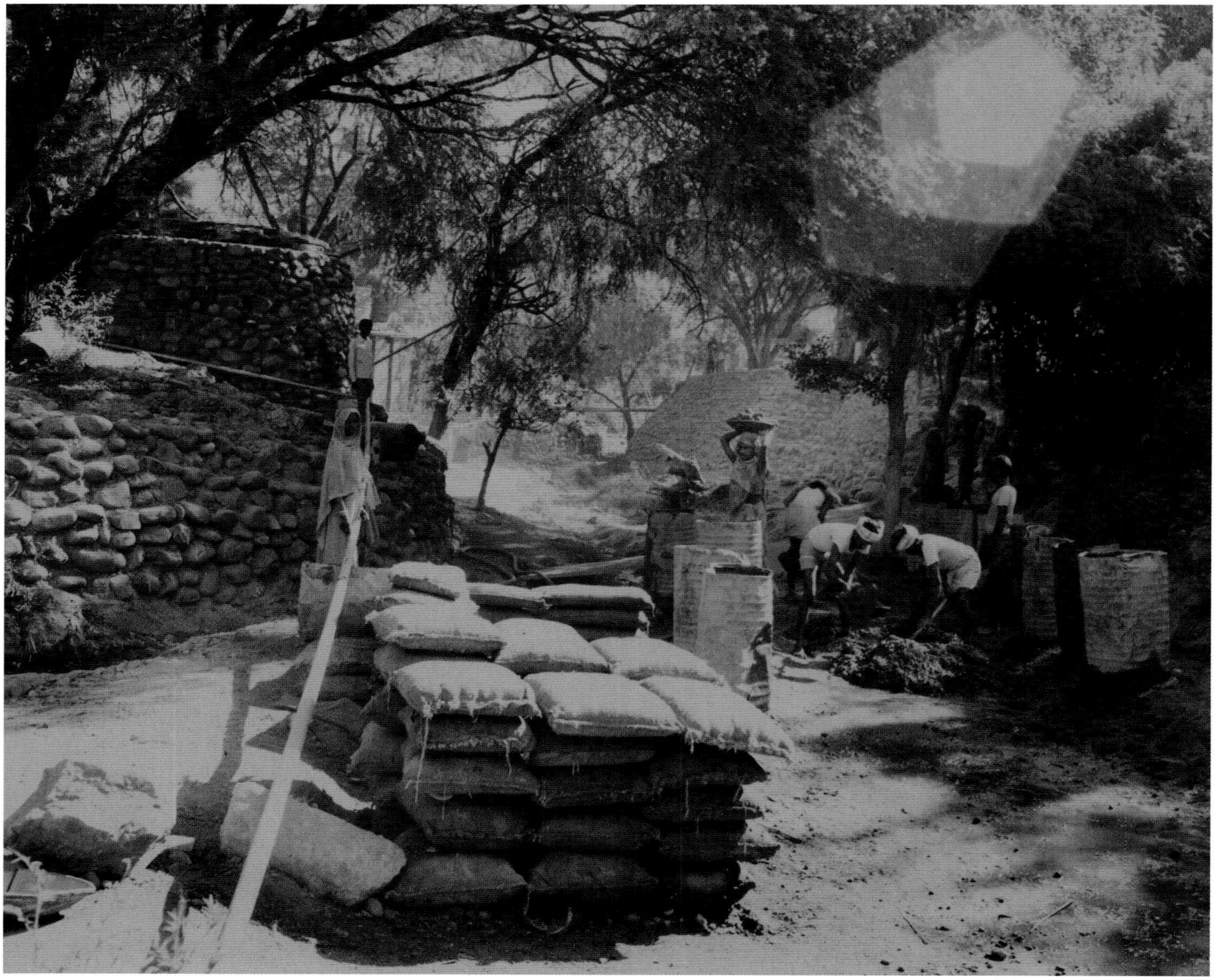

Nek Chand, Rock Garden, *Chandigarh, photograph, ca. 1970s. The Nek Chand Foundation.* Under construction in the late 1970s, this photograph documents the development of the *Rock Garden*'s Phase II, which was realized with the assistance of additional labor.

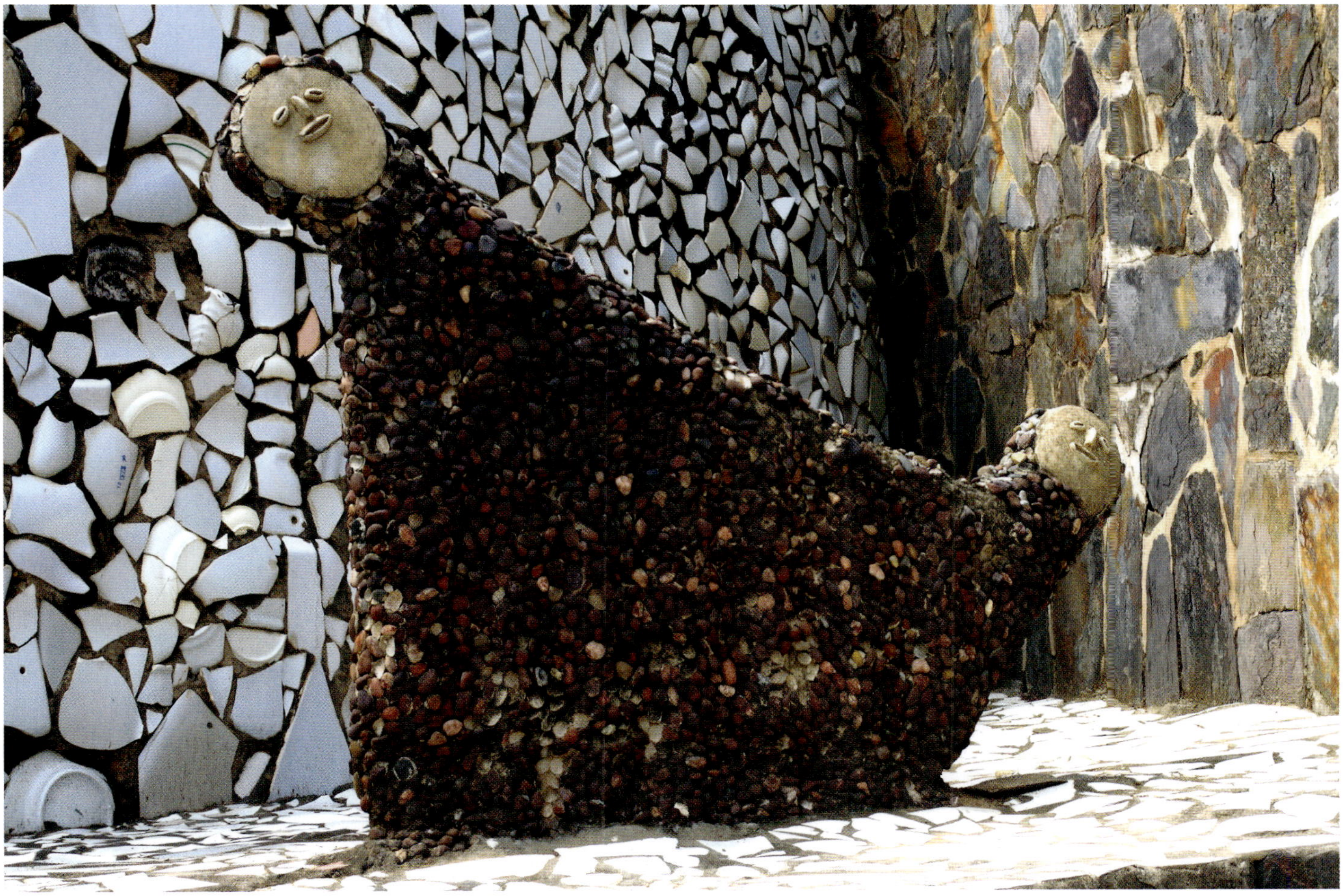

Nek Chand, Rock Garden, *Chandigarh, photograph, n.d. The Nek Chand Foundation.* This playful two-headed character, modeled with a bicycle frame as its base, demonstrates Chand's innovative use of recycling material; this is also noticeable in the various white ceramics covering the wall behind the sculptural form.

Chand had trepidation over his illegal development on public land and, in 1969, he approached Chandigarh's chief architect, M.N. Sharma, to explain his pursuits.[3] This admittance was followed by a visit by Sharma to the site where he, rather unexpectedly for a government official, encouraged Chand to continue his illegitimate practice and did not report his unauthorized development. This early period of his creative environment, before its formal recognition as the *Rock Garden* is referred to as Phase I and was orchestrated by Chand alone. This phase has a predominant focus on the inherent aesthetics of existing forms, like the presentation of exceptionally shaped stones from the riverbed with natural deterioration. Mosaic work is also featured in the construction of Phase I but implemented primarily in support to present the eroding stones.

In 1973, Chand's environment was accidentally visited once again by crew workers. This led to an exposure of Chand's prodigious pursuits to chief commissioner M.S. Randhawa, who was influential to arts, culture, and park establishment for the city. With an initial awe of the site and municipal foresight of its cultural value, Randhawa not only encouraged Chand to continue, but also officiated over his environment. Named by Randhawa, the "Rock Garden" opened to the public on January 24, 1976. Significant growth and advancements were made to the property for decades following its public debut. Chand accordingly was given the title of "Creator and Director". He was also granted a salary, support team, and equipment to foster the future cultivation of his environment, now the *Rock Garden*.

Alongside its public opening, the anthology of the garden entered its next stage, which introduced the significant use of discarded materials to create new/unique sculptural forms. This stage was led by Chand with the construction and support of a team. Visually, Phase II is

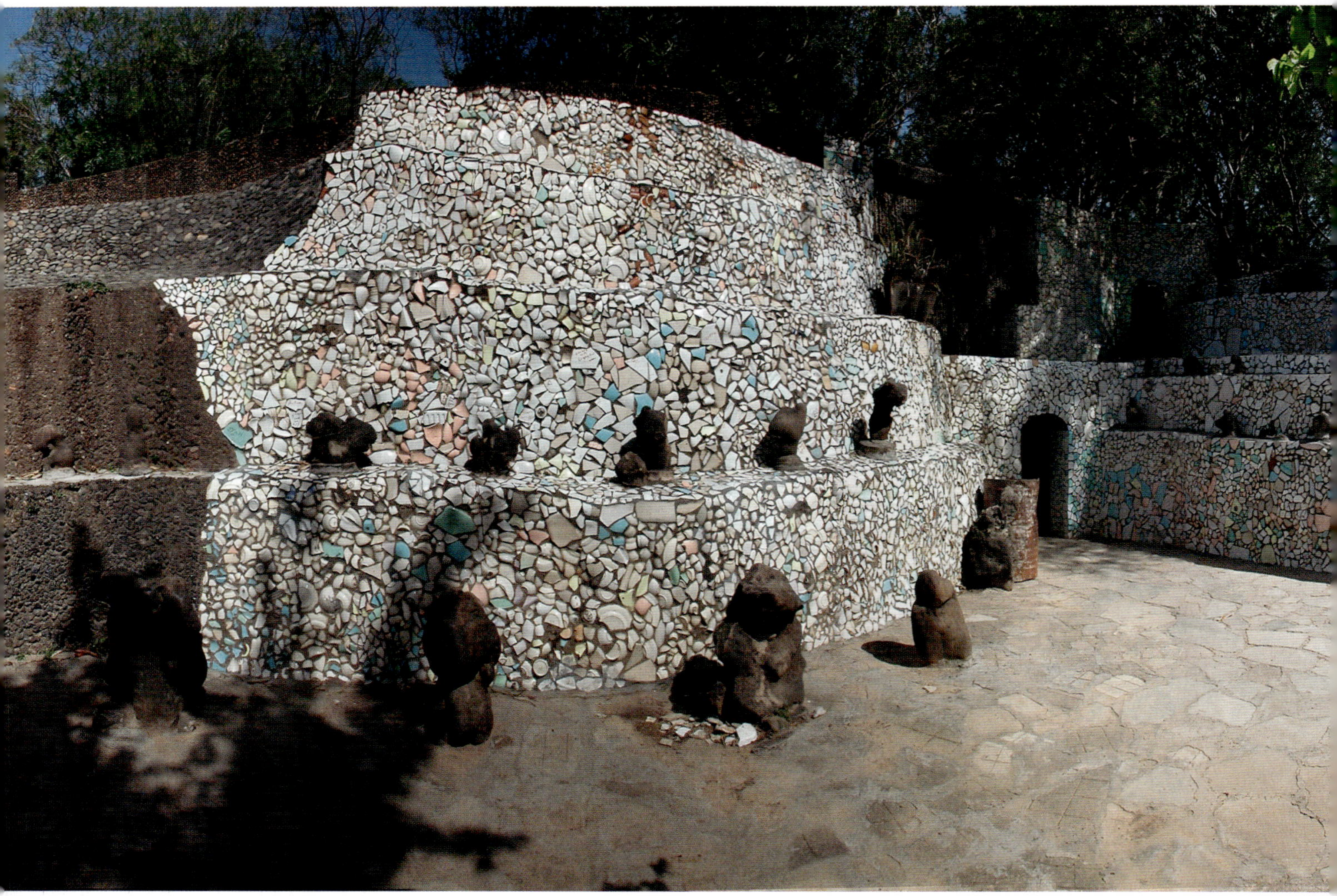

Nek Chand, Rock Garden, *Chandigarh, photograph, n.d. The Nek Chand Foundation.* This panoramic view of the *Rock Garden* shows how Chand's initial pursuits from Phase I are positioned within the larger garden. The sculptural forms here are naturally formed rocks, which were found and collected by Chand, triggering his initial intrigue.

widely identifiable for its fields of sculptures with multilevel planes, each with sets of specific sculptural characters repeated en masse.[4] A large consortium of sculpted women constructed from broken bangles presents a poignant example of a material vocabulary for assembling from recycled objects. The re-presentation of recognizable fragments creates a dialogue with Indian tradition and individual narrative. This material transition and transaction is also apparent in Chand's humanoid figures whose silhouettes were informed by their recycled substrates, such as a bike frame as the framework for a two-headed angular character. Phase II's echoing of local cultural history and the activation of a community through the garden's construction adds further enrichment to the development of the *Rock Garden* and presents a more multifaceted position of Chand.

The early 1980s brought significant recognition to Chand and his garden, which provided him with additional resources, such as collection centers for material throughout Chandigarh and assistance for more ambitious sculptures. In 1983, the *Rock Garden* was featured on an Indian postage stamp, and the following year Chand received the government's highest honor with the title Padma Shiri. Conversely, toward the end of the decade, the *Rock Garden* suffered funding cuts and staff reductions. In 1988, there was a threat of demolition to areas of the *Rock Garden* and activists in their thousands came to the site to protect it.

Marked by a commemorative sign, Phase III was inaugurated on September 23, 1993. The final and most continuous stage, it is recognized for its planning and construction with the viewer in mind. Strife struck the garden again in 1997, when Chand returned from a trip abroad to find that his staff and the budget had both been cut back. With the *Rock Garden* left unattended due to staff reductions,

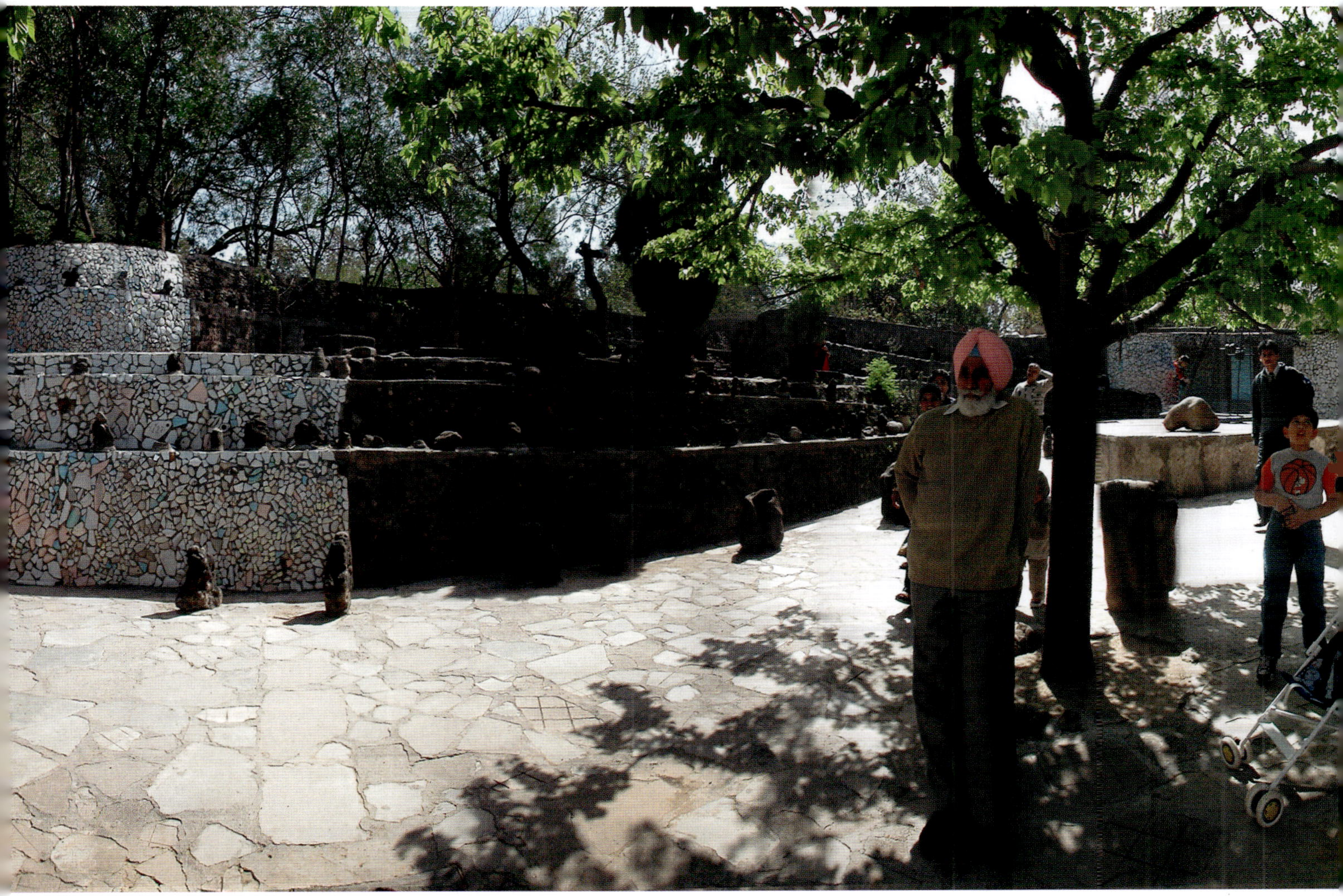

"It's a child's dream and not a garden of cold rocks . . . it is my poetry with rocks." – Nek Chand[5]

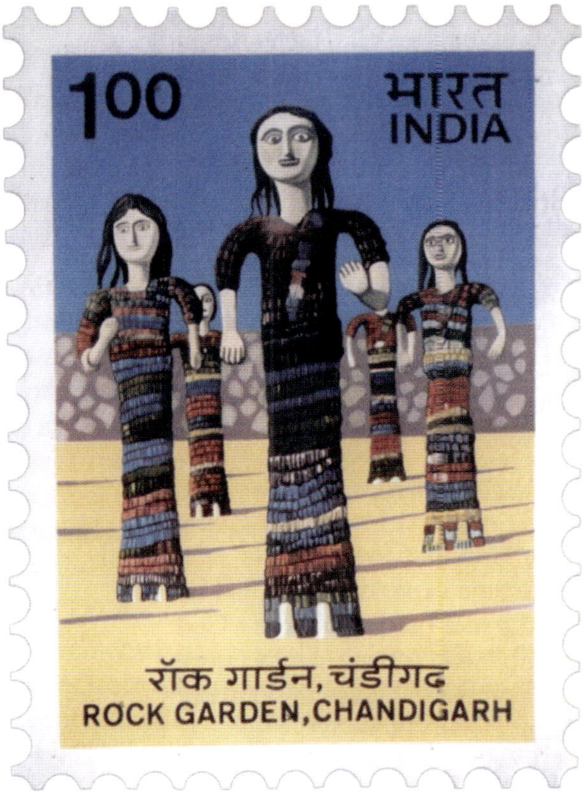

Indian postage stamp. The Nek Chand Foundation. With Nek Chand and the *Rock Garden* gaining recognition in the 1980s, this illustration of five female sculptures was featured on a 1983 Indian postage stamp.

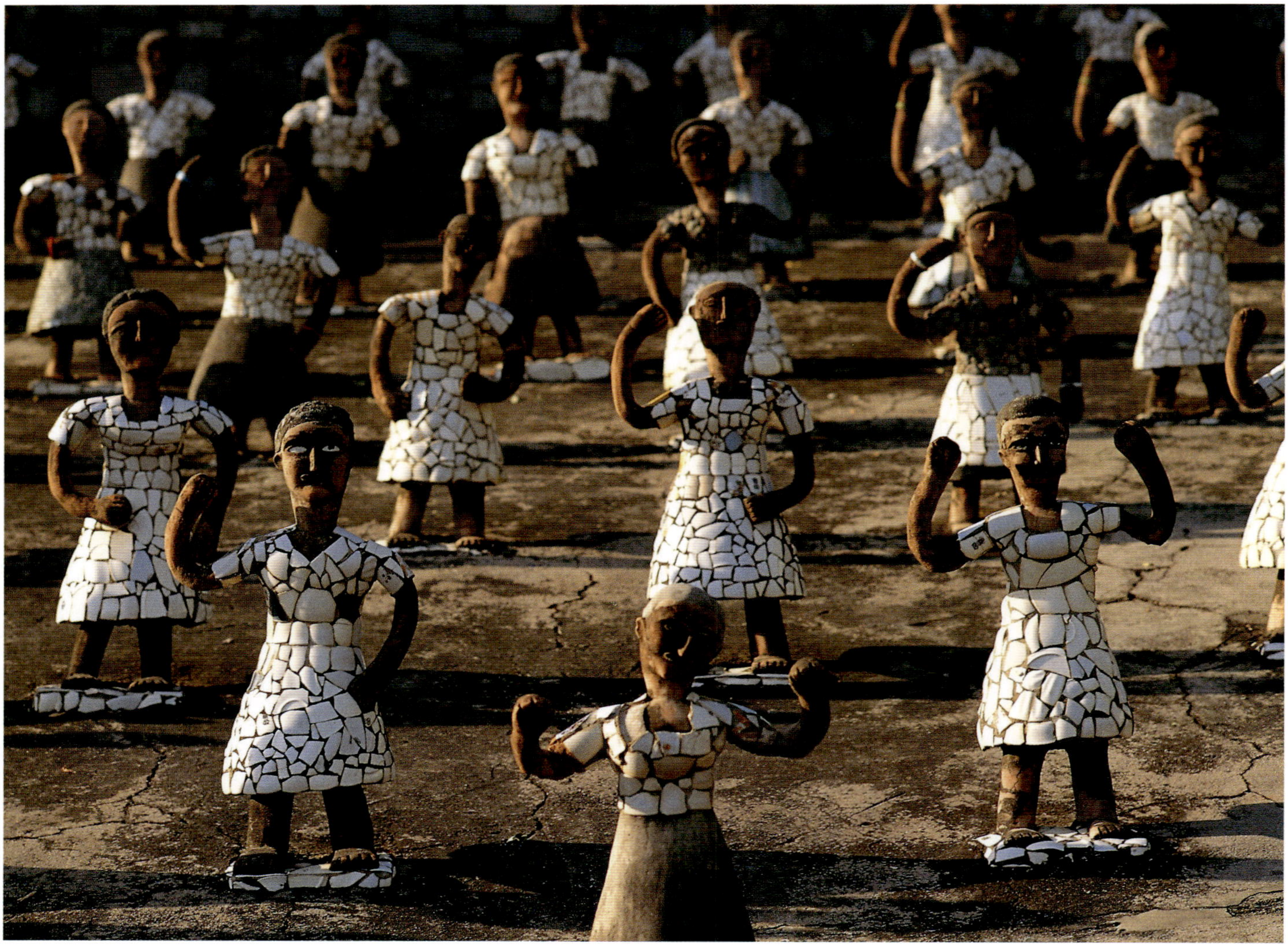

Nek Chand, Rock Garden*, Chandigarh, photograph, n.d. The Nek Chand Foundation.* This patterned plot of sculptures of young girls has impressive whimsy considering their cohesive scale and white clothing. Subtle, unique characteristics are employed by Chand in each, such as a bracelet, arm position, or colored top.

sculptures had been vandalized. Later that year, the international charity, the Nek Chand Foundation was formed to provide future preservation in direct response to this act of vandalism.

With Phase III still in development into the 2000s, the scope of community involvement further expanded to include international volunteers contributing to the site. Through the incorporated collective community, an established foundation, and the growing popularity of the garden, this phase included a major expansion of plazas, sculptures over 13 ft (4 m) tall, and a stone amphitheater. This stage caters directly to the public, with more commercial ventures, such as a gift shop and cafe.

Nek Chand passed away at the age of 90 in 2015, leaving behind an unprecedented legacy. Thousands of visitors attend the *Rock Garden* daily, which has received more than ten million visitors. While various commercial aspects have been incorporated over the years, the single hut Chand constructed privately in 1958 is still on display. The garden has over 2,000 sculptures and is considered one of the most significant and spectacular visionary environments ever created. From a clandestine endeavor to a multi-authored community, the cacophony of aesthetics and range of styles are at once forever unique and vibrating, a palpable cohesion from the power of recycled materials.

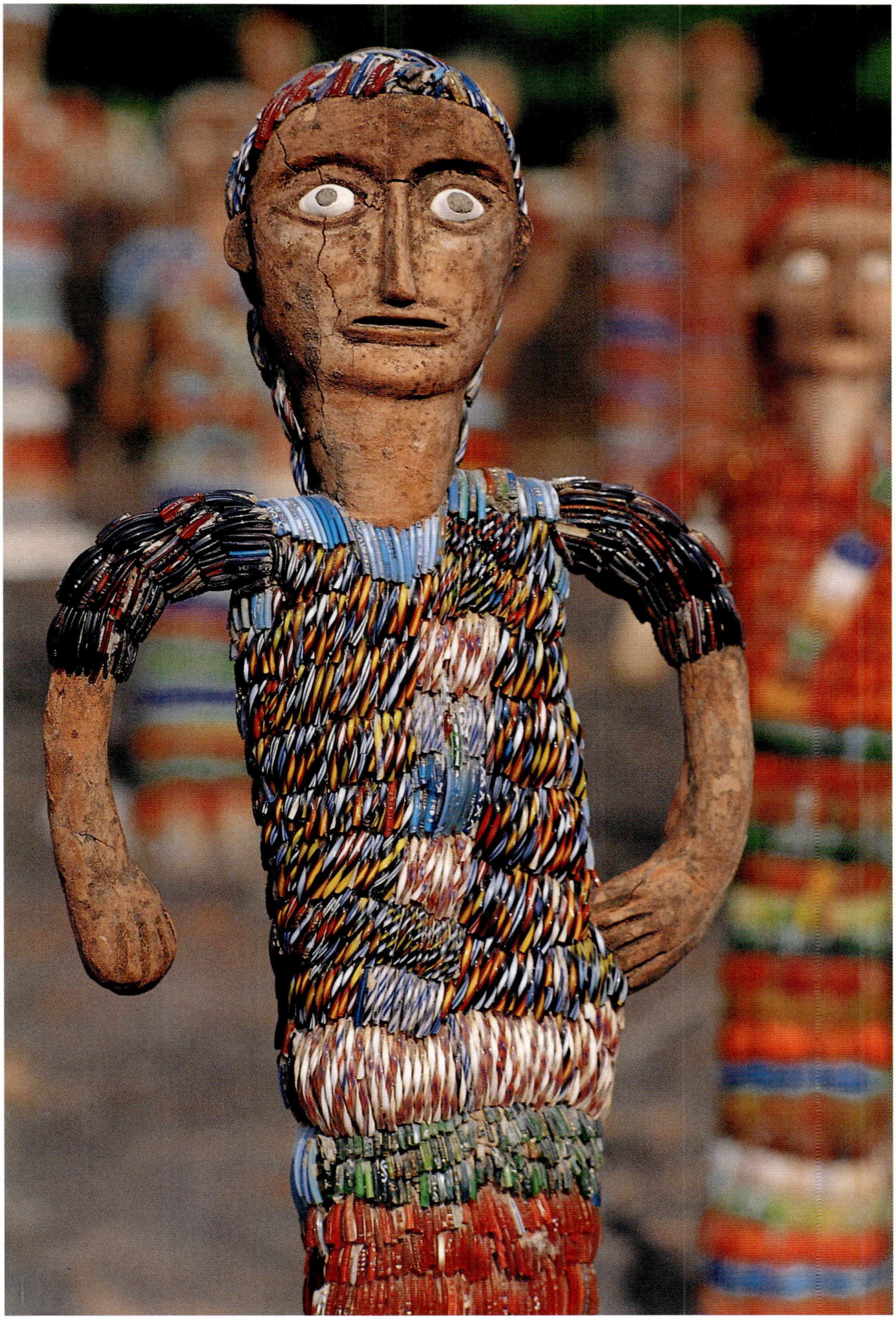

Nek Chand, Rock Garden, *Chandigarh, photograph, n.d. The Nek Chand Foundation.* A close-up of a queen after bathing from Phase II of the *Rock Garden*. This detail shows the colorful and intricate garments of this set of sculptural queens, which are constructed from broken glass bangles.

HELEN MARTINS

(b. 1897–1976 Nieu Bethesda, South Africa)
***Owl House*, Nieu Bethesda, South Africa**

The intimate cosmology of Helen Martins' *Owl House* evokes a deep sense of spirituality. An aura of sublime meditation floods through the environment, while the performative placement of objects and sculptures introduces an uncanny tension. Around the age of 30, Martins returned to her remote birthplace to care for her ill and aging parents. She was recently divorced when she moved back to the village of Nieu Bethesda and, in 1945, following the death of her father (her mother had passed away in 1941), she became liberated by her solitude. Martins initially began transforming her immediate environment to increase natural light in her domestic interior. This metamorphosis developed into an orchestra of reflective and translucent material interventions and the making of over 300 outdoor sculptures. As the creative director of her private setting, Martins formed continual collaborations with local workers to assist in the construction. Tragically, at the age of 78, after decades dedicated to her environment, she took her own life. The creative legacy of Martins has been preserved, which has allowed visitors up to the present day to experience the personal and universal spirituality of the *Owl House*.

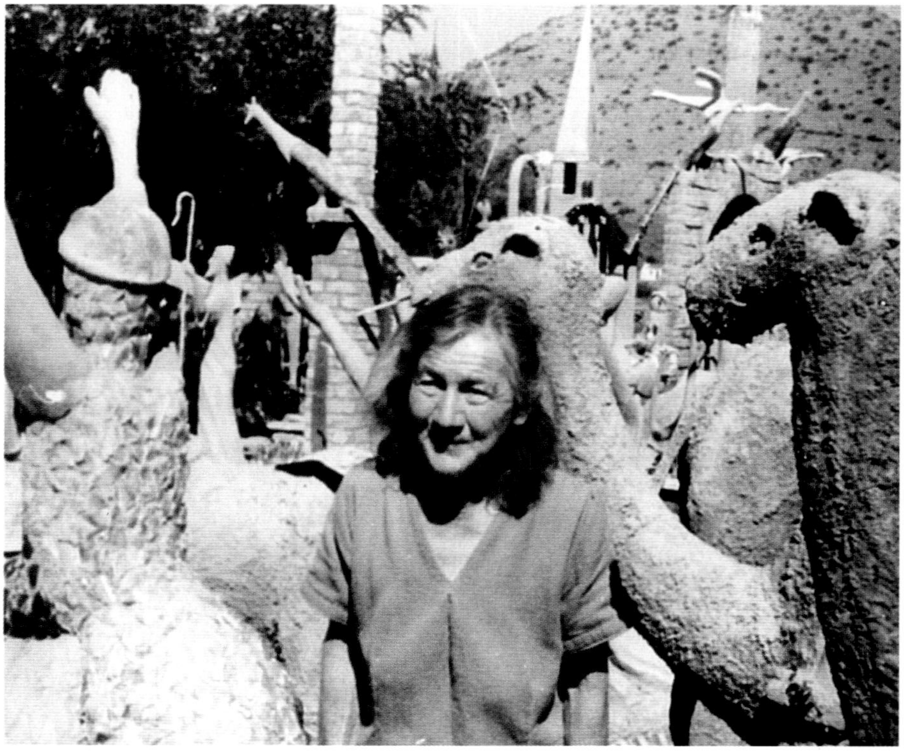

Helen Martins, n.d., photograph. The Owl House Foundation. A private person, and even considered reclusive by several in her community, photographs of Helen Martins at the *Owl House* are rare. Here, she is seen among her outdoor sculptures, surrounded by camels and figurative characters encompassing her sensuality, spirituality, and passion.

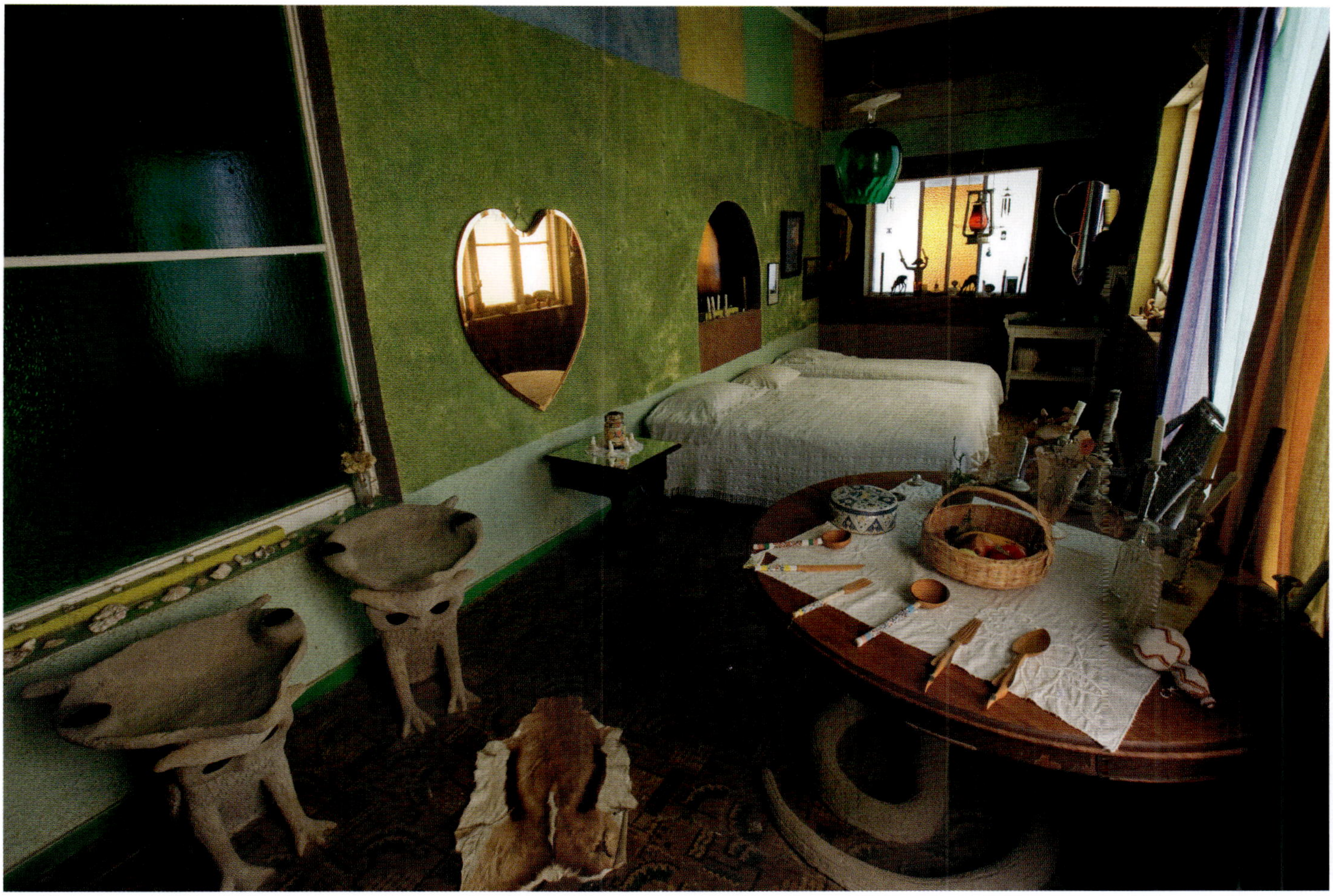

Helen Martins, Owl House*, Nieu Bethesda, photograph, n.d.* This interior view of the *Owl House* shows Martins' use of ground glass applied to the walls to achieve a shimmering effect, as well as her placement of mirrors to reflect and enhance the natural light.

Following her newfound sense of independence in 1945,[6] Helen Martins' creativity flourished in multifaceted ways as she drew from local materials and references. Her reclusive tendencies were remarked upon but she established close and long-term working relationships with a few workmen of the village, who assisted in the construction of the *Owl House* and sculptures of the adjacent *Camel Yard*. Koos Malgas (1937–2001) was her most significant collaborator and it is considered that they had a symbiotic creative relationship.

Martins' village of Nieu Bethesda is remotely located in the Karoo region of South Africa. Regional homes were built to be robust against the climate, and interiors often had limited natural light. With her earliest inspiration of creating a brighter environment with the materials she had available, the interior architecture of the *Owl House* was developed with vivid colored glass and repurposed translucent glass bottles. Mirrors, in whimsical shapes including crescents and hearts, were strategically placed as buoyant conductors to infuse the house with further natural light. Colored glass was ground in a coffee grinder and then applied to the walls, creating a glittering celestial effect. Martins' symbolic and visual motifs were developed from everyday references. Her sources included Christmas cards and packaging. For example, the sun from a brand of floor polish was appropriated as a spiritual visual emblem repeating throughout the house's interior. Dolls and other objects were also decisively placed throughout, in a manner evocative of both contemporary art installations and theater sets.

Expanding into an ornate and densely populated sculpture garden, Martins' environment became a spiritual journey adapting to her myriad of inspirations. Poetry, her dreams, and worldly faith practices all influenced her creative endeavors. Personal and universal, peaceful, interspersed with unsettlement, the legacy of Martins via the *Owl House* remains poignant for visitors attending this Eastern Cape tourist site where Martins' signage states: "This Is My World."

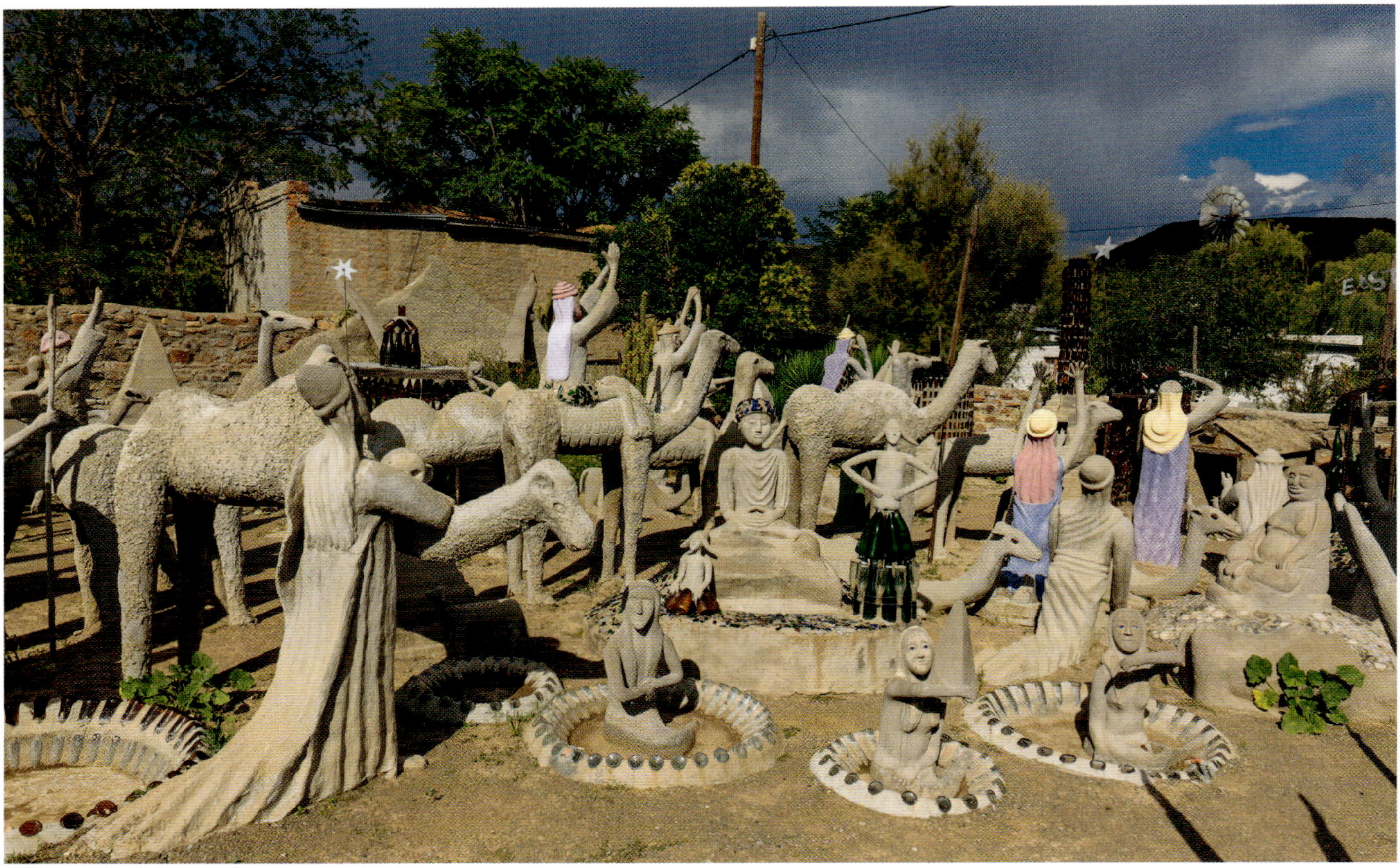

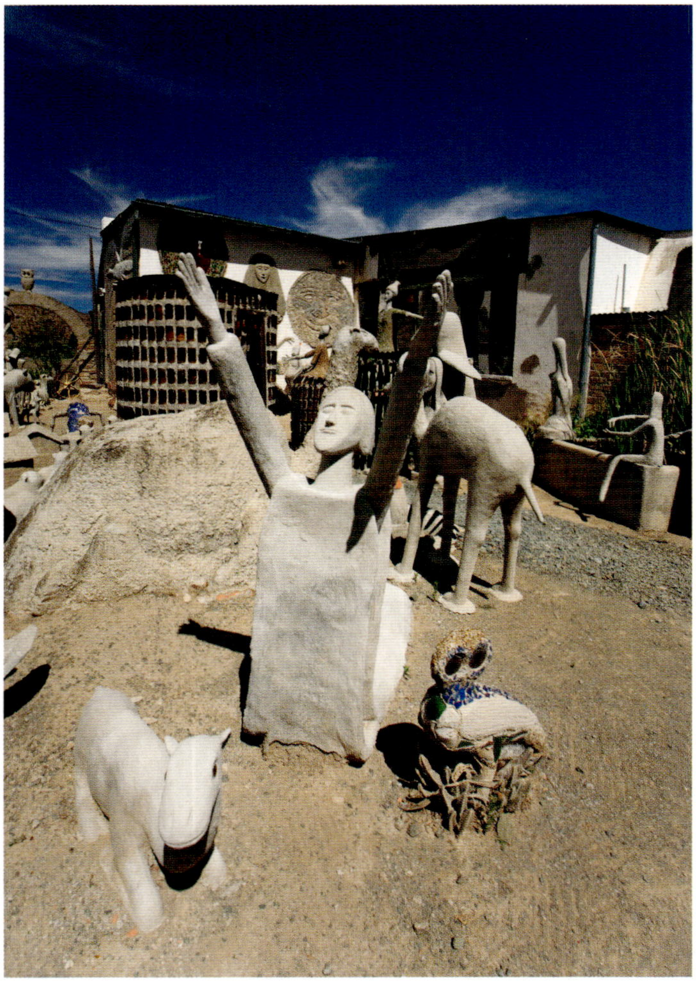

Helen Martins, Owl House*, Nieu Bethesda, photograph, n.d.* Sculptures of camels, Wise Men, birds, prophets, giraffes, donkeys, mermaids, babies, and angelic women are abundant in the *Camel Yard*—many of them facing a singular direction, giving the various sculptures a processional feel.

Helen Martins, Owl House*, Nieu Bethesda, photograph, n.d.* Both the *Owl House* and the *Camel Yard* exude a sense of deep spirituality, demonstrated here in a sculpture of a kneeling figure with its hands and head held toward the sky. It is accompanied by a mosaiced owl to its left.

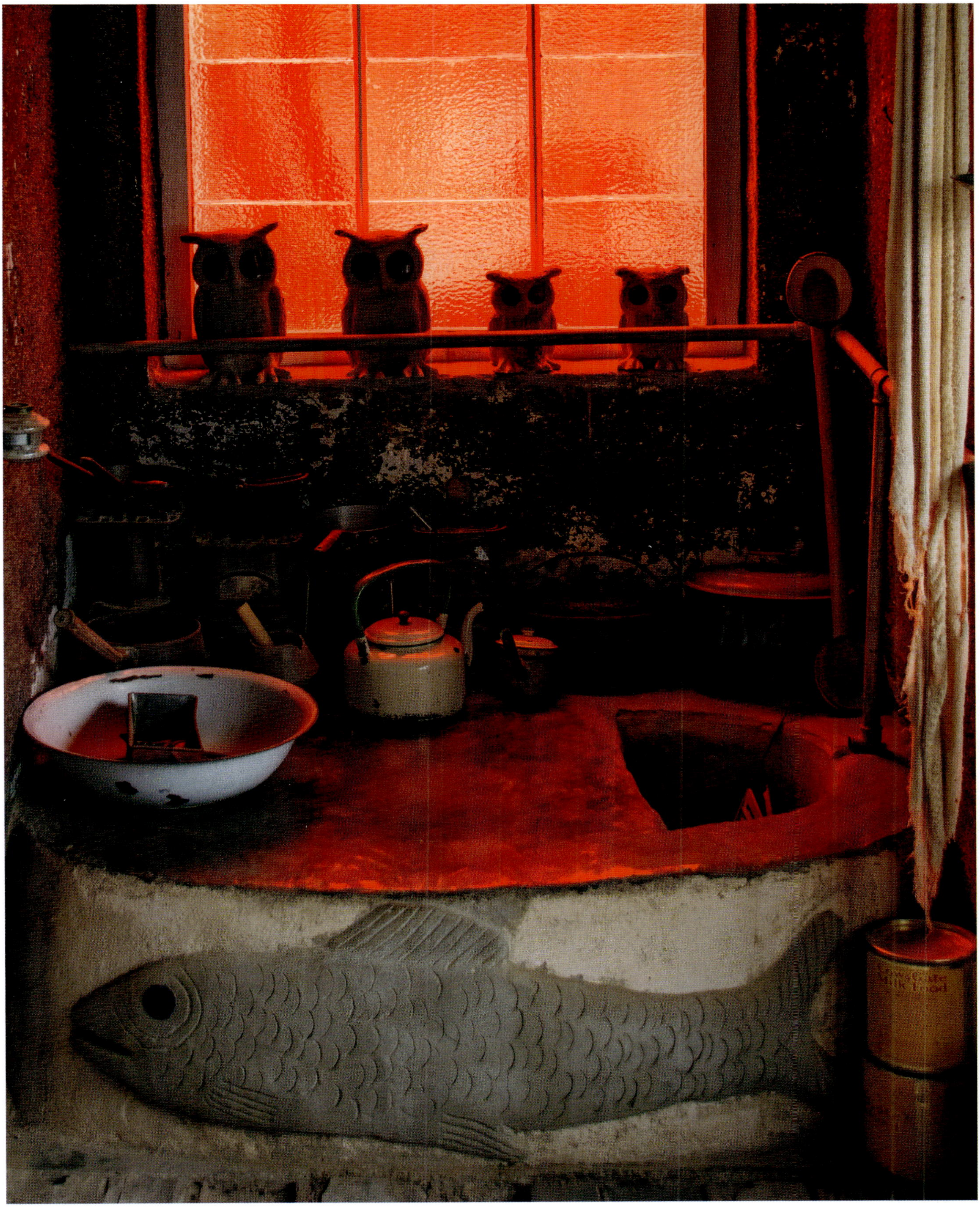

Helen Martins, Owl House, *Nieu Bethesda, photograph, n.d.* Martins' placement of domestic and sculptured objects within her home created a surreal effect that is both uncanny and sublime. Interested in light, her application of translucent red color over her window casts a powerful effect. Four owls seem to keep watch at the window.

PROPHET ISAIAH ROBERTSON

(1947, St. Thomas, Jamaica–2020, Niagara Falls, New York, USA)
***Second Coming House*, Niagara Falls, New York, USA**

Isaiah Robertson adorned his home, referred to as the *Second Coming House*, in response to a prophetic vision. From a young age, while living in Jamaica, Robertson's mother foresaw that her son would be led by God. He emigrated to Ontario, Canada, in 1972 and later to Niagara Falls, New York, where his prophecy-led ingenuity emerged via a carpentry job for a local church. Two main prophecies informed the spiritual and creative practice of Robertson. The first was a prediction of forgiveness and redemption. The following, and most crucial, was the second coming of Jesus Christ. Believing to be under the direction of God, Robertson spent years intricately and skillfully embellishing his home. The interior is abundant with intricate beaded patterns and bespoke woodwork, while its exterior and surrounding property is the utmost in fantastical. The facade is lush with symbolic forms while, adjacent, a mammoth cross stands in the driveway and the front yard features a rock garden.

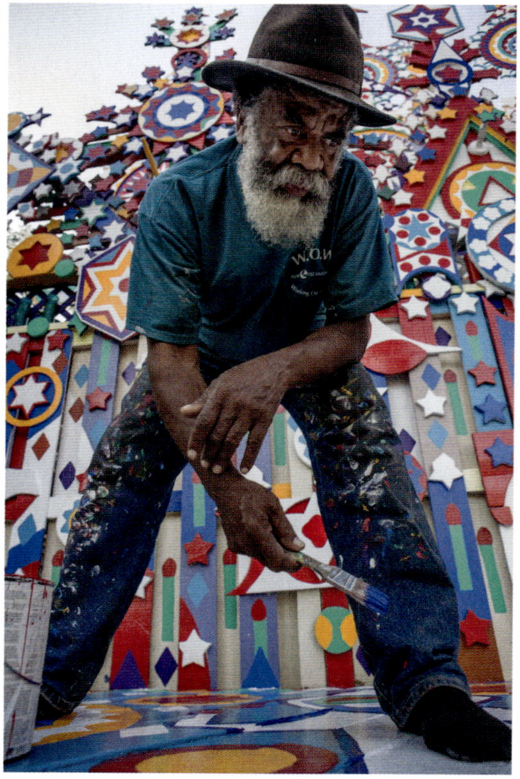

Prophet Isaiah Robertson, 2013, photograph by Fred Scruton. Courtesy Fred Scruton. With a paintbrush in hand and tin of paint by his side, this portrait of Robertson shows him at work on the *Second Coming House*. He continued to update and maintain the visuals of the house to keep its meticulous condition.

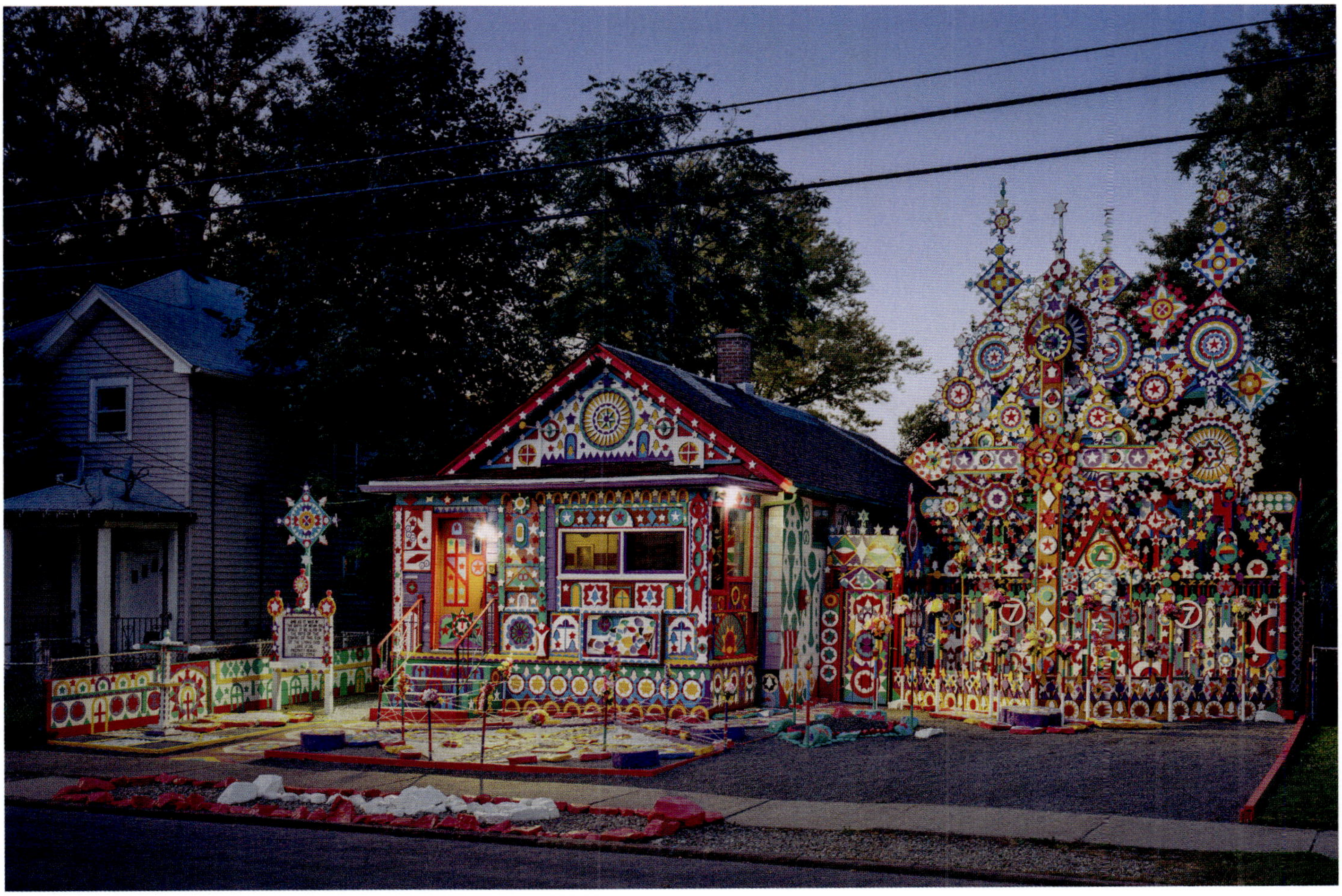

Prophet Isaiah Robertson, Second Coming House, *Niagra Falls, photograph by Fred Scruton, 2011. Courtesy Fred Scruton.* Robertson's transformation of his home, which became known as the *Second Coming House*, was led primarily by a prophetic vision of The Rapture. His vision and concept was specific to his locale of Niagara Falls, a setting magnificent enough for a biblical spectacle.

Despite the prophetic prediction of Isaiah Robertson's mother in 1960, his next 30 years were lived rather unexceptionally. He had been raised deeply Christian, even his profession of carpentry was a result of his admiration for Jesus. In 2004, Robertson moved to Niagara Falls, New York, from Canada, to pursue professional opportunities in building renovation. During a carpentry job for a local church, he experienced a directive from God that informed the materials used and symbols formed. The initial three-month job for the Mount Erie Baptist Church took three years to complete, resulting in oak-stained wood, bespoke symbols, and biblical visuals. Following this defining moment, Robertson received his personal prophecies and was directed by God to adorn his home.

The creative direction of Robertson's home in Niagara Falls was subjectively led by two prophecies: The Jubilee of 2006 and, predominantly, The Rapture of 2014. The interior of the house was ornamented with a multitude of candles and Byzantine-like beaded patterns on the floors illustrating Robertson's religious symbolism. The public-facing exterior of the house reads like a topological geometric quilt. Declaring his hands were led by God, the precision of the silhouetted 3-D forms and the boldness of the colors infer miraculous qualities. On a conceptual level, Robertson's symbolism references biblical narratives. The star, in various forms, appears to be the most recognizable and repeated symbol from scripture. Trumpets, doves, and suns present further exploratory visuals.

By the close of 2014, Robertson believed that Jesus had returned, but was waiting for the right moment to announce his presence on Earth. It was observed that this interpretation of The Rapture caused some distress to Robertson but did not discourage his belief in conveying God's messages. Robertson's health was in decline from 2017 and he passed away three years later. Following Robertson's death in 2020, advocates of the *Second Coming House* are working with aims to establish a legacy and preservation in perpetuity.

"This is not the work of man . . . no man could be capable of this." – Prophet Isaiah Robertson[7]

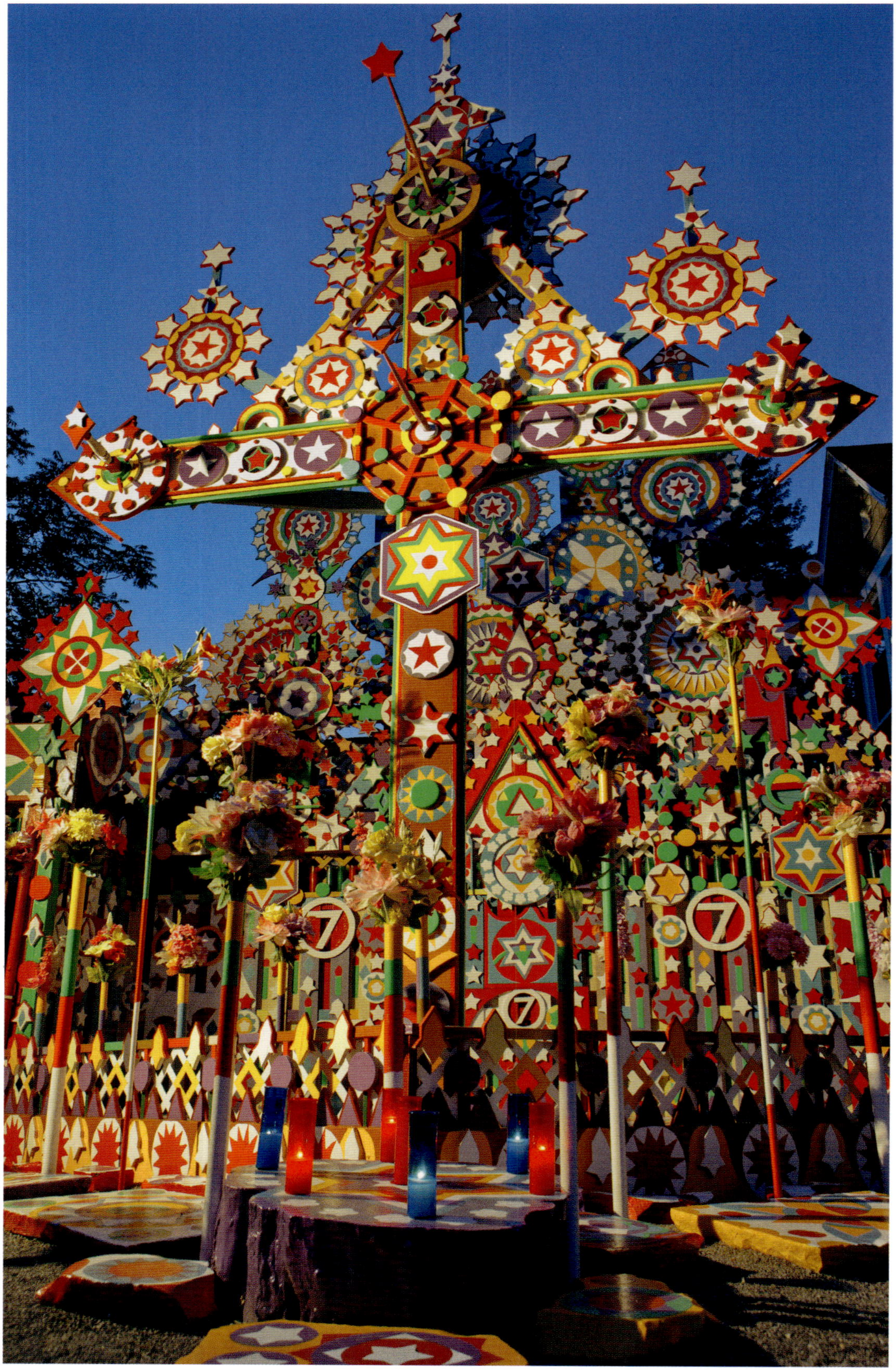

Prophet Isaiah Robertson, Second Coming House*, Niagra Falls, photograph by Fred Scruton, 2012. Courtesy Fred Scruton.* This detail of Robertson's exterior-mounted cross exemplifies his implementation of geometric symmetry and iconic symbolism, as well as his astute skill in producing silhouetted forms. Both five- and six-pointed stars and the number seven feature heavily on the cross.

Prophet Isaiah Robertson, Second Coming House*, Niagra Falls, photograph by Fred Scruton, 2017. Courtesy Fred Scruton.* The interior of the *Second Coming House* was as sacred and adorned as the exterior. From floor to ceiling, the entrance room is covered with multidimensional spiritual patterning and objects, such as flowers, candles, goblets, to serve worship.

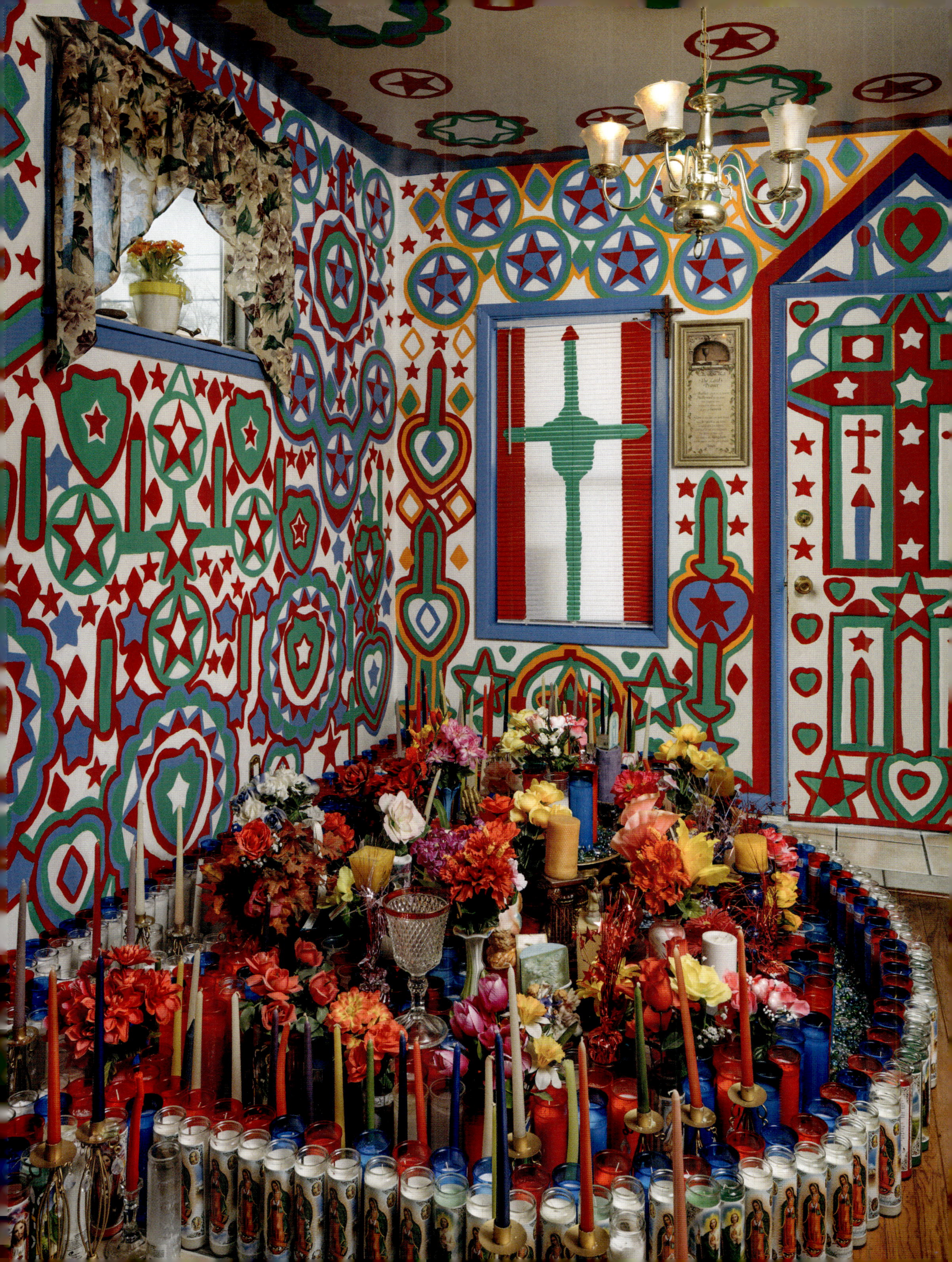

HUANG YONG-FU

(b. ca. 1921, Guangzhou, China)
***Rainbow Village*, Nantun District, Taichung, Taiwan**

When he was in his 80s, Huang Yong-Fu began painting frescos at 3.00 a.m. daily onto the facades of his small Taiwanese village. This routine of painting enigmatic characters before dawn has lasted 10 years, resulting in the fantastical *Rainbow Village*. Born in 1924, in Taishan City, China, Huang served in the air force for Kuomintang, the Chinese Nationalist Party, and later settled outside of Taichung in a veterans' village that was previously a military headquarters. In the early 2000s this temporary settlement was facing demolition and declining in population. In 2008, Huang had the desire to protect his home and preserve his universe by boldly painting the local exteriors, interiors, and pavement. His spirit of art activism received support from university students, followed by the local authority. Eventually, *Rainbow Village*—Huang's artistic transformation of his local architecture—gained the preservation status of an official Taichung public park. In 2019, *Rainbow Village* welcomed over a million visitors, with Huang and his wife (m. 2013) still living on-site as the sole residents.

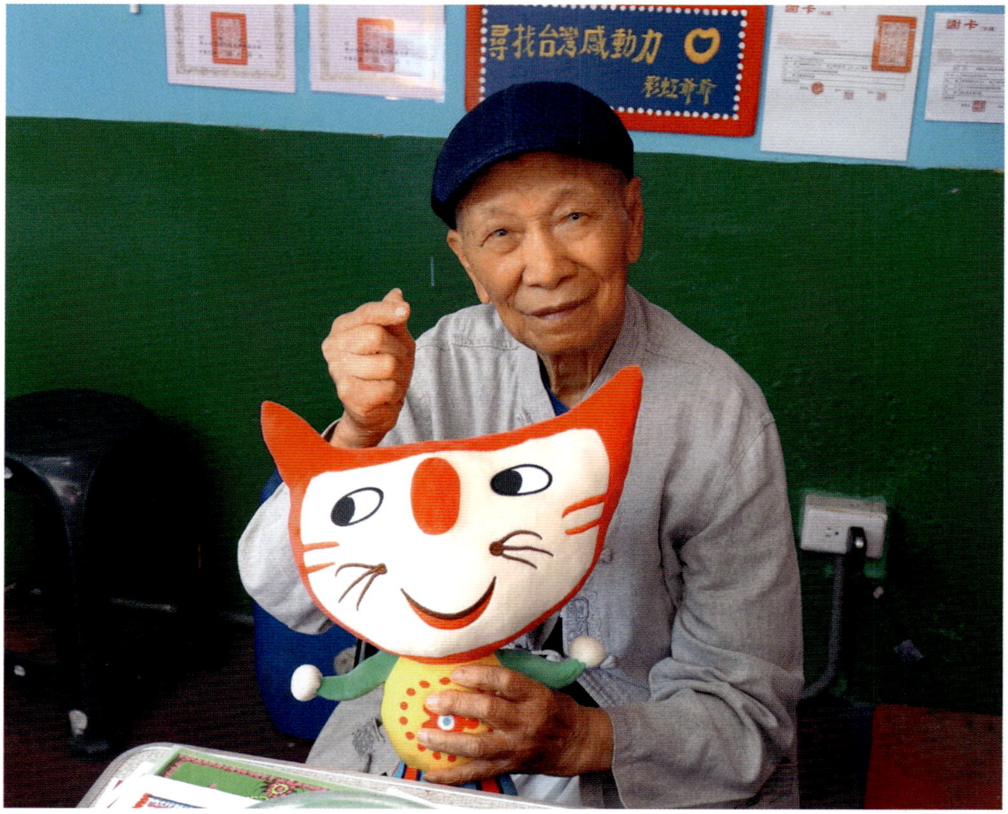

Huang Yong-Fu, 2019, photograph. Rainbow CreativeCo., Ltd. Known to his community and visitors to the village as "Rainbow Grandpa," Huang has been developing *Rainbow Village* for nearly 20 years. He enjoys spending time on-site during the day to watch and interact with visitors.

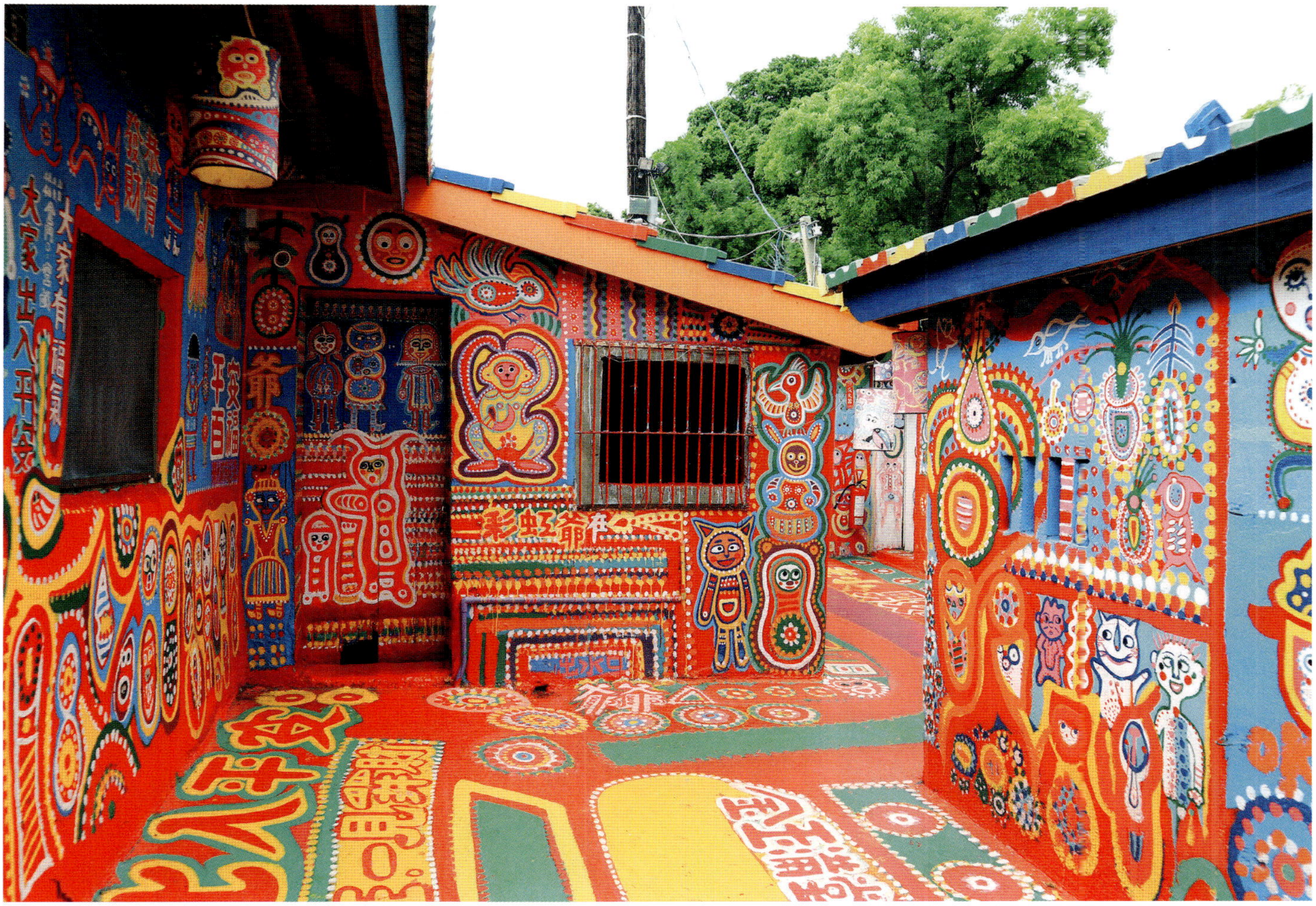

Huang Yong-Fu, Rainbow Village*, Taichung, photograph, n.d. Rainbow CreativeCo., Ltd.* In a bold and spirited aesthetic akin to the cartoon style of Japanese manga, Huang commenced on reinventing his village in 2008 by painting the facade and alleyways.

The settlement now established as *Rainbow Village*, located on the outskirts of Taichung, Taiwan, was part of a series of purpose-built military shelters from the 1950s. These structures initially served as headquarters for the Chinese Nationalist Army after Chiang Kai-Shek was defeated by Mao Zedong's Communist Party of China. Also known as military dependent's villages, they later served as long-term veteran housing when Huang moved to his particular settlement around 1996. However, from 2000, military dependents' villages were targeted under a Taiwanese redevelopment scheme, and the majority were demolished. *Rainbow Village* consists of only 11 houses, whereas the original settlement was comprised of over a thousand shelters.

Between 2000 and 2004 with the impediment of its demolition, Huang's village had become deserted, eventually rendering him the sole resident. In an act of creative resistance, Huang initiated a transformative practice of fresco painting: first within the interiors of his own bungalow, extending to its exterior, and then onto the facades of neighboring buildings. Perhaps his act of personal protest, Huang's creative urge was strong and regimented—abiding by the schedule of an 8.00 p.m. bedtime, 3.00 a.m. rise to paint frescos, followed by breakfast and completing exactly two drawings on paper.

First championed by a local university student, who had encountered these creative interventions, Huang quickly gained the support of the larger community, even adopting the name "Rainbow Grandpa." In 2010, Taichung's mayor announced the preservation of the alleyway and buildings frescoed by Huang. *Rainbow Village* is the first of its kind in the municipality and, according to the Taichung city government, welcomed over 1.25 million visitors in 2016.

Huang's frescos have an exuberant and colorful aesthetic. He was once described by a nearby neighbor as being in a trancelike state while painting by street light. Perhaps reflecting this state between consciousness and unconsciousness, Huang refers to many of his rendered characters as otherworldly. These cartoon-spirited figures encompass humans, gods, animals, and amalgamations thereof. In 2019, at almost 100 years old, Huang continues to illustrate the site when in good health—*Rainbow Village* has become a living entity, accessible and alluring.

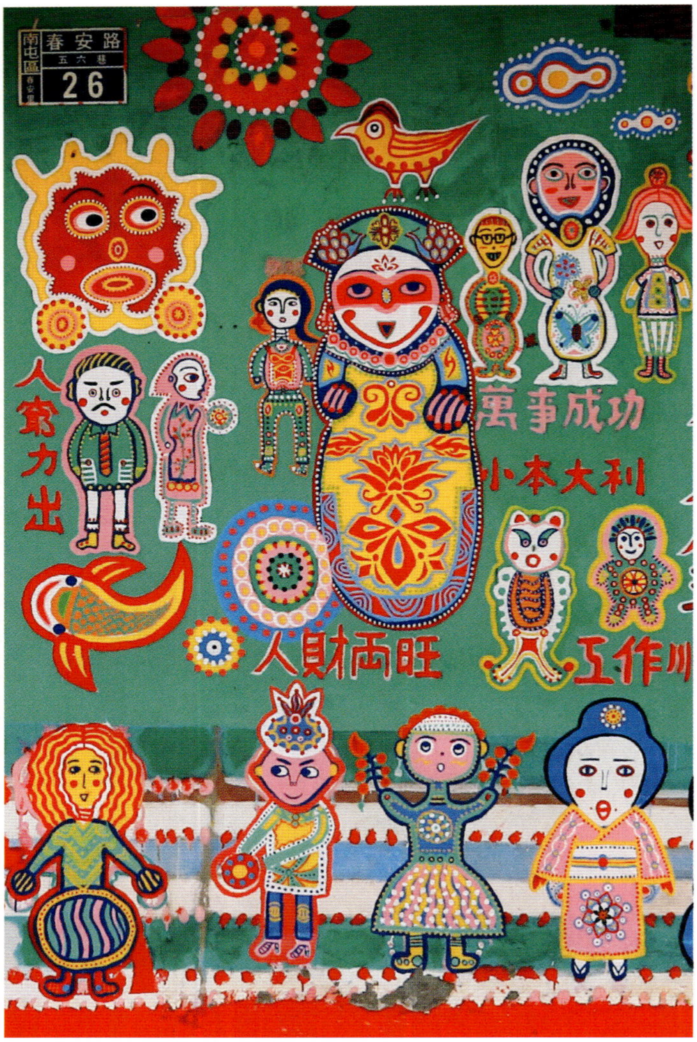

Huang Yong-Fu, Rainbow Village*, Taichung, photograph, n.d. Rainbow CreativeCo., Ltd.* Huang often incorporates positive and reflective Chinese idioms into his fantastical designs. This detail includes the proverbs "Wish you prosperity both in family and purse," "Wish you have a little bait that catches a large fish," and "May you achieve anything your heart desires."

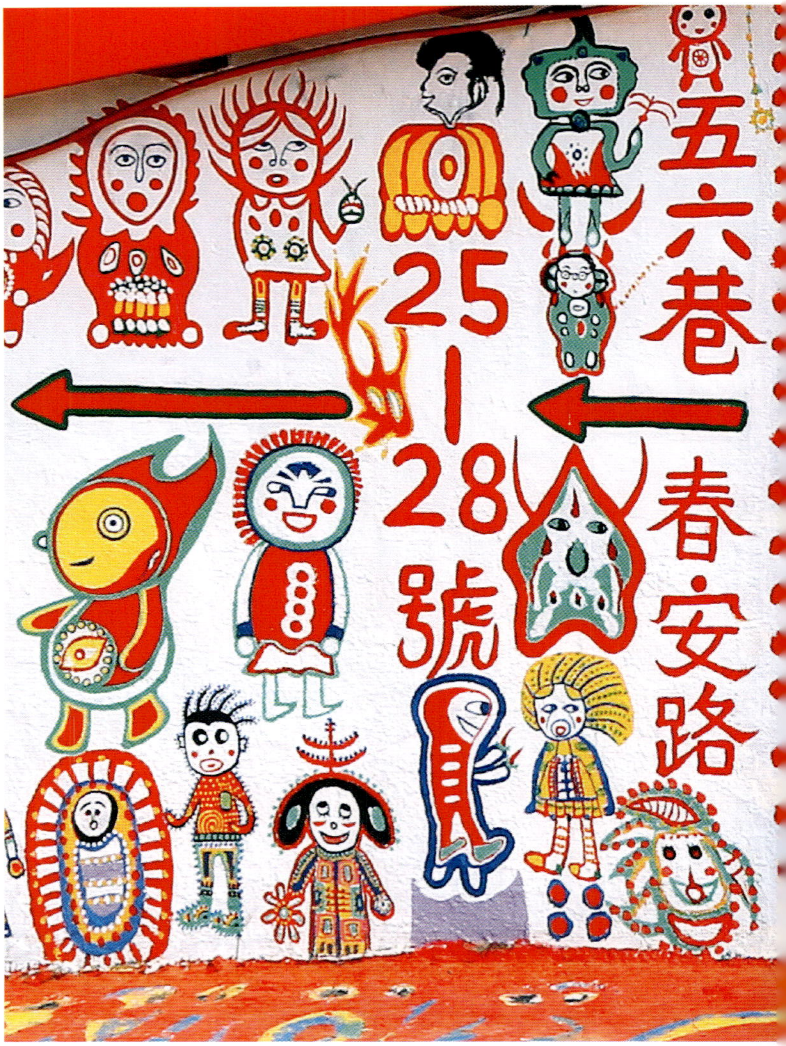

Huang Yong-Fu, Rainbow Village*, Taichung, photograph, n.d. Rainbow CreativeCo., Ltd.* Exemplary of his bold use of color, Huang's vibrant palette on this village wall is appealing and mesmerizing to visitors. Emboldened and spirited by the creative process, he often sings folk songs, as well as talks with his characters while painting.

"There are many things I can't do anymore, but I can still paint. It keeps me healthy, and adding a little color can turn something old into something beautiful."
– Huang Yong-Fu[8]

Huang Yong-Fu, Rainbow Village*, Taichung, photograph, n.d. Rainbow CreativeCo., Ltd.* Referred to by Huang as otherworldly, his figurative and animalistic characters take on a variety of forms and scale. These details show cats, birds, and cows interspersed with smiling people and ornate decoration, while other characters appear to be hybrids between human and otherworldly creatures.

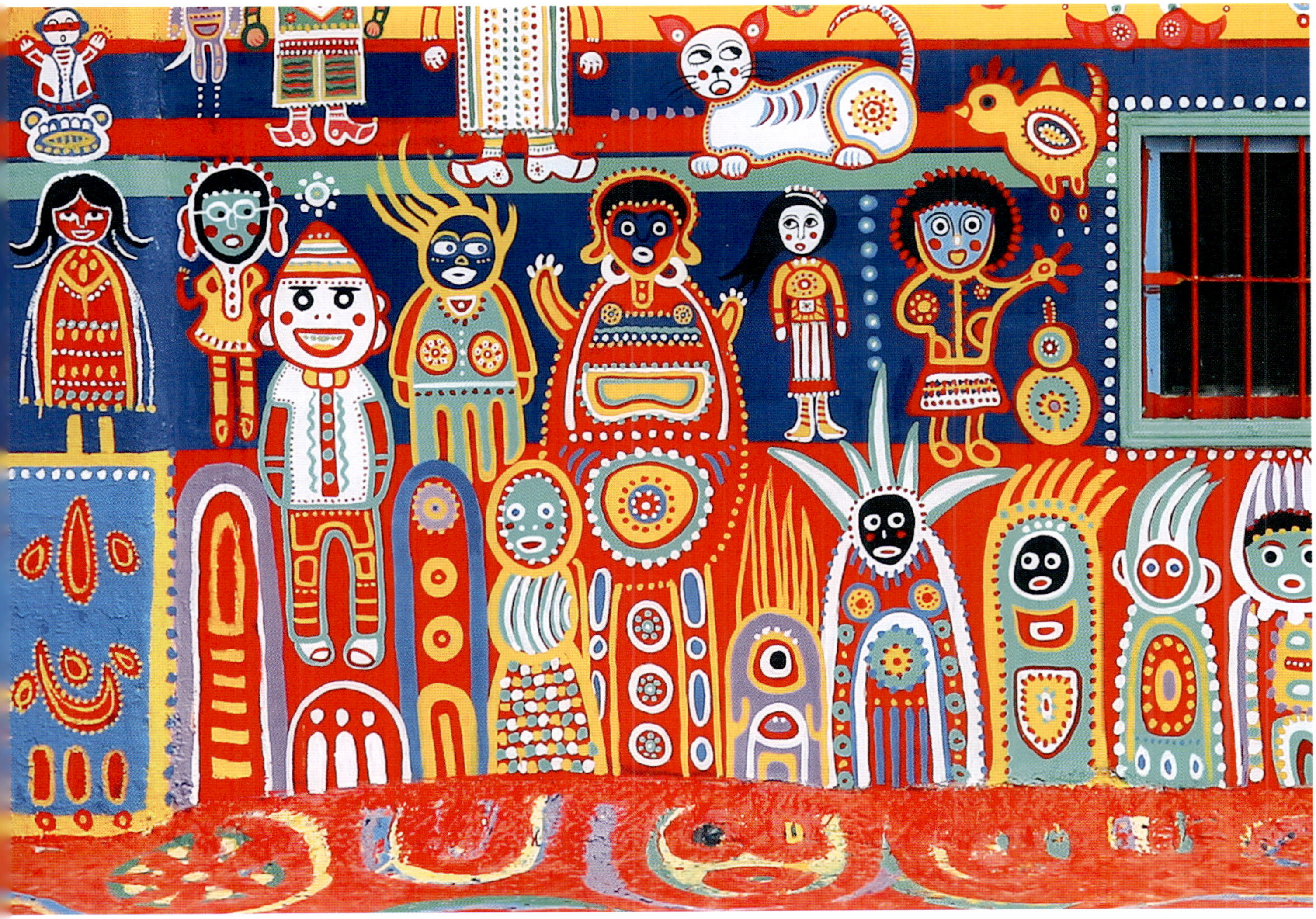

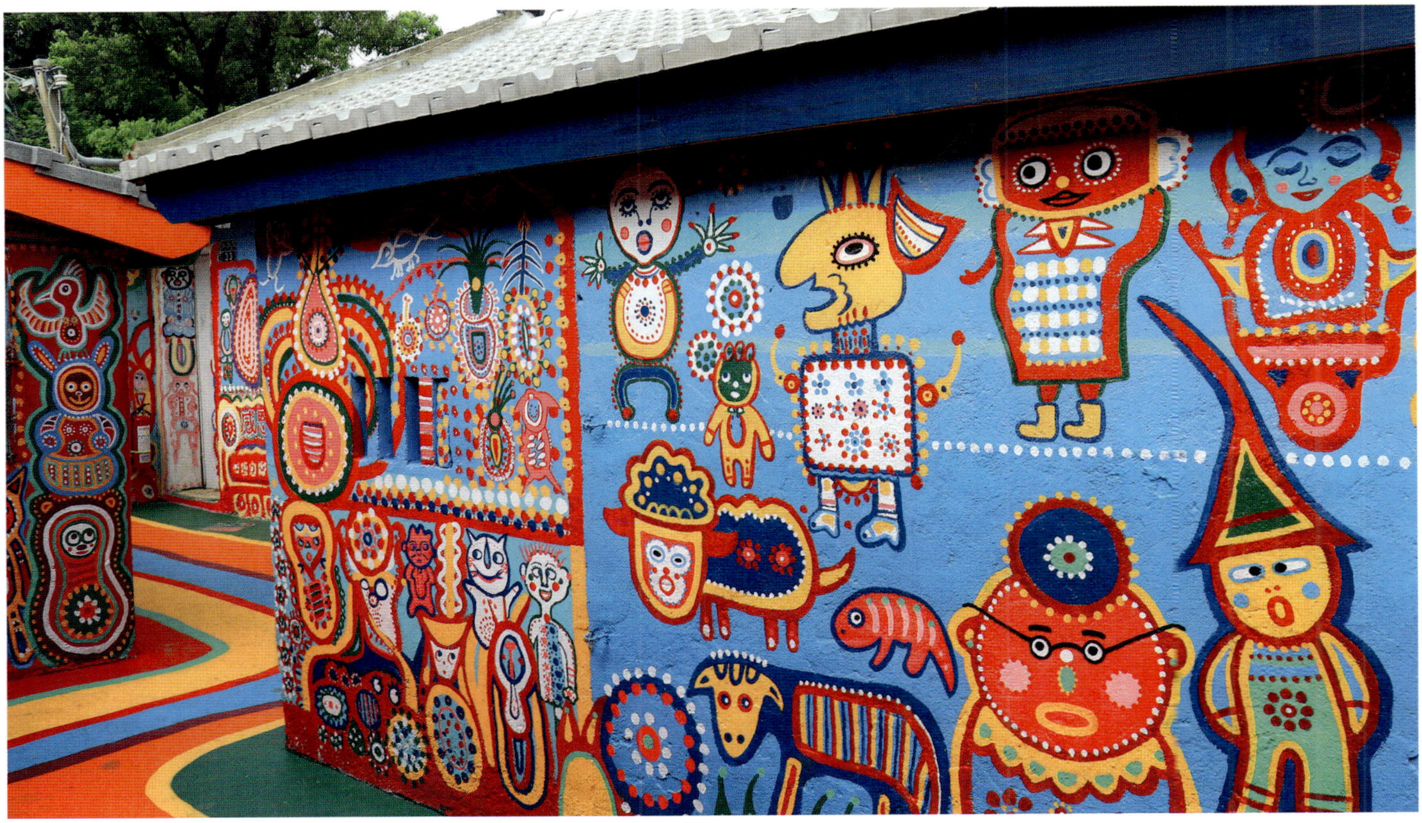

JOSEP PUJIULA I VILA

(1937–2016 Argelaguer, Spain)
***Poblat Salvatge* (Wild Village), Argelaguer, Catalonia, Spain**

The improvisation and perseverance of Josep Pujiula i Vila produced one of Spain's most intriguing artist-built environments. His initial pursuits were for purely personal satisfaction but evolved into an interactive architectural feat greatly driven by its communal participation and enjoyment. Pujiula began constructing his environment in the 1970s—what became known as *parc salvatge* (wild park) or *poblat salvatge* (wild village)—and worked on it until his death. By constructing on property that he did not own, Pujiula endured setbacks and demolition during his near half-century creative practice but continued to be emboldened by determination. The site's extraordinary evolving existence included tree-top towers, labyrinths, cabins, walkways, fountains, pools, and caves with heights of over 100 ft (30 m), and mile-long labyrinth routes. His use of pliable twigs was his most recognizable technique. While later specific forms incorporated more durable materials, Pujiula returned to working with branches in his final years. Furthermore, he ornately carved out a hillside cave that now holds his ashes after his death from a heart attack while constructing on-site in 2016.

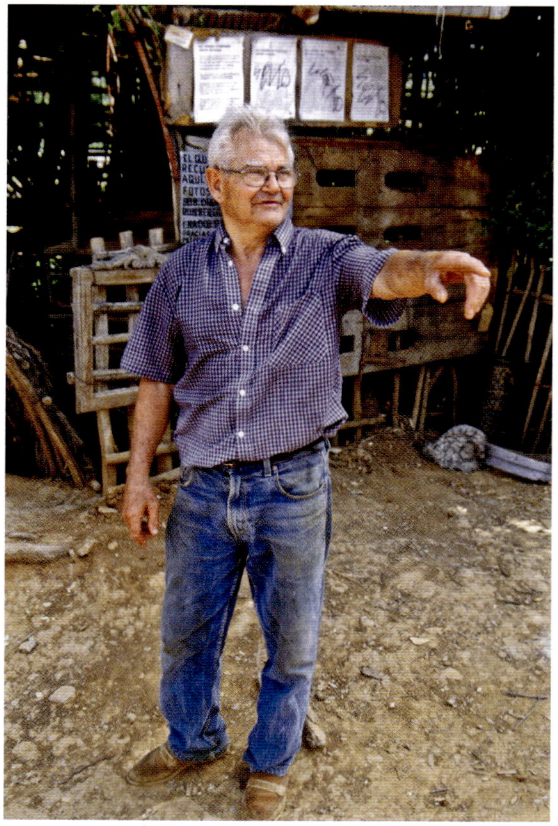

Josep Pujiula i Vila, *2002, photograph by Jo Farb Hernández.* Known for his perseverance, Pujiula is shown on-site here in 2002—a significant year in the demolition, evolution, and dedication to his environment.

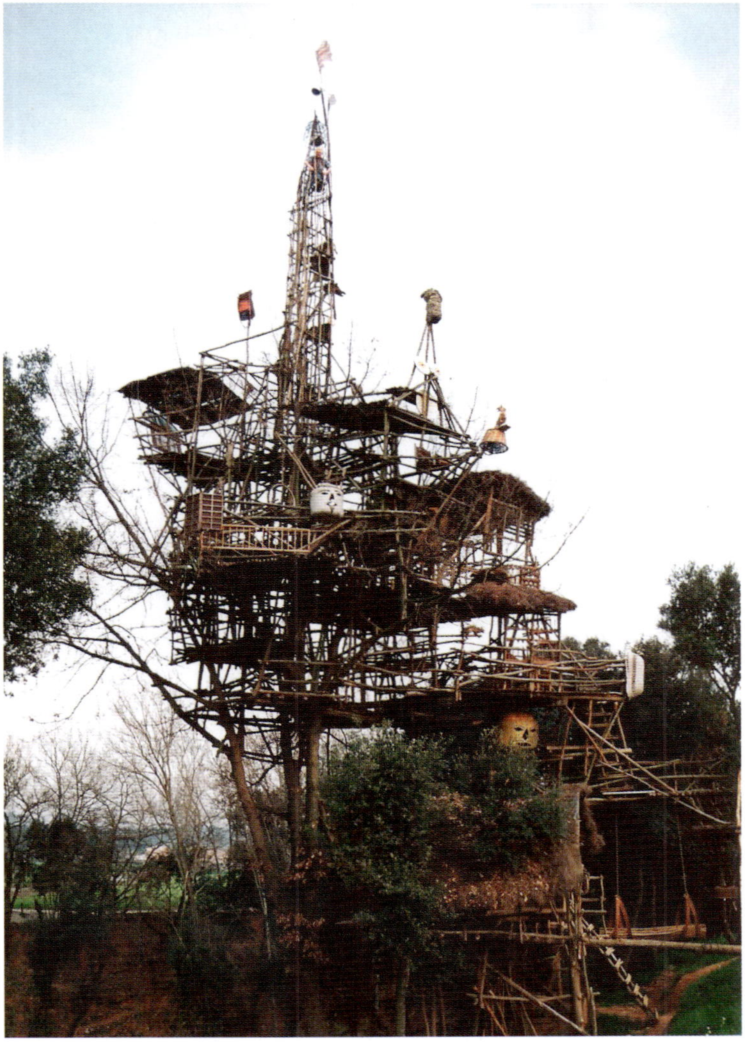

Josep Pujiula i Vila, Poblat Salvatge (Wild Village)*, Argelaguer, photograph, 1997. Courtesy Carles Vila and the archives of the artist.* Following the demolition of earlier works, this historical image documents the early second phase of Pujiula's constructions. Unforunately, this ornate structure with ladders, levels, and tower was deemed a public hazard by local authorities.

Perhaps influenced by horseback riding with friends, some of Josep Pujiula's earliest structures were reminiscent of ranches in the American West. He developed his signature style of weaving and assembling wood branches on a plot of land (inadvertently owned by the mayor of Argelaguer) that surrounded a nearby pond. As his cabins evolved into dwellings and towers, they were punctuated with repurposed architectural elements such as doors and windows. In the 1990s, Pujiula faced issues with the authorities concerning the height of certain towers and incidents of vandalism by careless individuals. These circumstances inspired a focus on horizontal expansion in addition to vertical. He used supple twigs and branches to create archways, ladders, and mazelike paths, which meant only the dedicated would have the patience to make it to his site.

By the early 2000s, when Pujiula was in his 60s, the realization of his environment was reaching its climax with seven astonishing towers, surrounded by the circuitous and playful labyrinth. He was also receiving international encouragement; however, following concerns from multiple authorities (road, electric, and forest), the Department of Public Works confirmed a highway project that would require demolition of the site. Between June and November 2002, Pujiula dismantled his entire creation.

With palpable perseverance, in 2003, Pujiula began a new iteration of his environment on nearby land, this time tapping into resources via the highway expansion project's surplus of concrete and steel. More ornamental and even introducing kinetic elements, this phase eventually featured another labyrinth with peaks, valleys, deadends,

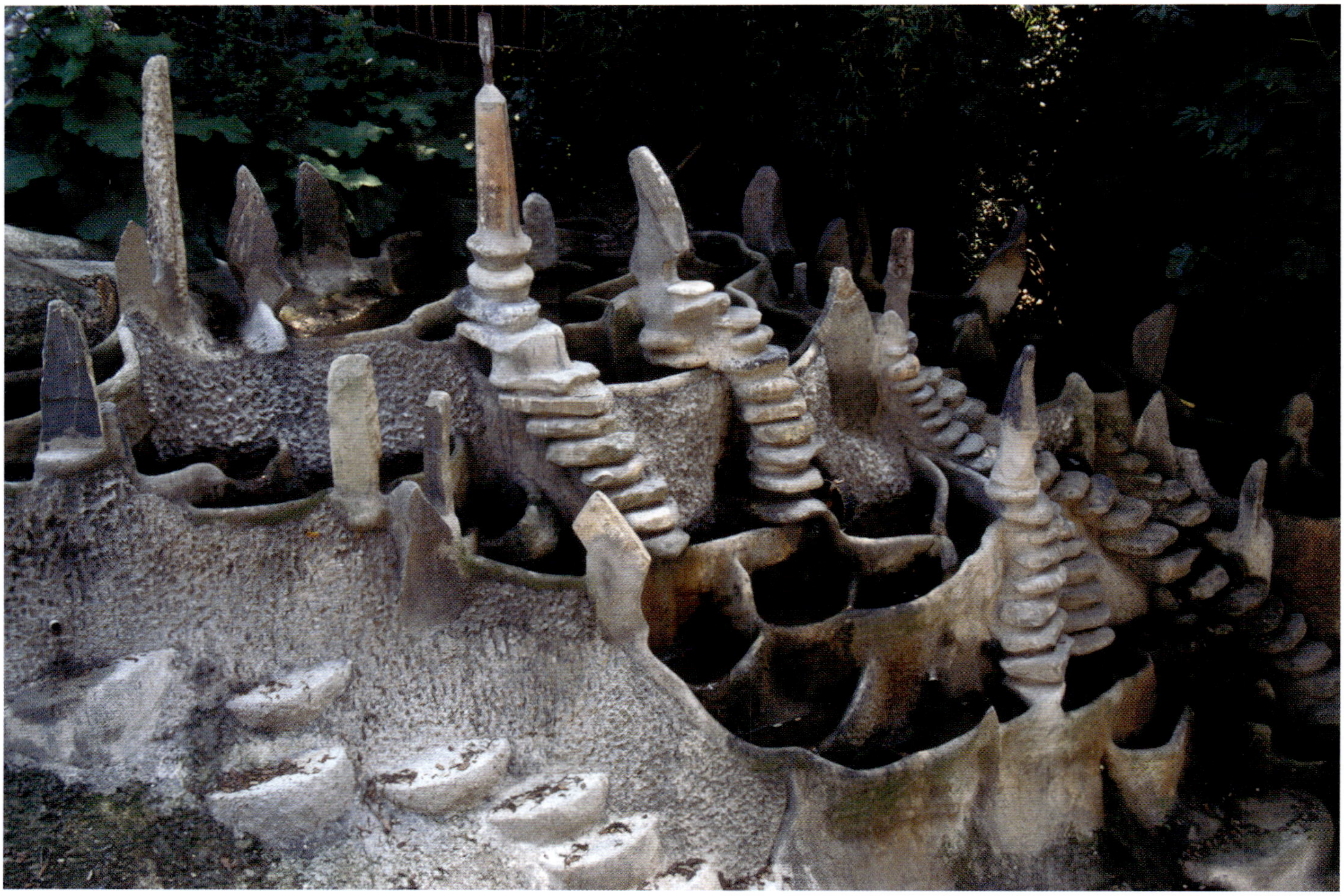

Josep Pujiula i Vila, Poblat Salvatge (Wild Village), *Argelaguer, photograph by Jo Farb Hernández, 2007.* Known for this elaborate sculptural network of ponds, Pujiula utilized stone, concrete, and found objects to construct these cascading ponds alongside spillway underneath Route 260. This beautifully complicated water feature feels both organic and architectural.

and mysterious walkways; erected tall towers; and ornate water features. Unfortunately, in March 2012, numerous authorities again formalized concerns over the site. They ordered Pujiula to demolish all wooden components of his environment. Following another discouraging dismantling, he began expanding and developing the fountain area with durable materials, but this faced further concern from the water authorities. This time, however, the threat was met with opposition from the community and strengthened by international support so that in the fall of 2014 Pujiula's environment was designated as a local heritage site (Bé Cultural de Interés Local). Echoing his tenacity, Pujiula continued erecting towers on adjacent sites until his sudden death in 2016.[9]

"Documenting Pujiula's art environment over some 22 years—through three demolitions, four iterations, his death, and now its gradual deterioration—has taught me much about perseverance and the ability to creatively pivot in order to reframe challenges as opportunities. I also witnessed his challenge to local societal standards as he led both the Argelaguer community and his supporters worldwide to broaden their understanding of what art can be, and to celebrate and value the wit, rebellion, and irrepressibility of his monumental and engagingly interactive *Poblat Salvatge*." – Jo Farb Hernández, curator, art historian, and writer[10]

"When you want to do something that pleases you, you always find the time to do it." – Josep Pujiula i Vila[11]

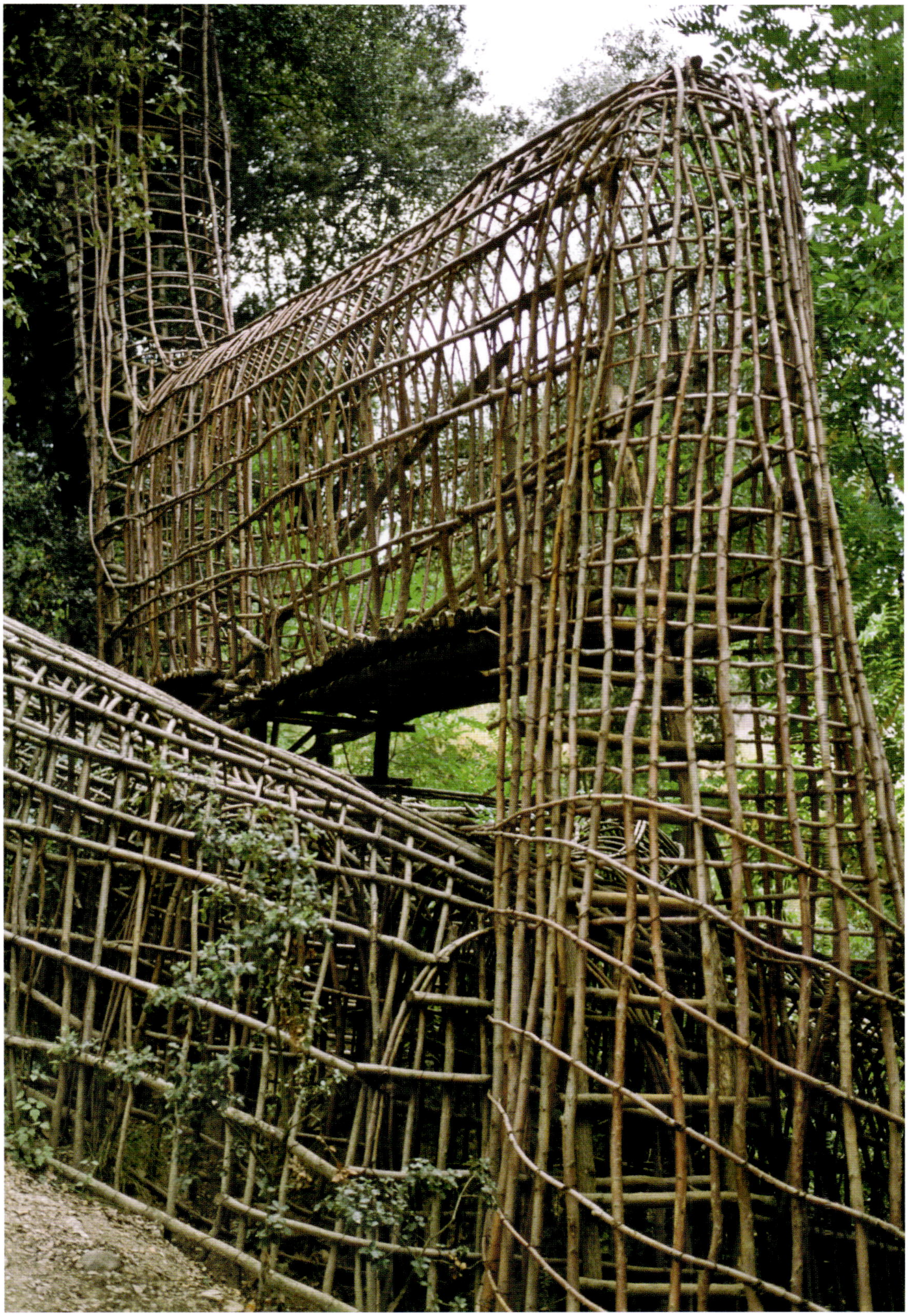

Josep Pujiula i Vila, Poblat Salvatge (Wild Village), *Argelaguer, photograph by Jo Farb Hernández, 2000.* Wood and wire bands were used by Pujiula to create this three-level enclosed ladder inside the labyrinth. His skill at building and sculpting shapes from twigs is evident, and demonstrates his playful penchant for labyrinths and mazes.

NIKI DE SAINT PHALLE

(1930, Neuilly-sur-Seine, Paris, France–2002, La Jolla, CA, USA)
***Tarot Garden*, Capalbio, Tuscany, Italy**

Prior to her artistic awakening, Parisian-born Niki de Saint Phalle was raised in New York, modeled for *Vogue* magazine, and then married at 18. While in recovery after experiencing extreme mental health challenges at a psychiatric hospital in France, she had an unexpected emergence of creativity and continued, throughout her life, to perpetually evolve her artistic production. Her therapeutic discovery of painting in 1953 led to her inclusion with artists of nouveau réalisme and opportunities to exhibit. Throughout the 60s, de Saint Phalle became an established artist most notably for *Nanas*—colorful, patterned sculptures embodying her idea of the feminine spirit. In 1978, she embarked on her most ambitious endeavor, the *Tarot Garden*, an immersive outdoor sculptural environment in Tuscany, Italy, representing tarot's major arcana cards. De Saint Phalle continued to gain notoriety during the development of the *Tarot Garden*, including a retrospective at the Musée National d'Art Moderne, Centre Georges Pompidou (1980) in Paris. She dedicated over ten years to the environment. The vivid and whimsical sculptures of the *Tarot Garden* are esoteric but monumental, feminine but bold—encompassing de Saint Phalle's long exploration of female identity.

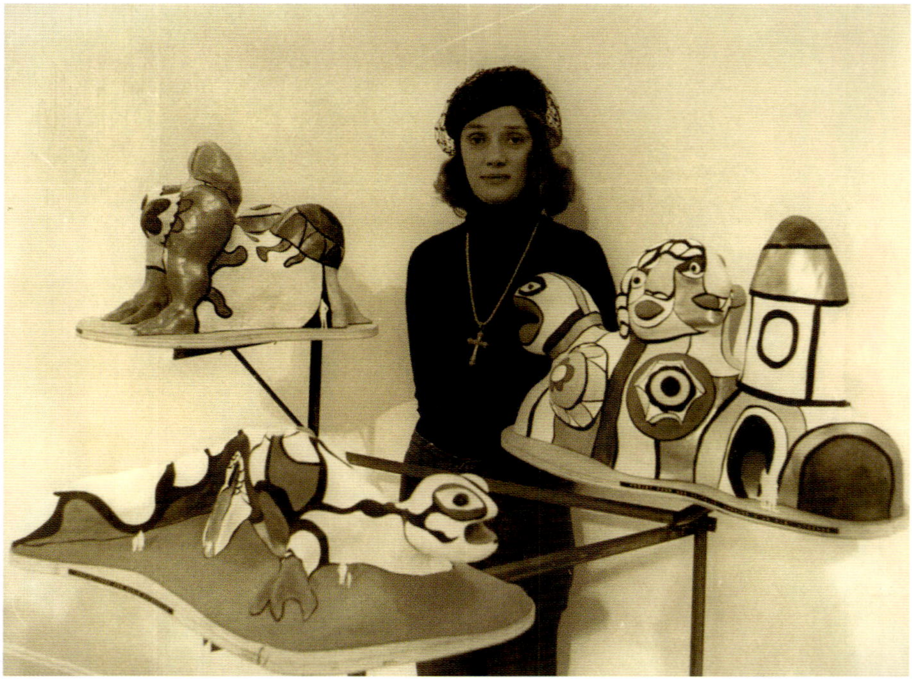

Niki de Saint Phalle, February 6, 1974, photograph. de Saint Phalle is seen here with her sculptures. Though a few years prior to her work on the *Tarot Garden*, the style and maquette-like forms of these featured sculptures aesthetically align with the development of her environment in Tuscany.

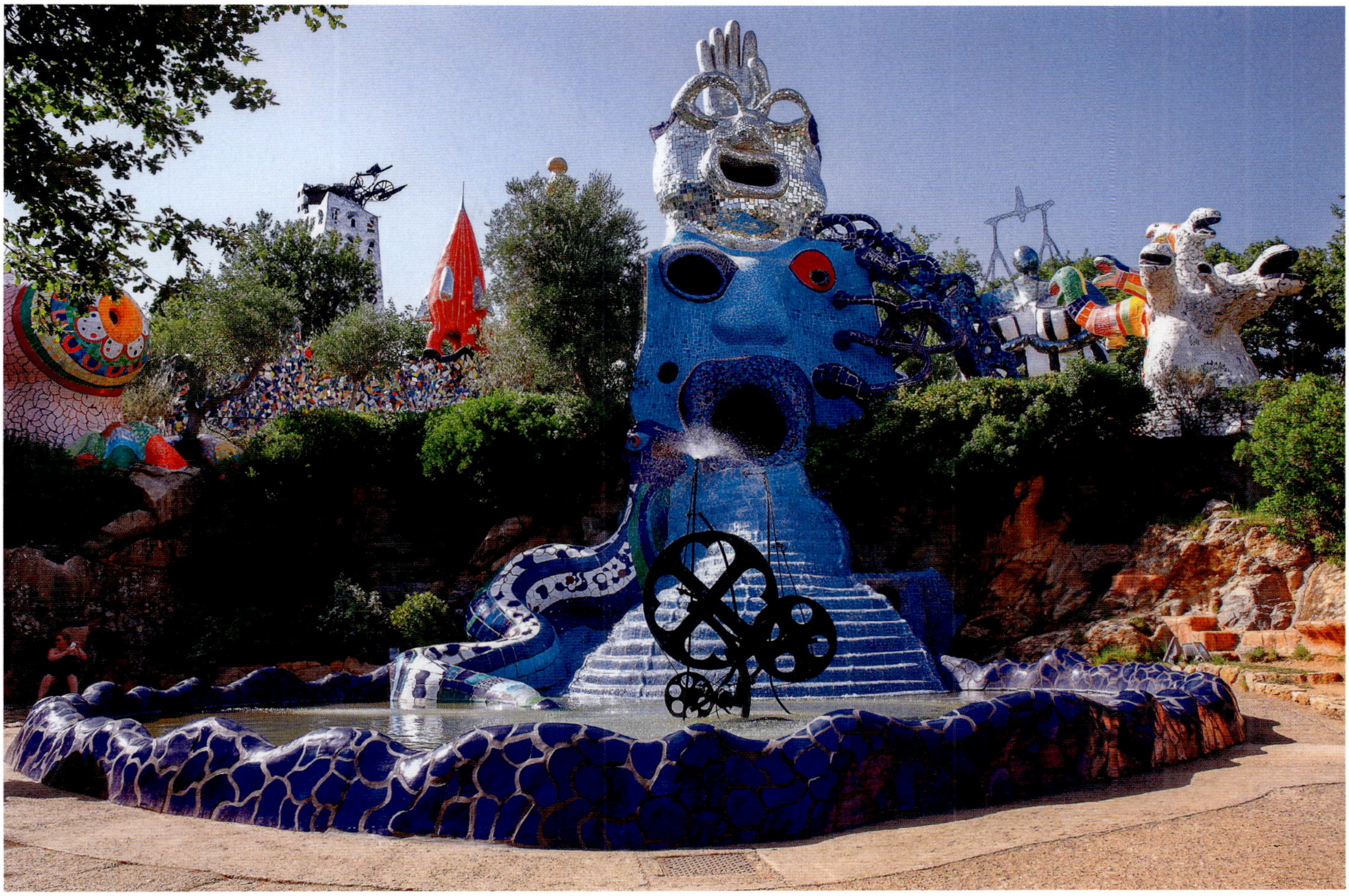

Niki de Saint Phalle, Tarot Garden, *Capalbio, photograph, 2016*. This expansive view of the *Tarot Garden* shows the High Priestess with the glittering Magician on top. The fountain flowing from the priestess's mouth was an homage to the historic sculptures found in the Garden of Bombarzo, a 16th-century garden in Italy. De Saint Phalle said of the sculpture: "The Magician represents primal energy in its most creative and active form. The Magician is the masculine principle of the universe . . . The Magician lives in the present—the High Priestess represents the feminine principle of the universe. She signifies inner wisdom at its deepest level."

Despite being self-taught and often referring to herself as an "Outsider," Niki de Saint Phalle was widely accepted into the modern and contemporary art curriculum. Her acceleration seemed to correspond to her early acceptance into the nouveau réalisme movement and collaborations with Swiss artist Jean Tinguely (whom she later married in 1971 and collaborated with until his death in 1991). Her initial recognition was through two bodies of work: *Shooting Paintings* and *Nanas*; nonetheless, the *Tarot Garden* is considered her most significant work.

She was an established artist with international acclaim at the time of conceptualizing the *Tarot Garden*. The planning and modeling for the garden began in 1978, and construction began in 1980 with support from her friends, family, and a team of assistants. Based on the 22 major arcana cards of the tarot, the first card to be completed was *The High Priestess*. A symbol of universal feminine principles, *The High Priestess*, juxtapositioned with the masculine representation of *The Magician* card positioned on top, is monumental in scale and was intricately mosaiced in a variety of materials. It also has a kinetic quality with a water fountain feature flowing out of the Priestess's mouth. From 1984 to 1987, de Saint Phalle spent most of her time at the *Tarot Garden*. She even began living on-site with the completion of *The Empress* sculpture, which was built with a studio inside.

The 22 immense sculptures were constructed from iron and steel that was covered in plaster and a myriad of mosaic materials. Their fabrication and scale exude permanence, yet clearly evoke the tarot's esoteric concepts and symbolism. De Saint Phalle's own playful quest for identity is reflected throughout her life-long practice. Her timely *Shooting Paintings* after her divorce were the aggressive result of shooting a rifle at canvas assemblages. Her later sculptures, *Nanas*, became overtly feminine and expressed balance. The execution of the *Tarot Garden* became de Saint Phalle's forceful, but poetic, gesture proving that women artists can work on a monumental and environmental scale, and reflected her continual interest in, and response to, the different societal roles for women.

"If life is a game of cards we are born without knowing the rules. Yet we must play our hand." - Niki de Saint Phalle[12]

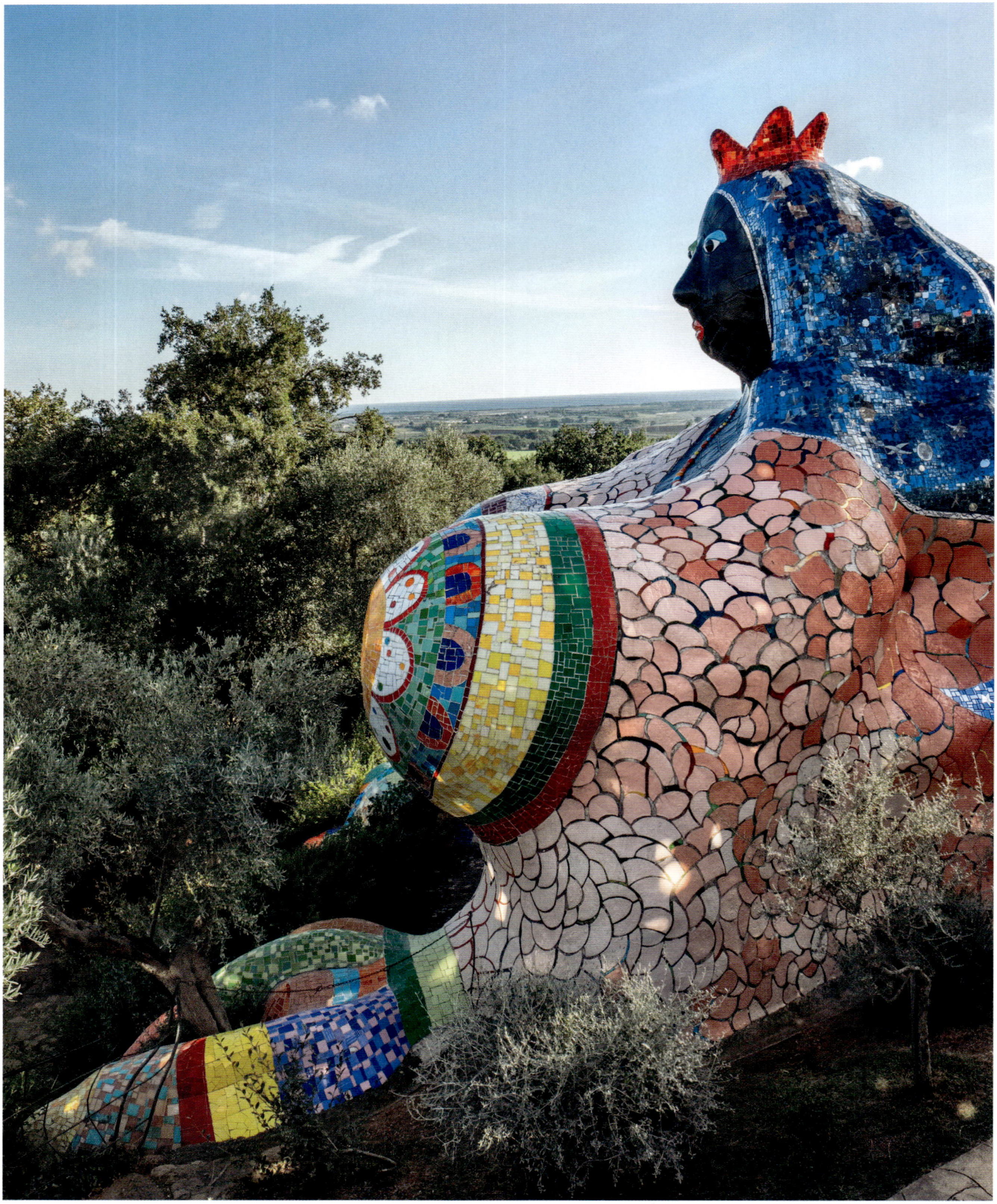

Niki de Saint Phalle, Tarot Garden*, Capalbio, photograph, 2019*. The inside of this powerful and overtly feminine representation of the Empress, seen here, was de Saint Phalle's home and studio while she completed the *Tarot Garden*.

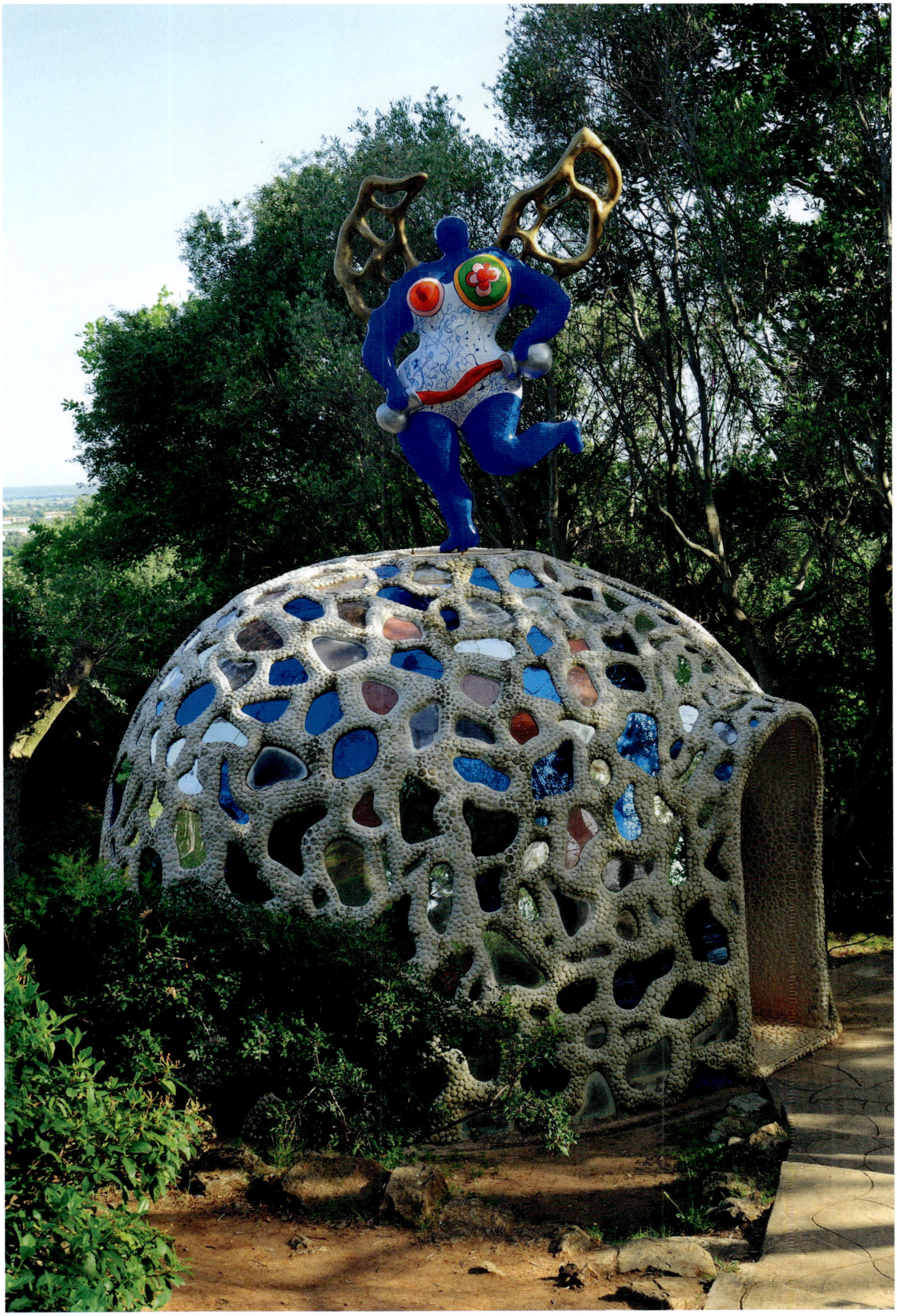

Niki de Saint Phalle, Tarot Garden*, Capalbio, photograph, 2009*. This flamboyant and stylized depiction of Temperance echoes de Saint Phalle's larger oeuvre of *Nanas*. She compared herself to a devouring mother, consuming culture and history like Giotto, early Sienese paintings, temples, and even artists from Rousseau to Picasso—digesting them, then producing her work.

CHAPTER 8

ABILITY: ADVOCATING FOR ARTISTIC DEVELOPMENT

SHIFTING FOCUS, A BRIEF HISTORY OF DISABILITY ART IN GLOBAL CONTEXTS

Tom di Maria

If you have studied art history, perhaps you've read a paragraph on the Swiss artist Adolf Wölfli (see page 64), tucked away in a small section about nonacademically trained artists. Our story starts here, with the first widely recognized instance of a person with a psychiatric illness being accepted into the fringes of the art historical canon. If we use Wölfli's life and art as a starting point for our narrative, how do we arrive at a place where people with disabilities are increasingly being accepted as culturally relevant contemporary artists?

To study this advancement, we can look to the emergence of art studios designed to support the creativity of people with disabilities. Their growth, from very few in the 1970s, to more than 50 today, parallels the increased participation of people with disabilities in society, and curatorial shifts that have accompanied this advancement. Influenced by a few individuals, the field has been impacted by notable contributors including Walter Morgenthaler (1882–1965), Hans Prinzhorn (1886–1933), Jean Dubuffet (1901–1985), Roger Cardinal (1940–2019), Elias Katz (1901–1947), and numerous contemporary curators and collectors.

One of the first significant publications in the field, *Artistry of the Mentally Ill*, was published in 1922 by Hans Prinzhorn. A doctor in a psychiatry hospital in Heidelberg, Germany, he was familiar with the pioneering work of Walter Morgenthaler, who found Wölfli's work to be artistically relevant and protected it for future generations. He, too, considered these objects to be more than personal expressions and saw them as works of art in their own right. His attempts to exhibit these works in galleries, and to seek critical reviews of them, was met with initial success. But these efforts were interrupted by the rise of the Nazi Party in Germany. The Third Reich not only condemned the existence of people with mental health issues and disabilities, but of artists in general. This was a serious setback to the emergence of these artists: Their work was banned and many pieces destroyed.

Despite Hitler's condemnation of art by people with disabilities, many works were safely returned to Heidelberg after World War II, where they are now housed in a museum named in honor of Prinzhorn. The postwar continuation of psychiatric art practices commenced again, and continued at venues such as the Gugging House of Artists in Austria (see page 112) with it pioneering work to offer artistic opportunities to those seeking personal and artistic advancement. Postwar thinking on the subject is considered to be principally led by the French artist Jean Dubuffet. He expanded his interest in nonacademic artists under the genre Art Brut (see Chapter 2). Similar ideas came to a greater readership in the 1970s with Roger Cardinal's book *Outsider Art* (see Chapter 3).

While artists with disabilities are included in such books, at the time of these publications there was not a concept of disability as a culture or class, as most people with disabilities were either institutionalized, hidden away with families, or worse. Increasing independence for people with disabilities started to take root in countries around the world as historical norms of social isolation were challenged. While these changes made way for the social and cultural advancements of people with disabilities, it is worth considering how forward-looking artists also contributed by considering artistic opportunities for people with disabilities.

By the early 1970s, the San Francisco Bay Area was an epicenter for the emergence of new social ideals. A coming together of several important occurrences that included the deinstitutionalization of people with disabilities in California, new cultural freedoms, and social changes proposed by groups such as the Black Panther Party, and movements supporting feminism, lesbian and gay rights, and free speech. As these movements advanced, an updated view of social diversity eventually came to include rights for people with disabilities. This helped form the basis of the idea of disability as a culture and set the stage for the emergence of artists with disabilities. Creative Growth Art Center, in Oakland,

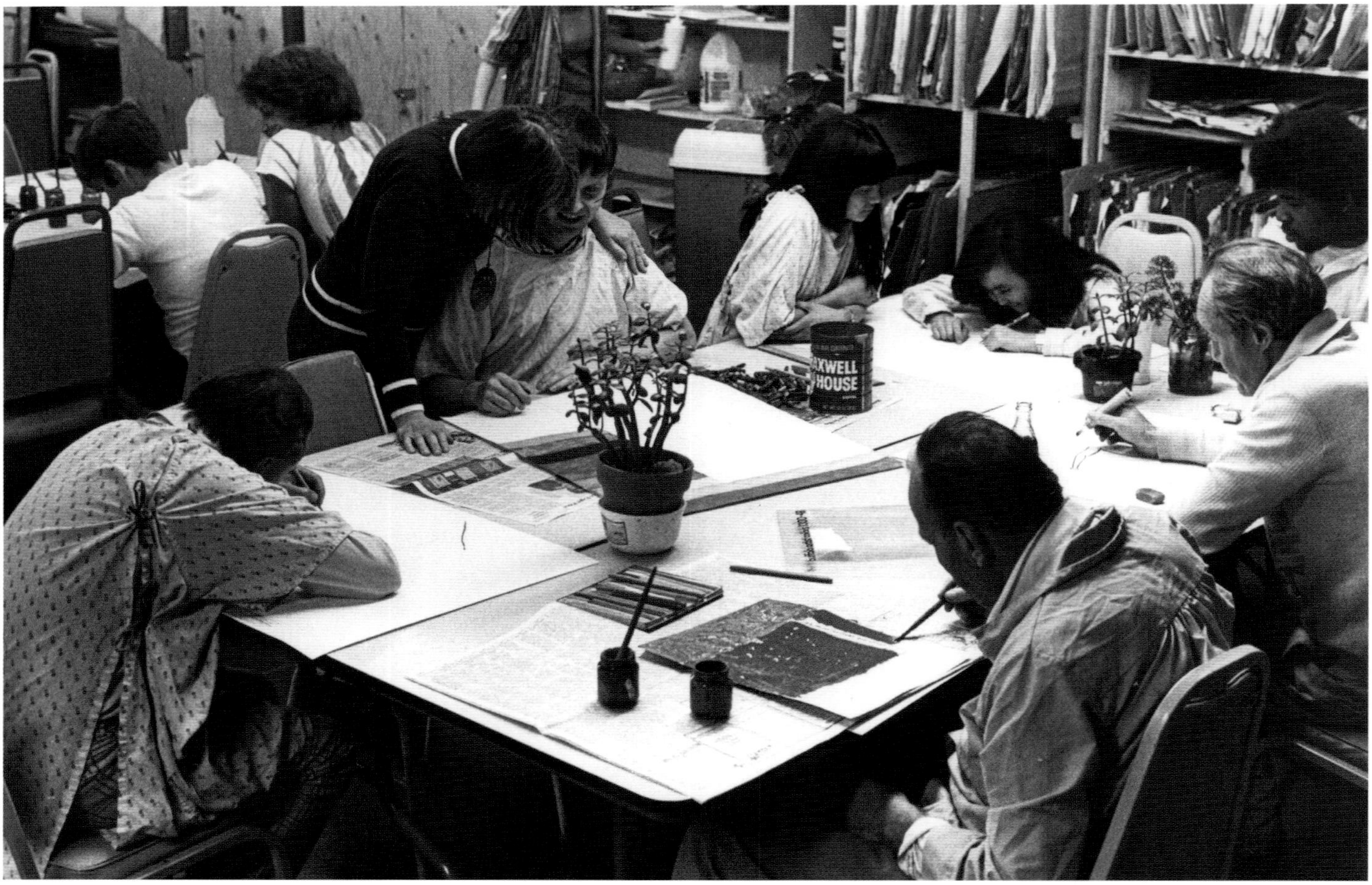

Artists working at Creative Growth Art Center, photograph, 1976. Courtesy Creative Growth Art Center. Founded in Oakland, California, in 1974, by Elias Katz and Florence Ludins-Katz, this early photograph demonstrates the center's focus on a communal and supportive development of artists with disabilities.

California, is one of the first stand-alone art centers for people with disabilities and was premised on these ideas.

Founded in 1974, by psychologist Elias Katz, and his wife, artist Florence Ludins-Katz, the couple started a radical social experiment to empower people with disabilities to grow personally, socially, and aesthetically through the process of making art. Carefully considered in his publication, *Art & Disabilities: Establishing the Creative Art Center for People with Disabilities*, the Katz model has become a primary influence for dozens of similar centers in North America and worldwide.

The culture of creative growth, as an independent art center not associated with any other program for people with disabilities, is notable. Influenced by a new social order and personal freedoms of the times, a radical model was put forth; the opening of an artist-led space with a hands-off approach to foster the inherent creative potential of every individual. From the very start, it was designed as a non-judgmental studio and gallery to provide creative freedom for individuals in a wide variety of visual arts media. Artists are offered endless amounts of time to do their work, and to develop and exhibit significant bodies of artistic expression that often take decades to create.

It is interesting to make note of a few leading centers in the field and understand their genesis. Across the globe, new social attitudes about disability helped these centers take form, often reflecting the social/cultural traditions of their locations. In Melbourne, in the 1970s, Arts Project Australia was created by a mother seeking a better opportunity for her son, at a time when new ideas were percolating about how people with disabilities should have better opportunities for growth. That prolific center is now home to notable artists including Julian Martin (see page 264) and Alan Constable (b. 1956).

In the United Kingdom, ActionSpace creates innovative opportunities for people with intellectual disabilities to engage in the arts by partnering with a range of contemporary arts organizations. Emerging in the 1960s, and becoming an independent organization in 1984, their programs have allowed for the professional development of artists such as Andrew Omoding (see page 268) and Nnena Kalu (see page 310). There are also numerous examples of studios emerging in Europe: the vibrant Belgian programs of La S Grand Atelier and Creáhm, and in Frankfurt, Germany, Atelier Goldstein, where artist Julia Krause-Harder (see page 272) works.

In North America, early centers devoted to this work include the Tierra del Sol Foundation in Southern California where Helen Rae (see page 370) worked for 30 years, and Pure Vision Arts, in Manhattan, home to the artist Walter Mika (see page 276). Many centers grew from the Katz model, including Visionaries and Voices, Cincinnati, Creativity Explored, San Francisco, Arts of Life, Chicago, and the Center for Creative Works, Philadelphia. In Canada, the National accessArts Centre is bringing together art and disability programs from across the country for collegial support and mutual advancement.

In Japan, in 2005, a new law gave people with disabilities the right to choose programs and activities on their own. This resulted in the formation of Atelier Incurve, supporting multiple artists including Tomoyuki Shinki (see page 280) and Katsuhiro Terao (see page 346) both of whom have been working at the studio since it opened.

These studios, and dozens of others worldwide, have become an informal association of centers and practitioners, whose work is often based upon similar missions, but whose practices draw both from the culture in which they are immersed, and the ethos of their respective founders. If a center is founded and managed by artists, it may have a studio program that fosters artistic independence using a non-directive approach. Programs organized by multipurpose centers for people with disabilities, vocational programs, or similar programs for social integration that also include artmaking, may favor practices that encourage the acquisition of social or vocation skills over the advancement of a unique artistic voice.

When the work from an artist crosses the threshold from a disability art studio to the contemporary art world, it changes the lens through which we see the work. It raises questions about its relationship to the thinking of Dubuffet and Cardinal, and about how work by artists with disability relates to Art Brut, Outsider Art, and contemporary art.

Lucienne Peiry, former director of the Collection de l'Art Brut, pondered: If Dubuffet's definition is based on the artist being isolated from cultural influence, could a person working in such a communal studio be considered Art Brut? After visiting Creative Growth in 2001, Peiry put forth that the studio's hands-off approach to artmaking for artists who, due to disability or circumstance, experience personal isolation, could indeed be considered under the remit of Art Brut. Artists Judith Scott (see page 256) and Dwight Mackintosh (1906–1999), following decades isolated within institutions, each came to Creative Growth lacking basic literacy, isolated from the world, and without any creative outlets. Despite that history, each formed signature bodies of work: Mackintosh's obsessive drawings based upon an invented language and X-ray vision and Scott's compulsive gathering and bundling of accumulated objects, have both become accepted into the Art Brut canon.

Similarly, during a visit to Creative Growth in 2005, Roger Cardinal responded to what he described as the necessary and compelling need to create witnessed among the artists. These urgent acts of creation resonated with his definition of Outsider Art. While the words Outsider Art are not embraced by Creative Growth, there are advantages for artists with disabilities to align themselves with the collectors and galleries that do use the term. Take, for example, the annual Outsider Art Fair. It serves as a meeting place for viewers in a field driven largely by collectors. The fair is also one of the few marketplaces where self-taught artists with disabilities can bring their work to a venue to be seen by a

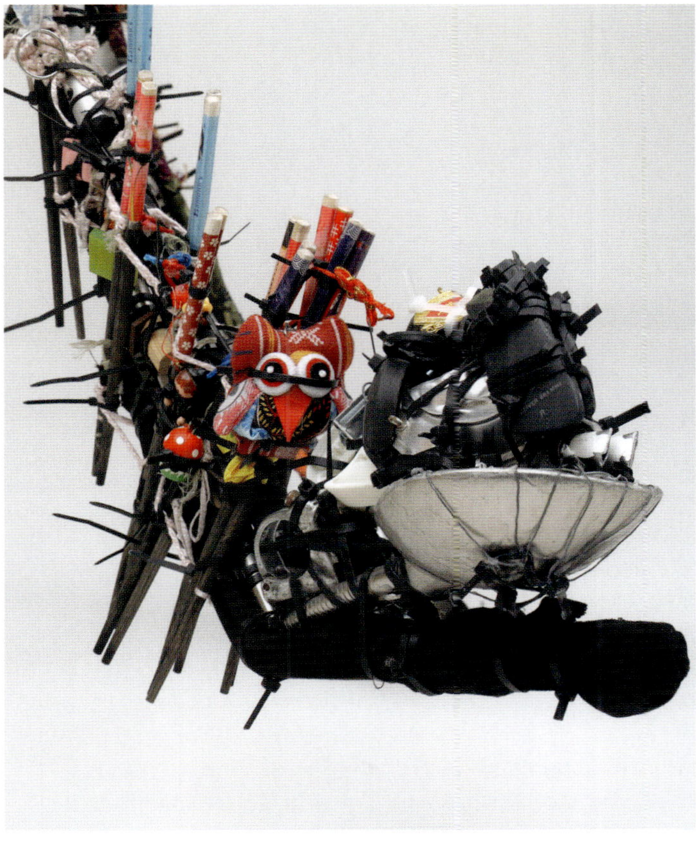

Julia Krause-Harder, Singapursaurus (Hypsilophodon) *(detail), 2019, various materials, 47 × 39 × 98½ in (120 × 100 × 250 cm). Courtesy Atelier Goldstein.* Working from Atelier Goldstein in Frankfurt, Krause-Harder's practice is dedicated to recreating every dinosaur species discovered to date. This detail of a head based on the Hypsilophodon, demonstrates both her accuracy and use of divergent materials, including an audio receiver, metal hardware, keychains, and chopsticks.

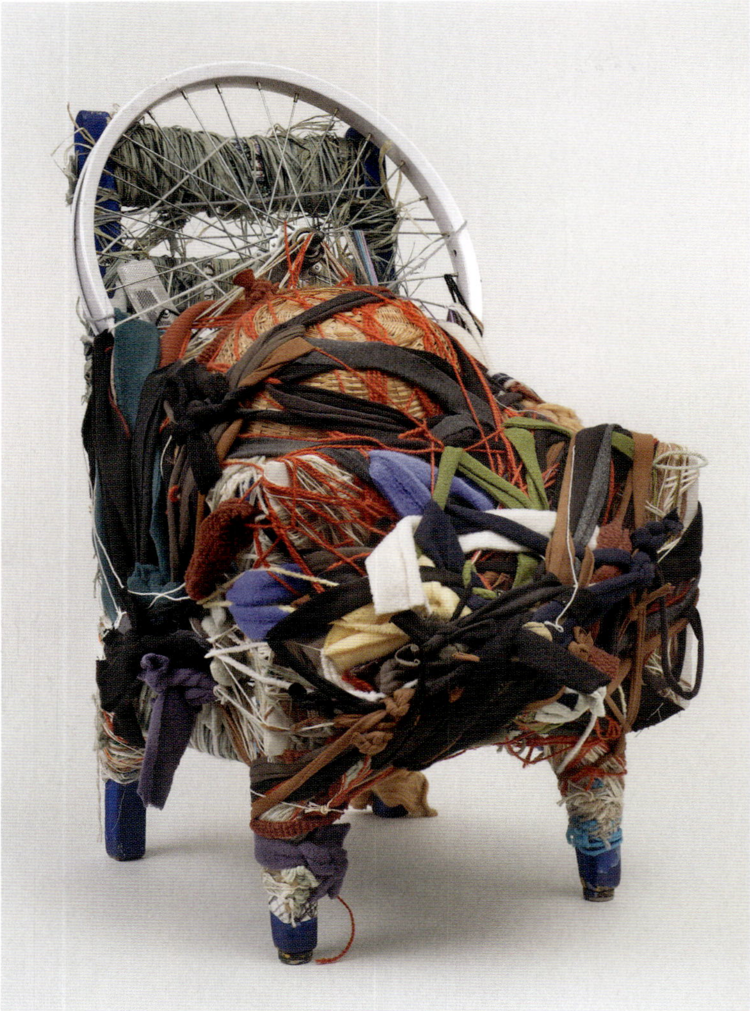

Judith Scott, untitled, *2004, fiber and found objects, 29 × 16 × 21 in (73.6 × 40.6 × 53.3 cm). Courtesy Creative Growth Art Center.* This colorful sculpture by Scott reveals or exposes the objects informing its structure. Erected by the four legs of a chair, an upside-down basket is viewable through the bounds of red yarn, while a bicycle wheel is attached to the seat back of the chair.

large audience. The downside to using the label of Outsider Art, is that such artists might become relegated only to this arena of the self-taught, and excluded from advancing into the more globalized art markets and contemporary art galleries. The term can be useful, however, the word also has negative connotations as it denotes how the maker, in this case a person with a disability, can be seen as being "other." It also delegates the work to a niche market, perhaps a lesser division of the art world, where it might only appeal to a narrow segment of specialized collectors.

As an example of an artist whose work exists in a variety of contexts, we consider the artist Dan Miller (b. 1961). As a boy on the autism spectrum, Miller's reduced interest in verbalization led family members to spell words with him to encourage language. These "spelling lessons" led him to develop a form of communication that was specific to him; a language that developed artistically, not verbally, into an aesthetic output formed by the repetition of letters, words, and glyphs.

Miller found in Creative Growth a community that allowed his expressiveness to find its own path. After years of working in the Creative Growth studio, Miller's drawings were first shown in the Outsider Art Fair in 2002, then at Art Brut galleries in Paris and New York. His career benefitted from Creative Growth's ability to have his work be seen by curators such as Matthew Higgs, and to present it in contemporary art fairs. The curator Christine Macel, who selected his work for the 2017 Venice Biennale, was unaware

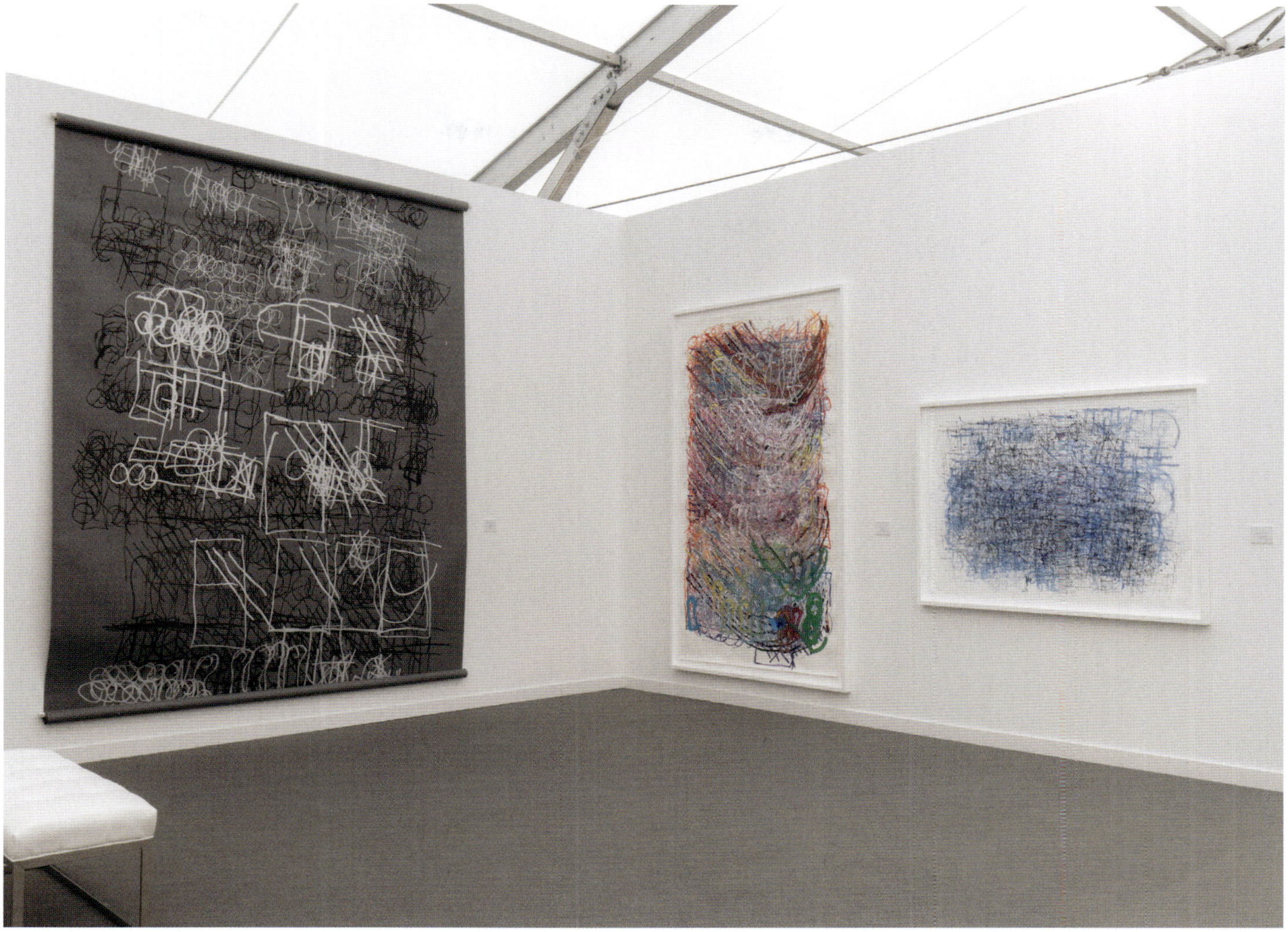

Installation view of work by Dan Miller, Frieze New York, 2019. Courtesy Andrew Edlin Gallery. Presented by New York's Andrew Edlin Gallery, this solo presentation of Creative Growth artist Dan Miller demonstrates the integrity of Miller's aesthetic to transcend the boundaries of self-taught or "Outsider."

of the conditions under which Miller's work was made, having selected it solely on its merits as contemporary drawing. Miller has become recognized as both an artist on the autism spectrum, and a notable contemporary artist.

The art and disability movement is becoming a recognized segment within the contemporary art world. It is driven both by the public's interest in self-taught art, and an increasing curatorial interest in the field. Continued advancement requires additional thinking about aesthetic and curatorial concerns, disability culture, and whether centers for art and disability might also serve to cocoon their artists or isolate them from the larger art world. Equally, as movements such as Black Lives Matter bring greater awareness to struggles for social equity and disability justice, urgent attention must be paid to issues of race, diversity, class, and intersectionality as we work to broaden artistic access and opportunities for people of color with disabilities.

Overall, the number of people with disabilities who are able to access creative expression remains exceedingly small. It is imperative to understand that creative growth is a fundamental human right. If we truly recognize and support creativity as a powerful tool for people with disabilities to find aesthetic, personal, and communicative growth, we all will share in the magnificent results of that vision.

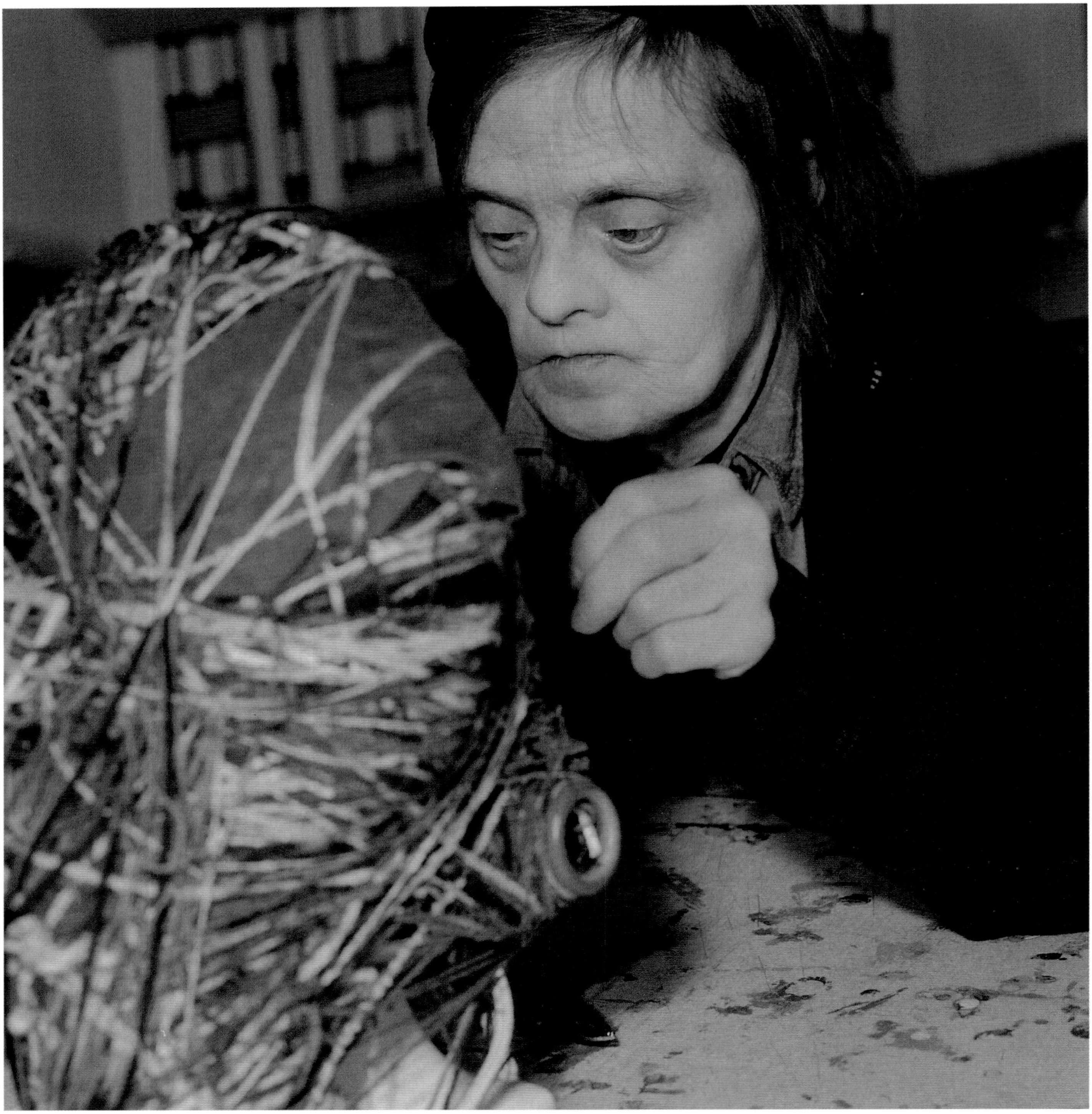

Judith Scott, 2003, photograph by Leon Borenzstein. Courtesy Creative Growth Art Center. Portrait of Judith Scott working in the studio of the Creative Growth Art Center.

JUDITH SCOTT

(1943, Cincinnati, Ohio–2005, Dutch Flat, California, USA)

The creative practice of Judith Scott commenced when she was 43 years old and began attending the supported studio Creative Growth Art Center in Oakland, California. Through her work in the studio for 18 years, Scott produced an oeuvre of three-dimensional forms revered by the international art world; recognizable for their implementation of wrapping and binding a conglomerate of objects. They are powerful but enigmatic. Scott was born deaf and with Down syndrome and, due to her circumstances in 1940s Ohio, she was institutionalized for over 30 years. She was not positioned to learn sign language and remained predominantly nonverbal her entire life. Her twin sister, Joyce, gained custody of Scott in adulthood and enrolled her at Creative Growth in 1987. Interest in Scott's sculptures developed from the 1990s with key achievements including *Metamorphosis,* her first monograph by art historian John MacGregor (1999), her retrospective *Judith Scott: Bound and Unbound*, Brooklyn Museum (2014), and her inclusion in *Viva Arte Viva*, 57th Venice Biennale (2017), curated by Christine Macel. Her sculptures are in the collections of MoMA, New York, and the Smithsonian American Art Museum, Washington, D.C.

The question between dichotomy and duality permeates existing examinations of the artist Judith Scott. The dichotomy lies within simultaneous calls for independent observations of Scott's personal biography and of her sculptures. There lies concern over the speculations that allow her personal narrative to inform the concept of her sculptural forms. Scott never articulated what her sculptures were about, so assumptions that her abstract textile forms are twins, babies, or other, warrants criticism. Authorities familiar with her practice, have set forth a curatorial establishment that Scott's sculptures should be read as formal art objects, however, a further concern arises: the urgency for institutions, curators, and viewers to abstain from a narrative-led presentation that predisposed Scott's biography to overshadow her practice. These apprehensions addressed by both art historians and curators urge keeping art and narrative completely separate. However, it is worth introducing the more permeable notion of duality, considering it is the human condition for our personal lived experiences to influence our work—be it creative or not. We are products of our environment and of our circumstances.

In respect to the concept of dichotomy, a concise account of Scott's biography establishes context to her arrival at Creative Growth Art Center: undoubtedly seminal to the initiation of her artistic practice. This reading proposes that it can be productive to acknowledge circumstances that prove tenacity in an artist. It also explores the proposition that examining Scott's creative process and production may serve as a respectful middle ground for a conceptual consideration of her practice.

Scott was born a fraternal twin with her sister Joyce in Cincinnati, Ohio in 1943. She was born with Down syndrome and profoundly deaf. Her deafness was not recognized until she was in her 30s and this lack of acknowledgment or diagnosis presented a problematic context for understanding Scott's abilities, rendering her below Ohio's threshold for special education for children with disabilities. She was very close with her sister Joyce and remained living with her family until the age of seven.[1] Without the communicative skills of signing or speaking (she never learned sign language and remained predominantly nonverbal for her entire life), on October 18, 1950, Scott was institutionalized and remained between two Ohio facilities until 1986.[2] Records are scarce of Scott's time in institutions, with a complete void of medical records between 1955 and 1976. It can be ascertained that she was not encouraged or fostered during this period. Records indicate disturbing incidents, including the extraction of all of her teeth and a general assessment that Scott was disobedient and disturbed. There is at least a single account of Scott expressing interest in drawing and being prohibited from doing so. A record from August 1984 also referred to Scott habitually tearing up pieces of clothing, an act which may have been a precursor to her later creative practice.[3]

In 1974, the Creative Growth Art Center was founded in California by psychologist Elias Katz and his wife, artist, educator Florence Ludins-Katz. As founders of one of the earliest supported studios in America, the Katzes' mission was to establish an open and nurturing environment to foster creative development. They stated: "The strength of people with disabilities can be brought out only if there are opportunities. Art Centers help these persons fulfill themselves and become contributors to society."[4] Principal to Creative Growth's establishment in Oakland (and Scott's later opportunities when a resident of the state) was California's 1969 passing of the Lanterman Developmental Disabilities Services Act, which grants individuals with developmental disabilities and their families rights to get the services and support required to live akin to people without disabilities.[5] This act provides funding for innovative and meaningful day programs and encompasses supported studios, like Creative Growth. In turn, California ensured rights that were not granted in Ohio for individuals with disabilities. Following the dedication of her sister to locate, emancipate, and engage with Scott's life, on November 16, 1986 Scott was released from the Ohio institution and boarded a plane to California, where Joyce had obtained legal custody.

On April 1, 1987, at 43 years old, the story of Scott's artistic practice began. In the absence of a direct artist statement, exploring Scott's creative process as a concept is considered. This look at production offers an alternative to the overreliance on biography in relation to her artistic output. For the first six months at Creative Growth, Scott was modest on production, with the development of an initial series of drawings. Her early compositions showed repetitive looping and mark-making. The active gestures seem to precede her later sculptural fiber techniques. There exists a visual rhythm in the drawings that reflects the physical process of her three-dimensional works. Curator Matthew Higgs also notes that these early drawings demonstrate Scott's inclination as a "natural colorist."[6]

Toward the end of 1987, Scott took an interest in textiles during a workshop at Creative Growth led by fiber artist Sylvia Seventy. This introduced Scott to a range of materials to explore and manipulate. In 1988, through workshops and engagement with Seventy, Scott made what is considered her first sculptural form. She combined, rather totteringly, wooden sticks bundled by twine that were further wrapped with various layers of textiles. Several seemingly indiscriminate, but carefully selected plastic components are further bound within the structure. Applied roughly, a final coat of blue paint acted as an outer layer. Scott also applied many push pins with multicolor round tops, giving the overall configuration a multi-textural quality. Noticeable in this work is that fact that particular aspects of experimentation are not later returned to (this is the only instance where Scott painted a sculpture), while other principle techniques suggest a starting point for her archetypal aesthetic. Her physical process of executing multiple layers of textiles to mitigate the severity of objects that serve as the sculpture's internal frame is resonant in this first work, as well as a penchant for stochastic objects assigned as concealed, obscured, and disclosed.

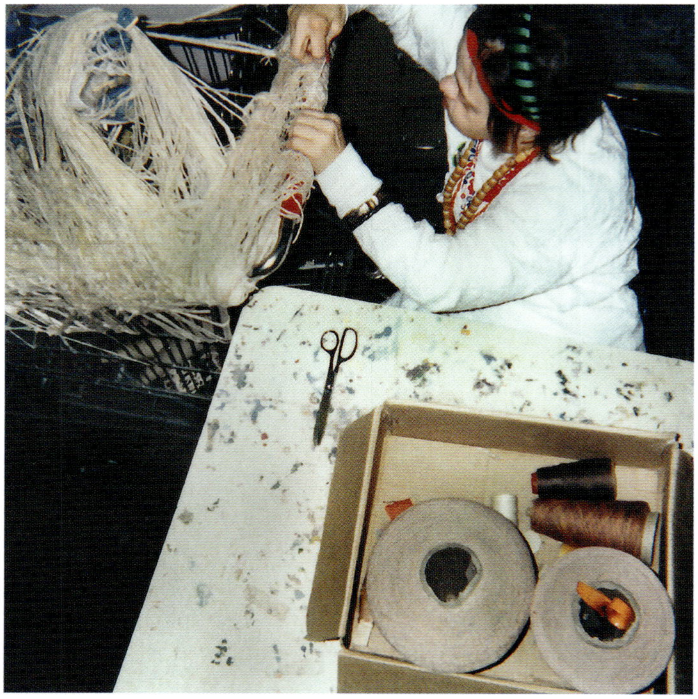

Judith Scott, 1999, photograph. Courtesy Creative Growth Art Center. Scott working on a sculpture that uses a shopping cart as its internal structure.

Scott continued her practice with a series of sculptures that developed chromatically and were more considered in construction. It seems, through her process, she was developing her own creative mandate and perimeters. These early forms are more loose and modest in scale. In 1989, following the close of her Arts Council grant, Seventy left the studio. That same year Seventy organized the exhibition *Crossed Parallels* at Creative Growth, which exhibited the work of Scott for the first time.

Around 1990, Scott's sculptures became more dynamic in shape. This development in configuration may have been, in part, as a result of another visiting artist at Creative Growth. Richard Elliot introduced (to all the studio artists) dimensionality and a variety of pliable materials within the discipline of textile or fiber art. Scott's sculptural practice became more exuberant and complex. The scale of her oeuvre continued to increase with a defining characteristic of her late sculptures as too large for her to carry herself. In addition to size, Scott's practice into the 1990s became more self-directed. The initial reception of her work was moderate, but by the late 1990s, her sculptures were of interest to international galleries and institutions. This decade closed with the publication of *Metamorphosis,* a key monograph on Scott written by art historian John MacGregor. By 2002 she had multiple solo exhibitions in America, Europe, and Asia.

Integral and consistent to her process was Scott's gathering of objects and ephemera that constituted the sculptures. She scavenged at Creative Growth Art Center, accumulating objects (these accounts are often playfully referred to as stealing). Domestic and industrial donations also provided materials. Larger objects (an umbrella frame, electric fan, skateboard, tree branch, even a shopping cart) served as the framework for her sculptures, while more modest objects (bottles, shoes, zippers) are submerged among the layers of yarn, string, and fabric that are wrapped, tied, and knotted in layers. The recognizability of these articles varies, some concealed completely as a skeleton or internal texture; others obscured, protruding through the fabric; others serving as external visual adornment. These various levels of recognition are all effects of Scott's various wrapping and binding methods. Through a conceptual contemplation of production, we see two physical processes in action: obscuring or concealing objects within a larger form and mitigating the properties of more substantial (hard) objects into a comfortable tactile and visual experience.

From 1987 until her death in 2005, Scott was resolutely dedicated to her practice at Creative Growth. She was assertive and confident when she completed a sculpture. When it was modest in scale, she would remove

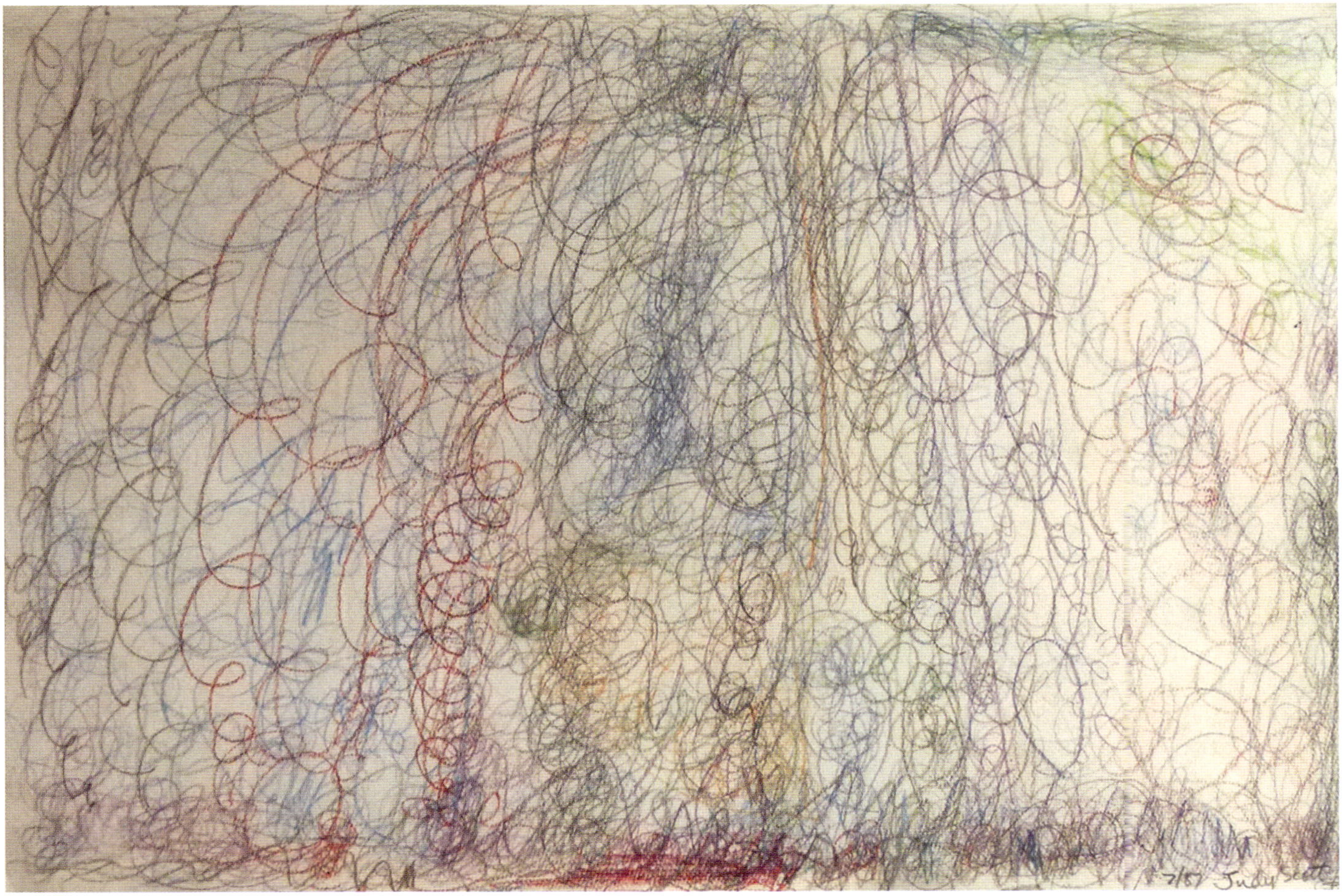

Judith Scott, untitled, *1987, mixed media on paper, 11½ × 17½ in (29.2 × 44.5 cm). Courtesy Creative Growth Art Center.* A precursor to her three-dimensional textile work, Scott's earliest artistic experiments at Creative Growth were drawings. In this abstract composition, her looping lines and colors are reminiscent of her later sculptural practice.

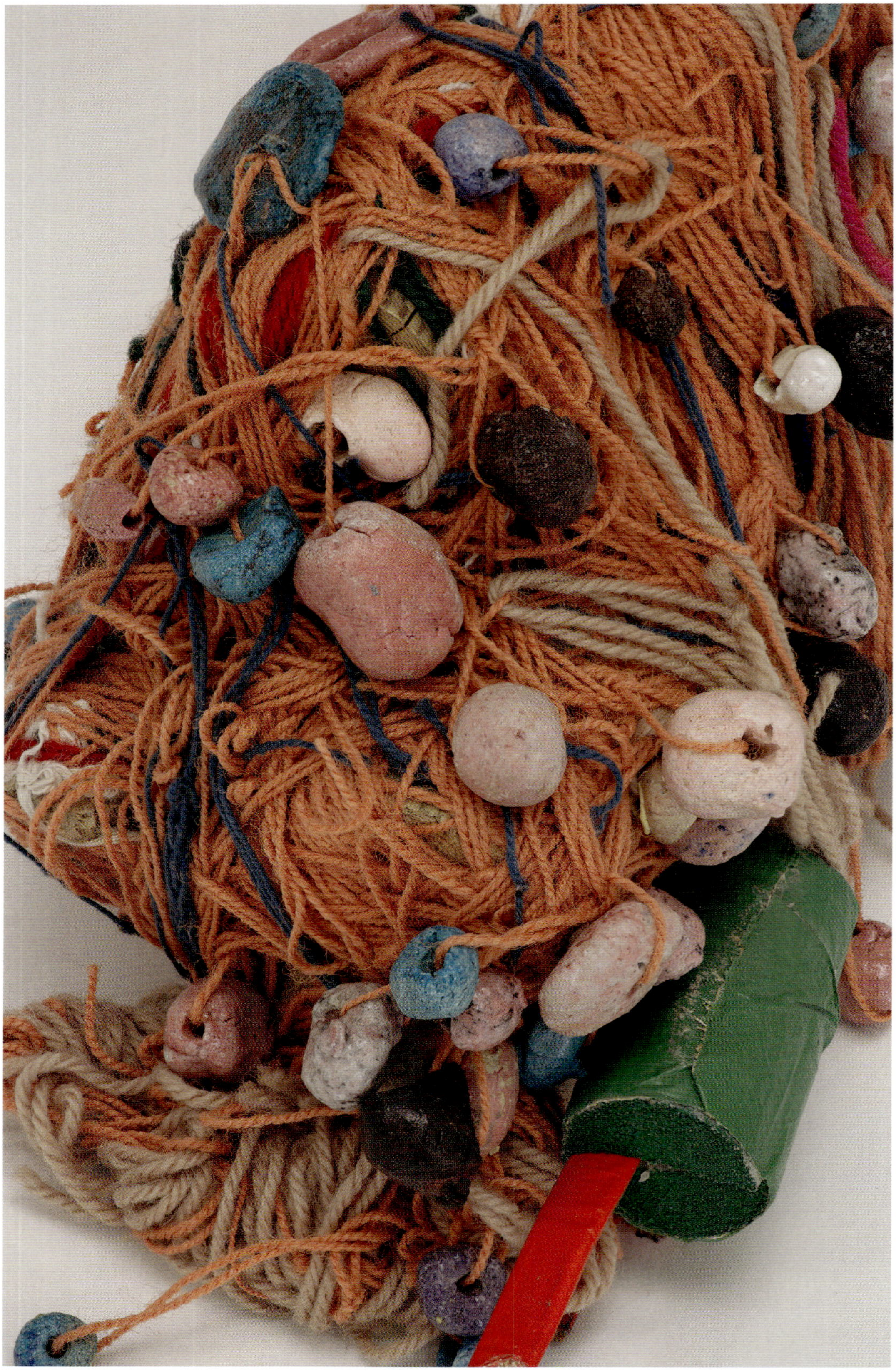

Judith Scott, untitled *(detail), 1993, fiber and found objects, 44 × 10 × 10 in (111.8 × 25.4 × 25.4 cm). Courtesy Creative Growth Art Center.* Detail of a Scott sculpture from 1993, showing her complex use of materials, and incorporation of found objects. This detail shows her specific threading of stone-like beads into the sculpture—like jewelry.

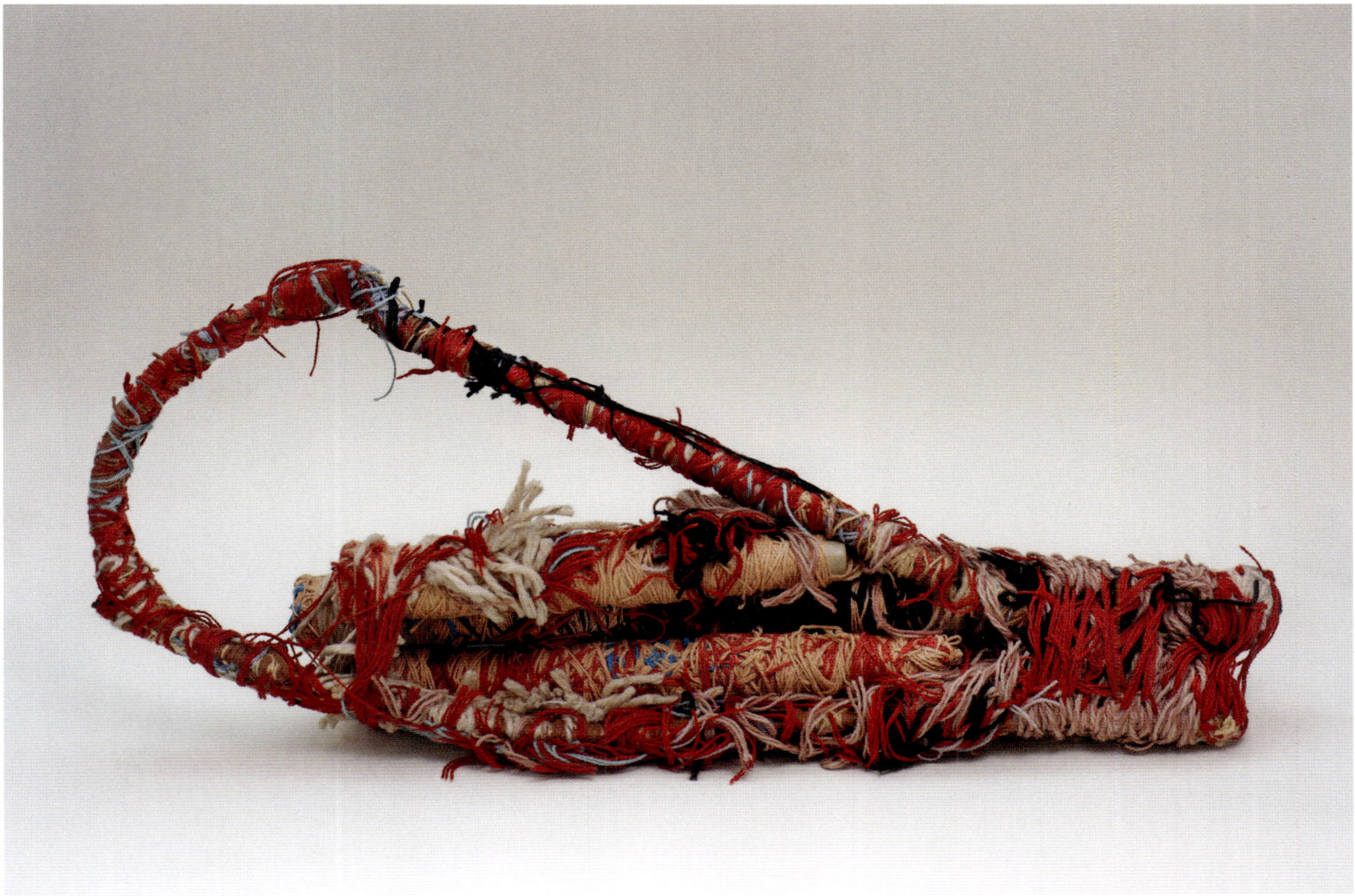

Judith Scott, untitled, *1992, fiber and found objects, 38 × 15 × 5 in (96.5 × 38 × 12.7 cm). Courtesy Creative Growth Art Center.* With the introduction of flexible and more expansive textile materials, this dynamic shape, which frames a void completely encompassed by the sculpture, shows the development of Scott's practice in the early 1990s.

the sculpture when finished, with an immediate interest in commencing the next. When she completed substantially larger works in her later practice, she developed a signature hand motion signifying to the Creative Growth staff when she was done. It appeared her interest was in making, not presenting. Questions exist surrounding whether Scott understood her activity of producing these three-dimensional forms as "art," against which it is important to pose the context of her making: an art studio where she was consistently surrounded in a creative environment and fellow artists developing their respective practices. Over the 18 years in the studio, completing approximately 160 sculptures, Scott worked at the same table, with astute dedication, for up to 6 hours a day. She appeared enthralled and enthusiastic about her routine. Implementing a range of autodidactic techniques—wrapping, binding, knotting, and sewing—Scott took from two weeks up to six months to make a sculpture. In the physical process, we see themes of repetition, concealment, mitigation, and security. In her practice, she established an intimate visual vocabulary through her creative mode of production. There can be no affirmation that Scott's idiosyncratic oeuvre was autobiographical or metaphorical, but its force is undeniably energetic, rhythmic, and alluring.

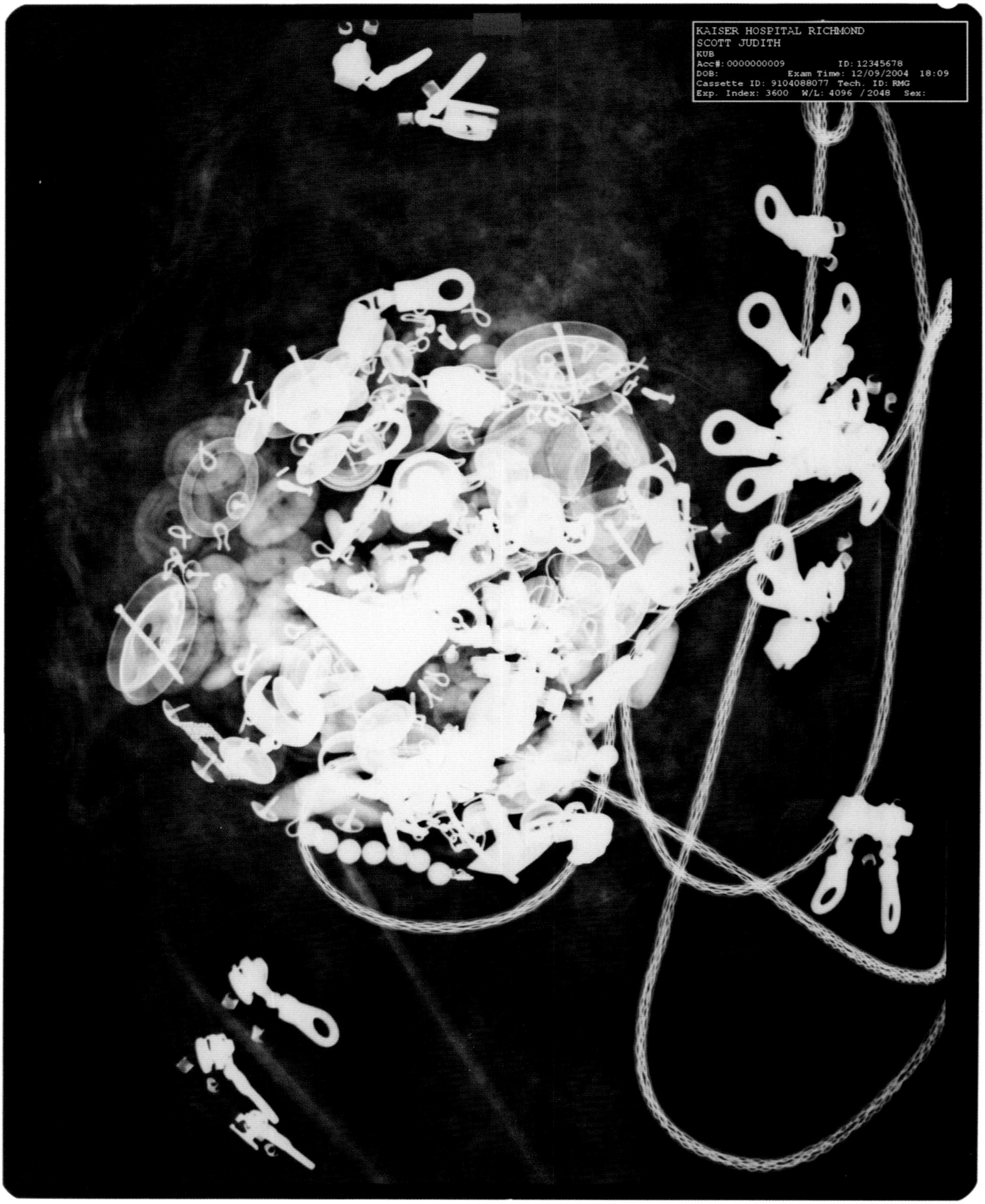

Judith Scott, 2004, X-ray result. Courtesy Creative Growth Art Center. Scott was known for gathering objects—donated, available, and covertly taken—at the studio and working them into the layers of her sculptures. This X-ray of one of her sculptures shows zippers, cords, jewelry, nails, and tacks all existing within, and all otherwise concealed by, the wrapping process.

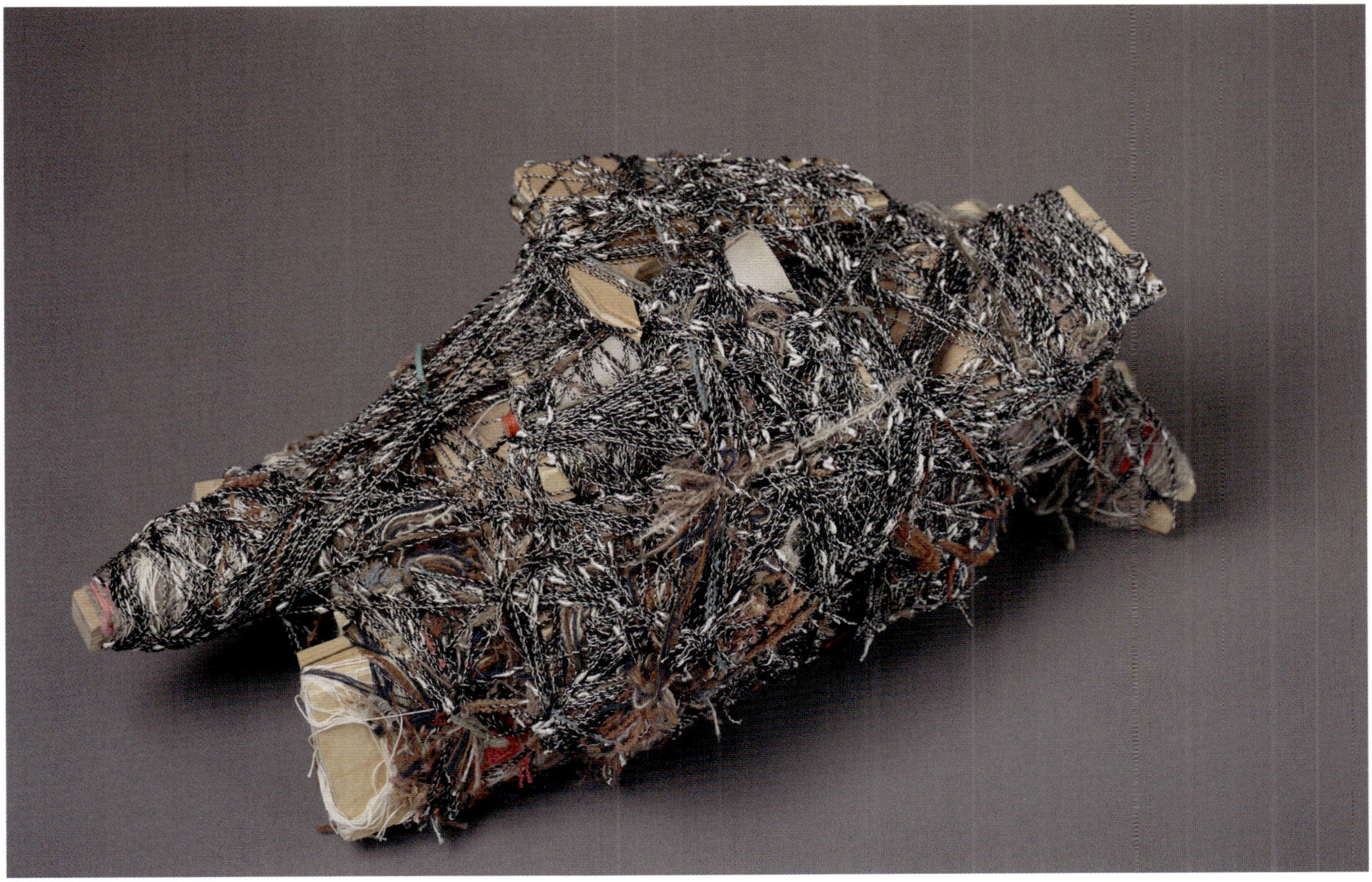

Judith Scott, untitled, *2005, mixed material, 11 × 25$\frac{3}{16}$ × 12$\frac{5}{8}$ in (28 × 64 × 32 cm). Collection de L'Art Brut, Lausanne.* This was the last work made by Scott prior to her death. With a distinguishably dark palette when compared to the totality of her oeuvre, one ponders if Scott was aware of her morality.

JULIAN MARTIN

(b. 1969, Melbourne, Australia)

The pastel drawings of Julian Martin transform everyday objects, places, and people into liminal compositions. Martin, who is autistic and nonverbal, started drawing at ten years old and since 1988 has been attending Arts Project Australia, a studio founded in 1974 that supports artists with intellectual disabilities. During his 30 years at the studio, Martin has developed a practice of densely covered pastel drawings that oscillate between abstraction and representation. Formally, his oeuvre enters an intriguing dialogue with a history of abstraction, contributing to his international emergence in contemporary art. Martin began exhibiting in Australia in 1990 and internationally in 1995. He received a significant retrospective titled *Transformer* with Arts Project Australia in 2014, featuring over 60 pastel drawings. Martin exhibits regularly in the United States through his representation by Fleisher/Ollman Gallery in Philadelphia. His drawings were included in the exhibition *Nicholas Party: Pastel*, The FLAG Art Foundation, New York (2019), and are part of the National Gallery of Victoria Collection.

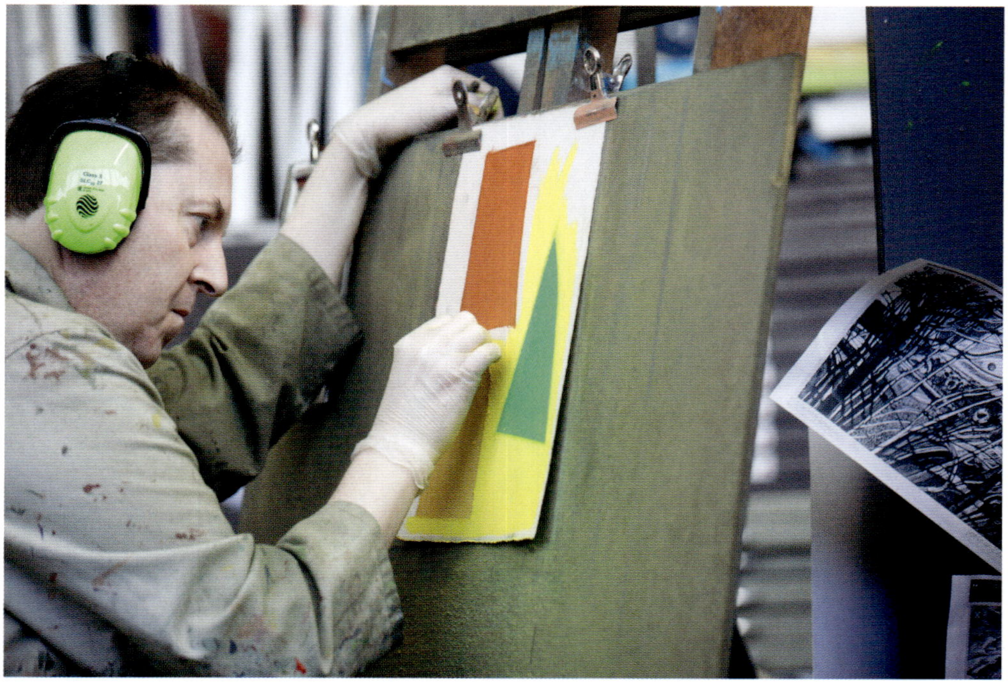

Julian Martin, 2017, photograph. Courtesy Arts Project Australia. Martin, who prefers a quiet and focused environment, often wears noise-reducing headphones while drawing.

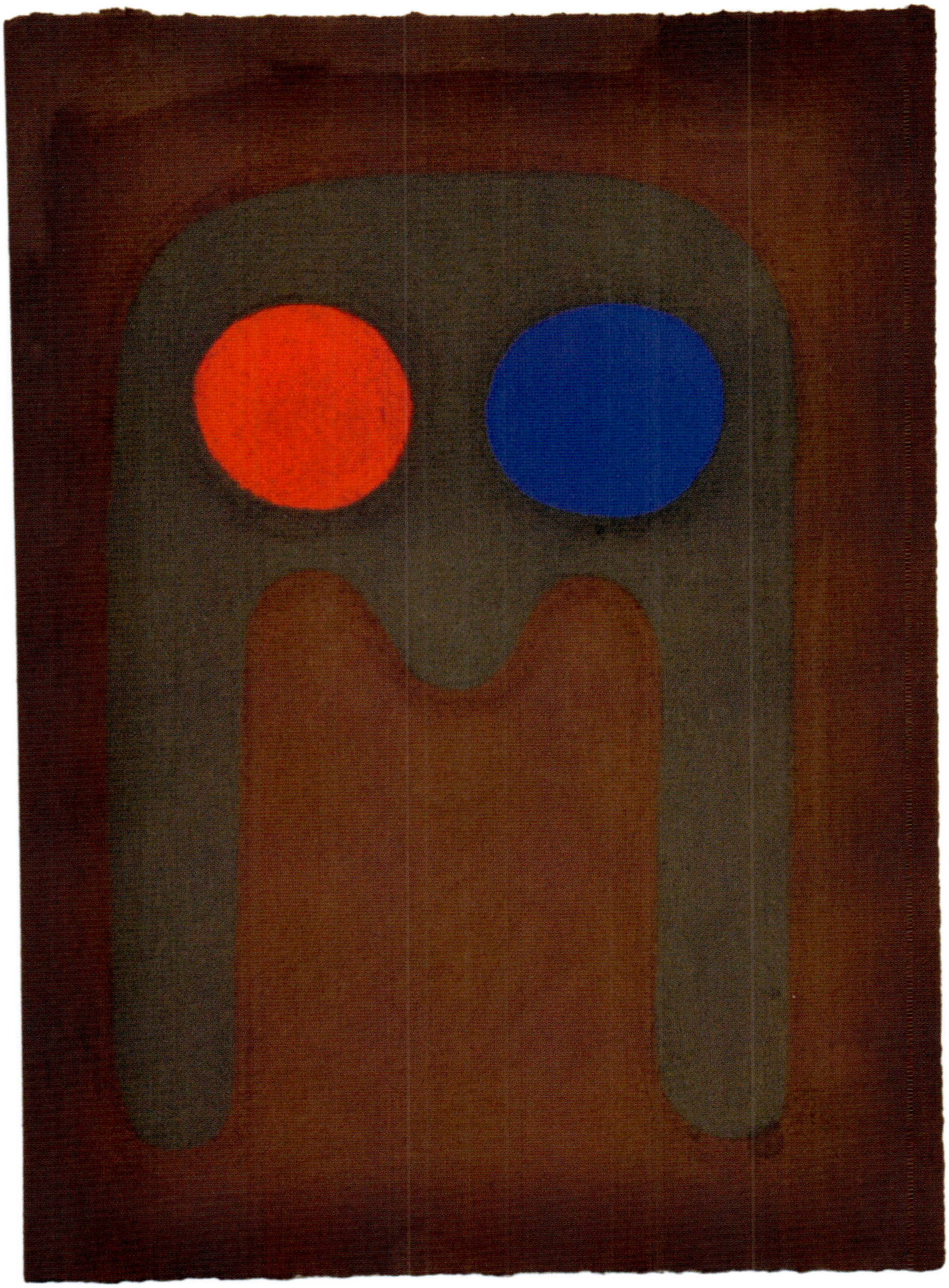

Julian Martin, untitled, *2012, pastel on paper, 15 × 11 in (38 × 28 cm). Courtesy Arts Project Australia.* This haunting composition by Martin borders between object abstraction and figuration. While the blue and red circles could refer to an array of features in inanimate objects, their particular placement sets up the potential of a facial reading.

Julian Martin likes rhythm and routine in his creative practice. His earliest works from Arts Project Australia were figurative, predominantly in profile, and drafted with monochromatic acrylic paint (see page 14). Around 1992, Martin's drawings began to shift toward a prevailing idiosyncratic aesthetic of abstracted compositions. He also adapted to using pastels (now ubiquitous to his oeuvre) and the initial conceptual reduction of his figures. Contributing to his evolution of figurative forms in the mid-1990s was Martin's use of a hand-held mirror to execute a series of self-portraits. A frontal reflection informed the development of his "mask" portraits. In these masked depictions, facial features are reduced to composition-specific elements, resonating a geometrical phantasmic feel.

Whether via his mirrored reflection, photographs, magazines, or directly examining real-life objects, Martin

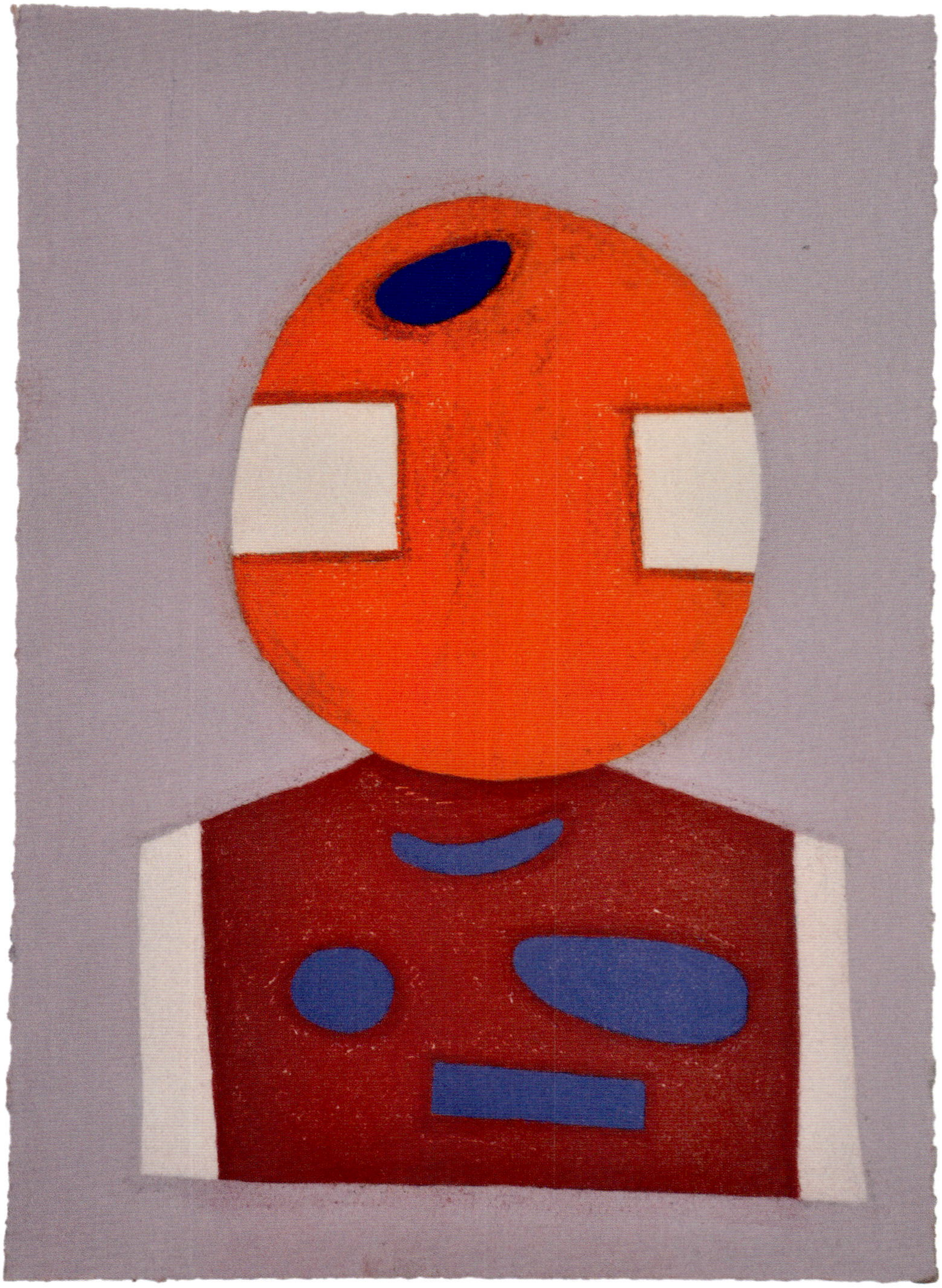

Julian Martin, untitled*, 2013, pastel on paper, 15 × 11 in (38 × 28 cm). Courtesy Arts Project Australia.* With formal elements indicative of a traditional portrait, where a figure is formally posed from the waist or chest, other compositional choices by Martin here leave the viewer joyfully puzzled on the representation.

works from existing visual sources. Within his observational compositions of objects, a simple tool or kitchen utensil keeps its semiotic integrity while also transcending into an enigmatic hieroglyph. His formal decisions ricochet between representative and committedly abstract.

There is an unspoken and undefined, but inviting and intriguing language in the drawings of Martin. Through his reductive aesthetic, the poignancy of line and bold color inform Martin's pictorial vernacular. The tones and hues of pastels are applied with severe intent. The chalky material blankets the paper with pastel, where it takes on more properties of pure pigment than that of paper. In certain circumstances, Martin will also use the point of a compass to deboss specific forms by pressured outline. Drills, forks, presidents, or himself, Martin takes the familiar and through abstraction, transforms their existence.

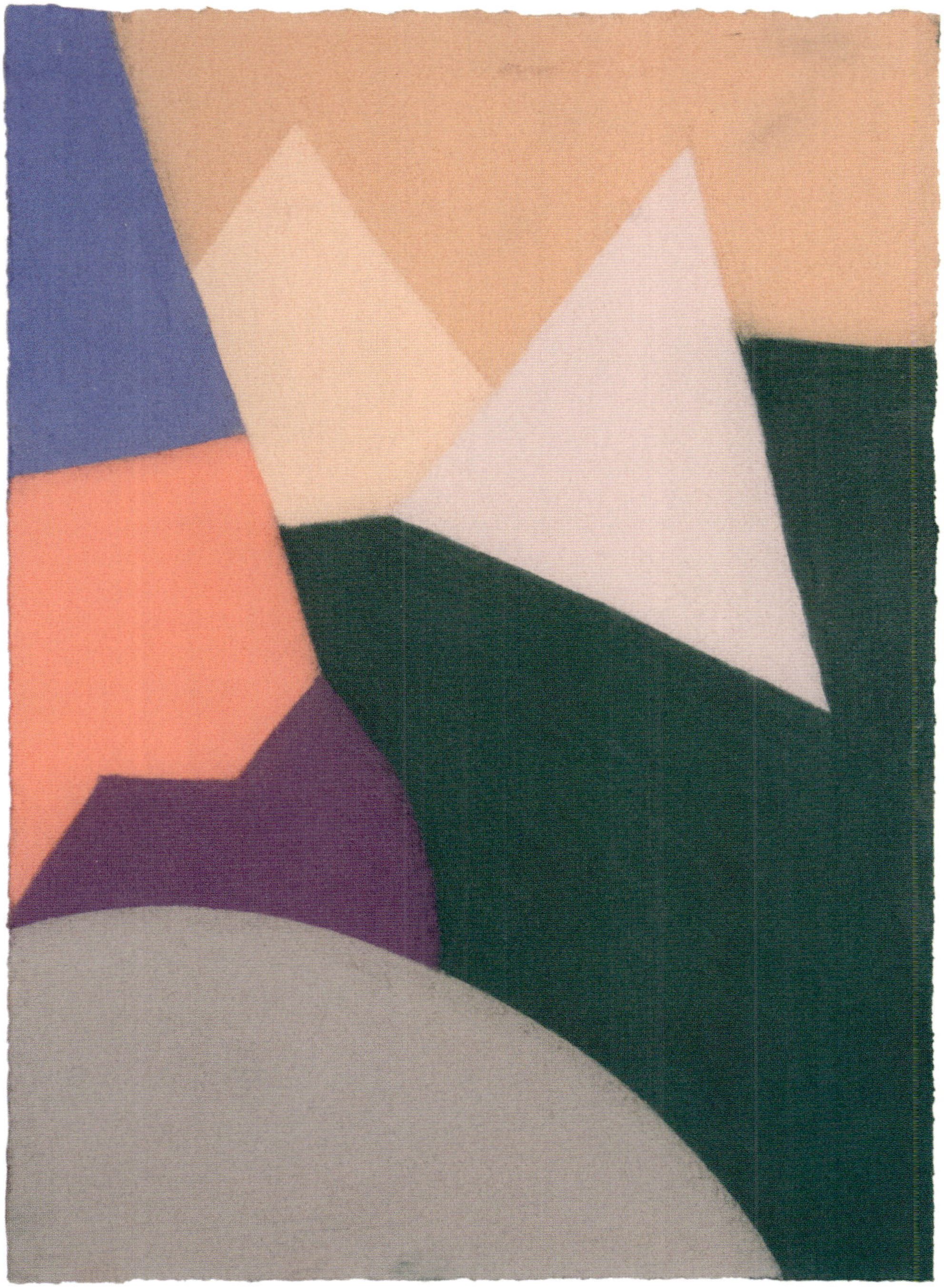

Julian Martin, untitled, *2016, pastel on paper, 15 × 11 in (38 × 28 cm). Courtesy Arts Project Australia.* This enigmatic set of geometric shapes scenically suggests a landscape. Here, Martin's thoughtful skill in implementing simple shapes to infer complex visual scenes is excellently demonstrated.

"Unlike Reinhardt and other artists of his generation, Martin has chosen to embrace a much more open-ended form of abstraction, exploring 'pure' abstraction in one drawing, representing letterforms or objects in others, and then falling back again on familiar sentient subjects like human figures or animals—all decidedly and idiosyncratically abstract, but not abstraction for its own sake." – Alex Baker, director, Fleisher/Ollman Gallery, Philadelphia[7]

ANDREW OMODING

(b. 1987, Eastern Region, Uganda)

Concepts of home, family, and Africa seem pivotal to the oeuvre of Andrew Omoding. Visually exploring soft and hard, monumental and intimate, even loud and quiet, his exuberant creative installations are abundant with colorful textiles and assemblages of repurposed materials. During his early childhood in Uganda, in what was considered a tumultuous time for the country, his grandmother imparted traditions that later appear as influential themes to his art-making. In 1999, Omoding and his sister relocated to the United Kingdom to join their mother, who had emigrated years prior to secure opportunities for her family. Living in London a decade later, he was accepted to ActionSpace. Launched in the 1960s and established as an independent charity in 1984, ActionSpace creates innovative opportunities for people with learning disabilities to engage with visual arts. An exceptional multidisciplinary art practice—sewing, sculpting, sound, and performance—emerged from Omoding, with observable reference to both his African heritage and his London relationships. In 2019, Omoding became the first neurodiverse artist to be awarded an artist-in-residence with Camden Art Centre, London. He was further awarded a residency with the Barbican Arts Group Trust, London (2021) and is the subject of a solo exhibition at The Woodend Gallery, Scarborough (2022).

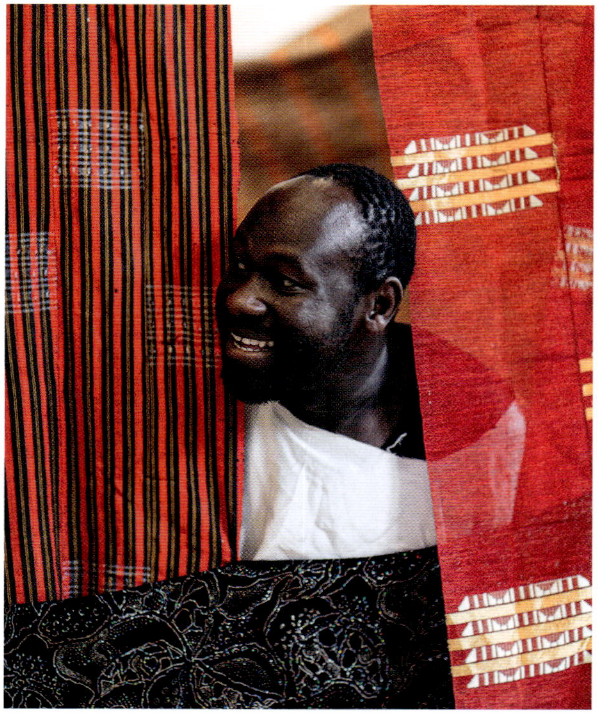

Andrew Omoding, 2019, photograph. Courtesy the artist and ActionSpace. A photograph taken during Omoding's summer residency at the Camden Art Centre, London, UK.

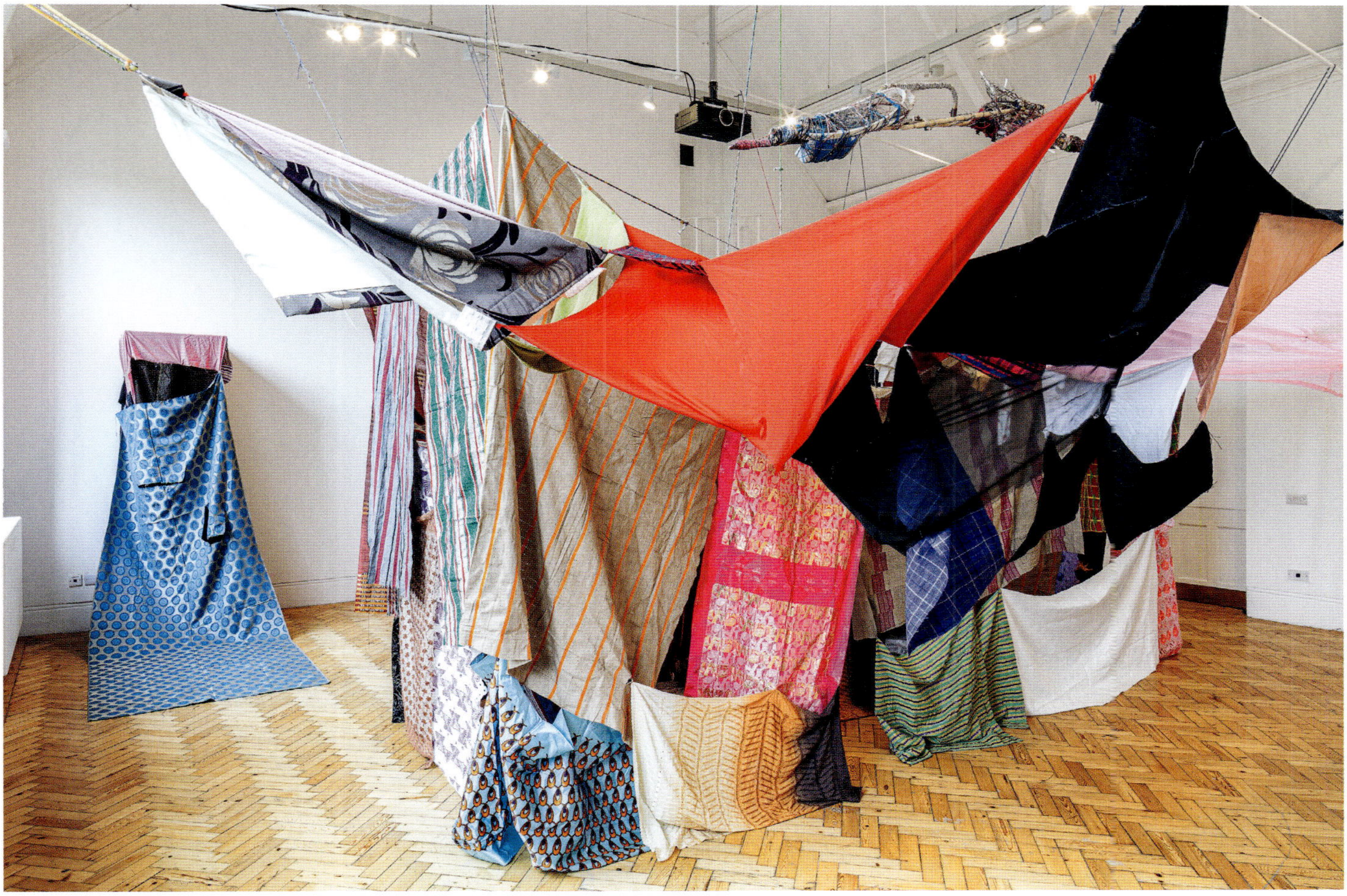

Andrew Omoding, It's my work, come see, come see *(installation view), 2019, Camden Art Centre, London. Courtesy the artist and ActionSpace.* Omoding's dwelling-like formation is central for his installation at the Camden Art Centre. His penchant for bright and colored fabrics is evident in its construction. With visitor participation important to him, the audience can enter the dwelling, walk around, and even enter inside the "sound pod" (left) to further engage with the work.

The 1990s brought tremendous violence, economic strife, and upheaval to Uganda succeeding Idi Amin's rule, followed by the civil Ugandan Bush War when Milton Obote regained power. Though the country was under traumatic circumstances, Andrew Omoding was surrounded by family, with his grandmother often telling stories that raised spirits while imparting an oral history. This African tradition of storytelling feels paramount to the development of Omoding's joyful practice of blending narratives into dimensional making. It was also his aunt and grandmother who taught him to sew. Sewing and adorning textiles is a significant component to his process, often combined with or informed by his narratives.

In the studio at ActionSpace, Omoding's often improvisational narratives are initially transcribed by an artist facilitator, then as a drawing exercise, Omoding will copy the story verbatim onto a textile. At other times the narrative is formalized post-creation to give context to a completed installation. His sculptural process transforms discarded and donated materials into vibrant compositions echoing his own jubilant character. These colorful, thoughtful, and inquisitive installations become celebratory and considered explorations of cultural identity and, possibly, what it means to be home.

In July 2019, Omoding completed his most ambitious work to date, a culmination from a summer residency with London's Camden Art Centre. This large-scale and multimedia narrative-led installation included a central domestic tent structure, sound electronically composed by Omoding, wall-based narrative textiles, and an abundance of sculptural objects throughout the space. *It's my work, come see, come see* also exemplified how his work operates on a macro and micro level. From afar it reads as a large domestic dwelling, even bordering on environmental, yet with the adornment and details worked in, the viewer can also experience moments of intimate interplay. An interactive performative evening was led by Omoding to conclude his residency—a procession of his peers and friends dressed in artist-made costumes, led through the building and grounds of the centre accompanied by a call-and-response chorus initiated by Omoding.

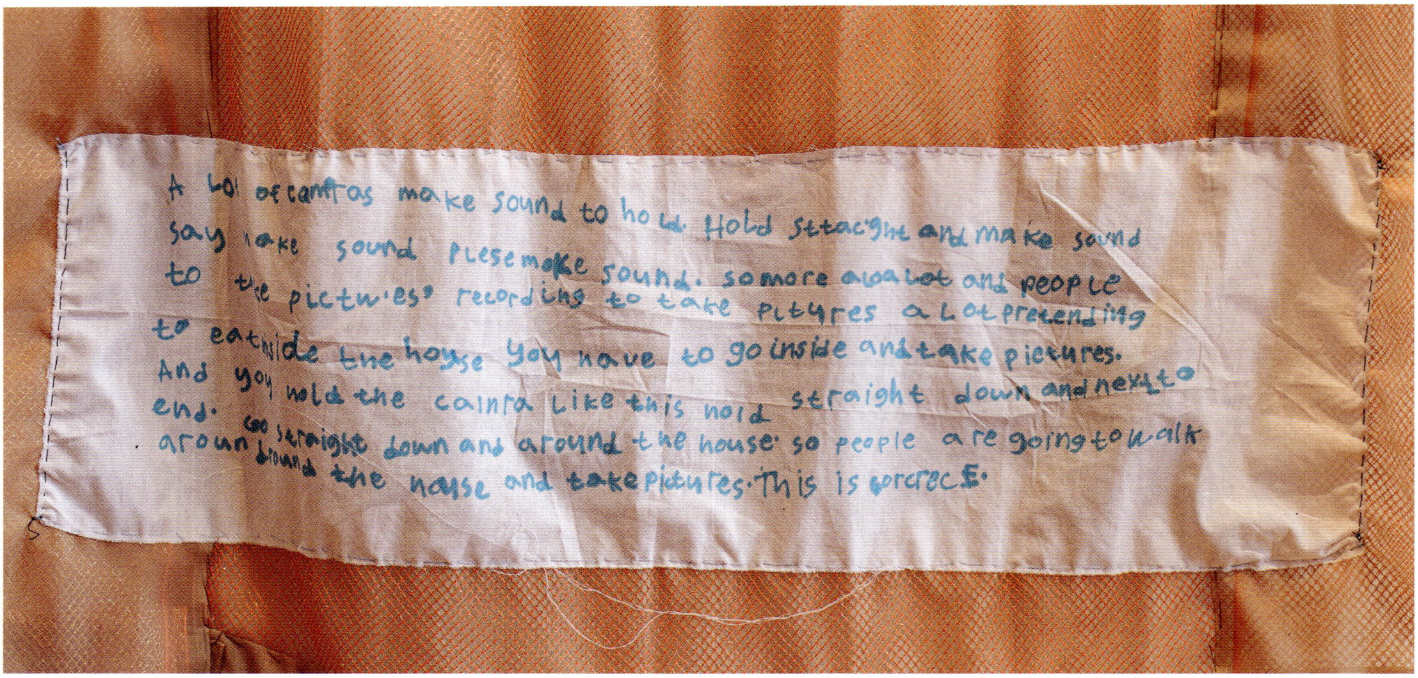

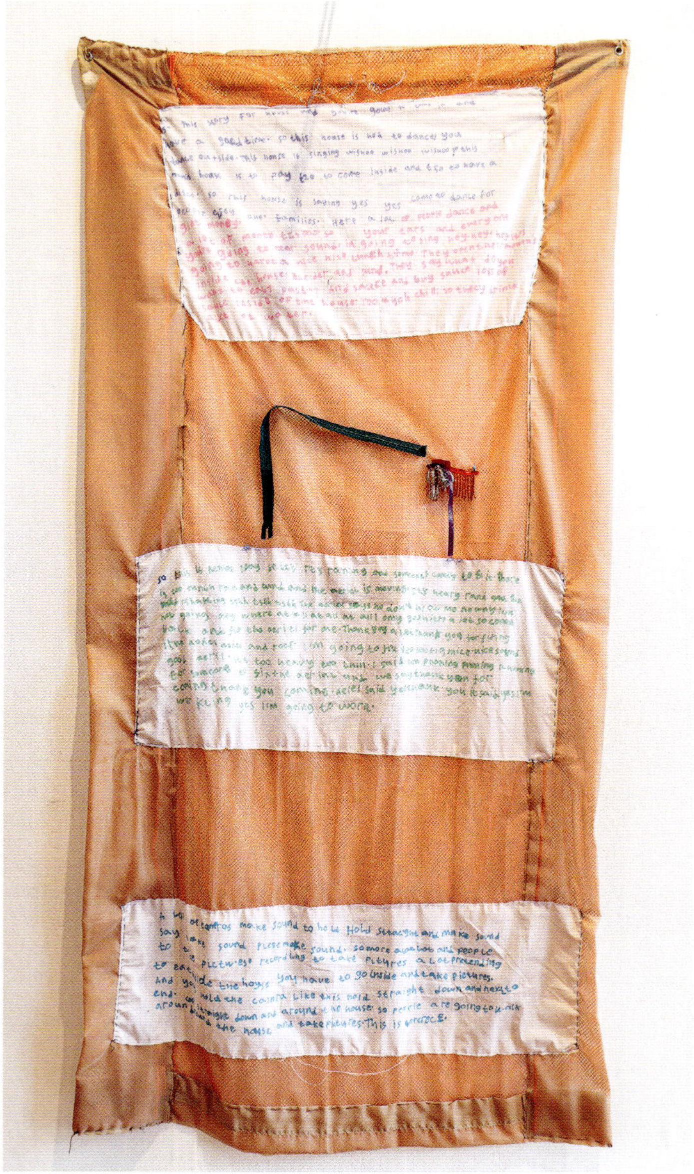

Andrew Omoding, It's my work, come see, come see *(installation detail) 2019, Camden Art Centre, London. Courtesy the artist and ActionSpace.* A segment from Omoding's narrative, this informs the audience on interacting with the installation with text including "please make sound," "eat inside the house You have to go inside and take pictures," and "Go straight down and around the house."

Andrew Omoding, It's my work, come see, come see *(installation detail) 2019, Camden Art Centre, London, embroidery and textiles. Courtesy the artist and ActionSpace.* Influenced by the tradition of storytelling from growing up in Uganda, Omoding's practice often presents direct, but improvisational, narratives to accompany his installations. Exhibited as part of *It's my work, come see, come see*, this provides further context directly from the artist.

"I'm doing sewing. I'm going to put beads on and stones very very heavy you can feel. You can hold it and feel. How do you feel? You ask me questions. How many hours sewing. It took a long time to finish it. It took a long long time. More than one, two hours." – Andrew Omoding[8]

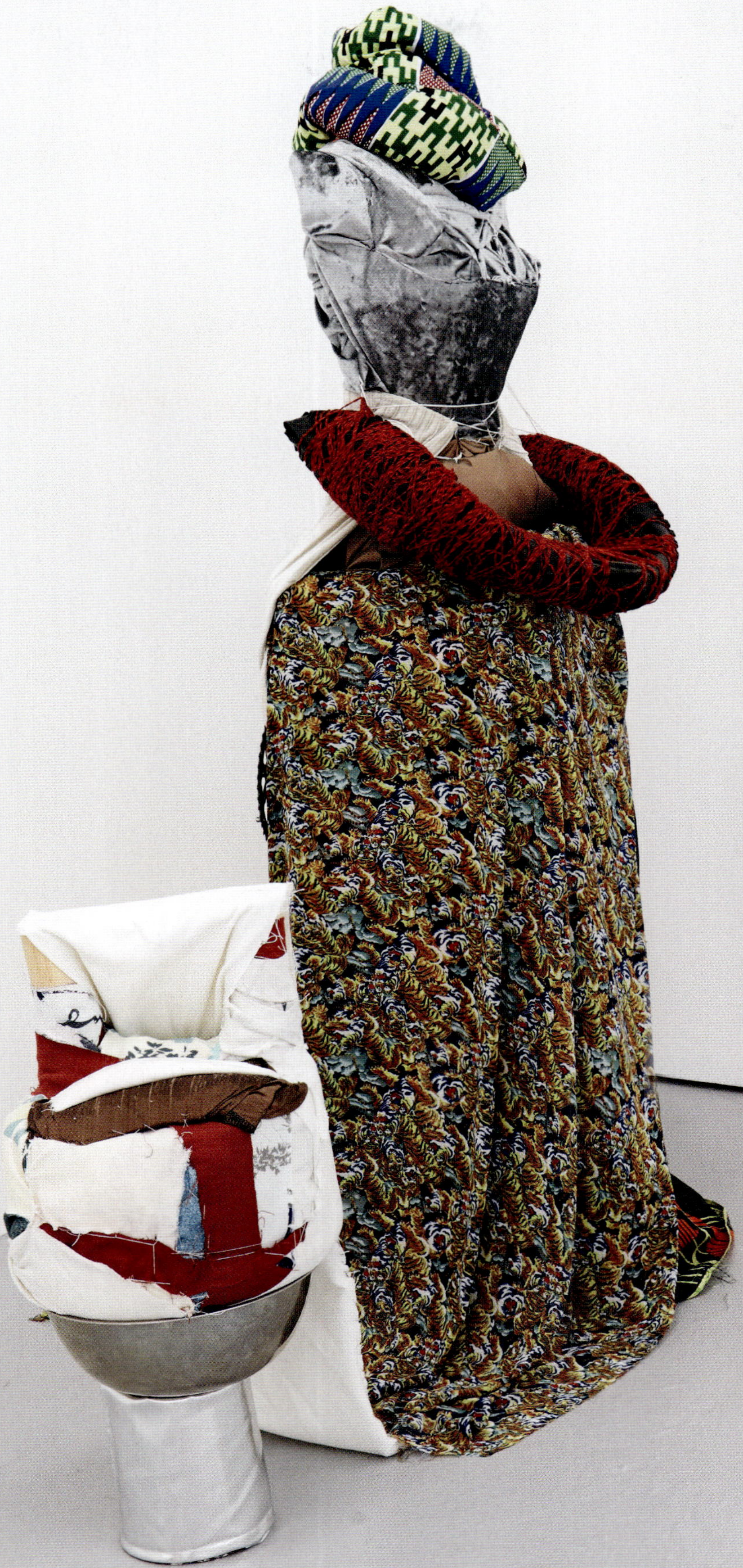

Andrew Omoding, Africa phoning me. It's my sweetheart wanting to see me*, 2018, fabric and found materials. Courtesy the artist and ActionSpace.* This installation detail from *Spring Syllabus*, J Hammond Projects, London (2018) shows a figurative form constructed by Omoding, exemplifying his skill at combining materials and textiles.

Omoding's narrative for this installation:
This is Mum and Dad. I am making pillows and is going to sleep on. They are going to relax and say something. They are planning, want to go holiday to Jamaica, to India. Want to go to shop to buy new clothes. Went out to have lunch together and "hello, come in!" Happy and make me happy. "Please talk to me please"
They say, "Yes please"
They came out on a bus. Get off and get aeroplane. Airport Heathrow and they get on another aeroplane very far. They meet their families, big, big families.
Families said, "Welcome back. Good to see you"
"Thank you for coming, please come again"
"Did you enjoy your holiday?"
I said "Yes"
They sent dinner, what you want to eat, want hot chocolate and big, big meat, beef and a like a big dinner please. And wine, maybe wine?
You don't want wine!
I say, "No, I don't want wine. I'm a Christian, don't drink wine"
And do relaxing.
"No, don't drink wine please and no thank you. I don't like drinking in case I get sick, not good to drink and fall down, up down, and hospital. Be safe. Thank you a lot"
What's the time? I go to the airport at 6 o'clock. I have to very early morning. I have to leave 8 o'clock. What's the time? I have to go. I have to leave house. Lock door need to be checked. Thank you lock door, in case someone go to somebody's house to take something. Check it's safe. Don't
talk to strangers, ask them where you going.
"Excuse me, where's the station please?"
All people ask me "Excuse me, wheres the station please? Where's the bus stop?"
Bus 29, 134 and C2. Camden Town.
I help them, I did help them and it was station Euston. It's a big station and they go inside straight on.
Said, "I did good job, thank you showed me"
"You are very kind and where's chicken shop?"
I'm from Uganda and he's from Kenya, all families come together.
Did you born here or Kenya?
Africa phoning me. It's my sweetheart wanting to see me."

JULIA KRAUSE-HARDER

(b. 1973, Kronberg im Taunus, Germany)

Julia Krause-Harder's artistic mission is to sculpturally reproduce the approximately 800 dinosaur species scientifically discovered to date. She collects varied but specific everyday materials for an anatomically precise approach to fully realizing her interest in skeletal forms. An artist with autism, Krause-Harder has been part of Atelier Goldstein since 2009. This Frankfurt studio supports artists with disabilities and was founded in 2001 by Christiane Cuticchio. Krause-Harder's research relating to a keen interest in paleontology, specifically anatomy and geographical history, began in 2005 as a precursor to establishing her visual language as a sculptor. From cassette tapes to chocolate bar wrappers, she uses repetitive materials to build skeletal forms that conceptually balance scientific inquiry and liminal playfulness. Krause-Harder regularly lectures about her studio practice and tutors art students through Atelier Goldstein's education initiative. She has exhibited internationally including *The Museum of Everything #7*, Museum of Old and New Art, Hobart (2017), Musée Visionnaire in Zurich (2019), and Kunstforum Wien, Austria (2019).

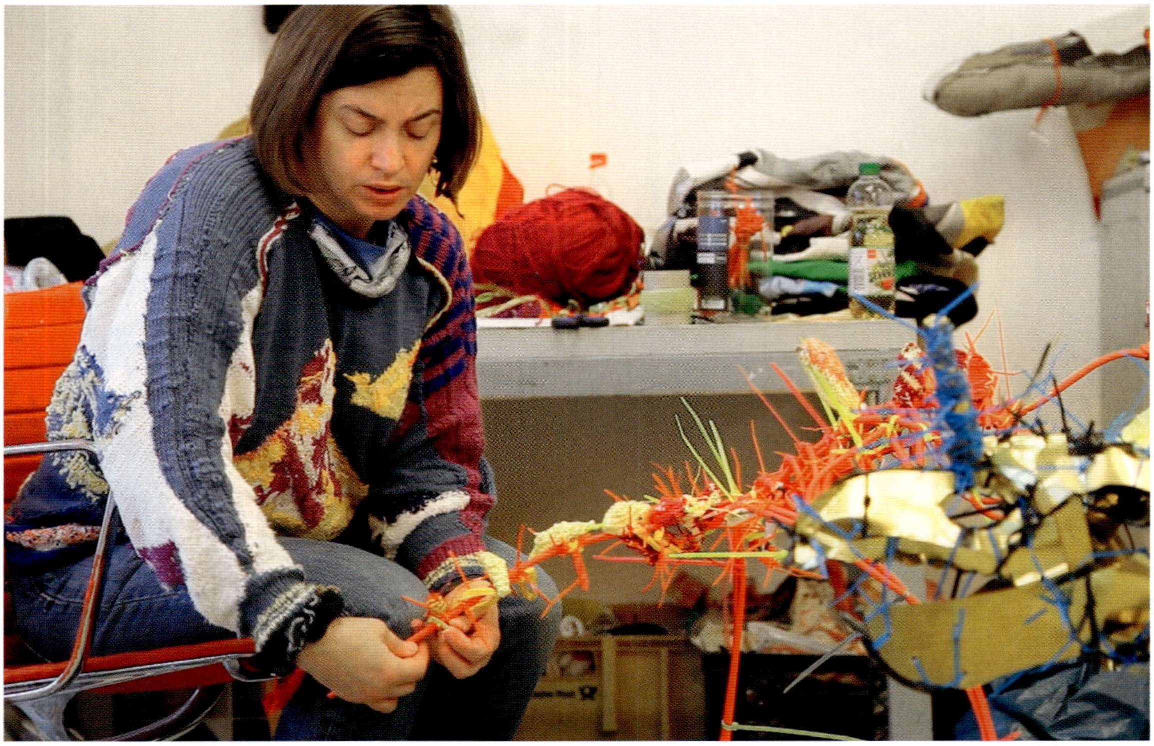

Julia Krause-Harder, 2021, photograph. Courtesy Atelier Goldstein. Krause-Harder has worked at the Frankfurt studio, Atelier Goldstein for over a decade, and here she is at the studio implementing her consistent method of binding her sculptural dinosaurs together with cable ties.

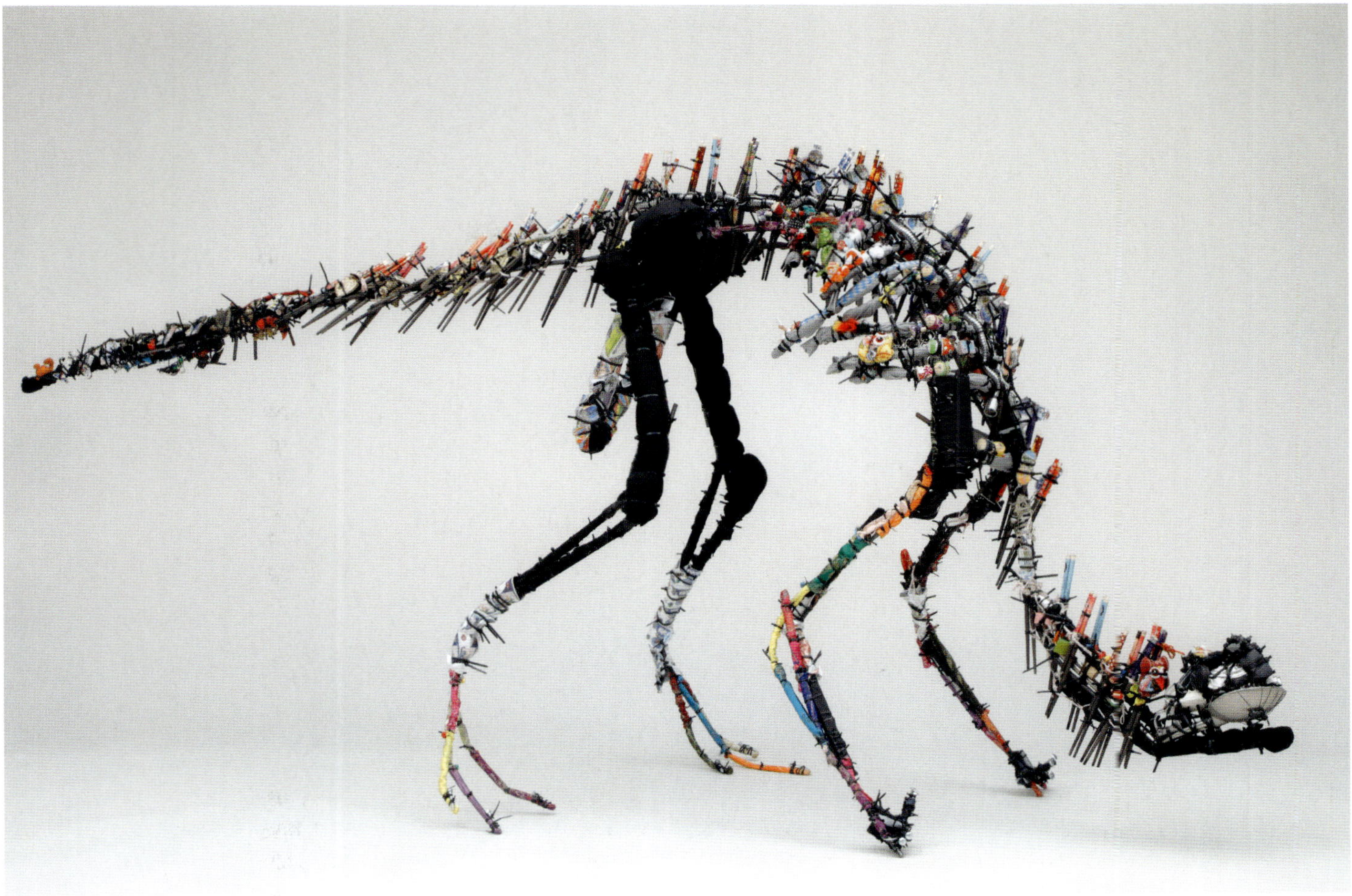

Julia Krause-Harder, Singapursaurus (Hypsilophodon), *2019, various materials, 47 × 39 × 98½ in (120 × 100 × 250 cm). Courtesy Atelier Goldstein.* Over 8 ft (2 m) in length, Krause-Harder's accuracy in scale and proportion is demonstrable here. Her sense of humor is also apparent in her titling of this dinosaur, which references the prehistoric species Hypsilophodon but also infers the use of her cultural materials (including chopsticks) with an additional name based on Singapore. See detail of head on page 253.

Before developing her artistic practice with Atelier Goldstein, Julia Krause-Harder trained as a tailor. The precision and three-dimensional consideration required in garment alterations seem relevant to her artistic methods. Though she is most recognized for her paleontological series, her oeuvre also includes working with textiles in large-scale installations and sewing machine drawings. Dedicated to constructing the over 800 known dinosaurs, each sculpture varies in scale and material, and can take up to 10 weeks to intricately construct and reflect anatomical proportions. *Maiasaura* (2016) is over 6½ ft (2 m) long and was constructed with hundreds of translucent plastic pockets with candy wrappers placed inside that were meticulously folded into animal shapes by Krause-Harder. While in *Singapursaurus* (2019), the bone formation is rendered from chopsticks and key chains adorned with small soft toys or plastic tags.

Material diversification is integral to Krause-Harder's practice and exercised by her paleontological research, which had led her to visit natural history museums internationally. For *Maiasaura,* she spent over a year collecting wrappers she deemed required for its construction. From sturdy hardware materials such as wood and metal to more ephemeral material like teabags, her divergent material choice is distinct.

Visually it is apparent that Krause-Harder's practice is influenced by a creative geometry beyond the parameters of strict scalable reproduction. In juxtaposition to the rigidity of anatomical precision, she also considers what is "unknown" about dinosaurs as a creative departure point. The inconclusive scientific data surrounding the color and texture of dinosaurs' skin becomes freedom for her to explore her own innovative archaeological decisions. One of Krause-Harder's consistent choice of materials is her use of plastic cable ties as a binding method, which gives this monumental series an aesthetic cohesiveness, while celebrating the uniqueness of each dinosaur species.

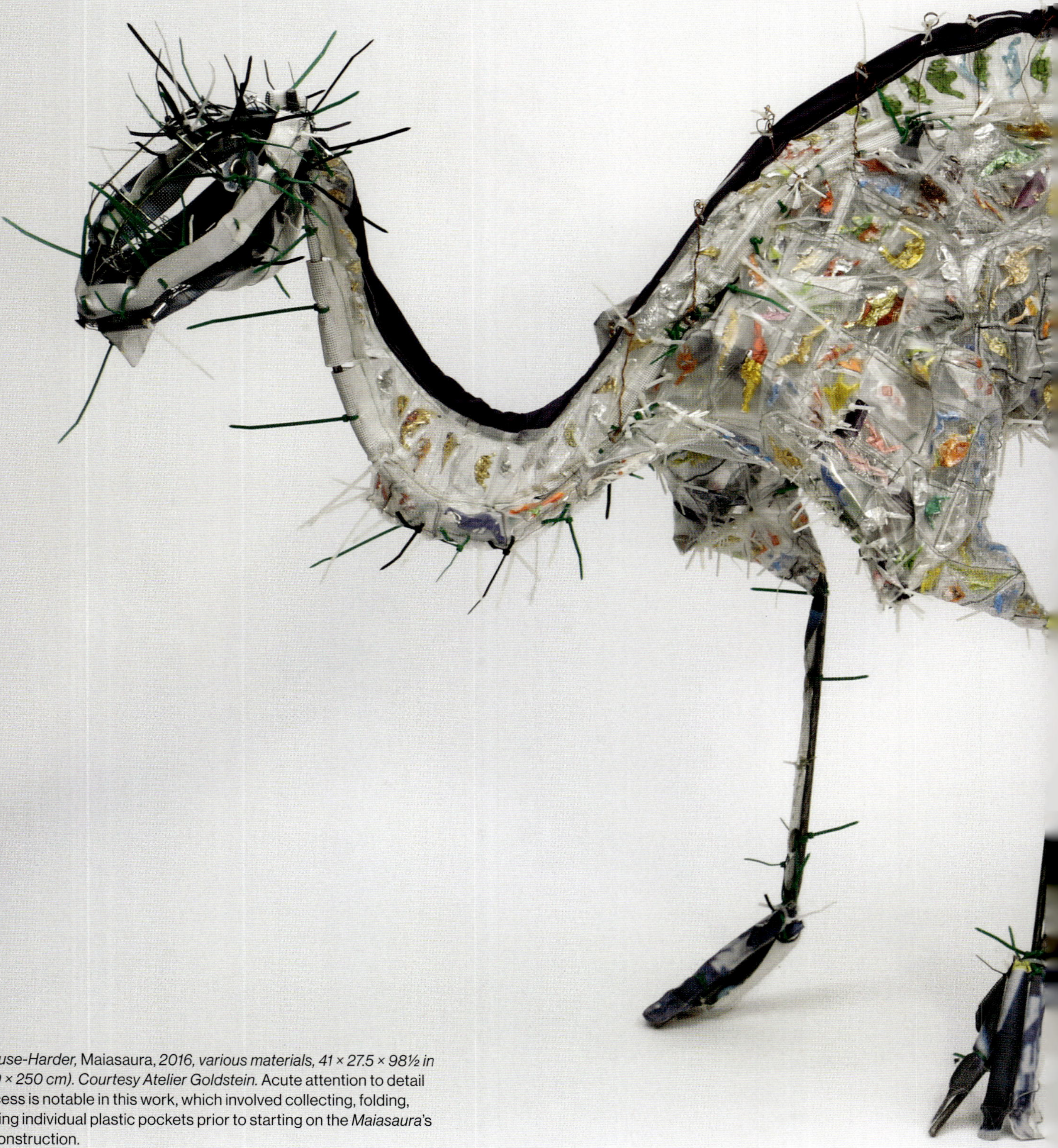

Julia Krause-Harder, Maiasaura, *2016, various materials, 41 × 27.5 × 98½ in (105 × 70 × 250 cm). Courtesy Atelier Goldstein.* Acute attention to detail and process is notable in this work, which involved collecting, folding, and making individual plastic pockets prior to starting on the *Maiasaura*'s overall construction.

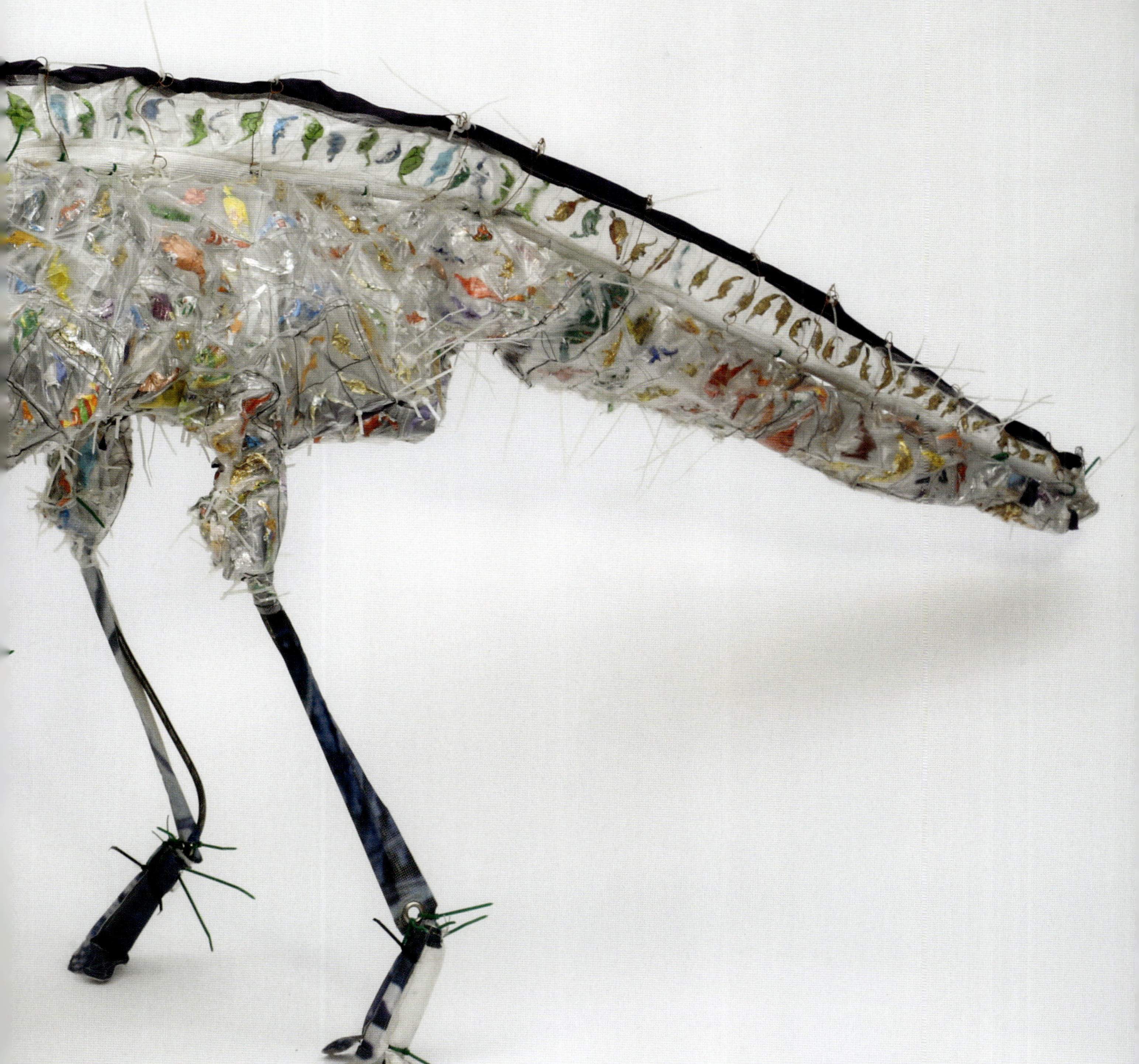

“It is important to me that I rebuild these animals from materials that didn’t even exist in the Mesozoic era. I alienate them a bit, but it’s important to me that they look realistic and anatomically analogous and that you can recognize the species.” – Julia Krause-Harder[9]

WALTER MIKA

(b. 1961, Queens, New York, USA)

Walter Mika chose Garfield the Cat—familiarly observed while watching cartoons with his parents—as one of the first characters featured in his drawings. Born with Down syndrome, Mika began attending the Shield Institute's Day Program in 1982. It was at Shield that his drawing practice was first observed, thus initiating the development of his figurative cartoon aesthetic. Since 1987, Mika has been living in a group residence, which resulted in expanded exposure to popular culture and topical discourse. This communal living, with its access to wider current events, particularly through television, went on to influence his creative subject matter. The attacks of September 11, 2001, the Iraq War, and the election of President Barack Obama each had a profound effect on Mika's practice. His illustrations of firemen, soldiers, and the former president, allowed Mika, who is verbally limited, to define and explore the significance of individuals in extraordinary circumstances. Mika has been attending the art studio Pure Vision Arts, New York's first dedicated studio and exhibition space supporting artists with developmental disabilities, since its inception in 2002. With expressive lines and vivid colors, his drawings are humorous and human. In 2020, Mika received his first solo exhibition with Shrine Gallery, New York.

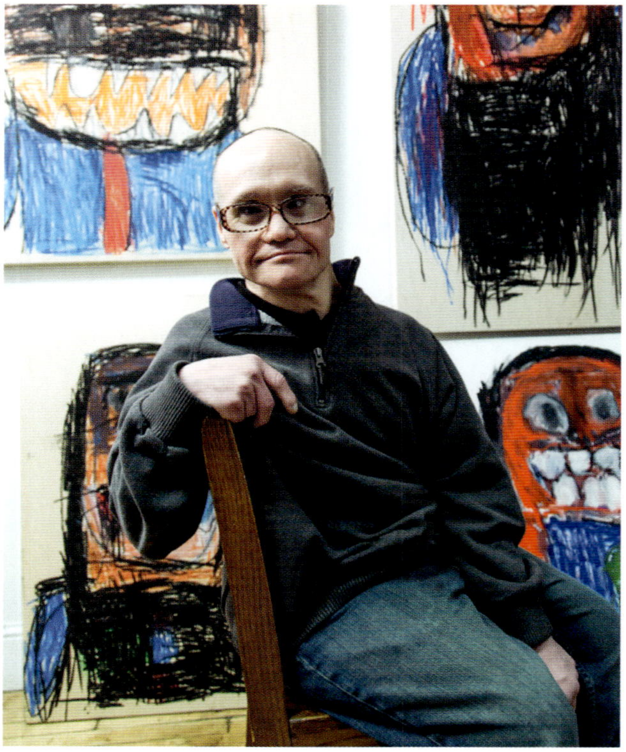

Walter Mika, 2014, photograph. Courtesy Pure Vision Arts. A portrait of Mika among his drawings in the studio at Pure Vision Arts, New York.

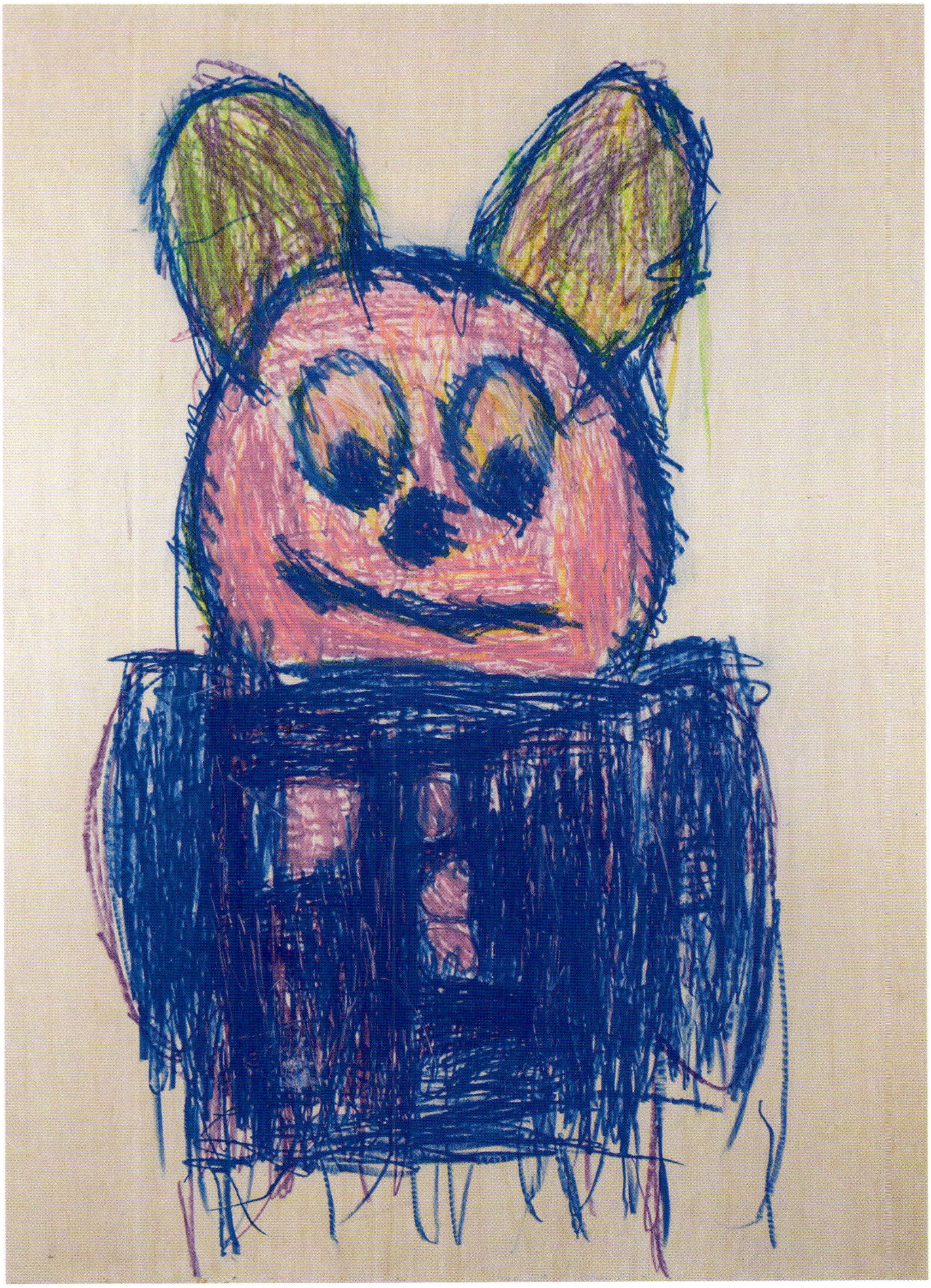

Walter Mika, untitled, *ca. 2002–2016, pastel and oil stick on wood, 48½ × 36½ in (123 × 93 cm). Courtesy Pure Vision Arts.* The combination of cartoon cuteness and frenetic lines creates a vibrating Easter Bunny. This drawing was the featured image for Mika's first solo show *Funny Bunny* at the Shrine Gallery, New York (2020).

Undoubtedly influenced by media and memory, Mika's drawing practice was first observed in the early 1980s at a day program for adults with developmental disabilities at Shield Institute in Queens, New York. Mika's initial subject matter was cartoon characters and benevolent figures from the American zeitgeist, like the Easter Bunny. Mika enjoyed watching cartoons on television when he lived with his parents while in his mid-20s. Following their death, he moved into a group home where television exposed him to a wider scope of current events. From Garfield the Cat to news stories about the NYPD, these media encounters inform his artwork.

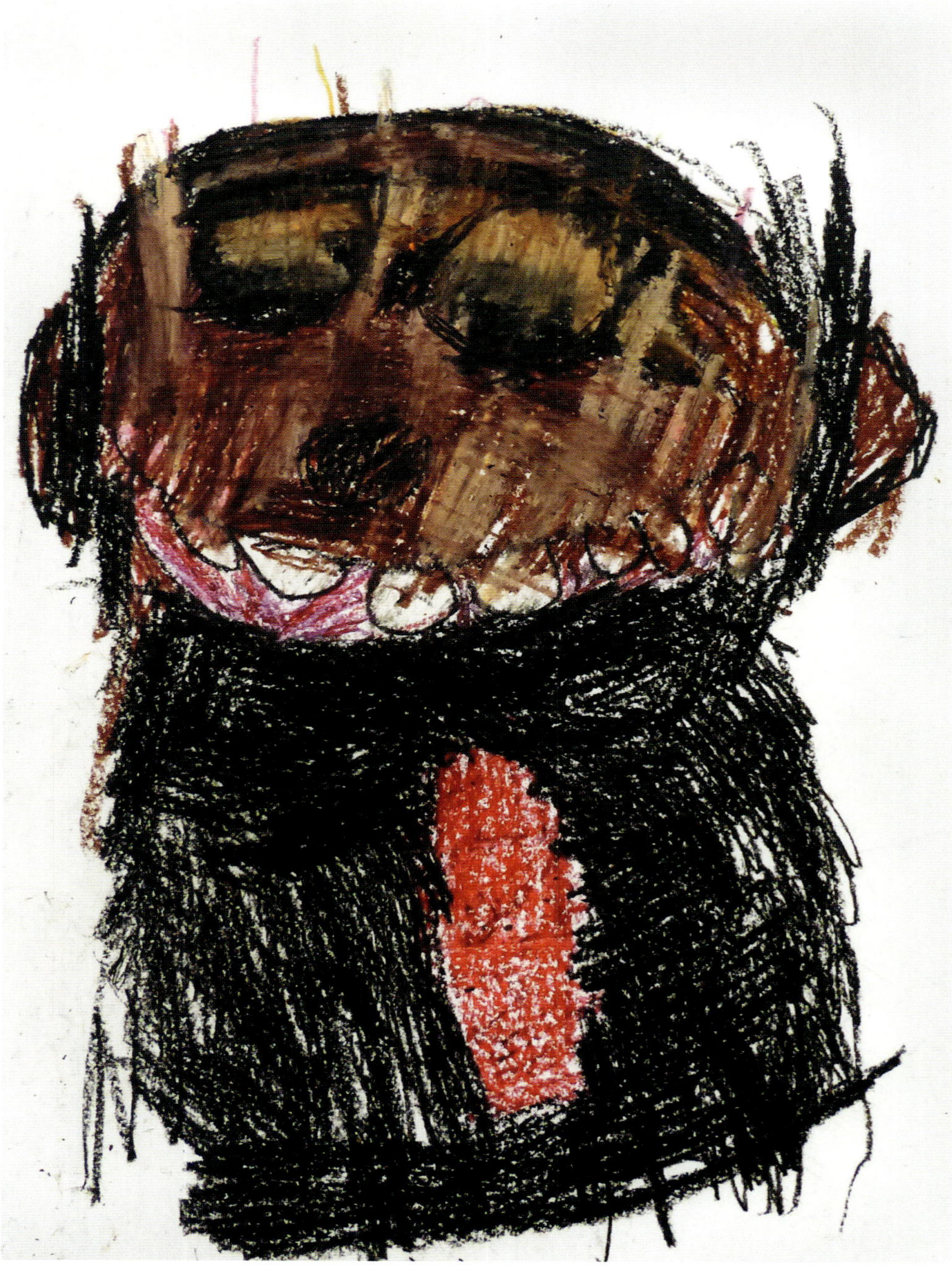

Walter Mika, Obama, *2012, oil pastel on paper, 18 × 24 in (46 × 61 cm). Courtesy Pure Vision Arts.* Mika's work developed in the early 2000s into referencing not only cartoons or fictional characters, but also figures from current events. This can be seen here with his depiction of US President Barack Obama.

Because it borrows visual cues from cartoons, some may dismiss Mika's aesthetic as childlike, but upon closer viewing, the complexity and emotion bestowed within begin to emerge. Ambidextrous, Mika employs both left and right hands in a process of repetitive rendering, using color pastels. His fluctuations of linear direction—vertical, horizontal, diagonal—create a vibrating representation of those influential to him.

Following the attacks of September 11, 2001, Mika, a New York native, began producing hard-lined renditions of firemen and police officers. A progression emerged from influential fictional characters from childhood to real-life figures. With his exposure to the media landscape, his figurative works became more referential as a means to process these current events. When the Iraq War started, Mika drew soldiers from the US Army; following the election of 2008, he drew numerous portraits of the president, Barack Obama. The combination of portraitures that include the Easter Bunny, Santa Claus, US soldiers in Iraq, and former President Obama create an uncanny, yet poignant, body of work.

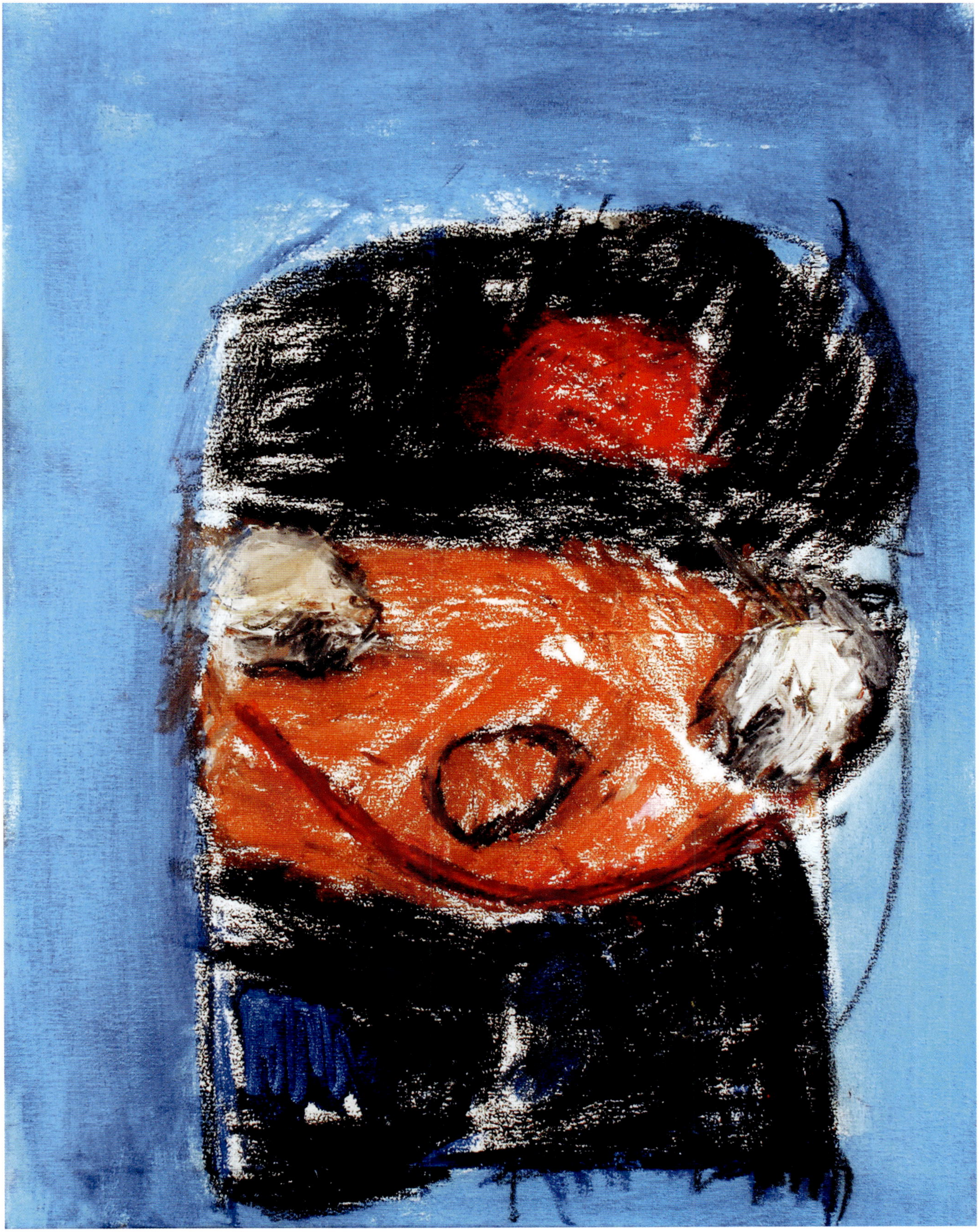

Walter Mika, untitled (Police)*, ca. 2002, acrylic and oil stick on canvas, 24 × 30 in (61 × 76 cm). Courtesy Pure Vision Arts.* A New York native, following the attacks of September 11, 2001, Mika began to draw heroic characters, such as this policeman.

"Walter was driven by a determined desire to make art on a daily basis as an important and necessary outlet for self-expression and communication." – Pamala Rogers Ed.D. NC PsyA, director, Pure Vision Arts[10]

TOMOYUKI SHINKI

(b. 1982, Osaka, Japan)

The compositional black outlines of Tomoyuki Shinki's physical psychedelic battles emulate stop-motion animation. His practice, which takes place at the studio Atelier Incurve in Osaka, Japan, encompasses drawing, painting, and digital illustration. Founded by Hiroshi Imanaka, Atelier Incurve was established in 2002 as the headquarters and art studio of the Social Welfare Foundation SOOHKAI, which fosters the artistic development of individuals with disability. Bodily fighting is axial to Shinki's oeuvre, but his creative and conceptual motivation is distinguished as that of athletic competition, not violence. Photographs of martial arts and combat sport matches serve as pictorial references transposed by Shinki into dynamic scenes. His compositions often merge the competitors into a singular humanoid form set against a stark, white background, which contributes to their evocative state of motion suspended. Exhibiting since 2005, Shinki's museum exhibitions include Atelier Incurve at the Tokyo Opera City Art Gallery (2012) and *The Museum of Everything #6*, Kunsthal Rotterdam (2016). Shinki was one of the artists commissioned to create an official poster for the Tokyo 2020 Olympics and Paralympics.

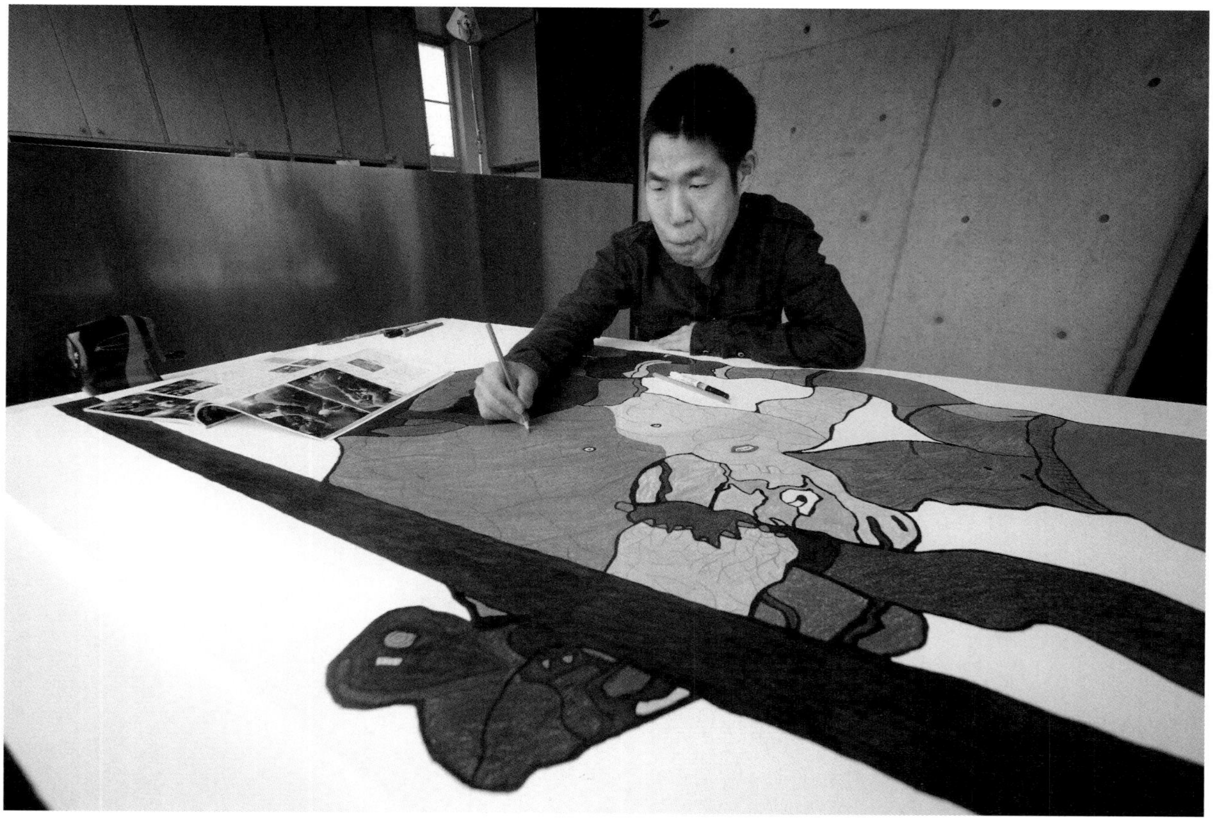

Tomoyuki Shinki, 2017, photograph. Courtesy atelier incurve. Tomoyuki Shinki working in the studio, Atelier Incurve in Osaka, Japan.

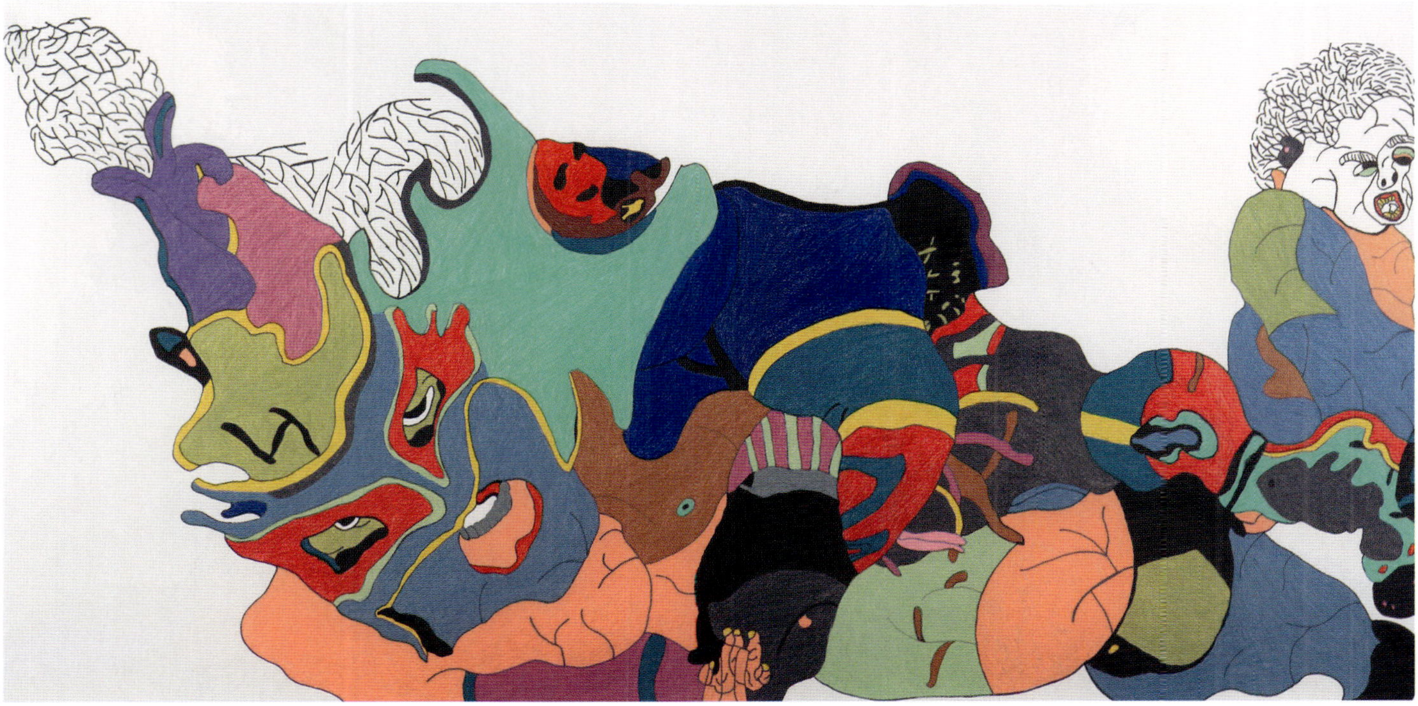

Tomoyuki Shinki, Reverse Half Boston Crab, *2007, pen and colored pencil on paper, 33¹¹⁄₁₆ × 70 in (86 × 178 cm). Courtesy atelier incurve.* With his oeuvre often referencing direct sporting and combat events, Shinki's representation of the reverse half Boston crab wrestling move captures the energy of physical competition through the ambiguous morphing of bodies.

Tomoyuki Shinki's art production is varied but informed by a singular conceptual framework led by his personal interest in bodybuilding and physical fitness. His earliest compositions were digitally composed via his self-taught approach to computer applications. Later, Shinki began to favor a process of first drawing directly onto large sheets of paper with a black marker pen, followed by densely saturating the forms with colored pencils, which produces a satisfying texture. Shinki has also further developed a series of monochromatic drawings on canvas using black pen only.

The departure points of Shinki's drawings are often scenes from pro-wrestling matches but also include boxing, judo, Muay Thai, and Shorinji Kempo. Referring back to their suspended motion quality, many drawings are titled after the relevant (strategic) move depicted, such as *Hook* (2014), *Left Upper* (2010), and *Yokozuna Impact* (2015). Titles from another series—*Curtis Stevens vs. Gennady Golovkin* and *Takashi Uchiyama vs. Daiki Kaneko*—highlight significant boxing matches.

In *Reverse Half Boston Crab* (2007), in reference to the strategic pro-wrestling move, Shinki both eccentrically and playfully morphs the wrestlers into a vibrant figurative amoeba. A green nipple and yellow fingertips surface among the unicellular form as signifiers of bodies. The rendering of a wrestling mask—with its tradition in Mexican lucha libre—addresses the viewer straight on. From there, the muscular forms and collision of bodies become indistinguishable from one another but united, emoting strength and impact. Shinki's use of black marker pen sets his parameters for designating color, while also drafting distinct moments of details. Selectively, there are moments when these details are left without the addition of pencil; this absence of color against the white background extenuates the details of the black line. In *Crab* this summons a wiry or branch-like patterning and a second figurative face appears to stare off the canvas.

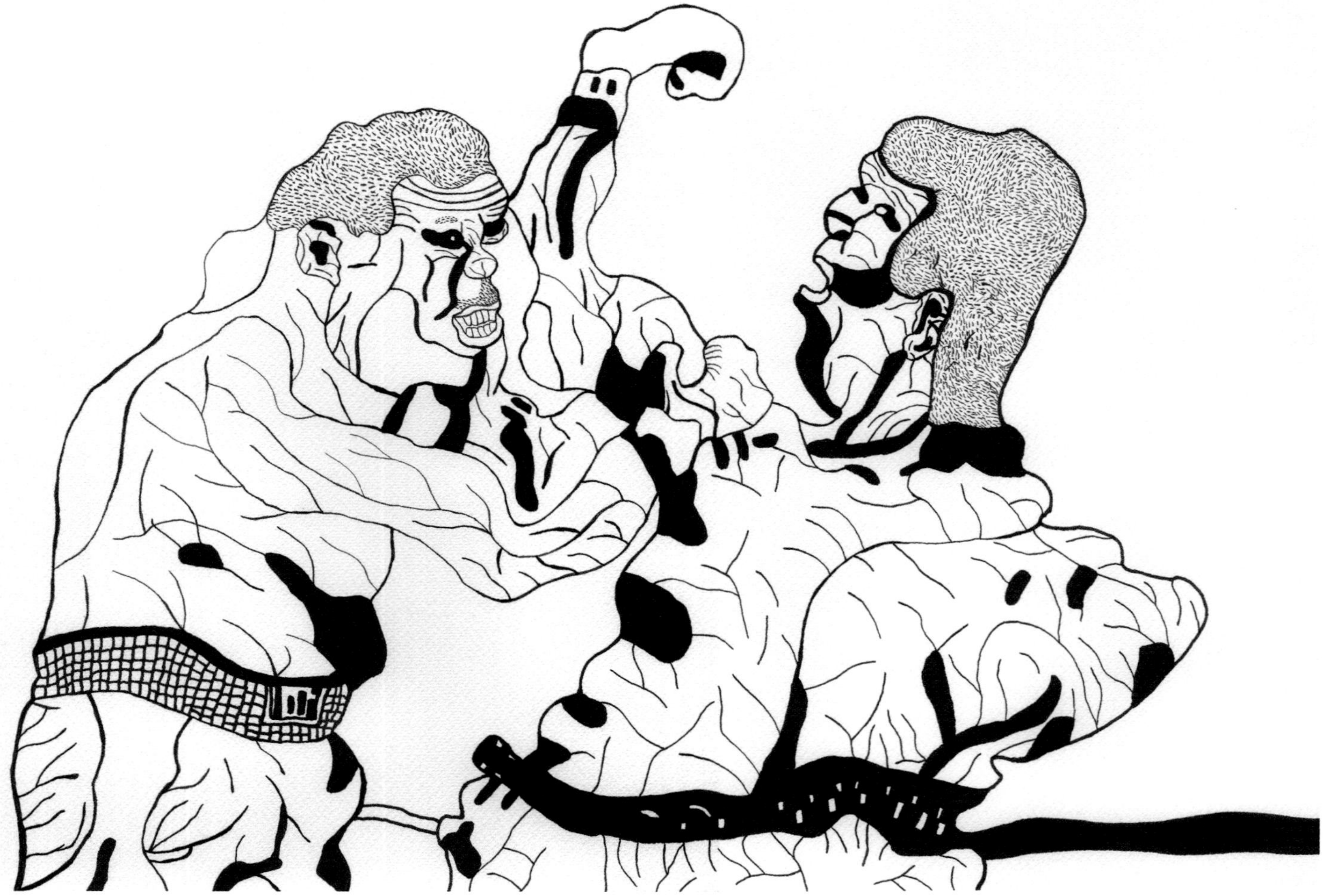

Tomoyuki Shinki, Left Upper, *2010, pen on paper, 16½ × 23⅝ in (41.9 × 59.9 cm). Courtesy atelier incurve.* Shinki's monochromatic rendering of an upper left shot accentuates and dramatizes the physicality of an athlete's body. Thin lines defining muscles also mimic veins or even a landscape, while the deep black shadows look topographical.

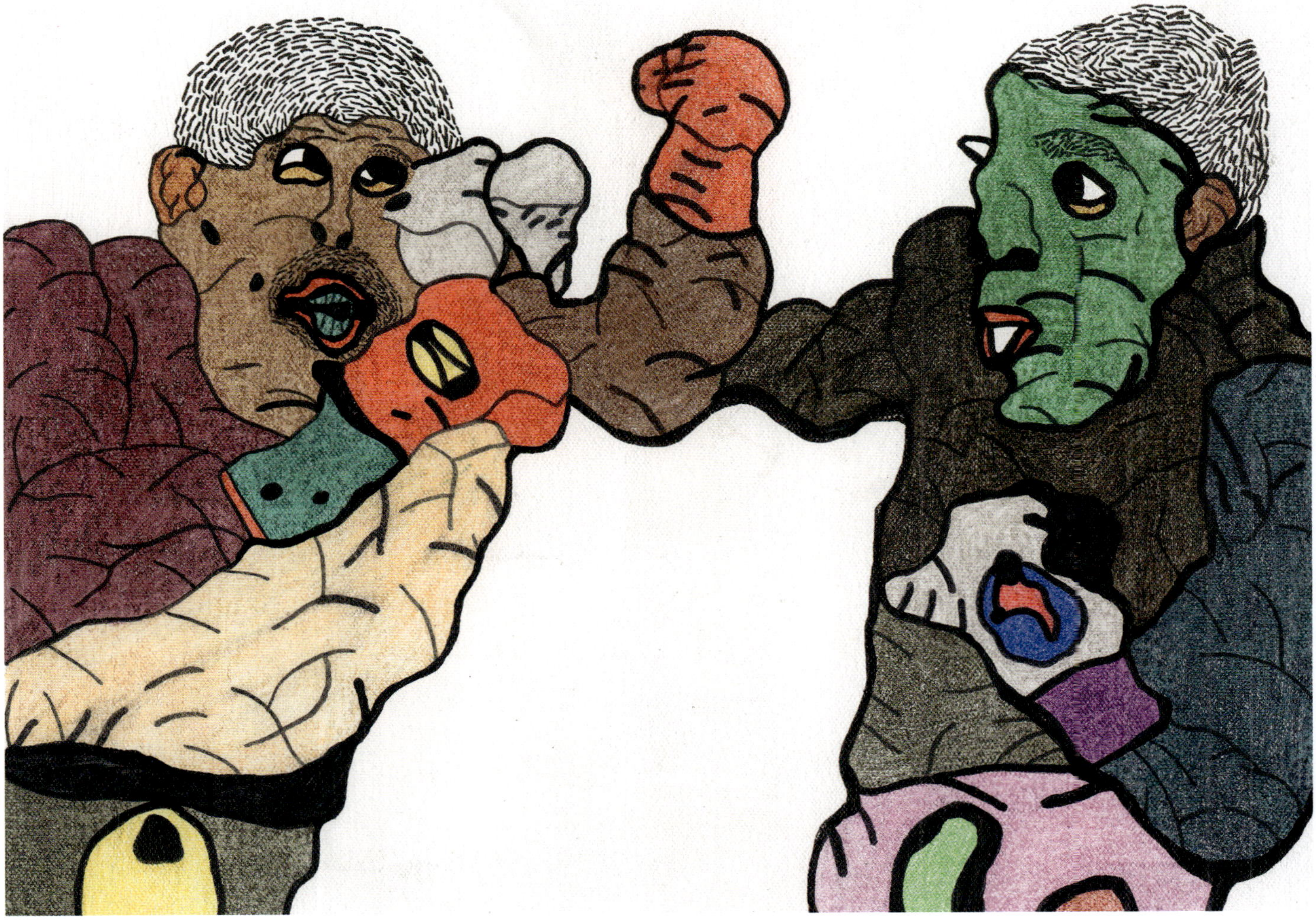

Tomoyuki Shinki, Hook, *2014, pen and colored pencil on canvas, 9½ × 13⅛ in (24.1 × 33.3 cm). Courtesy atelier incurve.* Drafted on canvas, *Hook* has an added textural quality to its overall composition. The impact of the punch is subtle, but effectively illustrated by Shinki in the eyes of the fighter (left), with his opponent's gray glove striking his face.

PART 3: COMPOSITIONS

Compositions is a future proposition for artists currently relegated as self-taught facing possible restrictions from labels and categories. It offers a reexamination of artists and their oeuvres through a formal curatorial lens, rather than circumstantial positioning. The chapter *Abstraction* explores artists whose visual output is nonrepresentational but bears distinct methods and intent. The creative practices in *Landscapes* are diverse and unique approaches to rendering our surroundings—natural, built, real, and imagined. The final chapter, *Figuration*, presents artists interested in the human form, figures, and faces.

Each chapter is curatorially contextualized by an introduction, and significant to *Compositions* are three artists' interviews that serve as advocations for an artist-led discussion in the field. George Widener, Mamadou Cissé, and William Scott directly address their practice, process, and identities as artists, reflecting an emblematic shift in categorizing, presenting, and discussing artists.

CHAPTER 9

ABSTRACTION: BEYOND REPRESENTATION

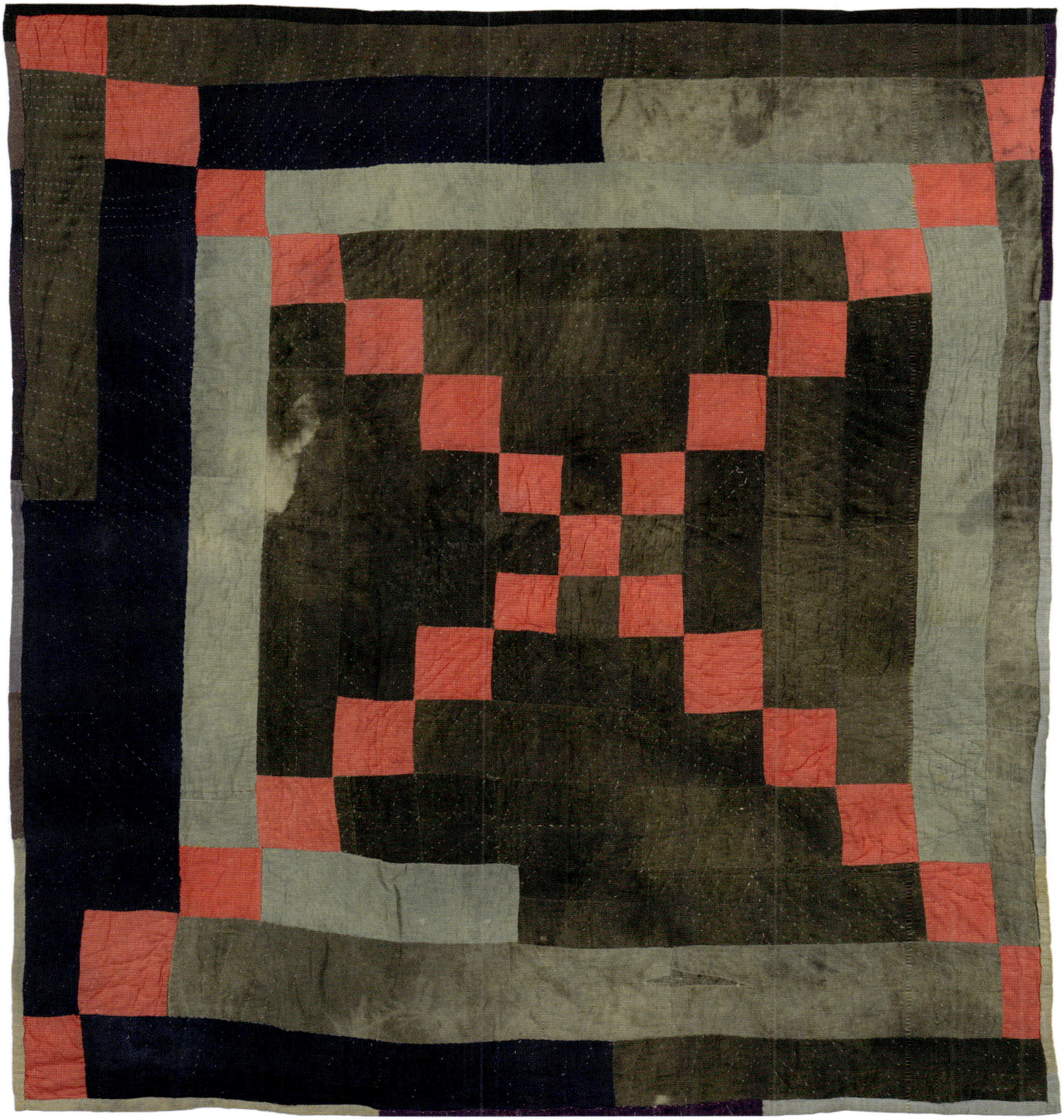

Martha Jane Pettway (American, 1898–2003), two-sided work-clothes quilt, 1920s, pieced cotton denim twill and corduroy, 67 × 72 in (170.2 × 182.9 cm). Philadelphia Museum of Art. Pettway was part of the community of African American women known as Gee's Bend. Existing since the mid-century in Boykin, Alabama, the quilts of Gee's Bend have a strong aesthetic connection to geometric abstraction. While pointing to a direct link between American abstract expressionism and the tradition of quilting can be problematic, these quilts and their formal relationship with abstraction is relevant and stands to recognize their visual contribution.

ALTERNATIVE EXPRESSIONS

Lisa Slominski

Abstraction surveys six artists who experiment with the boundaries of concept and process in nonrepresentational aesthetics. These artists explore direct and indirect narratives, influences, and ideas present in abstract compositions. This preface to the chapter establishes the relevance of Hilma af Klint (1862–1944) and Janet Sobel (1893–1968) to the history of abstraction. It sets forth the relationship between direct messaging and performative process within the practices of Thornton Dial (1928–2016) and Nnena Kalu (b. 1964). Furthermore, it presents geometric abstraction and information via the oeuvres of George Widener (b. 1962) and Junko Yamamoto (b. 1973).

In its rudimentary definition, "to abstract" means to separate or withdraw something from something else. Examining the term "abstraction" through the lens of an art historical framework creates a broad implication that the visual output has no direct subject matter. The broader genre of abstraction describes an extremely diverse range of canons and practices—contemporary and historical, self-taught or academic—that are considered nonrepresentational.

With his assertion of making the first abstract compositions in 1911, Wassily Kandinsky (1866–1944) has been considered the pioneer of abstract painting in Europe; however, more contemporary discourse has established Swedish artist, Hilma af Klint (see page 298) as his predecessor. During a seance af Klint was summoned by her spiritual guides, known as the High Masters (*De Höga*), who directed her to undertake a creative commission. In 1906, af Klint began a series of preparatory paintings, known as *Primordial Chaos.* These 26 paintings are her first exploration of abstraction, predating Kandinsky by five years.

In 1940s America, Jackson Pollock (1912–1956) was at the forefront of the painters establishing the movement of abstract expressionism. Pollock is specifically credited for his "drip paintings": lying canvases on the floor, then dripping and flinging enamel paint onto them. Before Pollock developed this distinguished style, Janet Sobel (see page 302) developed her own process of dripping enamel through glass pipettes (materials available to her through her husband's jewelry business), creating abstract "all-over" paintings. These densely covered abstract compositions were exhibited in 1944 and recorded by critic Clement Greenberg as influential to Pollock.

Sobel, along with Pollock, developed an art practice that was inherently driven by the physical process that was relevant to Gutai, an adjacent Japanese avant-garde movement intending to allow action and everyday life to lead creation. Their performative mark-making—a process of implementing ordinary materials and physical movement to form an abstract but communicative outcome—presents a context similar to the practice of British artist Nnena Kalu (see page 310). Building up temporal installations via physical and performative process, Kalu uses donated and sourced materials like VHS tapes, string, and cardboard, which are wrapped in a repetitive motion.

The set aesthetics of abstract expressionism defined in the 1940s are evoked in the oeuvre of Thornton Dial (see page 306), yet his implementation of subversive abstraction connected to his lived experience as an African American in the South, applying less representational signs and motifs to convey cultural and political meaning. His abstracted assemblages and sculptures integrate symbols and emblematic materials, demonstrating abstraction's ability to present concepts and be driven by narrative.

Commitment to inherent information within a seemingly abstract composition is evident in the work of American artist George Widener (see page 290), whose colorful geometric multimedia drawings are full of historic and mathematical information. Widener can visualize the polymorphous connections between numbers, dates, and history, through composing them into hypnotic abstract and geometric patterns. The practice of Japanese artist Junko Yamamoto (see page 314) implements the rigor of abstracted geometric forms informed by existing objects. Using felt as a material, her abstract cut forms are influenced by kitchen utensils, food, and everyday objects.

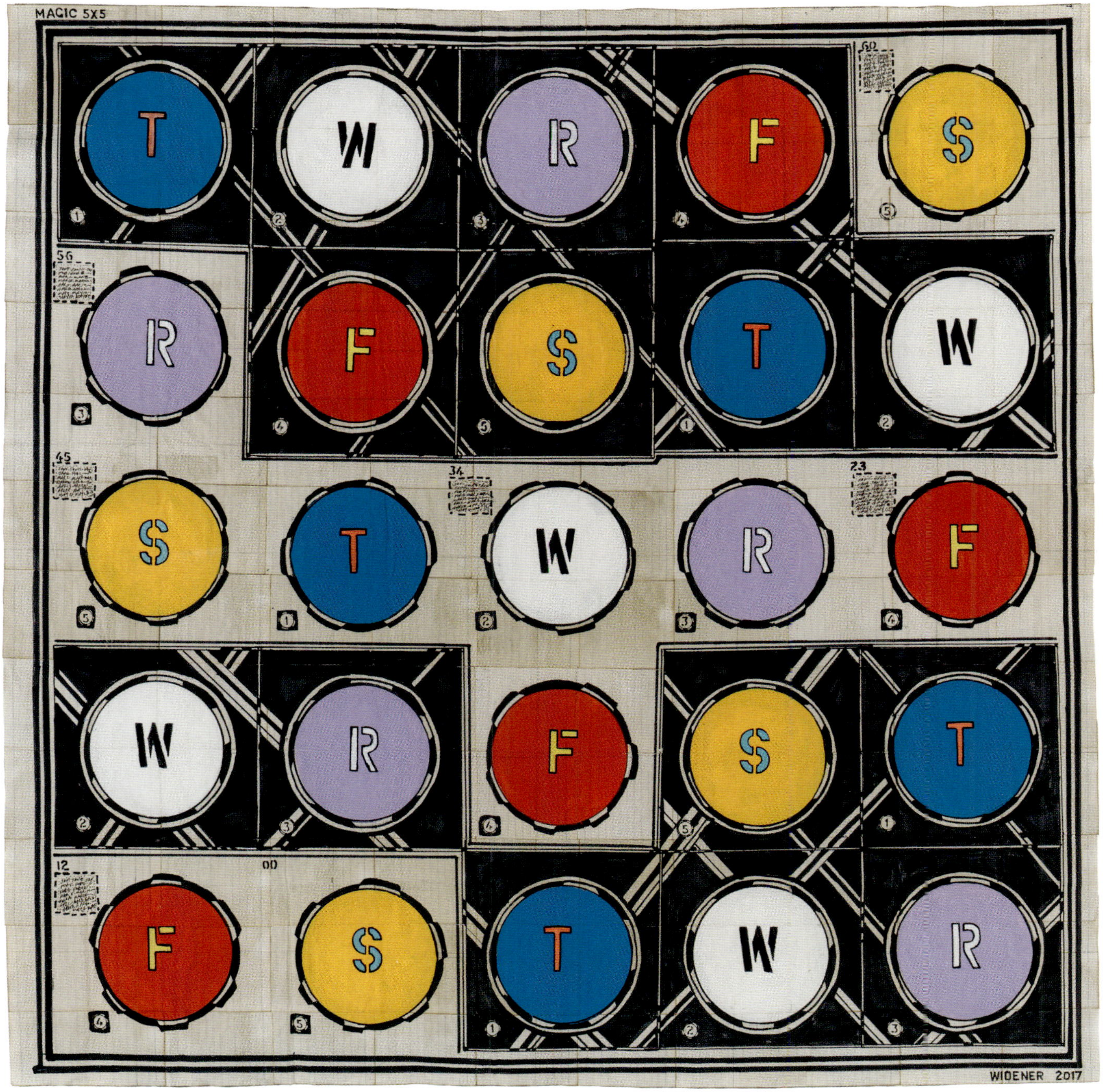

George Widener, Magic Circles, *2017, mixed media on paper, 46¼ × 48 in (117.5 × 121.9 cm). Courtesy Ricco/Maresca Gallery.* In his ongoing and developing series, Widener mathematically and conceptually expands the traditional magic circle/square (a grid of numbers with columns and rows all equaling an identical sum) by implementing his own observations of dates and time.

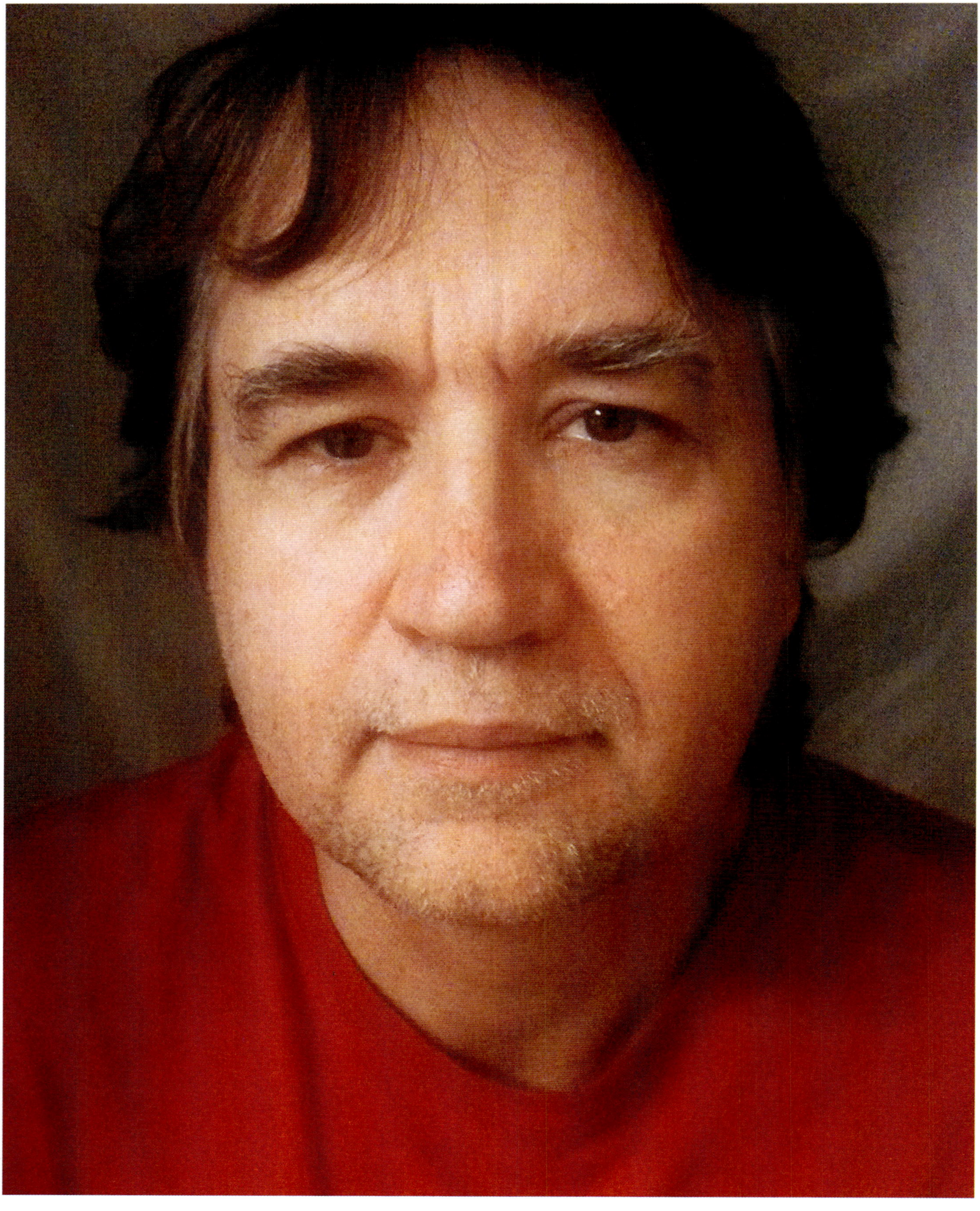

George Widener, n.d., photograph. Courtesy Ricco/Maresca Gallery.
Widener has exhibited his geometric and often abstract compositions since the early 2000s. His amalgamations of mathematics, history, and personal memory are extraordinary and compelling.

GEORGE WIDENER

(b. 1962, Covington, Kentucky, USA)

Dates, memories, historical catastrophes, and algorithmic magic squares inform the compositions of George Widener. Considered a numerical intellect, his compelling visual aesthetic presents complex calculations and data as mixed-media drawings. While growing up in Kentucky, his interest in numbers emerged at the age of six and he later used his fascination with dates to cope with anxiety by drawing regularly in notebooks. He served in the US Air Force in the early 1980s and then studied engineering in Texas. Following financial duress and mental instability, Widener left university and faced the circumstances of homelessness. In 2000, he was diagnosed with Asperger's syndrome, which introduced for Widener, a degree of validity for his numerical preoccupation. His ability to visualize the multifarious relationships between dates and occurrences is transposed into hypnotic compositions of critical numbers situated among abstract patterns and geometric forms. Widener has been exhibiting since the early 2000s and significant exhibitions include *The Alternative Guide to the Universe* at the Hayward Gallery (2013) and the retrospective *Secret Universe IV: George Widener* at Hamburger Bahnhof – Museum für Gegenwart in Berlin (2013).

Interview by Sophia Cosmadopoulos

Sophia Cosmadopoulos: Your work is often considered abstract or nonfigurative, how do you relate to abstraction?

George Widener: Well, I think that it's sort of a collection of graphic images and memories that I have. Ever since I was a child, I've had certain predilections or certain predispositions to do certain things. And in the beginning, I just did them automatically. And I didn't understand why or what it was about. And so I would do these activities, ever since I was a child, and it sort of evolved into exploring and a refuge, really, of things that I would explore. And they didn't have practical meaning in the sense of what they meant. Not an avenue to explore that would be traditional. I just explored them. And so in that way, I think that there was abstraction.

How would you describe your work?

My work exists in different ways. I have a certain memory capacity that's involved in making works and, for example, I was able to, as a child, mimic or imitate certain things. I can imitate graphic images or I could imitate the things I'd seen and produce them from memory. And so memory has played a part in the things I do. But I would say that I explore these inner processes that are things that are inside of me. And I have explored those. And I've just had a certain fascination with dates and certain numerical processes. And I never intended, I never started out to be an artist. I was originally going to be a scientist or an engineer, but that didn't work out. So I started doing some different activities. And that's how I came to be a working artist.

How did you start making art? Was there a specific moment or event that caused it?

I was the first person in my family to graduate high school. I had a small scholarship to Vanderbilt University to study engineering. But I was intimidated a little bit and didn't have money. So I said, well, I'm just going to join the Air Force and be a technician on these aircrafts. And then I'll leave the service and then I'll become an engineer. I went into the service on my 18th birthday and then upon my discharge, I enrolled in engineering school. But then I started having some difficulties about a year, a year and a half later. I had always drawn and I always had a sing-song thing with dates and numbers that relaxed me ever since I was a child. And I think what happened was that in those times, roughly 1985–1986 through 1988, when I was going through this sort of personal difficult time, what I did was I reverted back to the dates and the processes and the automatic drawing that relaxed me so much. I was having a personal difficulty when I was a young person. I was not sure what I was going to do or what was going to happen to me, like young people go through, like everybody goes through.

I was making art for myself of course, just keeping the notebooks and they had a science slant or a science twist to it. Because after all, I was going to be an engineer and so I was fascinated with science fiction and that sort of stuff. And it kind of got intertwined with some themes from that. But I just started keeping notebooks of dates and then I started to become more and more interested in the possibilities of different things that came to me. And it started to become a big part of my waking thoughts. And also when I slept, I would dream of certain patterns. Even though my circumstances back then were difficult at times. I was having a very active thought process. I sort of got lost in my things and that's how it came about. It wasn't planned or worked out or anything like that, it just happened naturally. I think partly it's that I have these things inside of me and also the circumstance that came about.

When did you first start considering yourself an artist?

I knew as a young person that I could draw things that other people couldn't. I knew that I could do that, that I had a facility for doing it. But, boy, I had to sort of figure out what an artist was, beyond just being able to do something technical. It took much more time. I kind of knew it in a superficial sense in my teen years. But, I wasn't being really creative, I was just producing because, if you have a technical ability with stuff you'll explore that. And I think it took me defining an artist as somebody that has a personal vision, you know? And that took much later—into my 20s. Even when I was doing my dates and my notebooks, I didn't share them with other people, but I knew it was something that was unique. And it was really something that I was doing that gave me confidence, and I knew it was probably something that had never been done.

Tell me why numbers first started to fascinate you.

In my family there were a couple of people that had obsessions. There has been some autism in my family and there was classic autism in some people and they had to be taken care of. And they had fascinations. And I think it comes a little bit from that. But I just had a fascination. As I was going to school, I would do a rhythmic repeating of numbers as I was walking. In Kentucky there was a certain way that we would go to school. So I just had a ritual that I would do as I was going to school with these dates and numbers, it just came from that. I would pick a certain year and then I would say the Wednesdays of a certain year. Like if I look at the year 2028, for example, like the Wednesdays. I know—January 5, 12, 19, 26, February 2, 9, 16, 23, March 1, 8, 15, 22, 29. And I would do this in a rhythmic sort of sense as I was walking and it was very relaxing. The powers of two, for some reason—1, 2, 4, 8, 16, 32, 64, and I would go on and on. And that was something that I did a lot as a kid too. The powers of two are somewhat related to prime numbers. I think some of the kids that have a lot of disability, but have a real gift with numbers, often do prime numbers. It may have been a cousin to that, you know, what I was doing?

Are there specific dates that are particularly significant to you?

Well, I have these markers, and I divide things up using them. Like the year 1972 and the year 2000, for example, I use them in certain ways to divide up the other dates. They're sort of like reference years or marked dates. You know, as far as dates and historical events, I got fascinated. But I don't keep them the way that I used to because I have become aware that I don't want to be seen as a person that's making something that's connected to disability. I want to be seen as a creative person.

I've been put on a stage before for my ability with dates, and I've also been brought out, like the Elephant Man. I was brought out in front of a group of medical students at the Institute of Neurology, where they had me behind the curtain and then they opened the curtain. That stuff actually happened. And then I met Kim Peek and they took him on stage, and Kim was amazing, but

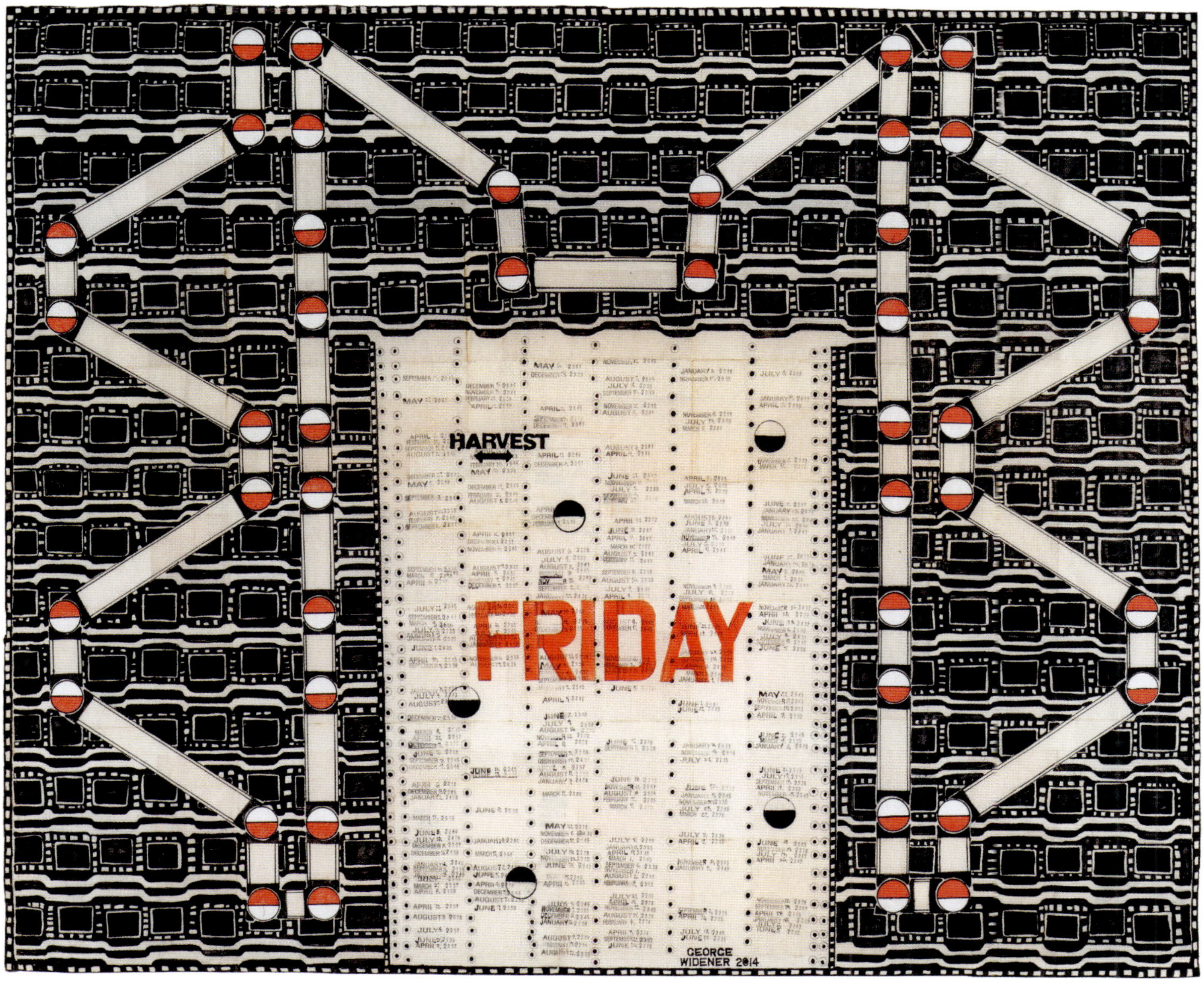

George Widener, Harvest, *2014, mixed media on paper, 47½ × 59½ in (120.7 × 151.1 cm). Collection of Victor F. Keen.* Friday is a consistent and significant day in the work of Widener, implementing a day of the week to explore historical phenomena, and in this specific composition conceptually "harvesting" the various Fridays together.

he was very disabled in a lot of ways. And so, I shy away from reeling off certain dates. I could do it, but I shy away from it. Because I'm trying to be recognized as just a creative artist, you know. Not to be doing tricks. Those are connected to a creative process. Mozart would do little musical tricks with a cloth laid on the keys that people find amazing and fascinating. But that's not what it's all about. Do you know what I am trying to say? In my own way, I have tried to be recognized as a creative artist. I hope eventually, that someday my fans are going to evolve.

Can you explain the motif of magic squares in your compositions?

A magic square is basically a grid of numbers that all add up to the identical sum in all directions, whether it's horizontal, vertical, or diagonal. The classic one, the top is 16, 3, 2, 13, and that adds up to 34, but it adds up to 34 in all directions. And serious mathematicians, they've said they don't really know what that means. Because, you see, everything in mathematics has generally got a connection to a condition in nature.

I made the first where I sort of mixed in dates. I made a hybrid between the Magic Square and I mixed it with dates. Often, theoretical mathematicians are generally decades ahead of any process that becomes discovered, any practical use or the mathematics or theoretical math or math equations for physics was discovered and then decades later, the practical applications and the engineering applications came about. There's a time difference. So it's possible that some of the things that I do, that I'm demonstrating in my work, that someday it's going to have some sort of relevance in a bigger way than it does today. Today it's abstract, but who knows?

What is the significance of Friday in the work *Harvest* (2014)?

It was me finding these particular connections, I think you could say, these particular connections between the day of Friday and different years and listing those out. Then the drawing that's around it is from when I was exploring, sort of trying to find mechanical or symmetrical images that sort of give me a feeling of the dates as I was finding them. The dates came out of my notebook. Now, the circles that are drawn on there were a reference to the yin and the yang concept, the on or off concept. As I recorded dates in my notebooks, sometimes I would find symmetrical patterns or things that were very odd, sort of like when you're walking along the beach and you're looking at all these rocks and sometimes something stands out, some shiny, unusual rock. I would find the first day of the second month and then the other one would be the second day of the first month. And so you see, it was sort of like a mirror image, sort of a symmetrical thing that I was doing. And some of the dates in that particular piece, there are Fridays and I was finding these odd connections and stuff that popped up in my head. And then, the word "harvest" implies that I was sort of harvesting these particular Fridays. The structure of it that's drawn in the background, it's mechanical or a graphic feeling, a representation of what I was doing with those dates.

How would you describe yourself as an artist?

Well as far as "self-taught" or, of course, the term "Outsider"—I'm no longer an Outsider, of course. I think it does apply in certain times. If you look at Henry Darger or Adolf Wölfli, they were in particular circumstances and their circumstances never changed during their lifetime. They were pretty much isolated. I get that, but I feel fortunate that my circumstances changed.

I make the statement that I was an Outsider Artist from roughly 1986 until 1994. I fit that description of somebody doing it for themselves and not sharing it. And it was coming from something internal. And, at times it was very secretive. And so I did fit some of those

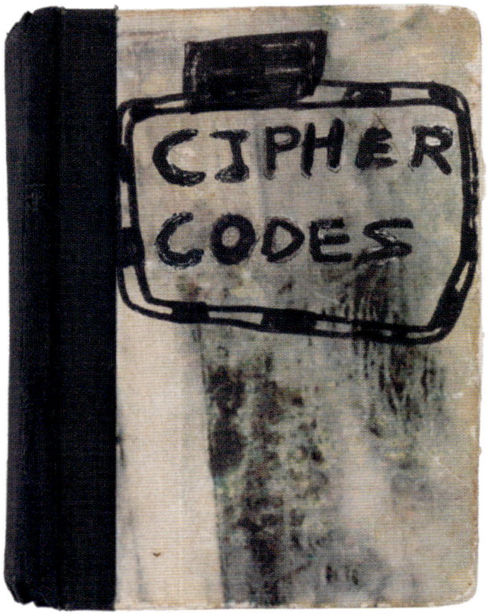

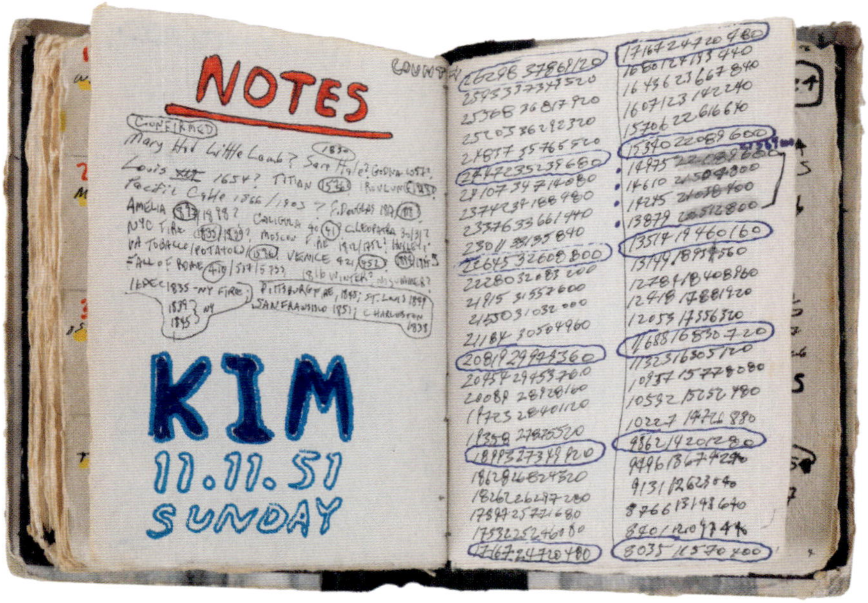

George Widener, Cipher Codes: Book III. The Final Word. Short Stories + Notes, *2006, felt-tip pen and tape on paper, 6⅛ × 4¾ × 1 in (15.6 × 12.1 × 2.5 cm). American Folk Art Museum, Gift of the Artist.* Widener has long kept notebooks recording numbers, dates, and concepts. In this notebook from 2006, the left page shows, "NOTES" and below the name "KIM," in reference to numerical savant Kim Peek. Below, Widener records Peek's birthdate, November 11, 1951.

definitions of an Outsider. But, things changed. So it is what it is. People can make of it what they want. You can't control that or whatever people are going to think of me. I just do my work and try to stay true to myself and that's it. I'm aware now of this stuff. Before, I wasn't even aware. I wasn't aware of what an Outsider was.

But I have evolved and I have explored things that were interesting for me. And now I interact with galleries and I'm aware that people see my artwork. And, you know, it's true that I'm somewhat influenced by that. I don't think you can have an audience and not be influenced.

Tell me about your interest in the Titanic.

As a teenager, I was looking over the passenger list of the Titanic, and happened to see my name, George Widener, and it was George D. Widener of Philadelphia. And it was a little bit fascinating, it was very fascinating for me for different reasons. My mom was from a poor Appalachian family, but she married James Widener and parts of his family were sort of gentry. He died when I was young and I always had this in my head. These very nice parts of my family. And so it was sort of a positive thing to think that I was connected to this famous and rich Widener, riding around on the Titanic. And like a lot of people, I had sort of a macabre fascination with disasters. I'm not a person to stop and look at a car wreck or something like that. But I did witness in Mannheim, Germany, for example, a big helicopter crash. I was too close to that. And I was in an explosion and fire when I was a teenager in the Air Force. So, I witnessed, and I felt this emotion that comes with an accident or disaster. And so, as I went into my 20s, I sort of attributed bad luck in my life back then to natural disasters. I said, "Well it happens, bad stuff can happen to the best of people, to people that you wouldn't expect."

The people on the Titanic, some of them had great lives to look forward to, and this thing happened. It shows the fragility of our existence. And so I was thinking about all this. And so the Titanic, became a theme for me. I had won awards and everything as a child in Appalachia, and I was considered somebody who was going to be successful. And then I went into service and I did a very good job in the service as a technician and I won medals. When I got out I had some difficulty. I became homeless, and I was in shelters with people with a lot of drug and alcohol issues. And I started feeling like a failure. I was wondering, what the hell? What's happening? I kind of had the idea of the disaster that happens, which people have no control over. It can happen to anyone. We feel like we're in control of our lives, but then things happen and you realize you're not in control of your life always. I mean, you can be in control of your life as best as possible, try to make plans or preparations and stuff, but things can still happen that are fate. I think the Titanic is connected with these kind of ideas. It was sort of like the 9/11 of its day, something that people never imagined.

What are your goals for your work in the future?

I have a fantasy idea that someday they might put a small piece of mine on a spacecraft, and it might go out into space. Yeah, they can look at it and sort of be reminded of Earth because I'm using Earth dates, you see? I keep up with the Perseverance rover and all of that stuff. I love that stuff. It's pretty amazing what they're doing. They're going to find life and it's gonna change a lot of stuff. The idea is that they find it on Mars and then my God, it's gonna exist everywhere, throughout the galaxy. And so what that means is, because our system is only 4.5 billion years old and the universe is roughly 14 billion years old, that there are civilizations out there. There are intelligent species out there that are way more advanced than us, that are evolved hundreds of thousands of years, or millions of years ahead of us. So it's a fascinating idea, isn't it?

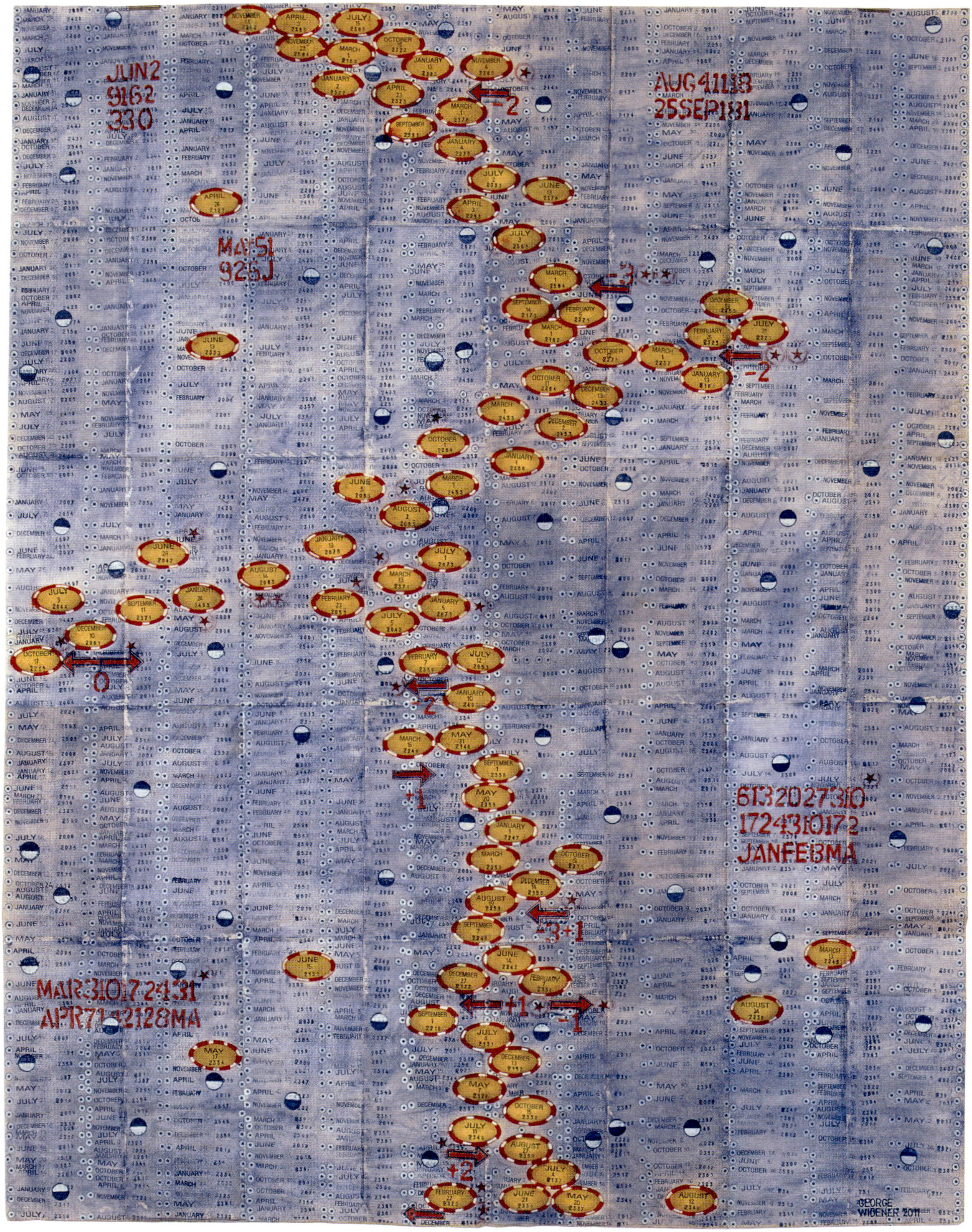

George Widener, Robot Puzzle, *2011, mixed media on paper, 60¹⁄₁₆ × 47 ⅝ in (152.5 × 121 cm). Courtesy Delmes & Zander, Cologne.* Structured according to Widener's own algorithms, his *Robot Puzzles* are composed for future, more highly developed and intelligent, computers or robots to solve. This drawing is visually complex and patterned, featuring hundreds of stamped dates of the future December 21, 2122 and March 13, 2371.

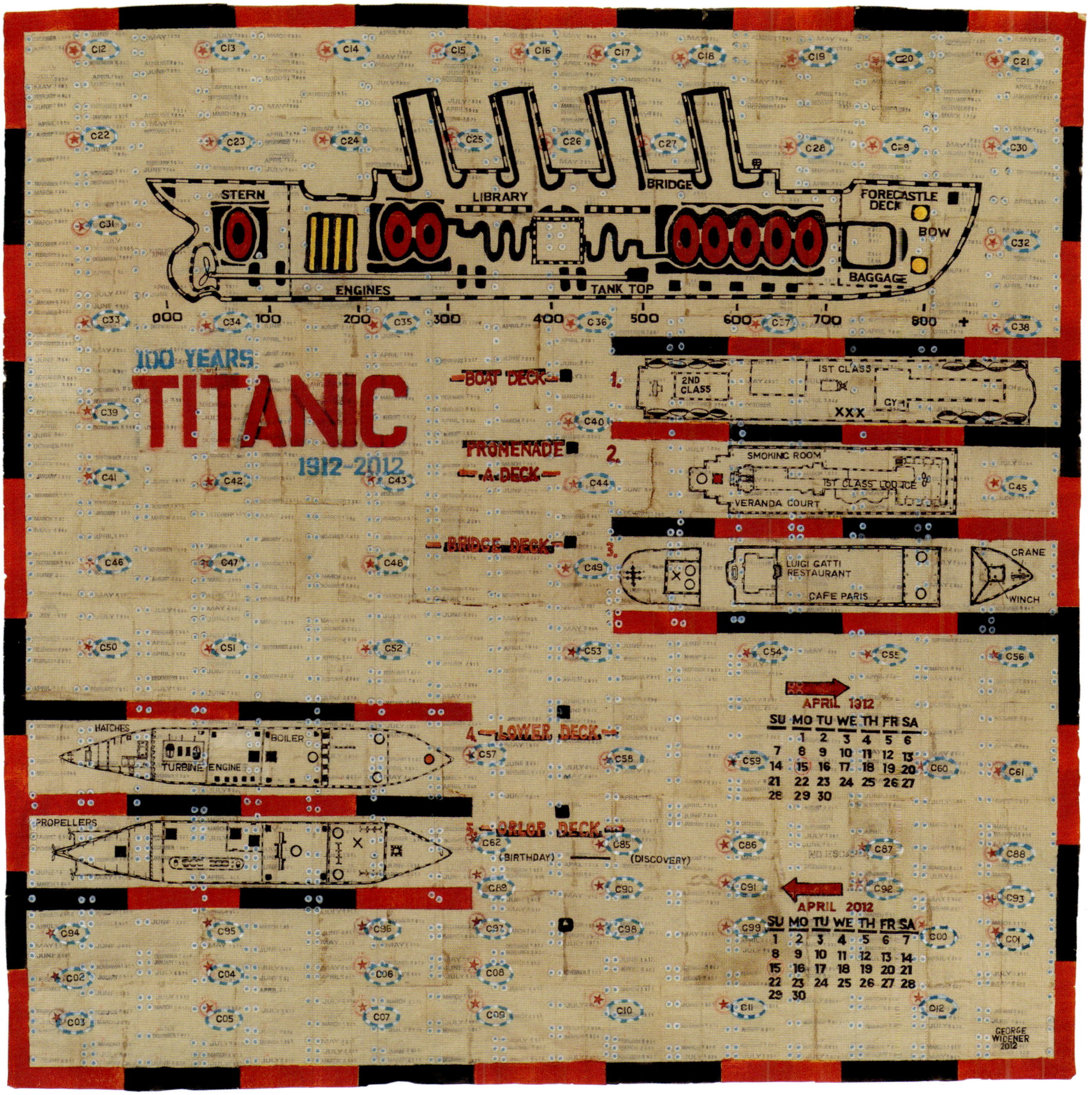

George Widener, 100 Years Titanic, GW/P 01, *2012, mixed media on paper, 58¹¹⁄₁₆ × 59¹³⁄₁₆ in (149 × 152 cm). Collection of Victor F. Keen.* Widener has been interested in the Titanic since he was a teenager. This work from 2012 references the 100th anniversary of the Titanic disaster and diagrammatically presents the levels of the ship among more cryptic information.

HILMA AF KLINT

(1862–1944 Stockholm, Sweden)

During a seance on January 1, 1906, a spirit named Amaliel summoned Hilma af Klint to undertake an extensive creative commission, which became her most significant body of work. By its completion in 1915, *Paintings for the Temple* was conceived in several series and comprised of 193 individual paintings. Af Klint's first abstract compositions were also produced for this commission. Born in Stockholm to a prominent naval family, she attended the Royal Academy of Fine Arts, where she was trained in representational illusionism. In 1889 at the age of 27, she joined the Theosophical Society, an emerging esoteric religion, and in 1896, af Klint coformed a spiritual group called The Five (*De Fem*), which led to the relationship with powerful spirits. At nearly 70 years old, she drafted an architectural design to hold *Paintings for the Temple*. She instructed that her paintings and notebooks should not be made public until 20 years after death. Following her first posthumous inclusion in the exhibition *The Spiritual in Art: Abstract Painting 1890–1985*, Los Angeles County Museum of Art (1986), af Klint's reception has been momentous, including retrospectives with Serpentine Galleries, London (2016), and Solomon R. Guggenheim Museum, New York (2018–19).

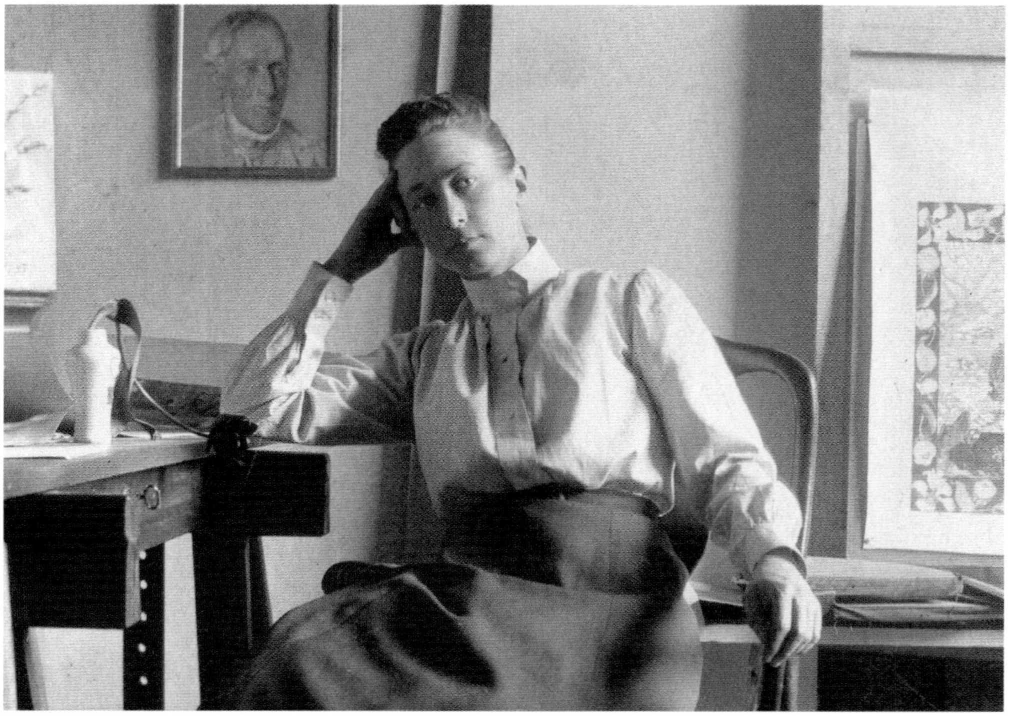

Hilma af Klint, ca. 1895, photograph. Taken in her studio at Hamngatan, Stockholm, af Klint is in her early 30s, just a few years after joining the Theosophical Society, which developed and informed her later spiritual and mediumistic artmaking.

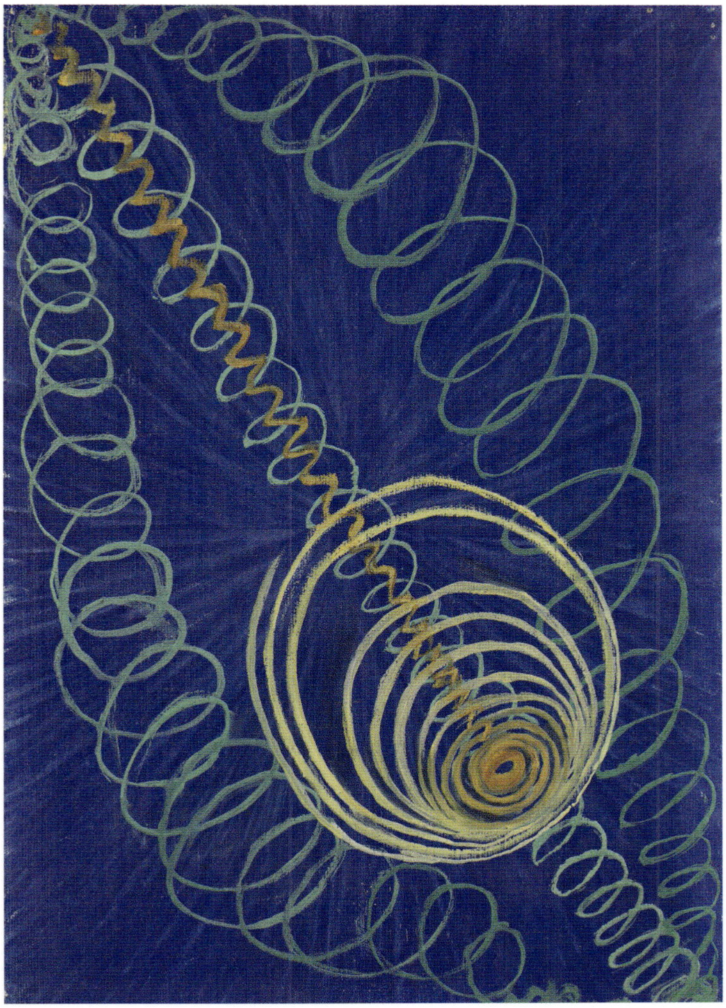

Hilma af Klint, Primordial Chaos, No. 16, Group I, *from The WU/Rose Series, 1906–1907, oil on canvas, 20⅞ × 14⅝ in (53 × 37 cm). Hulton Fine Art Collection.* From af Klint's *Primordial Chaos*, these preparatory paintings are her first abstract series. Composed primarily in yellows and blues, *Primordial Chaos* explored the birth of the world and the concepts of duality.

Hilma af Klint participated in seances as early as 1879, at the age of 17, when her initial interest in Spiritualism and the occult formed. A year later, following the death of her younger sister, af Klint's mystic interest furthered to communicating with the dead and spirits. It was through the activities of The Five (*De Fem*) that she came to be led by a group of spirits. Referred to as the High Masters (*De Höga*), the group included four spirit entities: Gregor, Clemens, Ananda, and Amaliel. The influences of the High Masters and activities with The Five aided the development of af Klint's own aesthetic and visual language.

Following Amaliel's proposal, The Five warned af Klint that accepting a commission informed by an intense extended engagement with spirits could cause personal duress. Regardless, she accepted and in 1906 began a year of preliminary work before commencing on *Paintings for the Temple*. Af Klint first completed *Primordial Chaos*—26 preparatory paintings. These were compositionally her earliest examinations of abstraction and conceptually she explored the Theosophical framework, including duality and earthly inception. *Primordial Chaos* introduced her catalog of conceptual visuals, such as the spiral and gender color assignment of masculinity (yellow) and femininity (blue).

Between 1907 and 1908, af Klint completed 111 works for *Paintings for the Temple,* including a distinct series known as *The Ten Largest.* The series, created in 60 days, is abundant with organic abstraction eluding to botanical form. Through af Klint's transcendental lens, these ten paintings journey through life from birth to old age. After taking a four-year hiatus, in 1912 af Klint re-engaged her work on the commission with a greater artistic agency, directed less by the spirits, than previously. The final three paintings are known as *Altarpieces* and are distinguishable by their geometric abstraction and implementation of metallic leaf that reinforces their significance.

From recording her automatic writing and sketches from The Five to later in life, af Klint was an avid note-taker. The temple design described for the *Paintings for the Temple*

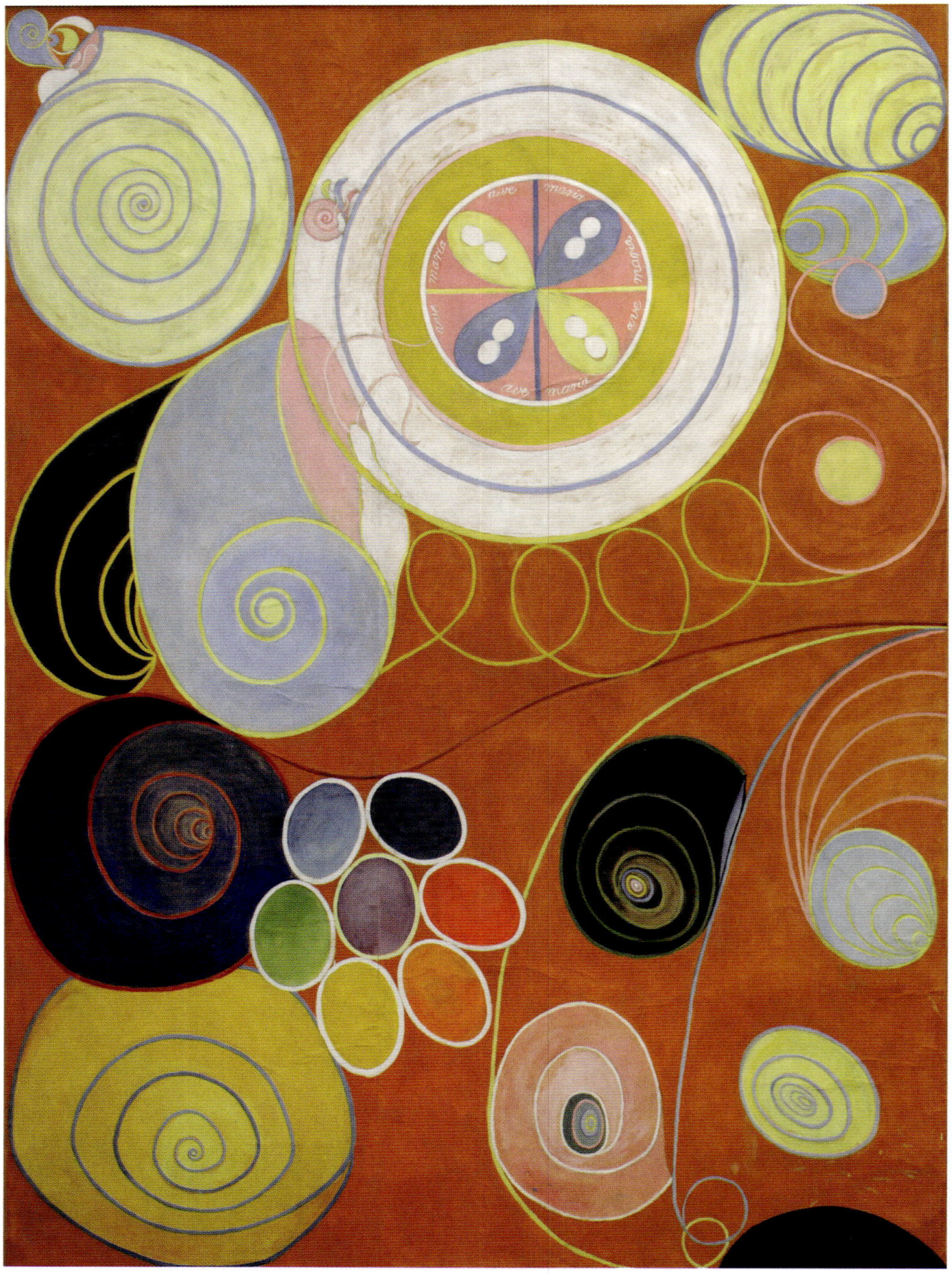

Hilma af Klint, The Ten Largest, No. 3, Group IV, Youth*, 1907, tempera on paper, mounted on canvas, 130 × 94½ in (330 × 240 cm). The Hilma af Klint Foundation, Stockholm.* This organic and botanical abstraction is part of af Klint's series from *Paintings for the Temple* titled *The Ten Largest*. This series presents the stages of life from infantry to adulthood to old age. Here, is af Klint's representation of Youth.

included details of three-levels, a spiral staircase, and a four-story tower with an altar. She also organized and edited notes of The Five to ensure its comprehension by future generations. These recordings aid in the recognition of her studies into abstraction as some of the earliest in Europe. Abandoning her academic rigor of representation, af Klint's abstract compositions were not intended to challenge the canon via an avant-garde movement, but more purely to use abstraction as an innate device to navigate existence.

"The pictures were painted directly through me, without any preliminary drawings and with great force. I supposed to depict; nevertheless, I worked swiftly and surely, without changing a single brushstroke ."
– Hilma af Klint[1]

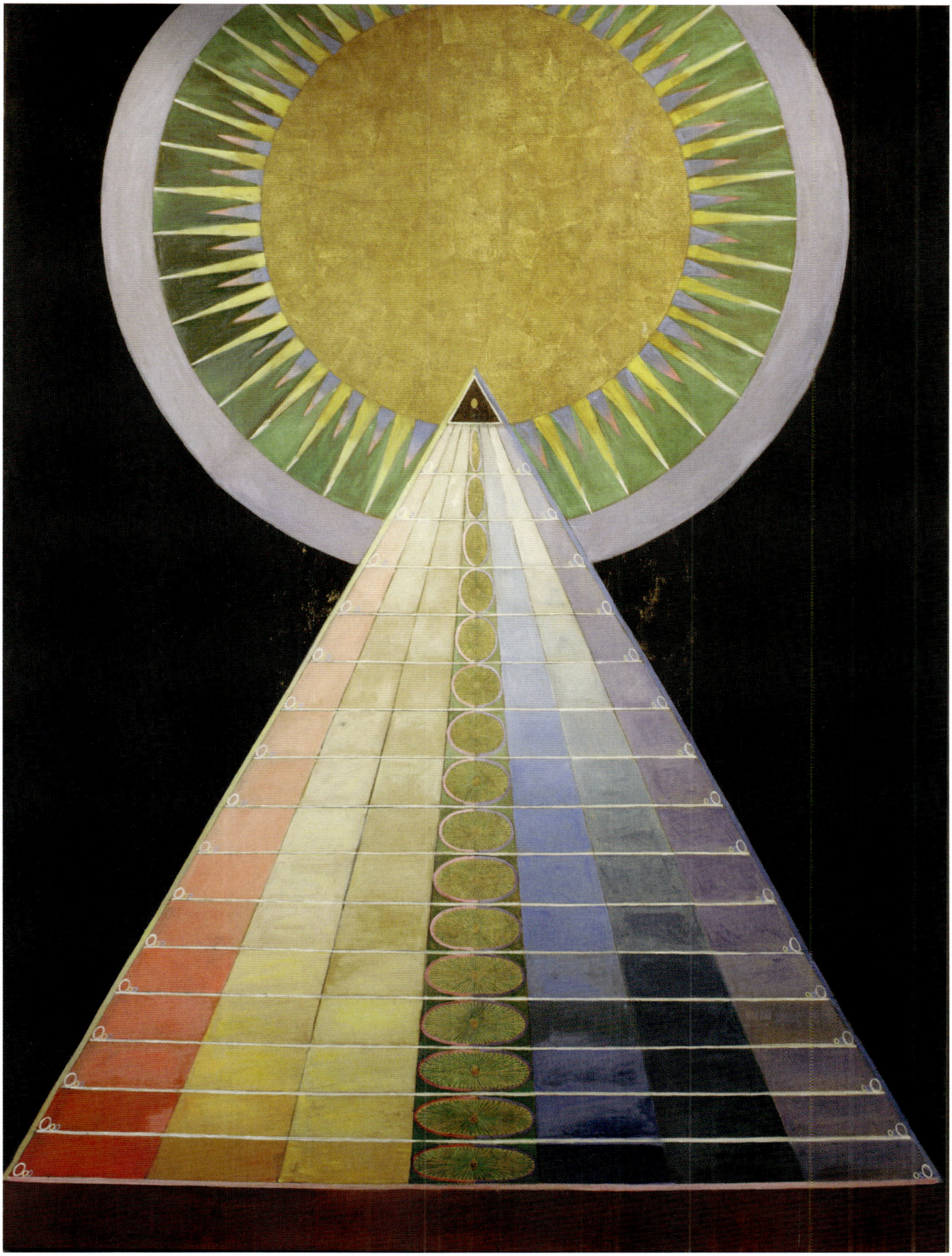

Hilma af Klint, Altarpieces, Group X, Altarpiece No. 1, *1915, oil and metal leaf on canvas, 93½ × 70¹¹⁄₁₆ in (237.5 × 179.5 cm). The Hilma af Klint Foundation, Stockholm.* The final series from *Paintings for the Temple* are three large paintings that af Klint referred to as *Altarpieces*. Theosophical theories of bilateral evolution between the physical and spiritual world seem to be explored in this geometric series.

JANET SOBEL

(1894 Ekaterinoslav, Ukraine–1968 Plainfield, New Jersey, USA)

Janet Sobel's presence in the mid-century American art scene was brief but impactful. She was written into art history by critic Clement Greenberg when he referenced her "all-over" drip paintings from 1944 as influential to Jackson Pollock. Revered by the surrealists and championed by curator Sidney Janis, Sobel's artistic identity metamorphosed from "naive" and "primitive" to recognition as a surrealist and a forerunner of abstract expressionism. Born Jennie Lechovsky in Ukraine, she emigrated to the United States following her father's death in an anti-Semitic pogrom. Married, a mother of five, and living in Brooklyn, she only began her artistic practice in her mid-50s. With her son's support, Sobel's paintings were soon recognized by New York art circles. Janis featured Sobel in her first of numerous significant exhibitions from 1943 until 1947, when Sobel relocated to New Jersey. Her oeuvre was magnetic and compelling to viewers, from her initial folk motifs to her enigmatic abstract dip paintings. Sobel's paintings are in the collections of Los Angeles County Museum of Art, The Museum of Modern Art, New York (MoMA), and The Whitney Museum of American Art, New York.

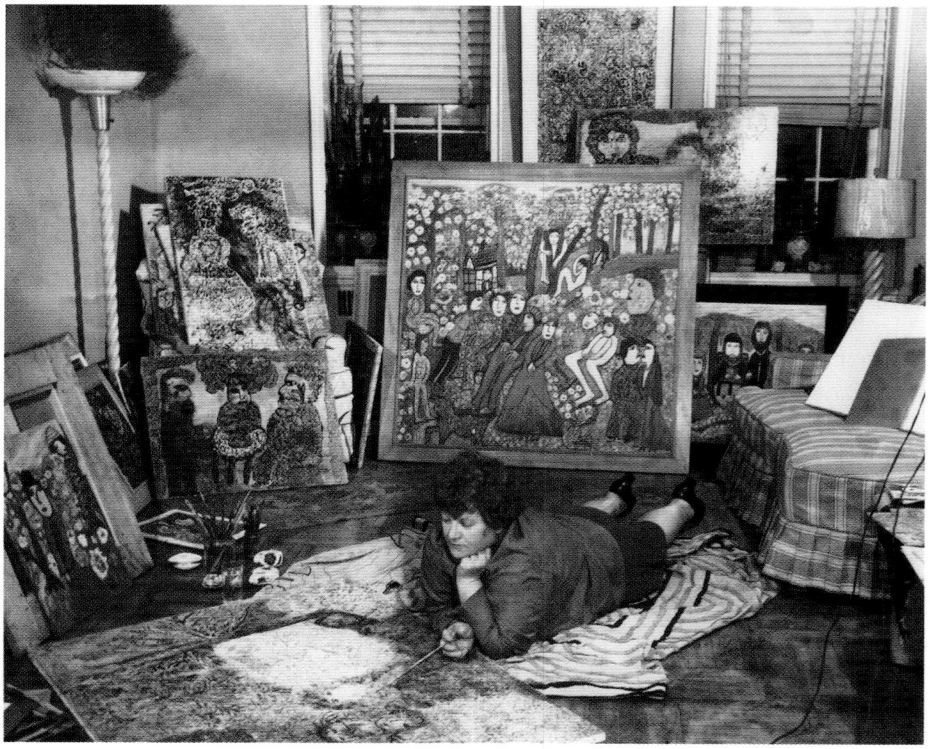

Janet Sobel, ca. 1944, photograph by Ben Schnall. Courtesy Gary Snyder Fine Art. Taken in her Brooklyn apartment, Sobel is shown here among her paintings. Featured in the background is Sobel's more figurative style, while the year this photograph was taken, 1944, was the year she was first recognized for her signature "all-over" drip aesthetic.

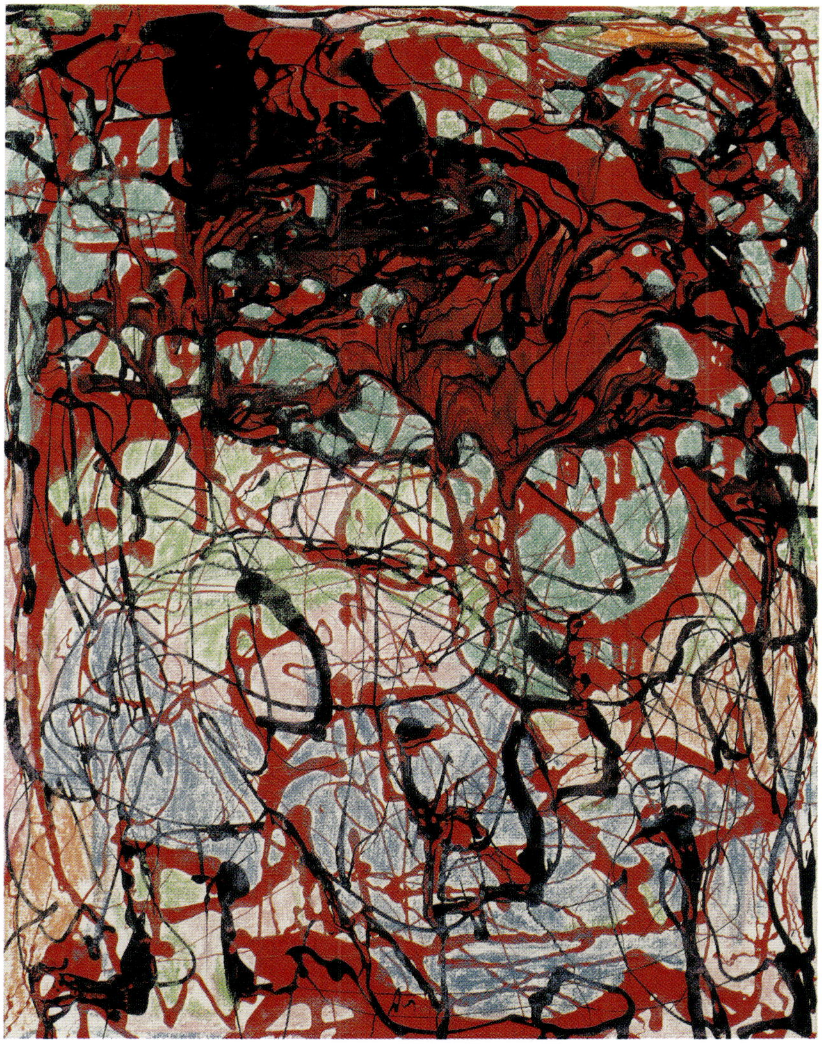

Janet Sobel, untitled, *ca. 1946–1948, oil and enamel on canvas, 18 × 14½ in (45.7 × 36.8 cm). San Diego Museum of Art.* This dynamic abstract drip painting by Sobel has an expressive application of black and red enamel on top of lighter washes of the color in hues of blues, pinks, and greens.

Likely through the support of her son, Sol, to pursue a creative practice, Janet Sobel's initial aesthetic was more akin to Ukrainian folk art, prior to the rapid development of her abstract, all-over compositions. Her husband manufactured costume jewelry, which consequently informed her drip process: she used enamel and glass pipettes—materials from his profession—to drip colors onto the surface in all-over motion. The outcome was densely covered paintings with a fluidity echoing spontaneous and improvisational mark-making. These paintings were distinguished for their abstract qualities and their kinship, in process, to surrealist automatism.

Sobel's brief but forceful career followed a unique path from primitive to surreal to abstract expressionist legacy. In 1943, Sidney Janis included Sobel in *American Primitive Painting of Four Centuries* at the Arts Club of Chicago and she received her first solo exhibition the following year at Puma Gallery, New York. In 1945, Peggy Guggenheim included

"Back in 1944, however, he [Jackson Pollock] had noticed one or two curious paintings shown at Peggy Guggenheim's by a 'primitive' painter, Janet Sobel (who was, and still is, a housewife living in Brooklyn). Pollock (and I myself) admired these pictures rather furtively: they showed schematic little drawings of faces almost lost in a dense tracery of thin black lines lying over and under a mottled field of predominantly warm and translucent color. The effect—and it was the first really 'all-over' one that I had ever seen, since Tobey's show came months later—was strangely pleasing. Later on, Pollock admitted that these pictures had made an impression on him." – Clement Greenberg, art critic[2]

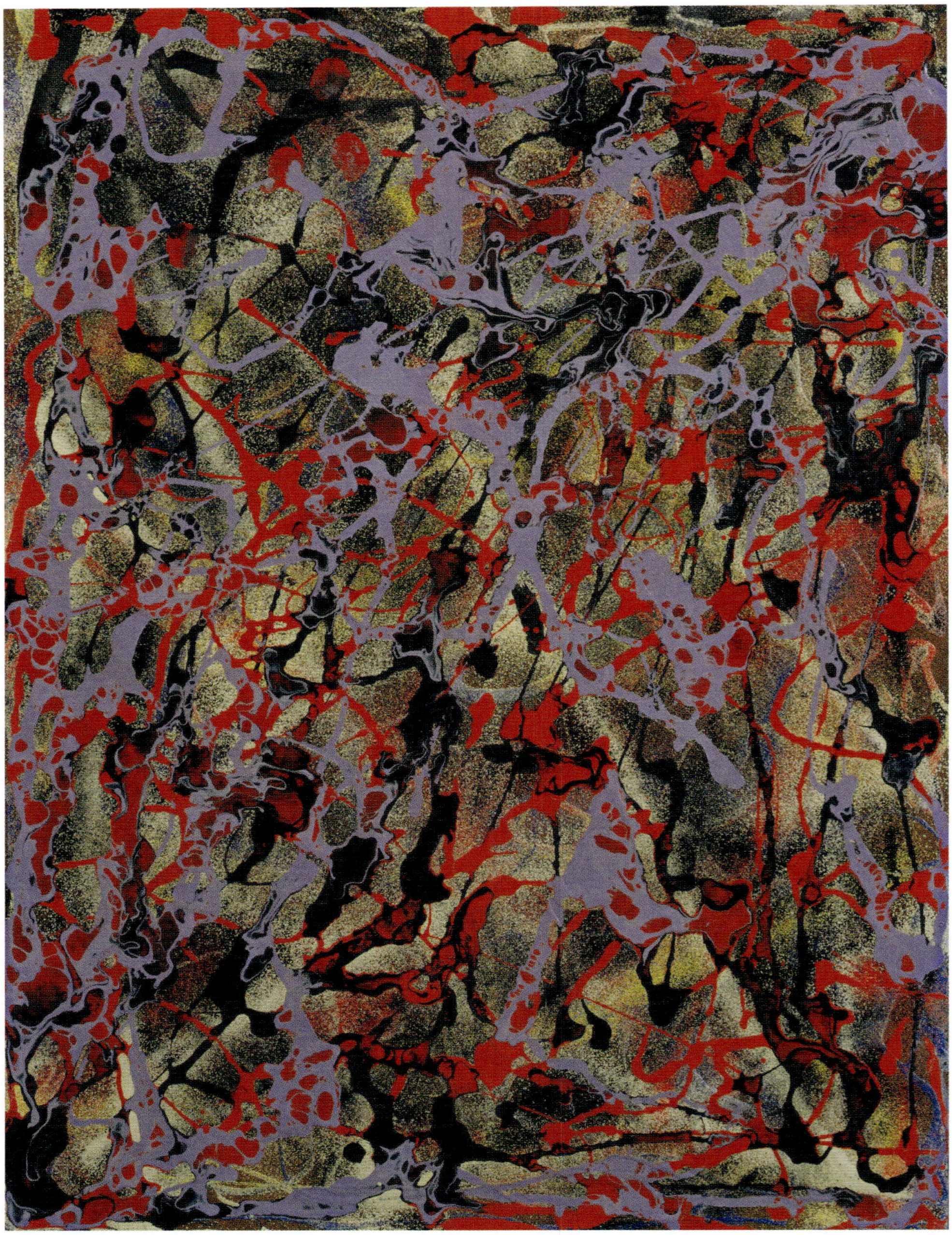

Janet Sobel, untitled, *ca. 1946, oil and enamel on composition board, 18 × 14 in (45.5 × 35.5 cm). Museum of Modern Art (MoMA), New York.* Archetypal of Sobel's drip painting, here black, purple, and red enamel are expressively applied across the board. This painting was shown in Sobel's solo exhibition at Peggy Guggenheim's gallery, The Art of This Century, New York in 1946.

her in *The Women,* alongside Louise Bourgeois and others. This was succeeded by another solo exhibition the following year, also at Guggenheim's gallery Art of This Century. In the exhibition catalog, Janis wrote: "Mrs. Sobel's work is no longer primitive . . . her paintings are filled with unconscious surrealist phantasy." Further exhibitions and notoriety flourished until 1947 when the Sobel family moved to New Jersey, distancing her from the burgeoning art scene.

It was not until 1990 that Sobel was reintroduced critically into the discussion of American modernism. Her first solo exhibition after her departure from New York only emerged posthumously in 2001 at Gary Snyder Fine Art, New York. In 2018, she was included in *Outliers and the American Vanguard Art*, National Gallery of Art, Washington, D.C., curated by Lynne Cooke. Her painting *Milky Way* (1945) was part of MoMA's collection display, "Architecture for Modern Art" from 2019 through 2021. While her potential influence on Jackson Pollock and abstract expressionism still percolate, her paintings have gained independent notoriety.

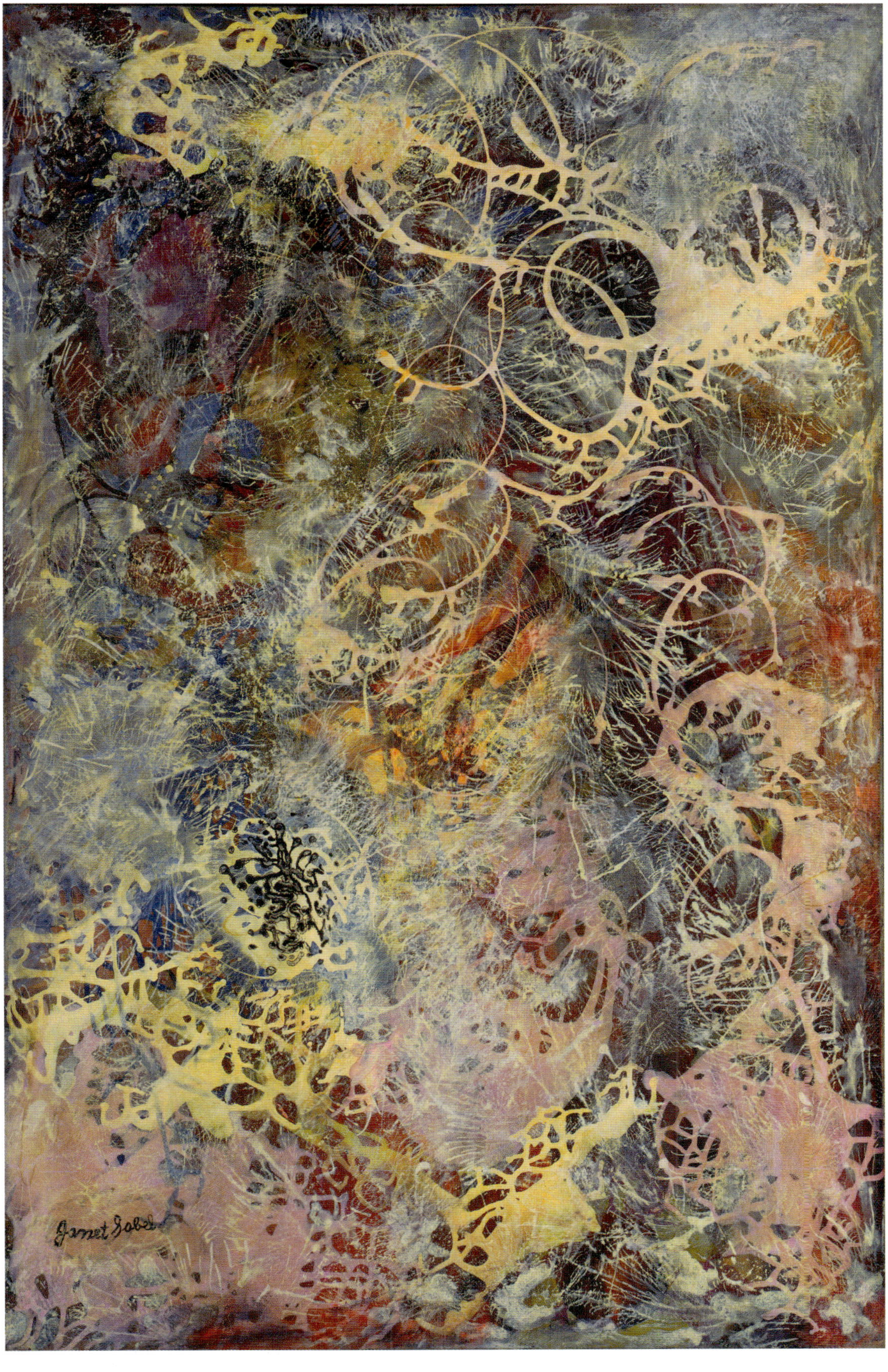

Janet Sobel, Milky Way, *1945, enamel on canvas, 44⅞ × 29⅞ in (114 × 75.9 cm). Museum of Modern Art (MoMA), New York.* One of her best-known drip paintings, this is in the permanent collection of The Museum of Modern Art (MoMA). Shortly before her death, curator William Rubin visited Sobel in New Jersey and acquired the painting for MoMA, which was exhibited at the Museum in 1970.

THORNTON DIAL

(1928, Emelle–2016, McCalla, Alabama, USA)

Following the 1981 closure of the Pullman's Standard Company Plant where he worked for nearly 30 years, Thornton Dial began sculpting furniture with his sons out of found material. His practice expanded into the making of freestanding sculptures and assemblages. In the late 1980s, Dial began painting, which he developed into an abstracted aesthetic implementing non-representational symbolism. Born in rural Alabama, Dial worked from the age of five. He remained illiterate throughout his life; however, he engaged with social and political issues through his creative production. From his perspective of an African American in the South, he examined the position of race, oppression, and poverty with overt and subversive symbolic tactics. Dial used everyday objects, including old tires, chains, roots, and scrap metal, as material and as metaphors. His position challenged the barriers between "self-taught" and "contemporary." In 1993, Dial was the subject of dual New York solo exhibitions at the New Museum of Contemporary Art and the American Folk Art Museum. His work is included in numerous significant collections, including the Metropolitan Museum of Art, New York; Philadelphia Museum of Art, Philadelphia; and Smithsonian American Art Museum, Washington, D.C.

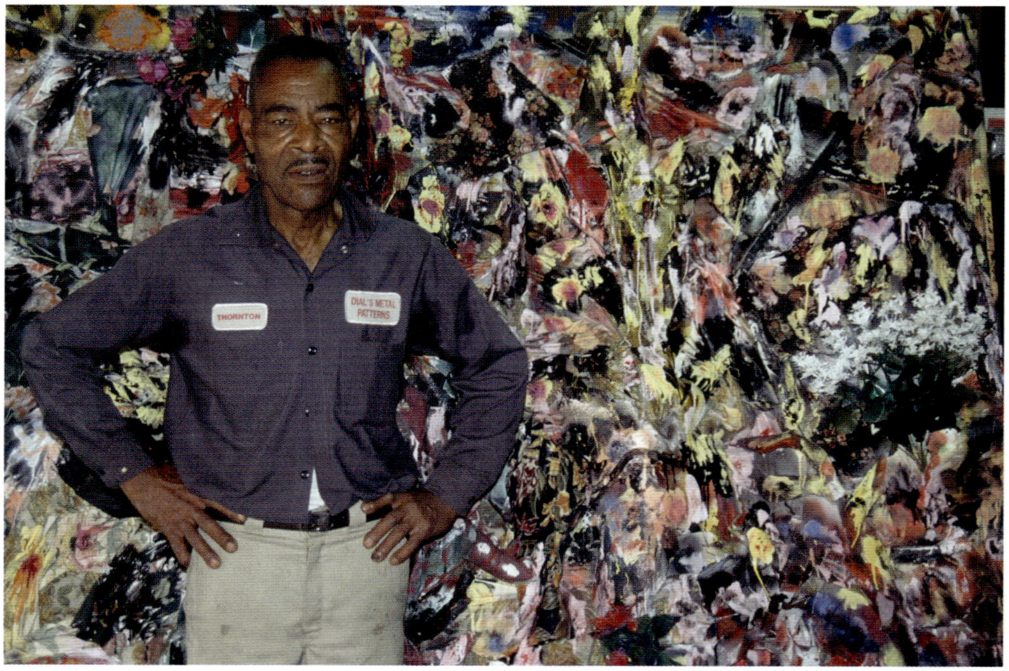

Thornton Dial, ca. 1997, photograph. Souls Grown Deep Foundation. Here, Dial poses in front of one of his painted assemblages. Among the abstract composition floral elements emerge, illustrating the poetic tension often found in his oeuvre.

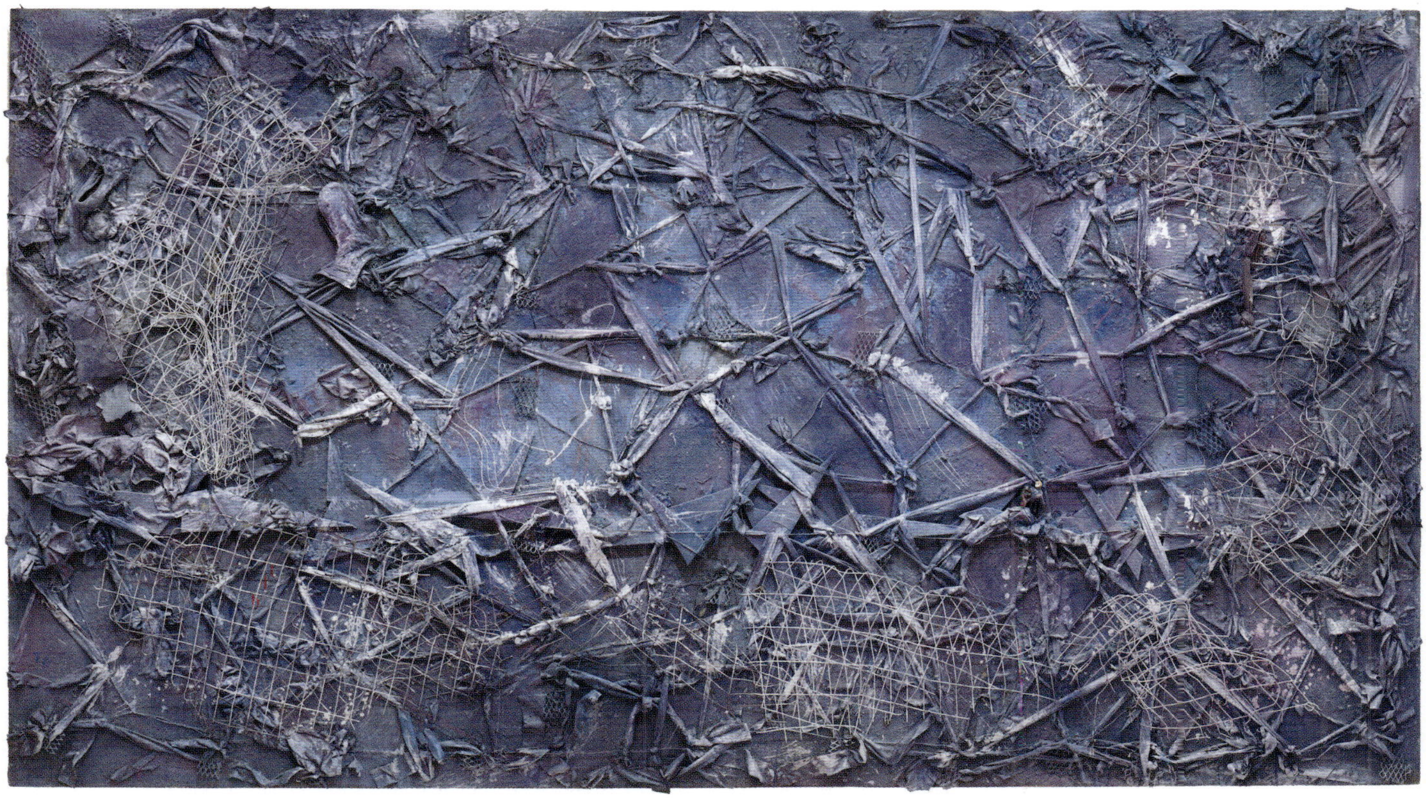

Thornton Dial, Crossing Waters, *2006–2011, wire fencing, clothing, cloth, wood, metal, corrugated tin, shoe, ceramic figurines, and paint on canvas on wood, 96 × 169 in (243.8 × 429.3 cm). High Museum of Art, Atlanta.* In this composition of fencing and found materials that are redolent of tumultuous waters, Dial confronts the legacy of the transatlantic slave trade. *Crossing Waters* evokes the Middle Passage and larger metaphors of water as deliverance in African American cultural traditions.

From furniture to sculptures, assemblages, and paintings, the scope of Thornton Dial's practice was at times functional, figurative, representational, and abstract. Consistently his nonrepresentational compositions were informed by a direct message. His commentaries reflected his immediate environment and personal experience—examining slavery, race relations, and poverty. In Dial's later works he broadened to national social and political issues, like the attacks of September 11, 2001, and the Iraq War.

Dial made objects most of his life, he just didn't categorize them as "art" until 1987, coinciding with his introduction to curator and patron Will Arnett by fellow Southern artist, Lonnie Holley. Arnett, the founder of Souls Grown Deep, emerged as a key supporter of his art practice. In the 1970s, while still employed by the Pullman Plant in Bessemer, Alabama, Dial was constructing animals and figures from scrap metal and found materials. Undoubtedly, his exposure to materials through Pullman and his myriad of prior trades (welder, carpenter, painter) informed the diversification of his artistic production.

Heterogeneity is also found in Dial's allegories and symbolism. Discoverable throughout his oeuvre is his implementation of materials serving as metaphors and quiet commentary devices. Roots, in particular, have served as an important and flexible symbolic mechanism for Dial. Their emblematic responsibilities included representing nostalgia for his childhood; notions of heritage and tradition fostering the future; and more ominously, referencing an "unburied" past. Dial's multilayer narratives balanced representation and abstraction woven with symbolism. His use of repurposed and nontraditional materials bore a history of intimate and universal meaning that addressed America, articulated through his lens.

"When I start making something, I gather up the pieces I want to work with. I only want materials that have been used by people, the works of the United States, that have did people some good but once they got the service out of them they throwed them away." – Thornton Dial[3]

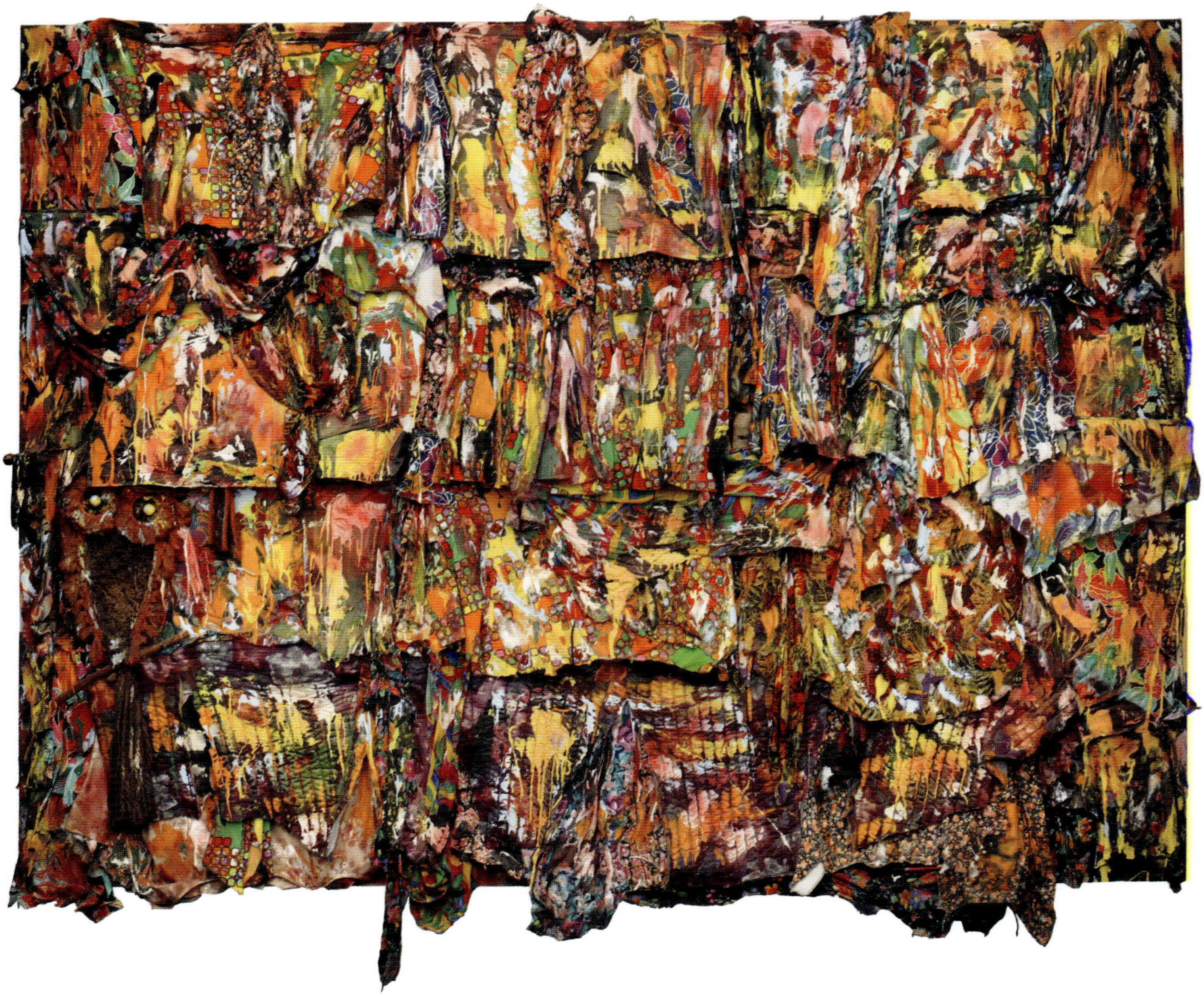

Thornton Dial, Birmingham News*, 1997, wood, rope, fabric, rope carpet, enamel, spray paint, and Splash Zone compound on canvas on wood, 83 × 100 × 7 in (210.8 × 254 × 17.8 cm). High Museum of Art, Atlanta.* Dial made this work shortly after discovering the quilts of his deceased great aunt. Titled after his local newspaper, this abstract assemblage explores the dichotomy between the representation and the reality of African American culture.

"Dial's life is inseparable from history because he made it his business as an artist to be a historian. Dial lived history, then he represented it." – John Beardsley, art historian and curator[4]

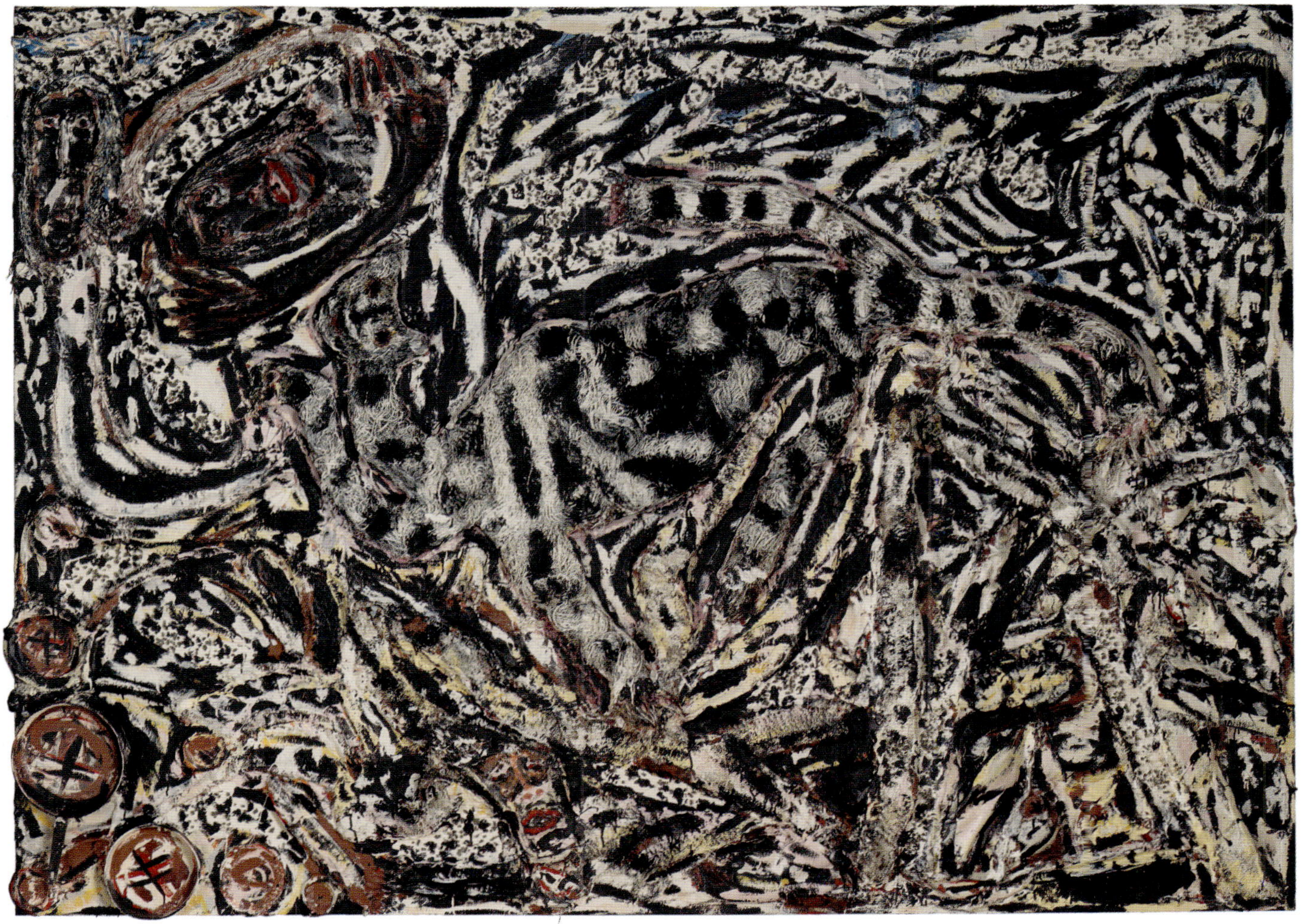

Thornton Dial, The Last Day of Martin Luther King, *1992, wood, carpet, rope carpet, wire screen, metal pans, broken glass, broom, mop cords, cloth, string, enamel, and Splash Zone compound on canvas on wood, 80 × 113½ × 4½ in (203.2 × 288.3 × 11.4 cm). Philadelphia Museum of Art.* In this semi-abstracted composition, the form of a tiger emerges. For Dial, his various representational use of the tiger is iconic. Comprised of twisted mop cords, here the tiger is emblematic of the great civil rights activist, Dr. Martin Luther King, Jr.

NNENA KALU

(b. 1966, Glasgow, Scotland)

The extraordinary practice of Nnena Kalu consists of monumental installations and her drawn series known as *Vortex* drawings. Her sculptural installations are temporal and constructed durationally, which, when observed, also have a performative quality. Both aspects of her work are rhythmic and undulate with magnetism. The *Vortex* drawings demonstrate the repetitive drive behind her process with densely and ferociously drawn circular motifs, while in her sculptural work, repetition is prevalent in the action of wrapping existing sculptural forms or the architecture itself. Kalu, who has a complex learning disability (she is autistic and has limited verbal communication), has been developing her art practice with ActionSpace, London since 1999. Launched in the 1960s and established as an independent charity in 1984 to support artists with learning disabilities, ActionSpace creates innovative opportunities to engage with visual arts. An integral part of the development of her practice is her long-term working relationship with artist facilitator Charlotte Hollinshead. Her oeuvre is abstract but communicative, without narrative or representation. Kalu has been the subject of several significant solo presentations, including her exhibition with *Project Ability* for Glasgow International (2018) and her *elsewhere* commission with Studio Voltaire, London (2020).

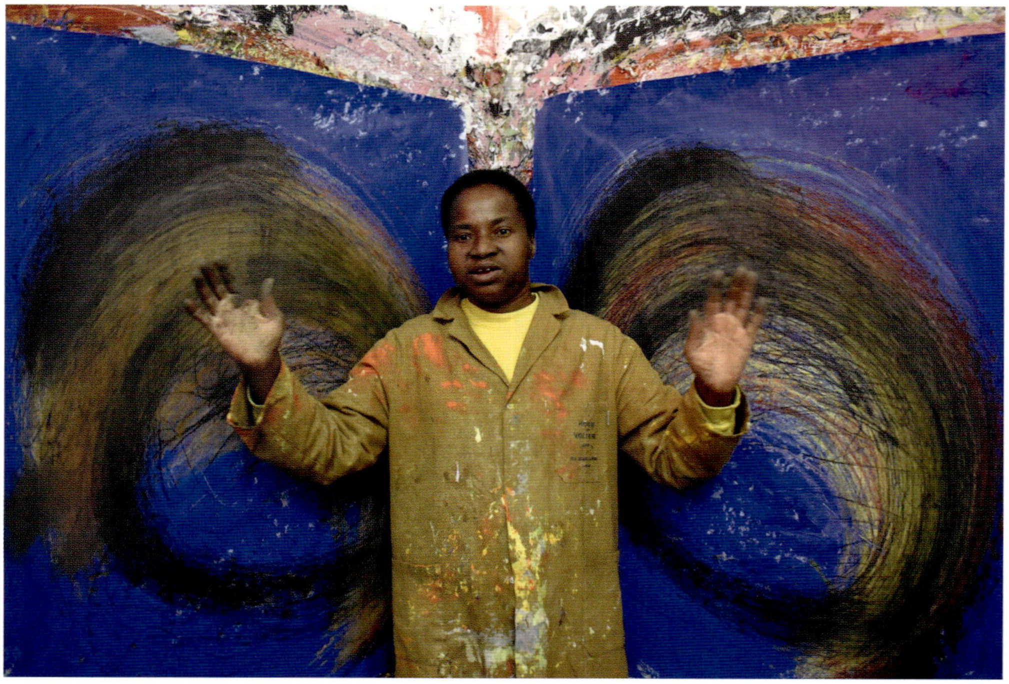

Nnena Kalu, 2019, photograph. Courtesy the artist and ActionSpace. This portrait of Nnena Kalu at her ActionSpace studio in London shows two of her *Vortex* drawings in progress.

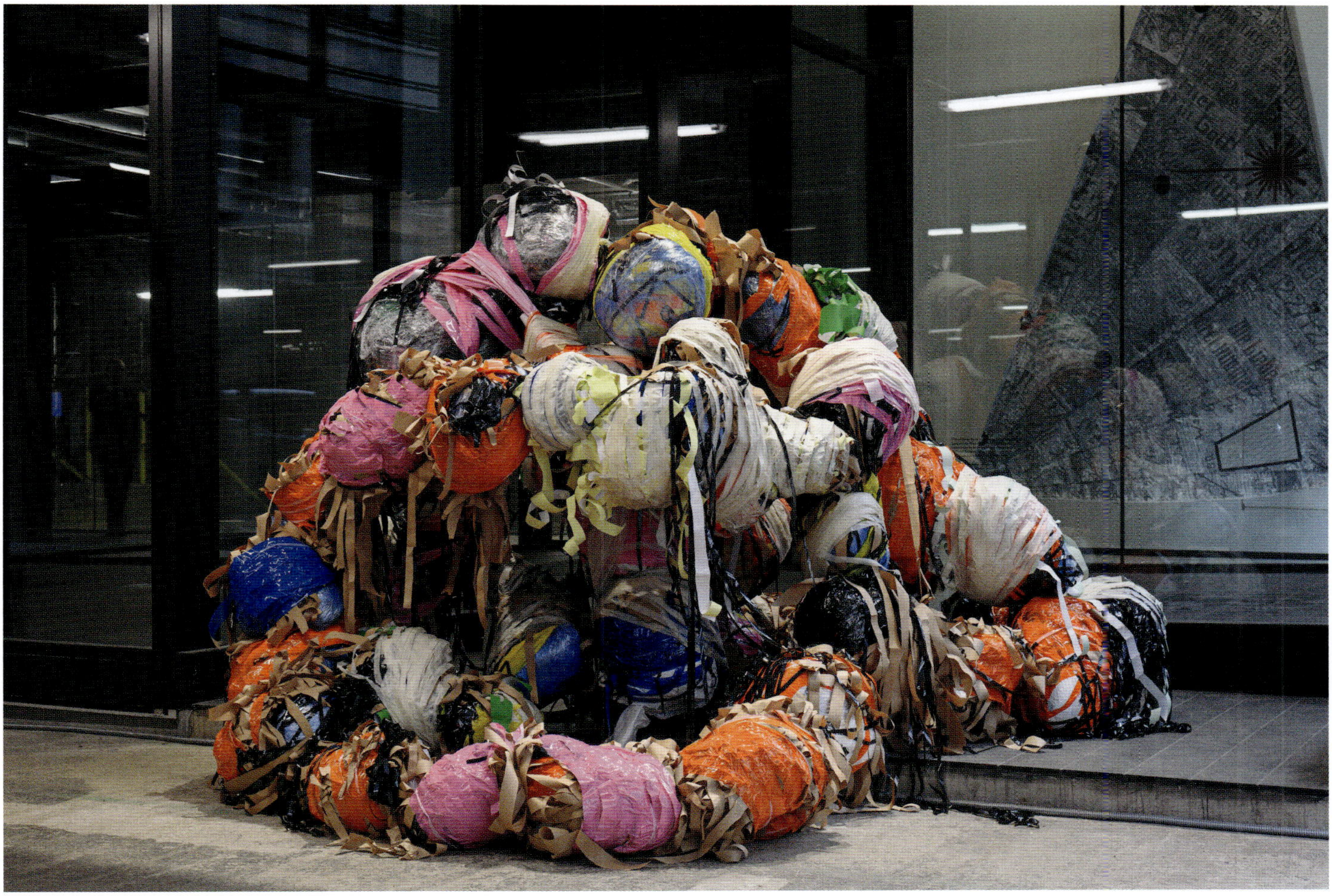

Nnena Kalu, installation view of Nnena Kalu: elsewhere*, a commission by Studio Voltaire, London in partnership with ActionSpace, 2020, mixed media including tape, VHS tape and plastic. Courtesy of the artist and Studio Voltaire.* This sculpture demonstrates Kalu's process of building sculptures from existing and reused small boulder-like sculptures that were made in her studio. Here, they give this looping sculpture a silhouette evocative of a beaded or pearl necklace.

In 2010, as part of an ActionSpace project for London's Wandsworth Arts Fringe, Nnena Kalu first began developing the live or durational aspect of her creative practice. She is continually able to evolve, refine, and reinvent various methods to her performative build, and often the initial building blocks are smaller cocoon-like forms made in the studio and repurposed over multiple sculptural iterations. Pillars and armatures are also integral, pending on the existing or specially constructed architecture.

The concept of repurposing is important to Kalu's process. The materials used to build up her installations are often found and donated materials. These supplies include old VHS tapes, yarn, string, cardboard, and various adhesive tapes and her engagement with materials is physical and textural, rather than visual. A particular favorite of Kalu's is the metallic black tape from video cassettes; its desired copious length is implemented in multiple installations. On-site Kalu is dedicated and steadfastly moving with purpose to select, wrap, and repeat, allowing the elected material to leave a performative trace.

In her *Vortex* drawings, her performative rhythm is documented by the trace circular layers of pen, pencil, and ink. In one aspect, her drawings are visually abstract, in another, they evoke the body and movement through the scale of spherical marks relating to Kalu's arm length. Working on two drawings affixed in her corner studio space, repetitive strokes and an intimate routine of mark-making is observed. Kalu's oeuvre presents physical and instinctual repetitive motions that are at once elaborate but simple, expressive but restrained.

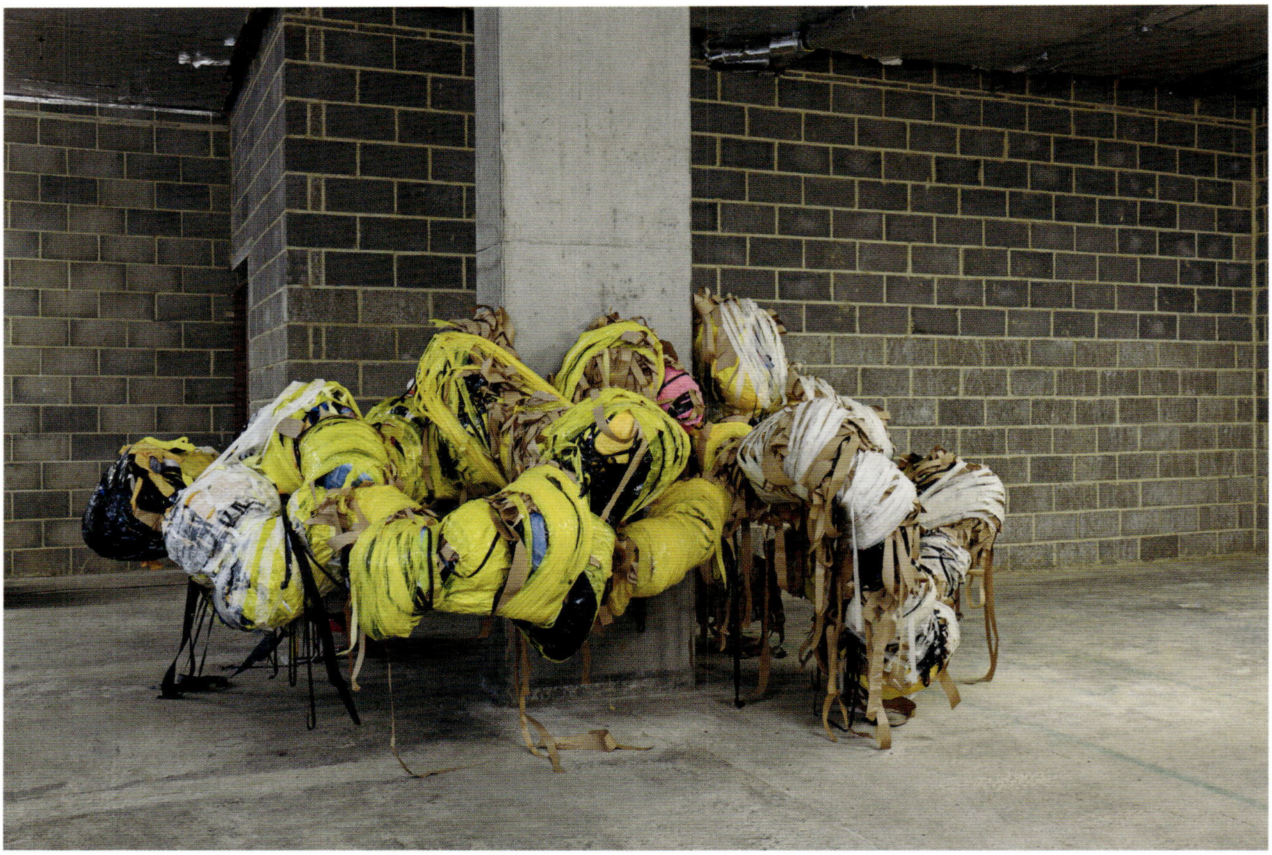

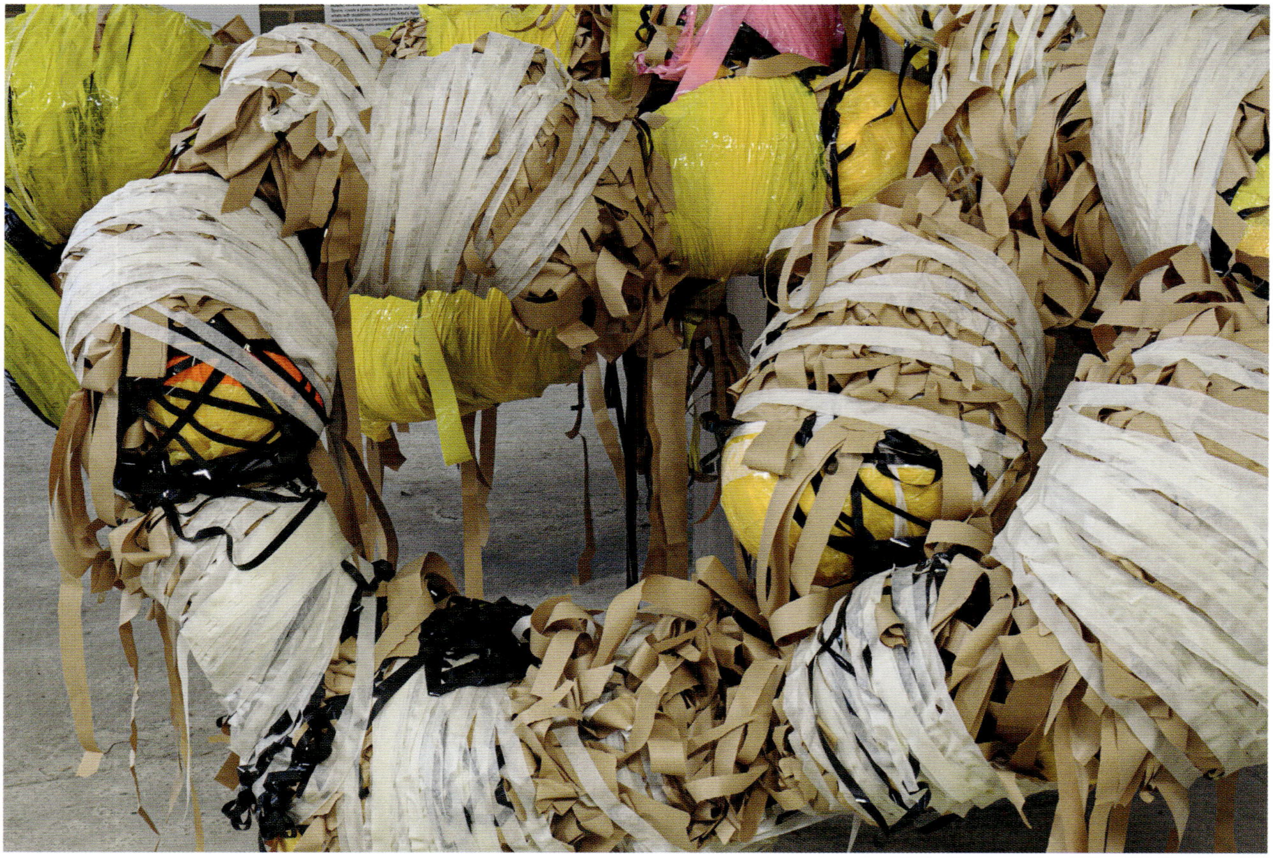

Nnena Kalu, installation view (and detail) of Nnena Kalu: elsewhere, *a commission by Studio Voltaire, London in partnership with ActionSpace, 2020, mixed media including tape, VHS tape, and plastic. Courtesy of the artist and Studio Voltaire.* This exhibition view from *elsewhere* shows one of Kalu's sculptures where a wooden substrate was provided for her to wrap and expand upon with a variety of materials, including plastic wrap, packing tape, and tape from inside a VHS cassette.

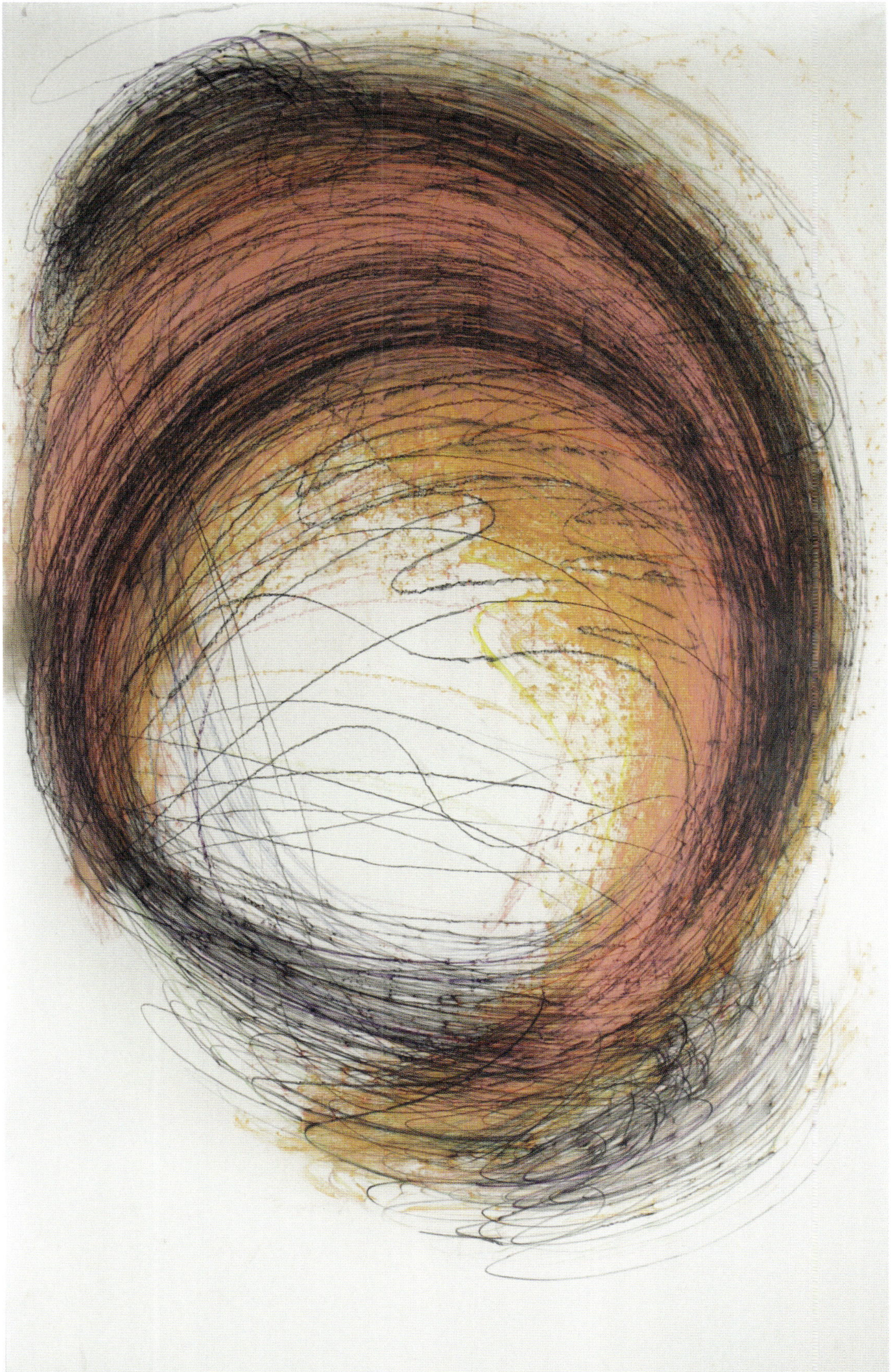

Nnena Kalu, untitled (Vortex drawing), *2018/19, pencil, pastel, marker on paper, 63¾ × 39¾ in (162 × 101 cm). Courtesy the artist and ActionSpace.* The layers of color and material in this *Vortex* drawing create a rhythmic poeticism. Kalu's compositional process for each *Vortex* drawing follows the same structure. She begins with a back-and-forth motion from the top left into the overall circle and finally markings on the bottom right.

JUNKO YAMAMOTO

(b. 1973, Hyogo Prefecture, Japan)

In the late 1990s, Junko Yamamoto's art practice materialized spontaneously after she unexpectedly acquainted herself with the material, felt. While this was not her first introduction to textiles (her mother was a seamstress), something about the tactile quality of felt inspired Yamamoto creatively. Observations of her mother's trade also seem prominent in the development of Yamamoto's process within her actions of folding and stitching felt, then positioning it as a considered conceptual arrangement. Oscillating between abstraction and potential representation, her colorful arrangements are a response to her surroundings. An autistic artist and limited verbally, Yamamoto's recollections of everyday objects—kitchen utensils, foods, and domestic objects—become communicative and documentation of her experience. Yamamoto was part of *The Museum of Everything #6* at the Kunsthal Rotterdam (2016) and she has exhibited in Paris and New York through projects with Tokyo gallery Yukiko Koide Presents.

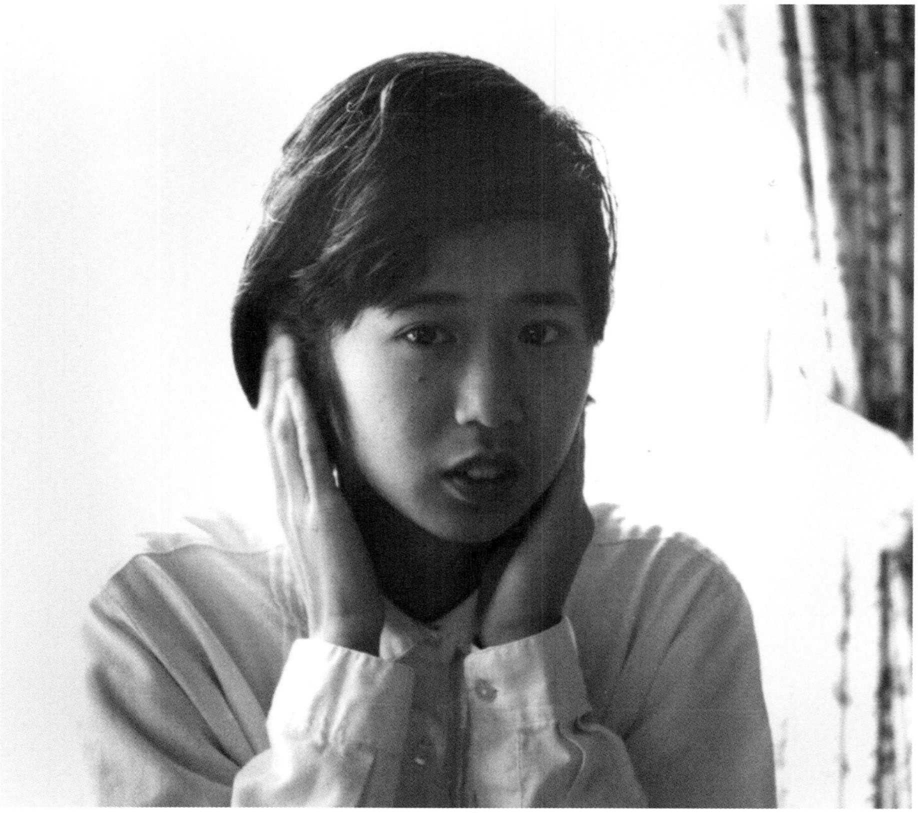

Junko Yamamoto, ca. 1994, photograph. Courtesy Yukiko Koide Presents, Tokyo. An intimate and candid portrait of the artist, Yamamoto's felt compositions are colorful and exuberant.

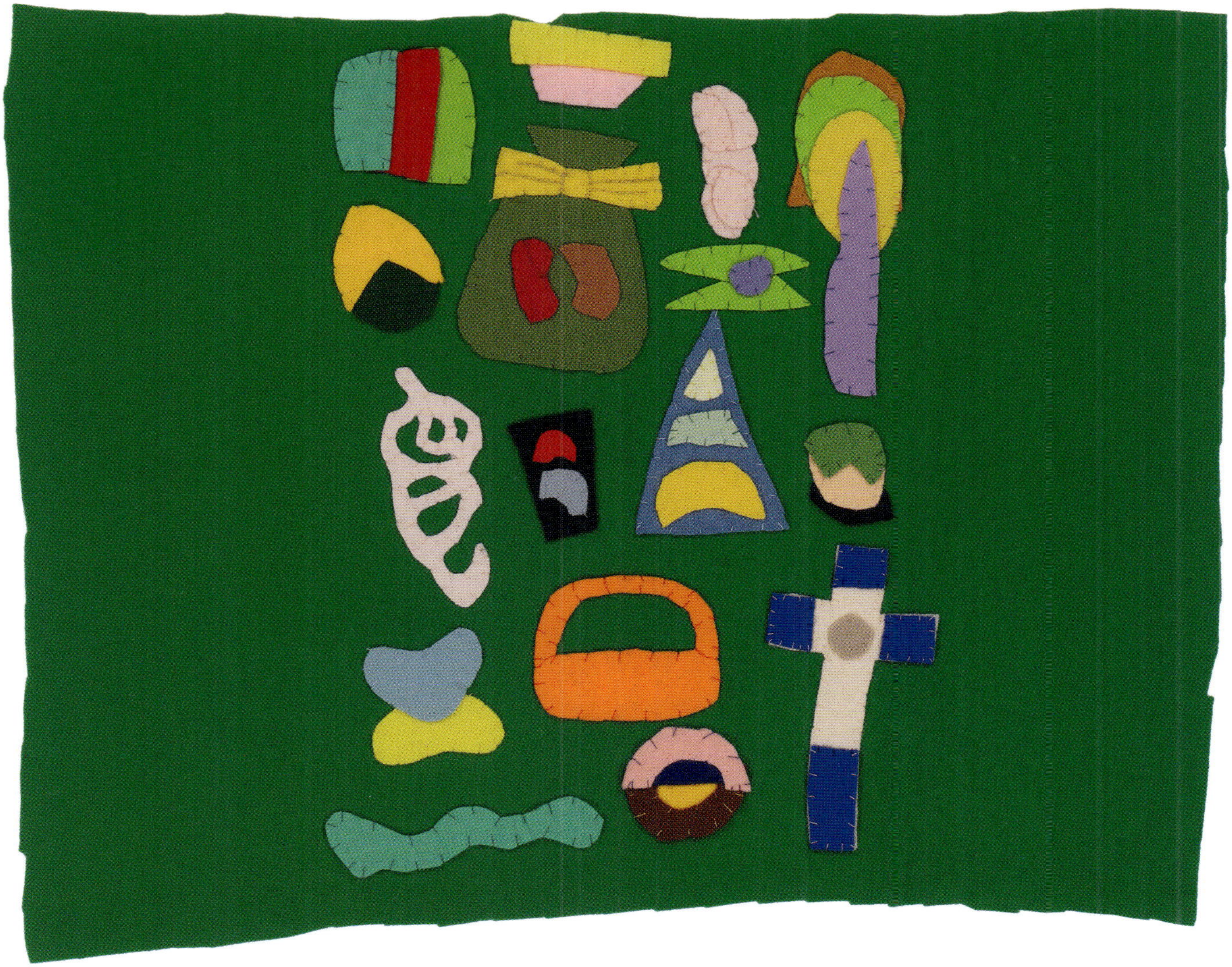

Junko Yamamoto, untitled (unknown objects)*, ca. late 1990s, felt appliqué, 16 9⁄16 × 20 7⁄8 in (42 × 53 cm). Private collection.* This embroidered felt composition by Yamamoto combines layers of felt to create more complex multicolored icons positioned in dialogue with one another. Among the abstract shapes, recognizable objects such as a bow tie and a cross are revealed.

Junko Yamamoto works without hesitation, selecting her palette for each aesthetic arrangement from an array of colors. Her chosen hues sometimes evoke nature with organic tones of browns and greens, while at other times fluorescent pinks and radiant yellows summon a synthetic impression. Regardless of a bright or subdued palette, the tactile texture is consistent because of Yamamoto's invariable use of material. Her introduction to this textile happened when a felt manufacturer, who was also a friend of the family, sent her a large quantity of surplus felt. Without an explanation of the fabric or instructions on how to use scissors, Yamamoto began to cut, sew, and position felt in a completely idiosyncratic method.

Felt is a unique textile because it is produced not by weaving or knitting, but by condensing and constraining fibers together. It is not constructed of interconnected loops or crisscrosses, therefore, its bound quality for cutting and morphing, as Yamamoto does, is ideal. Her process of stitching the felt adds both formal qualities through demarcation of lines like drawing and tactile layers through securing folds in the fabric.

Invariably, the visual objects that surround Yamamoto serve as her departure point, as well as references to art books and magazines, which allow her to share her experience through her felt language. The transformative reduction from what she sees into shapes that she cuts, folds, stitches, and arranges, places her oeuvre in dialogue with abstraction: shifting the prosaic into essential elements. There also seems to be a reference to memory; perhaps Yamamoto's traces are her visual recollections transposed into silhouettes and isolated colors. The outcome is selectively distinguishable to its references, while at other times her transformation through abstraction becomes purely exploratory.

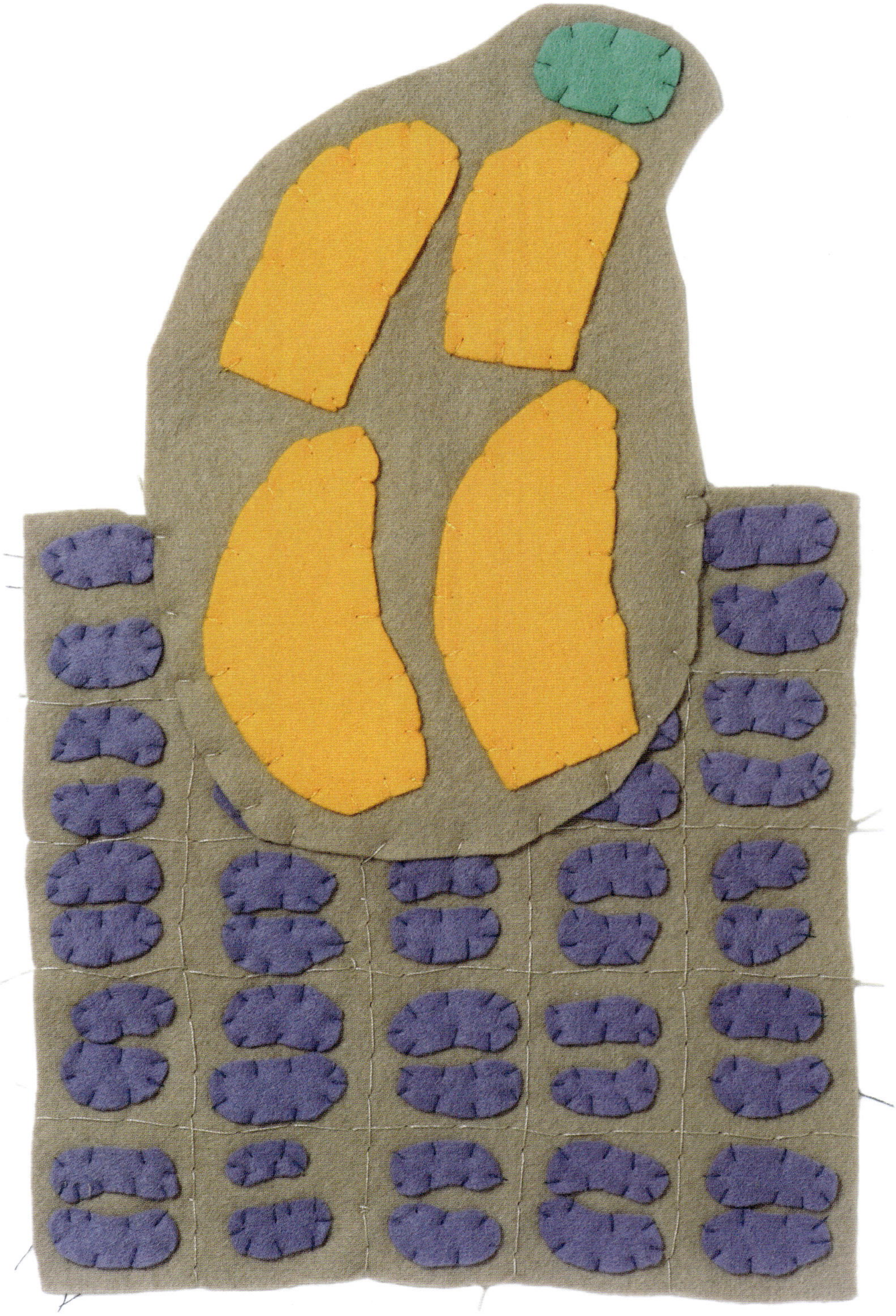

Junko Yamamoto, untitled (Banana and Bean), *ca. late 1990s, felt appliqué, 10 13⁄16 × 7 in (27.5 × 17.8 cm). Courtesy Yukiko Koide Presents, Tokyo.* In this composition, Yamamoto worked within an organic color palette, while her interpretation of a banana takes on fractal characteristics formed through four parts.

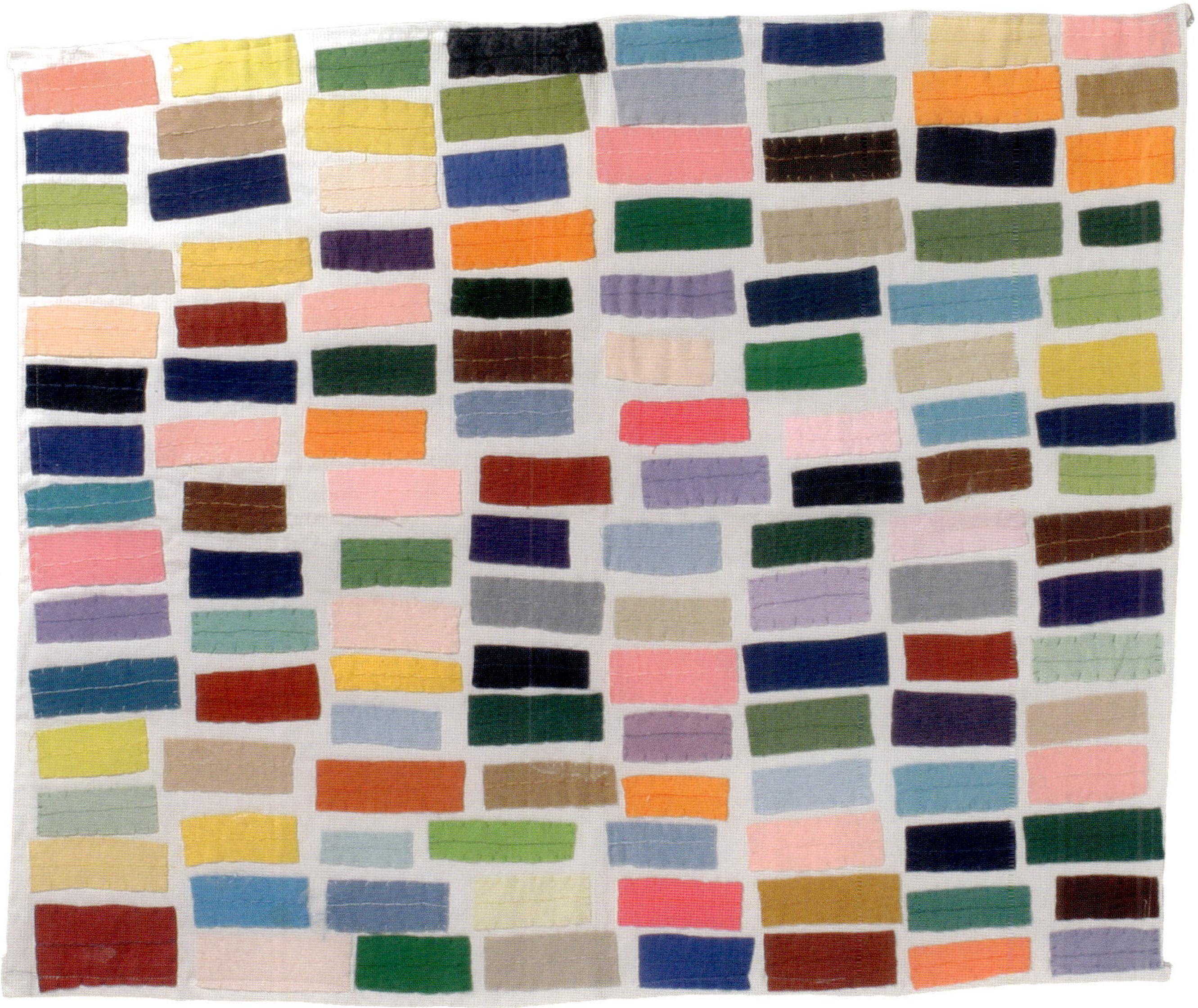

Junko Yamamoto, untitled (Lunchbox), *ca. late 1990s, felt appliqué on cotton,* $25\frac{9}{16} \times 31\frac{1}{8}$ *in (65 × 79 cm). Private collection.* Here, a colorful selection of felt rectangles is positioned in a brick-like pattern. Each rectangle is meticulously applied by Yamamoto with horizontal stitching down the centerline and radially around the border.

CHAPTER 10

LANDSCAPES: DOCUMENTING THE REAL AND THE IMAGINED

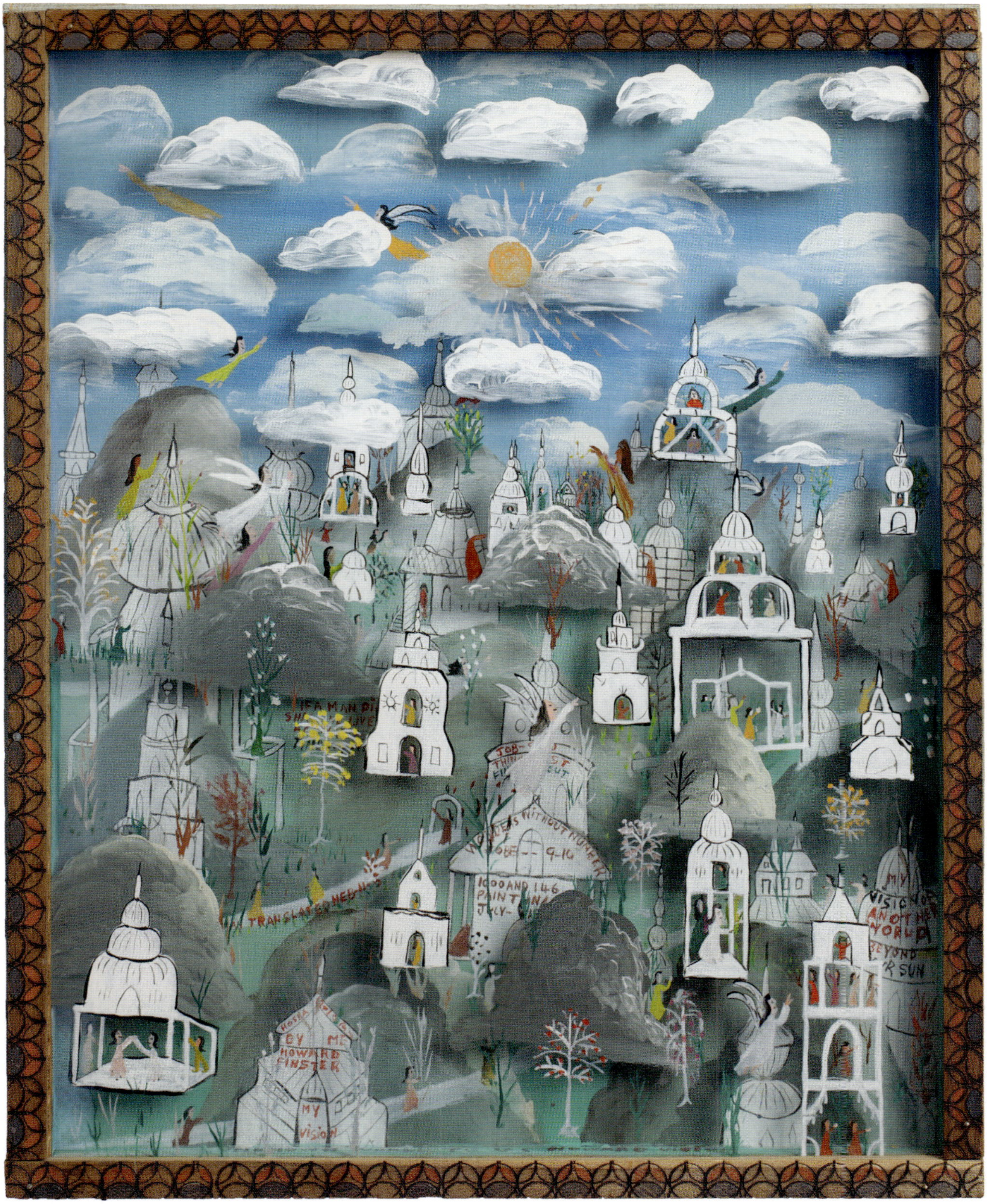

Howard Finster (American, 1916–2000), My Vision of Another World #1,146, *1978, shadowbox construction of plywood and glass, both painted inside and out; artist-made frame of Douglas fir, carved and branded with artist-made metal stamps, 22¾ × 18¾ × 2½ in (57.8 × 47.6 × 6.4 cm) (framed). Philadelphia Museum of Art.* Finster was an artist and minister whose prolific practice produced nearly 50,000 artworks including his extraordinary built environment, *Paradise Garden*. His exuberant oeuvre straddles both biblical and pop-cultural references. Numbering his work as part of his production, here, #1,146 is a visionary landscape with a three-dimensional quality created through layers of painted glass.

SEEING SCENES

Lisa Slominski

Landscapes examines the multifarious approaches and shared influences of six artists in relation to depictions of their surroundings. Whether real, remembered, or imagined, these artists' compositions transform the concept and elements of traditional landscape from background to foreground. This chapter introduction proposes the potential connection between environment, memory, and landscape through three divergent mid-century American practices: Grandma Moses (1860–1961), Martín Ramírez (1895–1963), and Minnie Evans (1892–1987). It further considers three international contemporary artists, Katsuyoshi Takenaka (b. 1987), Katsuhiro Terao (b. 1960), and Mamadou Cissé (b. 1960), whose creative processes are more reflective of the architectural and urban interjections upon landscape.

Until the 17th century, landscape in art was confined to the background of portraits and scenes dedicated to a central subject matter. From the mid-20th century, the definition of landscape has been challenged and its perimeters expanded. This conceptual and compositional repositioning into the foreground—encompassing cityscapes, botanicals, and architecture—continues to be a significant theme in many modern and contemporary practices. Representations of landscape and environment, be they traditional, surreal, or invented, are explored by the artists in this chapter.

The compelling relationship between memory and environment is resonant in the oeuvres of the following mid-century producers. Their disparate American locales and idiosyncratic practices manage to present a connective thread of influence. The scenic landscapes of Anna Mary Robertson Moses, better known as Grandma Moses (see page 330), emote nostalgia and a sense of intimacy that distinguished her traditional compositions from other contemporaneous regionalist painters. Moses only began painting in her late 70s, and the profound quality in her paintings connects to Moses' lived experience and inherent memories. Simultaneous to Moses' work, and with seemingly similar influences of memory and place, are the surreal and uncanny landscapes of Martín Ramírez (see page 334). Ramírez emigrated from Mexico in 1925, but only started drawing while confined to California state psychiatric hospitals. His repetitive and ornately patterned scenes of trains and tunnels infer connection and transition. Particular drawings suggest conceptually his journey from his Mexican past to his American present.

While Moses and Ramírez seemed to fuel their landscapes with the power of memories, Minnie Evans (see page 338) referenced her immediate environment. Through her drawings and paintings, her surroundings transcended into otherworldly and spiritual spaces. Evans lived and worked on the Pembroke Park Estate in the Southern state of North Carolina, and from 1948 to 1974, she was the gatekeeper for the property's Airlie Gardens. She drew on-site at the Gardens, where the lush botanical atmosphere paired with her spirituality informed her alternative landscapes of capricious horizon lines brimming with leaves, flowers, and beings.

The concepts of memory and environment continue to inform the oeuvres of artists into the 21st century. Further, the influences of industry, architecture, and urbanism are present within the compositional genre of landscape. For the following three artists the fluidity of perspective is also evident in their practices. Japanese artist Katsuyoshi Takenaka (see page 342) implements a structural approach to his drawings, mimicking the physical building process of architecture. His complex structuring presents futuristic drawings, where the concept of perspective shifts to a notion of weightlessness. A contemporary of Takenaka is Osaka-based Katsuhiro Terao (see page 346), who visualizes his environment and memories in terms of metal structures. An aesthetic compelled by 20 years of working with his father, a welder, Terao's "plan-like" drawings introduce an elaborate perspective of considering a landscape in all directions. Perspective shifts from the all-encompassing to birds-eye in the elaborate imaginary cityscapes of Senegalese artist Mamadou Cissé (see page 322). Working as a night watchman and informed by the chaos of condensed hyper-urban cities, Cissé began drawing in France in 2001, producing highly detailed and energetic futuristic city plans during his long work shifts.

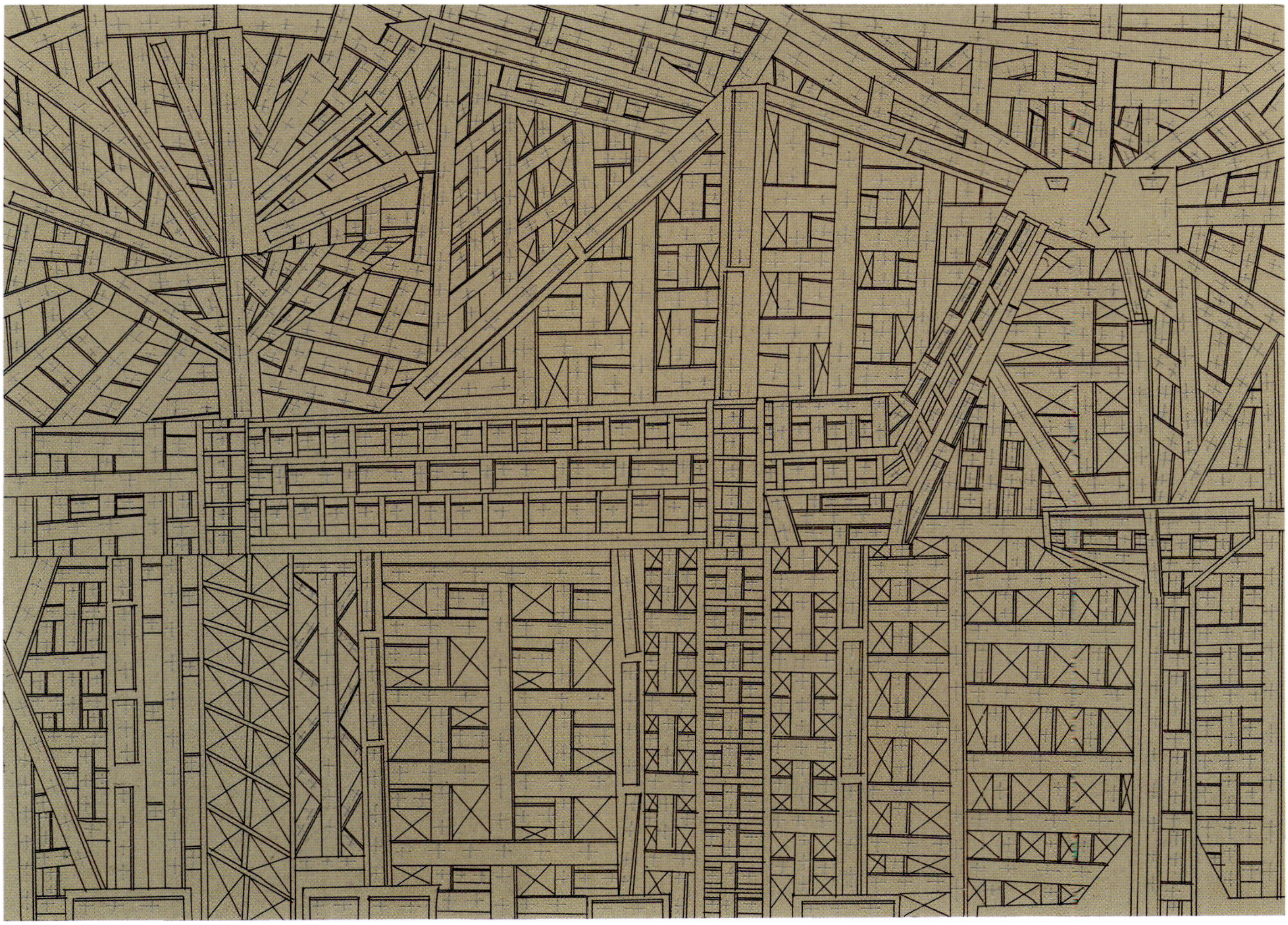

Katsuhiro Terao, Dog-shaped Robot, *2005, pen on paper board, 11⅞ × 16⅝ in (30.2 × 42.2 cm). Courtesy atelier incurve.* Terao, who visualizes the world around him as metal structures, uses the aesthetic of beams and girders to create this architectural composition. His use of multidirectional lines creates the profile of a dog looking right.

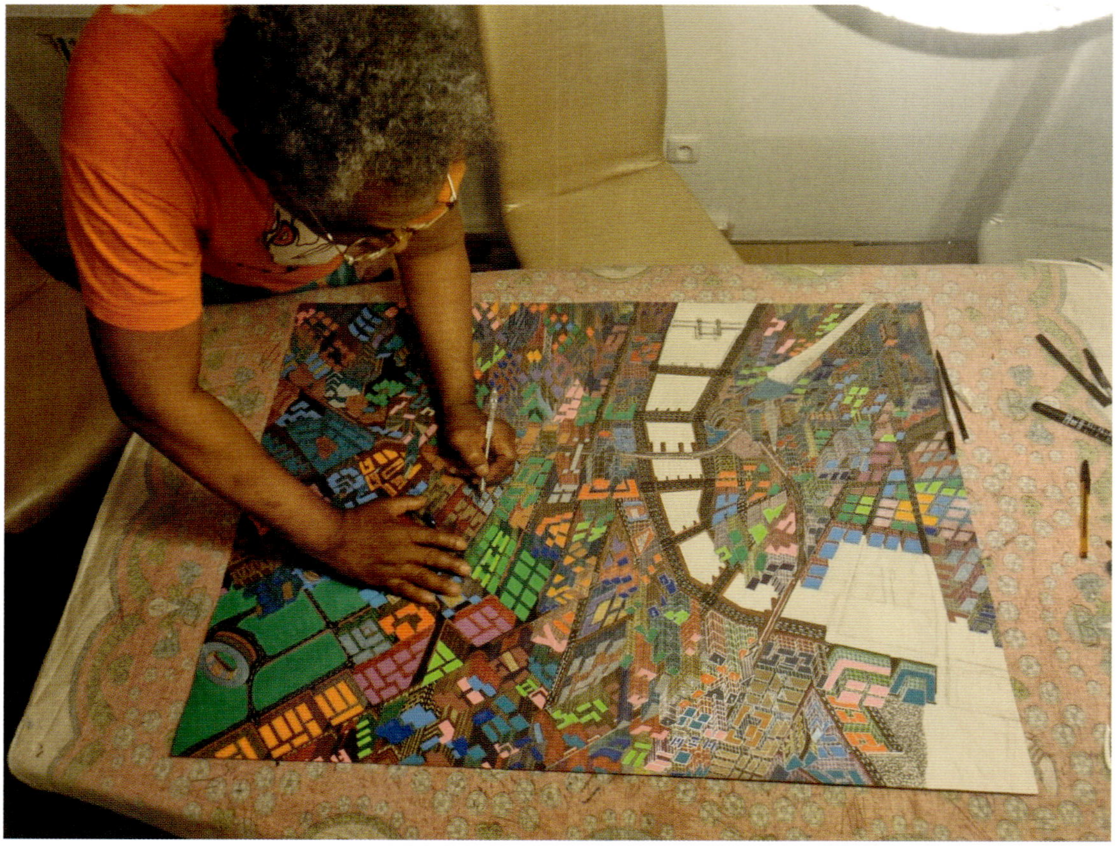

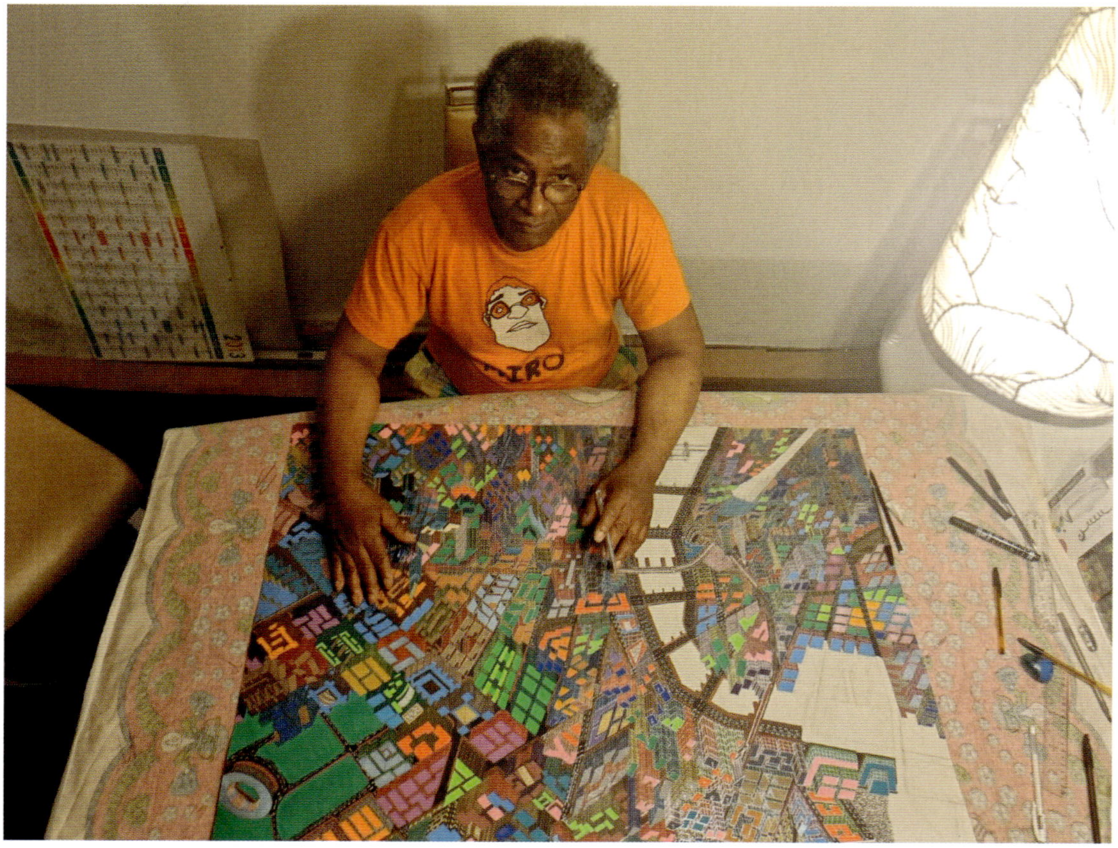

Mamadou Cissé, 2021, photograph. Courtesy Mamadou Cissé studio. These intimate portraits of Cissé show him at work developing a new futuristic city. The candid shots allow a glimpse into his working process.

MAMADOU CISSÉ

(b. 1960, Baghagha, Senegal)

The fantastical perspectives of a futuristic bird's-eye view in Mamadou Cissé's drawings overlook kaleidoscopic and complex megacities. His urban landscapes merge built structures referenced from across the globe into his own imagined utopian principles. At age 18, Cissé moved from Senegal to France, where he worked a variety of jobs in the upholstery and textile industries, followed by 20 years at a bakery. In 2001, he returned to his childhood interest in drawing as an activity to stay awake during long night shifts as a watchman. Cissé's detailed and colorful drawings are highly structured; he makes a grid in pencil first to inform perspective, then begins to explore depth and height. His vibrant colors are influenced by his African identity, while his utopian compositions are informed by his admiration for architecture. Cissé has exhibited internationally, including the 10th Dakar Contemporary Art Biennale, Senegal (2012) and *The Museum of Everything #6*, Kunsthal Rotterdam (2016). His works are in the permanent French collections of Fondation Blachère, Apt, and Fondation Cartier, Paris.

Interview by Sophia Cosmadopoulos

Sophia Cosmadopoulos: Before you moved to Paris, you grew up in Senegal, did those surroundings inspire your work?

Mamadou Cissé: Yes, I grew up in Senegal and I arrived in France at the age of 18. You know, I always practiced drawing, painting, and other mediums. I was of course inspired by the colors of my birth place, La Casamance.

What did the view from your home looking outward look like?

The view from my house is not atypical. But my house is modern, square, big, and spacious as Le Corbusier architecture.

What did those surroundings look like?

Senegal is a developing country like many other African countries.

How old were you when you started making work? What stage in your life were you at when you started drawing?

I began to draw at a very young age, at three years old [laughs]. In the beginning, I drew portraits and African villages.

What was your life like when you first moved to Paris?

When I arrived in Paris it was not for drawing. I first did a lot of odd jobs in upholstery, in the denim industry, and I worked in a bakery for 20 years. Now, I work as a security agent in Roissy Charles de Gaulle Airport and, of course, I'm also an artist. I was so lucky to meet Marcel Lubac, Director of la Maison d'art contemporain Chaillioux de Fresnes (94). Thanks to his support the artworld opened its doors to me.

Why did you move to France?

I came to France because it's the dream of all African people. I came to join some family and because the education was better here. I think I came here too because I'm an adventurer and I like to travel.

In Paris you started drawing on your job as a night watchman, can you tell me about that? Can you describe this environment?

As I always say, drawing doesn't allow me to sleep. Time becomes very long at night when we work alone in a deserted area. Before, I tried to do crosswords or read but nothing worked. Nothing apart from drawing.

Did you work from images or references?

Yes, I often begin with a postcard when I am drawing a city or outlining a monument or a symbolic building, but I also create my own imaginary and utopian cities.

How did your very first drawing come to you and what did it look like?

I became interested in cities by collecting postcards of cities of the world. I have also traveled extensively in different places throughout Europe and the United States. New York City was one of the most inspiring cities for me. My first drawing as a security agent is *Le Pont de Normandie* (a bridge in Normandy, France). My model was a postcard, very far from the final result.

Have your varied professions influenced your work at all?

Yes. I was an apprentice in upholstery decoration and worked in the denim industry. For me, all these crafts are linked to aesthetics, color, and craftsmanship. Also discipline. All these elements are reflected in my drawings.

It is evident from the intricacy of your compositions that you have a real fascination with urban environments. What draws you to landscapes/cityscapes?

Our urban environment is a very important subject, so it is important for me to build smart, clean, well-organized, and less polluted and polluting cities. It's my dream.

I find your vantage points so interesting. Where do you picture yourself when you are making this work?

I imagine myself inside my drawings.

You use such vibrant, radiant, and varied colors in your work, while cities are so often monochromatic. How do you make your color choice?

My colors, of course, are inspired by my native Africa. I wanted to break the standard of monochromatic colors we find in many cities. Since I began to draw in 2001, urban landscapes have become more colorful. We find a lot of colors in new constructions of buildings in France. I'd like to think that I influenced this change through my drawings because I have been approached by architects, even though no contracts were signed.

How do you construct these drawings (from start to finish)?

I have always said, I behave like a photographer. I zoom in on a monument or a building that interests me, and then create a dressing, a covering. Technically, I am more specialized in markers, ballpoint pens, and gels, sometimes I like to vary a bit and use gouache and paint on some drawings. However, all the beginnings of my drawings start with a pencil, an eraser, and a ruler.

How long does it take for you to complete a piece?

Between 10 days and 12 months.

When did you first consider yourself an artist? (Was it an event, exhibition, moment?)

When I started living off my art. Exhibitions like La Fondation Cartier and others allowed me to gain more confidence in my art and to feel more comfortable. The recognition of my work and my art helps me gain confidence since I am self-taught in this field.

What does your practice look like now? How has your artmaking/studio practice changed/evolved?

When I started, I copied the cities I saw in postcards and I tried to make them as realistic as possible. Now I create whole imaginary and utopian cities and most of my drawings are composed of a mixture of cities copied and imagined.

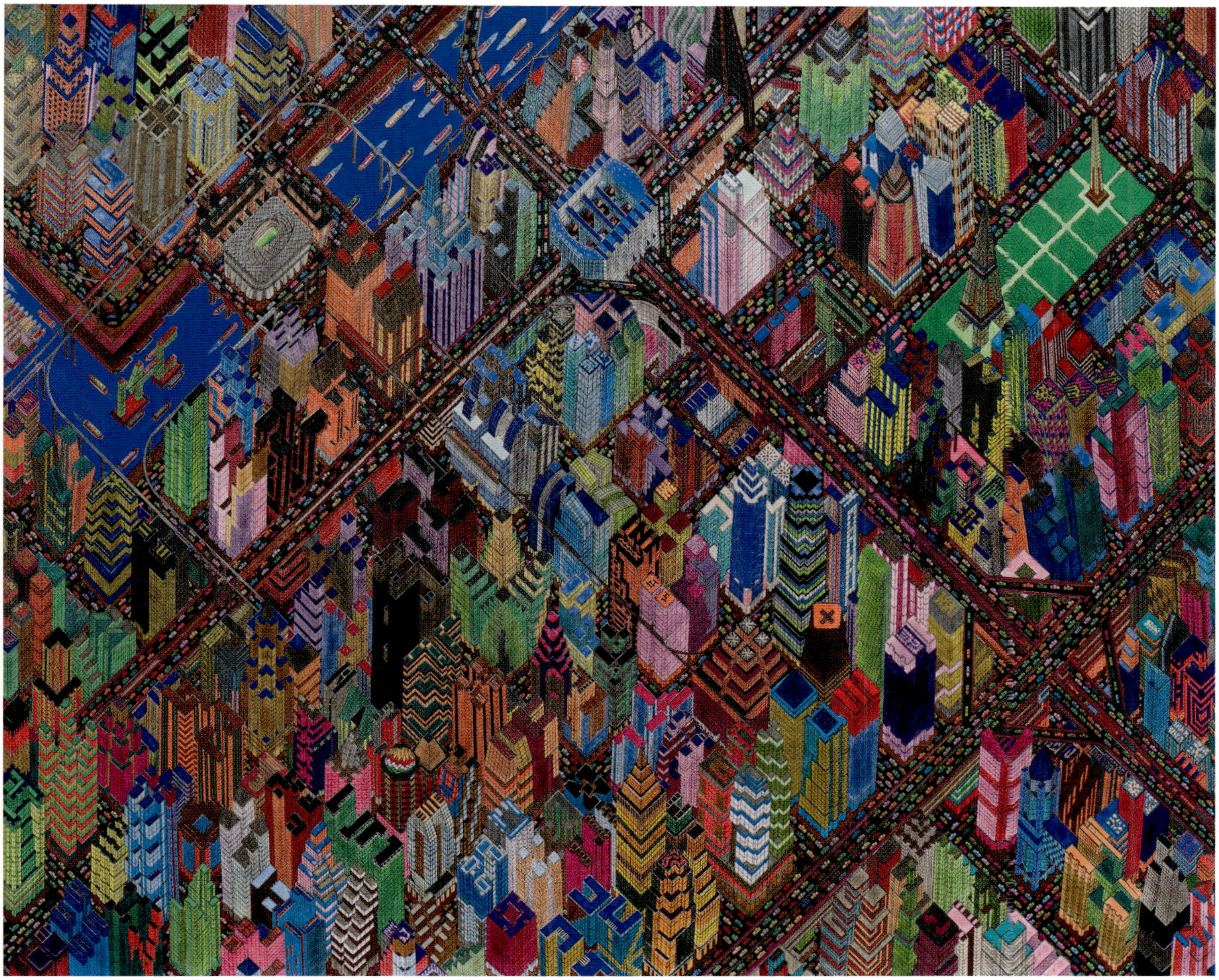

Mamadou Cissé, untitled, *2015, ink, pen on paper, 47¼ × 59⅛ in (120 × 150 cm). The Museum + The Gallery of Everything.* This extremely detailed work by Cissé is abundant with modes of transportation in movement, inferring a very active human presence within the cityscape.

How would you describe your work to someone who had never seen it before?

I draw urban landscapes, very colorful, imaginary, utopian, modern, and clever cities where mobility is central.

You have been described as a self-taught and a visionary artist, how would you identify your artistic practice?

I am in fact a self-taught artist because I didn't go to art school. I make my own creations and don't follow norms. I like to say I am a visionary artist because I like to think I am creating futuristic cities.

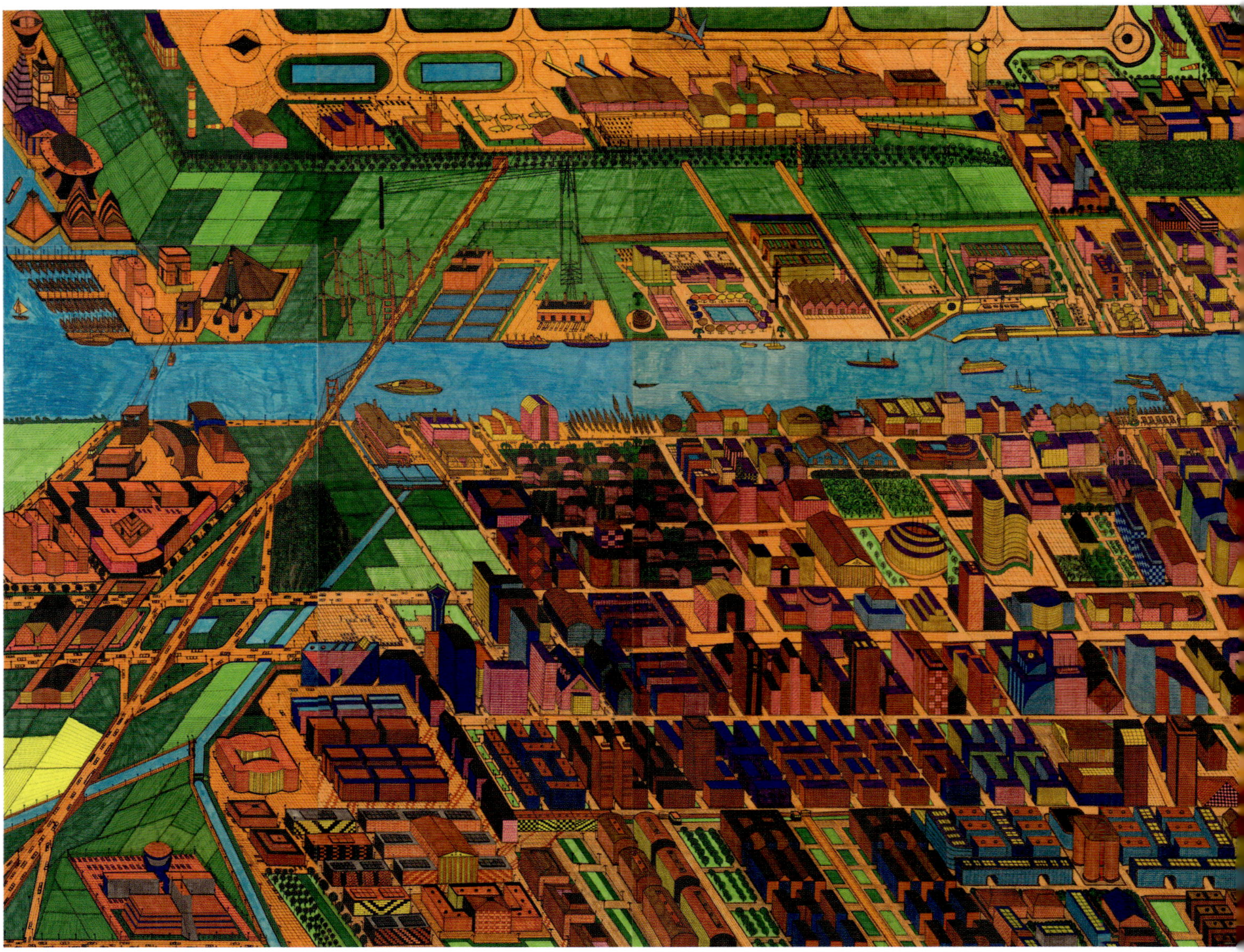

Some might consider your cityscapes utopian, what is your definition of utopia?

Utopia is creations and dreams. This concept inspired great architects Gustave Eiffel, Le Corbusier, and others.

How did you become aware of such architects? Could you tell me more about your work's relationship with Le Corbusier?

I knew Le Corbusier through documentaries and I had the chance to exhibit some of my works near his. I like his futurist approach and his drawings of utopian cities. I think my work joins him in these points; future and utopia. I have the same vision of architecture and especially of his space management; he constructs squares, rectangles and never loses a square meter.

Your ornate infrastructure and complicated transportation systems have a very futuristic quality to them. How do you envision the future?

I believe the future is bright for humans because we will have smart cities that will be nice to live in, with adapted and intelligent transportation systems.

Cities have suffered so much during the pandemic of 2020, do you believe they will be resilient?

You know, the lockdowns will push humans to be even more ingenious because we will have this ability to adapt. Of course, it is a difficult moment for humanity but I have hope for a better future. Life will resume little by little and cities will continue to progress.

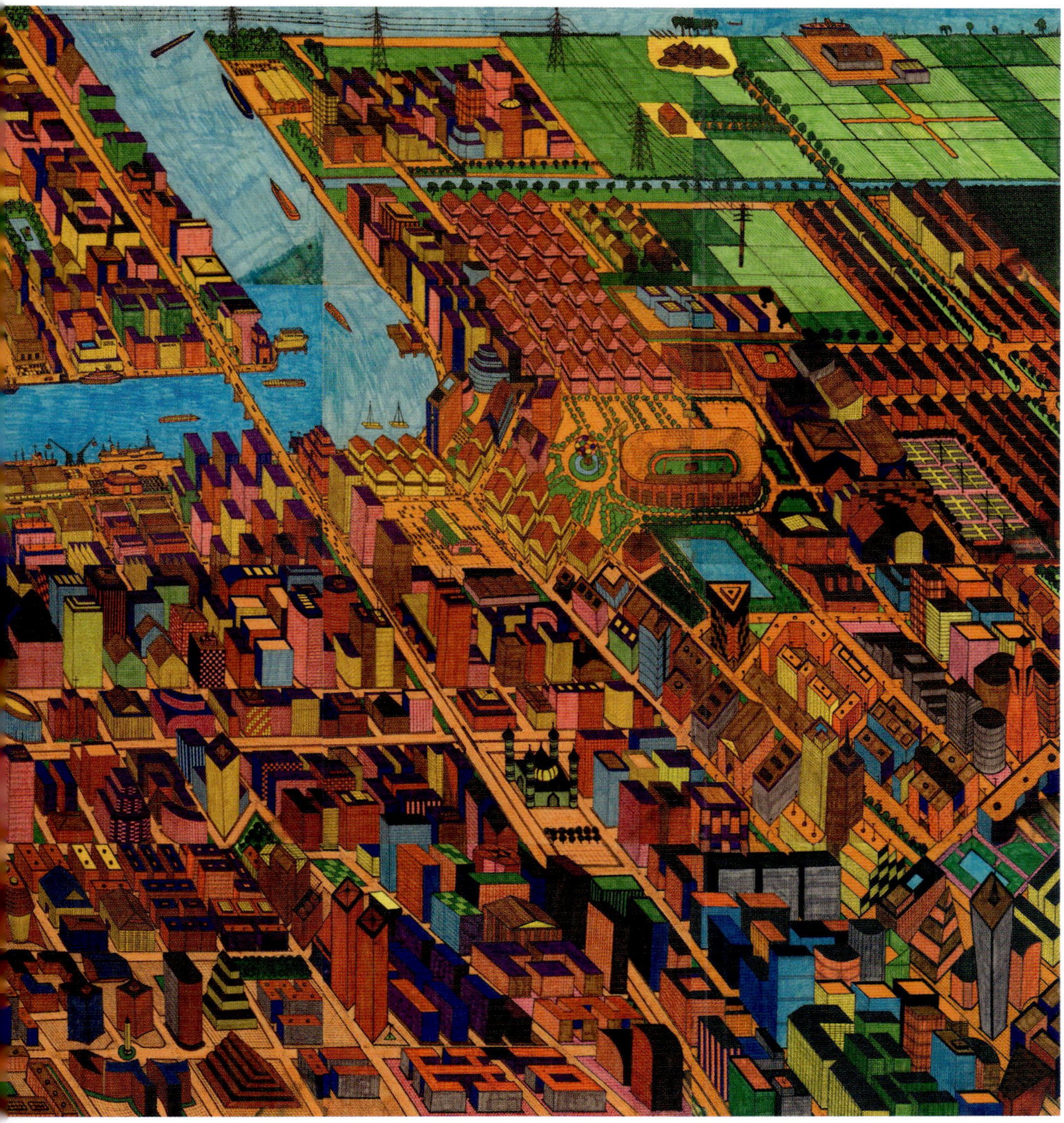

Mamadou Cissé, untitled, *n.d., 47¼ × 59⅛ in (120 × 150 cm). The Museum + The Gallery of Everything.* This monumental work by Cissé, almost 12 ft (3 m) in length, presents an intriguing perspective and his growing interest in the link between waterways and African cities.

Your compositions seem to be void of citizens, do you envision these environments unpopulated?

Humans are in the center of my drawings. You just need to look closer!

What are your hopes for the future of your work?

I will always focus on cities. But, I would like to work on African cities and the connection between African rivers and the creation of artificial rivers to prevent flooding, and the best distribution of water in the continent so there will always be futuristic cities.

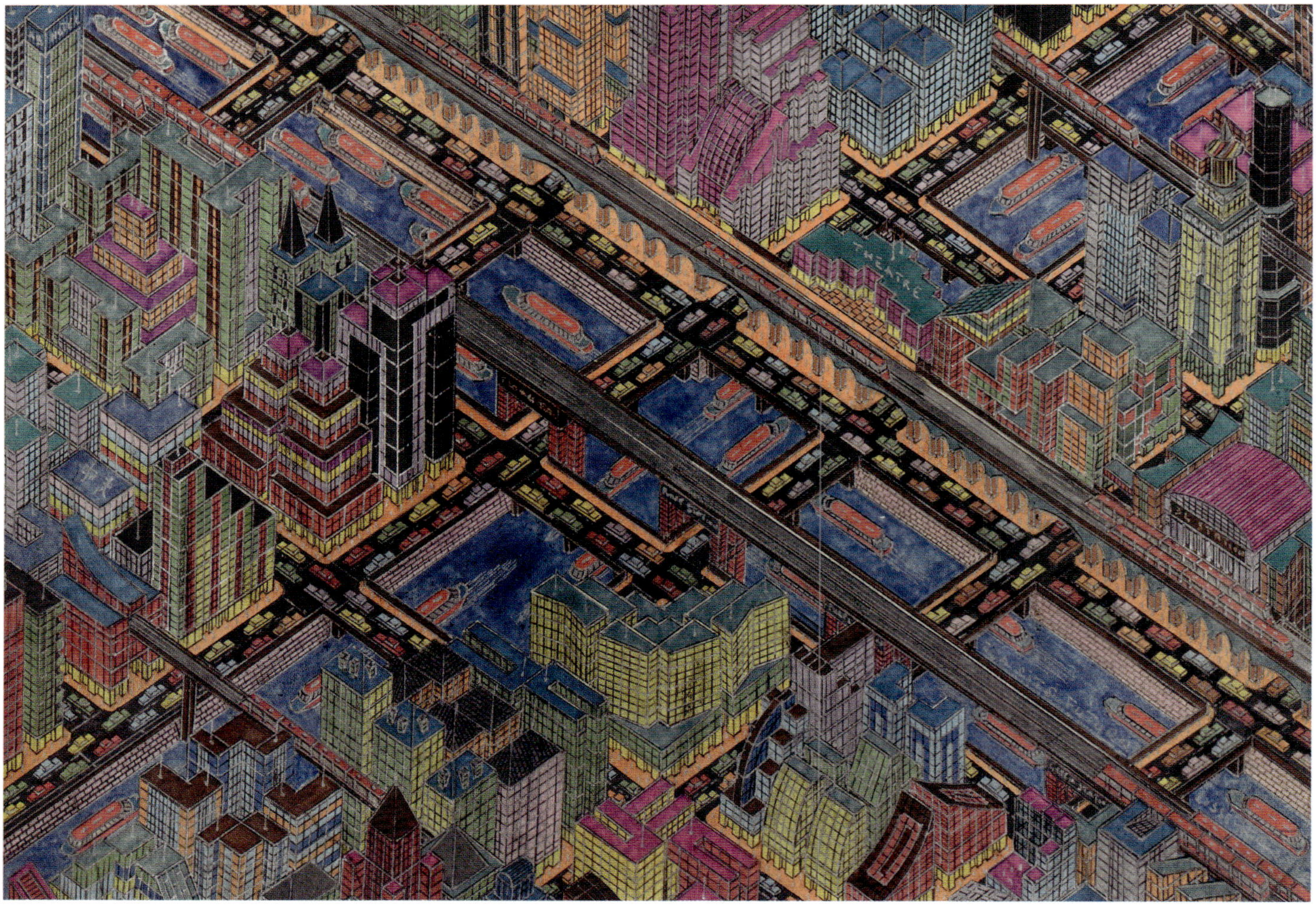

Mamadou Cissé, Venise futuriste (Futuristic Venice), *2019, ink, pen on paper, $11\frac{13}{16} \times 15\frac{3}{4}$ in (30 × 40cm). Courtesy the artist and Art-Z Gallery.* Through the lens of a city planner, here Cissé proposes a futuristic Venice with alternative canals and details including his markings of where the theater and station are located.

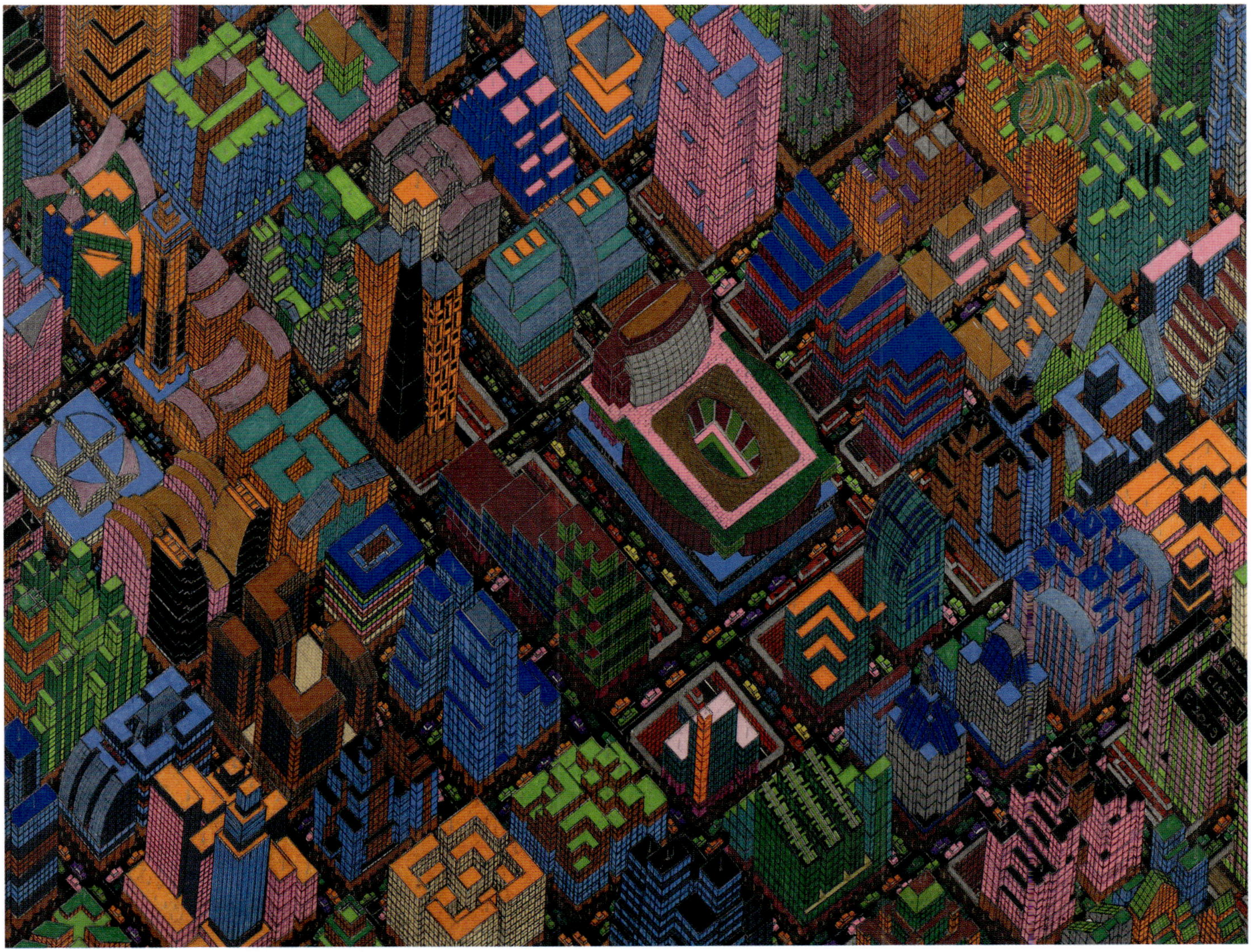

Mamadou Cissé, New Town, 2019, ink, pen on paper, 19 11/16 × 25 9/16 in (50 × 65 cm). Courtesy the artist and Art-Z Gallery. Here, Cissé's use of flat color shapes to reflect the tops of buildings creates an additional sense of geometric composition, reminiscent of early video games such as Tetris.

GRANDMA MOSES

(1860, Easton–1961, Hoosick Falls, New York, USA)

Anna Mary Robertson Moses grew up on a farm in upstate New York. Unaware of her future mastery of intimate pastoral paintings and notoriety as Grandma Moses, she was encouraged by her father to draw at a young age. However, her mother prioritized practical pursuits and Moses worked from the age of 12. She was married at 27 and raised five children on a rural farm in Virginia. In 1937, following her husband's death and in need of a constructive purpose, Moses began intuitively painting nostalgic scenes and, by 1938, she gained the attention of a local collector. Her undeniably American landscapes were painted with an inherent instinct, especially evident when considering that Moses had likely never been to an art museum when she began painting. By 1947, Moses had had several significant exhibitions, and Hallmark purchased the licensing to reproduce her landscapes as greeting cards. Considered the anti-Pollock, Moses' rebellion through traditionalism gave her an interesting position within modernism, as demonstrated by the inclusion of her serene stylistic paintings in a promotional campaign of American culture abroad during the Cold War.

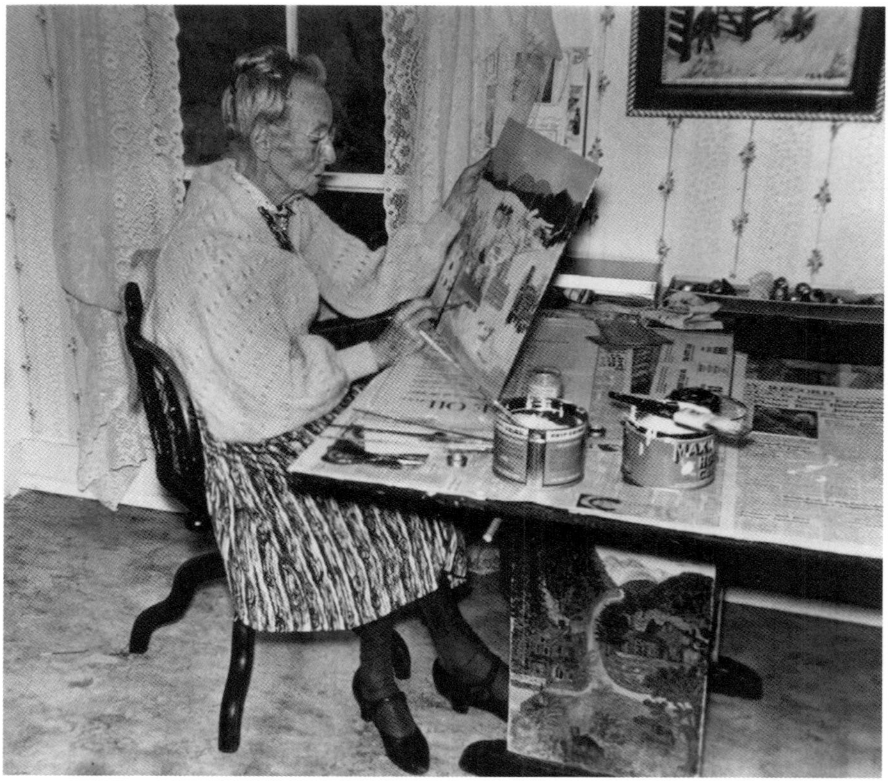

Grandma Moses, June 1, 1948, photograph by Otto Kallir. Only beginning to paint at the age of 77, here Robertson, better known as Grandma Moses, is shown painting one of her iconic, scenic landscapes. This intimate portrait was likely taken at her kitchen table in upstate New York.

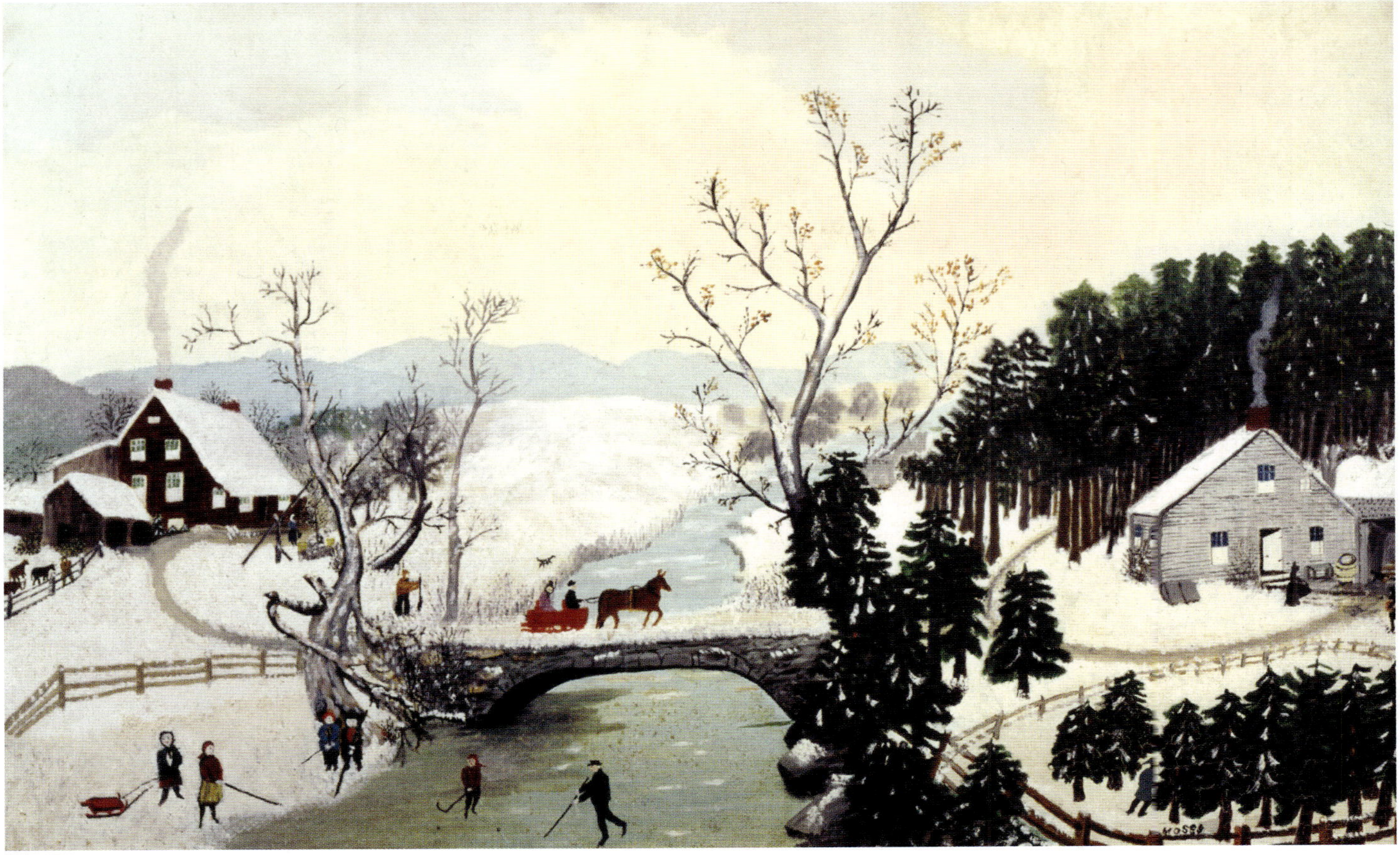

Grandma Moses, Over the River to Grandma's House, *1941, oil on pressed wood, 20½ × 30¾ in (52.1 × 78.1 cm). Private collection.* Moses' landscapes can be identified and studied in groups that correspond with the four seasons. Each season has a prevailing color, as seen here, in this winter scene dominated by white. Other seasons are defined with light green for spring, deeply saturated green for summer, and hues of brown for fall.

Grandma Moses's oeuvre consists mostly of scenic landscapes, that are balanced in composition between diagrammatic and stage setting. Anonymous figures are innately rendered as a pictorial language articulating the scene. Figures, animals, land, and sky are all painted with an intimate appeal. Moses painted with a true sense of satisfaction and appreciation. Her paintings had a resonant quality that set her apart from other contemporaneous landscape painters. The source of this reverberation was linked to her lived experience on the farm and her inclination to paint entrenched memories and references.

Moses' overt and subversive activity in the mid-20th century American zeitgeist was remarkable. Her paintings on Hallmark greeting cards were a catalyst for further accessible merchandise, including household commodities like ceramics and upholstery. Her presence became so ubiquitous that Norman Rockwell included in one of his paintings an armchair upholstered in one of her textiles. The painting, depicting a young boy practicing the trumpet, was then published on a *Saturday Evening Post* cover in 1950. Thus, coincidently and perhaps inadvertently, a Grandma Moses painting was also presented on the cover. In 1955, she appeared on the first color episode broadcast of the CBS' "See It Now," alongside Louis Armstrong. Her 100th birthday was celebrated by *Life* magazine, placing Grandma Moses on the cover.

Her paintings were introduced to a European audience with the eponymous exhibition *Grandma Moses*, in 1950. However, the motive of this touring exhibition extended beyond unadulterated traction for the artist. The tour was a US government-backed initiative to promote a curated vision of America abroad, through the idyllic and modest landscapes of Moses. The exhibition toured to six international locations, including the US Embassy in Paris, where her paintings were responsible for executing a key cultural initiative within the Cold War objective. By projecting serene idealism, Moses' landscapes actively fought against the image of an overly capitalistic and luxury driven America.

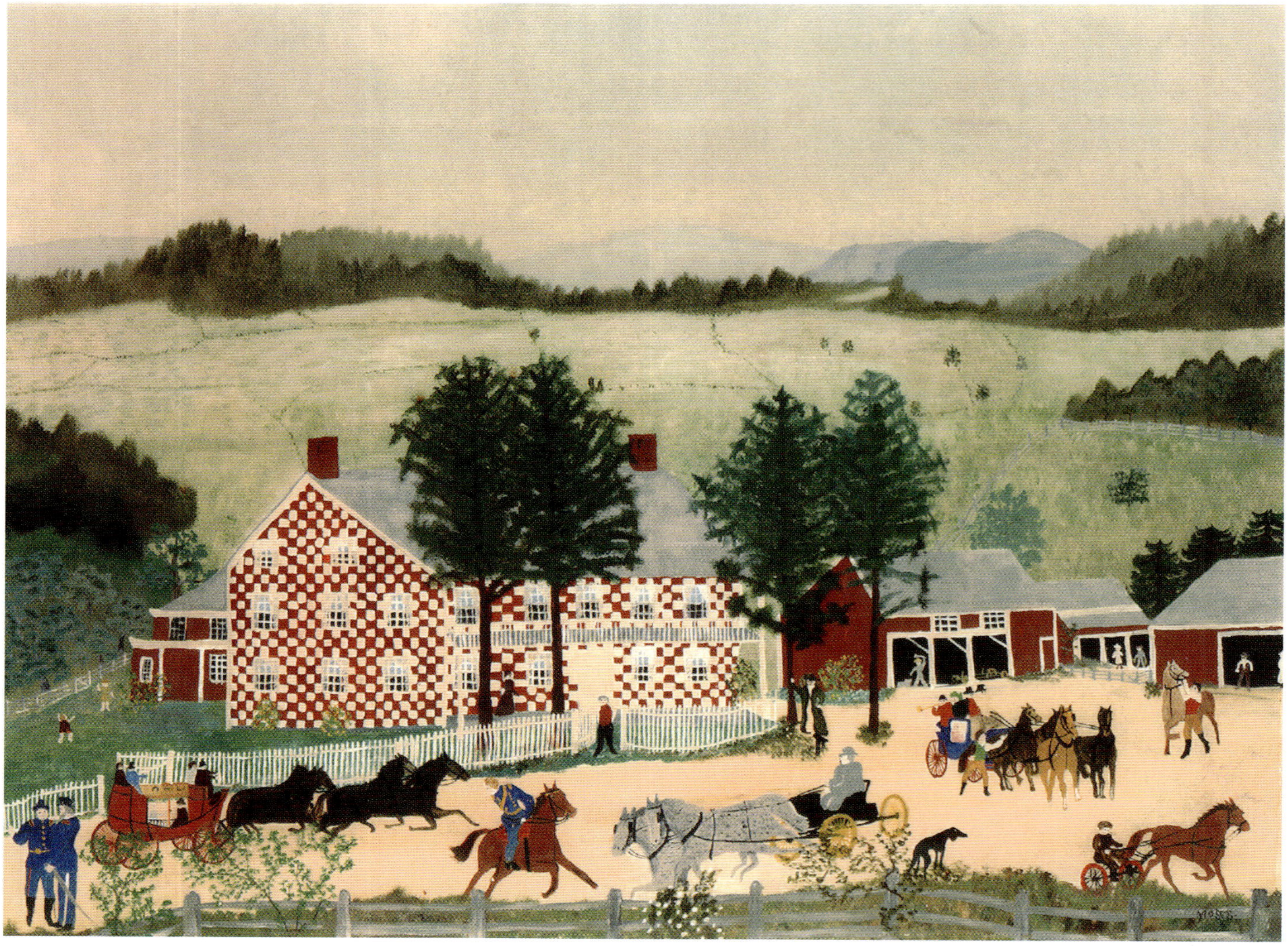

Grandma Moses, The Old Checkered House, 1853, *1944, oil on pressed wood, 20¾ × 28 in (52.7 × 71.1 cm). Bennington Museum*. The mesmerizing red-and-white checkering of the house draws immediate attention in this painting of a local landmark in Cambridge, New York. The house is surrounded by the buzzing activity of horses and people. This checkered house was revisited in Moses' oeuvre, and over the years she completed more than 20 versions.

"It's like looking out at the same landscape from various windows, it is the same landscape always, but it looks a little different every time." – Grandma Moses[1]

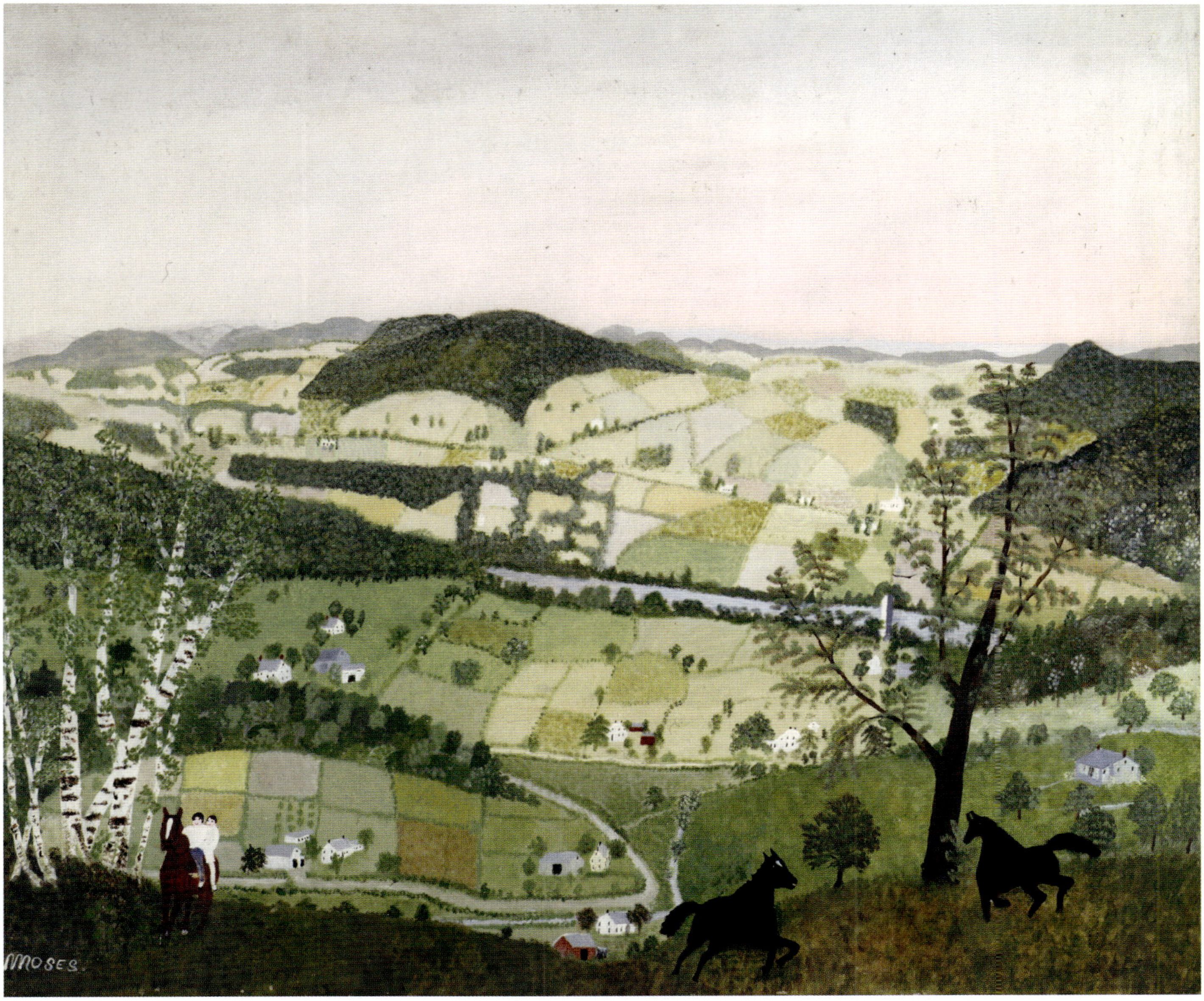

Grandma Moses, Black Horses, *1942, oil on pressed wood, 20 × 24 in (50.8 × 61 cm). Private collection.* This scenic landscape is considered one of Moses' most notable paintings. Her compositions of a condensed foreground and a sprawling background with multiple perspectives seen here, is archetypal and lauded in her paintings.

"But what struck me . . . was the way the artist handled the landscape . . . though she had never heard of any rules of the perspective, Mrs. Moses had achieved an impression of depth [with color] . . . creating a compelling truth and closest to nature." – Otto Kallir[2]

MARTÍN RAMÍREZ

(1895, Tepatitlán, Mexico–1963, Auburn, California, USA)

Martín Ramírez's drawings hold extensive psychological landscapes of trains and tunnels with reverberating concentric lines. Open-armed Madonnas and horseback riders surrounded by ornamental confinement are other emblematic subjects. Ramírez left his native Mexico and his family behind in 1925, when he emigrated to California for job opportunities, but discouragingly the Great Depression caused him to lose employment and lodgings. In 1931, observed by police to be disorientated, Ramírez was admitted to a California state hospital; he remained under institutional care until his death. While in the hospital, Ramírez began to draw on discarded paper with a pencil and crayons. His work was recognized by Tarmo Pasto after he was transferred to DeWitt State Hospital in 1948. A professor of art and psychology, during a visit to the hospital Pasto saw the inherent caliber of Ramírez's drawings. In turn, he fostered the development of Ramírez's practice and exposed his work to a larger audience. Recounting experiences—lived, imagined, and cross-cultural—appear to be at the core of his oeuvre. Ramírez has received significant exposure and appreciation in the 21st century, including a retrospective at the Museo Nacional Centro de Arte Reina Sofia, Madrid (2010).

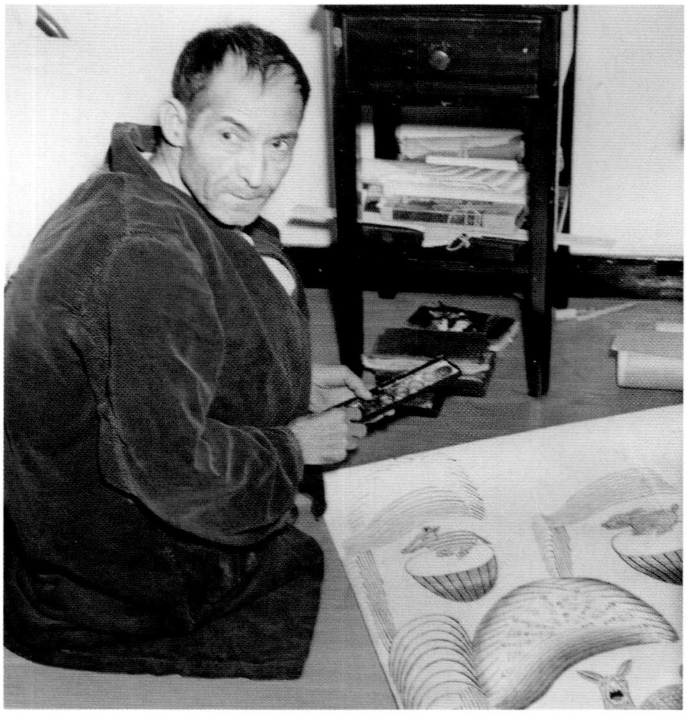

Martín Ramírez, ca. 1952, photograph. Courtesy of Matthew Pasto. This photograph of Ramírez from the early 1950s shows him drawing at the DeWitt State Hospital.

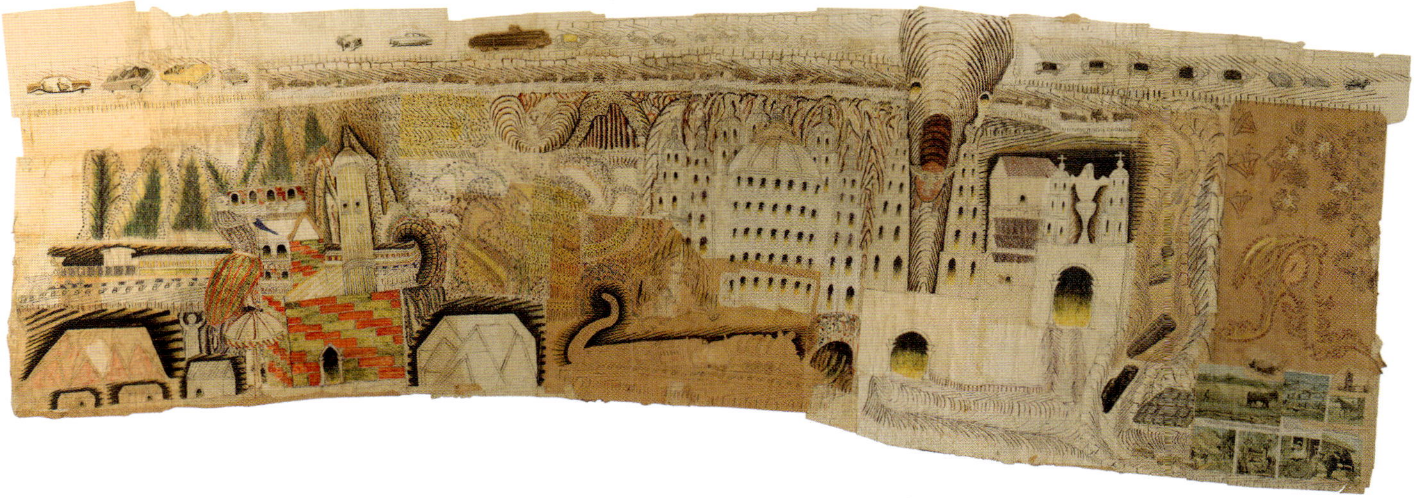

Martín Ramírez, untitled (landscape), *ca. 1950–1960, crayon, pencil, watercolor, and collage on paper, 40 × 105 in (102 × 267 cm). Courtesy the Estate of Martín Ramírez.* This dense and complex drawing seems to point to the journey between Mexico and the United States more directly than many of Ramírez's drawings. Here, a moving train is central, while the collage, iconography, and drawn landscape on the left, seem overtly American. These same elements on the right seem to indicate his native Mexico.

Historically, Martín Ramírez has been referred to as nonverbal. Records about his behavior and mental health are incomplete, nonetheless more recent research indicates that while he was limited verbally while under institutional care, the language barrier could have been an integral factor. This circumstance renders a reading of his work without the support of interviews with Ramírez or notes by him.

Ramírez would have traveled from Mexico to the United States by train. He also worked on the railroads while in California—pointing to his symbolic use of trains, rails, and transportation. Further, the Cristero War would have prevented Ramírez from returning to Mexico, which proposes the concept of nostalgia when understanding his practice. Transition seems evident in his work, in the form of tunnels and activated transportation. Are these tunnels leading to or from disparate cultures? Inferred in instances to be Mexico and the United States, particular visuals imply a direct polarity of locale between the constellated patterned tracks. His uncanny perspectives present isolated moments of surreal gravity. Ornamental and art deco are clear adjectives, but they add complex aesthetic intrigue to Ramírez's drawings. More hypnotic than disorienting, his oeuvre activates dialogue between representation and abstraction.

Research demonstrates that Ramírez was drawing from the mid-1930s and achieving a larger format by assembling found papers together with a glue composite of saliva and starches. He is also referenced to have used a tongue depressor for achieving concentric uniformity. With support from Tarmo Pasto, the 1950s and 1960s were prolific years for Ramírez. Posthumously in 1968, Chicago Imagist Jim Nutt encountered Ramírez's work among Pasto's reference materials while teaching at Sacramento. With art dealer Phyllis Kind, Nutt went on to acquire 300 drawings, which aided their extensive appreciation and reach in the 21st century. In 2015, he was commemorated by the United States Postal Service with the release of five "Martín Ramírez" forever stamps.

"First and last, Martín Ramírez was a master of space—both measured and mysterious, psychological and decorative. The primary tool of this mastery was line, just as its primary purpose was the creation of settings that would both protect and valorize his figures, animals, and machines." – Roberta Smith, co-chief art critic of the *New York Times*[3]

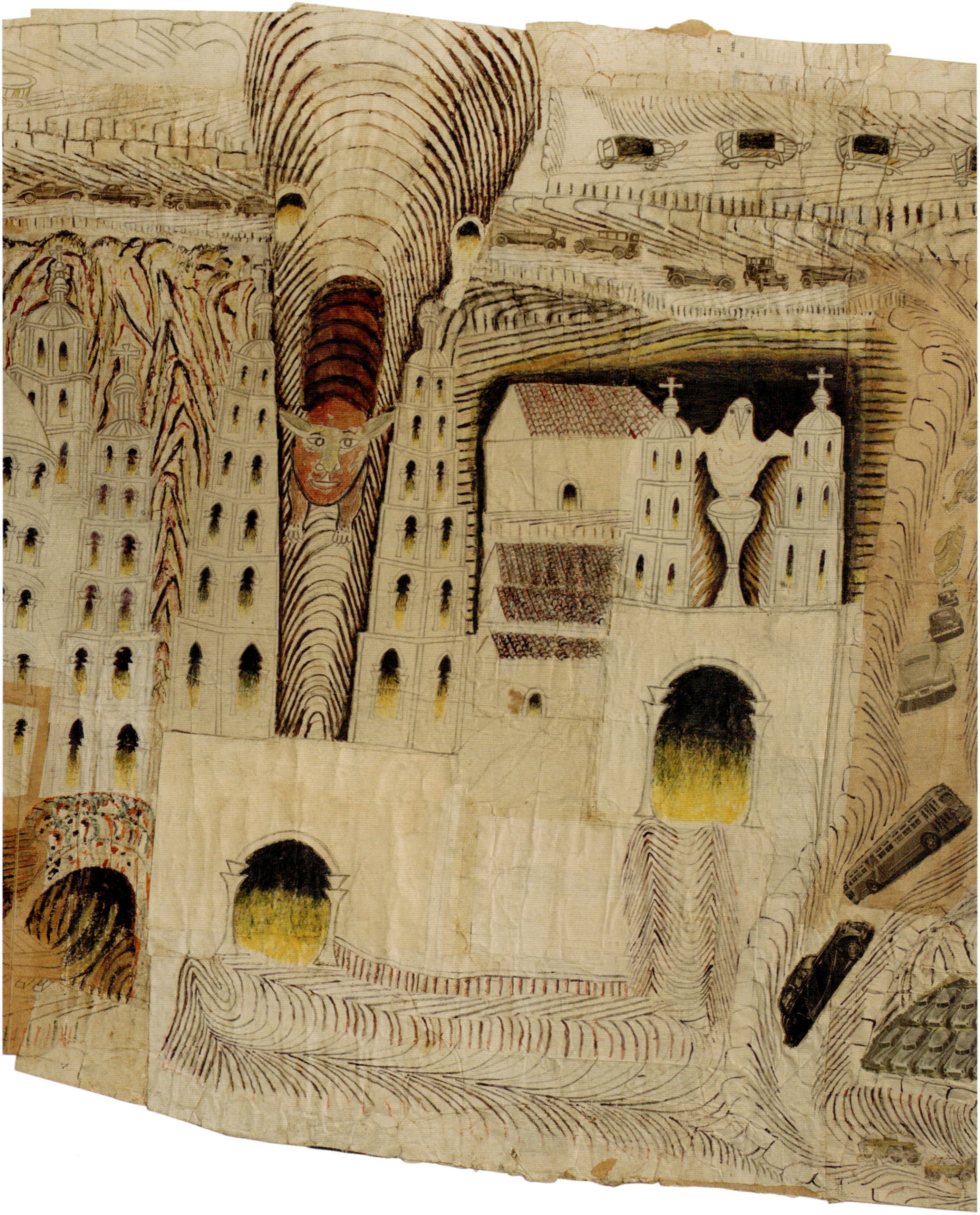

Martín Ramírez, untitled (landscape) *(detail), ca. 1950–60, crayon, pencil, watercolor, and collage on paper, 40 × 105 in (102 × 267 cm). Courtesy the Estate of Martín Ramírez.* This detail exemplifies Ramírez's aesthetic of concentric lines of exquisite details. Conceptually, it shows his penchant for tunnels, suggesting transportation and perhaps a sense of dislocation; collaged cars and buses also travel up a path, right.

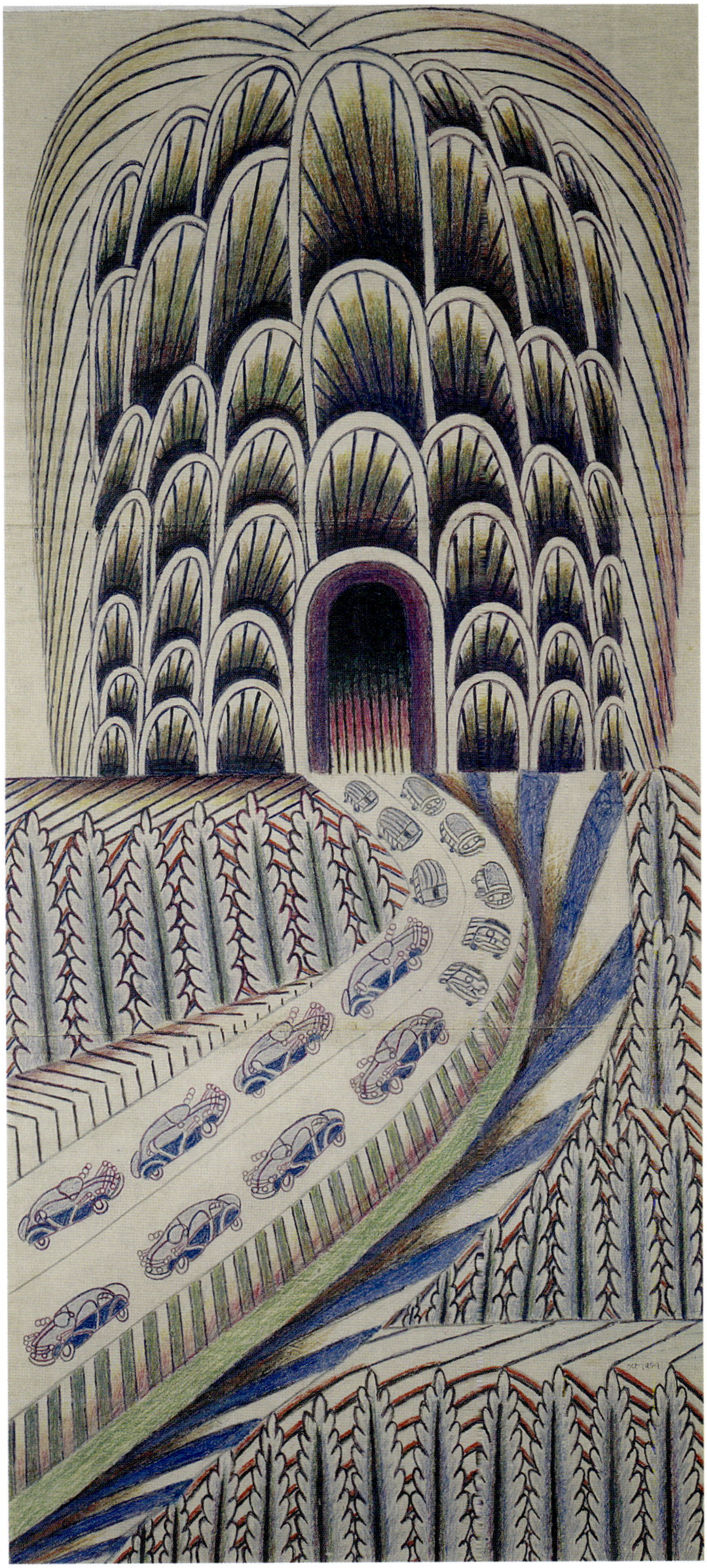

Martín Ramírez, untitled (Tunnel with Cars and Buses), *1954, pencil, colored pencil, watercolor, and crayon on paper,* $52\frac{3}{16} \times 23\frac{15}{16}$ *in (132.6 × 60.8 cm). Solomon R. Guggenheim Museum, New York.* Art deco elements are abundant in this patterned landscape by Ramírez. Automobiles appeared to be both entering and departing from the tunnel. However, the void beyond the tunnel's archway may conceptually suggest a threat or the unknown.

MINNIE EVANS

(1892, Long Creek–1987 Wilmington, North Carolina, USA)

The lush phantasmagoric compositions of Minnie Evans exhibit the space between waking vision and lucid dream. Raised by her grandmother, Evans attended school until sixth grade, when she began working to help provide for her family. From a young age, she was noted as having vivid recurring dreams and formed a strong connection with religion. In 1908, Evans moved to the Pembroke Park Estate, working first as a domestic servant and then as a gatekeeper for almost 30 years. Beginning with a drawing in 1935, then defining her style into the 1950s, Evans' oeuvre was undoubtedly emboldened by her botanical surroundings. She was driven by her evangelical community and spiritual higher powers to create divine drawings. Evans' first exhibition was at the Little Gallery, Wilmington, NC, (1961) and following the support of photography student Nina Howell Starr, Evans began exhibiting in New York in 1966. Her work entered the collection of the Smithsonian Museum of American Art in 1972 and she had a solo exhibition at the Whitney Museum of American Art in 1975.

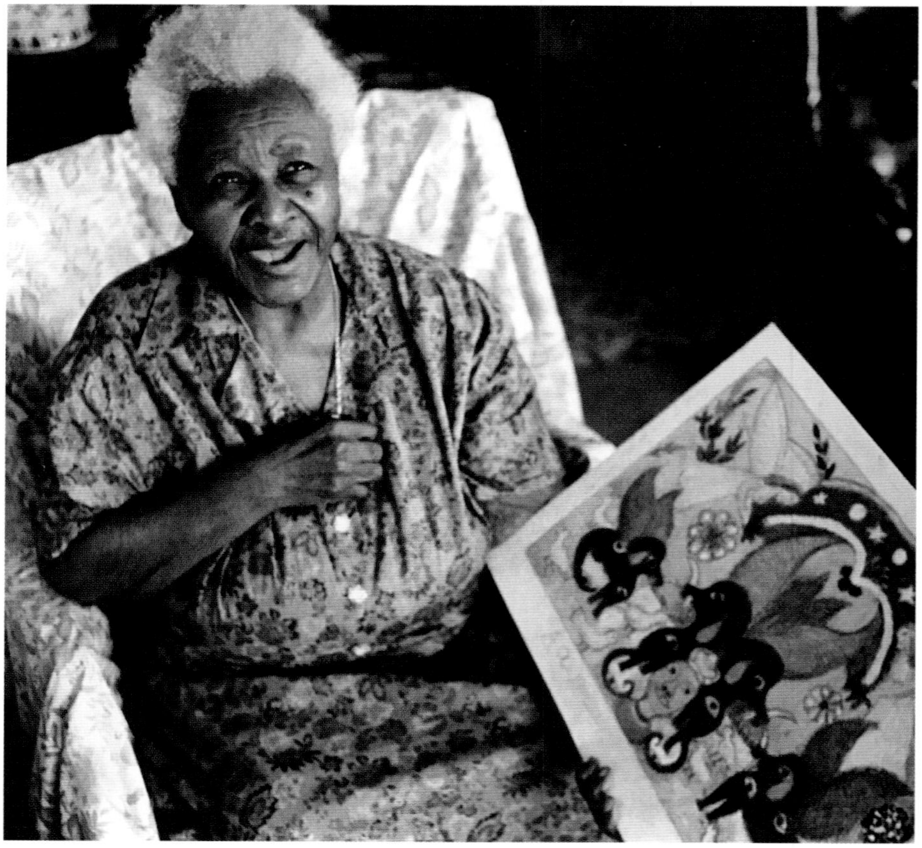

Minnie Evans, 1980, photograph by Susan Mullally. Here, Evans sits comfortably while she shows one of her fantastical botanical compositions.

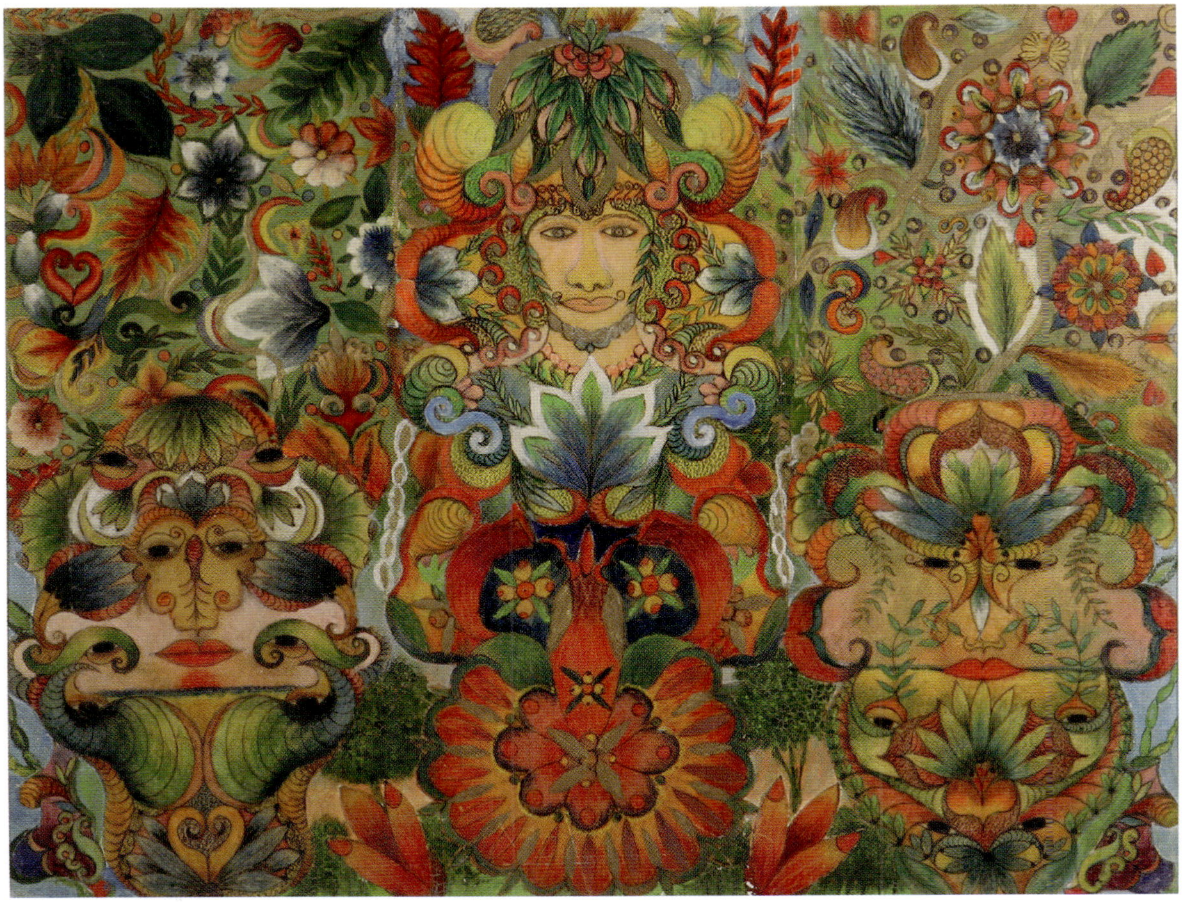

Minnie Evans, untitled, *1946, 1962–1963, 1968, oil pastel, pencil and paper mounted on board artwork, 20½ × 26⅛ in (52 × 66.5 cm). The Museum + The Gallery of Everything.* This intricate botanical composition exemplifies Evans's representation of God's presence through the visual of eyes. Here, they are introduced cryptically and mysteriously, in particular appearing on the left side of the painting, featuring eight sets of eyes.

Minnie Evans' first drawing was composed on Good Friday, 1935. Her early drawings were abstract and uncomplicated; later, symmetry, faces, and nature were introduced. Her practice involved drawing with ink, crayon, and pencil on discarded materials such as window shades, scrap paper, and boards. Adding watercolor and oil paints later into her practice, Evans' aesthetic developed into a more defined style from the 1950s. At Pembroke Park Estate, she worked as a domestic servant between 1918 and 1948 and then as a gatekeeper at the property's Airlie Gardens until 1974. She drew on-site at the gardens, an environment that contributed to her style of interweaving flowers and leaves into whimsical horizons emotive of entering an alternative landscape of a heavenly dimension.

Evans' work suggests a surreal collision of biblical and mythological departure points, and a historical cacophony of cultural traditions. She formed a strong relationship with the African American evangelical church community on the estate. The abundance of rich herbaceous visuals is signature, but Evans' compositions also often featured pairs of eyes, sometimes multiples, to represent God's omnipresence. God is often portrayed with wings and a rainbow halo, while depictions of spiritual mystics and wise people introduce Evans' more visionary influences. Evans credited her dreams and deciphered visions for her composed suns, moons, and stars that elude to a cosmological landscape.

The conceptual and ornamental influences worked into her verdant botanical shapes infer that Airlie Gardens was her foremost visual inspiration. It is also worth considering the decorative aesthetics Evans would have encountered while working as a domestic on the estate: Persian carpets, Asian and European porcelain, and English silverware all provided visual reference points to cultural traditions as well as ornamental influence. Certain visual elements that Evans used also seem connected to African traditions, specifically, Evans' use of symmetry could be placed in dialogue with Yoruba divination trays. Despite this

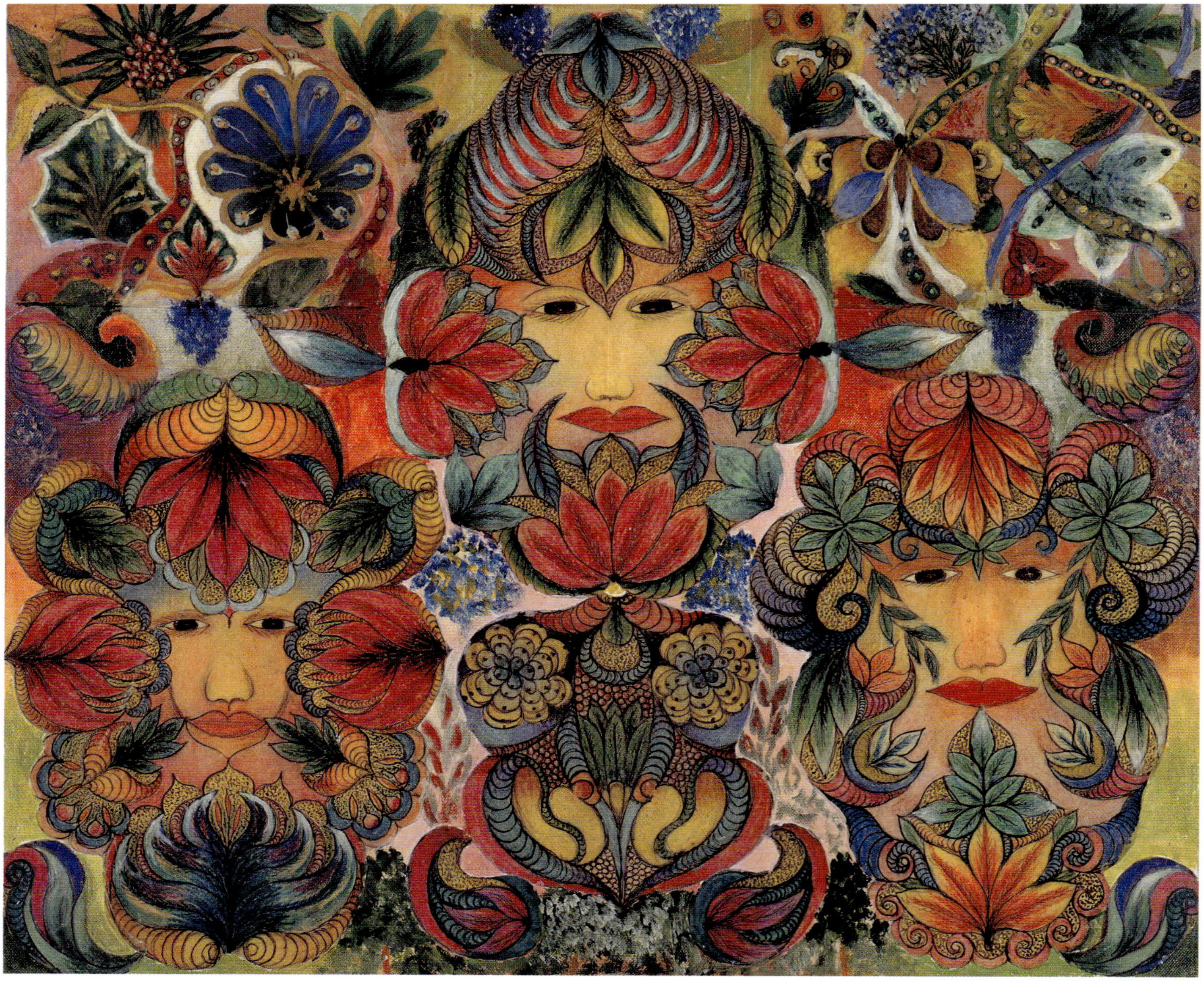

Minnie Evans, untitled, *1959, oil on canvas with collage, 20 × 24 in (50.8 × 61 cm). American Folk Art Museum.* This work from the 1950s shows Evans' signature aesthetic beginning to develop. Here, three mythical characters are framed by various floral and herbaceous motifs, creating an otherworldly landscape.

myriad of plausible global commands, her work transcends cultural boundaries, much like an unselfconscious dream landscape—a kaleidoscopic state of metamorphosis.

"My work is just as strange to me as they are to anyone else." – Minnie Evans[4]

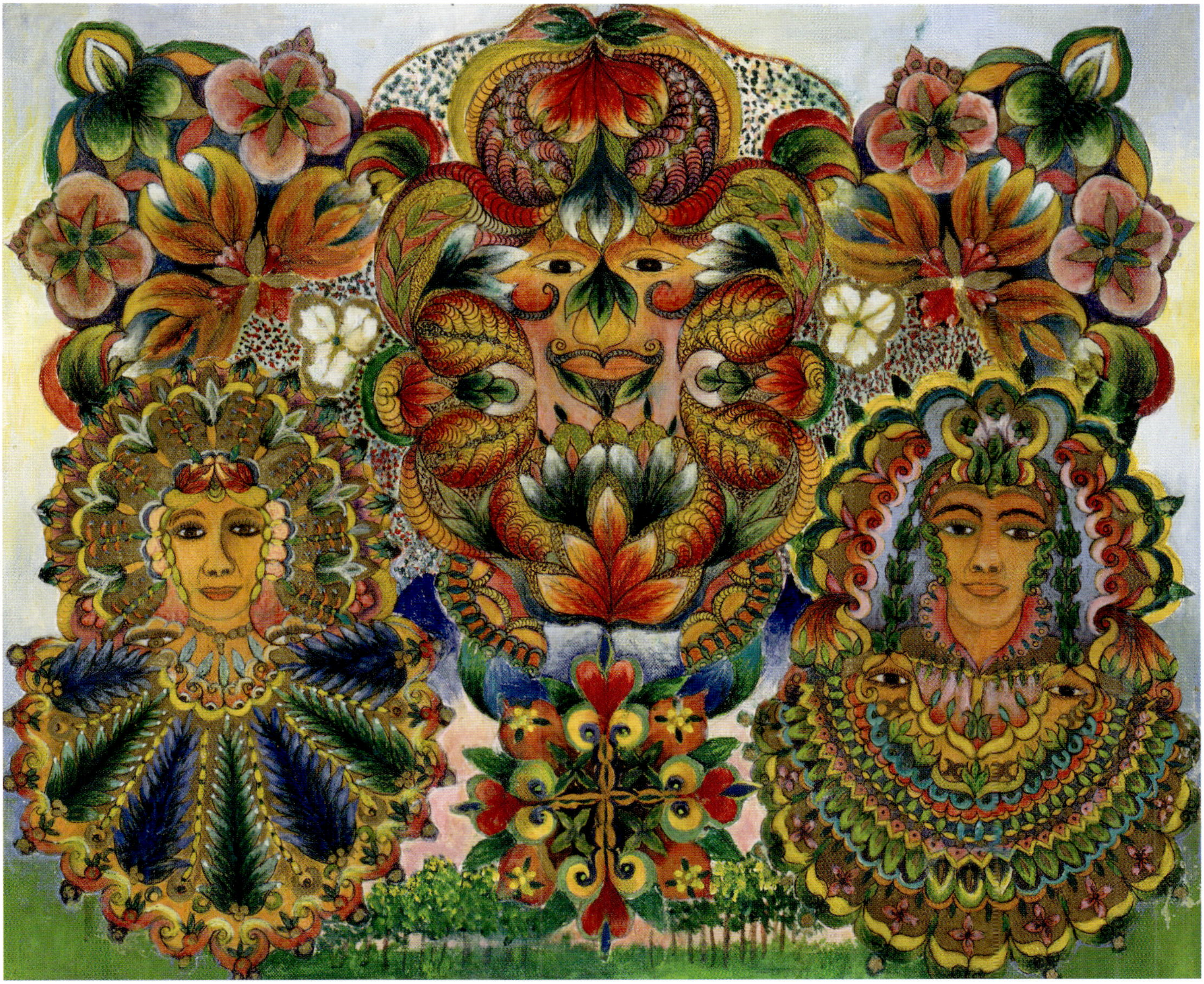

Minnie Evans, Design Made at Airlie Gardens, *1967, oil and mixed media on canvas mounted on paperboard, 19⅞ × 23⅞ in (50.5 × 60.6 cm). Smithsonian American Art Museum, Washington, D.C.* This painting is named after the site that Evans both drew and gained inspiration from, Airlie Gardens. Among the three main figurative beings, she painted botanical forms that are composed into semi-symmetrical kaleidoscopic shapes. The lower fanlike patterns illustrate the possible influence of international cultural ornamentation, observed while working inside of the estate's home.

KATSUYOSHI TAKENAKA

(b. 1987, Mie Prefecture, Japan)

Katsuyoshi Takenaka assumes a structural approach to drawing architectural buildings and forms. Metaphorically building a base, he draws cellular squares through repetitive crisscrossing with his pen. These pixelated cells multiply vertically and horizontally, constructing dense monumental structures. Takenaka, often referred to simply as Katsu, has been attending the studio Atelier Yamanami since 2014. Founded in 1986 and growing from three to ninety artists, Atelier Yamamani is a studio in Kōka that supports artists with intellectual, mental, or physical challenges. Takenaka works on several creative compositions at once, simultaneously drawing in the studio alongside his sculptural practice, which primarily focuses on constructing emblems of mechanical transportation (trains, planes, and helicopters) out of found material. It is for his oeuvre of complex and domineering architectonic structures that he is most recognized. Takenaka's drawings were part of *Eye, Eye, Nose, Mouth* at Harvard University, Asia Center (2019) and *Art Brut from Japan, Another Look*, Collection de l'Art Brut, Lausanne (2019).

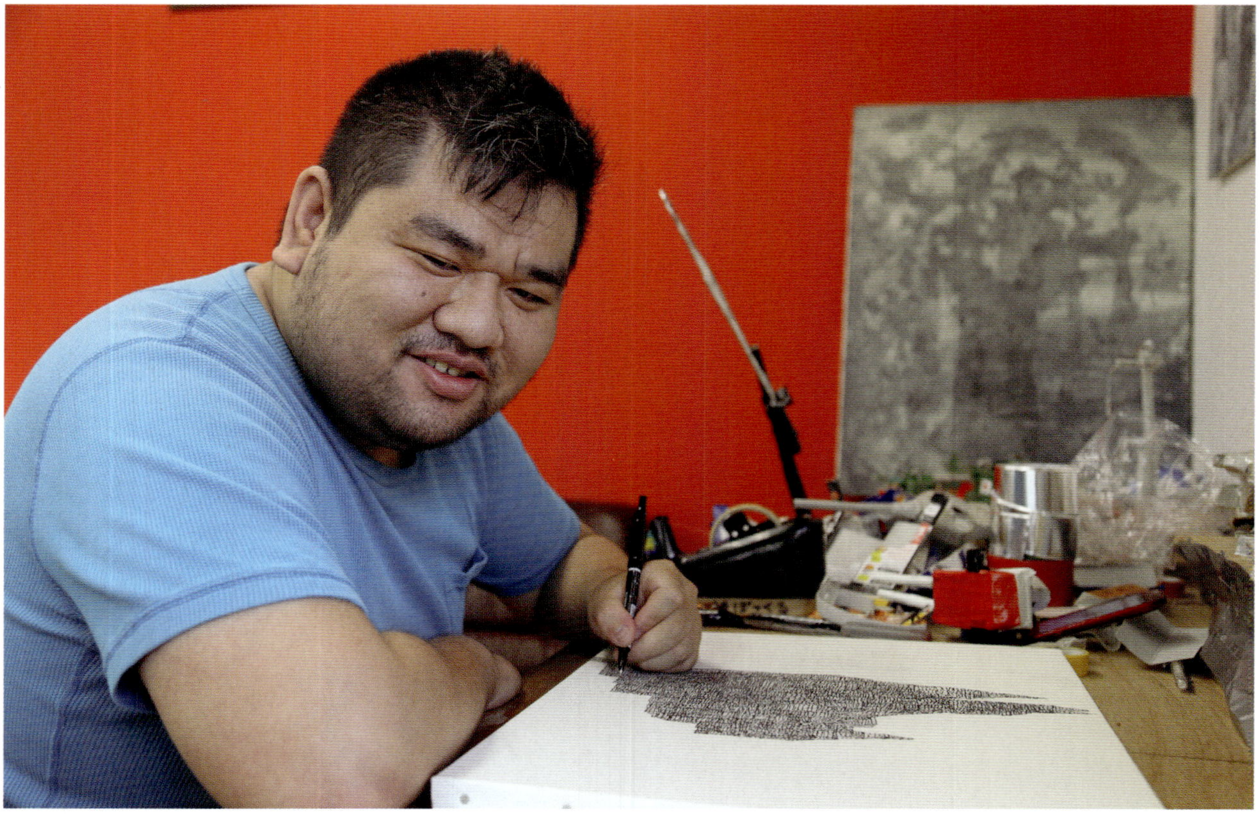

Katsuyoshi Takenaka, 2017, photograph. Courtesy Atelier Yamanami, Shiga. Taken at the studio Atelier Yamanami in Kōka, Takenaka is shown working on one of his detailed architectural drawings on canvas, while components of this three-dimensional practice are also evident on the table.

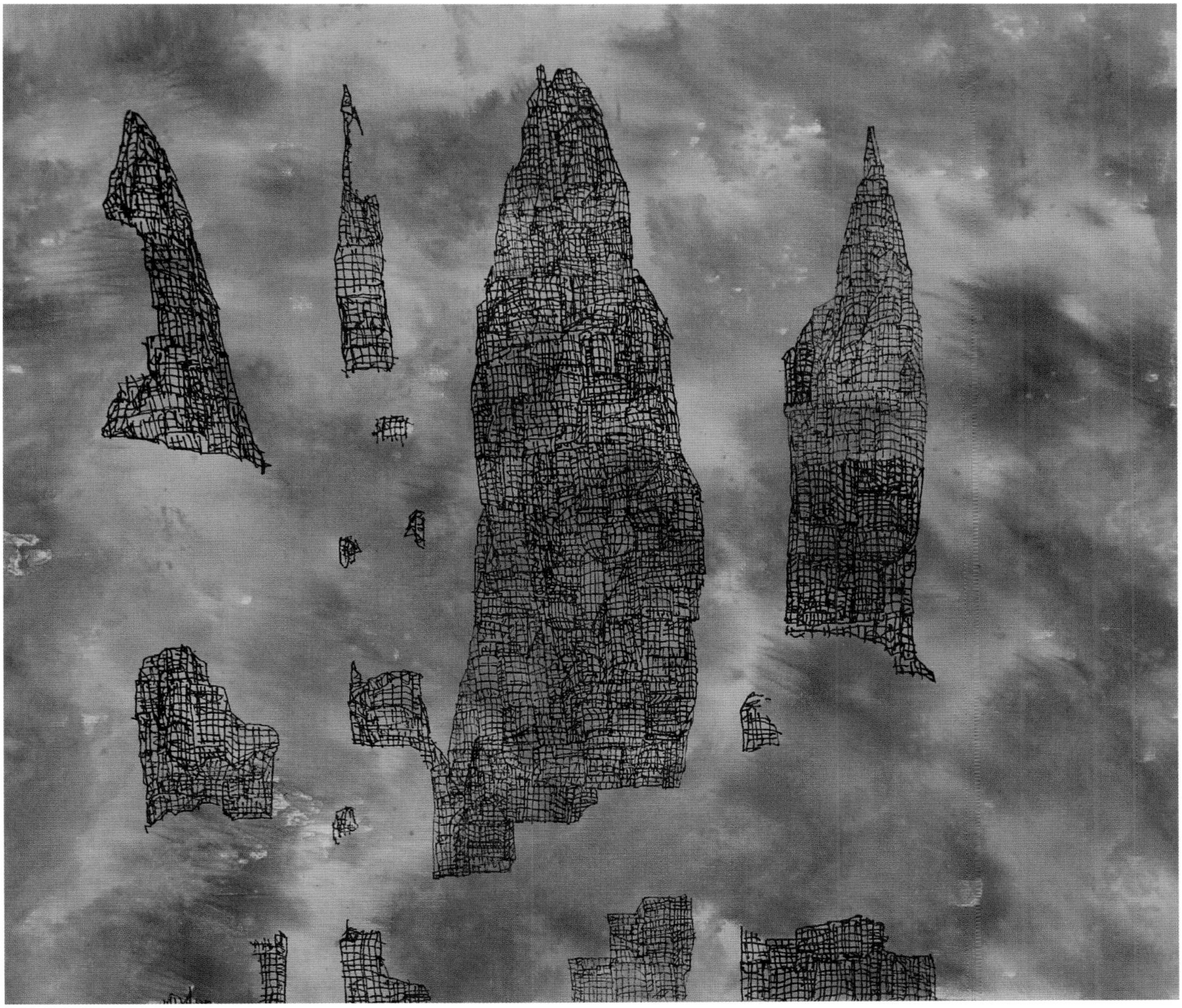

Katsuyoshi Takenaka, Mist City, *2017, acrylic paint, marker pen on canvas, 14 15⁄16 × 17 15⁄16 in (38 × 45.5 cm). Courtesy Atelier Yamanami, Shiga.* In *Mist City*, Takenaka draws fragmented buildings among his delicate wash of paint to compositionally play between foreground and background.

Katsuyoshi Takenaka's art practice is defined by elaborate perspective and complex structuring. His three-dimensional work follows the same principles as his drawings, which are more predominantly known. These highly detailed sculptural forms mimic mechanical structures of sophisticated machinery with acute precision and dimensional consideration. His combination of everyday materials—adhesive tape, cardboard, and cellophane—becomes his geometrical building blocks. Conversely, these building blocks remain two-dimensional cellular pixels in his remarkable body of drawings. Takenaka's almost bitmap approach could feel retro or rudimentary, but the sophistication in his slight shifts of cellular shape and outline density (seemingly from varying the pressure of the pen) produces a distinct futuristic aesthetic.

This futuristic aesthetic develops characteristics of science fiction when Takenaka applies a painted wash of color over the canvas before building up his architectural forms. In *Mist City* (2017), part of a larger series, the all-over wash is evocative of a galaxy. The buildings are rendered in a

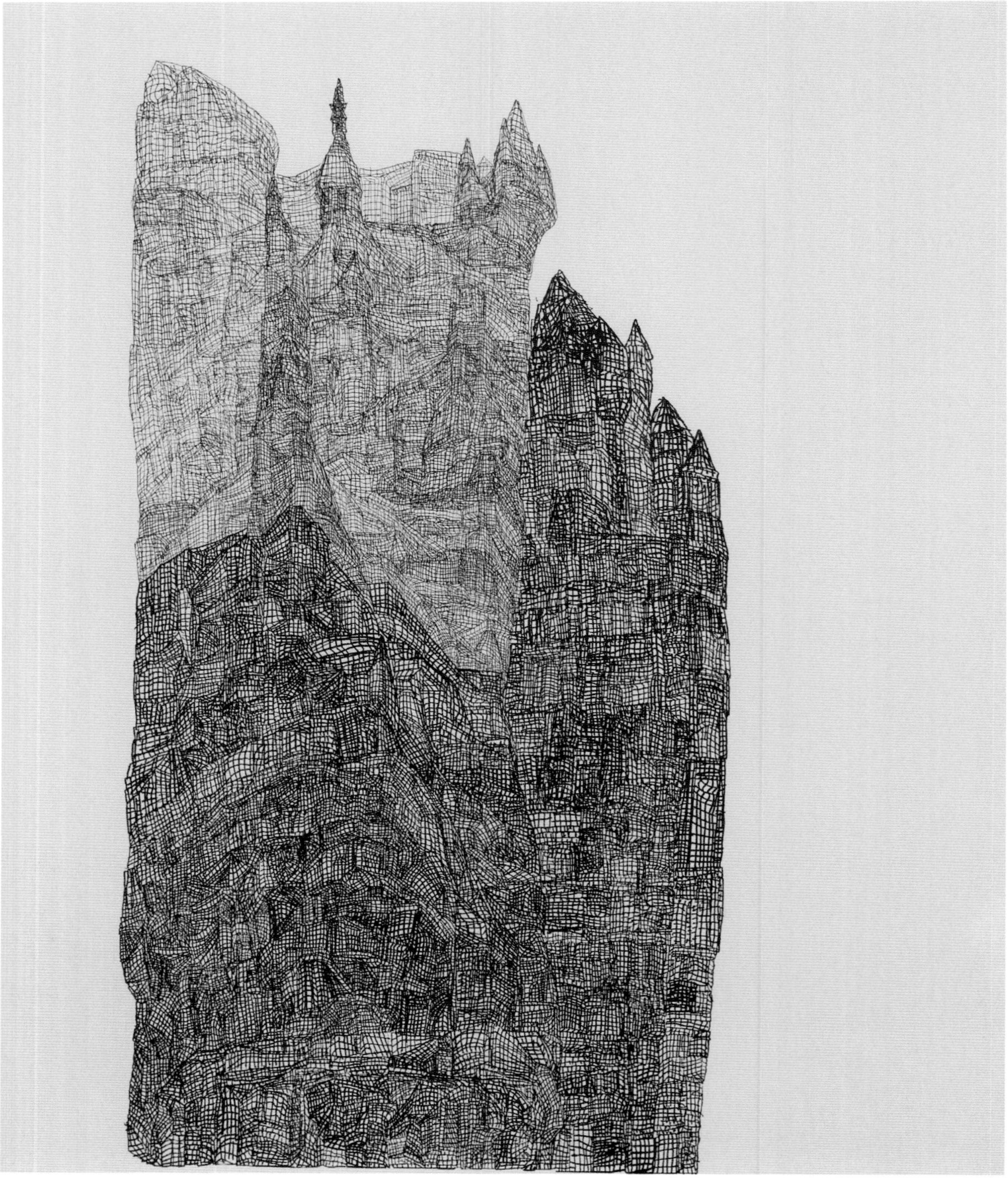

Katsuyoshi Takenaka, Metropolis, *2014, marker pen on canvas, 35¹³⁄₁₆ × 28¾ in (91 × 73 cm). Courtesy Atelier Yamanami, Shiga.*
The variation of pen pressure creates subtle tonal variations in this plotted cityscape with a detailed spired dome at the top.

position popularly considered to be floating and fractal in the atmosphere of the canvas, inviting the consideration of *Mist City* as a vast cosmos, while a more inherent reading of the composition could be that of four tall skyscrapers. The wash applied by Takenaka is the foreground, not the background. It is, as the title implies, a mist, or fog looming in the landscape, obscuring elements of the buildings from view.

This interplay between foreground and background is also present in drawings from his *Tower* series. In *Tower Series II* (2015) he worked in a reverse color palette with white architectural forms reading as almost skeletal against a black background. Takenaka's truly unique perspective renders him a creative architect and atmospheric planner.

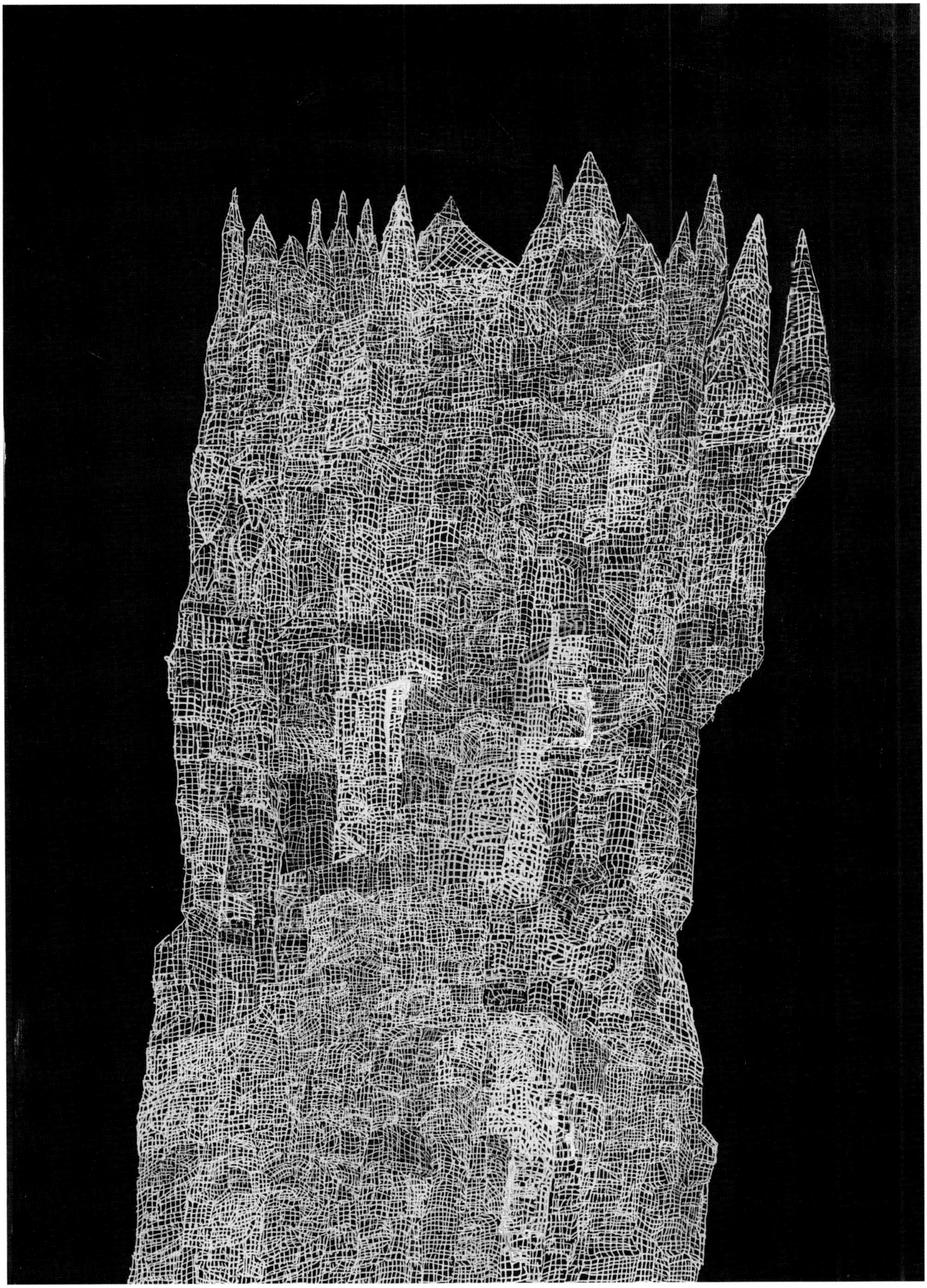

Katsuyoshi Takenaka, Tower Series II, *2015, acrylic paint, marker pen on canvas, 35 13/16 × 28¾ in (91 × 73 cm). Courtesy Atelier Yamanami, Shiga.* Drawing from the bottom and building upward, much like the physical erection of a building, the white lines on black background here feels both architectural and skeletal.

KATSUHIRO TERAO

(b. 1960, Osaka, Japan)

For his artistic practice, Katsuhiro Terao visualizes his environment, memories, and thoughts in terms of metal structures. His drawings present an anti-gravity architectural landscape with a craving for viewing from all directions. After graduating from high school, Terao worked with his father for 20 years as a welder. Following his parents' deaths and the closing of the iron factory, he began attending Osaka's Atelier Incurve when it opened in 2002. Founded by Hiroshi Imanaka, Atelier Incurve was established as the headquarters and art studio of the Social Welfare Foundation SOOHKAI, which fosters the artistic development of individuals with disability. Terao's highly dense, often monochromatic, detailed drawings evoke architectural blueprints while inherently echoing the steel beams of his welding experience. Terao is one of the most renowned artists working at Atelier Incurve. He has been exhibiting in museums, galleries, and art fairs internationally since 2004, including in New York, London, and Tokyo.

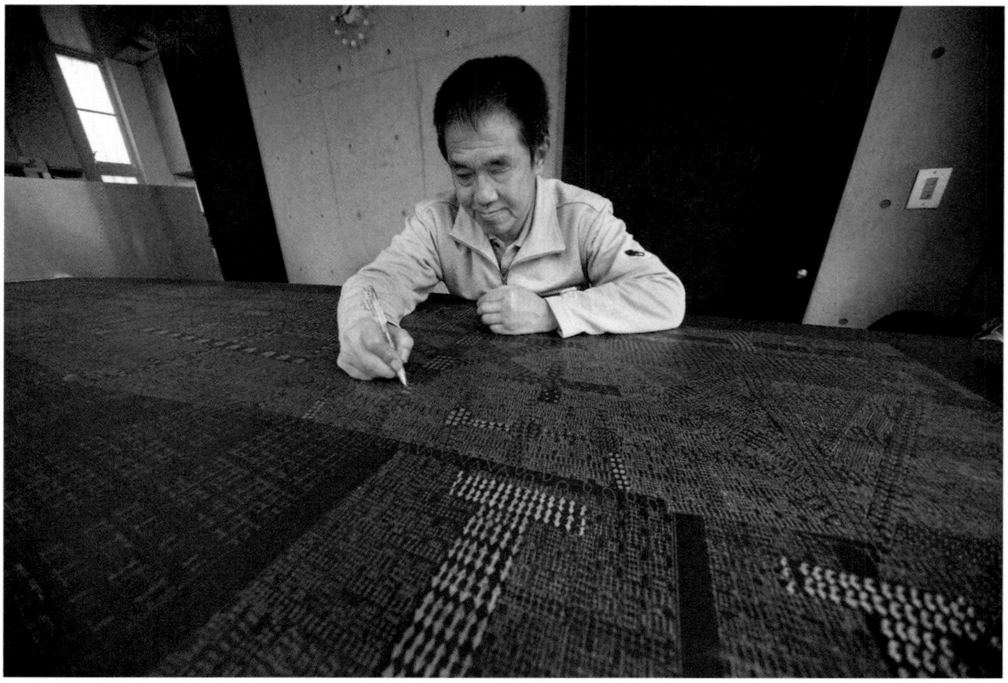

Katsuhiro Terao, 2017, photograph. Courtesy atelier incurve. A studio member since its opening, this portrait shows Terao working on one of his large-scale drawings at Atelier Incurve in Osaka, Japan.

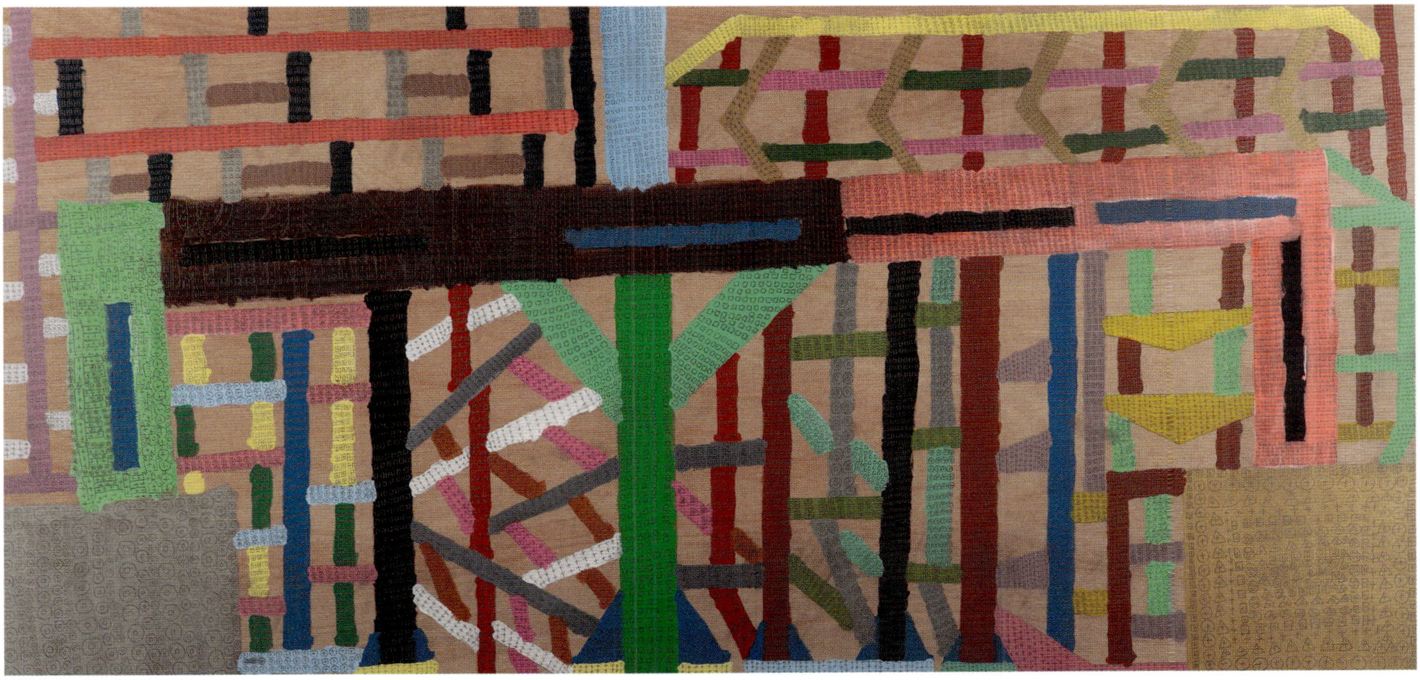

Katsuhiro Terao, Bridge Design 5, *2007, pencil and acrylic on wood board, 33¹³⁄₁₆ × 70 in (85.9 × 177.8 cm). Courtesy atelier incurve.* In this drawing from the 2000s, Terao applies various flat shapes of paint to create the design of a bridge. Layered on top of each designated color, are minutely plotted rows, in pencil, of symbols that include plus signs, squares, and concentric circles.

Katsuhiro Terao draws on his former career and experience as a welder to inform his creative compositions, resulting in a complex structure plan that is nostalgic to him, yet feels present, and almost futuristic. There is a tension in his mark-making between the ethereal quality of the lines and the weight evoked from his representation of steel structures. He refers to his drawings as "plans," reflecting their blueprint-like properties.

His initial drawings, from the early 2000s, presented simpler forms more topographical than architectural, but are recognizable within their developed vivid color palettes. In the decades proceeding, Terao's style matured into his definitive blueprint aesthetic, made with ballpoint pen acutely applied in scrupulous detail and repetition. His monumental work, *New York Past and Present, and Flag of the United States* (2015) demonstrates the archetypal and exemplary character of his compositions.

Terao is meticulous and measured about the pressure he enforces to control the amount of ink applied, which covers this black canvas edge-to-edge with metallic ballpoint pen. The monochromatic patterned forms introduce various perspectives for his invented steel structures. The upper left depicts inferred checkered pillars from a traditional landscape point of view, while representational steel girders zigzagging throughout the remainder of the canvas, from street map to building, take on multiple purposes and vantage points.

Extremely focused and fully committed to production while working at the studio at Atelier Incurve, Terao often will prepare paper to address his smaller-scale drawings when he is required to pause on a larger work to allow areas to dry. His smaller drawings are often on paper while his large drawings, over 6 ft (2m), are composed on canvas. For these substantial canvases, Terao works on them in sections in a scroll-like fashion, only seeing the totality of his invented structural schemas after completion.

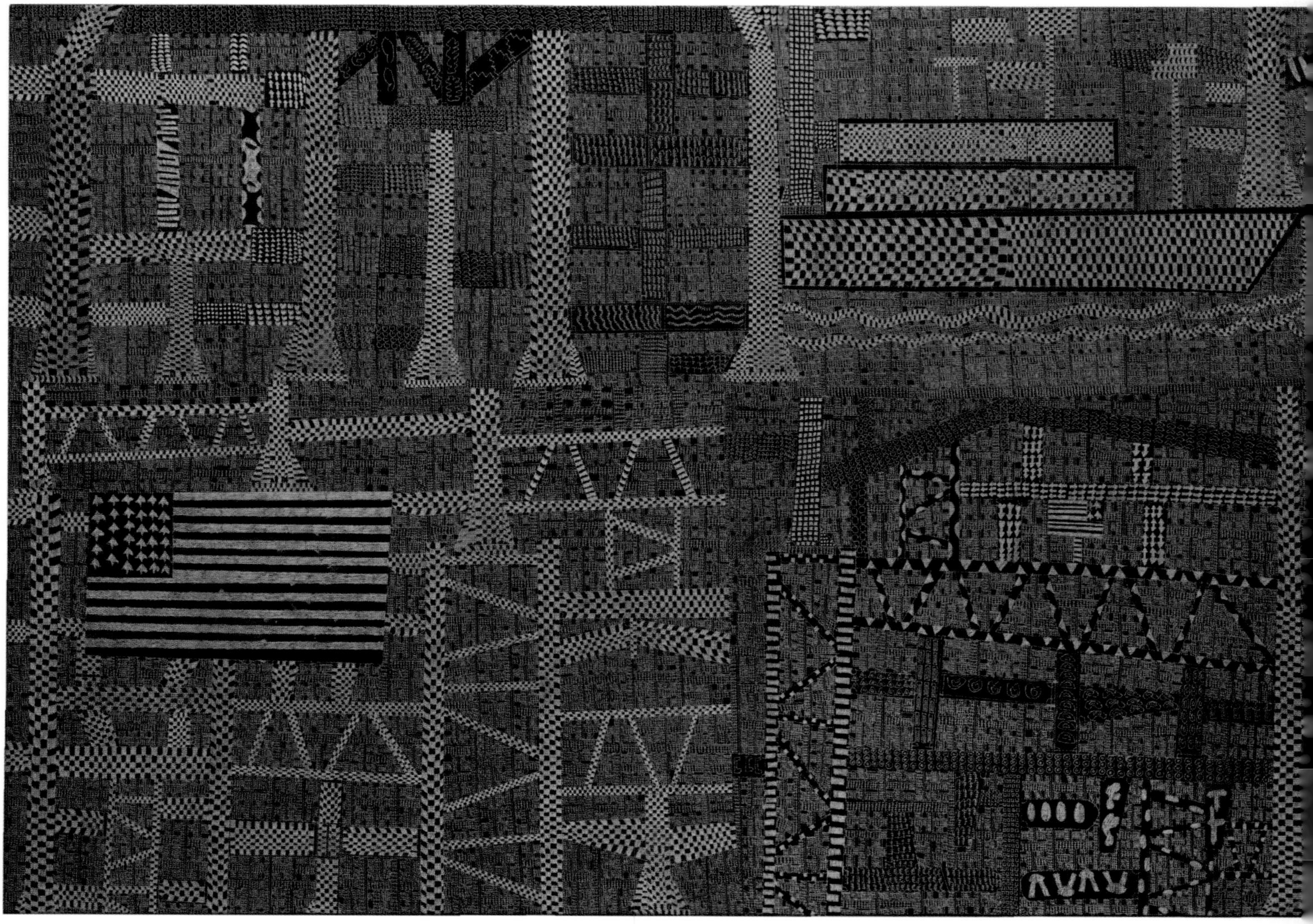

Katsuhiro Terao, New York Past and Present, and Flag of the United States, *2015, pen on canvas, 51⁵⁄₁₆ × 152¹¹⁄₁₆ in (130.3 × 387.9 cm). Courtesy atelier incurve.* This large-scale drawing of New York, abundant with checkered and patterned girders, seems to have multiple horizon lines and vantage points. Buildings, bridges, boats, and an American flag all emerge within the landscape.

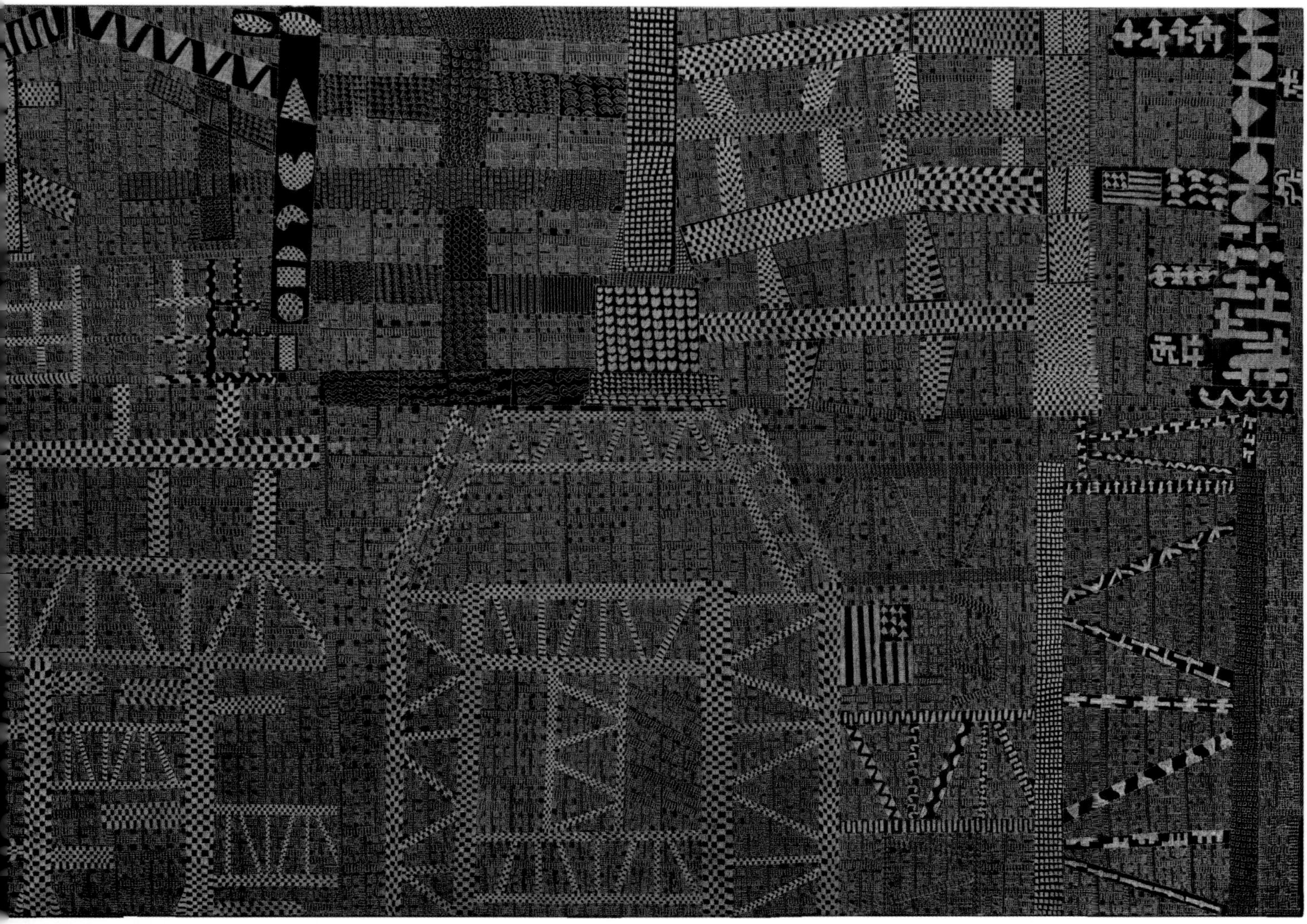

CHAPTER 11

FIGURATION: MEMORY, REPRODUCTION, AND DOCUMENTATION

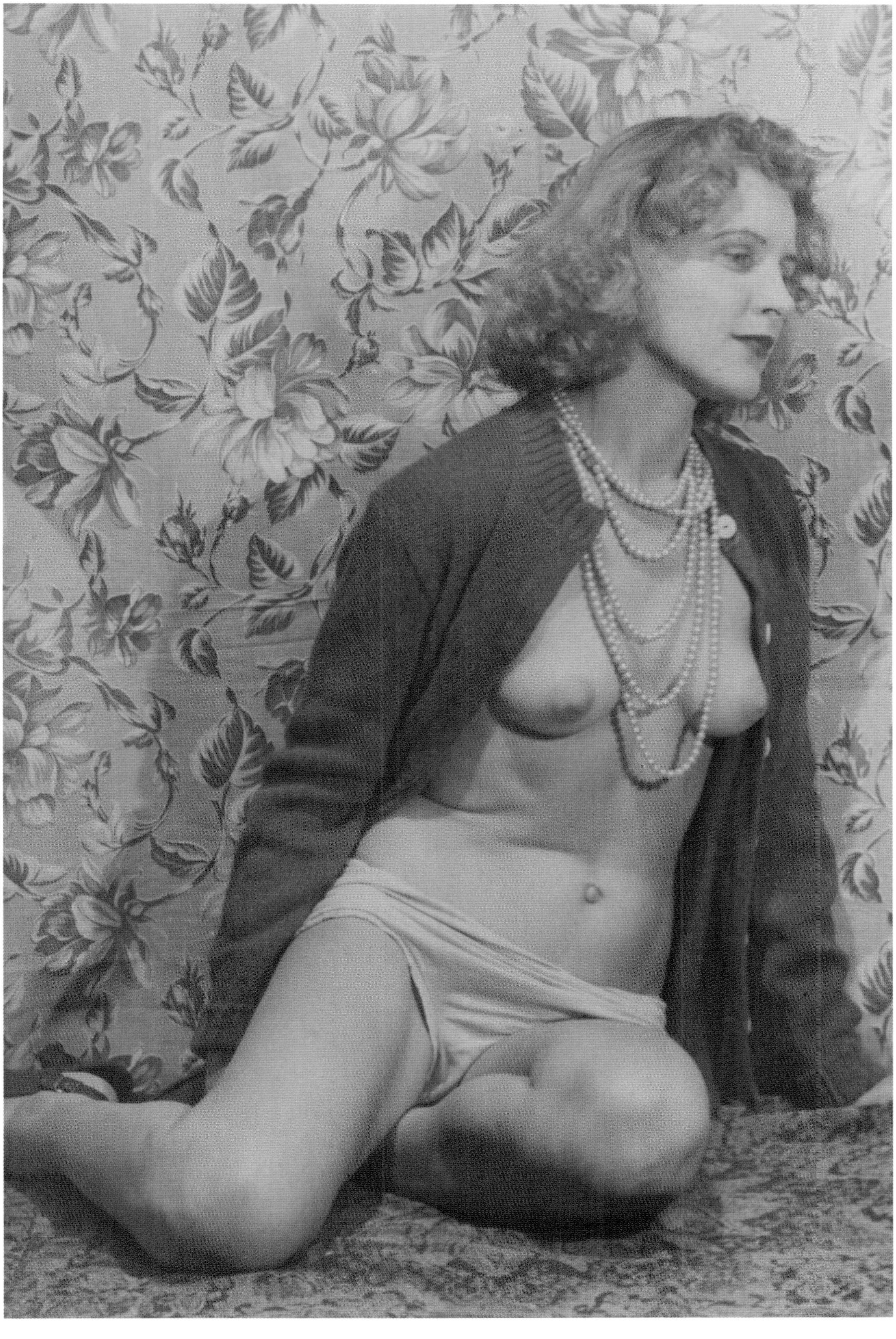

Eugene Von Bruenchenhein (American, 1910–1983), untitled, *1940s, photograph. Philadelphia Museum of Art.* From the 1940s onward, Von Bruenchenhein produced thousands of photographic images featuring his muse, his wife Marie (born Evelyn Kalka). Floral backdrops, handmade costumes, and elaborate accessories paired with Marie's commitment to the pose contribute to this effective body of work. The compositions range from pinup to surreal, often a collision of both.

CLOSE ENCOUNTERS

Lisa Slominski

Figuration explores the diverse representation of the human form through six distinct art practices. These various practices consider how the representation of the figure, or signifiers thereof, relates to messaging—whether personal, universal, invented, or documented. This introduction to the chapter presents the potential for figurative hybrids to express intimate visions within the practices of Shinichi Sawada (b. 1982) and Davood Koochaki (1939–2020). It examines figuration's potential as a communicative and visual relationship to experience within the work of Carlo Zinelli (1916–1974) and Helen Rae (1938–2021); and it raises the self-reflective decisions integral to the self-portraits of William Scott (b. 1964) and Chéri Samba (b. 1956).

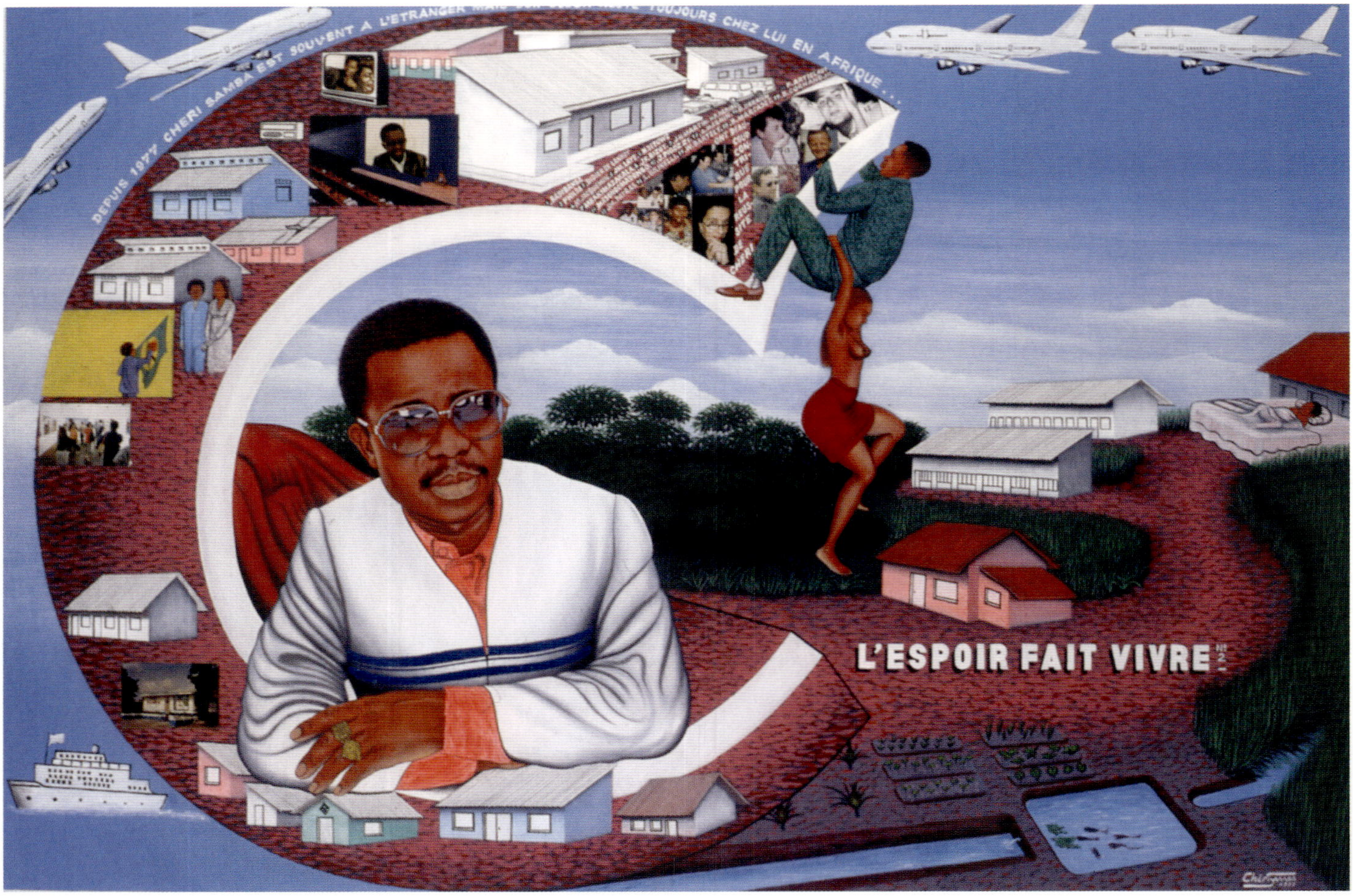

Chéri Samba, Hope Keeps You Going #2*, 1997, acrylic, sequins, photographs, and glue, 51³⁄₁₆ × 76⅜ in (130 x 194 cm). Courtesy Galerie MAGNIN-A, Paris.* In this surreal self-portrait, Samba is confidently positioned toward the viewer surrounded by a dreamlike landscape that merges into a graphically abundant letter "C." Text surrounding this illustrative graphic states "*despuis 1977 Cheri Samba est souvent a l'etranger mais son coeur reste toujours chez lui en afrique . . .*" (since 1977 Cheri Samba is often abroad but his heart always stays at home in Africa . . .).

The context of *Figuration* refers to a composition with visual language that relates to the human form and, often more broadly, infers visual elements of the "real world." In 20th-century art history, the term "figurative" was established in regular dialogue as a category broadly in juxtaposition to the development of abstract art. Onward, figurative notions of traditional and realistic representation have evolved dramatically, allowing unrestricted experimentation within retention of the essence of the human form. The creative practices explored in this chapter balance reference and recognition, metaphorical and memory, by using the human form as an experiential tool.

The implementation of invention and imagination via an artist's inner world is introduced by the sculptural forms of Japanese artist Shinichi Sawada (see page 362). His detailed and intimate ceramics combine figurative elements that are fantastically merged with spiritual and animal characteristics. This hybridization is also present in the oeuvre of Iranian artist Davood Koochaki (see page 366), whose stark colored-pencil drawings depict isolated and merged humanoid forms. Though Sawada and Koochaki have disparate practices, their aesthetics share a synthesis of human and enigmatic creature qualities. In particular, their implementation of recognizable fundamental facial elements—eyes, nose, and mouth—create familiarity and connection to the figurative amid the otherworldly and mysterious.

Unrestricted experimentation with the human form is an integral device in the drawings of American artist Helen Rae (see page 370). She drew from referencing fashion editorial photographs of models pulled from magazines, yet her compositional decisions seem intimately communicative: an inference of her experience over mere reproduction. Rae, who was limited verbally, reworked the figures in her composition, challenging the parameters of figuration by transcending the original's visual into a personal editorial. Italian artist Carlo Zinelli (see page 374) used repeated figurative forms and representational symbols in his drawings, suggestive that this creative act was communicative of his experiences. Limited on verbal communication following a decline in mental health, Zinelli was first observed drawing on the hospital walls while medically institutionalized. Following the provision of adequate materials, his practice flourished with figurative silhouettes—perhaps echoing his institutional environment—among a dense background of cryptic and emblematic signifiers. Through appropriation of images, from memory or from experience, both Rae and Zinelli rendered power in the depiction of the human form as means of expression.

Portraiture has been a creative tool used to express characteristics beyond strict documentation, aesthetically and symbolically attributing power, beauty, and prestige to its subjects. In his series of self-portraits, *J'aime la couleur (I like color)*, Congolese artist Chéri Samba (see page 378) emblematically confirms his identity as an artist by positioning a paintbrush between his teeth. His colorful and surreal oeuvre is often figurative, responding critically with wit to African stereotypes. The self-portraits of American artist William Scott (see page 354) present reinvented versions of himself as nostalgic icons such as Billy the Kid or a professional basketball player. A conceptual thread of Scott's practice is the reinterpretation of his environment and internal experiences as utopian propositions. Often figure-focused, the narrative of his paintings has the opportunity to invent, imagine, and memorialize without the restrictions of linearity.

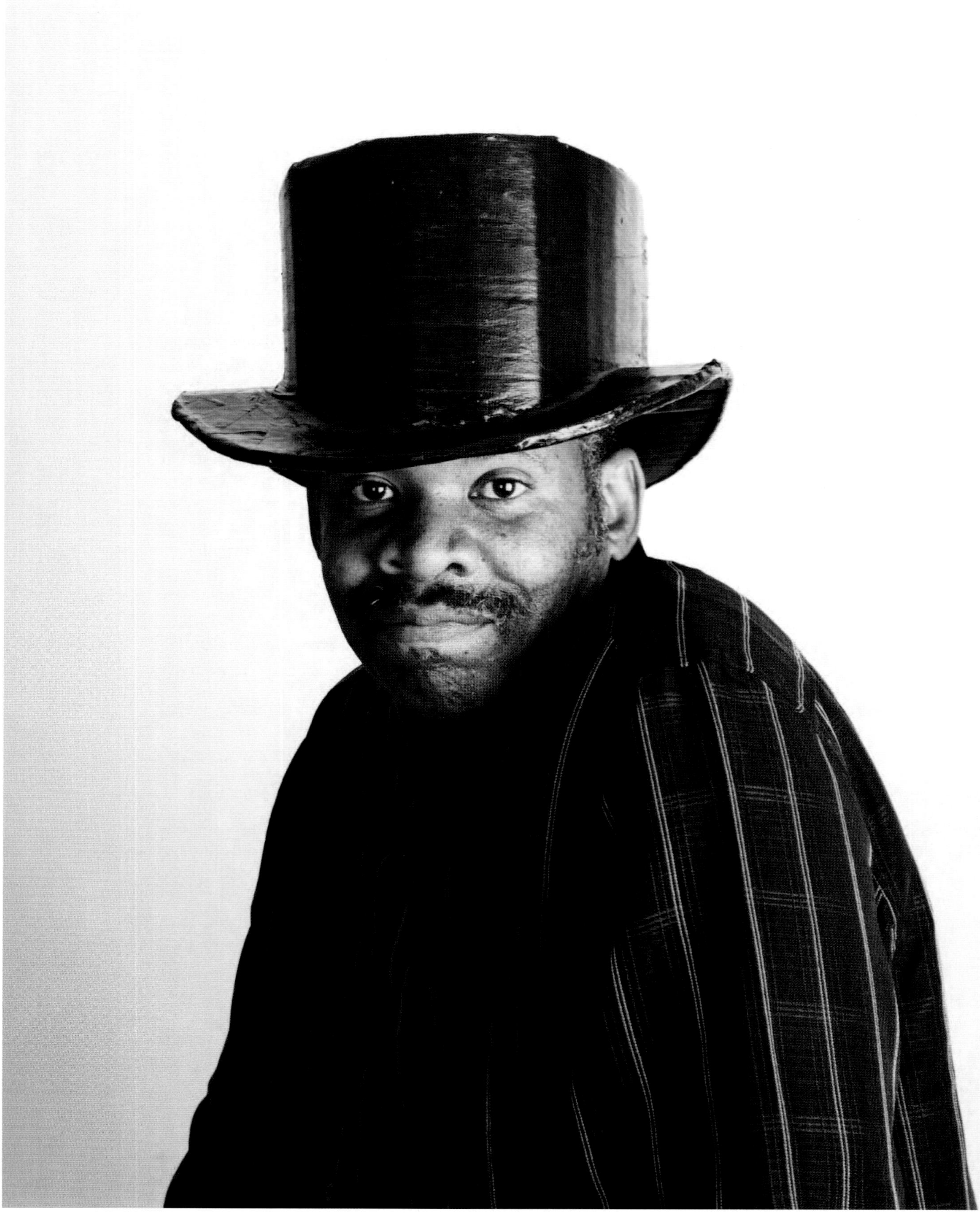

William Scott, 2018, photograph by Daniel Trese. Courtesy of the artist and Creative Growth Art Center. In this portrait of Scott he wears an artist-made hat. Scott considers himself as both an artist and a social theorist.

WILLIAM SCOTT

(b. 1964, San Francisco, California, USA)

The vivacious paintings of William Scott conceptually reassess his private and public world, resulting in utopian proposals. Evocative of memorials, his figurative and architectural oeuvre—encompassing past, present, and future—intimately connects to his history. In his series of self-portraits, Scott emulates alternate personas: a professional basketball player, Billy the Kid, or simply a modified version of himself. These transformations allow him to creatively circumvent a linear history. He has been developing his practice at Creative Growth in Oakland since 1992. Founded in 1974, Creative Growth is a nonprofit that serves artists with disabilities by providing a professional studio environment for artistic development, gallery exhibition, and representation. Scott is interested in the culture of community, specifically as it relates to memory and place, and therefore is referred to as a social theorist and an artist. He has had solo exhibitions with White Columns, New York (2006), Ortuzar Projects, New York (2020), and Studio Voltaire, London (2021). In addition to his works' inclusion in museum collections, Scott is celebrated by renowned contemporary artists in the private collections of Cindy Sherman and Chris Ofili.

Interview by Sophia Cosmadopoulos

Sophia Cosmadopoulos: William, tell me about figuration and portraiture in your work?

William Scott: My self-portraits are of Billy the Kid, because I will be reborn as Billy the Kid, to be in a new life of 1960s and 70s, to be a basketball player in 1974, to help those kids, teach them how to play basketball, to show them how to play basketball, when I will be a teenage kid. I draw myself as a church choir kid. To be in a church choir in 1981, in another life of 1981.

Did you play basketball and sing in a church choir when you were a child?

I wasn't playing basketball. In another life, I would play basketball. In another life, I will be having professional health, without disability. Without disability, to have no disability. To be having a professional health, to play basketball. I would be born a professional kid, a professional guy. To be born good. That's right.

So, you dream of being a professional basketball player, like Billy the Kid? How do you paint yourself looking?

I would have an Afro, a big round Afro. While playing basketball, I will be having a real round-hair Afro. The big Afro back in the 70s, like in the 1970s. I did not want no Afro in the first life. In the first life I did not want no Afro. I had short hair in the first life. But the next life I will be wearing an Afro, the round-hair Afro when I will be a kid, in the next life. To be wearing a Jheri curl in 1981, to be wearing a Jheri curl, to be in a church choir and wearing a Jheri curl, with the curly hair. In another life. With the professional health, in a basketball outfit. In a basketball outfit, with the new body. With the new body, with no burns, no scars. Never again. In another life of 1970s and 80s in my whole, new life.

Would you like to elaborate on the story of your scars? I know they are a common theme in your paintings.

I was playing with fire on the stove and accidentally caught on fire. I put the T-shirt on the stove and accidentally caught on fire. By accident. Because I did not learn no lessons, but I won't do that again. Won't be eight years old again. I would not do that again. I would not be hospitalized again. I will not be in the burn center, never again in 1972. I will stay off the stove, to stay away from that stove. Still, when I will be eight years old again in another life, when another life comes one day. And I will become a basketball player in 1973. To grow up to be a basketball kid in 1973.

Sometimes you paint yourself with scars and sometimes without scars. Why is that?

That's right. Because the torso with no scars, that's the new life. That's the new life. I will be a choir kid, to be a church man, to grow up to be in a church choir in 1981, to be making some friends at church in 1981. When another life comes again, when another life comes. In 1981, I will be meeting a girlfriend, Michelle, in 1981, at the Rose Olivet Baptist Church on Bayshore, to be in the choir with her.

Besides your self-portraits, who else do you like to paint?

I like to paint my family and my mom, and me as a kid, my young family. To be painting my young family, of the 70s, my young family of the 1970s. So they can bring the lives back from the 70s, bring them back so they can bring the world back.

Yes, can you explain that William? How will you bring people back with your paintings?

To bring back, as a reborn of the family. Reborn the family. To rebuilding the new family lives, family members. To rebuild the family members of Arterberry families. My sister Nadine and my grandfather and my uncle. My Uncle Calvin. And Auntie Helen. And my great uncles, of Uncle General, grandaddy's brothers who lost their lives. My Uncle Tack, to bring him back to life. And draw a picture of them to bring them back to life. Because I was missing Uncle Tack Arterberry, of the preacher man. I am going to bring him back to life, to draw a picture of Uncle Tack and Aunt Jessie-Mae. I lost my great auntie, Aunt Jessie-Mae Arterberry. I'm going to bring her back to life. In another life, to draw a young Aunt Jessie-Mae. The young men and the young women, the young church women, the younger ones of the new generations. To bring them back to life. Who lost the lives to illness.

You also bring back celebrities in your paintings, is that right?

The famous people too. Aretha Franklin, Mary Wilson, and Diana Ross, who is still living. Because Mary Wilson passed away. That's why I do Diana Ross, because Mary Wilson passed away. Because I make Diana Ross into a new Diana Ross of a young Diana Ross, into Wholesome Encounters to make her into a humorous woman, wearing a blue shirt and a blue jeans. And Vivica Fox and Halle Berry and Rosie Perez with the city, Hollywood City. City of Hollywood. So they can bring people's lives back. I did En Vogue of Cindy Herron, who brings them back to life, of the dead people, to raise the dead people back to life. To bring them back to life, to bring them back alive.

How would you define "Wholesome Encounters"?

Wholesome Encounters means, it's kind of a humorous creature. Kinds of humans, of wholesome humans, of good people, of outer space. We need to cancel the scary stuff. We need to cancel the aliens and monsters and evil, we need to cancel all of those. So they can hire the Wholesome Close Encounters (WCE). Hiring the new creatures of wholesome because they are humorous people of Interskyline, new art space. So they can bring people's lives back. Because Inner Limits is the name of the Skyline People who bring lots of people back to life from the dead.

Will you explain what "Inner Limits" are?

In another life, the Skyline Friendly Organization (SFO) is a spaceship that tours the world. The Inner Limits is a name of the skyline people of SFO, that's the name of the people. The name of the Wholesome Encounters. That's the name of it, it's called Inner Limits. That's the name of the people. Of a good people, without aliens, without monsters, without evils. People in outer space and everywhere, Interskyline everywhere. SFO people, wholesome Skyline Friendly Organization.

What do the wholesome people do?

They would take away the evils and aliens, take away the monsters, to take away the horrors. Take away all kinds of scary things, take it away. To cancel all of those. To put Wholesome Encounters into humorous people. And the humorous inside the world, inside the planet. To make people feel good, feel happy, feel excited. And feel very nice. With no attitude, no mean, no worrying, no bad stuff. No. They bring 20th century back, who lost their lives in the 20th century of the 1960s and 70s,

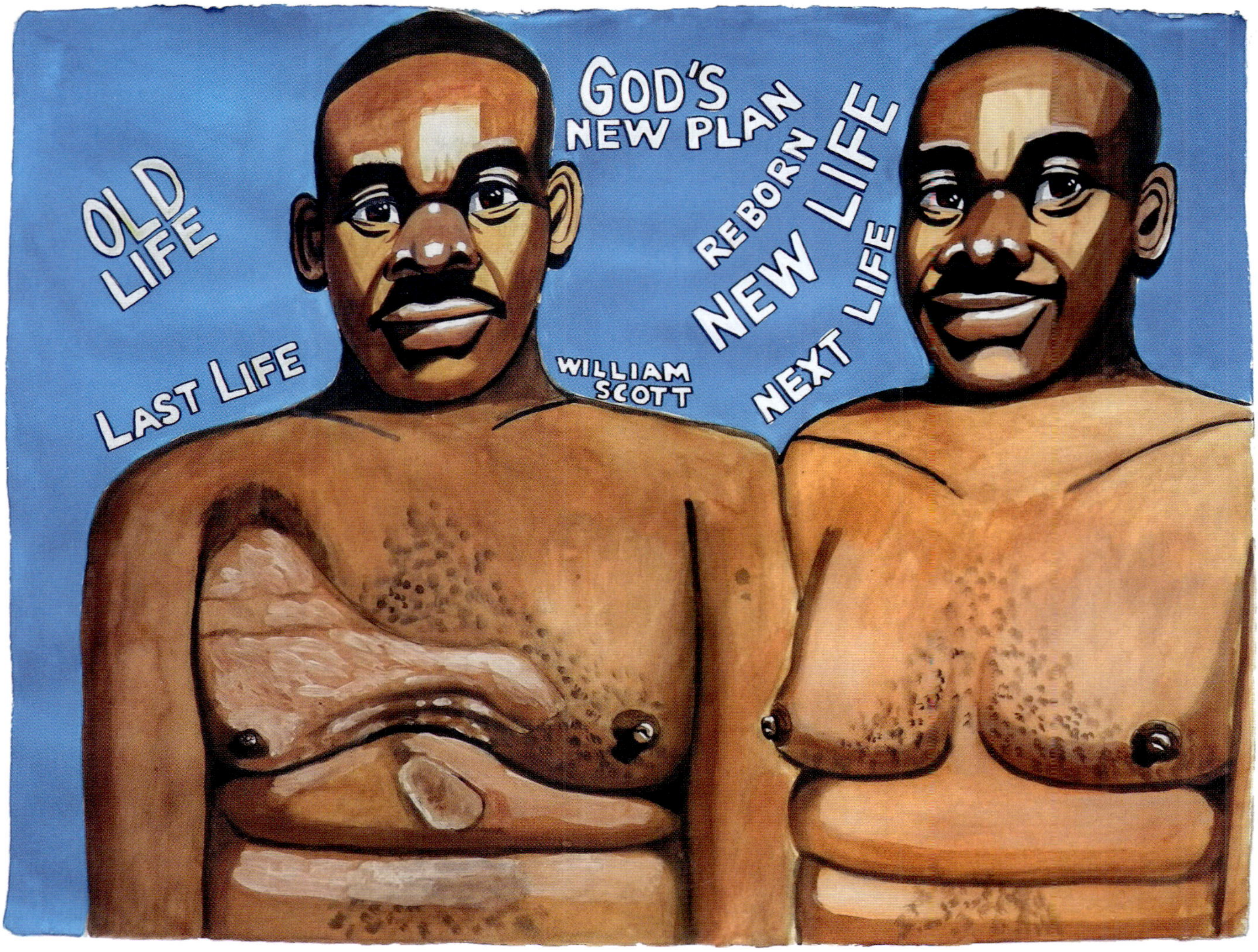

William Scott, untitled, *2012, acrylic on paper, 20 × 28 in (51 × 71 cm). Courtesy of the artist and Creative Growth Art Center.* This double portrait of Scott represents his proposal for "new life," where his scars from a childhood accident illustrated on his torso and chest on the left ("OLD LIFE") are removed in his depiction of his new life on the right ("REBORN NEW LIFE").

killings and gun violence. Because Martin Luther King was assassinated in 1968. We need to bring Martin Luther King back to life in another life of 20th century. Martin Luther King has not been alive for a long time. He's been dead for years. He died young. He got shot by James Earl Ray. Plus Inner Limits will be hiring the new people of the good people who bring people back to life, who lost their lives. Aliens and evil causes crimes, it causes bad stuff. And killings and gun violence, it was the aliens who caused that. The horror movies cause that, we need to take away the horror movies, cancel all those horror movies, cancel all those aliens and evils and monsters. So it will stop the crimes and killings and gun violence and hate crime, to stop the bad stuff.

William, what materials do you use when making your work?

I use acrylics and brushes. I use brushes and acrylic paints.

Do you start with a sketch or do you go straight to acrylic on canvas?

I started drawing before gesso. Before acrylics. I draw something before acrylic paints, before I put the acrylics on the canvas.

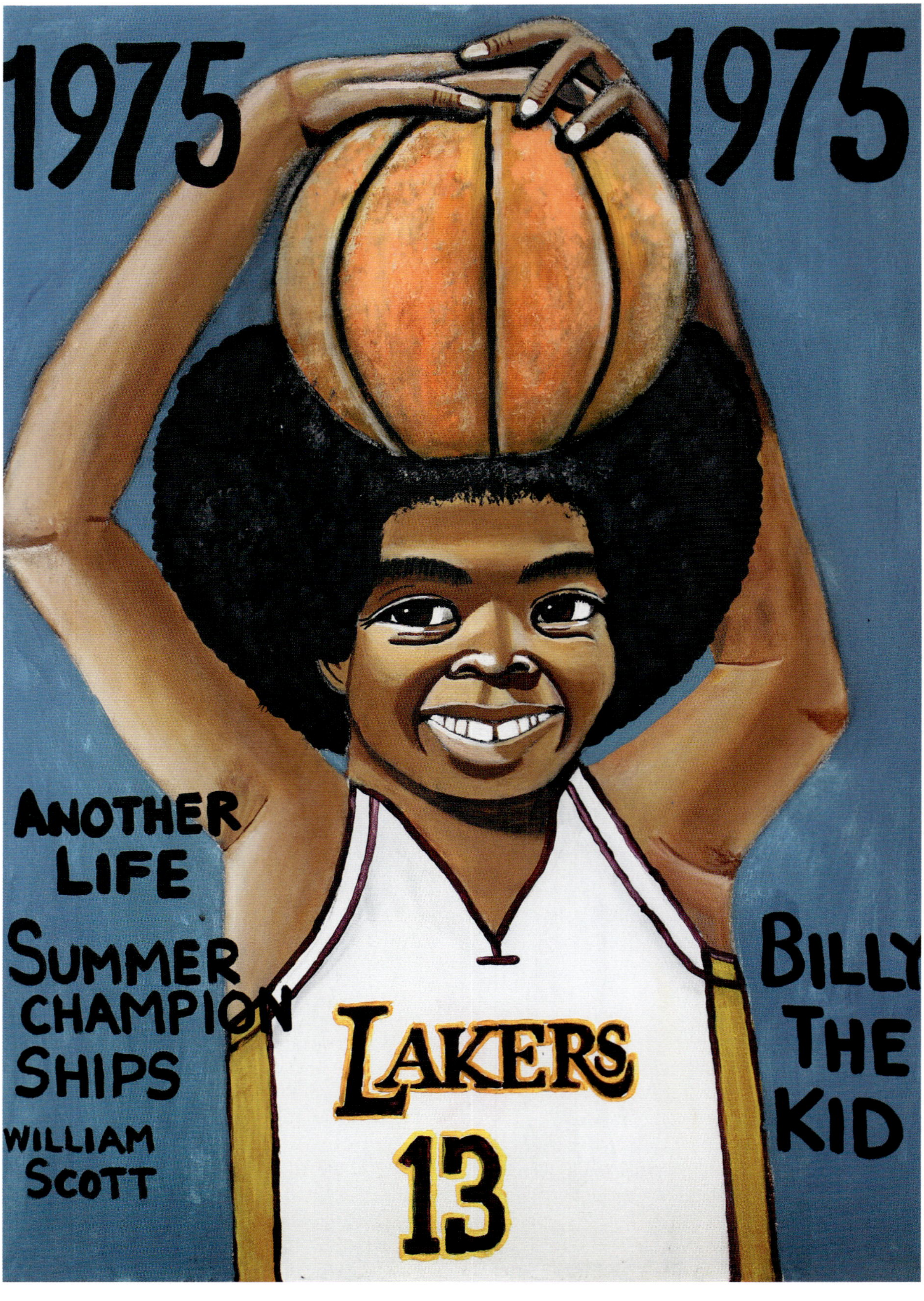

William Scott, untitled, *2013, acrylic on paper, 30 × 40 in (76 × 101 cm). Courtesy of the artist and Creative Growth Art Center.* Though Scott never played basketball, in this version of him as a child, he is both an LA Laker basketball player and Billy the Kid. The painted text "ANOTHER LIFE" confirms his placement across dimensions and the proposal for alternate lives.

And do you work from photographs or from your memory?

I work from photographs and from my memory too. And then I paint Halle Berry of the Cleopatra woman, the Cleopatra-zilla sexy woman of the big woman of Halle Berry, who is hiring the peace and good people to create good people in the future. Of the good, healthier lives.

Your work is very nostalgic, capturing a very specific era, can you tell me about that era? Where and when did you grow up?

I grew up in Hunters Point in San Francisco. It was back in the 60s. Back in the 60s and 70s, I was a kid back in the 60s and 70s. I did like it good, I did like 1970. I used to ride a bicycle, I used to ride a bike. I was a kid. I was a teenager. I used to skate a lot. Roller skates. I used to skate with my little sister Kim. I fell on the ground and my teeth was broke. I had a crack in my teeth back in 1976 and I had to go to the dentist. And it was in this life. It was in the first life, the first one. But in another life I would not have no broken teeth, never again. When 1976 comes again, I will not have no more broken teeth. No more dentist, no more dental appointments. I will be wearing an Afro. To be keeping playing basketball. To grow up to be a basketball player.

What was San Francisco like when you were a kid?

It looked like a skyscraper, like the Bank of America building. It would look back in the 70s, like a new skyscraper. It would look like the Transamerica pyramid. The Geneva Towers, I remember the Geneva Towers. So I drew the Geneva Towers, and the Martin Luther King Towers. Of the new towers.

You regularly wrote to your local politicians about how to improve San Francisco. Did you ever have any ideas for how San Francisco could change?

It can change into “Praise Frisco.” Rename it Praise Frisco like a new city, with the balconies, high rise of the Hawaii city. With the balconies. Change San Francisco into a balconies city with the high rise balconies, lots of ones. For the praise town of the Gospel people who live in a praise town. Of a healthier place of a good place. And the Bahamas and Disney World will be in Hunters Point with the two story houses in the War Town Housing, the new ones. Like it was back in the 60s up on the hills, because we need to bring the vintage housing back up on the hill when they tore them down. It’s gonna be called “Disneywood.” Would change into a new Fox Plaza, the new shape of the new balcony shape. Reshaping the Fox Plaza with the new penthouse on top. With the new shaped penthouse of Praise Frisco.

It seems like you paint things as you wish they would be or how you wish you were, or other people were. Can you tell me about your wishes in your paintings?

I wish for there to be a superstar gospel town. With the church people who lives in a new city without original San Francisco, original city, into a new city.

You have an entire series of police men and women, what interests you about them?

I paint the dancing police officers who helps the good people with the new uniforms. Helps the good people without no crimes, without no crime no justice, no jails. Into a new hall of justice and to Praise Jails of the dancing centers. Like a new building. Into a new Hall of Justice of the Community Dancing Center.

Do you paint police officers like you wish they would be?

Yeah, I do. I paint police like I wish. Like good, like musical cops, like the new TV series, *Musical Cop*, the new TV series. Terry and my sister were police officers. They are working families. They work with the prisons. Terry and Kim. They used to work, they are retired. The police officers I paint are wholesome people.

What are some of your favorite pieces of art?

My favorite is Inner Limits. Wholesome Encounters, science-fiction drawings. Science-fiction paintings, that’s my favorite of my artwork. Of my family members, of my Billy the Kid, of my self-portrait. The architects, in the new architects drawings.

How do you identify as an artist?

I describe myself good. To stay good, and to keep up the good artist. To stay that way of my memory, to be staying that way of the good memory, to keep up the good artists for a long time. For a long life. Keep up the good artists for a long life, until another life comes, to keep up my memory until another life comes. To keep it up, to keep the things up. Because I made with the pencil and acrylic paint on the canvas, to draw something on the canvas, to make into a masterpiece. Because I’m the star artist, I’ve been at Creative Growth a long time. I’d like to stay at Creative Growth for a long time.

You have been working at Creative Growth since 1992. Would you describe what your days at the studio are like?

I'd like to stay at Creative Growth for a long time. The studio looks like more an art center. The materials and equipment and supplies, they have my favorite supplies at the studio in Creative Growth.

What would you say is the most important aspect of your work? Why should everyone see it?

Because we need the community, that's very important, the community. We need art for the community, so they can bring lots of people back to life. We need lots of people who lost their lives, the Coronavirus, gun violence, and hate crimes. Killings of Asian people need to bring Asian people back to life to get rid of those hate crimes. Because hate crime is dangerous. We need to take the hate crimes of the world off the planet. We need to take them off the planet, take those crimes off the planet, so we can hiring the peace of the wholesome humoring people, so they can bring people's lives back from the dead, who lost their lives.

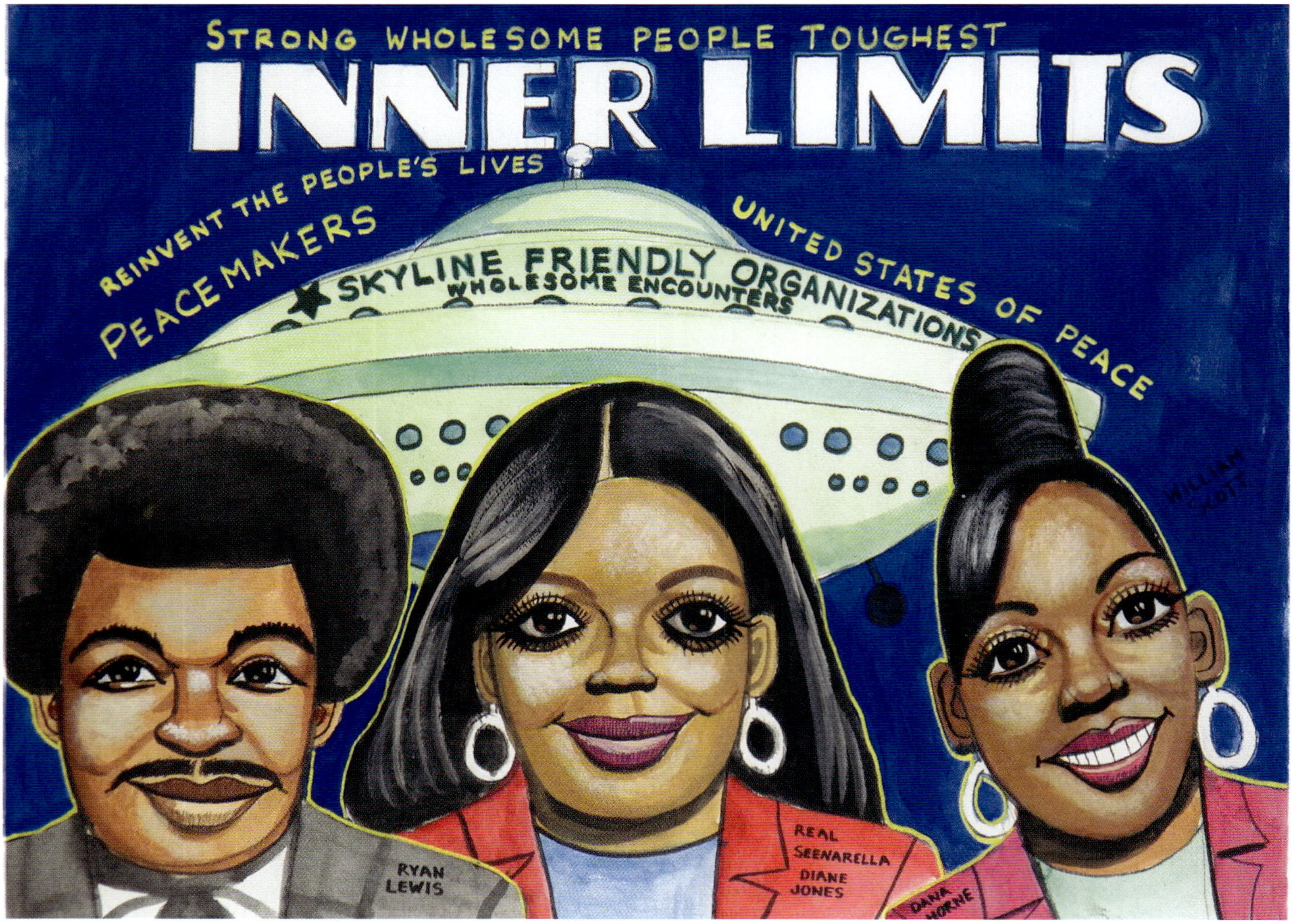

William Scott, untitled, *2012, acrylic on paper, 18 × 24 in (46 × 61 cm). Courtesy of the artist and Creative Growth Art Center.* In this utopian painting, Scott's concepts of both "Inner Limits" and "Wholesome Encounters" are presented. The Skyline Friendly Organization (SFO) is the spaceship in the background, which pursues worldly travel.

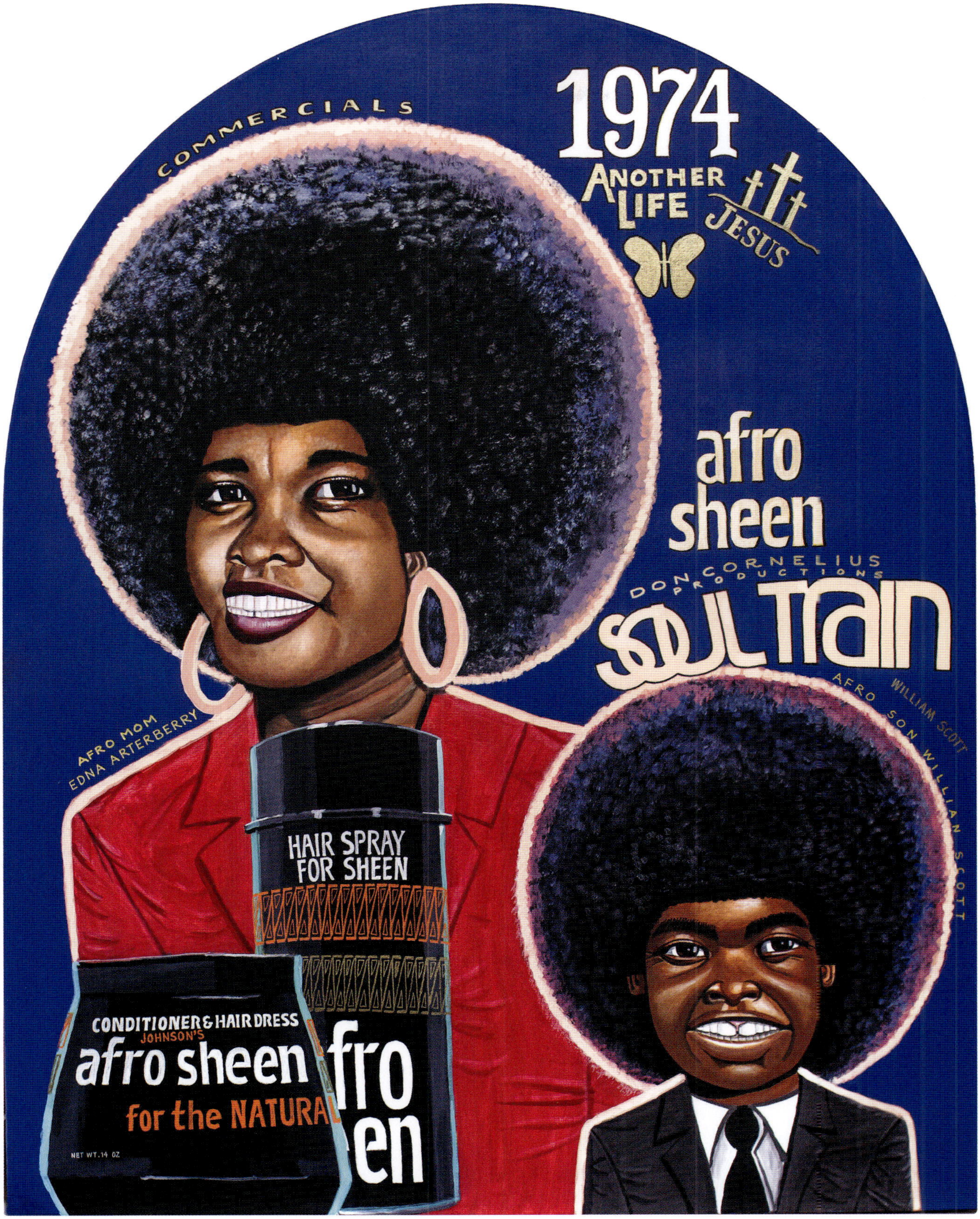

William Scott, untitled, *2016, acrylic on canvas, 42¼ × 60½ in (107.3 × 153.7 cm). Courtesy of the artist and Creative Growth Art Center*. This painting shows Scott's interest in portraying his family in the era of the 1970s, emphasized by cultural references to Soul Train and Afro Sheen. Scott has a penchant for featuring figures with Afros, seen here with young Scott and his mother both donning the iconic hairstyle.

SHINICHI SAWADA

(b. 1982, Shiga Prefecture, Japan)

Shinichi Sawada's perhaps unexpected inclusion in the 55th Venice Biennale (2013), curated by Massimiliano Gioni, facilitated an international introduction to his tactile, anthropomorphic ceramics. Since 2000, Sawada has been attending Nakayoshi Fukushikai, a social welfare organization supporting individuals with intellectual disabilities. This center, located in western Japan, has fostered his intricately detailed creative ceramic practice. Predominantly figurative but with elaborate fanaticism, his oeuvre combines the repetitive placement of orderly raised spikes with more biotic formations. Sawada is autistic with limited verbal communication, so while his poetic confidence is observable when he is working, the specific concepts of his ceramics remain thoughtful, suggestive readings made by others. Following the Venice Biennale, Sawada was part of *The Doors of Perception* at the Frieze Art Fair, New York (2019) and solo exhibitions including the Museum Lothar Fischer in Neumarkt (2020), Georg Kolbe Museum, Berlin (2020), and Venus Over Manhattan, New York (2021).

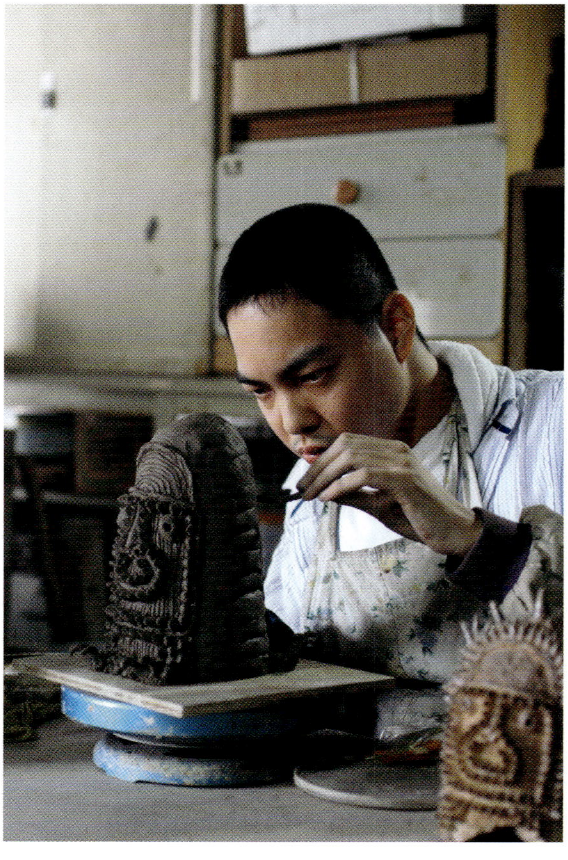

Shinichi Sawada, n.d., photograph. Courtesy the artist and Nakayoshi Fukushikai. Here Sawada is working on one of his ceramic forms at the Nakayoshi Fukushikai studio in Japan. His attention to detail in his creative practice concerns the entire sculpture: front, back, sides, and top.

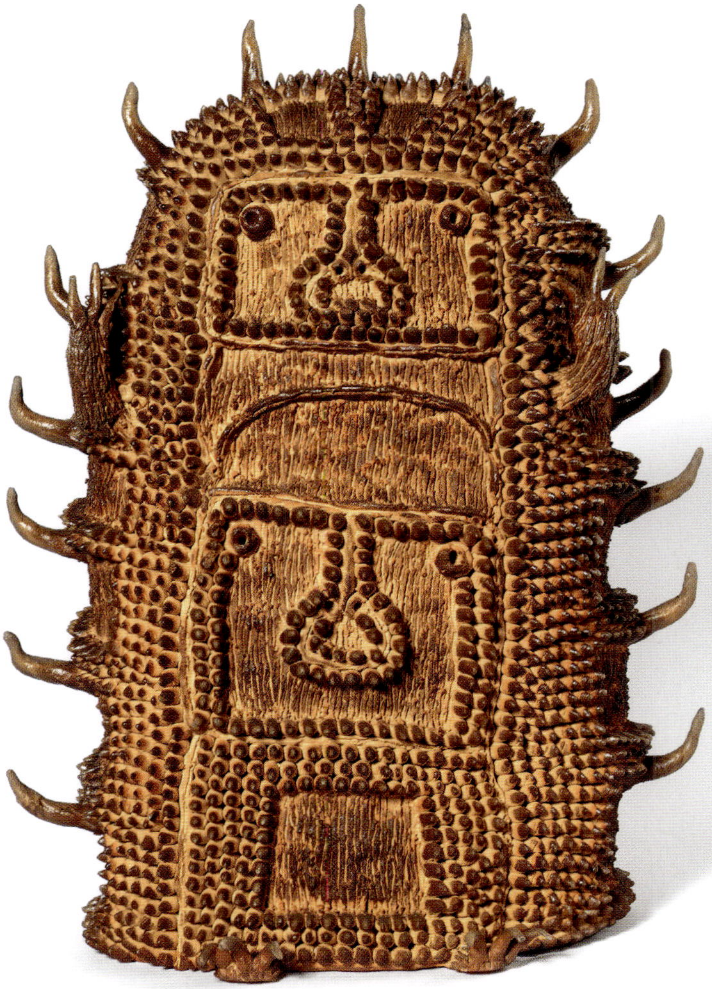

Shinichi Sawada, untitled (116), *2006–2010, ceramic, 13 × 9⅞ × 16½ in (33 × 24 × 42 cm). Courtesy Jennifer Lauren Gallery.* In this double-faced sculpture, Sawada's process of applying small raised ceramic bumps or spikes is so intricately dense that the effect is almost of hair or fur. The spikes are juxtapositioned with a vertical brushlike texture for areas defining faces.

The ceramic process of Shinichi Sawada at Nakayoshi Fukushikai is in line with the Shigaraki tradition—the region housed one of Japan's six ancient kilns. Sawada's technical elements of tools, clay, kiln, and wood are based on tradition, yet his forms and modeling methods are a departure of noticeable innovation. Prior to ceramics, Sawada engaged with *sashiko*, a traditional embroidery method dating back to Japan's Edo period (ca. 1603-1868). The *sashiko* stitching, with its characteristics of densely detailed rows and columns, seems to be dimensionally reflected in the spikes of Sawada's ceramics. The sculpture's gaze appears to be an entrance to Sawada's private world, with a visual aesthetic that resonates with figures from Japan's Neolithic Jōmon period.

Sawada works with steadfast confidence in preferred silence or with a low-humming radio while in the studio, and completes the sculpting of clay for an individual ceramic in about four days. Since the age of 18, Sawada has been attending Nakayoshi Fukushikai in the Shiga prefecture of Japan on Mondays, Tuesdays, and Thursdays. Seemingly interested in activities that are tactile, he spends these mornings in the center's bakery making bread and afternoons in the ceramic studio.

Sawada's ceramics teeter between ancient and contemporary anime but simultaneously elude to a ritualistic authority and prescribed whimsy. Initially, Sawada responded to approximately 15 themes Then in 2017, he expanded his schematic execution rendering each ceramic uniquely via his own formal language. Modest in scale, the ceramics' ornamental beauty requires substantial time from the viewer, especially considering their cylindrical point of view that allows all-encompassing viewpoints.

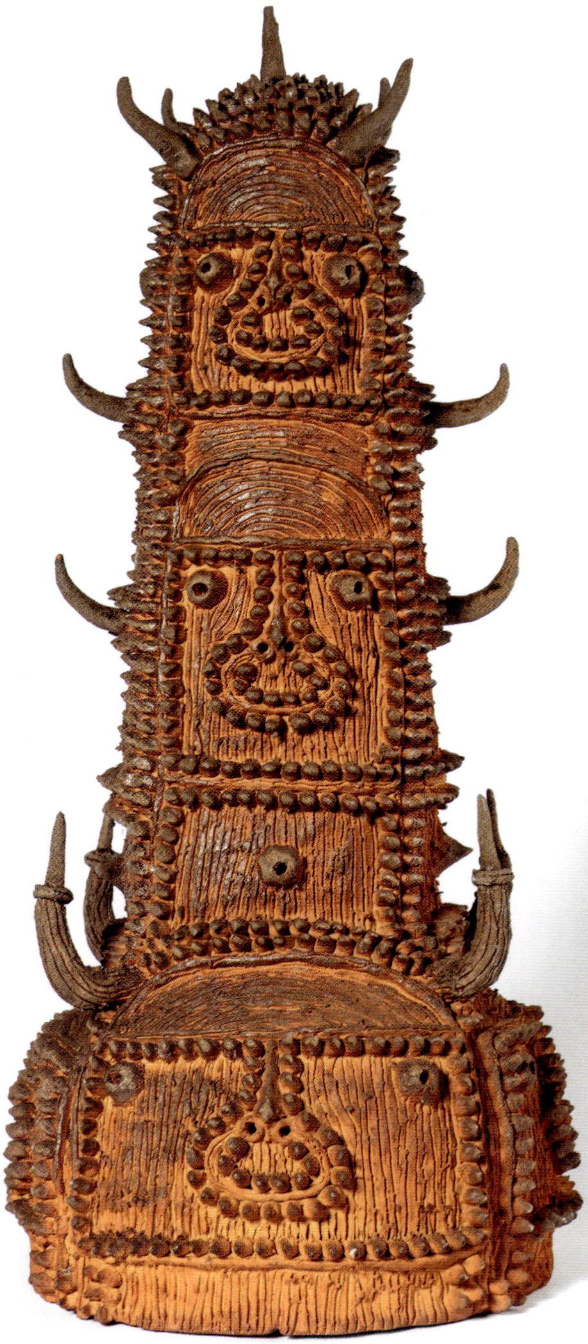

Shinichi Sawada, untitled (114), *2006–2010, ceramic, 9 13/16 × 9 13/16 × 20 7/8 in (25 × 25 × 53 cm). Courtesy Jennifer Lauren Gallery.* This totemic form demonstrates the orderly and systematic approach applied by Sawada. Three symmetrically stacked faces are flanked by energetic protruding shapes that give the overall work a powerful but delicate silhouette.

"I chose them as they seemed to contain so many variations of things I had seen before. I liked how they connected to centuries of depictions of imaginary beings (which immediately complicates any reductive reading of self-taught art as developing outside traditions and art history). [. . .] they displayed a faith in the power of imagination, depicted with absolute precision, that I had rarely encountered before." – Massimiliano Gioni, curator, contemporary art critic, and artistic director of the New Museum, New York[1]

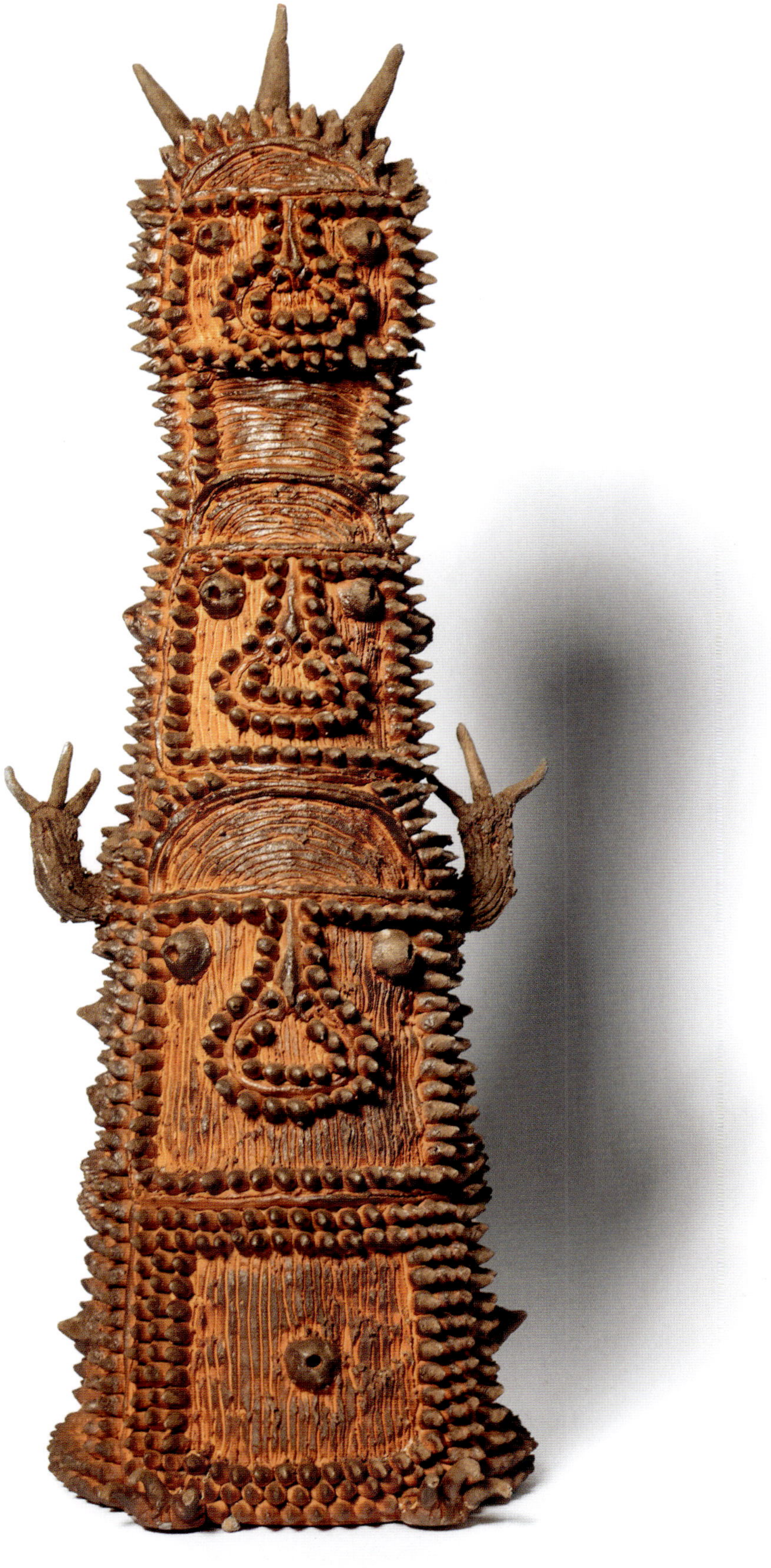

Shinichi Sawada, untitled (122), *2006–2010, ceramic, 9⅜ × 9⅜ × 22¹³⁄₁₆ in (24 × 24 × 58 cm). Courtesy Jennifer Lauren Gallery.* While this work features three stacked faces, it emotes a singular character through its sole pair of hands and trio of hornlike shapes at the top.

DAVOOD KOOCHAKI

(1939 Rasht–2020 Tehran, Iran)

The hovering and confluent beings in the drawings of Davood Koochaki evoke mysterious, whimsical, and humorous qualities. His oeuvre is recognizable by his figurative forms that brim with heavy-handed pencil markings against the natural white of the paper. Koochaki was raised in an agricultural region of Iran in the northern province of Gilan. He left school at a young age to help his family of rice growers. As a teenager, he moved independently to Tehran where he worked as an auto-mechanic but also engaged with the city's progressive intellectual circles. He married, started a family, opened his own automobile garage and in around 1980, Koochaki began to experiment with drawing. This cursory creative interest developed into a dedicated full-time art practice in his 60s, following retirement. In 2010, his drawings began gaining popularity within the arts community, initially in Europe, which preceded their appreciation in Iran. Koochaki passed away at the age of 81 in 2020, but his work continues to be exhibited globally, including in Iran, France, the Netherlands, America, and the United Kingdom.

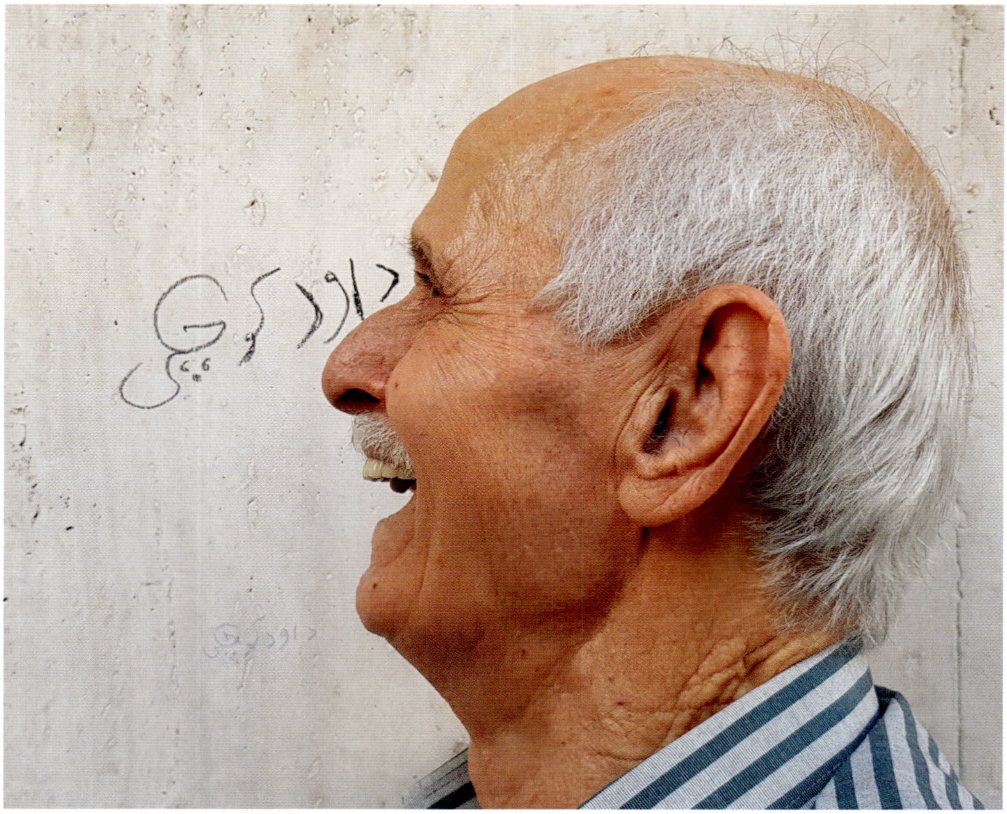

Davood Koochaki, 2019, photograph by Morteza Zahedi. Courtesy Gallery Outsider Inn. This portrait is of Koochaki at age 80, posed candidly in front of a wall that has his name scribed in Arabic.

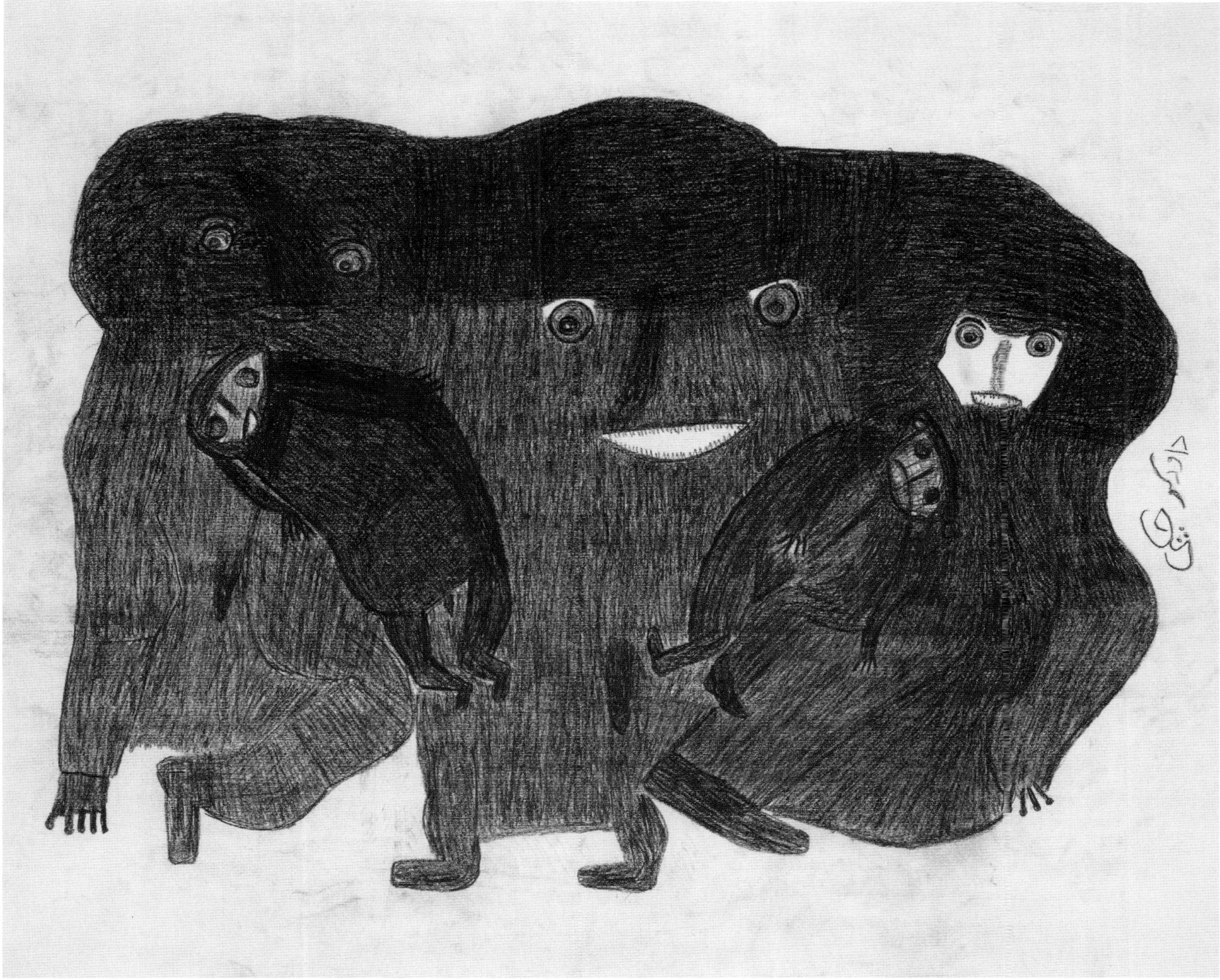

Davood Koochaki, untitled, *2019, graphite on paper, 39 × 27½ in (100 × 70 cm). Courtesy Gallery Outsider Inn.* This drawing first appears as a flat silhouette, but Koochaki's layering of smaller beings to the sides of the central smiling face infers dimensionality and depth.

In 2010, in Tehran, Davood Koochaki's son-in-law, Ali Zakeri, who is also an established painter in Iran, was being interviewed by Morteza Zahedi. An artist, curator, and writer, Zahedi had an emerging interest in artists within the self-taught remit. After becoming interested in some of Koochaki's drawings on Zakeri's laptop, Zahedi met with Koochaki himself a week later to discuss his practice. Another avenue for Koochaki's exposure relates to a documentary made by an Iranian filmmaker that featured Koochaki among other self-taught and street artists. Dutch art dealer Nico van der Endt learned about his work from the filmmaker, later giving Koochaki his first European exhibition in 2012. A pivotal exhibition for Koochaki, which also aided his recognition with a later American audience, was his inclusion in *L'envol* at La Maison Rouge, Paris (2018), which also included work by Robert Rauschenberg and Yves Klein.

Upon first viewing a drawing by Koochaki, one could be deceived by its seeming simplicity; however, longer engagement with his mysterious figurative forms presents complex aesthetics and concepts. Aesthetically, Koochaki's dedicated application of pencil establishes a substantial presence for the figures. The contrast creates a pronounced demarcation between *something* and *nothing*. His process is subtly documented through the trace of his fingerprints in the untouched white areas of the paper. The sheen of the metallic graphite (though occasionally Koochaki used coloured pencil) filling the figures with minuscule lines produces a synesthesia effect.

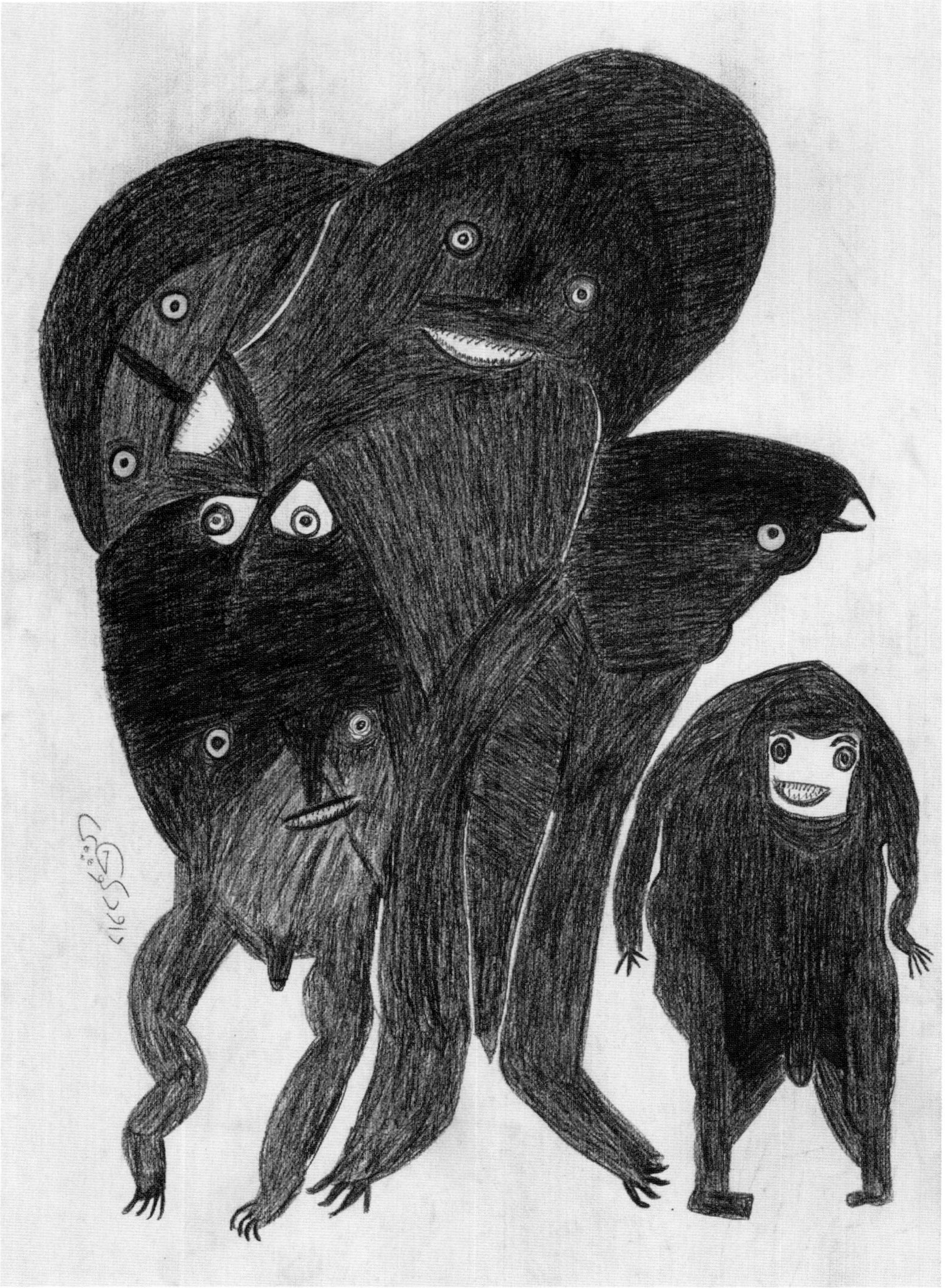

Davood Koochaki, untitled, *2019, graphite on paper, 39 × 27½ in (100 × 70 cm). Courtesy Gallery Outsider Inn.*
The dynamic main form hints at a hybrid creature with multiple sets of eyes, smiles (that feel human), and a protruding profile with birdlike characteristics. A smaller independent being accompanies to the right.

Art dealer and scholar Randall Morris referred to Koochaki as a storyteller. Are these narratives interpretations of Koochaki's lived environment or more influenced by forms witnessed through his inner imagination? Clear renditions of eyes, noses, and mouths present forms teetering between independence and amalgamation, human and beast, or altogether otherworldly hybrids.

"I try to draw perfectly, but this is what comes out!"
– Davood Koochaki[2]

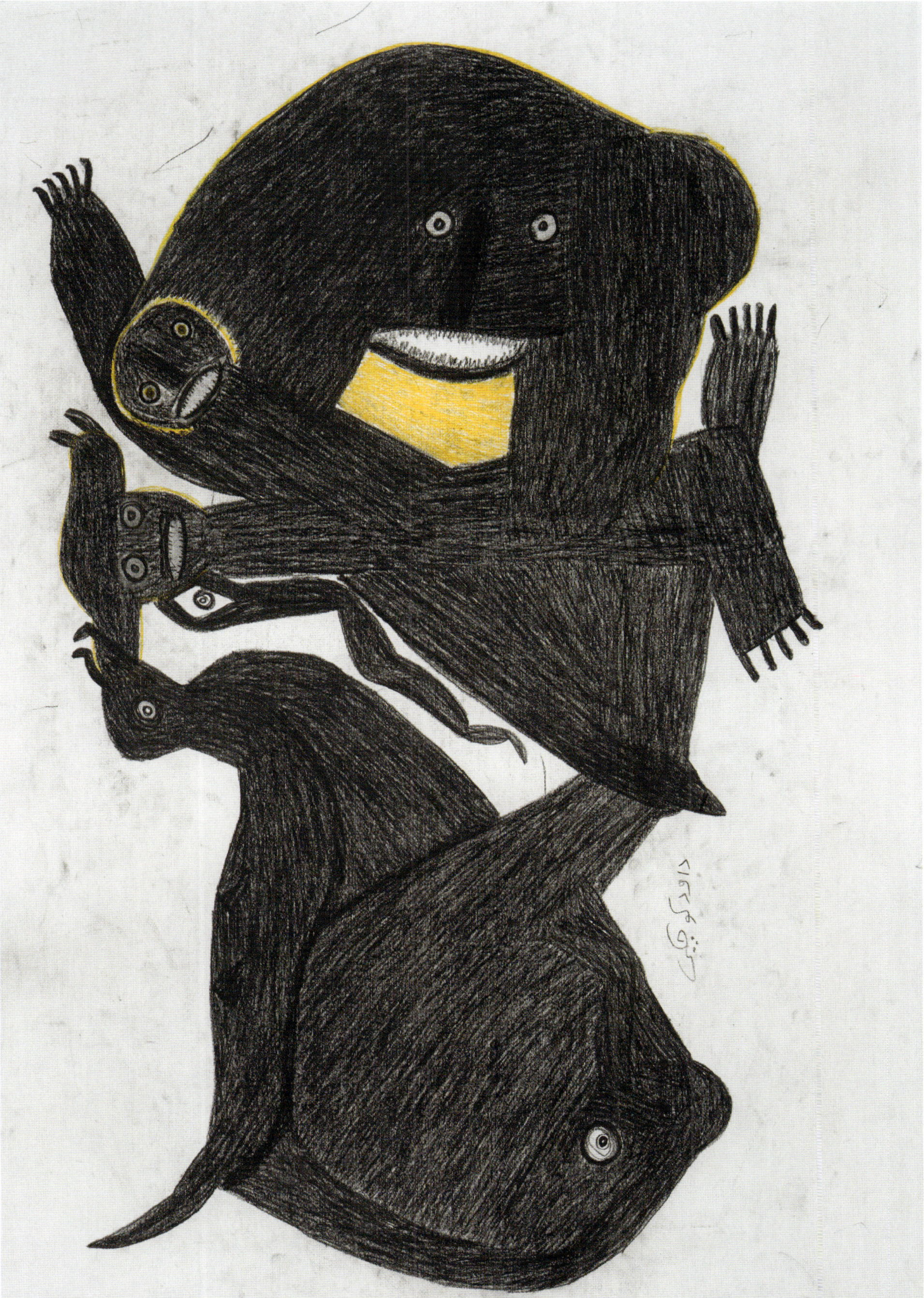

Davood Koochaki, untitled, *2019, graphite on paper, 39 × 27½ in (100 × 70 cm). Courtesy Gallery Outsider Inn.* This complex amalgamation stacks and merges various figures. The bottom double-faced being appears birdlike on one end and more beastly on the other. An emblematic snake seems rapped among the convergence of two main forms.

HELEN RAE

(1938–2021, Claremont, California, USA)

Helen Rae's art practice challenged preconceived notions of ability and age. Evocative of sophisticated psychedelia, her signature pencil drawings of fashion editorials are aesthetically complex and intricate. Rae, who was born deaf and limited verbally, only began drawing in her 50s, communicating through her creative practice of audacious colors and intricate delineation. Rae received critical acclaim following her first solo exhibition in 2015 at the age of 77. From this seminal debut at The Good Luck Gallery, Los Angeles, she rapidly established an advocacy of gallerists, collectors, and supporters. Subsequently, her singular interpretations of pop culture and high-fashion spreads were the subject of a solo exhibition at White Columns, New York (2017), and a focus at the Claremont Museum of Art, California (2020). In 2021, through a donation by collectors Martin and Rebecca Eisenberg, two drawings by Rae entered the permanent collection of The Museum of Modern Art, New York.

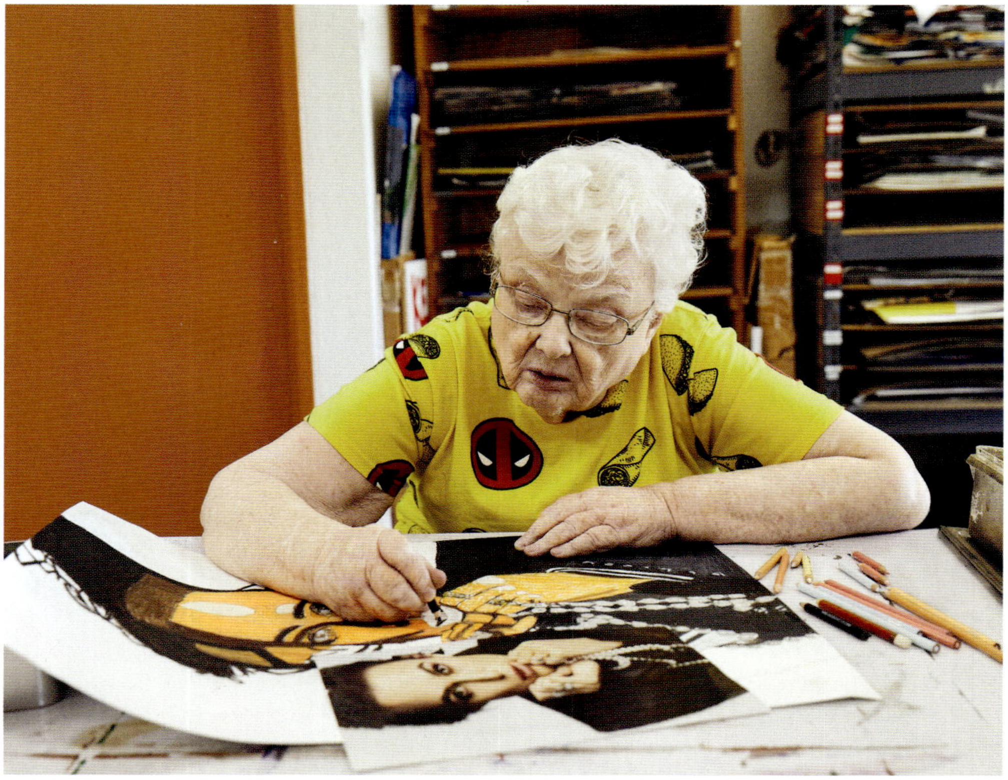

Helen Rae, 2019, photograph by Sami Drasin. Courtesy Galerie Magazine. Helen Rae at the studio at Tierra del Sol. Taken when she was in her early 80s, Rae is shown working on one of her archetypal fashion illustrations.

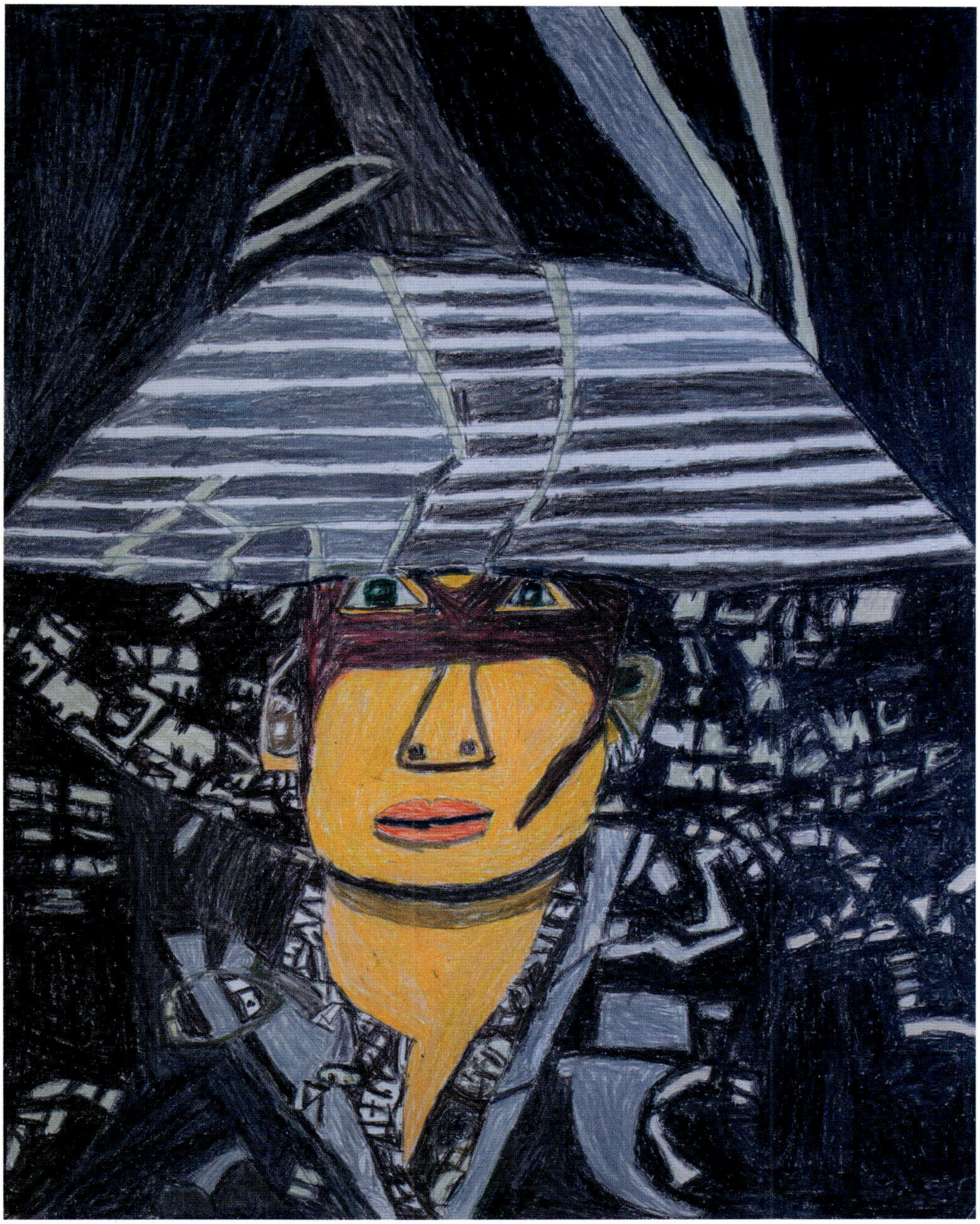

Helen Rae, untitled (April 3, 2020)*, 2020, colored pencil and pencil on paper, 24 × 18 in (61 × 45.7 cm). Estate of Helen Rae.* Here, the figure's hat assumes the form of an architectural element, while the shadowing of the face renders the components indistinguishable between shadow, face, the brim of the hat, collar, and background.

Helen Rae's practice developed over 30 years to evolve into the distinct style for which she is now recognized. When Rae first commenced on her creative endeavors, it appeared she initially focused on learning how to draw, and perhaps more significantly, how to look. Her earliest drawings were still-lifes and self-portraits, then her mark-making converged on reinterpreting pages from magazines. Originally, the source material was varied advertisements and ultimately progressed to her prominent and signature use of fashion editorials, including *Vogue* and fashion houses Celine and Sonia Rykiel.

Rae's shortlisted source material, previously ripped from magazines, was on file. Very focused and steadfast, when she began a drawing, Rae initiated a process that involved electing her researched magazine reference, delineating a diagram of intentions with graphite pencil, and finally Prismacolor pencils to occupy the outlined forms. Rae worked on a single dedicated drawing at a time, and a typical drawing took a number of weeks to complete. With her signature scope of works on paper, her departure point of fashion editorials transpires into an elaborate balance of figurative and kaleidoscopic.

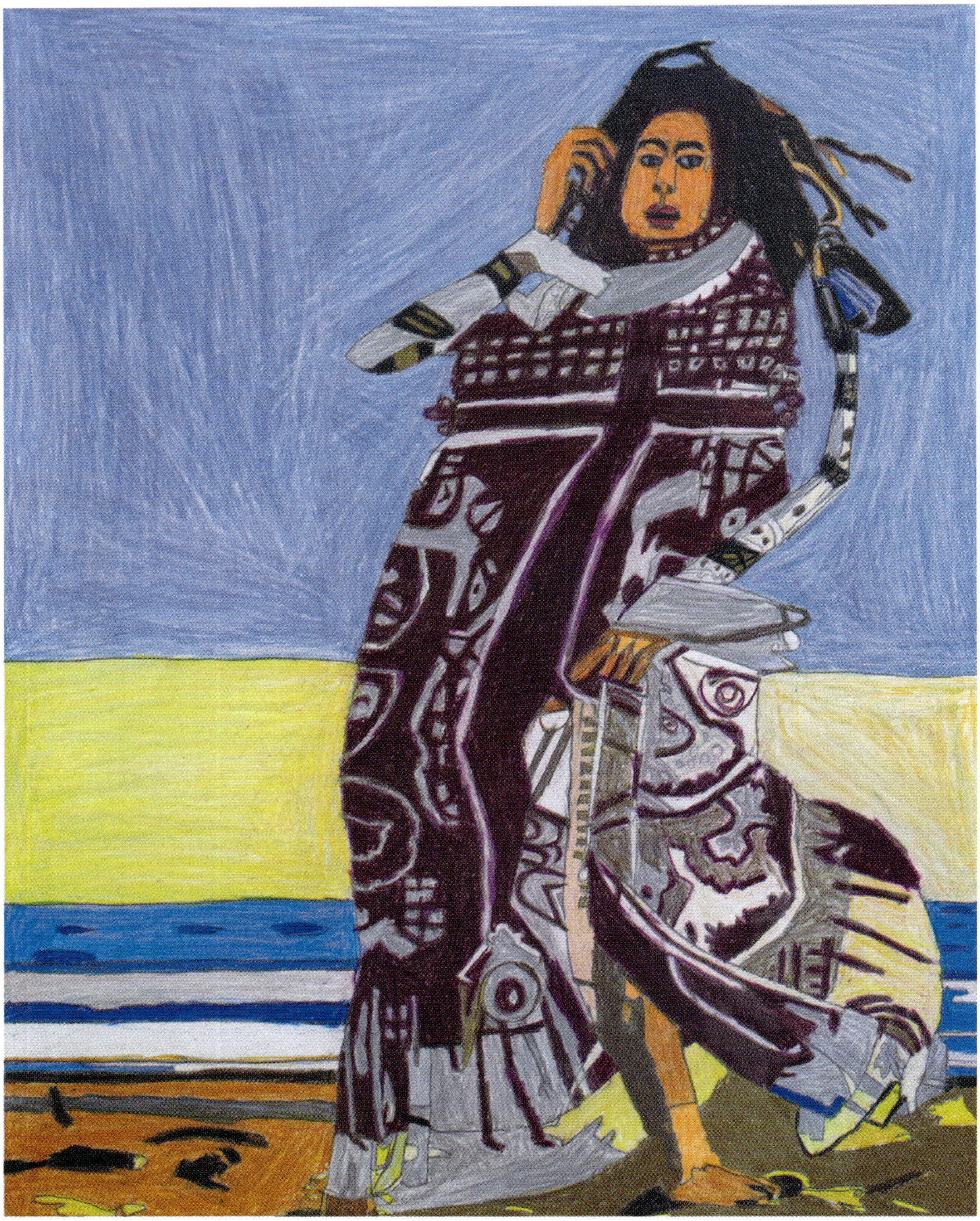

Helen Rae, untitled (March 19, 2019), *2019, colored pencil and pencil on paper, 24 × 18 in (61 × 45.7 cm). Estate of Helen Rae.* With extraordinary detail in the patterned garment worn by the figure, here Rae subtly plays with the fluidity of the body by rendering the arm as if an extension of her hair rather than from the model's shoulder.

Variables on pictorial emphasis are present in the drawings. In particular, Rae's underwater series has a stylized fractal democracy. The figures are prominent but the background competes, or complements, with equal interest. Composed with detailed intent, the background nearly morphs into the body and in instances suggests further beings in the shadows. In contrast, other drawings present the model figures with more power and demarcation between themselves and the background, assuming the characteristics of an architectural monument.

Rae's aesthetic decisions transformed her referenced magazine page, thereby transcending it beyond its initial intent. From erecting architectonic figures to the surreal blurring of subject and scene, Rae emancipated the models, fashion, and props from their intended cultural significance into her personal experience.

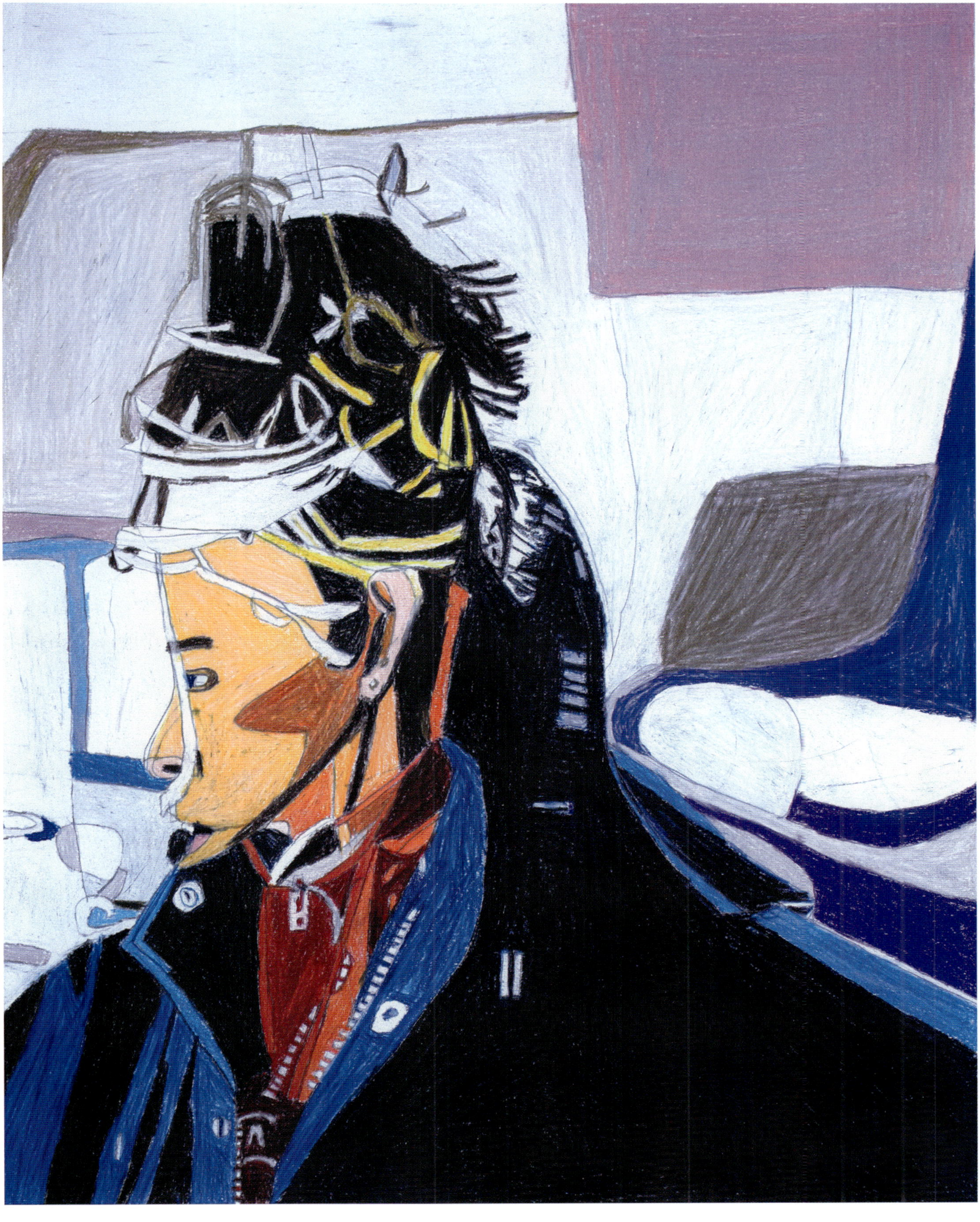

Helen Rae, untitled (March 10, 2020), *2020, colored pencil and pencil on paper, 24 × 18 in (61 × 45.7 cm). Estate of Helen Rae.* This drawing is archetypal for the equal attention given to both the rendering and composition of the background and the intricate detail in the figure. With the figure profiled left, the feather, or tassel on the headwear is matched with zipper detailing on the garment.

CARLO ZINELLI

(1916–1974 Verona, Italy)

Carlo Zinelli was observed drawing on the walls of San Giacomo alla Tomba psychiatric hospital after he had been admitted by his family in 1947. His urge to develop his own enigmatic graphic mode of communication was fostered within the hospital's art studio, where Zinelli worked from 1957 until 1971. In his early life, Zinelli lost his mother when he was two and worked during much of his childhood before being conscripted into military service. Amid the Spanish Civil War, his service led to an infantry post that supported the Nationalist forces in 1939. This experience was brief and traumatic, and consequently his mental health and verbal communications declined when he returned to Verona. During his 14 years in the art studio, Zinelli formed a distinct and cohesive oeuvre of predominantly double-sided gouache compositions. His drawings are often figurative-focused, surrounded by symbolic devices and visual puzzles. In the 1960s, with his innate and superb talent observed by the studio/hospital staff, Zinelli became the first Italian painter whose work was collected as part of the Compagnie de l'Art Brut and this established him as a significant artist defining the genre in Europe. Zinelli was also the subject of a solo presentation with The Museum of Everything for the 55th Venice Biennale (2013).

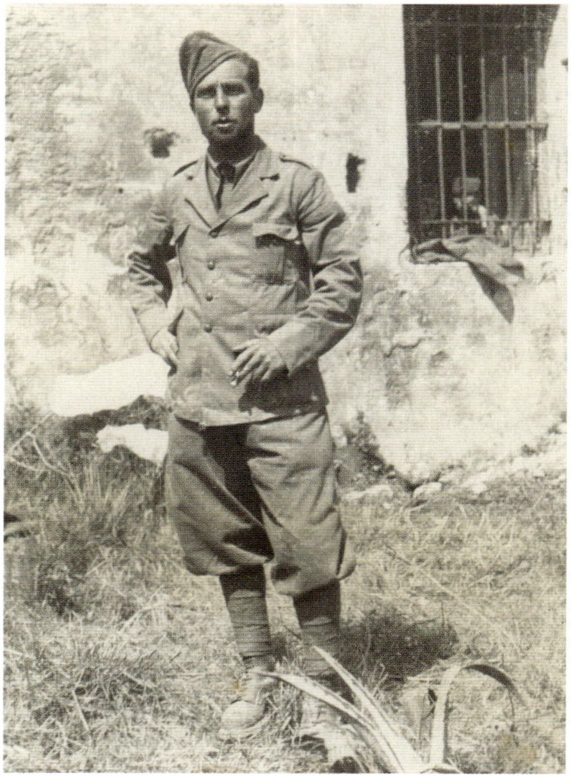

Carlo Zinelli, ca. 1938–1939, photograph. Courtesy Galerie Christian Berst.
Zinelli served in the military, which both affected his mental health post-1939 and influenced select symbolism in his later artistic practice.

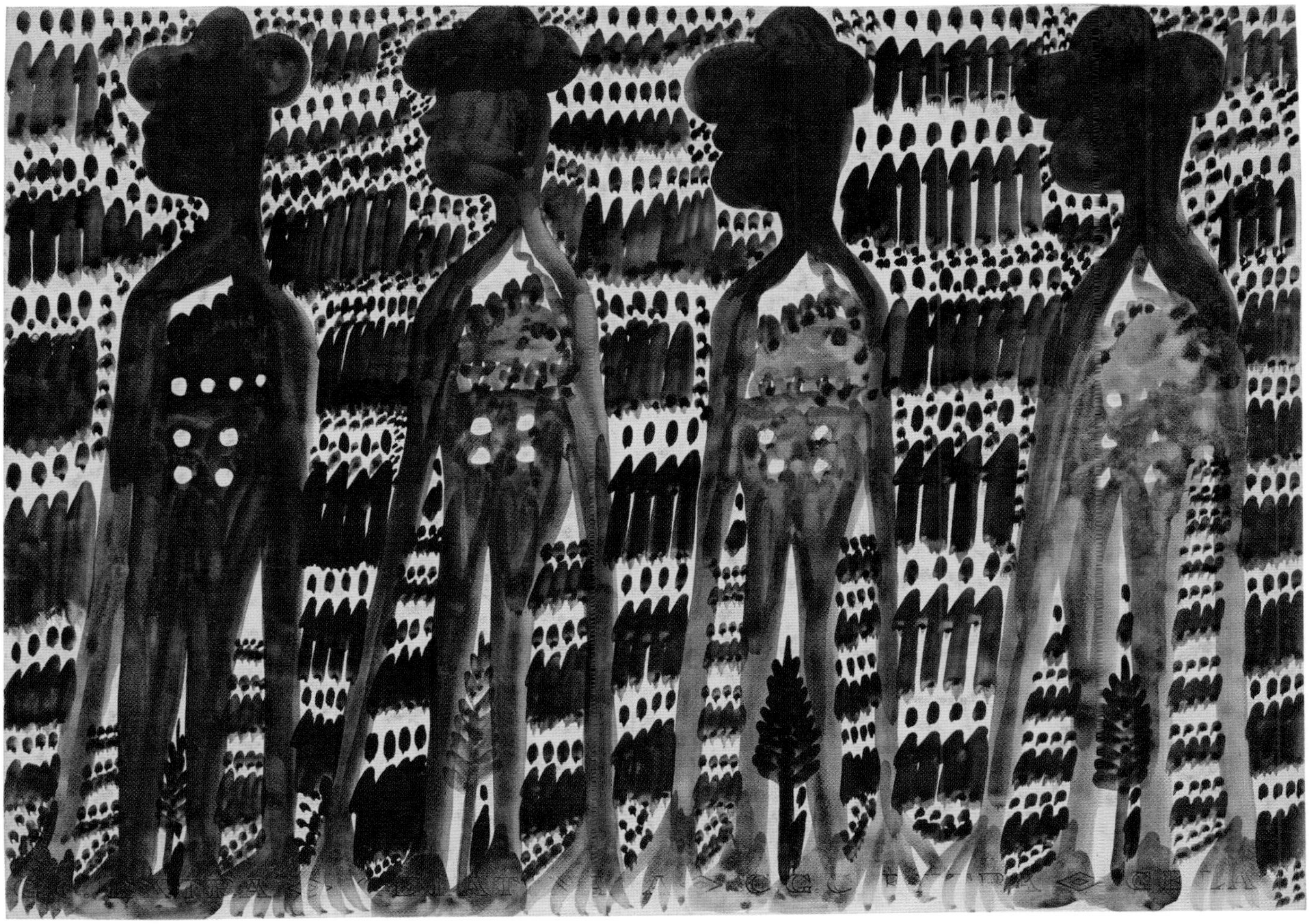

Carlo Zinelli, untitled, *1965, gouache, pencil and ink on paper, 14 × 19¾ in (35.5 × 50 cm). The Museum + The Gallery of Everything.* Sequencing of four was executed consistently in Zinelli's compositions, with animals, objects, and, as seen here, with the row of four human figures. Familiar with Zinelli's life at the studio and hospital, Vittorino Andreoli also observed that this predilection of four carried over to his actions and behaviors too.

In his youth, Carlo Zinelli engaged in drawing and developed an interest in music. In his late 20s, following his military engagements and return to Verona, Zinelli's mental decline included hallucinations and experiences of delusion, in addition to difficulties with cohesive verbal communication. After his family admitted him to San Giacomo alla Tomba hospital, he was rendered a permanent resident there.

In 1957, Zinelli was admitted to the hospital's painting and sculpture studio. Set on creating a nondidactic creative environment, the studio was initiated by Scottish sculptor Michael Noble with support from psychiatrist Dr. Mario Marini, and hospital director, Professor Cherubino Trabucchi. Zinelli was one of 12 artists and worked up to 8 hours a day in the studio, creating approximately 2–3,000 works. Medical student Vittorino Andreoli visited the studio in 1959 and the following year introduced Zinelli's practice to Jean Dubuffet and André Breton, who became interested in Zinelli's oeuvre in dialogue with their establishment of Art Brut. Discouragingly, the hospital closed in 1969, causing Zinelli to be relocated to a facility in the Veronan province of Marzana. Following this upheaval, Zinelli's steadfast art practice ceased in the final years of his life.

Zinelli's implementation of objective silhouettes and symbols introduces an implied personal graphic vocabulary. Most established in his body of work is the grouping of four figurative silhouettes and it is suggested these grouped men refer to Zinelli's surroundings of the hospital. His emblematic use of a gestural syringe also echoes a likely connection to his experience of being medically institutionalized. Tangentially, traditional Veronan sandolo boats, farming machinery, and sets of symbols relating to Alpine hunters and religious devotion were also regularly featured. Abundant with visual clues to his pictorial puzzle, the oeuvre of Zinelli is as autobiographical as it is mysterious.

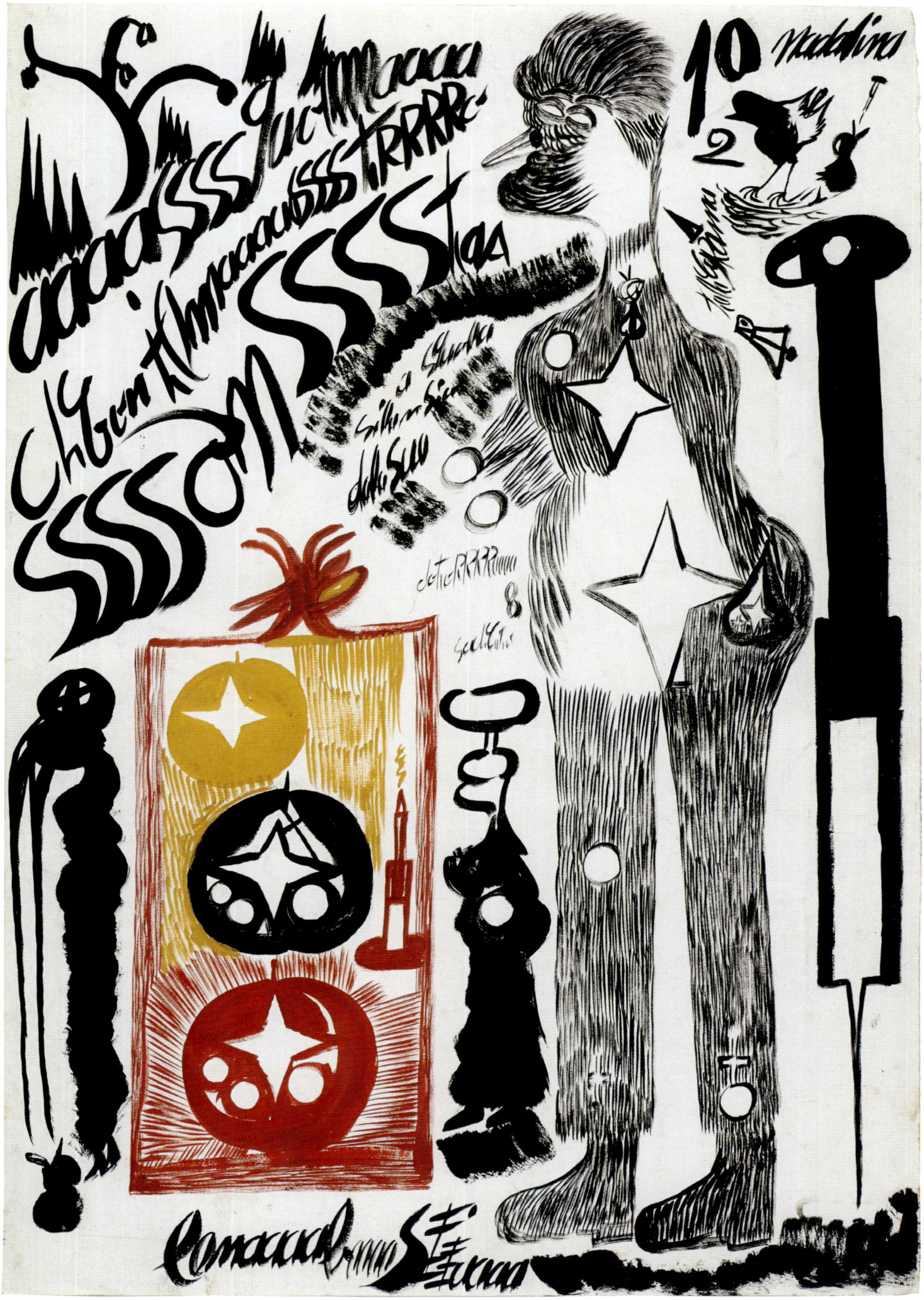

Carlo Zinelli, untitled, *1967, gouache on paper, 27½ × 19¾ in (70 × 50 cm). The Museum + The Gallery of Everything.* In this painting, the main figure is paired with a large-scale syringe to the right—one of Zinelli's symbols that seemingly referred to his larger experience of being institutionalized.

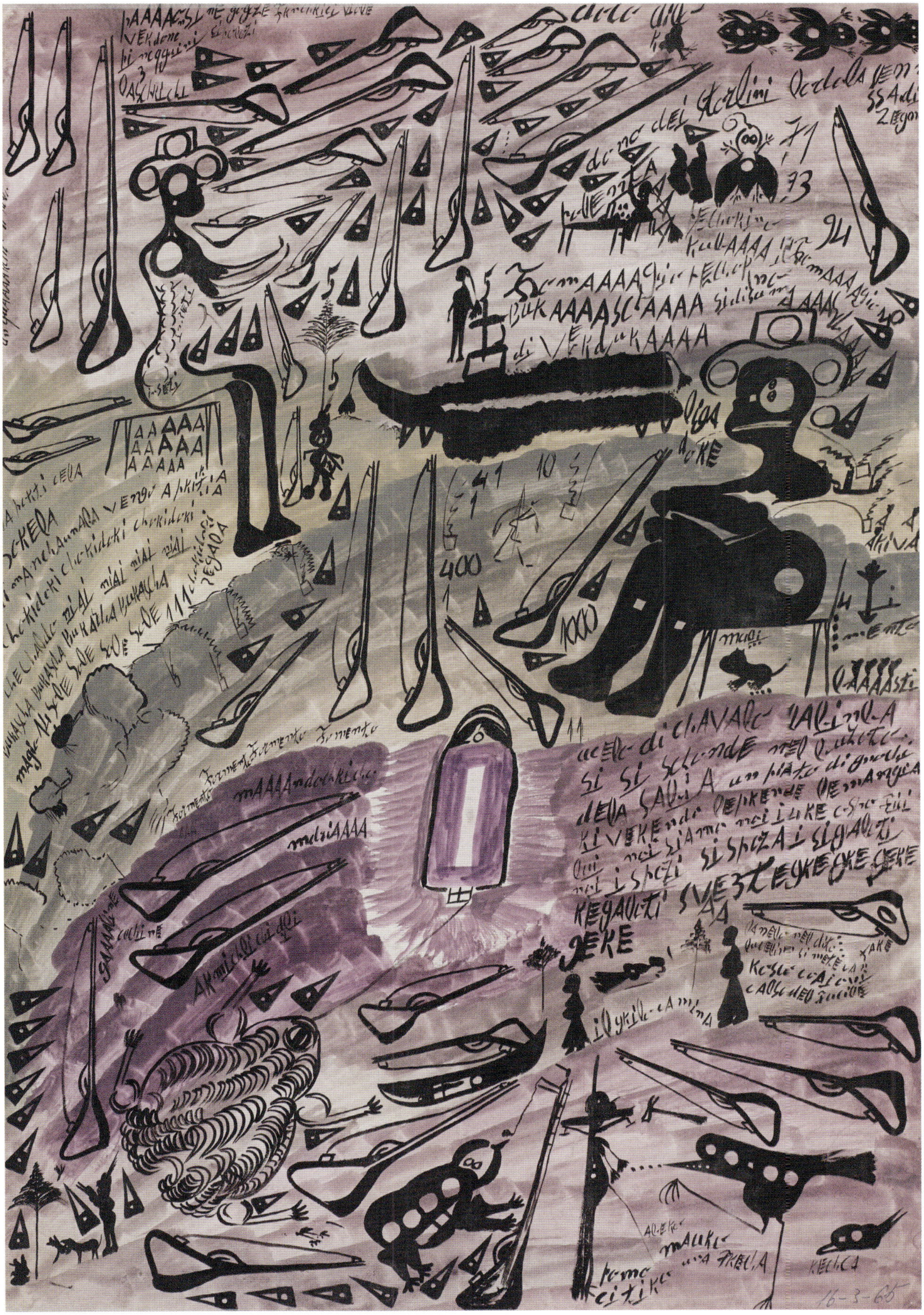

Carlo Zinelli, untitled, *1968, gouache, pencil, ink on paper, 27½ × 19¾ in (70 × 50 cm). The Museum + The Gallery of Everything.* Demonstrating his style from the 1960s of applying a light wash to the background of his compositions, here, two main figures are surrounded by a wealth of Zinelli's iconography, including his heavy repetition of rifles.

CHÉRI SAMBA

(b. 1956, Kinto M'Vuila, Democratic Republic of Congo)

The juxtaposition of realism and surrealism satirically collide in the politically driven paintings of Chéri Samba. After leaving school at the age of 16, he apprenticed with a sign painter in Kinshasa. Within a few years, Samba had set up his own workshop and began painting as an artistic practice alongside his business trade. By the mid-1970s, he formed the "School of Popular Painting" with his peers. Samba's inclusion in *Magiciens de la Terre,* curated by Jean Hubert-Martin at the Pompidou Centre, Paris (1989), introduced his paintings to an expanded European audience. Subsequently, he emerged internationally as a significant contemporary African painter, establishing an artworld identity beyond the confines of the "self-taught" genre. Samba's bold colors and emphatic comic-like style address his African experience from a personal and sociocultural point of view. He has had solo exhibitions at the Centre Culturel Congolais Le Zoo, Kinshasa (2000) and Fondation Cartier, Paris (2004). His paintings are included in the collections of the Museum of Modern Art, New York, and the Centre Pompidou, Paris.

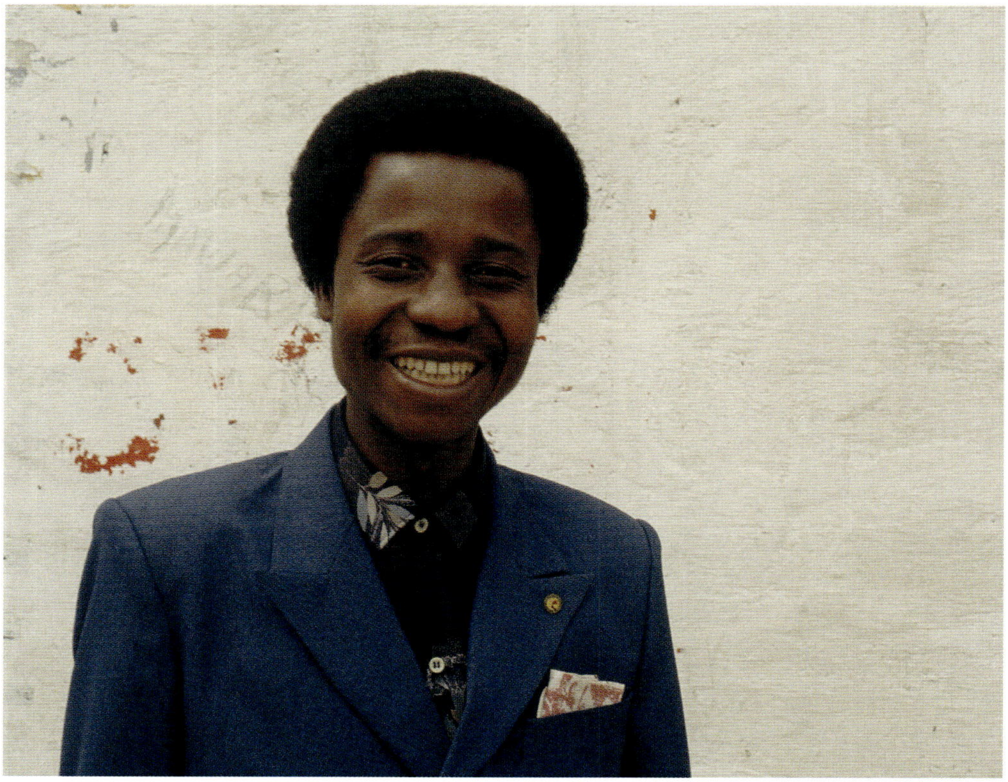

Chéri Samba, 1987, photograph by André Magnin. Courtesy Galerie MAGNIN-A, Paris. Taken in the 1980s, this portrait of Samba aligns with the same time period in which he was establishing his identity as "Chéri Samba: Artiste Populaire."

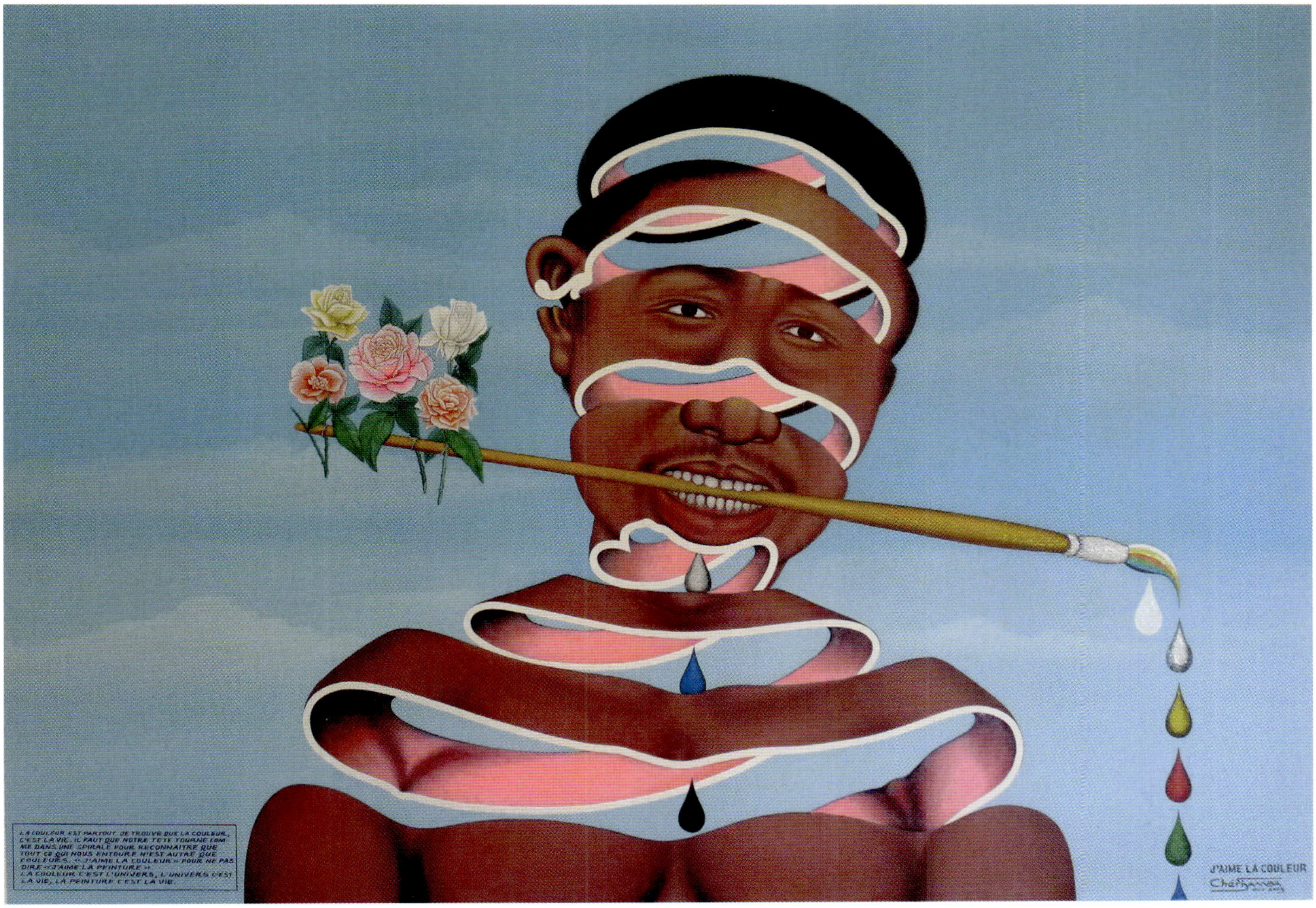

Chéri Samba, J'aime la couleur, *2003, acrylic and glitter on canvas, 53⅛ × 78¾ in (135 × 200 cm). Courtesy Galerie MAGNIN-A, Paris.* In this self-portrait series, Samba affirms his identity as an artist through his placement of a paintbrush in his mouth. His figurative form is ribboned, providing glimpses of the immense sky behind. His inscription confirms his affinity for color including: "*Il faut que notre tête tourne comme dans une spirale pour reconnaître que tout ce qui nous entoure n'est autre que couleurs.*" (Our head must turn like in a spiral to recognize that all that surrounds us is nothing but colors.)

Chéri Samba (born Samba wa Mbimba N'zingo Nuni Masi Ndo Mbasi) founded the "School of Popular Painting" in 1972, after relocating to Kinshasa. Like Samba, his fellow school painters were Congolese (formerly Zairean) and largely self-taught, including Camille-Pierre Bodo, Moke, Chéri Cherin, and later Samba's brother Cheik Ledy. In 2007, these five artists were exhibited at Tate Modern, London. Their exhibition *"Popular Painting" from Kinshasa* was Tate's first collection display of works by artists who were born (and working) in Africa.

For Samba—who in the 1980s began to sign his paintings "Chéri Samba: Artiste Populaire"—the term "popular" related to his interest in addressing the life of everyday African people. This interest was not in reflecting the banality of common life, rather, Samba's agenda was to explore globalization and geopolitics through the lens of his sub-Saharan locale. His hypnagogic style of painting, combined with contextualizing statements on the canvas, became a critical voice for addressing African stereotypes against a utopian potential.

Self-portraiture is a central theme for Samba and he has often painted variations on individual motifs. Examining his self-portraits from the 2000s titled *J'aime la couleur (I like color),* it appears Samba is embracing the identity of "the artist" by positioning a paintbrush between his teeth. This motif is consistently surreal with Samba's head and upper body spiraling like ribbon against a crisp sky. The singularity of each composed derivative is punctuated by variable objects, be it a plate of food, bouquet of flowers, or nothing at all, balanced on the left side of the paintbrush.

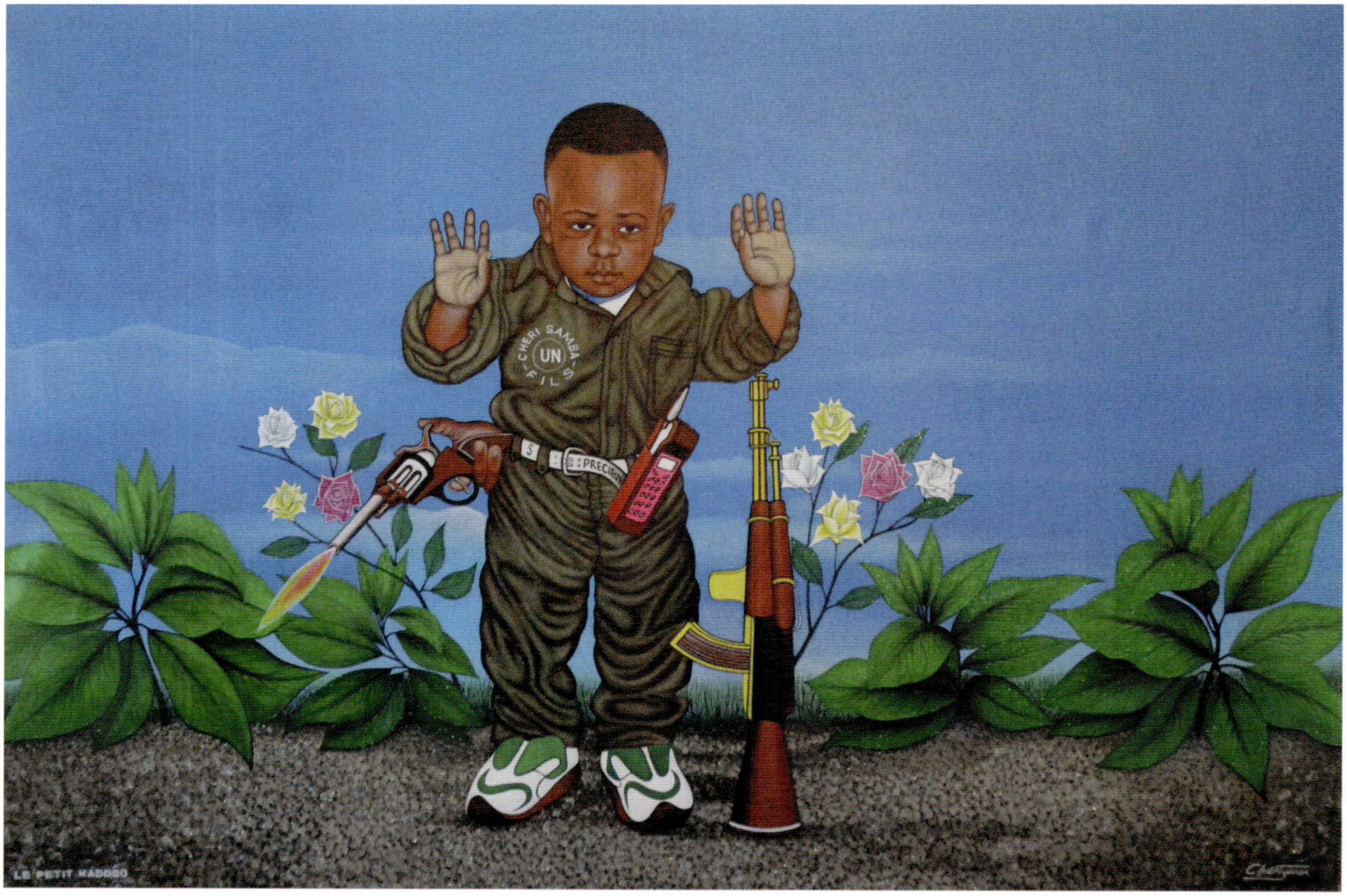

Chéri Samba, Le petit Kadogo, *2009, acrylic on canvas, 53⅛ × 78¾ in (135 × 200 cm). Courtesy Galerie MAGNIN-A, Paris.* Satirical, yet critical, a small child wears a labeled uniform identifying him as Samba's son and a belt that reads "*PRECIEUX*" (precious). He is posed surrendering with his hands up, yet a third hand emerges from behind him, shooting a gun from his waist. "Kadogo" refers to a child soldier.

"I had noticed that people in the street would walk by paintings, glance at them and keep going. I thought that if I added a bit of text, people would have to stop and take time to read it, to get more into the painting and to admire it. That's what I called 'the Samba Signature.' From then on, I put text in all my paintings." – Chéri Samba[3]

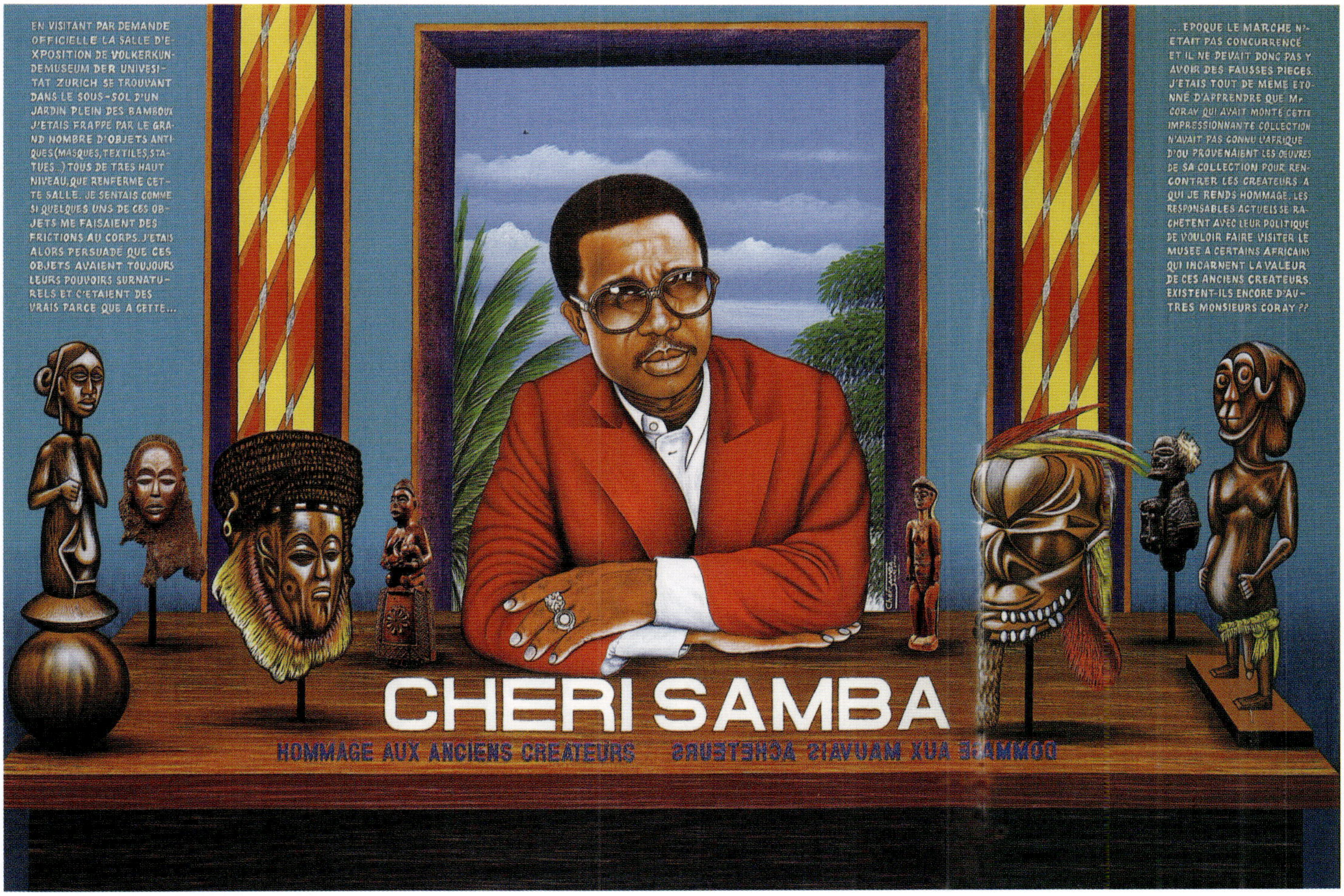

Chéri Samba, Hommage aux anciens créateurs, *2000, acrylic on canvas, 53⅛ × 78¾ in (135 × 200 cm). Courtesy Galerie MAGNIN-A, Paris.* Often exploring African culture in a global context, here Samba poses himself with authority at a desk surrounded by African antiques and objects (most modified with rods or plinths that confirm they are meant for display). Beneath his name, he proclaims: "*HOMMAGE AUX ANCIENS CREATEURS, DOMMAGE AUX MAUVAIS ACHETEURS*" (TRIBUTE TO THE ANCIENT CREATURES, DAMAGE TO BAD BUYERS).

ENDNOTES

INTRODUCTION

1. "Self-taught" is considered by many as the least troubling of labels—in comparison to "folk," "naive," and the most marketable, but perhaps the most problematic, "Outsider." I tend to agree, but also confirm that self-taught is far from perfect or necessary. I also use the noun or descriptor of "artist" plurally at times, but recognize that some individuals featured in *Nonconformers* likely did not self-identify as artists.
2. *Nonconformers* does include artists Hilma af Klint and Horst Ademeit, who studied in art academia, however neither of their recognizable oeuvres were created within the remit of their academic training.
3. Cubbs, "Rebels, Mystics and Outcasts: the Romantic Artist Outsider," 89.
4. This approach applied the theories of American educational philosopher Maxine Greene ("Diversity and inclusion: Toward a curriculum for human beings." *Teachers College Record* Volume 95 Number 2, 1993, 211–221). Kelly W. Guyotte, in respect to Greene, asserts that while the process of othering can be perceived as a negative, Green's concept of social imagination is different and proclaims revisiting "blurring over the differences." Guyotte: "[T]he problems in collapsing bodily boundaries, where such collapsing actually reinforces oppressive normative and hegemonic structures. In other words, the unwillingness to see color or to acknowledge the systemic issues of racial violence and oppression, fold such underrepresented groups into the majority, rendering them, once again, invisible . . . When one refuses to acknowledge difference, the majority subsumes the minority and voices that need to be heard are silenced." (Kelly W. Guyotte, University of Alabama, *Aesthetic Movements of a Social Imagination: Refusing Stasis and Educating Relationally/Critically/Responsibly*, Section: A Question of Relationally in, Critical Questions in Education 9:1 Winter 2018, 65. Looking at the educational theories of Maxine Greene.) My conclusion being that, until there are no longer distinct barriers facing artists who are considered self-taught that may be staked due to larger societal conceptions of race, gender, mental health, and disability, it is worth discussing the restrictive past and current obstacles, alongside commending progress.
5. Kort, "Friedrich Schröder-Sonnenstern: From Barefoot Prophet to Avant-Garde Artist," 2.
6. Kort, 22. It was Baselitz alongside artist Eugen Schonebeck; Schröder-Sonnenstern turned down their offer.
7. https://www.thebroad.org/art/ed-ruscha/where-are-you-going-man-do-you-dig-me
8. https://ropac.net/exhibitions/40-alvaro-barrington-artists-i-steal-from/
9. MacFarquhar, "Is It Art?," 542.
10. With the exception of the contextualization and landmark exhibitions, events, and publications of self-taught artists framing the chapters of *20th-Century Origins and Representation.*
11. It included a single oeuvre of sculpture by Karl Brendel (1871–1925).
12. Rexer, *How to look at Outsider Art*, 36.
13. Located at Rice University Houston and now called the Moody Center for the Arts.
14. Cooke, "Boundary Trouble," 16.
15. A supported studio is a creative environment for individuals with specific health or social needs that encourages and supports the different art practices of artists. Supported studios facilitate professional development and career-building opportunities for artists—individually, or as a group or collective. Supported studios provide technical artistic support, promote artists in the marketplace and within galleries, and develop networks and audiences outside of health and social care settings. Supported studios share a commitment to producing and presenting work of high artistic quality, (https://artetal.org/faqs accessed June 25, 2022).
16. Fine, *Everyday Genius: Self-taught art and the culture of authenticity*, 29.
17. Maclagan, *Outsider Art: From the Margins to the Marketplace*, 168.
18. Fine, 8.
19. Roberta Smith, "Art in Review," *New York Times*, January 28, 1994, https://www.nytimes.com/1994/01/28/arts/art-in-review-011215.html
20. Di Maria, *Nonconformers*, 251–255.
21. ibid.
22. McCollum, *Exhibitions of Outsider Art Since 1947*, 227. (Lawrence Ritter, *Create*, ex.cat. (University of California, Berkeley Art Museum, 2011), 9.
23. Fullerton, "Lonnie Holley—Interview."
24. George Widener interviewed by Sophia Cosmadopoulos, *Nonconformers*, 290–297.
25. Daic, *Gaston Chaissac*, Paris, 2000. Exhibition catalog (cited in MacLagan, 130).
26. Quote by Andrew Edlin in https://news.artnet.com/market/jim-carrey-outsider-art-fair-1406356
27. https://fewocious.com/art/; https://onlineonly.christies.com/s/hello-im-victor-fewocious-my-life/lots/2048
28. Lamb, "A brief (but possibly too long) account of my experiences with Lee Godie."

CHAPTER 1

1. Diane Tepfer, "Edith Gregor Halpert and The Downtown Gallery Downtown: 1926–1940; a Study in American Art Patronage." (Volumes I and II) (Ph.D., United States—Michigan, University of Michigan, 1989), 171–72.
2. When folk art from artists' collections was shown in *Early American Art* (1924) at the Whitney Studio Club in New York, a critic noted the affinity that the pre-20th weathervanes, limner portraits, and woodcarving on view had with 20th century modernist innovations: "The strange thing is that most of these very old-fashioned pictures give one vividly the sense of exactly the thing our most modern painters are doing." Quoted in Wanda Corn, "The Return of the Native: The Development of Interest in American Primitive Painting," (Master's Thesis, New York, N.Y., New York University, 1965), 16.
3. Barr's orange, black, and white tree diagram, which has been updated by artist Hank Willis Thomas to clarify its implicit biases, was featured on the catalog's cover. See Alfred Barr, Jr., *Cubism and Abstract Art* (New York: The Museum of Modern Art, 1936).
4. Holger Cahill and Maximilien Gauthier, eds., *Masters of Popular Painting: Modern Primitives of Europe and America* (New York: The Museum of Modern Art, 1938); for the letter that Miller wrote to Christian Brinton inquiring about Pippin in 1937, see Judith Stein, "An American Original," in *I Tell My Heart: The Art of Horace Pippin*, ed. Judith Stein (Philadelphia, PA: Pennsylvania Academy of the Fine Arts, 1993), 11.
5. This installation was on view through the first half of 1944, and its complete title was *Modern Primitives: Artists of the People*. Although Barr did not often engage in the populist and often nationalistic rhetoric around self-taught artists favored by his collaborator Holger Cahill, he did invoke it here by borrowing the title of Cahill's essay from the *Masters of Popular Painting* catalog as the subtitle of this installation.
6. Sidney Janis, *They Taught Themselves: American Primitive Painters in the 20th Century* (New York: The Dial Press, 1942), 11.
7. For more on the relationship between self-taught artists of different ethnic origins and changing ideas about whiteness and Americanness between the wars, see Katherine Jentleson, *Gatecrashers: The Rise of the Self-Taught Artist in America* (Oakland, C.A.: University of California Press, 2020), 59–73.
8. The Federal Art Project (FAP) in America was created as a branch of the New Deal in 1935 generating creative work relief to counteract the Great Depression.
9. Alfred Barr, Jr., "Preface and Acknowledgment," in *Masters of Popular Painting; Modern Primitives of Europe and America*, ed. Holger Cahill and Maximilien Gauthier (New York, N.Y., The Museum of Modern Art, 1938), 9.
10. Alfred Barr, Jr., "Foreword," in *They Taught Themselves: American Primitive Painters in the 20th Century*, ed. Sidney Janis (New York: The Dial Press, 1942), xx.
11. One critic compared Janis's didactic displays to "the hunting down of butterflies with the aid of caterpillar tractors." Howard Devree, "To Show Paintings by M. Hirshfield," *New York Times*, June 23, 1943, sec. BOOKS, http://search.proquest.com.proxy.lib.duke.edu/docview/106626680/abstract?accountid=10598
12. Boswell, Peyton, "Master of the Two Left Feet," *Art Digest*, July 1943.
13. Much weight had been put on the Hirshfield debacle as the end of the mainstream art world's interest in self-taught artists during the interwar period.

MoMA actually did not stop showing self-taught artists from its collection; the *Modern Primitives* gallery remained on view well into 1944 and Hirshfield even went on appearing in exhibitions as soon as 1946. Moses, meanwhile, was just achieving her status as an international phenomenon; although she never had a major exhibition at MoMA, her work was exhibited widely and embraced by many tastemakers dedicated to modern art. For a long view of how self-taught artists continued to operate within spheres of modern and contemporary art, see Lynne Cooke's exhibition catalog, *Outliers and American Vanguard Art* (National Gallery of Art and University of Chicago Press, 2018).

14. Aline B. Louchheim, "Americans in Italy: Venice Sees a Marin Show," *New York Times*, September 10, 1950, sec. Arts & Leisure.
15. Robert Goldwater, "Letter from Paris," *Magazine of Art* 44, no. 5 (May 1951), 185.
16. Darby and Barat, "Blackness at MoMA: A Legacy of Deficit," 23.
17. Likely between 1872 and 1874.
18. Fuller, *Visions in Stone*, 8.
19. His religious vision was in line with the Southern Baptist tradition of the time, however, contemporary research, discussed by Jennifer Jane Marshall, suggests a consideration of whether Edmondson felt his output would be more palatable to a white audience if linked to a vision from God.
20. Marshall, " 'Ever Not Quite': Empathy, Experience, and Williiam Edmondson," 112.
21. MoMA Press Release: Sculpture by William Edmondson (October 18, 1937) https://assets.moma.org/documents/moma_press-release_333062.pdf?_ga=2.74315163.887142772.1617013436-1841041169.1611249119
22. Marshall, 115.
23. Stabenow, *Rousseau*, 25.
24. Originated by Henry McBride, a critic for *The New York Sun*, cited in Jentleson, "The Most Truly American: John Kane's Naturalized Appeal," 47.
25. Jentleson, 52.
26. Rouvalis, *Carnegie Magazine* (accessed online).
27. Jentleson, *Gatecrashers*, 27.
28. Janis, *They Taught Themselves: American Primitive Painters of the 20th Century*, 16.
29. Bearden and Henderson, *A History of African American Artists: From 1792 to the Present*, 356.
30. Morang, "Some Artists of New Mexico."

CHAPTER 2

1. Jean Dubuffet interviewed by Franck Jotterand, "Jean Dubuffet: 'J'offre les collections de l'Art Brut à la Ville de Lausanne'," *La Gazette littéraire*, May 22–23, 1971.
2. Jean Paulhan, *Guide d'un petit voyage en Suisse*, (Paris: Les Cahiers de la Pléiade, 1946).
3. From 1948 onward, Dubuffet visited Aloïse Corbaz several times at La Rosière.
4. See the archives of the Collection de l'Art Brut (CAB).
5. Dubuffet then drafted a *collection annexe* (ancillary collection) register, but it was undated. In the list of works, we find entries stamped "Collection annexe." However, the real sorting out would take place around 1970, when he drew up a catalog of the Collection de l'Art Brut, with a view to donating the entire collection to the City of Lausanne in 1971.
6. In 1951 the Compagnie de l'Art Brut was dissolved owing to lack of space, a crucial shortage of funds, and disagreements between Dubuffet and its members, in particular André Breton.
7. Catalogue Raisonné Electronique (online archive) / in *Lettre au pere interne*.
8. Russell, *Groundwaters: A Century of Self-Taught and Outsider Artists*, 92.
9. Catalogue Raisonné Electronique (online archive) / Jean Dubuffet.
10. Porret-Forel, "Le Cloisonné de Théâtre-Aloïse Corbaz," 52.
11. Ibid.
12. The Adolf Wölfli Foundation, "Writings by Adolf Wölfli."
13. The belief system of Spiritualism was burgeoning in the late 19th and early 20th centuries. It was fundamentally focused on the belief of otherworldly dimensions; a world that was accessible under certain conditions. The concept of mediumship or mediumistic arose from Spiritualism, defining a medium as a person with power or ability to access this *other world*. For art to be defined as mediumistic implies the work was created by a power or spirit beyond the earthly realms and the person (artist), the medium, is merely a vessel.
14. Cardinal, *Outsider Art*, 116.
15. Breton, Dubuffet, Bounoure, Lanoux, Pierre, Seguin, Godberge, Deroux, *Fleury-Joseph Crépin, 1875–1948*, 213.
16. Archive of André Breton (online archive).
17. Thevoz, Michel, *Art Brut*, 147–8 (cited in Maizels, *Raw Creation*, 56.)
18. Oury, *Auguste For.*, 1956 (cited in Faupin, "Auguste Forestier's unbroken wanderlust.")
19. Bellemare and Le Guen, "La robe de mariée de Mlle S," 13.

CHAPTER 3

1. Cardinal, *Outsider Art*, 51.
2. Cardinal, 9.
3. Cardinal accepted, although he only received less than one third of Musgrave's fee.
4. "The Art Council does not normally invoke the cautionary note that 'the views expressed in this publication are those of the authors and not necessarily of the editors' in its exhibition catalogs. But in this case as one of the major cultural institutions in the brightly-lit centre of our city (cf Dr Cardinal's introduction) we have been invaded, at our own invitation, by 'outsiders', and we cannot be expected to accept entirely claims of artistic and spiritual dominance made on their behalf." Excerpt from the Foreword by Joanna Drew, Director of Art. *Outsiders* exhibition catalog, 1979.
5. John McEwan, *Spectator,* 3/3/79.
6. Marina Viazey, BBC 3, *Critics Forum*.
7. Terrance Mullaly, *Daily Telegraph*, 3/17/79.
8. William Feaver, *Observer* 2/23/79.
9. Cardinal, Roger, *Marginalia*, 2000, Museum de Stadshof, NL.
10. Dubuffet's original definition of *l'art brut* is jealously guarded by the Fondation Dubuffet and the Collection de l'Art Brut. It is a protected name, almost like a trademark, and thus has been able to keep its full meaning as the purest and most direct form of Outsider Art.
11. Norman Giradout, "Some Scarlet Thoughts on the Cardinal of Outsider Art," *Folk Art Messenger* #98, Vol 29 (Winter 2019), 12–13. Richmond VA.
12. Cardinal, Roger, *Outsider Art*, 179.
13. The concept of mediumship or mediumistic arose from Spiritualism, defining a medium as a person with power or ability to access this *other world*. For art to be defined as mediumistic implies the work was created by a power or spirit beyond the earthly realms and the person (artist), the medium, is merely a vessel.
14. Similar interpretations include "my inner rest" or "my innerest," perhaps alluding to the soul.
15. Ayad, Sara, "Borderlands – Dr Boyle and the Genesis of Gill's Art," 108.
16. Ibid.
17. Gill, Laurence W. "Myrninerest the Spheres" broadsheet issued March 1926
18. Gill corresponded with journalist Louise Morgan
19. Automatic writing, in Spiritualism is writing produced involuntarily when the subject's directed by external, esoteric, or religious entity. The phenomenon may occur when the subject is in an alert waking state or in a hypnotic trance, usually during a séance. The results include words in unexplainable arrangements, and foreign and invented languages transcribed.
20. Ayad, 110.
21. Cardinal, 144.
22. The name change from Louis Freeman to Scottie Wilson took place during his years in Canada, likely 1936 or 1937 according to Murrell, Katherine and Anthony Petullo, *Scottie Wilson; Peddler Turned Painter*, 24.
23. *Evening Citizen* (Glasgow), "Pictures Paid for Meals: Now Glasgow Man Holds Exhibition," October 6, 1948.
24. Maclagan, David, *Line Let Loose : Scribbling, Doodling and Automatic Drawing*, Reaktion Book, 2013.
25. Bihalji-Merin, Oto. *Das naive Bild der Welt*, Verlag M DuMont Schauberg, Cologne, 1959 (cited in Cardinal, *Outsider Art*, 74).
26. Cardinal, 154.
27. Schröder-Sonnenstern, "Autobiographie," in *Exposition Internationale du Surrealisme*, exhibition catalog, December 15–February 29, 1960, trans. Hans Bellmer (Paris: Galerie Daniel Cordier, 1959); via Kort, "Fredrich Schroder-Sonnenstern: From Barefoot Prophet to Avant-Garde Artist."
28. Outsider Art Fair. "Anna Zemánková."
29. Cardinal, "Johann Hauser," 24.

30. When founded by Navratil in 1981, it was under the name "Center for Art and Psychotherapy," but changed to its current name "House of Artists" under his successor, Johann Feilacher, in 1986.
31. *Raw Vision*, issue 75.

CHAPTER 4

1. *Missing Pieces: Georgia Folk Art 1770–1976* was organized for the Georgia Council for the Arts and Humanities with assistance from the National Endowment for the Arts, and was shown in Georgia in 1976–1977 at the Atlanta Historical Society, the Telfair Academy of Arts and Sciences in Savannah, and the Columbus Museum of Arts, before traveling to the Library of Congress in Washington, D.C., in 1978, where it opened as part of the two-part *Folk Art and Folk Life* exhibition. See https://www.loc.gov/folklife/news/pdf/FCN_Vol01_2.pdf accessed September 12, 2021. *Two Centuries of Black American Art* was on view at LACMA from September 30–November 21, 1976. It subsequently traveled over the next 11 months to the High Museum of Art, Atlanta, the Dallas Museum of Art, and the Brooklyn Museum. See https://www.lacma.org/art/exhibition/two-centuries-black-american-art accessed July 10, 2021.
2. *Black Folk Art in America, 1930–1980,* was on view at the Corcoran Museum of Art in Washington, D.C., from January 15–March 28, 1982. A scaled-down version of the show traveled nationally to the following venues: the Speed Museum of Art, Louisville, Kentucky, April 26–June 14; the Brooklyn Museum, July 4– September 12; the Craft and Folk Art Museum, LA, November 30, 1982–February 6, 1983; and Rice University Institute of the Arts, Houston, March 4–April 15, 1983.
3. Ibid, 11.
4. Mary Schmidt Campbell. "Black Folk Art in America." *Art Journal* (New York, 1960) 42, no. 4 (1982), 345–346.
5. Eugene W. Metcalf, "Black Art, Folk Art and Social Control." *Winterthur Portfolio* 18, no. 4 (1983): 271–89, 273. Accessed July 20, 2021. http://www.jstor.org/stable/1180989. Metcalf goes on to say, "To neglect a sense of community is to deny the very essence of folk culture."
6. Kinshasha Holman Conwill, *Testimony: Vernacular Art of the African American South: The Ronald and June Shelp Collection*, Schomburg Center for Research in Black Culture and Harry N. Abrams, 1990, 54
7. Ibid, 55.
8. Campbell, "Black Folk Art," 346.
9. Michael Brenson, "New Home and Life for Studio Museum in Harlem," *New York Times*, June 17, 1982, Section C, 16, National Edition. https://www.nytimes.com/1982/06/17/arts/new-home-and-life-for-studio-museum-in-harlem.html accessed July 10, 2021. The Studio Museum moved into a newly restored building designed by renowned African American architect J. Max Bond, Jr., at 144 West 125th Street in Harlem, its current location. That building was demolished in 2019 to make way for the new museum building designed by Sir David Adjaye. Foregrounding the scholarly mission of the Studio Museum, the illustrated catalog featured writing by leading African American art historians, including Hammond, Campbell, and Driskell.
10. Kellie Jones, "Ancient to the Future," *Studio*, Fall 2018/Winter 2019, 13. https://studiomuseum.org/article/ancient-future accessed July 10, 2021.
11. Studio Museum in Harlem, Exhibition Poster for *Harlem Heyday, Ritual and Myth and Images of Dignity*, 1982.
12. Perry, Regenia A. "Contemporary African American Folk Art in America: An Overview." *The International Review of African American Art* 11, no. 1 (1993): 4.
13. The Outsider Art Fair was pioneered by art fair impresario Sanford L. Smith in 1993, appearing at the iconic Puck Building in New York City's Soho in its initial years. Julie Dash's Daughters of the Dust premiered at the nearby Film Forum the same year.
14. The author wishes to acknowledge with gratitude the timely and thorough research assistance of Ms. Jade Flint, MA Candidate, Art History, Tulane University.
15. Umberger's research in relation to the exhibition and catalog *Between Worlds: The Art of Bill Traylor*, Smithsonian American Art Museum, 2018.
16. Umberger, *Between Worlds: The Art of Bill Traylor*, 59.
17. Umberger, 212.
18. Umberger, Leslie; 2021. *Between Worlds: The Art of Bill Traylor*, (online) Smithsonian American Art Museum, (Symposium delivered February 22, 2019 (22 minutes)).
19. Umberger, 247.
20. Barr on behalf of MoMA offered the small amount of between $1 and $2 per work. Shannon did not accept this offer according to Darby and Barat, "Blackness at MoMA: A Legacy of Deficit," 27.
21. DePasse, *Traveling the Rainbow: The Life and Art of Joseph E. Yoakum*, 14.
22. Livingston and Beardsley, *Black Folk Art in America 1930–1980*, 18.
23. Moore, "The Vision of Elijah," 30.
24. "Elijah Pierce Biography" on Folkstreams accessed on March 5, 2021 https://www.folkstreams.net/film-context.php?id=1068
25. Kent, Rosemary, "Sister Gertrude Morgan," *Andy Warhol's Interview* 1, no. 1, (September 1973), 40.
26. Livingston and Beardsley, *Black Folk Art in America 1930–1980*, 18.
27. Arnett (ed), *Souls Grown Deep: volume 1: African-American Vernacular Art of the South*, 298.

CHAPTER 5

1. In his mature work, Darger attempted to incorporate such things as diminishing perspectives and, less frequently, shading into his compositions, but even these devices were subject to his own peculiar interpretations.
2. It is possible that more than half of Darger's *Realms* saga consists of passages lifted from other literary works, which he then embroidered to a greater or lesser degree to fit his own purposes, while his remaining text contains completely original writing. In his artwork, most elements are traced or collaged from other sources, while fewer aspects are drawn freehand (such as scales on Blengins, grimacing mouths on faces, or diminutive penises on intersex children).
3. https://folkartmuseum.org/news/melvinway/
4. "I found that manneristic characteristics were there in the schizophrenic patient and I made this connection between mannerism in art and culture and mannerism evident in the expressions of my schizophrenic patients. (…) [W]hen a patient who has no knowledge of the forms of modern art draws such a drawing, you can conclude he is schizophrenic," Leo Navratil quoted in "John Maizels Interviews Dr. Leo Navratil, Founder of the Gugging House of Artists," *Raw Vision* #34, Spring 2001, 43.
5. Navratil demonstrated precisely the sort of attitude that is considered offensive by today's standards when he quoted Dubuffet as saying: "Heinrich Muller manifestly loved nothing so much as his madness. This was his reason for living and nothing enchanted him more than to project it onto living sheets of paper which he then fixed to the wall and gazed at," ibid, 44.
6. Patrick Harpur, *The Philosopher's Secret Fire: A History of the Imagination*, Ivan R. Dee, Publisher, Chicago, 2003, 35.
7. Biesenbach (ed), *Henry Darger*, 283.
8. Darger, Henry, *The History of My Life* (Published in Biesenbach (ed), 307).
9. Darger, Henry, *The History of My Life* (Published in Biesenbach (ed), 282).
10. Bonesteel, "Henry Darger's Great Crusade, Crisis of Faith and Last Judgement" in Beisenbach (ed), *Henry Darger*, 271. Further research on abuse and neglect in the Darger's boys' home can be found in Bonesteel, *Henry Darger: Art and Selected Writings*, 9.
11. These attempts to run away have been more related to Darger's summers spent away from the asylum working on at The State Farm, then being in the asylum itself (Bonesteel, 9–10).
12. Darger, Henry, *The History of My Life* (published in Biesenbach (ed)), 290.
13. Biesenbach, 23.
14. Darger, Henry, *The History of My Life* (published in Biesenbach (ed)), 283.
15. MacGregor, *Henry Darger: In the Realms of the Unreal*, 17.
16. Bonesteel, "Henry Darger's Great Crusade, Crisis of Faith and Last Judgement" in Beisenbach (ed), *Henry Darger*, 273.
17. Davis Anderson "An Artist's Studio at 851 Webster Avenue," in Beisenbach (ed), *Henry Darger*, 91.
18. MacGregor, 25.
19. Darger, Henry. *The History of My Life* (published in Biesenbach (ed)), 288.
20. Biesenbach, 13.
21. Darger, Henry. *The Realms*, vol. 1 "Predictions and threats," 295–304 (cited in MacGregor, 495).
22. Nathan Lerner (1913–1997) was a respected photographer and designer in Chicago. Lerner, along with his wife Kiyoko Lerner, were important advocates for both promoting and preserving the oeuvre from Henry Darger.

23. Quoted in Gordon W. Kirby, "Deaf Mute Boise Artist Work Acclaimed in West," *Idaho Daily Statesman*, 1962 (from Bell, Nicholas R., and Umberger, Leslie, *Untitled: The Art of James Castle*, Smithsonian American Art Museum, Washington, D.C., 2014, 40).
24. From Dellschau's *Recollections*, 2–3 (cited in Baker-White, "To Cross the Plains: The Art and Life of Charles A.A. Dellschau," 33).
25. *Melvin Way*, 2017 [online] Directed by Bruno Decharme, and produced by Barbara Safavora. YouTube.
26. Saltz "Studying the Masterpieces of Visionary Melvin Way."
27. *Melvin Way*, 2017 [online] Directed by Bruno Decharme, and produced by Barbara Safavora. YouTube.
28. Guo Fengyi, interview by Xu Tan, January 27, 2007, unpublished transcript prepared in conjunction with the exhibition *China Welcomes You... Desires, Struggles, New Identities* at Kunsthaus Graz, Austria, 2007 (cited in Drawing Papers 142, 13).
29. In 1975, Blagdon was intrigued to acquire "elements" leading to his introduction to pharmacist Dan Dryden who emerged as key to preserving the Healing Machine, which is now majoritively with the John Michael Kohler Arts Center, Sheboygan.
30. Yau, "The Wondrous Story of Emery Blagdon's Healing Machine."

CHAPTER 6

1. From the last paragraph of Holley's chapter in Arnett, William, *Souls Grown Deep: African American Vernacular Art of the South*.
2. Washington, *Up From Slavery*, 56.
3. Arnett, William, *Souls Grown Deep: African American Vernacular Art of the South*.
4. Bonesteel, *Artist—Lee Godie: A 20-Year Retrospective*, 10.
5. This biographical information was provided by Kapra Fleming for the documentary "Lee Godie, Chicago French Impressionist."
6. All quotations by Godie are from Bonesteel, *Artist-Lee Godie: A 20-Year Retrospective* (Noted by Bonesteel from the catalog: "All of Lee Godie's quotations used in this essay are derived from the recollections of her various friends and acquaintances, or taken from her writings. In the latter case, misspelled words and faulty grammar have been corrected.").
7. Bonesteel, 24.
8. Bonesteel, *Artist-Lee Godie: A 20-Year Retrospective*, 10.
9. Fullerton, "Lonnie Holley—Interview", June 6, 2020
10. Arnett, "Her Name is Someone."
11. Allamel, "Royal Robertson's Contribution to the Scriptures," 53–57.
12. *Raw Vision*, Issue 99, 35.

CHAPTER 7

1. The notion of community in relation to Chand's essay is broad to consider international advocates and local civlians, not directly infer an authoritive community (government).
2. Maizels, John, *Raw Creation: Outsider Art and Beyond*, 215.
3. Considering the research of Bonfitto, including her contribution to SPACES: Saving + Preserving Arts + Cultural Environments, Kohler WI (online archive).
4. Commencement of Phase II varies.
5. Bandyopadhyay and Jackson, *The Collection, the Ruin, and the Theatre: Architecture, Sculpture, and Landscape in Nek Chand's Rock Garden, Chandigarh*.
6. These creative alterations followed the death of her father whom she had a complicated and implied hostile relationship with. Researchers have suggested possible sexual abuse and such circumstances could have contributed to the select unsettling visuals of the *Owl House*.
7. Scruton, "Artist of the Universe," 57–65.
8. Stein, "The 96-year-old painter who saved a village."
9. Curator and historian Jo Farb Hernández visited the site in the summer of 2021 confirming that of his final iteration towers constructed only one is still standing.
10. Email communication with Hernández, September 2021.
11. Hernández, *Singular Spaces*, 542.
12. Schulz-Hoffmann (ed.), *Niki de Saint Phalle: My Art, My Dreams*, 140.

CHAPTER 8

1. It is actually quite rare for the time and place to have lived with her family that long.
2. Her first residence was the Ohio Asylum for Education of Idiotic and Imbecilic Youth (now Columbus State School), then the Gallipollis Developmental Center.
3. MacGregor, *Metamorphosis*, 51.
4. Ludins-Katz, Florence and Elias Katz. *Art and Disabilities: Establishing the Creative Art Center for People with Disabilities*, 14.
5. https://lanterman.org/lanterman_act#.YMMu9jZKjao
6. Higgs, "Judith Scott: Creative Growth," 31.
7. Baker, "Julian Martin's Abstraction with a lower-case "a"," 16–20.
8. Provided by ActionSpace, London, UK.
9. Krause-Harder interviewed by Atelier Goldstein, 2020. (Translated from German)
10. Rogers, "Up with Down Syndrome: The Art of Walter Mika."

CHAPTER 9

1. Müller-Westermann, "Paintings for the Future: Hilma af Klint—A Pioneer of Abstraction in Seclusion," 3.
2. Greenberg, "American-Type Painting," 218.
3. "Thornton Dial". Souls Grown Deep, accessed March 27, 2021, https://www.soulsgrowndeep.org/artist/thornton-dial
4. "Thornton Dial." Bill Lowe gallery, accessed March 27, 2021, https://lowegallery.com/about-thornton-dial

CHAPTER 10

1. Kallir, *Grandma Moses, American Primitive*, 28.
2. Kallir, *Grandma Moses* (New York: Harry N. Abrams, 1973), 35; cat 42. / Marling, Karal Ann, Designs on the heart: the homemade art of Grandma Moses, Harvard University Press, Cambridge MA, 2006, 127.
3. Elsa Longhauser et al. *The Heart of Creation: The Art of Martín Ramírez*, Philadelphia Galleries at Moore College of Art and Design, 1985, 6–14.
4. Howell Starr, Minnie Evans.

CHAPTER 11

1. Kobayashi, "Shinichi Sawada," 59.
2. Gómez, *Raw Vision*, (accessed online).
3. Spring, Angaza Afrika: African Art Now, 288.

BIBLIOGRAPHY

General

Alison Jacques Gallery. "The Gee's Bend Quiltmakers." Accessed May 28, 2021, https://www.alisonjacquesgallery.com/exhibitions/192/overview/

Arnett, Paul, and Arnett, William. *Souls Grown Deep: African American Vernacular Art of the South*. 1st ed. Atlanta, Ga.: [New York]: Tinwood Books; In Association with the Schomburg Center for Research in Black Culture, the New York Public Library, 2000.

Art et al. "FAQs." Accessed June 27, 2021, https://artetal.org/faqs

Brenson, Michael. "New Home and Life for Studio Museum in Harlem." *New York Times*, June 17, 1982, Section C, 16, National Edition. https://www.nytimes.com/1982/06/17/arts/new-home-and-life-for-studio-museum-in-harlem.html accessed July 10, 2021.

Campbell, Mary Schmidt. "Black Folk Art in America." *Art Journal* 42, no. 4 (1982): 345–46. Accessed March 25, 2021. doi:10.2307/776698

Cardinal, Roger. *Outsider Art*. New York: Praeger, 1972.

Collection de l'Art Brut. *L'Art Brut de Jean Dubuffet, aux origines de la collection*.Paris: Flammarion, 2016. Exhibition catalog.

Conwill, Kinshasha Holman. Schomburg Center for Research in Black Culture, Kalamazoo Institute of Arts, Genevieve Donald Gilmore Art Center, and KIA. *Testimony: Vernacular Art of the African American South: The Ronald and June Shelp Collection*. New York: Harry N. Abrams in Association with Exhibitions International and the Schomburg Center for Research in Black Culture, 2001.

Corcoran Gallery of Art. *Black Folk Art in America: 1930–1980*. Jane Livingston and John Beardsley. Jackson: University Press of Mississippi, and Center for the Study of Southern Culture, 1982. Exhibition catalog.

Dubuffet, Jean (ed). *L'Art Brut préféré aux arts culturels*. Paris: Compagnie De L'Art Brut, 1949.

Fine, Gary Alan. *Everyday Genius: Self-Taught Art and the Culture of Authenticity*. Chicago: University of Chicago Press, 2004.

Gundaker, Guy and Judith McWillie. *No Space Hidden: The Spirit of African American Yard Work*. Knoxville: University of Tennessee Press, 2005.

Hall, Michael D. and Eugene W. Metcalf, Jr., eds. *The Artist Outsider: Creativity and the Boundaries of Culture*. Washington, D.C.: Smithsonian Institution, 1994.

Hammond, Leslie King. *Ritual and Myth: A Survey of African American Art*, (New York: Studio Museum in Harlem, 1982).

Hayward Gallery. *Outsiders*. London: Arts Council of Great Britain, 1979. Exhibition catalog.

Indrisek, Scott. "Why 'Outsider Art' Is a Problematic but Helpful Label." *Artsy*, October 18, 2019. https://www.artsy.net/article/artsy-editorial-outsider-art-problematic-helpful-labe

Intuit: The Center for Intuitive and Outsider Art. *Outsider & Vernacular Art: The Victor F. Keen Collection*. Philadelphia: The Bethany Mission Gallery, 2019. Exhibition catalog.

Janis, Sidney. *They Taught Themselves: American Primitive Painters of the 20th Century*. New York: The Dial Press, 1942.

Jones, Kellie. "Ancient to the Future," *Studio*, Fall 2018/Winter 2019, 13, https://studiomuseum.org/article/ancient-future (accessed July 10, 2021).

Maclagan, David. *Outsider Art: From the Margins to the Marketplace*. London: Reaktion Books, 2009.

Maizels, John (ed). *Outsider Art Sourcebook: International Guide to Art Brut and Outsider Art*, 2002 (accessed electronic PDF versions by Raw Vision).

Maizels, John. *Raw Creation: Outsider Art and Beyond*. London: Phaidon, 1996.

McCollum, Christina. "Exhibitions in Outsider Art Since 1947," PhDdiss., The City University of New York, New York, 2017.

Metcalf, Eugene W. "Black Art, Folk Art, and Social Control." *Winterthur Portfolio* 18, no. 4 (1983): 271–89, 273.

Milwaukee Art Museum. *Common Ground / Uncommon Vision: The Michael and Julie Hall Collection of American Folk Art*. Milwaukee: Milwaukee Museum of Art, 1993. Exhibition catalog.

National Gallery of Art. *Outliers and American Vanguard Art*. Edited by Lynne Cooke. Washington: Chicago University Press, 2018. Exhibition catalog.

Peiry, Lucienne. *Art Brut: The Origins of Outsider Art*. Translated by James Frank. Paris: Flammarion, 2001.

Perry, Regenia A. "Contemporary African American Folk Art in America: An Overview." *The International Review of African American Art* 11, no. 1 (1993): 4.

Prinzhorn, Hans. *Artistry of the Mentally Ill*, 2nd edition. Translated by Eric von Brockdorff. Eastford: Martino Fine Books, 2019.

Rexer, Lyle. *How to Look at Outsider Art*. New York: Harry N.Abrams, 2005.

Russell, Charles. *Groundwaters: A Century of Self-Taught and Outsider Artists*. London, Munich, New York: Prestel, 2011.

Slominski, Lisa. "These Centers Are Helping with Disabilities Break into the Mainstream (and the Market)." *Artsy*, December 1, 2017, https://www.artsy.net/article/artsy-editorial-centers-helping-artists-disabilities-break-mainstream-market

Smith, Roberta. "Art in Review." *New York Times*, January 28, 1994, https://www.nytimes.com/1994/01/28/arts/art-in-review-011215.html

Tate. "Landscape." Accessed May 22, 2021, https://www.tate.org.uk/art/art-terms/l/landscape

Tate. "Figurative Art." Accessed June 15, 2021, https://www.tate.org.uk/art/art-terms/f/figurative-art

The Metropolitan Museum of Art. "Geometric Abstraction." Accessed May 18, 2021, https://www.metmuseum.org/toah/hd/geab/hd_geab.htm

The Metropolitan Museum of Art. *My Soul Has Grown Deep: Black Art from the American South*. London, New Haven: Yale University Press, 2018. (Catalog published in conjunction with "History Refused to Die: Highlights from the Souls Grown Deep Foundation Gift").

Thompson, Robert Farris. *Flash of the spirit: African & Afro-American Art & Philosophy*. New York: 1st Vintage Books, Random House, 1984.

Vlach, John Michael. *By the Work of Their Hands: Studies in Afro-American Folklife*. Charlottesville: University Press of Virginia, 1991.

Wardlaw, Alvia. *Black Art Ancestral Legacy: The African Influence in African American Art*, Dallas Museum of Art and Harry N. Abrams, 1990.

Wojcik, Daniel. *Outsider Art: Visionary Worlds and Trauma*. Jackson: University Press of Mississippi, 2016.

Yau, Elaine Y. "Post Black Folk Art in America 1930–1980–2016." *Panorama* 3, no. 1 (2017): Panorama, 01 June 2017, Vol.3 (1).

By Artist

Horst Ademeit

Bauer, Michael and Marcus Werner Hed, dirs. *ADEMEIT*. London: Pundersons Gardens, 2010.

McLaughlin, Rosanna. "Collection Study, Horst Ademeit, 4725, 4274, and Untitled." *The Roberts Institute of Art*, July 8, 2020.

Nationalgalerie im Hamburger Bahnhof – Museum für Gegenwart. *Secret Universe – Horst Ademeit*. Berlin: Verlag der Buchhandlung Walther König, 2011). Exhibition catalog.

Zander, Susanne: e-mail communication, January 26, 2021.

Kwame Akoto

Brown, Kate and Naomi Rea. "Here are 10 of the Most Exciting Artists to Discover at FIAC and Its Satellite Fairs in Paris." *Artnet*, October 19, 2018, https://news.artnet.com/art-world/10-top-artists-fiac-paris-2018-1374709?fbclid=IwAR1hfmRSbClBniQVYQQ4WO0AdoCqWzIpTBxma19eTCFi1B1SiHS6mThZAYA#.W8pZlaMvwv8.facebook

Ross, Doran H. "The Art of Almighty God, in his own words." *African Arts*, vol. 47, no. 2 (summer 2014): 8–27.

Seisser, Jean. "Kwame Akoto: Said Almighty God." *Raw Vision*, issue 99, (Autumn/Fall 2018): 33–37.

Emery Blagdon

Dryden, Dan. Dan Dryden to Seymour Rosen, SPACES, Inc., Los Angeles, CA 90028, April 2, 1987.

Kohler Foundation. "Emery Blagdon." Accessed August 31, 2021, http://www.kohlerfoundation.org/preservation/major-collections/emery-blagdon/

Umberger, Leslie and Erika Doss. *Sublime Spaces & Visionary Worlds: Built Environments of Vernacular Artists*. New York & Sheboygan: Princeton Architectural Press & Johan Michael Kohler Arts Center, 2007.

Umberger, Leslie. "Earthly Power." *Raw Vision*, issue 59, (Summer 2007): 22–19.
Yau, John. "The Wonderous Story of Emery Blagdon's Healing Machine." *Hyperallergic*, June 30, 2013.

James Castle
Bell, Nicholas R. "Being James Castle: Experiencing Place, Time, and Memory." In *Untitled: The Art of James Castle*, 19–34. Washington, D.C.: Smithsonian American Art Museum, 2014.
Kirby, Gordon W. . "Deaf Mute Boise Artist Work Acclaimed in West." *Idaho Daily Statesman*, 1962.
Museo Nacional Centro de Arte Reina Sofia. *James Castle Show and Store*. Madrid, 2011. Exhibition text by Lynne Cooke.
The James Castle Collection and Archive (JCCA). "Art." *James Castle*, Accessed November 18, 2020, https://jamescastle.com/james-castle-biography/
The James Castle Collection and Archive (JCCA). "Biography." *James Castle*, Accessed November 18, 2020, https://jamescastle.com/art/
Umberger, Leslie, "James Castle: Vanishing Point." In *Untitled: The Art of James Castle*, 35–-52. Washington, D.C.: Smithsonian American Art Museum, 2014.

Pedro Cervantes
Morang, Alfred. "Some Artists of New Mexico." Fiesta Issue of *The Santa Fean*. Santa Fe: The Santa Fe Press, inc., 1941.
Nunn, Tey Marianna, "All this Beauty and Colour Should Have a Place in Every Home." In *Sin Nombre: Hispana and Hispano Artists of the New Deal Era*, 43–74. Albuquerque: University of New Mexico Press, 2001.

Nek Chand
Anderson Davis, Brooke. "Concrete Kingdom: Sculptures by Nek Chand," in *Folk Art* (Spring/Summer 2006): 42–49.
Bandyopadhyay, Soumyen and Iain Jackson. *The Collection, the Ruin, and the Theatre: Architecture, Sculpture, and Landscape in Nek Chand's Rock Garden, Chandigarh*. Liverpool: Liverpool University Press, 2007.
Bonfitto, Tracy Ann Buck. "The Rock Garden of Chandigarh." *SPACES: Saving + Preserving Arts + Cultural Environments*. Accessed February 18, 2021, http://spacesarchives.org/explore/search-the-online-collection/nek-chand-rock-garden-of-chandigarh/
Cox, Paul, dir. *Kingdom of Nek Chand*. Australia: Ulli Beier and Paul Cox, 1980
Goswani, BN. "Rock Garden creator Nek Chand dead." *The Tribune India*, June 12, 2015.
Maizels, John. "Nek Chand Obituary." *The Guardian*, Art and Design, June 15, 2015.
Nek Chand Foundation. "About Nek Chand." *Nek Chand Foundation*. Accessed February 19, 2021, https://nekchand.com/about-nek-chand
Reeve, Phillip. "A Visit with the Master: The Creative Genius of Nek Chand." *Raw Vision*, issue 9 (Summer 1994): 34–42.
Visvanathan, Shiv. "Rethinking Waste: Time, Obsolescence, Diversity and Democracy." In *Arts and Aesthetics in a Globalizing World* edited by Raminder Kaur and Parul Dave-Mukjerji, 99–118. London, New Delhi, New York, Sydney: Bloomsbury, 2014.

Mamadou Cissé
Bidouzo-Coudray, Joyce. "Mamadou Cissé: a modern griot." *The Guardian*, November 13, 2012.
Marie Finaz Gallery. "Mamadou Cissé." Accessed June 29, 2021, https://www.mariefinazgallery.com/mamadou-cisse

Aloïse Corbaz
Lombardi, Sarah. "Aloïse Corbaz: Untitled." *Raw Vision*, issue 100 (December 2018): 65.
Muzelle, Céline. "'La Cantatrice'. A biography of Aloïse." *Swiss Institute for Art Research (SIK-ISEA), Aloïse Corbaz (1886–1964), catalogue raisonné électronique*. Accessed November 16, 2020, https://www.aloise-corbaz.ch/content.aspx?id=Q13
Porret-Forel, Jacqueline Forel and Jean Gagnebin. *Aloyse*. Paris: Compagnie de l'Art Brut, 1948.
Porret-Forel, Jacqueline. "Le Cloisonné de Théâtre-Aloïse Corbaz." *Raw Vision*, issue 57 (December 2006): 46–53.
Swiss Institute for Art Research (SIK-ISEA). "Bibliography." Aloïse Corbaz (1886–1964), *catalogue raisonné électronique*. Accessed November 16, 2020, https://www.aloise-corbaz.ch/literatur.aspx
Swiss Institute for Art Research (SIK-ISEA). "Documents." Aloïse Corbaz (1886–1964), *catalogue raisonné électronique*. Accessed November 16, 2020, https://www.aloise-corbaz.ch/dokumente.aspx
Swiss Institute for Art Research (SIK-ISEA). "Exhibitions." Aloïse Corbaz (1886–1964), *catalogue raisonné électronique*. Accessed November 16, 2020, https://www.aloise-corbaz.ch/ausstellungen.aspx
Swiss Institute for Art Research (SIK-ISEA). "Works." Aloïse Corbaz (1886–1964), *catalogue raisonné électronique*. Accessed November 16, 2020, https://www.aloise-corbaz.ch/werke.aspx

Fleury-Joseph Crepin
Archive of André Breton. "No.110." *André Breton. The Collection*. Accessed November 28, 2020, https://www.andrebreton.fr/fr/work/56600100805650?back_rql=Any%20X%20ORDERBY%20FTIRANK%28X%29%20DESC%20WHERE%20X%20has_text%20%22Fleury-Joseph%2A%20Cr%C3%A9pin%2A%22&back_url=https%3A%2F%2Fwww.andrebreton.fr%2Ffr%2Fview%3F_fsb%3D1%26rql%3DFleury-Joseph%25C2%25A0Cr%25C3%25A9pin%26subvid%3Dts
Breton, André. *Le Surréalisme et la peinture, Nouvelle édition revue et corrigée*, 1928–1965. Paris: Gallimard, 1979.
Breton, André, Jean Dubuffet, Vincent Bounoure, Jean-Louis Lanoux, Jose Pierre, Louis Segiun, Pierre Godberge, Didier Deroux. *Fleury-Joseph Crépin: 1875–1948*. Paris: Idée'Art, 1999.
Cardinal, Roger. "The Art of Entrancement." *Raw Vision*, issue 2 (Winter 1989/90): 22–31.

Henry Darger
Biesenbach, Klaus. "Introduction: American Innocence." In *Henry Darger*, edited by Klaus Biesenbach, 11–44. Munich, London, New York: Prestel, in cooperation with the American Folk Art Museum, 2019. (3rd edition).
Bonesteel, Michael. *Henry Darger: Art and Selected Writings*. New York: Rizzoli, 2000.
Bonesteel, Michael. "Henry Darger's Great Crusade, Crisis of Faith and Last Judgement." In *Henry Darger*, edited by Klaus Biesenbach, 271–276. Munich, London, New York: Prestel, in cooperation with the American Folk Art Museum, 2019. (3rd edition).
Darger, Henry. "The History of My Life." In *Henry Darger*, edited by Klaus Biesenbach, 281 – 314. Munich, London, New York: Prestel, in cooperation with the American Folk Art Museum, 2019. (3rd edition).
Davis Anderson, Brooke. "An Artist's Studio at 851 Webster Avenue." In *Henry Darger*, edited by Klaus Biesenbach, 87–99. Munich, London, New York: Prestel, in cooperation with the American Folk Art Museum, 2019. (3rd edition).
Kerr, Debra, Leisa Rundquist. "A Closer Look into Henry Darger's World." Lecture, Intuit: The Center for Intuitive and Outsider Art presented by The Outsider Art Fair, Chicago, February 3, 2021). (Attended virtually).
MacGregor, John. *Henry Darger: In the Realms of the Unreal*. New York: Delano Greenidge Editions, 2002.
Szremski, Ania. "Henry Darger: Andrew Edlin Gallery." *Artforum*. Accessed May 10, 2021, https://www.artforum.com/print/reviews/202101/henry-darger-84681
Watson, Carl. "The Metaphysics of Wreckage: Introduction to the Autobiography of Henry Darger." In *Henry Darger*, edited by Klaus Biesenbach, 277–280. Munich, London, New York: Prestel, in cooperation with the American Folk Art Museum, 2019. (3rd edition).
Yu, Jessica, dir. *In the Realms of the Unreal*. POV, Public Broadcasting Systems, 2004. (Accessed YouTube).

Charles A.A. Dellschau
Baker-White, Tracy. "To Cross the Plains: The Life and Art of Charles A.A. Dellschau." In *Charles A.A. Dellschau, 1830–1923*, 29–45. Seattle: Marquand Books, Inc., 2013.
Cardinal, Roger. "The Art of Interpolation: Charles A.A. Dellschau's Inscriptions and Airo Cutts." In *Charles A.A. Dellschau, 1830–1923*, 47–59. Seattle: Marquand Books, Inc., 2013.
Rosen, Rebecca J. "The Airship Club That Might Never Have Existed." *The Atlantic*, March 21, 2013.
Wehnert, Jay. *Outsider Art in Texas: Lone Stars*. College Station: Texas A&M University Press, 2018.

Thornton Dial

Andrew Edlin Gallery. "Thornton Dial." Accessed on March 15, 2021, https://www.edlingallery.com/artists/thornton-dial

Arnett, William. "The Root Sculptures Thornton Dial: A Network of Ideas." In *Souls Grown Deep: volume 1: African-American Vernacular Art of the South*, edited by Paul Arnett and William Arnett, 176–188. Atlanta: Tinwood Books, 2001.

Beardsley, John. *Art and Landscape in Charleston and the low country: a project of Spoleto Festival USA*. Washington, D.C.: Spacemaker Press, 1998.

Williams, Paige. "Composition in Black and White." *The New Yorker*, August 5, 2013.

Sam Doyle

Arnett, William. "Sam Doyle: The News from Frogmore." In *Souls Grown Deep: volume 1: African-American Vernacular Art of the South*, edited by Paul Arnett and William Arnett, 320–329. Atlanta: Tinwood Books, 2001.

Atwell, Mary Stewart. "Searching Out the Hidden Stories of South Carolina's Gullah Country." *New York Times*, April 15, 2019, https://www.nytimes.com/2019/04/15/travel/south-carolina-gullah-geechee-low-country.html

Bailey, Gordon. "Sam Doyle: Haints and Saints." *Raw Vision*, issue 61 (Winter 2007): 28–35.

Opala, Joseph A. "Introduction: Gullah: Rice, Slavery, and the Sierra Leone American Connection." *Yale University*, Macmillan Canter, Gilder Lehrman Center for the Study of Slavery, Resistance, and Abolition. Accessed July 1, 2021, https://glc.yale.edu/gullah-rice-slavery-and-sierra-leone-american-connection

William Edmondson

Barat, Charlotte; and Darby English. "Blackness at MoMA: A Legacy of Deficit." *Among Others: Blackness at MoMA*, 14–99. New York: The Museum of Modern Art, 2019.

Barat, Charlotte, and Darby English. "The Artist Wasn't Present: On MoMA's Fumbled First Showing of Black American Art." *ArtNews*, July 17, 2019, https://www.artnews.com/art-news/news/among-others-blackness-at-moma-excerpt-12972/

Fuller, Edmund L. *Visions in Stone*. Pittsburgh: University of Pittsburgh Press, 1973, https://archive.org/details/visionsinstonesc0000edmo/page/n5/mode/2up

Jentleson, Katherine. "Both New Negro and American: Horace Pippin's Crossover Appeal." *Gatecrashers: The rise of the self-taught artist in America*, 75–125. Oakland: University of California Press, 2020.

Marshall, Jennifer Jane. " 'Ever Not Quite': Empathy, Experience, and William Edmondson." *Experience (Volume 4)*, 102–133. Chicago: Terra Foundation for American Art with The University of Chicago Press, 2017.

Marshall, Jennifer Jane. "'Find-and-Seek: Discovery Narratives, Americanization, and Other Tales of Genius in Modern American Folk Art." *Outliers and American Vanguard Art*, 52–63. Washington: Chicago University Press, 2018.

Marshall, Jennifer Jane; Ghenete Zelleke. "The Carved Legacy of William Edmondson." Lecture, Minneapolis Institute of Art, Minneapolis, February 27, 2020. (Accessed on YouTube)

MoMA. "1929: Alfred Barr Chosen as First Director." *MoMA Through Time*. Accessed March 25, 2021, https://www.moma.org/interactives/moma_through_time/1920/alfred-h-barr-jr-selected-as-first-director/

MoMA. 1937. "Exhibition of Sculpture by William Edmondson." Press Release, October 18, 1937.

Minnie Evans

Arnett, William. "Minnie Evans." In *Souls Grown Deep: volume 1: African-American Vernacular Art of the South*, edited by Paul Arnett and William Arnett, 308–309. Atlanta: Tinwood Books, 2001.

Perry, Regenia A. *Free within Ourselves: African-American Artists in the Collection of the National Museum of American Art*. Washington, D.C.: National Museum of American Art in Association with Pomegranate Art Books, 1992.

Puchner, Edward M. "Faith and War: Wilmington, World War II and the art of Minnie Evans." *Raw Vision*, issue 92 (Winter 2016/17): 32–37.

Wellington B. Gray Gallery. *Minnie Evans: Artist*. Charles Muir Lovell Greenville: East Carolina University, 1993. Exhibition catalog.

Whitney Museum of American Art. *Minnie Evans*. New York, 1975. Nina Howell Starr. Exhibition text.

Guo Fengyi

Fengyi, Guo. Unpublished transcript prepared in conjunction with the exhibition *China, Welcomes You ... Desires, Struggles, New Identities* at Kunsthaus Graz, Austria, 2007. Interview by Xu Tan, January 27, 2007.

Guiraldes, Rosario. "The Ungovernable Images of Guo Fengyi." In *Guo Fengyi: To See from a Distance*, 25–39. New York: Drawing Papers 142, 2020.

Hoptman, Laura "To See from a Distance Is Still to Be Seen: Guo Fengyi at The Drawing Center." In *Guo Fengyi: To See from a Distance*, 9–16. New York: Drawing Papers 142, 2020.

Jie, Lu. "Who is Guo Fengyi?" In *Who is Guo Fengyi*, edited by Liu Jie. Beijing: 25000 Transmission Centre and Long March Foundation, 2005.

Ryor, Kathleen M. "Guo Fengyi and the Embodied Cosmos." In *Guo Fengyi: To See from a Distance*, 46–58. New York: Drawing Papers 142, 2020.

Tan, Xi. "The Story of Guo Fengyi." In *Guo Fengyi: To See from a Distance*, 72–79. New York: Drawing Papers 142, 2020.

Auguste Forestier

Borum, Jenifer P. "ABCD: A Collection of Art Brut," Folk Art (Spring 2001): 26.T, https://issuu.com/american_folk_art_museum/docs/folkart_26_1_spr2001

Faupin, Savin. "Auguste Forestier's unbroken wanderlust." *Epidemiology and Psychiatric Sciences* 26, issue 3 (June 2017): 228–230, https://doi.org/10.1017/S2045796016000901

Oury, Jean. *Auguste For.* Bizarre VI., 1956.

Madge Gill

Ayad, Sara. "Borderlands – Dr Boyle and the Genesis of Gill's Art." In *Madge Gill by Myrninerest*, edited by Sophie Dutton, 107 –110. London: Rough Trade Books, 2019.

Ayad, Sara. "Madge Gill: A Biography." In *Madge Gill by Myrninerest*, edited by Sophie Dutton, 235–244. London: Rough Trade Books, 2019.

Cardinal, Roger. "The Art of Entrancement." *Raw Vision*, issue 2 (Winter 1989/90): 22–31.

Cardinal, Roger. "Visions of Myrninerest." In *Myrninerest by Madge Gill* edited by Henry Boxer and David Tibet, 8–12. Chippenham: The Spheres, 2013.

Gill, Laurence E. "Myrninerest the Spheres." Broadsheet for *Theosophical Society* (March 1926).

Gill, Madge. Interview. *Prediction Magazine*, 1937.

Madge Gill. "Biography." Accessed January 11, 2021, http://madgegill.com/biography

Madge Gill. "Chronology." Accessed January 11, 2021, http://madgegill.com/chronology

Roberts, Vivienne. "Stare of Destiny: Madge Gill and Spiritualism." *In Madge Gill by Myrninerest*, edited by Sophie Dutton, 73–77. London: Rough Trade Books, 2019.

Lee Godie

Bonesteel, Michael. *Artist – Lee Godie: A 20-Year Retrospective*. Chicago: City of Chicago, Department of Cultural Affairs, 1993.

Bonesteel, Michael. "The Mysterious Master of Michigan Ave." *Chicago Reader*, January 8, 1982.

Fleming, Kapra and Tommy Palazzolo, dirs. *Lee Godie, A Chicago French Impressionist*. Chicago: Pandora Lobo Estepario Productions, 2021.

Kaplan, Isaac. "Searching for Lee Godie, One of Chicago's Most Collected Artists." Artsy, April 28, 2016, https://www.artsy.net/article/artsy-editorial-searching-for-lee-godie-one-of-chicago-s-most-collected-artists

Lamb, Joe, "A brief (but possibly too long) account of my experiences with Lee Godie." *Slominski Projects*, September, 2020, https://slominskiprojects.com/lee-godie

Monem, Nadine. "Before Cindy Sherman, There Was Lee Godie and the Bus Station Photo Booth." *Elephant*, 21 October, 2019, https://elephant.art/cindy-sherman-lee-godie-bus-station-photo-booth/

Johann Hauser

Cardinal, Roger. "Johann Hauser." *Raw Vision*, issue 91 (Fall 2016): 18-70.

Feilacher, Johann (ed). *Johann Hauser . . . I am the artist!* Wein: Residenz Verlag, 2016.

Museum Gugging. "Johann Hauser." Accessed March 6, 2021, https://www.museumgugging.at/en/gugging-art/gugging-artists/johann-hauser

Navratil, Leo. "The history and prehistory of the Artists' House in Gugging." In *The Artist Outsider: Creativity and the Boundaries of Culture* edited by Hall, Michael D. and Eugene W. Metcalf, Jr., 199–211. Washington, D.C.: Smithsonian Institution Press, 1994.

Wexler, Alice and John Derby. "Art in Institutions: The Emergence of (Disabled) Outsiders." *National Art Education Association Studies in Art Education: A Journal of Issues and Research*, 56, no. 2 (2015): 127–141.

Lonnie Holley

Arnett, Paul. "Lonnie Holley: Pulling on the Root." In *Souls Grown Deep: volume 1: African-American Vernacular Art of the South*, edited by Paul Arnett and William Arnett, 190–195. Atlanta: Tinwood Books, 2001.

Arnett, William. "Out-Outgribing the Momraths." In *Souls Grown Deep: volume 2: African-American Vernacular Art of the South*, edited by Paul Arnett and William Arnett, 575–583. Atlanta: Tinwood Books, 2001.

Curran, Maris, dir. *The Man is Music*. Nightshade Films, 2016.

Holley, Lonnie. "Lonnie Holley." In *Souls Grown Deep: volume 2: African-American Vernacular Art of the South*, edited by Paul Arnett and William Arnett, 538–574. Atlanta: Tinwood Books, 2001.

Holley, Lonnie. "Lonnie Holley – Interview: ' I started doing my work with a knife, fork and a spoon on sandstone'." Interview by Elizabeth Fullerton. *studio international*, June 6, 2020, https://www.studiointernational.com/index.php/lonnie-holley-interview-i-started-doing-my-work-with-a-knife-fork-and-spoon-art

Lonnie Holley. "Bio." Accessed on March 21, 2021, https://www.lonnieholley.com/blog/2018/1/26/bio

McWillie, Judith. "Lonnie Holley's Moves." *Artforum*, volume 30, no. 8 (April 1992): 80–84.

Nnena Kalu

ActionSpace. "Nnena Kalu." Accessed March 15, 2021, https://actionspace.org/artists/nnena-kalu/

Benson, Louise. "Nnena Kalu Weaves a Wild Web of Sellotape and Wool." *Elephant*, March 9, 2020.

Slominski Projects. "Nice to Meet You: Nnena Kalu." Accessed March 16, 2021, https://www.theguardian.com/artanddesign/2019/nov/11/nnena-kalu-compulsive-art-disabled-artist

John Kane

Galerie St Etienne. "Biography." John Kane (1860–1934) Accessed March 5, 2021, https://www.gseart.com/artist/john-kane/bio

Jentleson, Katherine. "The Most Truly American: John Kane's Naturalized Appeal." *Gatecrashers: The rise of the self-taught artist in America*, 23–73. Oakland: University of California Press, 2020.

Rouvalis, Cristina. "Pittsburgh Painter" *Carnegie Magazine*, spring 2018, https://carnegiemuseums.org/carnegie-magazine/spring-2018/pittsburghs-painter/

Susmann, Warren I. "The Useless Past: American Intellectuals and the Frontier Thesis, 1910–1930." *Bucknell Review II*, no. 2 (1963): 3.

Hilma af Klint

Birnbaum, Daniel. "Introduction – The Incredible Legacy of Hilma af Klint." In *Hilma af Klint: Visionary*, edited by Kurt Almqvist and Louise Belfrage, 13–17. Stockholm: Bokforlaget Stople, 2020.

Henderson, Lynda Dalrymple. "Hilma af Klint and the Invisble in Her Occult." In *Hilma af Klint: Visionary*, edited by Kurt Almqvist and Louise Belfrage, 71–82. Stockholm: Bokforlaget Stople, 2020.

Isenberg, Sarah. "The Future is Now: Hilma af Klint and the Esoteric Imagination." In *Bowdoin Journal of Art*, Bowdoin College, 2020.

Müller-Westermann, Iris."Paintings for the Future: Hilma af Klint—A Pioneer of Abstraction in Seclusion." In *Hilma af Klint—A Pioneer of Abstraction*, ed. Müller- Westermann with Jo Widoff, 3. Stockholm: Moderna Museet; Oftfildern, Germany: Hatje Cantz, 2013.

Spretnak, C. *The Spiritual Dynamic in Modern Art: A History Reconsidered, 1800 to the Present*. New York: Palgrave MacMillan US, 2014.

The Hilma af Klint Foundation. "About Hilma af Klint." Accessed Februrary 8, 2021, https://www.hilmaafklint.se/en/

Voss, Julia. "Five Things to Know About Hilma af Klint." In *Hilma af Klint: Visionary*, edited by Kurt Almqvist and Louise Belfrage, 21–39. Stockholm: Bokforlaget Stople, 2020.

Davood Koochaki

Gilbert, Jennifer, Randall Morris, and Morteza Zahedi. 'Monochromatic Minds." Prerecorded artist talks, Jennifer Lauren Gallery, July 13, 2020. (Accessed on Jennifer Lauren Gallery website).

Raw Vision. "Davood Koochaki 1939–2020." Accessed on June 18, 2021, https://rawvision.com/news/davood-koochaki-1939–2020.

Julia Krause-Harder

Fritz, Sven and Lutz Pillong. "Julia Krause-Harder: Portrait-Text." Provided by Atelier Goldstein, Frankfurt.

Kunstforum Wien. *Flying High - Kunstlerinnen der Art Brut*. " Wien, 2019. Production methods of contemporary Art Brut artists." Exhibition text by Hanna Rieger and Veronika Rudorfer.

Krause-Harder, Julia. An interview with Atelier Goldstein for Goldstein Academy Educational work. Frankfurt, 2020.

Krause-Harder, Julia. An interview with Atelier Goldstein, 2020. Provided by Atelier Goldstein, Frankfurt.

Rieger, Hannah. "Die Dinosaurier-Spezialistin." A text by Hannah Rieger, published on the occasion of the exhibition *Himmelstürmer innen auf Kurs*, Musée Visionnaire, Zürich, 2020.

Augustin Lesage

Cardinal, Roger. "The Art of Entrancement." *Raw Vision*, issue 2 (Winter 1989/90): 22–31.

La Maison Rouge. *Elmar Trenkwalder and Augustin Lesage: Inspired Artists*. Paris: Fondation Antoine de Galbert, 2008. Digital exhibition catalog.

Thevoz, Michel, "Augustin Lesage and Spiritualism." *Raw Vision*, issue 1 (1989): 5

Julian Martin

Baker, Alex. "Julian Martin's Abstraction with a lower-case 'a'." In *Julian Martin: Transformer*, 16–20. Northcote: Arts Project Australia, 2014.

Gomez, Edward. "Bold Essays in Colour and Form." *Raw Vision*, issue 84 (Winter 2014/15): 34–38.

Roff, Sue. "Julian Martin. Abstracting the Shape." *Epidemiology and Psychiatric Sciences* 24, issue 5 (October 2015): 376–378. doi:10.1017/S2045796015000499

Helen Martins

Graaf, Anne. "The Mystic Imagination." *Raw Vision*, issue 99 (Autumn/Fall 2018): 26–31.

Gotthardt, Alexxa. "The South African Teacher Who Turned Her Home into a Sanctuary of Color and Light." *Artsy*, June 13, 2018.

Karvellas, Greg and Daniel Rutland Manners, dirs. "The Owl House." The Fugard Theatre in association with The Owl House Foundation, 2019.

Lyster, Rosa. "A Visit to South Africa's Strange, Astonishing Owl House." *The New Yorker*, February 1, 2018.

Owl House. " History." Accessed May 8, 2021, https://theowlhouse.co.za/helen-martins/

Walter Mika

Rogers, Pamala: e-mail communication with author, November 25, 2020– January 25, 2021.

Rogers, Pamala, "Up with Down Syndrome: The Art of Walter Mika." New York: Pure Vision Arts, 2008.

Shrine. *Funny Bunny: Walter Mika*. Scott Ogden. New York: Shrine, 10 January–February 9, 2020. Exhibition text.

Sister Gertrude Morgan

Fagaly, William A. *Tools of Her Ministry: The Art of Sister Gertrude Morgan*, New York: American Folk Art Museum, with Rizzoli International, 2004.

Yau, Elaine Y. "Acts of Conversion: Sister Gertrude Morgan and the Sensation of Black Folk Art, 1960–1982." PhD., University of Berkeley, 2015.

Yau, Elaine Y. "Sister Gertrude Morgan's Material Performances and the Sensory Cultures in New Orleans, 1960–1983." *National Gallery of Art, Members' Research Report Archive*. Accessed on June 6, 2021, https://www.nga.gov/research/casva/research-projects/research-reports-archive/yau-2013-2014.html

Grandma Moses

Jentleson, Katherine. "Goodwill Grandma: Anna Mary Robertson Moses's Cold War Appeal." In *Gatecrashers: The rise of the self-taught artist in America*, 127–170. Oakland: University of California Press, 2020.

Jentleson, Katherine. "How the US Government Deployed Grandma Moses Overseas in the Cold War." *Smithsonian Magazine*, March 2020.

Kallir, Otto (ed). *Grandma Moses, American Primitive*. New York and Garden City: Doubleday and Company Inc., 1947.

Kallir, Otto (ed). *Grandma Moses*. New York: Harry N. Abrams, 1973.

Marling, Karal Ann. *Designs on the heart: the homemade art of Grandma Moses*, Cambridge: Harvard University Press, 2006.

Smithsonian American Art Museum. "Grandma Moses." Accessed December 9, 2021, https://americanart.si.edu/artist/grandma-moses-5826

Andrew Omoding

Catto, Sheryll: e-mail communication with author, November 29 –January 26, 2021.

It's my work, come see, come see, Andrew Omoding artist residency, Camden Art Center, July 17–28, 2019. Lisa Slominski spent several days with Andrew during his residency.

J Hammond Projects. *Spring Syllabus*. Lisa Slominski. London: Slominski Projects, 2018. Exhibition text.

Marchand, Trevor H.J. *Ducks and Daughters: Story-Making with Andrew Omoding*. Birmingham: Craftspace, 2016.

Marchand, Trevor H.J. "Explorations in Creativity with Andrew Omoding: artist, maker and raconteur." In *Radical Craft: alternative ways of making*, 48–59. Birmingham: Craftspace, 2016.

Elijah Pierce

Allport, Carolyn, dir. *Elijah Pierce: Wood Carver*. Columbus: WBNS-TV, The Ohio State University, 1974.

Folkstreams. "Elijah Pierce Biography." Accessed March 5, 2021, https://www.folkstreams.net/film-context.php?id=1068

Moore, Gaylen. "The Vision of Elijah." *New York Times Magazine*, August 26, 1979.

Promey, Sally M. "Elijah Pierce and Material Conversions." In *Reflections: The Columbus Museum of Art's American Collection*. Athens: Columbus Museum of Art in Association with Ohio University Press, 2019. Accessed March 4, 2021, https://mavcor.yale.edu/mavcor-journal/elijah-pierce-and-material-conversions

Sayej, Nadja. "Elijah Pierce: the wood carver who grappled with civil rights and racism." *The Guardian*, September 28, 2020.

Horace Pippin

Bearden, Romare and Harry Henderson. *A history of African-American artists : from 1792 to the present*. New York: Pantheon Books, 1993, https://archive.org/details/historyofafrican00bear

Jentleson, Katherine. "Both New Negro and American: Horace Pippin's Crossover Appeal." In *Gatecrashers: The rise of the self-taught artist in America*, 75–125. Oakland: University of California Press, 2020.

The National Gallery of Art. "Horace Pippin." NGA Online Editions. Accessed December 7, 2020, https://www.nga.gov/collection/artist-info.25.html

Josep Pujiula i Vila

Farb Hernández, Jo. "Josep Pujiula i Vila, Poblat Salvatge ("Wild Village"), Towers, and Labyrinth," *SPACES: Saving + Preserving Arts + Cultural Environments*. Accessed April 6, 2021, http://spacesarchives.org/explore/search-the-online-collection/poblat-salvatge-wild-village-towers-and-labyrinth/

Farb Hernández, Jo. *Singular Spaces – from the Eccentric to the Extraordinary in Spanish Art Environments*. San Jose: Raw Vision, SPACES, San Jose State University, 2013.

Raw Vision. "Josep Pujiula i Vila (1937–2016)." Accessed April 14 2021, https://rawvision.com/news/josep-pujiula-i-vila-1937-2016

Helen Rae

Slominski Projects. "Nice to Meet You: Helen Rae." Accessed July 8, 2020, https://slominskiprojects.com/nice-to-meet-you

Tierra del sol. "Rest in Peace & Power Helen Rae (1938–2021)." Accessed March 15, 2021, https://www.tierradelsol.org/rest-in-peace-power-helen-rae-1938-2021/

Wery, Paige, David Pagel, and Rebecca Hamm. "Unique Vision of Helen Rae." Panel discussion, Claremont Museum of Art, January 26, 2020. (Accessed on YouTube).

Wery, Paige: e-mail communication with author July 1–7, 2020.

Martín Ramírez

Anderson Davis, Brooke. "Martín Ramírez: Motifs and Memory" *Folk Art*, volume 32, number 1 (winter 2007): 46–55.

Anderson Davis, Brooke, Kristin Espinosa, and Matt Pasto. "Three Perspectives: Martín Ramírez." San Jose Museum of Art. Podcast audio. July 20, 2007.

Moore College of Art. *The Heart of Creation: The Art of Martín Ramirez*. Goldie Paley Gallery at Moore College of Art and Design, 1985. Exhibition catalog.

Reina Sofía. *Martín Ramírez: Reframing Confinement*. Madrid: Museo Nacional Centro de Arte Reina Sofía, 2010. Exhibition catalog.

Prophet Isaiah Robertson

Adly, Jack, dir. *The End of the World 2014 in Niagara Falls*. Niagara Falls: Jack Adley, 2011.

Scruton, Fred. "Artist of the Universe." *Raw Vision* issue 80 (Winter 2013): 57–65.

Scruton, Fred: e-mail communication with author, March 8–9, 2021.

Scruton, Fred, dir. *Rivers of Fire and Redemption*. Niagara Falls: Fred Scruton, 2014.

Scruton, Fred. "Second Coming House: Prophet Isaiah Robertson (1947–2020)." *SPACES: Saving + Preserving Arts + Cultural Environments*. Accessed March 8, 2021. http://spacesarchives.org/explore/search-the-online-collection/prophet-isaiah-robertson/

Prophet Royal Robertson

Allamel, Frederic. "Royal Robertson's Contribution to the Scriptures." *Raw Vision*, issue 13, (Winter 1995/1996): 53–57.

Arnett, Paul. "Night Vision: Royal Robertson" In *Souls Grown Deep: volume 1: African-American Vernacular Art of the South*, edited by Paul Arnett and William Arnett, 444–457. Atlanta: Tinwood Books, 2001.

Ogden, Scott and Malcolm Hearn, dirs. *MAKE*. Austin: Make Skateboards, Juju NYC, Asthmatic Kitty, 2011.

Webb, Julie: e-mail communication with author, January 26, 2021

Henri Rousseau

Alley, Ronald. *Henri Rousseau: portrait of a primitive*. Oxford: Phaidon, 1978. Ware: Omega, 1984. https://archive.org/details/henrirousseaupor0000alle/page/n7/mode/2up

Bihalji-Merin, *Oto. Das naive Bild der Welt*. Cologne: Verlag M DuMont Schauberg, 1959.

Stabenow, Corneli. *Rousseau*. London: Taschen, 2001. https://archive.org/details/henrirousseau1840000stab/page/n99/mode/2up

The National Gallery of Art. "Henri Rousseau: Jungles in Paris." Accessed April 11, 2021, https://www.nga.gov/features/slideshows/henri-rousseau.html#slide_1

Nellie Mae Rowe

Arnett, William. "Nellie Mae Rowe: Inside the Perimeter." In *Souls Grown Deep: volume 1: African-American Vernacular Art of the South*, edited by Paul Arnett and William Arnett, 290–307. Atlanta: Tinwood Books, 2001.

Augustine, Judith Alexander: e-mail communication, 5–26 January, 2021.

Cohen, Joyce. "Home Sweet Home – A Feminist Look at Nellie Mae Rowe." Lecture, The High Museum of Art, Atlanta, March 11, 2010. (Accessed on YouTube)

Lippard, Lucy. "The Word In Their Hands." In *Souls Grown Deep: volume 1: African-American Vernacular Art of the South*, edited by Paul Arnett and William Arnett, 282–285. Atlanta: Tinwood Books, 2001.

Niki de Saint Phalle

Il Giardinodei Tarocchi. "Chronology." http://ilgiardinodeitarocchi.it/en/about/chronology/#1955-1977 Accessed January 28, 2020.

Il Giardinodei Tarocchi. "In Niki's Words." http://ilgiardinodeitarocchi.it/en/about/materials-crew/ Accessed January 28, 2020.

Johnston, Jill; Marella Caracciolo Chia; Giulio Pietromarchi. *Niki de Saint and the Tarot Garden*. Zurich: Benteli Publishers, 2010.

Niki Charitable Art Foundation. "Life & Work: Bibliography." http://nikidesaintphalle.org/niki-de-saint-phalle/biography/#1930-1949 Accessed January 27, 2020.

Schulz-Hoffmann, Carla (ed.). *Niki de Saint Phalle: My Art, My Dreams*. Munich, Berlin, London, New York: Prestel, 2003.

Chéri Samba
Chéri Samba. Accessed March 9, 2021. CheriSamba.net
Mullins, Charlotte. *Painting people: figure painting today*. London: Thames and Hudson, 2006.
Rosen, Miriam. "Cheri Samba: Griot of Kinshasa and Paris." *Artforum*, March 1990: 137–140.
Smee, Sebastian. "Thirsty for solutions: African artist Chéri Samba speaks to the theme of scarcity amid abundance." *The Washington Post*, Sept 23, 2020.
Spring, Chris. *Angaza Afrika: African Art Now*. London: Laurence King, 2008.
Tate. "'Popular Painting' from Kinshasa." Accessed March 9, 2021, https://www.tate.org.uk/press/press-releases/popular-painting-kinshasa

Shinichi Sawada
Dornacher, Pia and Julia Wallner (eds.) *Inner-Lif. Shinichi Sawada Ceramic*. Oberpfalz: Museum Lothar Fischer, 2020.
Jennifer Lauren Gallery, provided biography and resume to author, February 25, 2020.
Kobayashi, Mizue. "Shinichi Sawada." *Raw Vision*, issue 102 (Summer 2019): 59.
Shinichi Sawada: No art, No life, NHK World-Japan OnDemand, 2020.

Friedrich Schröder-Sonnenstern
Gorsen, Peter. "The Fabulous Co-Equality of Man and Animal." *Raw Vision*, issue 80 (Winter 2013): 43–64.
Karlins, N.F. "Friedrich Schröder-Sonnenstern: The Snake Seduction." *Artnet Magazine*, April 14, 2011.
Kort, Dr. Pamela. "Friedrich Schröder-Sonnenstern: From Barefoot Prophet to Avant-Garde Artist." In *Friedrich Schröder-Sonnenstern*, New York: Michael Werner Gallery, 2011.

Judith Scott
Barrera, Lola and Iñaki Peñafiel, dirs. *¿Qué tienes debajo del sombrero?* Spain: Alicia Produce, 2006.
MacGregor, John M. *Metamorphosis: The Fiber Art of Judith Scott*. Oakland: Creative Growth Art Center, 1999.
Morris, Catherine, and Matthew Higgs, eds. *Judith Scott; Bound and Unbound*. Brooklyn: Elizabeth A. Sackler Center for Feminist Art, Brooklyn Museum, with DelMonico Books-Prestel, 2014.
Wallace Scott, Joyce. *Entwined: Sisters and Secrets in the Silent World of Artist Judith Scott*. Beacon Press: Boston, 2016.

William Scott
Creative Growth, *William Scott: Painting Utopia*. Creative Growth Arts Center, 2016.
Creative Growth. "William Scott." Accessed May 20, 2021.

Tomoyuki Shinki
Gallery Incurve | Kyoto. "Tomoyuki Shinki." Accessed May 15, 2021, http://g-incurve.jp/english/artist_shinki.html
Gomez, Edward M. "Japanese Self-Taught Artists Emerge." *Raw Vision*, issue 62, (Autumn/Fall 2008): 42–47.
Imanaka, Hiroyoshi; Kamitani, Kozue; Saki, Wakako; Ishikawa, Yuta (ed). *Atelier Incurve in Art Fairs*. Kyoto: atelier incurve, 2017.
Slominski, Lisa. "These Centers Are Helping with Disabilities Break into the Mainstream (and the Market)." *Artsy*, December 1, 2017, https://www.artsy.net/article/artsy-editorial-centers-helping-artists-disabilities-break-mainstream-market
Yukiko Koide Presents. "Tomoyuki Shinki." Accessed May 20, 2021, http://www.yukikokoide.com/eng/artist/tomoyuki.html

Marguerite Sirvins
Bellemare, Pierre and Véronique Le Guen. "La robe de mariée de Mlle S." *Curieux obets, étranges histoires*, 10–15. Paris: Flammarion, 2016.

Mary T. Smith
Arnett, William. "Mary T. Smith: Her Name is Someone." *Souls Grown Deep Foundation*. Accessed November 22, 2020, https://www.soulsgrowndeep.org/artist/mary-t-smith
Cardinal, Roger. "Vernacular Art: A Palpable Expression." In *Souls Grown Deep: volume 1: African-American Vernacular Art of the South*, edited by Paul Arnett and William Arnett, 13. Atlanta: Tinwood Books, 2001.
Gomez, Edward. "The Bold, Blessed Paintings of a Sharecropper's Daughter." *Hyperallergic*, June 18, 2019, https://hyperallergic.com/503923/the-bold-blessed-paintings-of-a-sharecroppers-daughter/
Lippard, Lucy. "The Word In Their Hands." In *Souls Grown Deep: volume 1: African-American Vernacular Art of the South*, edited by Paul Arnett and William Arnett, 282–285. Atlanta: Tinwood Books, 2001.
SPACES: Saving + Preserving Arts + Cultural Environments. "Mary Tillman Smith." Accessed November 24, 2020, http://spacesarchives.org/explore/search-the-online-collection/mary-tillman-smith/

Janet Sobel
Andrew Edlin Gallery. "Janet Sobel." Accessed April 19, 2021, https://www.edlingallery.com/artists/janet-sobel/biography
Art of this Century. *Paintings by Janet Sobel*. Sidney Janis. New York: Art of This Century, 1946. Exhibition catalog.
Gary Snyder Fine Art. "Janet Sobel." Accessed April 20, 2021, https://www.garysnyderfineart.com/janet-sobel/
Greenberg, Clement. "American-Type Painting." In *Art and Culture*. Boston: Beacon Press, 1961.
Levin, Gail. "Janet Sobel: Primitivist, Surrealist, and Abstract Expressionist." *Woman's Art Journal* 26, no. 1 (2005): 8–14. Accessed April 22, 2021. doi:10.2307/3566528.
Smith, Roberta. "Art in review: Janet Sobel," *New York Times*, February 15, 2002.
Solomon R. Guggenheim Museum. *Peggy Guggenheim's Other Legacy*. Melvin P. Ladder and Fred Licht. New York: Solomon R. Guggenheim Museum, 1987. Exhibition catalog.
Zalman, Sandra. "Janet Sobel: Primitive Modern and the Origins of Abstract Expressionism." *Woman's Art Journal* 36, no. 2 (2015): 20–29. Accessed April 22, 2021.

Katsuyoshi Takenaka
Atelier Yamanami. "KATSU." Accessed May 27, 2021, http://a-yamanami.jp/artworks/artists/334/
AYAW. Kōka: Masato Yamashita, and publishing house Atelier Yamanami, 2017.
Harvard University Asia Center. *Eye Eye Nose Mouth: Art, Disability and Mental Illness in Nanjing, China and Shiga-ken, Japan*. Raphael Koenig & Benny Shaffer. Cambridge: Blurb Publishing, 2019. Exhibition catalog.
Minchika, Kawashima. "A certain sanctuary sentence." *La Collina*, volume 14 (2019): 42–43.

Katsuhiro Terao
Gallery Incurve. "Katsuhiro Terao." Accessed May 15, 2021, http://g-incurve.jp/english/artist_terao.html
Imanaka, Hiroyoshi; Kozue Kamitani; Wakako Saki; Yuta Ishikawa (eds). "Art on paper: Katsuhiro Terao." In *Atelier Incurve in Art Fairs*, 38–51. Kyoto: atelier incurve, 2017.
Yukiko Koide Presents. "Katsuhiro Terao." Accessed May 16, 2021, http://www.yukikokoide.com/eng/artist/katsuhiro.html

Bill Traylor
Ausfield, Margaret Lynne, Leslie Umberger, William Ferris, Richard J. Powell, Randall Seth Morris, Diana Baird N'Diaye, and Radcliffe Bailey. "Between Worlds: The Art of Bill Traylor." Lecture, Smithsonian American Art Museum, Washington, D.C., February 22, 2019. (Accessed on YouTube
Barat, Charlotte; and Darby English. "Blackness at MoMA: A Legacy of Deficit." *Among Others: Blackness at MoMA*, 14–99. New York: The Museum of Modern Art, 2019.
Umberger, Leslie. *Between Worlds: The Art of Bill Traylor*. Princeton and Oxford: Smithsonian American Art Museum in association with Princeton University Press, 2018.

August Walla
Feilacher, Johann. "Artist of the Universe." *Raw Vision*, issue 75, (Spring/Summer 2012): 20–23.
Feilacher, Johann (ed) *august walla.!: weltallende*. Volumes 1–4. Wein: Residenz Verlag, 2012.
Museum Gugging. "August Walla." Accessed March 6, 2021, https://www.museumgugging.at/en/gugging-art/gugging-artists/august-walla

Melvin Way

Andrew Edlin Gallery. *Melvin Way: The Cocaine Files Dossier*. New York, February 23–March 25, 2018. Exhibition.

Decharme, Bruno, dir. *Melvin Way*. Bruno Decharme and Barbara Safavora, 2017. (Accessed on YouTube)

Gomez, Edward. "Melvin Way Holds the Keys to the Universe." *Hyperallergic*, March 3, 2018.

Karlins, N. F, "N. F. Karlins enters the cryptic world of Melvin 'Milky' Way." *Raw Vision*, issue 34 (Spring 2001): 50–53.

Saltz, Jerry. "Studying the Masterpieces of Visionary Melvin Way." *Vulture*, June 17, 2015.

Wortsman, Aurélie Bernard. "An Interview with Andrew Castrucci on Melvin Way." *Andrew Edlin Gallery*. January 19, 2021.

George Widener

Nationalgalerie im Hamburger Bahnhof – Museum für Gegenwart. *Secret Universe – George Widener*. Berlin: Verlag der Buchhandlung Walther König, 2013. Exhibition catalog.

Ricco Maresca Gallery. "George Widener." Accessed May 14, 2021, https://www.riccomaresca.com/artists/35-george-widener/biography/

Scottie Wilson

Maclagan, David. *Line Let Loose: Scribbling, Doodling and Automatic Drawing*. London: Reaktion Book, 2013.

Murrell, Katherine and Anthony Petullo. "Scottie Wilson: A new examination of a classic master of Outsider Art." *Raw Vision*, issue 47 (Summer 2004): 20–27.

Murrell, Katherine and Anthony Petullo. *Scottie Wilson; Peddler Turned Painter*. Milwaukee: Petullo Publishing, 2004.

Adolf Wölfli

Baumann, Daniel. "Adolf Wölfli (1864–1930): Writer, Poet, Draftsman, Composer." The Adolf Woelfli Foundation. PDF downloaded May 30, 2021. https://www.adolfwoelfli.ch/fileadmin/t8_jetpack/redaktion/dokumente/2020_09_02_Baumann_on_Adolf_Woelfli.pdf

Baumann, Daniel. Edward M.Gomez, Elka Spoerri, Gerard C, Wertkin and texts by Adolf Wölfli. *The Art of Adolf Wölfli: St. Adolf-Giant-Creation*. Translated by Andrew Shields. New York: Princeton University Press, 2003.

Miskin, Lionel. *St. Adolf II*. 1971, United Kingdom: Arts Council of Great Britain, Rosebrook Productions. BFI Player. https://player.bfi.org.uk/free/film/watch-st-adolf-ii-1971-online

Spoerri, Elka and Daniel Baumann. "St. Adolf-Giant-Creation: The Art of Adolf Wölfli." *Folk Art* (Winter 2002/03): 41–51.

The Adolf Woelfli Foundation. "Biographie." Accessed May 29, 2021, https://www.adolfwoelfli.ch/en/translate-to-english-leben#c505

The Adolf Woelfli Foundation. "Writings by Adolf Woelfi." Translated by Kiko Gaskel and Peter Jones. Downloaded May 30, 2021, https://www.adolfwoelfli.ch/fileadmin/t8_jetpack/redaktion/dokumente/2020_09_02_Writings_by_Adolf_Woelfli.pdf

Junko Yamamoto

Abcd / Art brut, Collection Bruno DeCharme. "Junko Yamamoto." Accessed May 27, 2021, https://abcd-artbrut.net/en/collection/yamamoto-junko/

Yukiko Koide Presents. "Junko Yamamoto." Accessed May 27, 2021. http://www.yukikokoide.com/eng/artist/junko.html

Yukiko Koide Presents. *Surface of Life: Junko Yamamoto*. Yukiko Koide Presents, Tokyo, 2004. Exhibition catalog.

Tokyo Metropolitan Foundation for History and Culture. *Open to Surprises*. Tokyo Shibuya Koen-dori Gallery, Museum of Contemporary Art Tokyo, 2020. Exhibition catalog.

Joseph E. Yoakum

DePasse, Derrel B. *Traveling the Rainbow: The Life and Art of Joseph E. Yoakum*. New York: Museum of American Folk Art, 2001.

Majeed, Faheem. "An Outsider to Outsider." In *Post Black Folk Art in America: 1930–1980,* 2016, 5–9. Chicago: Intuit: The Centre for Intuitive and Outsider Art, 2017.

Perry, Regenia A. *Free within Ourselves: African-American Artists in the Collection of the National Museum of American Art*. Washington, D.C.: National Museum of American Art in Association with Pomegranate Art Books, 1992.

Huang Yong-Fu

Hsiao, Sherry and Su Mang-chuan. "Rainbow Village in Taichung listed in global guidebook." *Taipei Times*, November 23, 2017.

Lin Yang-Kai, Creative Director and Fresco Painter in Rainbow Village (Su Meng-Pin as Translator and Administrative Staff in Rainbow Village), e-mail communication with author and picture researcher, March 21, 2021.

Lo, Barnaby. "Paintings of 'Rainbow Grandpa', 97, save Taiwan village," Produced by Culture, Beijing ICP. Aired May 1, 2019 on *CGTN*.

Ricordeau, Remy. "The Dreams of Three Taiwanese Pensioners." *Raw Vision*, issue 84 (Winter 2014/15): 61–70.

Ricordeau, Remy. "Rainbow Village: Huang Yongfu." *SPACES: Saving + Preserving Arts + Cultural Environments*. Accessed December 30, 2020, http://spacesarchives.org/explore/search-the-online-collection/huang-yongfu/

Stein, Eliot. "The 96-year-old painter who saved a village." *BBC, Travel*, November 29, 2018, https://www.bbc.com/travel/gallery/20181128-the-96-year-old-painter-who-saved-a-village

Anna Zemánková

Cavin Morris Gallery. "Anna Zemánková." Accessed on April 28, 2021, http://www.cavinmorris.com/anna-zemankova

Morris, Randall. "The exalted lark: Excerpts from an essay on Anna Zemánková." In *Anna Zemánková*, 7–8. New York: Cavin-Morris Gallery, 2013.

The Outsider Art Fair. "Anna Zemánková." Accessed on April 28, 2021, https://www.outsiderartfair.com/fr/artistes/anna-zemankova

Zemánková, Terezie. "Anna Zemánková: Twilight Before Dawn." In *TWILIGHT BEFORE DAWN: Anna Zemánková*, 4–9. New York: Cavin-Morris Gallery, 2016.

Zemánková, Terezie. "Anna Zemánková: The Flowers of Passion" in *Folk Art* (Winter 2004/2205): 58–65.

Carlo Zinelli

Gomez, Edward M. "In Carlo Zinelli and Eugen Gabritschevsky's Art, the Life Spirit Ensure." *Hyperallergic*, March 25, 2017.

Rosi, Daniela. *Carlo Zinelli: a convulsive beauty*. Paris: Christian Berst, 2011. Exhibition catalog.

Tansella, Carole. "The seminal work of Carlo Zinelli." *Epidemiology and Psychiatric Sciences* 22, issue 1, (March 2013: 15 – 16. https://doi.org/10.1017/S2045796012000728

The Collection de l'Art Brut. *Carlo Zinelli: recto verso*. Lausanne & Milan: The Collection de l'Art Brut & 5 Continents, 2019. Exhibition catalog.

The Museum of Everything. *The Museum of Everything presents Carlo Zinelli*. Venice& London: The Museum of Everything, 2013. Exhibition catalog.

IMAGE CREDITS

The publishers would like to thank the libraries, archives, galleries, photographers, and artists for their kind permission to reproduce the works featured in this book. Every effort has been made to trace all copyright owners but if any have been inadvertently overlooked, the publishers would be pleased to make the necessary arrangements at the first opportunity.

Key: top = t; bottom = b; left = l; right = r

2 Courtesy Gallery Outsider Inn. Photograph © Morteza Zahedi. **6** Courtesy of the artist and Creative Growth Art Center. Photograph by Cheryl Dunn, © Creative Growth Art Center. **8** Courtesy Galerie Brockstedt © DACS 2021. Photograph © Nicolai Stephan. **10** Archives of the Collection de l'Art Brut, Lausanne. Photograph © Claudine Garcia, Digitization workshop Ville de Lausanne. **13** Photograph by Soichi Sunami. Photographic Archive, The Museum of Modern Art Archives, New York. Object Number: IN76.18. New York, Museum of Modern Art (MoMA). © 2021. Digital image, The Museum of Modern Art, New York/Scala, Florence. **14** Courtesy the artist, Arts Project Australia and Fleisher/Ollman Gallery. **17** Photograph by Hydar Dewachi. Courtesy the artist, ActionSpace and Camden Art Centre. **21** Photographic Archive, The Museum of Modern Art Archives, New York. Object Number: IN234.10B. New York, Museum of Modern Art (MoMA). © 2021. Digital image, The Museum of Modern Art, New York/Scala, Florence. **22** Photograph by Soichi Sunami. Photographic Archive, The Museum of Modern Art Archives, New York. Object Number: IN153.8. New York, Museum of Modern Art (MoMA). © 2021. Digital image, The Museum of Modern Art, New York/Scala, Florence. **24** Collection Center for Creative Photography, University of Arizona. © Center for Creative Photography, Arizona Board of Regents, Louise Dahl-Wolfe Archive/Gift of the Louise Dahl-Wolfe Trust. **26** Philadelphia Museum of Art: Gift of Paul W. McCloskey in memory of Maris Madeira McCloskey, 1995, 1995-18-1. **27** Collection Center for Creative Photography. Photograph by Edward Weston © Center for Creative Photography, Arizona Board of Regents. **28** Bequest of Edmund L. Fuller Jr., 1985 (85.27). Newark, The Newark Museum of Art. © 2021. Digital image, The Newark Museum of Art/Art Resource/Scala, Florence. **29** Philadelphia Museum of Art: The Jill and Sheldon Bonovitz Collection, BST-95. **30** Philadelphia Museum of Art: The Jill and Sheldon Bonovitz Collection, BST-96. **31** Photographic Archive, The Museum of Modern Art Archives, New York. Object Number: IN76a.28B. New York, Museum of Modern Art (MoMA). © 2021. Digital image, The Museum of Modern Art, New York/Scala, Florence. **32** IanDagnall Computing / Alamy Stock Photo. **33** New York, Museum of Modern Art (MoMA), gift of Mrs. Simon Guggenheim. Digital image, The Museum of Modern Art, New York/Scala, Florence. **34** New York, Museum of Modern Art (MoMA), gift of Nelson A. Rockefeller. Digital image, The Museum of Modern Art, New York/Scala, Florence. **35** Philadelphia Museum of Art: The Louis E. Stern Collection, 1963, 1963-181-64. **36** Carnegie Museum of Art. Gift of the Carnegie Library of Pittsburgh. **37** New York, Museum of Modern Art (MoMA). Given anonymously. Acc. no.: 400.1941. © 2021. Digital image, The Museum of Modern Art, New York/Scala, Florence. **38** New York, Metropolitan Museum of Art. Bequest of Miss Adelaide Milton de Groot (1876-1967), 1967. Acc. no.: 67.187.165. © 2021. Digital image The Metropolitan Museum of Art/Art Resource/Scala, Florence. **39** New York, Museum of Modern Art (MoMA). Abby Aldrich Rockefeller Fund. Acc. no.: 6.1939. © 2021. Digital image, The Museum of Modern Art, New York/Scala, Florence. **40** Arnold Newman/Getty Images. **41** New York, Museum of Modern Art (MoMA). Abby Aldrich Rockefeller Fund. 328.1941. © 2021. Digital image, The Museum of Modern Art, New York/Scala, Florence. **42** New York, Museum of Modern Art (MoMA). The Sidney and Harriet Janis Collection. Acc. n.: 607.1967. © 2021. Digital image, The Museum of Modern Art, New York/Scala, Florence. **43** Collection Mickey Cartin. **44** Downtown Gallery records, 1824-1974. Archives of American Art, Smithsonian Institution. Photograph by Carl Van Vechten, 1880-1964. **45** Philadelphia Museum of Art: Gift of Robert Carlen, 1941, 1941-2-1. **46** Restricted gift in memory of Frances W. Pick from her children Thomas F. Pick and Mary P. Hines, 1990.417. Chicago (IL), Art Institute of Chicago. Digital image WBC ART / Alamy Stock Photo. **47** Gift of Mr. and Mrs. Meyer P. Potamkin, in Honor of the 50th Anniversary of the National Gallery of Art National Gallery of Art, Washington 1991.42.1. **48** Courtesy of the Palace of the Governors Photo Archives (NMHM/DCA), Negative Number, 020401. **49** Transfer from the General Services Administration (1985.65.13). Washington DC, Smithsonian American Art Museum. © 2021. Digital image, Smithsonian American Art Museum/Art Resource/Scala, Florence. **50** Oklahoma City Museum of Art. WPA Collection, 1942.024. **51** Sheldon Museum of Art, University of Nebraska–Lincoln, Allocation of the U.S. Government, Federal Art Project of the Works Progress Administration, WPA-115.1943. **53** Archives of the Collection de l'Art Brut, Lausanne. **55** Archives of the Collection de l'Art Brut, Lausanne. Photograph © Giuseppe Pocetti, Digitization workshop Ville de Lausanne. **56** © Henriette Grindat / Swiss Foundation for Photography. **58** © Archives cantonales vaudoises, ACV PP 1032/90 – T 504/3. **59** MCBA, Lausanne, on deposit at the Collection de l'Art Brut, Lausanne. © Aloïse Corbaz Foundation. Photograph © Amélie Blanc, Digitization workshop Ville de Lausanne. **60** Collection de l'Art Brut, Lausanne. © Aloïse Corbaz Foundation. Photograph © Arnaud Conne, Digitization workshop Ville de Lausanne. **61** Collection de l'Art Brut, Lausanne. © Aloïse Corbaz Foundation. Photograph © Olivier Laffely, Digitization workshop Ville de Lausanne. **62-3** Collection of Christine and Jean David Mermod. © Aloïse Corbaz Foundation. Photograph © Philip Bernard, Digitization workshop Ville de Lausanne. **64** Archives of the Collection de l'Art Brut, Lausanne. **65** Collection de l'Art Brut, Lausanne. Photograph © Arnaud Conne, Digitization workshop Ville de Lausanne. **66** LaM, Lille Métropole musée d'art moderne d'art contemporain et d'art brut, Villeneuve d'Ascq, n° inv. : 2010.5.2. Photograph © Philip Bernard. **67** Collection de l'Art Brut, Lausanne. Photograph © Arnaud Marie Humair, Digitization workshop Ville de Lausanne. **68** LaM, Lille Métropole musée d'art moderne d'art contemporain et d'art brut, Villeneuve d'Ascq, n° inv.: 2009.9.10. © Ervin Marton Estate. Photograph © Cécile Dubart. **69** Collection de l'Art Brut, Lausanne. Photograph © Claude Bornand. **70** The Museum + The Gallery of Everything. **71** Collection de l'Art Brut, Lausanne. Photograph © Claude Bornand. **72** LaM, Lille Métropole musée d'art moderne d'art contemporain et d'art brut, Villeneuve d'Ascq, n° inv. : 2011.5.4, gift of Philippe Mons. Photograph © Nicolas Dewitte / LaM. **73** Collection de l'Art Brut, Lausanne © ADAGP, Paris and DACS, London 2021. Photograph © Claude Bornand. **74** Dépôt du Musée régional d'ethnologie au LaM, Lille Métropole musée d'art moderne d'art contemporain et d'art brut, Villeneuve d'Ascq, n° inv. : D.991.9.2, © ADAGP, Paris and DACS, London 2021. Photograph © Thériez C. **75** LaM, Lille Métropole musée d'art moderne d'art contemporain et d'art brut, Villeneuve d'Ascq, n° inv. : 2000.5.7. © ADAGP, Paris and DACS, London 2021. Photograph © Nicolas Dewitte. **76** Collection de l'Art Brut, Lausanne, no inv. ni-5176. Photograph © Claude Bornand. **77** LaM, Lille Métropole musée d'art moderne d'art contemporain et d'art brut, Villeneuve d'Ascq, gift of L'Aracine in 1999, n° inv. : 999.43.11. Photograph © Philip Bernard. **78** LaM, Lille Métropole musée d'art moderne d'art contemporain et d'art brut, Villeneuve d'Ascq, gift of L'Aracine in 1999, n° inv.: 999.43.11. Photograph © Cécile Dubart. **79** Collection de l'Art Brut, Lausanne. Photograph © Philip Bernard. **80** © Succession Gérard Vulliamy. **81** Collection de l'Art Brut, Lausanne. Photograph © Charlotte Aebischer, Digitization workshop Ville de Lausanne. **82, 83** Collection de l'Art Brut, Lausanne. Photograph © Henri Germond. **85** Courtesy of the Hayward Gallery. Photograph © Mark E Edwards. **88** Paul Popper/Popperfoto/Getty Images. **90** Paul Popper/Popperfoto/Getty Images. **91** London Borough of Newham Heritage Service. **92** LaM, Lille Métropole musée d'art moderne d'art contemporain et d'art brut, Villeneuve d'Ascq, gift of L'Aracine in 1999, n° inv.: 999.10.149. **93** Collection de l'Art Brut, Lausanne, no inv. cab-3032. Photograph © Arnaud Conne, Digitization workshop Ville de Lausanne. **94** London Borough of Newham Heritage Service. **96** Mirrorpix / Getty Images. **97** Milwaukee Art Museum, Gift of Anthony Petullo M2012.236. Photograph © Larry Sanders. **98** Milwaukee Art Museum, Gift of Anthony Petullo M2012.238. Photograph © Larry Sanders. **99** Milwaukee Art Museum, Gift of Anthony Petullo M2012.237. Photograph © Larry Sanders. **100** © Dietmar Bührer. **101** Courtesy Galerie Brockstedt © DACS 2021. Photograph © Nicolai Stephan. **102** Courtesy Galerie Brockstedt © DACS 2021. Photograph © Nicolai Stephan. **103** Courtesy Galerie Brockstedt © DACS 2021. Photograph © Nicolai Stephan. **104** © Jan Reich. Courtesy of Anna Zemankova & Cavin-Morris Gallery. **105** © Terezie Zemankova. Courtesy The Museum + The Gallery of Everything. **106** © Terezie Zemankova. Courtesy Cavin-Morris Gallery. Work in the collection of The Museum of Everything. **107** © Terezie Zemankova. Courtesy The Museum + The Gallery of Everything. **108** © Private Foundation – Artists of Gugging. Photograph © J. Feilacher. **109** © Private Foundation – Artists of Gugging. Photograph © Christian Schindler, Pixelstorm Wien. **110** © Private Foundation – Artists of Gugging. Photograph © Christian Schindler, Pixelstorm Wien. **111** Galerie im Lenbachhaus, Munich. © Artists of Gugging. **112** © Art Brut KG. **113** © Art Brut KG. **114** © Art Brut KG. **115** © Art Brut KG, Landessammlung Niederösterreich. **117** The Museum + The Gallery of Everything. **118** Corcoran Gallery of Art archives department records, series 1.1 box 23. © Special Collections Research Center, George Washington University Libraries. **120** © Horace Perry, courtesy Alabama State Council on the Arts. **123** Gift of Micki Beth Stiller (2015.25). © 1994, Bill Traylor Family Trust. Washington DC, Smithsonian American Art Museum. © 2021. **124** The Museum of Modern Art, New York © Bill Traylor Family Trust. **125** Private Collection © Bill Traylor Family Trust. **126** Joseph Yoakum at "The Whole" in Chicago, 1967. Whitney Halstead papers, 1920-1982. Archives of American Art, Smithsonian Institution. **127** Collection of Christina Ramberg and Philip Hanson. Courtesy of the Art Institute of Chicago. **128** Bequest of Whitney Halstead (2019.1642), Chicago (IL), Art Institute of Chicago. © 2021 The Art Institute of Chicago / Art Resource, NY/ Scala, Florence. **129** Bequest of Whitney Halstead (1979.417). © 2021 Cooper-Hewitt, Smithsonian Design Museum/Art Resource, NY/Scala, Florence. **130** Columbus Museum of Art, Ohio: Gift of Carolyn Allport. © Kojo Kamau. **131** Columbus Museum of Art, Ohio: Museum Purchase. **132** Columbus Museum of Art, Ohio: Museum Purchase. **133** Milwaukee Art Museum, The Michael and Julie Hall Collection of American Folk Art M1989.253. **134** © Guy Mendes. **135** The Museum + The Gallery of Everything. **136** The Museum + The Gallery of Everything. **137** The Museum + The Gallery of Everything. **138** The Judith Alexander Foundation. © Judith Alexander Augustine. **139** Artwork © ARS, NY and DACS, London 2021. Souls Grown Deep Foundation/Atlanta/Georgia/USA. Photograph © Pitkin Studio / Art Resource, NY. **140** Artwork © ARS, NY and DACS, London 2021 Photo © High Museum of Art, Atlanta. Photograph © Mike Jensen. **141** Souls Grown Deep Foundation. © Lucinda Bunnen. **142** Courtesy Roger Manley Archive. © Roger Manley. **143** American Folk Art Museum, Gift of Leo and Dorothea Rabkin. Photograph © Gavin Ashworth. **144** American Folk Art Museum, Gift of Leo and Dorothea Rabkin. Photograph © Gavin Ashworth. **145** The Museum + The Gallery of Everything. **150** Collection of Intuit: The Center for Intuitive and Outsider Art, Henry Darger Room Collection and Archive, gift of Kiyoko Lerner, 2000.111.001 © ARS, NY and DACS, London 2021. Photograph © John Faier. **151** Collection of Dr. David Walega. Courtesy of the artist and Bullet Space. © Andrew Castrucci. **152** Long March Space. **154** Musée d'Art Moderne de la Ville de Paris Archive. © David Berglund. **156l** Collection of Intuit: The Center for Intuitive and Outsider Art, Henry Darger Room Collection and Archive, gift of Kiyoko Lerner, 2000.303. **156r** Collection of Intuit: The Center for Intuitive and Outsider Art, Henry Darger Room Collection and Archive, gift of Kiyoko Lerner, 2000.717a. **157** Musée d'Art Moderne de la Ville de Paris Archive. © Michaël Boruch. **158** Image ville de Paris. Paris, Musee d'Art Moderne de la Ville de Paris © 2021. RMN-Grand Palais /Dist. inv.: AMVP 3872. Photograph courtesy SCALA, Florence © ARS, NY and DACS, London 2021. **159, 160** American Folk Art Museum, purchased with funds generously provided by John and Margaret Robson. © Kiyoko Lerner (2004.1.3A). © ARS, NY and DACS, London 2021. Photograph © James Prinz. **162** Photo courtesy of James Castle Collection and Archive. **163** © James Castle Collection and Archive, all rights reserved. **164t** © James Castle Collection and Archive, all rights reserved. **164b** © James Castle Collection and Archive, all rights reserved. **165** © James Castle Collection and Archive, all rights reserved. **166** Courtesy of

Menil Archives, The Menil Collection, Houston. **167** The Menil Collection, Houston. Photograph © Paul Hester. **168** The Menil Collection, Houston. Photograph © Paul Hester. **169** The Menil Collection, Houston. Photograph © Paul Hester. **170** © Andrew Castrucci. **171** Private collection. Courtesy of the artist and Bullet Space. © Andrew Castrucci. **172** Collection of Daniel Klein. Courtesy of the artist and Bullet Space. © Andrew Castrucci. **173** Private collection. Courtesy of the artist and Bullet Space. © Andrew Castrucci. **174** Long March Space. **175** Long March Space. **176l** Long March Space. **176r, 177** Long March Space. **178** Sally and Richard Greenhill / Alamy Stock Photo. **179** Philadelphia Museum of Art: Gift of the Robert Alan Lewis Collection Palm Beach, 2014, 2014-208-27. **180** Sally and Richard Greenhill / Alamy Stock Photo. **181** Philadelphia Museum of Art: The Jill and Sheldon Bonovitz Collection, BST-71. **183** Souls Grown Deep Foundation Photographic Collection #20491, Southern Folklife Collection, The Wilson Library, University of North Carolina at Chapel Hill. **185** Souls Grown Deep Foundation Photographic Collection #20491, Southern Folklife Collection, The Wilson Library, University of North Carolina at Chapel Hill. **186** Courtesy françoise adamsbaum-victoire dirosa-artppol project. © Françoise Adamsbaum. **188** Courtesy Carl Hammer Gallery. **190** © Charles Dana Gibson. **191** Photograph © Michael Bonesteel. **192l** Collection of Orren Davis Jordan and Robert Parker. Photograph courtesy of John Michael Kohler Arts Center. **192r** Collection of Orren Davis Jordan and Robert Parker. Photograph courtesy of John Michael Kohler Arts Center. **193** Collection of Orren Davis Jordan and Robert Parker. Photograph courtesy of John Michael Kohler Arts Center. **194** Collection of Laura Wehrman. Photograph courtesy Summertime and Slominski Projects. **195** Collection of Robert Alter and Sherry Siegel. Photograph courtesy of John Michael Kohler Arts Center. **196** Souls Grown Deep Foundation Photographic Collection #20491, Southern Folklife Collection, The Wilson Library, University of North Carolina at Chapel Hill. **197** Baltimore Museum of Art Museum purchase and gift of the Souls Grown Deep Foundation © ARS, NY and DACS, London 2021. **198** Collection of Fine Arts Museums of San Francisco, museum purchase, American Art Trust Fund and gift of the Souls Grown Deep Foundation © ARS, NY and DACS, London 2021. **199** High Museum of Art, Atlanta, gift of William Arnett in memory of Lenore Gold, 2015.185. © ARS, NY and DACS, London 2021. **200** Souls Grown Deep Foundation Photographic Collection #20491, Southern Folklife Collection, The Wilson Library, University of North Carolina at Chapel Hill. **201** Souls Grown Deep Foundation. Photograph © Stephen Pitkin/Pitkin Studio. **202** Courtesy of SPACES–Saving and Preserving Arts and Cultural Environments. Photograph © Willem Volkersz. **203** Souls Grown Deep Foundation. Photograph © Stephen Pitkin/Pitkin Studio. **204** Courtesy The Orange Show Center for Visionary Art, Houston, Texas. **205** © ARS, NY and DACS, London 2021. Photograph © The Museum + The Gallery of Everything. **206** © ARS, NY and DACS, London 2021. Photograph © The Museum + The Gallery of Everything. **207** Gift of Chuck and Jan Rosenak and museum purchase through the Luisita L. and Franz H. Denghausen Endowment (1997.124.31). Washington DC, Smithsonian American Art Museum © ARS, NY and DACS, London 2021. Digital image © 2021 Smithsonian American Art Museum/Art Resource/Scala, Florence. **208** Courtesy françoise adamsbaum-victoire dirosa-artppol project. Photograph © Pierre Schwartz. **209** Courtesy françoise adamsbaum-victoire dirosa-artppol project. © Françoise Adamsbaum. **210** The Museum + The Gallery of Everything. © Françoise Adamsbaum. **211** Courtesy françoise adamsbaum-victoire dirosa-artppol project. © Françoise Adamsbaum. **212** © Estate of Horst Ademeit / Delmes & Zander, Cologne. **213l** © Estate of Horst Ademeit / Delmes & Zander, Cologne. **213r** © Estate of Horst Ademeit / Delmes & Zander, Cologne. **214l** © Estate of Horst Ademeit / Delmes & Zander, Cologne. **214r** © Estate of Horst Ademeit / Delmes & Zander, Cologne. **215l** © Estate of Horst Ademeit / Delmes & Zander, Cologne. **215r** © Estate of Horst Ademeit / Delmes & Zander, Cologne. **217** © Rainbow CreativeCo., Ltd. **218** Photograph © Jo Farb Hernández, 2000. **220** © The Nek Chand Foundation. **222** © The Nek Chand Foundation. **224** © The Nek Chand Foundation. Photograph © Suresh Kumar. **225** © The Nek Chand Foundation. **226** © The Nek Chand Foundation. **227** Courtesy The Nek Chand Foundation. **228** © The Nek Chand Foundation. **229** © The Nek Chand Foundation. **230** The Owl House Foundation. © Elbé van Heerden. **231** Ann and Steve Toon / Alamy Stock Photo. **232t** Grobler du Preez/Alamy Stock Photo. **232b** Ann and Steve Toon / Alamy Stock Photo. **233** Richard van der Spuy / Alamy Stock Photo. **234** © Fred Scruton. © Estate of Isaiah Robertson. **235** © Fred Scruton. © Estate of Isaiah Robertson. **236** © Fred Scruton. © Estate of Isaiah Robertson. **237** © Fred Scruton. © Estate of Isaiah Robertson. **238** © Rainbow CreativeCo., Ltd. **239** © Rainbow CreativeCo., Ltd. **240l** © Rainbow CreativeCo., Ltd. **240r** © Rainbow CreativeCo., Ltd. **241** © Rainbow CreativeCo., Ltd. **242** Photograph © Jo Farb Hernández, 2002. **243** Photograph courtesy Carles Vila and the archives of the artist. **244** Photograph © Jo Farb Hernández, 2007. **245** Photograph © Jo Farb Hernández, 2000. **246** Keystone Press / Alamy Stock Photo. **247** RealyEasyStar/Claudio Pagliarani / Alamy Stock Photo. © Niki de Saint Phalle Charitable Art Foundation / ADAGP, Paris and DACS, London 2021. **248** Alex Ramsay / Alamy Stock Photo. © Niki de Saint Phalle Charitable Art Foundation / ADAGP, Paris and DACS, London 2021. **249** yannick luthy / Alamy Stock Photo. © Niki de Saint Phalle Charitable Art Foundation / ADAGP, Paris and DACS, London 2021. **252** © Creative Growth Art Center. **253** Courtesy of Atelier Goldstein. Photograph © Uwe Dettmar. **254** © Creative Growth Art Center. Photograph © Benjamin Blackwell. **255** Courtesy Andrew Edlin Gallery. **256** Courtesy Creative Growth Art Center, Oakland. Photograph © Leon Borensztein. **258** © Creative Growth Art Center. Photograph © Stan Peterson. **259** © Creative Growth Art Center. Photograph © Mary K. O'Connor. **260** © Creative Growth Art Center. **261** © Creative Growth Art Center. Photograph © Benjamin Blackwell. **262** © Creative Growth Art Center. **263** © Creative Growth Art Center. © Collection de l'Art Brut, Lausanne. Photograph © Arnaud Conne, Digitization workshop Ville de Lausanne. **264** Courtesy the artist, Arts Project Australia and Fleisher/Ollman Gallery. **265** Courtesy the artist, Arts Project Australia and Fleisher/Ollman Gallery. **266** Courtesy the artist, Arts Project Australia and Fleisher/Ollman Gallery. **267** Courtesy the artist, Arts Project Australia and Fleisher/Ollman Gallery. **268** Courtesy the artist, ActionSpace and Camden Art Centre. Photograph © Hydar Dewachi. **269** Courtesy the artist, ActionSpace and Camden Art Centre. Photograph © Hydar Dewachi. **270t** Courtesy the artist, ActionSpace and Camden Art Centre. Photograph © Hydar Dewachi. **270b** Courtesy the artist, ActionSpace and Camden Art Centre. Photograph © Hydar Dewachi. **271** Courtesy the artist, ActionSpace and Camden Art Centre. Photograph © Nick Dehadray. **272** © Atelier Goldstein. **273** Courtesy of Atelier Goldstein. Photograph © Uwe Dettmar. **274** Courtesy of Atelier Goldstein. Photograph © Uwe Dettmar. **276** Courtesy of Pure Vision Arts. Photograph © Gerardo Somoza. **277** Courtesy of Pure Vision Arts. Photograph © Gerardo Somoza. **278** Courtesy of Pure Vision Arts. Photograph © Gerardo Somoza. **279** Courtesy of Pure Vision Arts. Photograph © Gerardo Somoza. **280** © atelier incurve. **281** © atelier incurve. **282** © atelier incurve. **283** © atelier incurve. **287** Philadelphia Museum of Art: Purchased with the Joseph E. Temple Fund, and gift of the Souls Grown Deep Foundation from the William S. Arnett Collection, 2017, 2017-229-8. © Estate of Martha Jane Pettway / ARS, NY and DACS, London 2021. **289** © Ricco/Maresca Gallery. **290** © Ricco/Maresca Gallery. **293** Collection of Victor F. Keen. © Ricco/Maresca Gallery. **294** Gift of the Artist. New York, American Folk Art Museum. © 2021. **296** Courtesy Delmes & Zander, Cologne. © Ricco/Maresca Gallery. **297** Collection of Victor F. Keen. © Ricco/Maresca Gallery. **298** Heritage Images / Getty Images. **299** Hulton Fine Art Collection Heritage Images / Getty Images. **300** The Hilma af Klint Foundation, Stockholm. Photograph © Jerry Hardman-Jones. **301** The Hilma af Klint Foundation, Stockholm. Photograph © Jerry Hardman-Jones. **302** Estate of Artist. Courtesy Gary Snyder Fine Art. Photograph © Ben Schnall. **303** © San Diego Museum of Art / Museum purchase with funds provided by Suzanne Figi and Mrs. Norton S. Walbridge / Bridgeman Images. **304** New York, Museum of Modern Art (MoMA). Gift of William Rubin. 00193.87 © 2021. Digital image © The Museum of Modern Art, New York/Scala, Florence. **305** Gift of the artist's family. Acc. no.: 1311.1968. New York, Museum of Modern Art (MoMA). © 2021. Digital image © The Museum of Modern Art, New York/Scala, Florence. **306** Souls Grown Deep Foundation Photographic Collection #20491, Southern Folklife Collection, The Wilson Library, University of North Carolina at Chapel Hill. **307** High Museum of Art, Atlanta, museum purchase, and gift of the Souls Grown Deep Foundation from the William S. Arnett Collection, 2017.42. © ARS, NY and DACS, London 2021. Photograph © Stephen Pitkin/Pitkin Studio. **308** High Museum of Art, Atlanta, museum purchase, and gift of the Souls Grown Deep Foundation from the William S. Arnett Collection, 2017.51. © ARS, NY and DACS, London 2021. Photograph © Stephen Pitkin/Pitkin Studio. **309** Philadelphia Museum of Art: Purchased with the George W. Elkins fund, and gift of the Souls Grown Deep Foundation from the William S. Arnett Collection, 2017, 2017-229-17. © ARS, NY and DACS, London 2021. **310** Courtesy of ActionSpace. **311** Courtesy of the artist and Studio Voltaire. Photograph © Francis Ware. **312t** Courtesy of the artist and Studio Voltaire. Photograph © Francis Ware. **312b** Courtesy of the artist and Studio Voltaire. Photograph © Francis Ware. **313** Courtesy the artist, ActionSpace and Slominski Projects. Photograph © Nick Dehadray. **314** Courtesy Yukiko Koide Presents, Tokyo. © Junko Yamamoto. **315** Private collection. Courtesy Yukiko Koide Presents, Tokyo. © Junko Yamamoto. **316** Courtesy Yukiko Koide Presents, Tokyo. © Junko Yamamoto. **317** Private collection. Courtesy Yukiko Koide Presents, Tokyo. © Junko Yamamoto. **319** Philadelphia Museum of Art: The Jill and Sheldon Bonovitz Collection, BST-109 © ARS, NY and DACS, London 2021. **321** © atelier incurve. **322t** Courtesy Mamadou Cissé studio. © Mamadou Cissé. **322b** Courtesy Mamadou Cissé studio. © Mamadou Cissé. **325** The Museum + The Gallery of Everything. © Mamadou Cissé. **326** The Museum + The Gallery of Everything. © Mamadou Cissé. **328** Courtesy of the artist and Art-Z Gallery. © Mamadou Cissé. **329** Courtesy of the artist and Art-Z Gallery. © Mamadou Cissé. **330** © Grandma Moses Properties Co., New York. Photograph © Otto Kallir. **331** Private collection. © Grandma Moses Properties Co., New York. Digital image © Galerie St Etienne. 332 Bennington Museum, Bennington, Vermont, USA. © Grandma Moses Properties Co., New York. Digital image © Galerie St Etienne. **333** Private collection. © Grandma Moses Properties Co., New York. Digital image © Galerie St Etienne. **334** Courtesy of Matthew Pasto, Estate of Martín Ramírez, and Ricco/Maresca Gallery. **335, 336** Courtesy Estate of Martín Ramírez. Photograph © Visko Hatfield. **337** Solomon R. Guggenheim Museum, New York. Gift of the Estate of Martin Ramirez, 2008 © Estate of Martín Ramírez Courtesy of Ricco/Maresca Gallery. **338** © Susan Mullally. **339** The Museum + The Gallery of Everything. © Christian Daniel. **340** Gift of Jacqueline Loewe Fowler (2018.19.24). New York, American Folk Art Museum. © 2021. American Folk Art Museum / Art Resource, NY/Scala, Florence. Photograph © Gavin Ashworth. © Christian Daniel. **341** Washington DC, Smithsonian American Art Museum. Gift of the artist (1972.44). © 2021. Photograph © Smithsonian American Art Museum/Art Resource/Scala, Florence. © Christian Daniel. **342** © Katsuyoshi Takenaka / Atelier Yamanami. **343** © Katsuyoshi Takenaka / Atelier Yamanami. **344** © Katsuyoshi Takenaka / Atelier Yamanami. **345** © Katsuyoshi Takenaka / Atelier Yamanami. **346** © atelier incurve. **347** © atelier incurve. **348** © atelier incurve. **351** Philadelphia Museum of Art: Gift of Lewis and Jean Greenblatt, 2013, 2013-147-17 © Estate of Eugene Von Bruenchenhein. Digital image © John Michael Kohler Arts Center. **352** © Galerie Magnin-A. Photograph © André Magnin. **354** © Creative Growth Art Center. **357** Courtesy of the artist and Creative Growth Art Center © Creative Growth Art Center. **358** Courtesy of the artist and Creative Growth Art Center © Creative Growth Art Center. **360** Courtesy of the artist and Creative Growth Art Center © Creative Growth Art Center. **361** Courtesy of the artist and Creative Growth Art Center © Creative Growth Art Center. **362** Courtesy the artist, Jennifer Lauren Gallery, Manchester, and Nakayoshi Fukushikai. **363** Courtesy the artist, Jennifer Lauren Gallery, Manchester, and Nakayoshi Fukushikai. Photograph © Ellie Walmsley. **364** Courtesy the artist, Jennifer Lauren Gallery, Manchester, and Nakayoshi Fukushikai. Photograph © Ellie Walmsley. **365** Courtesy the artist, Jennifer Lauren Gallery, Manchester, and Nakayoshi Fukushikai. Photograph © Ellie Walmsley. **366** Courtesy Gallery Outsider Inn. Photograph © Morteza Zahedi. **367** Courtesy Gallery Outsider Inn. Photograph © Morteza Zahedi. **368** Courtesy Gallery Outsider Inn. Photograph © Morteza Zahedi. **369** Courtesy Gallery Outsider Inn. Photograph © Morteza Zahedi. **370** Courtesy Galerie Magazine. Photograph © Sami Drasin. **371** © Estate of Helen Rae. **372** © Estate of Helen Rae. **373** © Estate of Helen Rae. **374** Courtesy of Galerie Christian Berst. **375** The Museum + The Gallery of Everything. © Dimitri Zinelli. **376** The Museum + The Gallery of Everything. © Dimitri Zinelli. **377** The Museum + The Gallery of Everything. © Dimitri Zinelli. **378** © Galerie Magnin-A. Photograph by André Magnin. **379** © Galerie Magnin-A. **380** © Galerie Magnin-A. **381** © Galerie Magnin-A.

EXHIBITION LIST

Salon des Indépendents, Paris, France (1886)
Henri Rousseau, 291 Gallery, New York, USA (1910)
The Armory Show, New York, USA (1913)
International Congress of Spiritualists, Château des Comtes de Méan, Liège, Belgium (1923)
Henri Rousseau, Whitney Studio Club, New York, USA (1924)
International Exhibition of Paintings, The Carnegie International, Carnegie Museum of Art, Pittsburgh, USA (1927)
Folk Art: The Art of the Common Man in American, 1750–1900, Museum of Modern Art, New York, USA (1932–33)
East End Academy, Whitechapel Gallery, London (1932–47)
Cubism and Abstract Art, Museum of Modern Art, New York, USA (1936)
New Horizons in American Art, Museum of Modern Art, New York, USA (1936)
Fantastic Art, Dada, Surrealism, Museum of Modern Art, New York, USA (1936–37)
Horace Pippin, solo exhibition, West Chester Community Center, West Chester, USA (1937)
Sculpture by William Edmondson, Museum of Modern Art, New York, USA (1937)
Masters of Popular Painting: Modern Primitives of Europe and America, Museum of Modern Art, New York, USA (1938)
Three Centuries of American Art, Musée du Jeu de Paume, Paris, France (1938)
Contemporary Unknown American Painters, Museum of Modern Art, New York, USA (1939)
Bill Traylor: People's Artist, The New South Gallery, Montgomery, USA (1940)
American Negro Art: 19th and 20th Centuries, Downtown Gallery, New York, USA (1941)
Modern Primitives: Artists of the People, Museum of Modern Art, New York, USA (1941–44)
Artists Aid Russia Exhibition, The Wallace Collection, Hertford House, London, UK (1942)
Bill Traylor: American Primitive (Work of an Old Negro), The Ethical Culture Fieldston School, Riverdale, USA (1942)
First Papers of Surrealism, private residence, New York, USA (1942)
Americans 1943: Realists and Magic Realists, Museum of Modern Art, New York, USA (1943)
The Paintings of Morris Hirshfield, Museum of Modern Art, New York, USA (1943)
American Primitive Painting of Four Centuries, The Arts Club of Chicago, Chicago, USA (1943)
Janet Sobel, Puma Gallery, New York, USA (1944)
The Women, Art of this Century Gallery, New York, USA (1945)
Janet Sobel, Art of this Century Gallery, New York, USA (1946)
Exposition Internationale du Surréalisme, Galerie Maeght, Paris, France (1947)
l'Art Brut, Galerie René Drouin, Paris, France (1949)
Grandma Moses, The Embassy of the United States, Paris, France (1950)
l'Exposition inteRnatiOnale du Surrealism, la galerie Cordier, Paris, France (1959–60)
Minnie Evans, Little Gallery, Wilmington, North Carolina, USA (1961)
A Voice of Silence: Drawings of James Castle, Image Gallery, Portland, USA (1962)
Swiss Society of Women Painters, Sculptors and Decorators at the Cantonal Museum of Fine Arts, Lausanne, Switzerland (1963)
Will Edmondson's Mirkels, Tennessee Fine Arts Center at Cheekwood, Nashville, USA (1964)
The Open House Day, Zemánková's private residence, Prague, Czech Republic (1964)
Joseph Yoakum, The Whole, Chicago, USA (1967) *The Guided Hand,* Grosvenor Gallery, London, UK (1968)
Joseph E. Yoakum: Recent Paintings, Edward Sherbeyn Gallery, Chicago, USA (1968)
Don Baum Sez: "Chicago Needs Famous Artists," Museum of Contemporary Art, Chicago, USA (1969)
The Sky is the Limit, University of St Thomas, Houston, Texas, USA (1969)
Dimensions of Black, La Jolla Museum of Art, California, USA (1970)
Joseph E. Yoakum, Whitney Museum of American Art, New York, USA (1972)
Lee Godie, Hyde Park Art Center, Chicago, USA (1975)
Minnie Evans, Whitney Museum of American Art, New York, USA (1975)
Two Centuries of Black American Art, Los Angeles County Museum of Art, Los Angeles, USA (1976)
Missing Pieces: Georgia Folk Art 1770–1976, Atlanta Historical Society, Atlanta, USA (1976)
Nellie Mae Rowe, Alexander Gallery, Atlanta, USA (1978)
Outsiders: An Art Without Precedent Or Tradition, Hayward Gallery, London, UK (1979)
Niki de Saint Phalle: exposition rétrospective, Centre Georges Pompidou, Paris, France (1980)
More Than Land and Sky: Art from Appalachia, Smithsonian Museum of American Art, Washington, D.C., USA, (1981–82)
Black Folk Art in America, 1930–1980, The Corcoran Gallery, Washington, D.C., USA (1982)
Ritual and Myth: A Survey of African American Art, The Studio Museum in Harlem, New York, USA (1982)
Kunstnerne fra Gugging, Museum of Modern Art , Wien, Vienna (1983)
The Spiritual in Art: Abstract Painting 1890–1985, Los Angeles County Museum of Art, Los Angeles, USA (1986)
Crossed Parallels, Creative Growth Art Center, Oakland, USA (1989)
Magiciens de la Terre, Centre Georges Pompidou, Paris, France (1989)
Thornton Dial: Image of the Tiger, New Museum of Contemporary Art, New York, USA (1993–94)
Thornton Dial: Image of the Tiger, American Folk Art Museum, New York, USA (1993–94)
Artist Lee Godie A Twenty Year Retrospective, Chicago Cultural Center, Chicago, USA (1993–94)
Chéri Samba une fois encore à Kinshasa, Centre Culturel Congolais le Zoo, Kinshasa, Democratic Republic du Congo (2000)
Hands Across the Sea, Phyllis Kind Gallery, New York, USA (2001)
Janet Sobel: Selected Works from the Artist's Estate Gary Snyder Fine Art, New York, USA (2001–02)
Long March Project: A Walking Visual Display, Long March Foundation, Lijiang, China (2002)
J'aime Chéri Samba, Fondation Cartier, Paris, France (2004)
White Room: William Scott, White Columns, New York, USA (2006)
The Power of Atelier Incurve, 21st Century Museum of Contemporary Art, Kanazawa, Japan (2006)
"Popular Painting"' from Kinshasa, Tate Modern, London, UK (2007–08)
James Castle: A Retrospective, Philadelphia Museum of Art, Philadelphia, USA (2008)
Horst Ademeit - Living in the Radiant Cold, Galerie Susanne Zander, Cologne, Germany (2009)
Martín Ramírez Reframing Confinement, Museo Nacional Centro de Arte Reina Sofía, Madrid, Spain (2010)
10,000 Lives, 8th Gwangju Biennale, South Korea (2010)
Davood Koochaki, Galerie Hamer, Amsterdam, The Netherlands (2012)
Secret Universe IV: George Widener, Hamburger Bahnhof Museum für Gegenwart, Berlin, Germany (2013)
The Encyclopedic Palace, 55th Venice Biennale, Venice, Italy (2013)
The Museum of Everything presents Il Palazzo di Everything, 55th Venice Biennale (2013)
The Alternate Guide to the Universe, Hayward Gallery, London, UK (2013)
Transformer, Arts Project Australia, Melbourne, Australia (2014)
Judith Scott: Bound and Unbound, Brooklyn Museum, New York, USA (2014–15)
Helen Rae, Good Luck Gallery, Los Angeles, USA (2015)
Hilma af Klint: Painting the Unseen, Serpentine Galleries, London, UK (2016)
The Museum of Everything #6, Kunsthal Rotterdam, The Netherlands (2016)
Viva Arte Via, 57th Venice Biennale, Venice, Italy (2017)
Watch This Space, Wandsworth Arts Fringe, London, UK (2017)
White Room: Helen Rae, White Columns, New York, USA (2017)
The Museum of Everything #7, The Museum of Old and New Art, Hobart, Australia (2017–18)

Nnena Kalu, Project Ability, Glasgow International, Glasgow, UK (2018)
L'envol, La Maison Rouge, Paris, France (2018)
Outliers and American Vanguard Art, Smithsonian American Museum of Art, Washington, D.C., USA (2018)
Between Worlds: The Art of Bill Traylor, Smithsonian American Art Museum, Washington, D.C., USA (2018–19)
Hilma af Klint: Painting for the Future, Solomon R. Guggenheim Museum, New York, USA (2018–19)
Art Brut from Japan, Another Look, Collection de l'Art Brut, Lausanne, Switzerland (2018–19)
Eye, Eye, Nose, Mouth: Art, Disability and Mental Illness in Nanjing, China and Shiga-ken, Japan, Harvard University, Asia Center, Massachusetts, USA (2019)
The Doors of Perception, Frieze Art Fair, New York, USA (2019)
Flying High: Women Artists of Art Brut, Kunstforum Wien, Austria (2019)
Andrew Omoding: It's My Work, Come See, Come See, Camden Art Centre, London, UK (2019)
Romantic Idealists, Musée Visionnaire, Zurich, Switzerland (2019–20)
Vanguard: Origins of Tierra del Sol Arts in Claremont featuring Helen Rae, Claremont Museum of Art, Claremont, USA (2019–20)
Nicholas Party: Pastel, The FLAG Art Foundation, New York, USA (2019–20)
Architecture for Modern Art, Museum of Modern Art, New York, USA (2019–21)
Funny Bunny, Shrine Gallery, New York, USA (2020)
We Will Walk – Art and Resistance in the American South, Turner Contemporary, Margate, UK (2020)
Nnena Kalu, Studio Voltaire elsewhere, London, UK (2020)
Inner Life, Museum Lothar Fischer, Neumarkt, Germany (2020)
It's a Beautiful Day Outside, Ortuzar Projects, New York, USA (2020)
Shinichi Sawada, Georg Kolbe Museum, Berlin, Germany (2020)
Shinichi Sawada, Venus Over Manhattan, New York, USA (2021)
William Scott, Studio Voltaire, London, UK (2021)
Really Free: The Radical Art of Nellie Mae Rowe, High Museum of Art, Atlanta (2021)
Gatecrashers: The Rise of the Self-Taught Artist in America, High Museum of Art, Atlanta (2021)
Joseph Yoakum: What I Saw, The Art Institute of Chicago, Chicago (2021)

CONTRIBUTOR BIOGRAPHIES

Lisa Slominski is an American curator, writer, and cultural producer based in London. She advocates for neurodiversity in the contemporary art current discourse, and the historical framework and placement of artists considered "self-taught" or "outsiders." She previously served as Head of Visual Culture for The Museum of Everything and lectures on the topic of 'Outsider Art' including for Queen Mary University of London. She is the co-founder of Art et al., a curatorial platform focusing on international commissions and collaboration between arts professionals with and without disability (2020), and published in the peer-reviewed international journal *Epidemiology* and *Psychiatric Sciences* for Cambridge University Press (2022).

Katherine Jentleson, PhD, is the Merrie and Dan Boone curator of folk and self-taught art at the High Museum of Art, Atlanta. Her recent publications and exhibitions include *Gatecrashers: The Rise of the Self-Taught Artist in America* and *Really Free: The Radical Art of Nellie Mae Rowe*.

Sarah Lombardi has been director of the Collection de l'Art Brut since March 2013. She gives priority to highlighting the museum collections with biennials presenting works from the institution's own holdings. She has also published numerous essays and directed several books on Art Brut.

John Maizels founded *Raw Vision* magazine in 1989, as a platform for the presentation and dissemination of Outsider Art and allied fields. He is the author of *Raw Creation* (Phaidon 1996) and *Fantasy Worlds* (Taschen 2002) as well as many articles and catalog essays on Outsider Art, including *Vernacular Visionaries* (Yale, 2003). He cofounded the Nek Chand Foundation, an international charity concerned with the support and protection of the world's biggest sculpture garden, the Rock Garden of Chandigarh, India.

Dr. Cheryl Finley is the director of the Atlanta University Center Art History + Curatorial Studies Collective and distinguished visiting professor in the Department of Art & Visual Culture at Spelman College. On leave from Cornell University, she is the author of *Committed to Memory: the Art of the Slave Ship Icon* (Princeton UP, 2018), and her work has appeared in numerous academic and popular publications, including *Aperture, Nka: Journal of Contemporary African Art, American Quarterly, Artforum*, and *Small Axe*; and in the co-authored publications, *My Soul Has Grown Deep: Black Art from the American South* (Yale University Press, 2018), and *Diaspora, Memory, Place: David Hammons, Maria Magdalena Campos-Pons, Pamela Z.* (Prestel, 2008).

Michael Bonesteel is an independent scholar, curator, and contributing editor to *Raw Vision*; author of *Henry Darger: Art and Selected Writings* (Rizzoli International, 2000); previously employed as adjunct professor at the School of the Art Institute (Chicago); art critic for *Art in America* and *Artforum* magazines (New York); and managing editor of the *New Art Examiner* (Chicago).

Phillip March Jones is an artist, writer, and curator. He served as the inaugural director of Atlanta's Souls Grown Deep Foundation. He is the founder and creative director of Institute 193, a nonprofit contemporary art space in Lexington, Kentucky. In 2020, Jones launched MARCH, a curatorial platform and gallery operating at the intersection of visual art and social justice.

Tom di Maria was hired as director of Creative Growth Art Center in January, 2000. He has developed partnerships with museums, galleries, and international design companies to help bring Creative Growth's artists with disabilities fully into the contemporary art world. He speaks around the world about the center's major artists and their relationship to both Outsider Art and contemporary culture. He was the 2019 recipient of the Visionary Award from the American Folk Art Museum in New York.

Jo Farb Hernández is director/curator emerita of SPACES Archives and professor emerita of San José State University. She has documented hundreds of environments created by self-taught artists across Europe and the US since 1973, and her exhibitions and scholarly publications are widely regarded as models for the field. A Fulbright Senior Scholar, her groundbreaking book, *Singular Spaces: From the Eccentric to the Extraordinary in Spanish Art Environments*, has been described as the ". . . most impressive single volume of research ever published in the field of self-taught art"; she is currently completing work on the second volume of this study.

Sophia Cosmadopoulos is the cofounder and gallery director of Summertime, an art studio and gallery where artists with and without intellectual disabilities create and display work alongside one another in New York City. Founded in 2019, Summertime was the recipient of an Andy Warhol Foundation for the Visual Arts grant, as well as a grant from the Shelley and Donald Rubin Foundation. Sophia has been a passionate proponent for artists with intellectual disabilities since 2005, working at HAI, Pure Vision Arts, AHRC, YAI Arts and LAND Studio & Gallery in NYC. She is also a freelancer writer.

ACKNOWLEDGMENTS

This opportunity and invitation to develop *Nonconformers* bittersweetly coincided with the COVID-19 pandemic. Living in London, I worked through the national lockdowns of 2020, followed by winter's Tier 4 restrictions of the southeast. Finally, in the summer of 2021, as the lingering restrictions eased, I completed my initial texts and received essays back from contributors. The effects of the pandemic inadvertently provided a situation enabling me to commit to *Nonconformers*, to which under normal circumstances, I may not have been able, or certainly not brave enough, to accept. It also created the utmost focused environment: reading, researching, and writing quietly in the confines of my Hackney flat. However, given the limits from the pandemic of physical visiting, seeing, and meeting, I am indebted to every author listed in the bibliography and for the technology allowing me to digitally access—whether live, recorded, or scanned—so many important lectures, discussions, and literature that informed this book.

Nonconformers is, in part, my response to, and participation with, an urgency for a more inclusive, diverse, and accessible art world. This includes a reexamination of the past, with implementations for the future. The examinations and critiques of terminology are not with contempt, but frame propositions of an outdated taxonomy. Archaic language is an undeniable effect of our human development, and I already acknowledge (with trepidation) that aspects of my writing here may reach a future expiration date.

Concepts and details regarding identity, biography, and personal agency are included with respectful consideration throughout *Nonconformers*. Language surrounding artists who identify with disability was checked with the artist, artist representative/family, or studio wherever possible. Their preferred language for addressing and identifying with disability (or not) is reflected in their respective features. With consideration and interest in the history of artists, development of international intersecting genres, and valued opinions, I have invited contributors whose essays preface the first eight chapters. To document the direct voices of artists, the final three chapters commence with an interview between a contributor and an artist.

The contextualizing, critical placement, and research of artists is an ongoing and developing responsibility. *Nonconformers* is an introduction with the hope to ignite further discussion and research in the 21st century. With the inclusion of creatives considered "classics" to the history of this field, as well as, more emerging artists, I hope it will be compelling for both new and existing audiences. I wish I could have included more artists, and more histories. Artists have been left out, of course, highlighting a selection of artists globally over roughly one 100 years—how could they not be? Please consider that this is not an exclusive total roster; rather, a diving board.

An intention of *Nonconformers* is to discuss these creatives in relation to the wider art historical canon and cultural mainstream. The four opening chapters present a historical 20th century context, via four key genre defining moments. Beyond this initial historical review of the artists, I aim to administer an integrative framework, demonstrating where possible, an artist's appeal in the wider canon, with recognition not limited to the remit of self-taught. This is seen in the referencing of select exhibitions and collections representing the artists. However, without a doubt, it is important to acknowledge and express gratitude to those dedicated institutions and platforms, as they were and continue to be integral to the development of this genre: notably, the Collection de l'Art Brut, Lausanne; the American Folk Art Museum, New York; The Museum of Everything, London; Intuit: The Center for Intuitive and Outsider Art, Chicago; the John Michael Kohler Arts Center, Sheboygan; Souls Grown Deep Foundation, Atlanta, and the international publication *Raw Vision*. The majority of artists presented in *Nonconformers* have been featured, exhibited, and supported through these platforms. I am also beholden to the significant contributions by dealers, writers, and curators, beyond the four pivotal moments introduced in *Origins and Representation* to the legacy of the artists in this book.

I am indebted to the contributors: Katherine Jentleson, Sarah Lombardi, John Maizels, Dr. Cheryl Finley, Michael Bonesteel, Phillip March Jones, Jo Farb Hernández, Tom di Maria, Sophia Cosmadopoulos, George Widener, William Scott, and Mamadou Cissé; especially those who, behind the scenes, contributed far more than an essay or interview.

I am grateful for all the individuals and organizations that helped facilitate artists' information and artworks including: Vincent Monod, Savine Faupin, Sarah Galender Meyer, Megan Mirro, Yukiko Koide, Frank Maresca, James Brett, Michelle Michael, Deborah Kerr, Alison Amick, Christina Stavros, Kozue Kamitani, Andrew Castrucci, Sheryll Catto, Sven Fritz, Jennifer Gilbert, Sim Luttin, Su Meng-Pin, Pamela Rogers, Fred Scruton, Morteza Zahedi. And to those who would answer my seemingly random research e-mails, including Judith Alexander Augustine, Jennifer Jane Marshall, Michael Thompson, Julie Webb, Jay Wehnert and Suzanne Zander.

I especially want to thank my all-women team! My editors Emma Harverson and Katherine Boller; art director Gemma Wilson and picture researcher Alexandrina Pereira; Rebecca Kressley for her immeasurable feedback and consideration, and Amy Berg for our fact-checking research sessions.

Lastly, I want to thank Eszter Karpati, for convincing me to take on such a daunting project and consistently believing in my point of view, and The Museum of Everything, my introduction to this incredible field.

INDEX

Illustrations and captions are in **bold**.

Produced by
Quintessence Editions
The Old Brewery
6 Blundell Street
London N7 9BH

Senior Commissioning Editor: Eszter Karpati
Project Editor: Emma Harverson
Design: Regular Practice
Art Director: Gemma Wilson
Picture Research: Alexandrina Pereira
Associate Publisher: Eszter Karpati
Publisher: Lorraine Dickey

Published in association with
Yale University Press
302 Temple Street
P.O. Box 209040
New Haven, CT 06520-9040
yalebooks.com/art

Library of Congress Control Number: 2021948869
ISBN 978-0-300-26022-9

10 9 8 7 6 5 4 3 2 1

Printed in Singapore

Cover front: Helen Rae, *untitled (June 15, 2016)*, 2016, colored pencil and pencil on paper, 24 × 18 in (16 × 45.7 cm). © Estate of Helen Rae. Photograph courtesy Good Luck Gallery.

FSC www.fsc.org MIX Paper from responsible sources FSC™ C007207